SWEDISH PRACTICAL
DICTIONARY

SWEDISH PRACTICAL DICTIONARY

Swedish-English
English-Swedish

Harald Hille

HIPPOCRENE BOOKS, INC.
New York

For information, address:
HIPPOCRENE BOOKS, INC.
171 Madison Avenue
New York, NY 10016
www.hippocrenebooks.com

Library of Congress Cataloging-in-Publication Data

Hille, Harald.
 Swedish-English, English-Swedish practical dictionary /
Harald Hille.
    p. cm.
 Text in Swedish and English.
 ISBN-13: 978-0-7818-1246-7 (pbk.)
 ISBN-10: 0-7818-1246-1 (pbk.)
 1. Swedish language--Dictionaries--English. 2. English
 language--Dictionaries--Swedish. I.Title.
 PD5640.H64 2011
 439.73'21--dc22

                                        2010046261

Printed in the United States of America.

Mixed Sources
Product group from well-managed
forests and other controlled sources
www.fsc.org Cert no. SW-COC-002283
© 1996 Forest Stewardship Council

Introduction

This practical English-Swedish and Swedish-English dictionary is intended for native speakers of American English and therefore follows American spelling and vocabulary practice. It joins a
long line of earlier dictionaries, most of which were compiled in
Sweden. What I hope to add with this effort is its practical size
(approx. 16,000 entries in each direction) intended for tourists and
students; the inclusion of terms germane to the new Sweden (i.e.
tourism, sports, immigration, education, the European Union and
information technology); and a bias towards American English. It
is probably unnecessary here to introduce English as a language
but a certain amount probably needs to be said about Sweden and
Swedish.

Sweden is a large North European country (about the size of
California) with about 9 million inhabitants (now about 15% foreign born) and a unique but very European culture based on a specific environment and political, economic and social history.
Sweden has not been at war since 1814 and maintains a policy of
non-alignment in peace and neutrality in war. It is one of a small
number of constitutional monarchies and is a member of the
Nordic (Scandinavian) group of countries, the European Union
(although not in the euro currency zone) and the United Nations.
Sweden is very active in many international organizations, both
in providing assistance and in policy formation. The country ranks
high on human development, democracy, immigration- and asy-
lum-friendly and human rights indices and has a well developed
social welfare system supported by high income and sales taxes.
The economy has long been heavily export-oriented (timber, hydro-
electricity, iron ore, pharmaceuticals, telecommunications and information technology, and motor vehicles) and benefits greatly
from a highly skilled labor force, a strong work ethic and a well-
developed transportation infrastructure.

Swedish is a North Germanic language, with many borrowings
from English and other European languages. From a grammatical
point of view, Swedish, like most Germanic languages, including
English, has a large stock of irregular verbs. Verb forms indicate

tense but not person or number, e.g. the verb form **går** shows that it is a present tense form but not whether it is singular or plural nor whether it is 1st, 2nd or 3rd person. Noun forms indicate number, i.e. singular or plural, and "definiteness (see below) but not case (**flicka** is singular, **flickor** is plural, but you can't tell whether they are serving as subjects or objects). What makes nouns complicated is the fact that there is an almost unlimited set of noun compounds written as one word (e.g. **administrationskostnader**: overhead costs). Like other Scandinavian languages, Swedish nouns have a basic or "indefinite" form (e.g. **hus**: house) along with a "definite" form (**huset**: the house), with the definite form marked in the singular by a definite article marker tacked on at the end (the article is attached as an ending of the noun: **huset**, **boken**). Word stress tends to fall on the initial syllable, particularly in native words, which is typical of Germanic languages, including the Anglo-Saxon word stock of English.

Swedish is notorious for its "sing-song" melody of rising and falling tones on many polysyllabic words (a feature called the grave and acute accents in Swedish). This feature is not uniformly pronounced in all regions of the country, and it is difficult for foreigners to get it right. It will not be indicated or dealt with in this dictionary. At the risk of offending purists, I would urge students to give this feature low priority and certainly not to exaggerate the pronunciation of tones, which often degenerates among learners into a caricature of Swedish. Listen to native speakers and imitate their tones cautiously, realizing that regional and personal differences exist.

Word stress, on the other hand, is pronounced by all native speakers in much the same way and is a concept familiar to English speakers. It must be rendered correctly. A simple word (not compounded) has a single stressed syllable, typically the initial syllable. Compound words (usually noun compounds) can be treated as having more than one stressed syllable, with a **primary stress** on or towards the beginning of the word and a **secondary stress** towards the end. Both primary and secondary stresses are marked in this dictionary (though not in standard Swedish texts). Take the word **folkskola**; the first syllable (closest to beginning of the word) has the primary stress and any later stressed syllables in the word have secondary stress by default. A primary stress

vii

marks the loudest syllable, and a secondary stress is less emphatic than a primary one but more emphatic than an unstressed syllable. Stress patterns have some relation to the tonal or acute & grave accent system mentioned above, but only in a very rough way. In marking secondary stresses I am not trying to present a disguised or simplified tone system. Tone patterns will eventually have to be learned. Swedish words can be lengthy and the secondary stress concept helps learners to manage to pronounce compound words.

Symbols and Abbreviations

The following symbols, type styles and abbreviations have been used in this dictionary:

/	variant, ("or")
~	the whole head word is used in a phrase, compound or word form
-	word form uses only part of the head word
( )	abbreviations and optional elements of words or phrases
[ ]	grammatical and reference information
bold	head words and other source language elements
underline	stressed syllable (primary first, then secondary if applicable)

abbrev.	abbreviation
adj.	adjective
adv.	adverb
art.	article
colloq.	colloquial
comp.	comparative [adjectives, adverbs]
conj.	conjunction
contr.	contraction
def.	definite [articles]
EU	European Union
exp.	expression
gram.	grammar
indecl.	indeclinable
indef.	indefinite [articles]
interj.	interjection
interrog.	interrogative [pron., adverbs]
intrans.	intransitive [verbs]
IT	information technology
n.	noun
ngn.	någon [someone]

ngt.	något [something]
num.	number
obj.	object case [pronouns]
o.s.	oneself
pl.	plural [nouns, pronouns]
poss.	possessive [pronouns]
prep.	preposition
pron.	pronoun
rel.	relative [pronouns, adverbs]
sing.	singular [nouns, pronouns]
s.o.	someone
sthg.	something
subj.	subject case [pronouns]
superl.	superlative [adjectives, adverbs]
trans.	transitive [verbs]
v.	verb
vul.	vulgar (indicates a word to be used with caution and sensitivity to appropriateness)

English grammar notes are given in brackets in the dictionary and show the following:

Part of speech

For adjectives: irregular comparative and superlative forms

For nouns: a plural form, if irregular or special in some way, i.e. doubling of the final stem consonant, or the -es ending after stems ending in -s, -x, -ch, -z and sometimes -o

For verbs: a present tense form (3rd sing.), where necessary; present participle (-ing form), where necessary; simple past and past participle forms where necessary

Swedish grammar notes are given in brackets in the dictionary and show the following:

Part of speech

For adjectives: neuter indefinite and plural/definite forms, and comparative and superlative forms where necessary

For nouns: singular definite ending and plural indefinite ending or form

For verbs: present tense ending or form, simple past and supine

Pronunciation

It is folly to try to capture the sounds of a language in chart form based on sounds taken from other languages. Nothing replaces listening to native speakers. There are also tapes and CDs in libraries and websites with sound files for Swedish learners. Having said that, I offer the following:

Vowels

Swedish vowels have **short** and **long** variants.

Short vowels come, generally speaking, in syllables that are closed by 2 or more consonants, e.g. **att, holm, hemskt**, or they occur in the unstressed syllables of a polysyllabic word, e.g. **tala** (first syllable is open, long and stressed, while the second syllable is short, albeit open, and unstressed).

Long vowels occur in stressed syllables where the syllable is open (not closed by a consonant), e.g. **bra, på**, or is closed by a single consonant, e,g, **hot, fat**.

Some **short** syllables ending in -m or -n are spelled with a single -m or -n when final, but the double consonants reemerge when endings are attached, e.g. **hem, hemmet**.

Vowel letter	Short	Long
a	short **ah**; rather like the vowel sound in: **cup**	like the **a** in: **father**
e	short **eh**; like: **bet**	long **eh**; like French é in: **café**
i	like: **bit, tip**	like: **keen, we** y off-glide at end
o*	like: **book**; short, with lip rounding	like: **moose** lip rounding, **w** off-glide at end
	see: short **å** below	see: long **å** below like: **awe, tall**, with lip rounding
u	like: **full** light lip rounding	long **ü** as in German: **über** or French: **tu** heavy lip rounding, **w** off-glide at end
y	like: **it**, but rounded and with **y** off-glide	long version of short y; **y** off-glide at end
å	short **aw**; British: **hot, cot**	like: **awe, talk** lip rounding
ä	like: **cat**, but short; tends towards short **eh**	like: **bad**; tends towards **eh**
ö	short version of long **ö**	like vowel sound in: **worse**; like French: **peu, jeux**

Note for o*: The letter **o** presents a problem for learners, as some syllables have the **oo**-like sound and others the **aw**-like sound. A rule of thumb, fraught with exceptions, would be that short syllables tend to favor the **aw** sound, whereas long syllables tend to favor the **oo** sound (a common environment for long **oo** is words ending in **-sion** and **-tion**).

Consonants

Some consonants are non-problematic for English speakers as they are pronounced more or less as in English (except as noted below): b, ck, d, f, h, k, l, m, n, ng, p, q, s, t, v, x.

The following consonants are problematic for English-speakers as there are some differences from English pronunciation:

Letter	Sounds like	Environment	Swedish examples
c	k	before a,o and u and before most consonants, except h	**cafeteria, coda, curry, crawl, clown**
	s	before e, i, y	**centimeter, cigarett, cykel**
	sh*	before h	**chalet, chic, choklad** except: **och** (pron. ock) **Bach**, etc. (pronounced as in German)
d	y	before j	**djungel, djävul**
g	g (hard, as in English **go**)	before a, o, u, å and consonants (except t) and when final (except -rg)	**gas, gott, gummi, gås, glas, gnist, gris; steg, nog**
	y	before e, i, y, ä, ö and j and after l and r	**genom, gissa, gynna, göra, gjuta, gjort; helg, älg, arg, borg** [note: borrowings with ge- and gi- may, contrary to the rule, have the hard g pronunciation above: **getto, gerilla,** or the sh* pronunciation below: **generell, geni**]
	sh*	before e, i in some borrowings from French	**gelé, gendarm, Genève**
	ng	before and after n	**ingen, pengar** (no g sound; like Eng. pinging, not like bingo, finger); **vagn** (pron. vang+n)
	k	before t	**lagt, sagt**
h	y	before j	**hjort, hjul, hjälp**
j	y		**jakt, je, jo, ju, jä,**
k	ç*	before e, i, y, ä, ö and j	**kedja, Kina, kyrka, källare, kök; kjol** [Exceptions: numerous borrowings where the hard k (as in **king**) is kept: **arkiv, monarki, bukett, kö, prekär, skeptisk, skelett;** note also **människa** (pron. with -sh*a)]
l	y	before j	**Ljus**

n	ng	before g, k	**många, sjunga, skinka**
r	rolled r [as in German, Italian]	most environments	**Rast, resa, ris, ros, brun, bröst**
	r as in Amer. Eng.	before d, l, n, t	**bord, farlig, barn, parti**
	sh*	before s	**borste, kors, Lars**
s	sh*	before ch, j, k, kj, tj and in -sion	**schack, schema, sjö, skepp, skida, skjorta, skjul, stjärna; vision**
t	sh*	in -tion	**realisation** [note: some words preserve a bit of the t sound, t + sh*: **portion**]
	ç*	before j	**tjugo**
w	v	all environments	foreign words and names: **Wilhelm**
x	ks	all	**box, exempel**
z	s	all	**Zoo**

Note for **sh*** and **ç***: These consonants present problems for learners as they are unique to Swedish:

In the case of **sh***, grouping all the environments under the one sound **sh*** is a rough approximation for beginners and its pronunciation has regional and individual variants and variants that depend on the vowel following (front vs. back). One variant (the easiest for English speakers) is a fairly straightforward **sh** sound, much like English, but with more lip protrusion (rounding). There is, however, a large group of Swedish speakers that use variants of a sibilant (hissing) sound rather like English **sh** but done with heavy lip rounding; the lips produce most of the hissing, not the teeth. To get it authentic, the learner must listen to a native speaker or to some of the sound recordings available in libraries and on the Internet.

In the case of **ç***, the sound is a sibilant formed by raising the tongue back in the mouth. It has been compared to the hiss of a cat and corresponds to the German **ch** in **ich** and **echt** (not the **ch** in **Bach** or **Buch**).

Note that the consonant clusters discussed above must be initial or final within a given syllable. With some exceptions, the fact that such consonants might come into contact across syllable boundaries does not trigger the "rules" in the chart.

SWEDISH-ENGLISH DICTIONARY

A

A [abbrev: amp<u>e</u>re] ampere (A)

A4 f<u>o</u>rmat [n.; ~en, ~er] A4 format [European standard letter paper size: 8.3" x 11.7"]

AA [abbrev: Anon<u>y</u>ma Alkoh<u>o</u>lister] Alcoholics Anonymous (AA)

AB [abbrev: <u>a</u>ktieb<u>o</u>lag; <u>A</u>ftonbl<u>a</u>det] corporation; Aftonbladet [major evening newspaper]

ABB [abbrev: <u>A</u>sea Brown Boveri] ABB Group [multinational corporation in power and automation technologies]

abb<u>o</u>rre [n.; ~n, abborrar] perch [fish]

AB<u>C</u>-str<u>i</u>dsmedel [n.; -medlet, ~] NBC weapons [nuclear, biological and chemical]

abdikat<u>i</u>on [n.; ~en, ~er] abdication

AB<u>F</u> [abbrev: <u>A</u>rbetarnas b<u>i</u>ldningsförb<u>u</u>nd] Workers Enlightenment League [workers education]

abn<u>o</u>rm [adj.; ~t, ~a] abnormal

abonnem<u>a</u>ng [n.; ~et, ~] subscription

abonnem<u>a</u>ngsavgift [n.; ~en, ~er] subscription fee

abonn<u>e</u>nt [n.; ~en, ~er] subscriber

ab<u>o</u>rt [n.; ~en, ~er] abortion

abs<u>i</u>d [n.; ~en, ~er] apse

absol<u>u</u>t[1] [adj.; ~a] absolute

absol<u>u</u>t[2] [adv.] definitely, really; ~ **inte** not at all, absolutely not

absorpt<u>i</u>onsförm<u>å</u>ga [n.; ~n] absorptive capacity

abstr<u>a</u>kt [adj.; ~a] abstract

abs<u>u</u>rd [adj.; absurt, ~a] absurd

accelerat<u>i</u>onsfält [n.; ~et] acceleration lane

acc<u>e</u>nt [n.; ~en, ~er] accent; stress

acc<u>e</u>nttecken [n.; -tecknet, ~] accent mark, diacritical mark

accept<u>e</u>ra [v.; ~r, ~de, ~t] accept [invitation]

accept<u>e</u>rad [adj.; -rat, ~e] accepted

acet<u>o</u>n [n.; ~et] acetone

ack [interj.] alas, oh dear

ack<u>o</u>rd [n.; ~et] chord

ackusat<u>i</u>v [n.; ~en, ~er] accusative [gram]; ~ **med <u>i</u>nfinitiv** accusative with the infinitive [gram; ex.: "I want him to go"]

<u>a</u>ckusativobj<u>e</u>kt [n.; ~et, ~] direct object [gram]

acqu<u>i</u>n [n.] Community acquis [total body of EU law adopted so far]

act<u>i</u>onfilm [n.; ~en, ~er] action film

ad<u>a</u>pter [n.; ~n, adaptrar] adapter

ADB [abbrev: autom<u>a</u>tisk d<u>a</u>tabeh<u>a</u>ndling] automatic data processing (ADP)

add<u>e</u>ra [v.; ~r, ~de, ~t] add

addit<u>i</u>on [n.; ~en, ~er] addition [IT]

<u>a</u>del [n.; ~n] nobility

<u>a</u>derton [num.; obsolete, see: **arton**] eighteen

adjekt<u>i</u>v [n,; ~et, ~] adjective [gram]

adj<u>u</u>nkt [n.; ~en, ~er] secondary school teacher

adj<u>ö</u> [interj.] goodbye

administrat<u>i</u>on [n.; ~en, ~er] administration, management

administrat<u>i</u>v [adv.; ~t, ~a] administrative

adopt<u>e</u>ra [v.; ~r, ~de, ~t] adopt

adopt<u>i</u>on [n.; ~en, ~er] adoption

adopt<u>i</u>vbarn [n.; ~et, ~en] adopted child

adopt<u>i</u>vför<u>ä</u>ldrar [n.pl.] adoptive parents

adr. [abbrev: adress] address

adr<u>e</u>ss [n.; ~en, ~er] address

adress<u>a</u>t [n.; ~en, ~er] addressee

adr<u>e</u>ssbok [n.; ~en, -böcker] address book

adr<u>e</u>ssfält [n.; ~et, ~] address bar, location bar [IT]

adr<u>e</u>sshuvud [n.; ~et, ~] address header [IT]

adr<u>e</u>ssik<u>o</u>n [n.; ~en, ~er] favicon [IT]

adr<u>e</u>sslapp [n.; ~en, ~ar] address label

adr<u>e</u>sslista [n.; ~n, -listor] address list

adr<u>e</u>ssruta [n.; ~n, -rutor] address box [IT]

adressymbol [n.; ~en, ~er] favicon [IT]

adressändring [n.; ~en, ~ar] address change

Adriatiska havet [n.] Adriatic Sea

advent [n.; ~et] Advent [4-week period before Christmas]

adventskalender [n.; -dern, -drar] Advent calendar

adventsljus [n.; ~et, ~] Advent candle

adventsstjärna [n.; ~n, -stjärnor] Advent star

adverb [n.; ~et, ~] adverb [gram]

adverbial [n.; ~et, ~] adverbial [gram]

adverbiell [adj.; ~t, ~a] adverbial [gram]

adversativ [adj.; ~t, ~a] adversative [gram]

advokat [n.; ~en, ~er] lawyer

advokatbyrå [n.; ~n, ~er] law office

advokatsamfund [n.; ~et, ~] bar association

AF [abbrev: Arbetsförmedlingen] employment office

affisch [n.; ~en, ~er] poster

affär [n.; ~en, ~er] store; business; ~**en upphör** the store/company is going out of business; **resa i ~er** travel on business

affärsbank [n.; ~en, ~er] commercial bank

affärsbiträde [n.; ~t, ~n] salesclerk

affärsbrev [n.; ~et, ~] business letter

affärscentrum [n.; ~et, ~] business district; shopping center

affärsgata [n.; ~n, -gator] shopping street

affärsgrafik [n.; ~en] business graphics [IT]

affärsklass [n.; ~en] business class

affärsinnehavare [n.; ~n, ~] storekeeper

affärskontakt [n.; ~en, ~er] business contact

affärskvarter [n.; ~et, ~] business district

affärskvinna [n.; ~n, -kvinnor] businesswoman

affärsman [n.; ~nen, -män] businessman

affärsresa [n.; ~n, -resor] business trip

affärssamtal [n.; ~et, ~] business discussion

affärssystem [n.; ~et, ~] accounting program [IT]

affärsvän [n.; ~nen, ~ner] business contact

affärsvärld [n.; ~en] business world

afghansk [adj.; ~t, ~a] Afghan

Afrika [n.] Africa

afrikansk [adj.; ~t, ~a] African

afton [n.; ~en, aftnar] evening; **god ~!** good evening!

Aftonbladet [n.] Aftonbladet [major evening newspaper]

aftonkläder [n.pl.] evening wear

aftonklänning [n.; ~en, ~ar] evening dress

aftonsång [n.; ~en, ~er] evening service [church], vespers

aga (barn) [v.; ~r, ~de, ~t] apply corporal punishment (to children), beat (children)

agat [n.; ~en, ~er] agate

Agenda 2007 [n.] Agenda 2007 [EU budget for 2007-2013]

agent [n.; ~en, ~er] agent; representative, traveling salesman

agera [v.; ~r, ~de, ~t] act

agerande [n.pl.] performers, actors; cast

agr. [abbrev: agronomi] agronomy

agronom [n.; ~en, ~er] agronomist, crop and soil specialist

aids [abbrev: förvärvat immunbristsyndrom] AIDS [abbrev: acquired immunodeficiency syndrome]

AIK [abbrev: Allmänna Idrottsklubben] General Sports Club

aioli [n.; ~n] aioli, garlic mayonnaise

aj! [interj.] ouch!

akademi [n.; ~n, ~er] academy

Akademibokhandel [n.; ~n, -handlar] university bookstore

akademiker [n.; ~n, ~] university graduate

akademisk [adj.; ~t, ~a] academic; university; ~ **examen** university degree; ~ **utbildning** university education

A-kassa [abbrev: arbetslöshets-kassa] unemployment benefits office

akrobat [n.; ~en, ~er] acrobat

akryl [n.; ~en] acrylic (fabric)

akt¹ [n.; ~en, ~er] act; document; ceremony; nude (artwork)

akt² [n.] attention, watchfulness, care; **ge ~** watch out, pay attention, be careful

akter [n.; ~n, aktrar] stern [boat]

akta [v.; ~r, ~de, ~t] be careful with, look out for, mind; take notice; respect; **~ sig för** watch out for

aktie [n.; ~n, ~r] share, stock

aktiebolag (AB) [n.; ~et, ~] company, corporation (Inc.)

aktiekurs [n.; ~en, ~er] stock price

aktiemarknad [n.; ~en, ~er] stock market

aktieutdelning [n.; ~en, ~ar] stock dividend

aktieägare [n.; ~n, ~] shareholder, stockholder

aktion [n.; ~en, ~er] action

aktiv [adj.; ~t, ~a] active; **~ form** active voice [gram]

aktivist [n.; ~en, ~er] activist

aktivitet [n.; ~en, ~er] activity, task

aktivitetsfält [n.; ~et, ~] icon tray, task bar [IT]

aktivitetshantare [n.; ~n, ~] task manager [IT]

aktsam [adj.; ~t, ~a] careful, prudent

aktuell [adj.; ~t, ~a] current, timely; **~t** news program

aktör [n.; ~en, ~er] actor; participant, operator; vendor [IT]

akut [adj., ~a] acute; urgent

akuten [n.] emergency center, trauma center, out-patient clinic, walk-in medical center

akutfall [n.; ~et, ~] emergency case

akutmottagning [n.; ~en, ~ar] out-patient department, emergency room

akutvård [n.; ~en] emergency treatment

akvarell [n.; ~en, ~er] watercolor

akvavit [n.; ~en, ~er] aquavit

al [n.; ~en, ~ar] alder [tree]

aladåb [n.; ~en, ~er] aspic

A-lag [n.; ~et, ~] A-team, first team

alarm [n.; ~et, ~] alarm

alarmera [v.; ~r, ~de, ~t] alarm, call; **~ brandkåren/polisen** call the fire department/police

Albanien [n.] Albania

albansk [adj.; ~t, ~a] Albanian

albanska [n.] Albanian language

album [n.; ~et, ~] album, scrapbook

aldrig [adv.] never; **~ i livet** not on your life

alfabet [n.; ~et, ~] alphabet

alg [n.; ~en, ~er] alga (pl. algae)

Alger [n.] Algiers

Algeriet [n.] Algeria

algerisk [adj.; ~t, ~a] Algerian

alibi [n.; ~t, ~n] alibi

alkohol [n.; ~en, ~er] alcohol

alkoholfri [adj.; ~tt, ~a] non-alcoholic

alkoholhaltig [adj.; ~t, ~a] alcoholic [beverage]

Alkoholsortimentsnämnden [n.] Alcoholic Beverage Assortment Board

alkoholtest [n.; ~et, ~] breath alcohol test

alkoläsk [n.; ~en, ~ar] bottled mixed drink [alcoholic]

alkov [n.; ~en, ~er] alcove

all¹ [adj.] out of supply, exhausted; over, ended

all² [pron.; ~t, ~a] all, every; **för ~ del** by all means, sure

alla [pron.pl.] everyone, all; **i ~ fall** in any case

Alla Helgons dag [see: **Allhelgon-dagen**]

alldeles [adv.] absolutely, completely

allé [n.; ~n, ~er] avenue

allehanda [adj.] all sorts of, miscellaneous

allemansrätt [n.; ~en] right of public access to private land

allergi [n.; ~n, ~er] allergy

allergiker [n.; ~n, ~] allergic person

allergisk (mot) [adj.; ~t, ~a] allergic (to)

allesammans [pron.] whole group, all together

Allhelgondagen [n.] All Saints Day [officially November 1, but celebrated on first Saturday after October 30]

allians [n.; ~en, ~er] alliance

alliansfri [adj.; ~tt, ~a] non-aligned

Allians för Sverige [n.] Alliance for Sweden [center-right coalition]

alliansring [n.; ~en, ~ar] wedding ring

allierad [adj.; -rat, ~e] allied, connected

allihop [pron.] all (of us, you, them)

allm. [see: **allmän**]

allmän [adj.; ~t, ~a] common, general, public; ~ **beredning** formal government meeting; ~ **betydelse** general meaning [gram]; ~ **byggnad** public building; ~ **försäkringskassa** regional social insurance office; ~ **handling** official document; ~ **helgdag** public holiday; ~ **post** general delivery, poste restante; ~ **rösträtt** universal suffrage; ~ **självdeklaration** income tax return; ~ **skolplikt** compulsory education; ~ **tilläggspension (ATP)** supplementary pension for retirees; ~ **toalett** public toilet [for both sexes]; ~ **värnplikt** compulsory military service; ~ **åklagare** public prosecutor

allmänheten [n.] the public

Allmänhetens pressombudsman (PO) [n.; ~en] Office of the Press Ombudsman

allmänläkare [n.; ~n, ~] general practitioner

Allmänna arvsfonden [n.] State Inheritance Fund

Allmänna reklamationsnämnden [n.] National Board for Consumer Complaints

Allmänna riktlinjer för den ekonomiska politiken [n.pl.] Broad Economic Policy Guidelines (BEPG) [EU]

Allmänna rådet [n.] General Affairs and External Relations Council (GAERC) [EU]

allmänna val [n.; ~et, ~] general election

allmänpraktiker [n.; ~n, ~] general practitioner

allmänpraktiserande läkare [n.; ~n, ~] general practitioner (GP)

allmänt [adv.] generally, widely

allmäntbråk [n.; ~et, ~] ordinary fraction

allmäntjänstgöring läkare [n.; ~n, ~] intern [doctor in training in hospital]

allra [adv.] of all

allra bäst [adj./adv.] best of all

alls [adv.]: **inte** ~ not at all

allsmäktig [adj.; ~t, ~a] almighty

Allsvenskan [n.] first division [Swedish sports leagues, usually soccer]

allt [adv.] everything, all; ~ **möjligt** all sorts of things, everything imaginable

alltför [adv.] all too

alltid [adv.] always

alltihop [pron.; see: **alltsammans**]

allting [pron.] everything

alltjämt [adv.] still

alltsammans [pron.] all of it, everything; every one

alltsedan [adv.] ever since

alltså [adv.] that is to say, you know; therefore

allvar [n.; ~et] seriousness; gravity; **på** ~ seriously

allvarlig [adj.; ~t, ~a] serious

allvarligare [adj. comp.] more serious

alm [n.; ~en, ~ar] elm

almanacka [n.; ~n, -ckor] almanac; diary, day planner

Alperna [n.pl.] Alps

alpin skidåkning [n.; ~en] downhill skiing

altan [n.; ~en, ~er] terrace, balcony

altare [n.; ~t, ~n] altar

altarduk [n.; ~en, ~ar] altar cloth

altarljus [n.; ~et, ~] altar candle

altartavla [n.; ~, -tavlor] altarpiece

alternativ [adj.; ~t, ~a] alternative, option

alternativ väg [n.; ~en, ~ar] alternate route
aluminium [n.; ~et] aluminum
aluminiumfolie [n.; ~n, ~r] aluminum foil, tin foil
Alzheimers sjukdom [n.; ~en] Alzheimer's disease
amalgam [n.; ~et, ~] amalgam [dentistry]
amatör [n.; ~en, ~er] amateur
Amazonfloden [n.] Amazon River
ambassad [n.; ~en, ~er] embassy
ambassadråd [n.; ~et, ~] counsellor [embassy]
ambassadör [n.; ~en, ~er] ambassador
ambition [n.; ~en, ~er] ambition
ambulans [n.; ~en, ~er] ambulance
Amerika [n.] America
amerikan [n.; ~en, ~er] American person
amerikansk [adj.; ~t, ~a] American
ametist [n.; ~en, ~er] amethyst
amiral [n.; ~en, ~er] admiral
amma [v.; ~r, ~de, ~t] breast-feed
amnesi [n.; ~n] amnesia
amnesti [n.; ~n, ~er] amnesty
amning [n.; ~en] breast-feeding, nursing [baby]
amortera [v.; ~r, ~de, ~t] pay off (a loan) in installments
amorteringsplan [n.; ~et] installment plan
ampere (A) [n.; ~en, ~] ampere (A)
amputera [v.; ~r, ~de, ~t] amputate
AMS [abbrev: Arbetsmarknadsstyrelsen] Labor Market Board
Amsterdamfördraget [n.] Treaty of Amsterdam [EU, 1999]
AMU [abbrev: arbetsmarknadsutbildning] vocational training
ana [v.; ~r, ~de, ~t] have a feeling/presentiment, suspect
analog [adj.; ~t, ~a] analogous, analog [IT]
analys [n.; ~en, ~er] analysis
analysera [v.; ~r, ~de, ~t] analyze
analytiker [n.; ~n, ~] analyst, analyzer
ananas [n.; ~en, ~] pineapple
anarki [n.; ~n] anarchy

anbud [n.; ~et, ~] offer, bid, quote
and [n.; ~en, änder] wild duck
anda [n.; ~n] breath; spirit; **hålla ~n** hold one's breath
andas [v.; ~, andades, andats] breathe
ande [n.; ~n, andar] spirit, mind; ghost
andel [n.; ~n, ~ar] share, interest
andelslägenhet [n.; ~en, ~er] condominium apartment
andetag [n.; ~et, ~] breath; **djupt ~** deep breath
andlig [adj.; ~t, ~a] spiritual; intellectual, mental
andningsapparat [n.; ~en, ~er] breathing apparatus
andningssvårigheter [n.pl.] breathing difficulties
andra [pron./num.] second; other(s); February; ~ **klass** second class
andrahandslägenhet [n.; ~en, ~er] sublet apartment
anfall [n.; ~et, ~] attack, fit
anfalla [n.; -faller, -föll, -fallit] attack, attack
ang. [abbrev: angående] concerning (re:)
ange [v.; -ger, -gav, -givit] indicate, state; inform
angelägen [adj.; -get, -gna] eager, interested
angelägenhet [n.; ~en, ~er] matter, affair, concern; significance, urgency
angenäm [adj.; ~t, ~a] pleasant
angenämt [adv.] nice; pleased to meet you
angrepp [n.; ~et, ~] attack
angripa [v.; -griper, -grep, -gripit] attack, assault; tackle, deal with
angränsande [adj.] adjoining
angå [v.; -går, -gick, -gått] concern; **det ~r dig inte** it's no business of yours
angående [prep.] concerning
anhålla [v.; -håller, -höll, -hållit] take into custody, arrest; request, apply for
anhållande [n.; ~t, ~n] arrest, apprehension

anhållen [adj.; ~a] taken into custody, arrested, apprehended
anhängare [n.; ~en, ~] follower, adherent, supporter
anhörig [adj.; ~a] relative, related
animerad [adj.; ~t, ~a] animated [IT]
animering [n.; ~en, ~ar] animation [IT]
aning [n.; ~en, ~ar] presentiment, hunch; notion, idea; a little bit
aningslös [adj.; ~t, ~a] unsuspecting; naive
ank. [abbrev: ankomst; ankommande] arrival; incoming
anka [n.; ~n, ankor] duck
ankare [n.; ~t, ~] anchor
ankel [n.; ~n, anklar] ankle
anklaga [v.; ~r, ~de, ~t] accuse
anklagade [n.] accused
anklagelse [n.; ~n, ~r] accusation, charge
anknytning [n.; ~en, ~ar] telephone extension; connection
anknytningsinvandring [n.; ~en, ~ar] immigration aimed at reuniting families
anknytningsnummer [n.; -numret, ~] extension number
ankomma (till) [v.; -kommer, -kom, -kommit] arrive (at)
ankommande [adj.] arriving, incoming
ankomst [n.; ~en, ~er] arrival
ankomstdag [n.; ~en] day of arrival
ankomsthall [n.; ~en, ~ar] arrival lounge
ankomsttid [n.; ~en, ~er] arrival time
ankring förbjuden [n.] no anchorage
ankunge [n.; ~n, -ungar] duckling
anlagstest [n.; ~et, ~] aptitude test
anledning [n.; ~en, ~ar] reason, occasion; **med ~ av** concerning, about, with reference to
anlita [v.; -litar, -litade, -litat] engage; use, make use of
anläggning [n.; ~en, ~ar] construction; establishment, premises, works; building

anlända [v.; -länder, -lände, -länt] arrive
anm. [abbrev: anmärkning] comment
anmäla [v.; -mäler, -mälde, -mält] announce, report; review; ~ **sig** **(till)** apply (for), enroll (in)
anmälan [n.; ~, anmälningar] announcement; report, review; declaration
anmäld [adj.; -mält, ~a] announced, reported
anmälning [n.] [see: **anmälan**]
anmälningsavgift [n.; ~en, ~er] application fee
anmälningsblankett [n.; ~en, ~er] application blank
anmälningstid [n.; ~en, ~er] application period
anmärkning [n.; ~en, ~ar] note, comment, remark
anmärkningsvärd [adj.; -värt, ~a] remarkable, noteworthy
annan [pron.; annat, andra] other, else
annandag [n.] the day after; ~ **jul** December 26; ~ **pingst** Monday after Pentecost [7 weeks after Easter]; ~ **påsk** Easter Monday
annanstans [adv.] elsewhere
annars [adv.] otherwise
annat [pron.] other; **något** ~ something else
annons [n.; ~en, ~er] advertisement, announcement
annonsbilaga [n.; ~n, -lagor] advertising supplement
annonsera [v.; ~r, ~de, ~t] advertise
annorlunda (än) [adj./adv.] different (from)
annullerad [adj.; ~rat, ~e] canceled
anonym [adj.; ~t, ~a] anonymous
anorak [n.; ~en, ~er] anorak [hooded pullover jacket]
anorexi [n.; ~n] anorexia
anpassa [v.; ~r, ~de, ~t] adjust, adapt, customize
anpassad (till) [adj.; -ssat, ~e] suitable (for), adapted (to)
anpassning [n.; ~en, ~ar] adjustment, accomodation, adaptation

anpassningsprogram [n.; -gram-met, ~] middleware [IT]
anropa [v.; ~r, ~de, ~t] call, call on
anse [v.; ~r, -såg, ~tt) think, be of the opinion
anseende [n.; ~t] reputation; esteem, respect
ansikte [n.; ~t, ~n] face
ansiktsbehandling [n.; ~en, ~ar] facial
ansiktskräm [n.; ~en, ~er] face lotion
ansjovis [n.; ~en, ~ar] anchovies
anslag [n.; ~et, ~] notice, placard; grant, subsidy; impact
anslagsskrivare [n.; ~n, ~] impact printer [IT]
anslagstavla [n.; ~n, -tavlor] message board, bulletin board
ansluta [v.;-sluter, -slöt, -slutit] connect; join
anslutande land [n.; ~et, -länder] acceding country [EU]
ansluten [n.; -slutna] being a member of, being affiliated with; connect [IT]
anslutning [n.; ~en, ~ar] connection; accession; **i ~ till** in connection with
anslutningsbarhet [n.; ~en, ~er] connectivity [IT]
anslutningsflyg [n.; ~et, ~] connecting flight
anslutningsförhandlingar [n.pl.] accession negotiations [EU]
anslutningskontakt [n.; ~en, ~er] connector [IT]
anslutningskriterier [n.pl.; see: **Köpenhamnskriterierna**] association criteria [EU]
anspråk [n.; ~et, ~] claim, demand
anspråkslös [adj.; ~t, ~a] unpretentious, modest
ansträngande [adj.] tiring, strenuous
anstränga sig [v.; -stränger, -strängde, -strängt] exert oneself, make an effort
ansträngning [n.; ~en, ~ar] effort
anställa [v.; -ställer, -ställde, -ställt] employ
anställas [v. ; -ställes, -ställdes, -ställts] be recruited, be hired

anställd [n.; ~a] employee
anställning [n.; ~en, ~ar] employment; job, position
anställningsbetyg [n.; ~et, ~] employment reference(s)
anställningsintervju [n.; ~n, ~er] job interview
anställningsstopp [n.; ~et, ~] hiring freeze
anställningstrygghet [n.; ~en] job security
anställningsvillkor [n.; ~et, ~] terms of employment
ansvar [n.; ~et] responsibility; **ta ~ för** take responsibility for, accept responsibility for
ansvara (för) [v.; ~r, ~de, ~t] be responsible (for)
ansvarig [adj.; ~t, ~a] responsible, liable
ansvarsfull [adj.; ~t, ~a] responsible
ansöka (om) [v.; -söker, -sökte, -sökt] apply (for)
ansökan [n.; ~, ansökningar] application
ansökansblankett [n.; ~en, ~er] application form
ansökarland [n.; ~et, -länder] applicant country
ansökning [n.; ~en, ~ar; see: **ansökan**]
ansökningstid [n.; ~en, ~er] application period
anta [v.; ~r, -tog, -tagit] take, accept; consent to, approve; assume, take; engage, appoint
antaga [v.; see: **anta**]
antagligen [adv.] probably
antal [n.; ~et, ~] number
Antarktis [n.] Antarctica
antarktisk [adj.; ~t, ~a] Antarctic
antasta [v.; ~r, ~de, ~t] harass
anteckna [v.; ~r, ~de, ~t] take notes, jot down
anteckningsbok [n.; ~en, -böcker] notebook
antenn [n.; ~en, ~er] antenna
antibiotika [n.pl.] antibiotics
antibiotisk medel [n.; -medlet, ~] antibiotic

Antici [n.] Antici Group [EU, COREPER]
antidiskrimineringsbyrån [n.; -byråer] anti-discrimination office
antik [adj.; ~t, ~a] ancient, antique
antikaffär [n.; ~en, ~er] antique store
antiken [n.] classical antiquity
antikva [n.; ~n] Roman, serif [type style]
antikvariat [n,; ~et, ~] used book store
antikvitet [n.; ~en, ~er] antique
antikvitetsaffär [n.; ~en, ~er] antique store
antilop [n.; ~en, ~er] antelope
antingen [adv.] ~ A eller B either A or B
antirasistisk [adj.; ~t, ~a] antiracist
antirynkkräm [n.; ~en, ~er] anti-wrinkle cream
antisemitisk [adj.; ~t, ~a] anti-Semitic
antiseptisk medel [n.; medlet, ~] antiseptic
antiseptisk salva [n.; ~n, salvor] antiseptic cream
antitrust [adj.] antitrust [EU]
antivirusprogram [n.; -grammet, ~] anti-virus program [IT]
antog [v.past; see: **anta**]
antyda [v.; -tyder, -tydde, -tytt] suggest, hint at; imply; indicate
anvisningar [n.pl.] directions [map]
använda [v.; -vänder, -vände, -vänt] use; **använd gångtunneln** use the underpass; **använd helljus** use headlights; **använd innan** use before; **använd kedjor eller vinterdäck** use chains or snow tires
användaragent [n.; ~en, ~er] user agent [IT]
användardefinierad [adj.; -rat, ~e] user defined [IT]
användare [n.; ~n, ~] user
användargränssnitt [n.; ~et, ~] user interface [IT]
användarhjälp [n.; ~en] user assistance [IT]
användar-ID [n.; ett ~] user ID [IT]
användaridentitet [n.; ~en, ~er] user ID [IT]

användarlicens [n.; ~en, ~er] user license [IT]
användarnamn [n.; ~et, ~] user name [IT]
användarstöd [n.; ~et, ~] user support [IT]
användarvänlig [adj.; ~t, ~a] user-friendly [IT]
användbar [adj.; ~t, ~a] useful
användning [n.; ~en, ~ar] use
användningsområde [n.; ~t, ~n] area of application
apa [n.; ~n, apor] monkey
apatisk [adj.; ~t, ~a] apathetic
apelsin [n.; ~en, ~er] orange
apelsinjos [n.; ~en, ~er] orange juice
apelsinsaft [n.; ~en, ~er] orange drink, orange juice
AP-fonden [abbrev: Allmäna pensionsfond] National Pension Insurance Fund
apostel [n.; -steln, -stlar] apostle
apostrof (') [n.] apostrophe (')
apotek [n.; ~et, ~] pharmacy, drugstore
apotekare [n.; ~n, ~] pharmacist
apparat [n.; ~en, ~er] device, apparatus
apparatdykning [n.; ~en] scuba diving
appellativ [n.; ~et, ~] appelative, common noun [gram]
appletprogram [n.; -programmet, ~] applet [IT]
applicera [v.; ~r, ~de, ~t] apply, submit an application
applåd [n.; ~en, ~er] applause
applådera [v.; ~r, ~de, ~t] applaud
apposition [n.; ~en] apposition [gram]
apr. [see: **april**]
aprikos [n.; ~en, ~er] apricot
april [n.] April; **april!** April Fool!
aprilskämt [n.; ~et, ~] April Fool's joke
apropå [prep., adv.] with regard to; by the way, incidentally
aptit [n.; ~en] appetite
aptitlöshet [n.; ~en] loss of appetite
aptitretare [n.; ~n, ~] appetizer

A-punkt [n.; ~en] A item [EU, Council agenda]
arab [n.; ~en, ~er] Arab
Arabförbundet [n.] Arab League
Arabien [n.] Arabia
arabisk [adj.; ~t, ~a] Arabian
arabiska [n.; ~n] Arabic language
arabvärlden [n.] Arab world
arbeta [v.; ~r, ~de, ~t] work; vad ~r du med? what do you do for a living?
arbetare [n.; ~n, ~] worker
arbetarkvarter [n.; ~et, ~] working class district
Arbetarnas bildningsförbund (ABF) [n.] Workers Enlightenment League [educational and cultural section of the Swedish labor movement and Social Democratic Party]
arbetarpartiet [n.] Workers Party, Labor Party
arbetarrörelse [n.; ~n, ~r] labor movement
arbetarskyddslaget [n.] Occupational Safety and Health Law
arbete [n.; ~t, ~n] work
arbetsam [adj.; ~t, ~a] hard-working
arbetsbok [n.; ~en, -böcker] workbook
arbetsbänk [n.; ~en, -bänkar] workbench
arbetsdag [n.; ~en, -dagar] working day
Arbetsdomstolen (AD) [n.] Labor Court
arbetsförhållanden [n.pl.] working conditions
Arbetsförmedlingen (AF) [n.] employment office
arbetsgivaravgift [n.; ~en, ~er] payroll tax
arbetsgivare [n.; ~n, ~] employer
arbetsgivarorganisation [n.; ~en, ~er] employers association
Arbetsgivarverket [n.] National Agency for Government Employers
arbetsgrupp [n.; ~en, ~er] team, working group, working party
arbetskamrat [n.; ~en, ~er] fellow worker, colleague

arbetskraft [n.; ~en] labor, labor force
arbetskraftsinvandring [n.; ~en, ~ar] labor immigration
arbetslagstiftning [n.; ~en] labor legislation
arbetsliv [n.; ~et] working life
arbetslivserfarenhet [n.; ~en, ~er] work experience
Arbetslivsinstitutet [n.] National Institute on Professional Life
Arbetslivsminister [n.; ~n] Minister of Employment
arbetslivsorientering [n.; ~en] [see: PRAO]
arbetslös [adj.; ~t, ~a] unemployed
arbetslöshet [n.; ~en] unemployment
arbetslöshetsersättning [n.; ~en, ~ar] unemployment benefits
arbetslöshetskassa [n.; ~n, -kassor] unemployment benefit fund/office
arbetsmarknad [n.; ~en, ~er] labor market; ~ens parter [n.pl.] social partners [EU]
arbetsmarknadsdialog [n.; ~en] social dialogue [EU]
Arbetsmarknadsminister [n.; ~n] Minister of Labor, Secretary of Labor
arbetsmarknadspolitik [n.; ~en] labor policy
Arbetsmarknadsstyrelsen (AMS) [n.] Labor Market Board
arbetsmarknadsutbildning (AMU) [n.; ~en] vocational training [for unemployed and handicapped]
Arbetsmarknadsutskottet [n.] Committee on the Labor Market [in Parliament]
arbetsmiljö [n.; ~n, ~er] work environment
Arbetsmiljöverket [n.] Work Environment Administration
arbetsplats [n.; ~en, ~er] workplace
arbetsrum [n.; -rummet, ~] study, workroom
arbetsrätt [n.; ~en] labor law
arbetsstation [n.; ~en, ~er] workstation [IT]

arbetssökande [adj.] looking for work, applying for a job

arbetstagare [n.; ~n, ~] employee

arbetstagarsorganisation [n.; ~en, ~er] workers' union, employees' organization

arbetstid [n.; ~en, ~er] working hours

arbetstidsförkortning [n.; ~en, ~ar] shortening of working hours

arbetstillfälle [n.; ~t, ~n] work opportunity, job opening

arbetstillstånd (AT) [n.; ~et, ~] work permit

arbetsuppgift [n.; ~en, ~er] duties, tasks

arbetsutskott [n.; ~et, ~] working committee

arbetsvecka [n.; ~n, -veckor] work week

areal [n.; ~en, ~er] area

arena [n.; ~n, arenor] arena, stadium

arg [adj.; ~t, ~a] angry

Argentina [n.] Argentina

argentinsk [adj.; ~t, ~a] Argentinian, Argentine

argument [n.; ~et, ~] argument

arkadspel [n.; ~et, ~] arcade game [IT]

arkeologi [n.; ~n] archeology

arkitekt [n.; ~en, ~er] architect

arkitektur [n.; ~en, ~er] architecture

Arkitekturmuseet [n.] Museum of Architecture

arkiv [n.; ~et, ~] file [IT]

arkivera [v.; ~r, ~de, ~t] file away

arkivsystem [n.; ~et, ~] filing system [IT]

Arktis [n.] the Arctic

arktisk [adj.; ~t, ~a] Arctic

arm [n.; ~en, ~ar] arm

armband [n.; ~et, ~] bracelet

armbandsklocka [n.; ~n, -klockor] wristwatch, watch

armbandsur [n.; ~et, ~] wristwatch, watch

armbåge [n.; ~n, -bågar] elbow

armé [n.; ~n, ~er] army

Armémuseum [n.; -museet, -museer] Army Museum

Armenien [n.] Armenia

armenisk [adj.; ~t, ~a] Armenian

armeniska [n.; ~n] Armenian language

armhåla [n.; ~n, -hålor] armpit

armhävning [n.; ~en, ~ar] push-up

armkuddar [n.pl.] water wings

aromsmör [n.; ~et, ~] herb butter

arrangemang [n.; ~et, ~] arrangement; organization

arrangera [v.; ~r, ~de, ~t] arrange, organize

arrangör [n.; ~en, ~er] arranger, organizer

arrende [n.; ~t, ~n] tenancy; leasing; lease; rent

arresteringsorder [n.] arrest warrant

arsenal [n.; ~en, ~er] arsenal, armory

arsle [n.; ~t, ~; colloq.] ass, backside; jerk [colloq.], asshole [vul.]

art [n.; ~en, ~er] kind, type; species

artificiell intelligens [n.; ~en] artificial intelligence [IT]

artificiellt neuronnät [n.; ~et, ~] neural network [IT]

artig [adj.; ~t, ~a] polite, courteous

artikel [n.; ~n, artiklar] article; commodity

artikelnummer [n.; -numret, ~] part number, item number

artist [n.; ~en, ~er] artist, actor, musician

artnamn [n.; ~et, ~] species name

arton [num.] eighteen

artonde [num.] eighteenth

artonhundratalet (1800-talet) [n.] nineteenth century

artonhålsbana [n.; ~n, -banor] 18-hole golf course

artrit [n.; ~en] arthritis

artär [n.; ~en, ~er] artery

arv [n.; ~et, ~] inheritance, heritage, legacy

arvinge [n.; ~n, arvingar] heir/heiress

arvode [n.; ~t, ~n] remuneration

ASEA [abbrev: Allmänna svenska elektriska] General Swedish Electric Co.

asfaltbana [n.; ~n, -banor] asphalt court [sports]

asiatisk [adj.; ~t, ~a] Asian
Asien [n.] Asia
ask [n.; ~en, ~ar] box; ash [tree]
A-skatt [n.; ~en, ~er] tax withheld at source
askfat [n.; ~et, ~] ashtray
askkopp [n.; ~en, ~ar] ashtray
aspekt [n.; ~en, ~er] aspect
assembler [n.; ~n] assembler language, assembler code [IT]
assiett [n.; ~en, ~er] side plate
assistent [n.; ~en, ~er] assistant; clerical person
assistera [v.; ~r, ~de, ~t] assist, help; act as an assistant
associerad (med) [adj.; -rat, ~e] linked (to) [IT]
assurera [v.; ~r, ~de, ~t] insure
astma [n.; ~n] asthma
astmaanfall [n.; ~et, ~] asthma attack
astmatiker [n.; ~n, ~] asthmatic person
astronomisk [adj.; ~t, ~a] astronomical
asyl [n.; ~en, ~er] asylum
asylansökan [n.; ~, -ansökningar] application for asylum
asylkommittén [n.] Asylum Committee [non-governmental organization that helps asylum seekers]
asylpolitik [n.; ~en] asylum policy
asylrätt [n.; ~en] right of asylum
asylskäl [n.; ~et, ~] grounds for requesting asylum
asylsökande [n.; ~n, ~] asylum seeker
asynkron [adj.; ~t, ~a] asynchronous [IT]
AT [abbrev: arbetstillstånd; allmäntjänstgöring] work permit; intern, doctor in training
ateist [n.; ~en, ~er] atheist
ateljé [n.; ~n, ~er] workshop, studio
Aten [n.] Athens
Atlanten [n.] Atlantic Ocean
atlas [n.; ~en, ~er] atlas
AT-läkare [n.; ~n, ~] intern [doctor in training at a hospital]
atmosfär [n.; ~en, ~er] atmosphere
atom [n.; ~en, ~er] atom
atombomb [n.; ~en, ~er] atom bomb

ATP [abbrev: allmänstilläggspension] general supplementary pension
att¹ [infinitive marker, often pronounced: å] to
att² [conj.] that
attack [n.; ~en, ~er] attack
attackera [v.; ~r, ~de, ~t] attack
attityd [n.; ~en, ~er] attitude
attitydadverbial [n.; ~et, ~] sentence adverbial [gram]
attraktion [n.; ~en, ~er] attraction, event
attraktiv [adj.; ~t, ~a] attractive
attribut [~et, ~] feature, attribute
att-sats [n.; ~en, ~er] that-complement clause [gram; e.g. I saw that …]
AU [abbrev: Arbetsmarknadsutskottet] Committee on the Labor Market
aubergine [n.; ~n, ~r] eggplant
audiovisuell politik [n.; ~en] audiovisual policy [EU]
aug. [see: augusti]
augusti [n.] August
augustpriset [n.] August Prize [literary prize]
auktion [n.; ~en, ~er] auction, sale
auktorisera [v.; ~r, ~de, ~t] authorize
auktoriserad [adj.; -rat, ~e] authorized, official; ~ **revisor** certified accountant
auktoritet [n.; ~en, ~er] authority
aula [n.; ~n, aulor] lecture hall
Australien [n.] Australia
australiensisk [adj.; ~t, ~a] Australian
australisk [adj.; ~t, ~a] Australian
autentisering [n.; ~en, ~ar] authentication [IT]
autism [n.; ~en] autism
automat [n.; ~en, ~er] vending machine; payphone
automatisk [adj.; ~t, ~a] automatic; ~ **dörr** automatic door
automatlåda [n.; ~n, -lådor] automatic transmission
automatväxel [n.; ~n] automatic shift, automatic transmission

av [prep.] of, by, off, made of, out of; **pjäsen är ~ Strindberg** the play is by Strindberg

av. [see: **aveny**]

avancera [v.; ~r, ~de, ~t] advance; be promoted

avancerad [adj.; -rat, ~e] advanced

avbeställa [v.; -ställer, -ställde, -ställt] cancel; **~ en tid** cancel an appointment

avbetalning [n.; ~en, ~ar] installment (buying/plan)

avbildning [n.; ~en, ~ar] mapping [IT]

avbitartång [n.; ~en, -tänger] diagonal cutting pliers

avboka [v.; ~r, ~de, ~t] cancel (a reservation)

avbrottsfri kraft [n.; ~en, ~er] uninterruptible power supply (UPS) [IT]

avbryta [v.; -bryter, -bröt, -brutit] cancel, interrupt

avbytare [n.; ~n. ~] substitute player

avböja [v.; -böjer, -böjde, -böjt] decline

avd. [abbrev: avdelning] department

avdelning [n.; ~en, ~ar] department; ward

avdelningschef [n.; ~en, ~er] department head/manager

avdrag [n.; ~et, ~] deduction; reduction; proof sheet, impression (printing)

avel [n.; ~n] breeding; stock

aveny [n.; ~n, ~er] avenue

avfall [n.; ~et, ~] waste

avfallskvarn [n.; ~en, ~ar] garbage disposal

avfart [n.; ~en, ~er] exit [highway], turnoff

avföringsmedel [n.; -medlet, ~] laxative

avföringsprov [n.; ~et, ~] stool sample

avg. [see: **avgång, avgående**]

avgas [n.; ~en, ~er] exhaust

avgasrör [n.; ~et, ~] exhaust pipe

avgick [see: **avgå**]

avgift [n.; ~en, ~er] charge, fee

avgiftsfri [adj.; -fritt, ~a] free of charge

avgjorde/avgjort [see: **avgöra**]

avgå [v.; -går, -gick, -gått] leave, depart, resign; **~ med pension** retire on a pension

avgående [adj.] outgoing

avgång [n.; ~en, ~ar] departure

avgångsbetyg [n.; ~et, ~] high school diploma, school finishing certificate

avgångsbidrag [n.; ~et, ~] severance payment

avgångsexamen [n.; ~, ~] final examination

avgångshall [n.; ~en, ~ar] departure lounge

avgångstid [n.; ~en, ~er] departure time

avgångsvederlag [n.; ~et, ~] severance pay

avgöra [v.; -gör, -gjorde, -gjort] decide, determine

avgörande[1] [adj.] decisive

avgörande[2] [n.; ~t, ~n] decision

avhandling [n.; ~en, ~ar] thesis, dissertation; paper

AV-hjälpmedel [n.; -medlet, ~] audio-visual aid

avhämtning [n.; ~en, ~ar] collection, pick-up

avi [n.; ~n, ~er] notice, notification

avkastning [n.; ~en, ~ar] proceeds, return, yield

avkodare [n.; ~n, ~] decoder [IT]

avkodning [n.; ~en] decoding [IT]

avkoppling [n.; ~en, ~ar] relaxation

avkunna [v.; -kan, -kunde, -kunnat] **~ dom** pronounce a sentence/ judgement [court trial]

avled (v.past; see: **avlida**)

avleda [v.; -leder, -ledde, -lett] carry off; drain; turn away, divert; derive

avlida [v.; -lider, -led, -lidit] die, decease

avliden [adj.; -lidna] deceased, dead; late

avlopp [n.; ~et, ~] drain, sewer; sewage

avlusning [n.; ~en] debugging [IT]

avlägga [v.; -lägger, -lade, -lagt] make, render, carry out; **~ examen** pass an exam; **~ vittnesmål** give testimony avlägsen [adj.; -set, -sna] remote, distant

avmarkera [v.; ~r, ~de, ~t] deselect [IT]

avokado [n.; ~n, ~r] avocado

avresa [n.; ~n, -resor] departure

avresedatum [n.; ~et] date of departure

avrundning [n.; ~en, ~ar] rounding off [IT]

avråda [v.; -råder, -rådde, -rått] advise against

avrätta [v.; ~r, ~de, ~t] execute, put to death

avs. [see: avsändare]

avsade/avsagt [v.past; see: avsäga]

avse [v.; -ser, -såg, -sett] mean, intend

avsedd [adj.] intended

avseende [n.; ~t, ~n] respect, regard

avsevärd [adj.; -värt, ~a] considerable

avsikt [n.; ~en, ~er] intention

avsiktligen [adv.] intentionally, deliberately

avsiktskonjunktion [n.; ~en, ~er] purpose conjunction [gram]

avskaffa [v.; ~r, ~de, ~t] abolish

avsked [n.; ~et, ~] dismissal, discharge; resignation; parting, leave-taking

avskeda [v.; ~r, ~de, ~t] dismiss, discharge, fire

avskedsansökan [n.; ~, -ansökningar] (letter of) resignation

avsky[1] [n.; ~n] hate, loathing

avsky[2] [v.; ~r, ~dde, ~tt] hate, detest

avskärning [n.; ~en] truncation [IT]

avslag [n.; ~et, ~] refusal, rejection

avsluta [v.; ~r, ~de, ~t] complete, finish; close; exit

avslutad [adj.; -tat, ~e] completed

avslutningsdag [n.; ~en, ~ar] last day of school/sports season

avslutningsfras [n.; ~en, ~er] complimentary closing [letter]

AVS-länder [n.pl.] ACP countries [abbrev: African, Caribbean and Pacific countries] [EU; Cotounou Agreement]

avslöja [v.; ~r, ~de, ~t] expose, unmask, disclose, reveal

avsmak [n.; ~en] distaste, dislike

avsmaka [v.; ~r, ~de, ~t] taste, sample

avsmalnande väg [n.] road that narrows

avsnitt [n.; ~et, ~] section, part, chapter

avspark [n.; ~en, ~ar] kickoff

avstavning [n.; ~en] division into syllables; hyphenation

avstigning [n.; ~en, ~ar] getting off [transport]

avstjälpning [n.; ~en, ~ar] dumping

avstå [v.; -står, -stod, -stått] give up, relinquish; ~ från give up, abandon, forgo, renounce

avstånd [n.; ~et, ~] distance

avstängd [adj.; -stängt, ~a] closed off

avstängningskran [n.; ~en, ~ar] shutoff valve

avsåg [v.past; see: avse]

avsäga sig [v.; -säger, -sade, -sagt] renounce

avsändare [n.; ~n, ~] sender

avtagsväg [n.; ~en, ~ar] side road

avtal [n.; ~et, ~] agreement, convention; contract

avtala [v.; ~r, ~de, ~t] make an appointment

Avtalet om socialpolitik [n.] Social Policy Agreement [EU]

avtalsvillkor [n.pl.] terms of agreement

avundsjuk [adj.; ~t, ~a] envious

avundsvärd [adj.; -värt, ~a] enviable

avvakta [v.; ~r, ~de, ~t] wait for, await

avvaktande [adj.] waiting, expectant

avveckla [v.; ~r, ~de, ~t] phase out

avveckling [n.; ~en, ~ar] winding up; liquidation

avvisa [v.; ~r, ~de, ~t] turn away, refuse, reject, dismiss

avvisning [n.; ~en, ~ar] rejection, denial, refusal

avvärja [v.; -värjer, -värjde, -värjt] prevent

axel [n.; ~n, axlar] axle; shoulder

axelband [n.; ~et, ~] (shoulder) strap [dress]

axelbandslös [adj.; ~t, ~a] strapless
axelvadd [n.; ~en, ~ar] shoulder
  pad
axelväska [n.; ~n, -veskor] shoulder bag
ayatolla [n.; ~n] ayatollah
Azerbajdzjan [n.] Azerbaijan
azerbajdzjansk [adj.; ~t, ~a]
  Azeri, Azerbaijani
azerbajdzjanska [n.; ~n] Azeri
  language

B

babord [n.] port (side) [left side of ship]

baby [n.; ~n, ~ar] baby

babykläder [n.pl.] baby clothing

babylarm [n.; ~et, ~] baby monitor

babylift [n.; ~en, ~ar] portable baby crib

babysitter [n.; ~n, ~] bouncy chair [for babies]

babysäng [n.; ~en, ~ar] baby crib

bacill [n.; ~en, ~er] germ

bacillskräck [n.; ~en] fear of germs

back [n.; ~et, ~] tray, crate; back; reverse gear

backa [v.; ~r, ~de, ~t] go back; reverse, go backwards, back; ~ **upp** back up, support

backe [n.; ~et, ~] slope, hill

backen [n.] reverse gear

backhoppning [n.; ~en] ski jumping

backljus [n.; ~et, ~] backup lights

backspegel [n.; ~n, -speglar] rearview mirror

backväxel [n.; ~n] reverse gear

bacon [n.; ~et] bacon

bad[1] [n.; ~et, ~] bath

bad[2] [v.past; see: **be**]

bada [v.; ~r, ~de, ~t] bathe; go swimming

badbyxor [n.pl.] swimming trunks

baddräkt [n.; ~en, ~er] swimsuit

badförbud [n.; ~et, ~] no swimming

badhandduk [n.; ~en, ~ar] bath towel

badhus [n.; ~et, ~] public baths; beach hut

badhytt [n.; ~en, ~er] bathing cubicle, beach hut

badkappa [n.; ~n, -kappor] bathrobe, bathing wrap

badkar [n.; ~et, ~] bathtub

badkläder [n.pl.] swimsuit

badlakan [n.; ~et, ~] (large) bath towel

badminton [n.] badminton

badmintonboll [n.; ~en, ~ar] shuttlecock

badmössa [n.; ~n, -mössor] bathing cap

badort [n.; ~en, ~er] seaside resort

badplats [n.; ~en, ~er] swimming area, beach, pool

badrock [n.; ~en, ~ar] bathrobe

badrum [n.; ~et, ~] bathroom

badrumsmatta [n.; ~n, -mattor] bathroom mat

badrumsskåp [n.; ~et, ~] bathroom cabinet

badrumsvåg [n.; ~en, ~ar] bathroom scales [pl.]

badsandaler [n.pl.] flip-flops

badskor [n.pl.] beach shoes, shower shoes, bathing shoes

badstrand [n.; ~en, ~er] beach

badvakt [n.; ~en, ~er] lifeguard

bag [n.; ~en, ~ar] bag, carry-all, travel bag

bagage [n.; ~et, ~] baggage, luggage

bagagehall [n.; ~en, ~ar] baggage claim area

bagageincheckning [n.; ~en] baggage check-in

bagagekarusell [n.; ~en, ~er] baggage carousel

bagagekvitto [n.; ~t, ~n] baggage check

bagagekärra [n.; ~n, -kärror] baggage cart

bagagelucka [n.; ~n, -luckor] trunk [car]

bagageutlämning [n.; ~en] baggage claim area

bagageutrymme [n.; ~t] trunk [car]

bagagevagn [n.; ~en, ~ar] baggage cart

bagare [n.; ~n, ~] baker

Bagdad [n.] Baghdad

bageri [n.; ~et, ~er] bakery

bagge [n.; ~en, ~ar] ram [male sheep]

bajsa [v.; colloq.; ~r, ~de, ~t] poop [colloq.]

bak [adv./prep.] behind, at the back of

baka [v.; ~r, ~de, ~t] bake

bakad potatis [n.] baked potato

bakben [n.; ~et, ~] hind leg

bakdörr [n.; ~en, ~ar] back door, rear door

bakelse [n.; ~en, ~er] pastry, cake
bakficka [n.; ~n, -fickor] back pocket, hip pocket
bakform [n.; ~en, ~er] baking tin
bakgrund [n.; ~en] background
bakgrundsbelyst [adj.] backlit [IT]
bakhjul [n.; ~et, ~] rear wheel
bakhjulsdrift [n.; ~en] rear-wheel drive
bakifrån [adv.] from behind
bakljus [n.; ~et, ~] rear light, tail-light
baklucka [n.; ~n, -luckor] trunk lid [car]
baklänges [adv.] backwards
bakom [prep.] behind
bakplåt [n.; ~en, ~ar] baking sheet/tray
bakruta [n.; ~n, -rutor] rear window [car]
baksida [n.; ~n, -sidor] back, rear
bakslag [n.; ~et, ~] rebuff; setback
baksmälla [n.; ~n, -smällor] hangover
bakspegel [see: **backspegel**]
bakstega [n.; ~n, ~-stegor] back-space [IT]
bakstreck [n.; ~et, ~] backslash [IT]
baksäte [n.; ~t, ~n] backseat
bakterier [n.pl.] bacteria [pl.]
baktill [adv.] at/in/on the back, behind
baktrappa [n.; ~n, -trappor] back-stairs
bakugn [n.; ~et, ~] oven
bakverk [n.; ~et, ~] pastries
bakåt [adv.] backwards, toward the back
bakåtkompatibel [adj.; ~t, -bla] backward compatible [IT]
bal [n.; ~en, ~er] ball [dance]
balans [n.; ~en] balance
balansgång [n.; ~en] tightrope walk, balancing act
balett [n.; ~en, ~er] ballet
balettdansör/-dansös [n.; ~en, ~er] ballet dancer [m./f.]
Balkan [n.] Balkans
balkong [n.; ~en, ~er] balcony
ballong [n.; ~en, ~er] balloon
balsam [n.; ~en] balsam, balm; conditioner

baltikum [n.] Baltic area, Baltic states
baltisk [adj.; ~t, ~a] Baltic
bambu [n.; ~n] bamboo
bana [n.; ~n, banor] way, course, track, orbit, trajectory; line
banan [n.; ~en, ~er] banana
band[1] [n.; ~et, ~] band; binding, tie; tape
band[2] [v.past; see: **binda**]
bandbredd [n.; ~en, ~er] band-width [IT]
banderoll [n.; ~en, ~er] banner [IT]
bandspelare [n.; ~n, ~] tape recorder
bandy [n.; ~et] bandy [Swedish form of ice hockey]
bangolf [n.; ~en] miniature golf
banhoppning [n.] show jumping
bank [n.; ~en, ~er] bank
bankbok [n.; ~en, -böcker] bank-book
bankfack [n.; ~et, ~] bank box, safe deposit box
bankgiro [n.; ~t, ~n] bank giro transfer [bank transfer system for individuals and businesses]
Bankinspektionen [n.] Bank Inspection Board
bankkonto [n.; ~t, ~n] bank account
bankkort [n.; ~et, ~] bank card
banklån [n.; ~et, ~] bank loan
bankomat [n.; ~en, ~er] automated teller machine (ATM), cash machine
bankrutt [adj.; ~a] bankrupt
banktjänsteman [n.; -mannen, -män] bank clerk
bankutgifter [n.pl.] bank charges
banta [v.; ~r, ~de, ~t] reduce, slim; diet, try to lose weight
bantare [n.; ~n, ~] dieter
Banverket (BV) [n.] National Rail Administration
bar[1] [adj.; ~t, ~a] bare, naked
bar[2] [n.; ~en, ~er] bar [drinking establishment]
bar[3] [v.past; see: **bära**]
bara [adv.] only, just; ~ **bra** just fine; ~ **frakt** freight only
barack [n.; ~en, ~er] barracks [pl.]
barbacka [adv.] bareback
Barcelonaprocessen [n.] Barcelona

Process [EU, re: Mediterranean region]

bardisk [n.; ~en, ~ar] bar counter

barfota [adj.] barefoot

barmästare [n.; ~n, ~] head bartender

barn [n.; ~et, ~en] child

barnadödlighet [n.; ~en] infant mortality

barnavårdscentral (BVC) [n.; ~en, ~er] children's clinic

barnbarn [n.; ~et, ~en] grandchild

barnbassäng [n.; en, ~er] childrens' pool

barnbegränsning [n.; ~en] birth control, family planning

barnbidrag [n.; ~et, ~] family allowance [for children]

barnbiljett [n.; ~en, ~er] child's ticket

barnbok [n.; ~en, -böcker] children's book

barndaghem [n.; -hemmet, ~] day care center

barndom [n.; ~en] childhood

barnfamilj [n.; ~en, ~er] family with children

barnförbjuden [adj.; ~t, -bjudna] for adults only, not for children

barnhage [n.; ~n, -hagar] playpen

barnkalas [n.; ~et, ~] childrens' party

barnkammare [n.; ~n, ~] nursery

barnkläder [n.pl.] children's clothing

barnkoloni [n.; ~n, ~er] children's vacation camp

barnkärra [n.; ~n, -kärror] child's stroller

barnlift [n.; ~en, ~ar] children's lift [skiing]

barnlås [n.; ~et, ~] parental controls [IT]

barnläkare [n.; ~n, ~] pediatrician

barnmat [n.; ~en] baby food, children's food

barnmeny [n.; ~n, ~er] children's menu

barnmisshandel [n.; ~n] child abuse

barnmorska [n.; ~n, -skor] midwife

Barnombudsmannen (BO) [n.] Children's Ombudsman

barnomsorg [n.; ~en, ~er] child care

barnportion [n.; ~en, ~er] children's portion

barnprogram [n.; -programmet, ~] children's program

barnrabatt [n.; ~en, ~er] children's discount

barnsits [n.; ~en, ~ar] child's seat [bicycle, car]

barnsjukdom [n.; ~en, ~ar] childhood illness

barnsjukhus [n.; ~et, ~] children's hospital

barnsköterska [n.; ~n, -skor] nanny

barnslig [adj.; ~t, ~a] childish

barnsoldat [n.; ~en, ~er] child soldier

barnstol [n.; ~en, ~ar] child's seat, high chair

barnsäker [adj.; ~t, -säkra] safe for children, childproof; ~t lock childproof cap [medicine jar]

barnsäng [n.; ~en, ~ar] crib, child's bed; childbirth

barntillåten [adj.; -tillåtet, -tillåtna] suitable for children, for general audiences [film]

barnuppfostran [n.] raising of children, upbringing

barnvagn [n.; ~en, ~ar] baby carriage

barnvakt [n.; ~en, ~er] babysitter, babysitting; **sitta ~** babysit

barnvaktsservice [n.; ~n, ~] babysitting service

barnvänlig [adj.; ~t, ~a] suitable for children, child friendly

barock [adj.; ~t, ~a] baroque; odd

barr¹ [n.; ~en, ~en] parallel bars; bar [gold]

barr² [n.; ~et, ~] pine needle

barservering [n.; ~en, ~ar] snack bar

bas [n.; ~en, ~ar] base; basis; boss

BA-samtal [n.; ~et, ~] collect call, reverse-charge call

basera [v.; ~r, ~de, ~t] base

basfiol [n.; ~en, ~er] double bass

basilika [n.; ~n, -kor] basilica; basil

basketboll [n.; ~en, ~ar] basketball

bassäng [n.; ~en, ~er] pool

basta [adv.]: **och dermed ~!** and that's that!

bastu [n.; ~n, ~r] sauna

basun [n.; ~en, ~er] trombone

batteri [n.; ~et, ~er] battery

batteriladdare [n.; ~en, ~] battery charger

baud [n.] baud [IT]

B-avdrag [n.; ~et, ~] leave on partial pay

BB[1] [abbrev: barnbördsavdelning, barnbördshus, barnbördsklinik] maternity ward/hospital

B.B.[2] [abbrev: Bäste broder] My Dear Friend [formal greeting in letter between male friends/relatives]

be [v.; ber, bad, bett] ask, request; **~ en bön** say a prayer; **~ om** ask for; **~ om lov att** ask permission to

bearnaisesås [n.; ~en] béarnaise sauce [egg yolks and butter]

béchamelsås [n.; ~en] béchamel sauce [rich white sauce]

bedraga [v.; -drager, -drog, -dragit] deceive, cheat, swindle

bedriva [v.; -driver, -drev, -drivit] run, manage; pursue [studies]

bedrägeri [n.; ~et, ~er] fraud, swindle; illusion

bedöma [v.; -dömer, -dömde, -dömt] judge, assess; grade

bedömare [n.; ~n, ~] judge; marker, grader; commentator

bedömning [n.; ~en, ~ar] judging, judgment; estimate

bedövning [n.; ~en, ~ar] anesthesia, sedation; unconsciousness

befinna sig [v.; -finner, -fann, -funnit] be; feel; find oneself

befintlig [adj.; ~t, ~a] existing

befogenhet [n.; ~en, ~er] authority, powers

befogenhetsfördelning [n.; ~en] distribution of competences [EU]

befolkning [n.; ~en, ~ar] population

befordra [n.; ~r, ~de, ~t] promote; transport

befria [v.; ~r, ~de, ~t] liberate

befrielsekrig [n.; ~et, ~] war of liberation

befäl [n.; ~et, ~] command; officer

begagnad [adj.; -gagnat, -gagnade] used

bege sig [v.; -ger, -gav, -givit] go, proceed; start a journey

begick [v.past; see: begå]

begrava [v.; ~r, ~de, ~t] bury

begravning [n.; ~en, ~ar] burial, funeral

begravningsakt [n.; ~en, ~er] burial ceremony, funeral

begravningsbyrå [n.; ~n, ~ar] funeral home, undertakers

begrep [v.past; see: **begripa**]

begrepp [n.; ~et, ~] conception, notion, idea

begripa [v.; -griper, -grep, -gripit] understand

begränsa [v.; ~r, ~de, ~t] limit, restrict, bound

begränsad [adj; -sat, -sade] limited; **~ last** limited load

begränsning [n.; ~en, ~ar] limitation

begå [v.; -går, -gick, -gått] commit, perpetrate; celebrate

begåvad [adj.; -gåvat, -gåvade] talented

begåvning [n.; ~en, ~ar] intelligence, talent, gift

begär [n.; ~et, ~] desire, longing, craving

begära [v.; begär, begärde, begärt] request, apply for

begäran [n.] request

behandla [v.; ~r, ~de, ~t] treat; deal with; consider; handle; process

behandling [n.; ~en, ~ar] treatment

behandlingsrum [n.; -rummet, ~] treatment room

behov [n.; ~et, ~] need

behå [abbrev: bysthållare] bra

behålla [v.; -håller, -höll, -hållit] keep; **behåll växeln!** keep the change!

behärska [v.; ~r, ~de, ~t] rule over, control; master

behörig [adj.; ~t, ~a] qualified, competent; **~ myndighet** competent authority

behörighet [n.; ~en, ~er] qualification; authority; access rights [IT]

behöva [v.; -höver, -hövde, -hövt] need, require; have to, need to

behövas [v.; - hövs, - hövdes, - hövts] be needed

beige [adj.] beige

bekant [n.; ~a] acquaintance

bekantskap [n.; ~en, ~er] acquaintance

beklaga [v.; ~r, ~de, ~t] regret; **jag ~r** I'm sorry, I regret

bekostnad [n.; ~en, ~er] expense, cost

bekräfta [v.; ~r, ~de, ~t] validate, confirm

bekräftelse [n.; ~n, ~r] confirmation

bekväm [adj.; ~t, ~a] comfortable

bekvämligheter [n.pl.] facilities, amenities

bekymmer [n.; -kymret, ~] worry, problem

bekymra sig (för/om/över) [v.; ~r, ~de, ~t] worry (about)

bekymrad [adj.; -rat, ~e] worried

bekämpa [v.; ~r, ~de, ~t] fight, combat

Belgien [n.] Belgium

belgisk [adj.; ~t, ~a] Belgian

belopp [n.; ~et, ~] amount, sum

ben [n.; ~et, ~] leg; bone

bena¹ [n.; ~n] part [hair]

bena² [v.; ~r, ~de, ~t] bone [fish]; dissect; part [hair]

benbrott [n.; ~et, ~] fracture

bensin [n.; ~en] gasoline

bensindunk [n.; ~en, ~ar] jerry can [gasoline]

bensinmack [n.; ~en, ~ar] gas station

bensinmätare [n.; ~n, ~] gas gauge, fuel gauge

bensinpris [n.; ~et, ~er] price of gasoline

bensinpump [n.; ~en, ~ar] gas pump; fuel pump [car]

bensinstation [n.; ~en, ~er] gas station

bensinstopp: få ~ [v.] run out of gas

bensintank [n.; ~en, ~ar] fuel tank, gas tank

benvaxning [n.; ~en, ~ar] waxing [legs]

beredd [adj.; -rett, ~a] prepared, ready

beredskap [n.; ~en] preparedness

beredskapsarbete [n.; ~t, ~n] relief work

berg [n.; ~et, ~] mountain

bergbana [n.; ~n, -banor] mountain railway, cable railway, funicular

bergbestigning [n.; ~en] mountain climbing, rock climbing

bergsby [n.; ~n, ~ar] mountain village

bergskedja [n.; ~n, -kedjor] mountain chain, mountain range

bergsklättring [n.; ~en] rock climbing

bergspass [n.; ~et, ~] mountain pass

bergstopp [n.; ~en, ~ar] summit

berikad [adj.; -rikat, ~e] enriched

berlock [n.; ~en, ~er] charm [for bracelet]

bero (på) [v.; ~r, -rodde, -rott] depend (on), be due (to)

beroende på [prep.] subject to, depending on

berusad [adj.; -sat, ~e] intoxicated, drunk

beräkna [v.; ~r, ~de, ~t] compute, calculate; estimate

beräknad [adj.; -knat, ~e] estimated

beräkning [n.; ~en, ~ar] calculation

berätta [v.; ~r, ~de, ~t] tell

berättelse [n.; ~en, ~er] story

beröm [n.; ~et] praise, credit

berömd [adj.; -römt, ~a] famous

beröra [v.; -rör, -rörde, -rört] touch, come into contact with; affect

berörd [adj.; -rört, ~a] affected, touched; upset

beröva [v.; ~r, ~de, ~t] deprive

besegra [v.; ~r, ~de, ~t] beat, conquer, defeat

besiktiga [v.; ~r, ~de, ~t] inspect, examine, view

besiktning [n.; ~en, ~ar] viewing, inspection

besk [adj.; ~t, ~a] bitter; sharp

besked [n.; ~et, ~] letter, message; news

beskriva [v.; -skriver, -skrev, -skrivit] describe

beskrivning [n.; ~en, ~ar] description

beslag [n.; ~et, ~] fittings; seizure, confiscation

beslagta [v.; -tar, -tog, -tagit] confiscate

beslut [n.; ~et, ~] decision, resolution

besluta [v.; ~r, ~de, ~t] decide, determine; ~ **sig för** decide to, make up one's mind to

besluten [adj.; -slutet, -slutna] determined, resolved

beslutsfattare [n.; ~n, ~] decision maker

besläktad [adj.; ~tat, ~e] related

besparing [n.; ~en, ~ar] saving(s)

besparingsåtgärd [n.; ~en, ~er] economy measure

bestick [n.; ~et, ~] cutlery

bestod [v.past; see: **bestå**]

bestulen (på) [adj.; -stulet, -stulna] robbed (of)

bestyr [n.; ~et, ~] work, task; cares

bestå [v.; -står, -stod, -stått] last, remain; go through, endure; pay for; ~ **av** consist of

bestående [adj.] lasting

beståndsdel [n.; ~en, ~ar] component, part

beställa [v.; -ställer, -ställde, -ställt] order; reserve, book; ~ **tid** make an appointment

beställning [n.; ~en, ~ar] order, request; appointment

beställningssydd [adj.; -sytt, ~a] tailored, made to order

beställvideo [n.; -videon, -videor] video on demand (VOD) [IT]

bestämd [adj.; -stämt, -stämda] determined, settled, definite, intended; ~ **artikel** definite article; ~ **form** definite form [gram]

bestämma [v.; -stämmer, -stämde, -stämt] decide

bestämmelse [n.; ~n, ~r] provision; purpose

bestämning [n.; ~en, ~ar] modification, qualification [gram]

besvikelse [n.; ~n, ~r] disappointment, disillusionment

besviken [adj.; -sviket, -svikna] disappointed

besvär [n.; ~et, ~] trouble, bother

besvärande [adj.] troublesome, annoying

besvärlig [adj.; ~t, ~a] troublesome; difficult

besättning [n.; ~en, ~ar] crew; herd

besök [n.; ~et, ~] visit; **få/ha ~ av** have a visit from

besöka [v.; -söker, -sökte, -sökt] visit

besökare [n.; ~n, ~] visitor

besökstid [n.; ~en, ~er] visiting hour(s)

besökt [adj.; ~a] visited

bet. [abbrev: betydelse; betalt] meaning; paid

bet [v.past; see: **bita**]

betala [v.; ~r, ~de, ~t] pay; ~**s till** be payable to

betalkort [n.; ~et, ~] charge card

betalning [n.; ~en, ~ar] payment

betalningsbalans [n.; ~en, ~er] balance of payment

betalningsmedel [n.; -medlet, ~] means of payment

betalt [adj.] paid; **ta ~ för** charge a fee for

betal-tv [n.] pay-TV

betaversion [n.; ~en, ~er] beta version [IT]

bete[1] [n.; ~t, ~n] bait

bete[2] [n.; ~n, betar] tusk

beteckna [v.; ~r, ~de, ~t] represent, designate, denote

beteende [n.; ~t, ~n] behavior

betjäning [n.; ~en] service [shop, restaurant]

betjäningsavgift [n.; ~en, ~er] service charge

betona [v.; ~r, ~de, ~t] stress, emphasize

betonad stavelse [n.; ~n, ~r] stressed syllable

betoning [n.; ~en, ~ar] emphasis

betr. [abbrev: beträffande] regarding (re:), in reference to

betrakta [v.; ~r, ~de, ~t] regard

beträda [v.; -träder, -trädde, -trätt] enter, set foot on, walk on

beträffa [v.; ~r, ~de, ~t] concern; **vad ~r** with regard to

beträffande [prep.] concerning, with regard to

betsel [n.; betslet, ~] bridle

betsla [v.; ~r, ~de, ~t] bridle; ~ **av** unbridle

bett [v.past; see: **be**]

betungande [adj.] burdensome

betyda [v.; -tyder, -tydde, -tytt] mean

betydande [adj.] important, substantial, notable

betydelse [n.; ~n, ~r] importance, significance, meaning

betydelsefull [adj.; ~t, ~a] meaningful, significant

betydlig [adj.; ~t, ~a] considerable, substantial

betyg [n.; ~et, ~] grade, mark; certificate

betygsskala [n.; ~n, -skalor] grading scale

betänketid [n.; ~en, ~er] time allowed for (re)consideration

beundra [v.; ~r, ~de, ~t] admire

beundran [n.] admiration

beundransvärd [adj.; -värt, ~a] admirable

bevaka [v.; ~r, ~de, ~t] guard, watch, look after

bevakning [n.; ~en, ~ar] supervision

bevara [v.; ~r, ~de, ~t] preserve, keep

bevis [n.; ~et, ~] proof, evidence; certificate

bevisa [v.; ~r, ~de,~t] prove

beväpna [v.; ~r, ~de, ~t] arm, fortify

bg. [abbrev: bankgiro] bank giro [transfer system for individuals and businesses]

bh [abbrev.; pronounced: behå; see: **bysthållare**] bra

bi [n.; ~et, ~n] bee

bibel [n.; ~n, biblar] Bible

bibliotek [n.; ~et, ~] library

bibliotekarie [n.; ~n, ~er] librarian

bidra [v.; ~r, -drog, -dragit] contribute; assist; promote

bidrag [n.; ~et, ~] support, grant, allowance; contribution

bidraga [see: **bidra**]

bidragsförskott [n.; ~et, ~] advance payment of maintenance allowance

biff [n.; ~en, ~ar] beef; ~ **à la Lindström** fried beef patties; ~ **à la Rydberg** fried cubed beef and potatoes

biffkor [n.pl.] beef cattle

biffkött [n.; ~et, ~] beef

biffstek [n.; ~en, ~ar] steak

bifoga [v.; ~r, ~de, ~t] enclose, insert, attach

bifogad [adj.; -gat, ~e] attached, annexed

bigarråer [n.pl.] whiteheart cherries

bihåla [n.; ~n, -hålor] sinus

bihåleinflammation [n.; ~en] sinusitis

bijouterier [n.pl.] costume jewelry, fashion jewelry

bikini [n.; ~n, ~] bikini

bikt [n.; ~en, ~er] confession [church]

bikupa [n.; ~n, -kupor] beehive

bil [n.; ~en, ~ar] car; **med ~** by car

bil. [abbrev: bilaga] enclosure, attachment

bila [v.; ~r, ~de, ~t] drive, go by car

bilaga [n.; ~n, -lagor] enclosure, attachment, supplement

bilateral [adj.; ~t, ~a] bilateral

bilbarnstol [n.; ~en, ~ar] child seat for car

bilbesiktning [n.; ~en, ~ar] car inspection

bilbälte [n.; ~t, ~] safety belt

bild [n.; ~en, ~er] picture, image

bilda [v.; ~r, ~de, ~t] form; educate

bildbehandling [n.; ~en] image processing [IT]

bildfil [n.; ~en, ~ar] image file [IT]

bildhantering [n.; ~en] image processing, imaging [IT]

bildhuggare [n.; ~n, ~] sculptor

bildläsare [n.; ~n, ~] scanner [IT]

bildpunkt [n.; ~en, ~er] pixel [IT]

bildredigerare [n.; ~n, ~] photo editor, image editor [IT]

bildskärm [n.; ~en, ~ar] monitor, display, video display unit [IT]

bildspel [n.; ~et,~] slide show, film strip [IT]

bildtext [n.; ~en, ~er] caption

bildäck [n.; ~et, ~] tire; car deck [ferry]

bildörr [n.; ~en, ~ar] car door
bilfärja [n.; ~n, -färjor] automobile ferry
bilförsäkring [n.; ~en] car insurance
bilism [n.; ~en] driving, use of cars
bilist [n.; ~en, ~ar] motorist
biljard [n.; ~en, ~er] billiards
biljardkö [n.; ~n, ~er] billiards cue
biljett [n.; ~en, ~er] ticket
biljettagentur [n.; ~en, ~er] ticket agency
biljettautomat [n.; ~en, ~er] ticket-vending machine
biljettdisk [n.; ~en, ~ar] ticket counter
biljetthäfte [n.; ~t, ~n] booklet of tickets
biljettinnehavare [n.; ~en, ~] ticket holder
biljettkassa [n.; ~n, -kassor] ticket office
biljettkontor [n.; ~et, ~] box office, ticket office
biljettkontrollant [n.; ~en, ~er] ticket checker
biljettlucka [n.; ~n, -luckor] ticket window
biljettmaskin [n.; ~en, ~er] ticket machine
biljettpris [n.; ~et, ~er] cost of a ticket, fare
biljon [n.; ~en, ~er] trillion [million millions]
bilkarta [n.; ~n, -kartor] road map
bilkörning [n.; ~en] driving
billarm [n.; ~et, ~] car alarm
billig [adj.; ~t, ~a] cheap, inexpensive; ~ **hyra** low rent
billigare [adj.comp.] cheaper
bilmekaniker [n.; ~n, ~] auto mechanic
bilmärke [n.; ~t, ~n] make of car
bilnyckel [n.; ~n, nycklar] car key
bilolycka [n.; ~n, -olyckor] automobile accident
bilprovning [n.; ~en, ~ar] automobile inspection; **AB Svensk Bilprovning** Swedish Motor Vehicle Inspection Co.
bilradio [n.; ~n, ~r] car radio
bilrally [n.; ~t, ~n] motor rally

bilregistreringsnummer [n.; -nummret, ~] car registration number
bilregistreringspapper [n.; ~et, ~] vehicle registration document
bilreparation [n.; ~en, ~er] car repair
bilruta [n.; ~n, -rutor] car window
bilskatt [n.; ~en] automobile tax
bilskola [n.; ~n, -skolor] driving school
biltur [n.; ~en, ~er] drive
biltvätt [n.; ~en, ~ar] car wash
biltåg [n.; ~et, ~] auto train, motor-rail
biltävling [n.; ~en, ~ar] car race
biluthyrning [n.; ~en] car rental
bilverkstad [n.; ~en, -städer] garage
binda¹ [n.; ~n, ~or] sanitary napkin
binda² [v.; binder, band, bundit] bind, tie
bindestreck [n.; ~et, ~] hyphen [IT]
bindeverb [n.; ~et, ~] linking verb, copula [gram]
B-inkomst [n.; ~en, ~er] unearned income
binär [adj.; ~t, ~a] binary [IT]; ~**a tal** binary numbers [IT]
bio [n.; ~n, ~] movies, movie theater
biograf [n.; ~en, ~er] movie theater
biolog [n.; ~en, ~er] biologist
biologi [n.; ~n] biology
biologisk [adj.; ~t, ~a] biological; ~**t genus** biological gender [gram]
biorytm [n.; ~en] biorhythm
biovagn [n.; ~en, ~ar] lounge car on train where movies are shown
bisats [n.; ~en, ~er] subordinate clause [gram]
bisatsordföljd [n.; ~en, ~er] word order in subordinate clauses [gram]
bisatstyp [n.; ~en, ~er] subordinate clause type [gram]
bisexuell [adj.; ~t, ~a] bisexual
biskop [n.; ~en, ~er] bishop
biskopssäte [n.; ~t, ~n] bishopric
bistånd [n.; ~et, ~] aid
biståndsminister [n.; ~n] Minister for Foreign Aid
bit [n.; ~en, ~ar] piece, bit, part; **i** ~**ar** diced, cubed, in chunks

bita [v.; biter, bet, bitit] bite
bitkarta [n.; ~n, -kartor] bitmap [IT]
bitkartafont [n.; ~en, ~er] bit-mapped font [IT]
bitmappad [adj.; -pat, ~e] bitmapped [IT]
biträdande [n.; ~n, ~] deputy
biträde [n.; ~t, ~n] assistance; assistant, shop assistant
bitsocker [n.; -sockret] lump sugar
bitter [adj.; ~t, bittra] bitter; acute, severe
bitterhet [n.; ~en] bitterness; embitterment
bitti [adv.] early; **i morgon ~** tomorrow morning (early)
biverkning [n.; ~en, ~ar] side effect
biväg [n.; ~en, ~ar] secondary road
bjuda [v.; bjuder, bjöd, bjudit] invite, offer; ~ **hem** invite home; ~ **in** invite in; ~ **någon på** invite someone for, offer
bjuden [adj.; bjudet, bjudna] invited
bjälke [n.; ~n, bjälkar] beam
bjöd [v.past; see: **bjuda**]
björk [n.; ~en, ~ar] birch
björkkvist [n.; ~en, ~ar] birch branch
björkris [n.; ~et, ~] birch twig
björn [n.; ~en, ~ar] bear
björnbär [n.; ~et, ~] blackberry
björnstek [n.; ~en, ~ar] roast bear
BK [abbrev: bollklubb] ball club, sports club
bl a [abbrev: bland annat] among other things, among others, inter alia
blad [n.; ~et, ~] leaf; page, piece of paper
bladspenat [n.; ~en, ~er] spinach
bland [prep.] among; ~ **annat (bl a)** among other things; ~ **andra** among others
blanda [v.; ~r, ~de, ~t] mix, blend; shuffle [cards]
blandad [adj.; -dat, ~e] assorted, mixed; ~ **sallad** mixed salad
blandfärs [n.; ~en, ~er] ground beef and pork
blandning [n.; ~en, ~ar] mixture, blend
blank [adj.; ~t, ~a] bright, shiny,

glossy [photo]; ~**t spel** love game [tennis]
blankett [n.; ~en, ~er] form, application form
blazer [n.; ~n, blazrar] blazer
blek [adj.; ~t, ~a] pale
bleka [v.; bleker, blekte, blekt] bleach; fade
blekmedel [n.; -medlet, ~] bleach
blekning [n.; ~en, ~ar] bleaching
blemma [n.; ~n, blemmor] pimple
blev [v.past; see: **bli**]
bli [v.; blir, blev, blivit] become, be; ~ **av med** lose; get rid of; ~ **kär i** fall in love with
blick [n.; ~en, ~ar] look, glance
blind [adj.; blint, ~a] blind; ~ **person** blind person
blindtarm [n.; ~en] appendix
blindtarmsinflammation [n.; ~en] appendicitis
blinkande [adj.] blinking, flashing
blinker [n.; ~n, blinkrar] blinker, indicator
blivande [adj.] future, prospective; expecting (a baby)
blixt [n.; ~en, ~ar] lightning; flash
blixtfotografering [n.; ~en] flash photography
blixtlås [n.; ~et, ~] zipper
block [n.; ~et, ~] block; group, coalition; writing pad, notebook, drawing pad
blockera [v.; ~r, ~de, ~t] block
blockeringsattack [n.; ~en, ~er] denial-of-service attack [IT]
blockflöjt [n.; ~en, ~er] recorder [musical instrument]
blod [n.; ~et] blood
blodbrist [n.; ~en] anemia
blodförgiftning [n.; ~en, ~ar] blood poisoning
blodgrupp [n.; ~en, ~er] blood type
blodig [adj.; ~t, ~a] bloody; rare [less cooked]
blodkorv [n.; ~en, ~ar] black pudding, blood sausage
blodomlopp [n.; ~et] blood circulation
blodpropp [n.; ~en, ~ar] blood clot
blodprov [n.; ~et, ~er] blood test

blodpudding [n.; ~en, ~ar] black pudding, blood sausage

blodtransfusion [n.; ~en, ~er] blood transfusion

blodtryck [n.; ~et, ~] blood pressure; **högt/lågt** ~ high/low blood pressure

blodtrycksmätare [n.; ~n, ~] blood pressure gauge

blogg [n.] blog [web log] [IT]

blom [n.; blommen, blommar] blossom; bloom

blombukett [n.; ~en, ~er] flower bouquet, bunch of flowers

blomkruka [n.; ~n, -krukor] flower pot

blomkål [n.; ~en] cauliflower

blomlåda [n.; ~n, -lådor] flowerbox

blomma [n.; ~n, blommor] flower

blomsteraffär [n.; ~en, ~er] florist

blomsterhandel [n.; ~n, ~] florist

blomsterkrans [n.; ~en, ~ar] flower garland

blomsterlök [n.; ~en, ~ar] flower bulb

blomsterrabatt [n.; ~en, ~er] flower bed

blomsterutställning [n.; ~en, ~ar] flower show

blomstra [v.; ~r, ~de, ~t] flower

blond [adj.; blont, ~a] blond

blott [adv.] merely, only

blotta [adj.] mere, bare

blues [n.; ~en] blues

bluffwebbplats [n.; ~en, ~er] spoof web site [IT]

bluffvirus [n.; ~et, ~] hoax virus [IT]

blus [n.; ~en, ~ar] blouse

bly [n.; ~et] lead

blyad [adj.; blyat, ~a] leaded

blybensin [n.; ~en, ~er] leaded gasoline

blyertspenna [n.; ~n, -pennor] pencil

blyfri [adj.; -fritt, ~a] unleaded; ~ **bensin** unleaded gasoline

blyg [adj.; ~t, ~a] shy, bashful

blå [adj.; ~tt, ~a] blue; ~**a vindruvor** black grapes

blåbär [n.; ~et, ~] blueberry, bilberry

blåklint [n.; ~en, ~ar] cornflower, bachelor's button

blåklocka [n.; ~n, -klockor] bluebell

blåmusslor [n.pl.] mussels

blåmärke [n.; ~t, ~n] bruise

blåsa¹ [n.; ~n, blåsor] blister; bladder; bubble

blåsa² [v.; blåser, blåste, blåst] blow; be windy

blåsig [adj.; ~t, ~a] windy

blåsippa [n.; ~n, -sippor] blue anemone

blåst [n.; ~en, ~ar] strong wind

blåtira [n.; ~n, -tiror] black eye

blått [see: **blå**]

blåvit [adj.; ~t, ~a] bluish white

bläck [n.; ~et, ~] ink

bläckfisk [n.; ~en, ~ar] octopus

bläckpatron [n.; ~en, ~er] ink cartridge [IT]

bläckstråleskrivare [n.; ~n, ~] inkjet printer [IT]

bläddra [v.; ~r, ~de, ~t] leaf through, browse

bläddrare [n.; ~n, ~] browser [IT]

bländare [n.; ~n, ~] aperture, diaphragm [camera lens]

blöda [v.; blöder, blödde, blött] bleed, lose blood

blödning [n.; ~en, ~ar] bleeding

blöja [n.; ~n, blöjor] diaper

blötsnö [n.; ~n] wet snow; slush

BNP [abbrev: bruttonationalprodukt] gross national product (GNP)

bo [v.; bor, bodde, bott] live

boardingkort [n.; ~et, ~] boarding pass

bob [n.; bobben, bobbar] bobsled

bock [n.; ~en, ~ar] billy goat; buck; mistake; checkmark [IT]

boende [adj.] resident

bofink [n.; ~en, ~ar] chaffinch

bog [n.; ~en, ~ar] shoulder [meat cut]

bogsera [v.; ~r, ~de, ~t] tow

bogserlina [n.; ~n, -linor] tow line

bogserskärmflygning [n.; ~en] parasailing

bohag [n.; ~et, ~] household goods/ furnishings

boj [n.; ~en, ~ar] buoy
bojkotta [v.; ~r, ~de, ~t] boycott
bok [n.; ~en, böcker] book; beech [tree]
boka [v.; ~r, ~de, ~t] book, reserve; ~ **en tid** make an appointment; ~ **om** change a reservation, change a booking
bokdator [n.; ~n, ~er] e-book reader [IT]
bokförlag [n.; ~et, ~] book publisher
bokhandel [n.; ~n, ~] bookstore
bokhylla [n.; ~n, -hyllor] bookshelf
bokmärke [n.; ~t, ~n] bookmark [IT]
bokmässa [n.; ~n, -mässor] book fair
bokning [n.; ~en, ~ar] reservation
bokstav [n.; ~en, -stäver] letter [alphabet]
bokstavera [v.; ~r, ~de, ~t] spell out
bokstavlig [adj.; ~t, ~a] literal
bokstavligen [adv.] literally
bolag [n.; ~et, ~] company
Bolagsverket [n.] Company Registration Office
boll [n.; ~en, ~ar] ball
bolla [v.; ~r, ~de, ~t] play ball
bollspel [n.; ~et, ~] ball game; ball-playing
bom [n.; bommen, bommar] gate, boom [RR crossing]
bomb [n.; ~en, ~er] bomb; bullet [word-processing]
bomba [v.; ~r, ~de, ~t] bomb
bomull [n.; ~en] cotton
bomullsfröolja [n.; ~n] cottonseed oil
bomullsspinne [n.; ~n, pinnar] cotton swab
bomullstopp [n.; ~en, ~ar] cotton swab
bomullsvadd [n.; ~en] absorbent cotton, cotton wool, cotton wadding
bondbönor [n.pl.] broad beans
bonde [n.; ~n, bönder] farmer; pawn [chess]
bondgård [n.; ~en, ~ar] farm
bondstuga [n.; ~n, -stugor] farmer's cottage
bonus [n.; ~en] bonus

boolesk logik [n.] Boolean logic [IT]
bord [n.; ~et, ~] table; board; **om** ~ on board; **sätta sig till** ~**s** sit down to lunch/dinner
borde [v.past; see: **böra**]
bordsdator [n.; ~n, ~er] desktop computer [IT]
bordsduk [n.; ~en, ~ar] tablecloth
bordservering [n.; ~en] table service
bordslampa [n.; ~n, -lampor] table lamp
bordsvin [n.; ~et, ~er] table wine
bordtennis [n.; ~en] table tennis
borg [n.; ~en, ~ar] fortress, castle
borgare [n.; ~n, ~] townsperson; non-socialist
borgarråd [n.; ~et, ~] city commissioner
borgen [n.] security; bail
borgensman [n.; -mannen, -män] guarantor, (bail) bondsman, surety
borgerlig [adj.; ~t, ~a] civil; middle-class; non-socialist; ~ **vigsel** civil marriage; ~**t block** center-right coalition
borgmästare [n.; ~n, ~] mayor
borr [n.; ~en, ~ar] drill; bit
borra [v.; ~r, ~de, ~t] drill
borsta [v.; ~r, ~de, ~t] brush; ~ **håret** brush one's hair
borste [n.; ~n, borstar] brush
bort¹ [adv.] away [motion]; **komma** ~ be missing; ~ **med händerna!** hands off!
bort² [v.past; see: **böra**]
borta [adv.] away [location], not here; missing, **mitt bagage är** ~ my baggage is missing; **där** ~ over there
bortamatch [n.; ~en, ~ar] away game, game not on home field
bortaplan [n.; ~et] sports field not your own, not the home field
bortifrån [adv.] from far away
bortkopplad [adj.; -lat, ~e] remote [IT]
bortom [prep.] beyond, past
bortsett från [prep./adv.] aside from, besides the fact that

borttagen [adj.; -get, -gna] deleted [IT]

borttagning [n.; ~en, ~ar] deletion, removal

bortåt [prep.] in the direction of, towards; along

bosatt (i) [adj.; ~a] resident (of), residing (in)

Bosnien [n.] Bosnia

Bosnien-Hercegovina [n.] Bosnia-Herzegovina

bosnisk [adj.; ~t, ~a] Bosnian

Bosporen [n.] Bosporus

bostad [n.; ~en, -städer] housing, accommodation

bostadsadress [n.; ~en, ~er] (residence) address

bostadsannons [n. ~en, ~er] housing advertisement

bostadsbidrag [n.; ~et, ~] housing allowance

bostadsbrist [n.; ~en] housing allowance

bostadsbolag [n.; ~et, ~] real estate agency

bostadsförmedling [n.; ~en, ~ar] housing agency, housing authority

bostadskvarter [n.; ~et, ~] residential area

bostadsområde [n.; ~et, ~en] housing area, housing district

bostadsort [n.; ~en, ~er] place of residence, home town

bostadsrättslägenhet [n.; ~en, ~er] cooperative apartment, tenant-owned apartment

bostadstillägg [n.; ~et, ~] housing subsidy

Bostadsutskottet [n.] Committee on Housing

bot [n.; ~en, böter] remedy, cure; penance; fine [punishment]

bota [v.; ~r, ~de, ~t] cure; remedy

botanik [n.; ~en] botany

botanisk [adj.; ~t, ~a] botanical; ~ **trädgård** botanical garden

botemedel [n.; -medlet, ~] remedy, cure

bott [v.past; see: **bo**]

botten [n.; bottnen, bottnar] bottom; awful

Bottenhavet [n.] Gulf of Bothnia [southern part]

bottenvåning [n.; ~en, ~ar] ground floor

Bottniska viken [n.] Gulf of Bothnia

bouquet garni [n.] mixed herbs

bourgognevin [n.; ~et, ~er] Burgundy wine

boutredningsman [n.; -mannen, -män] estate administrator [inheritance]

Boverket [n.] National Board of Housing, Building and Planning

bowlingbana [n.; ~n, -banor] bowling alley

box [n.; ~en, ~er] box, post office box

boxare [n.; ~n, ~] boxer [sportsman]

boxning [n.; ~en, ~ar] boxing

boxningsmatch [n.; ~en, ~er] boxing match

bra [adv./adj.indecl.; comp: bättre, bäst] good, well, fine; **det går ~** that's fine; I'm fine; **ha det ~!** take it easy!

bragt [v.past; see: **bringa**]

brand [n.; ~en, bränder] fire

brandbil [n.; ~en, ~ar] fire engine

branddörr [n.; ~en, ~ar] fire door

brandfara [n.; ~n] fire emergency; **vid ~** in the event of fire

brandförsäkring [n.; ~en, ~ar] fire insurance

brandgul [adj.; ~t, ~a] orange [color]

brandkår [n.; ~en, ~er] fire department

brandman [n.; -mannen, -män] fireman

brandredskap [n.; ~et,~] fire-fighting equipment

brandsläckare [n.; ~n, ~] fire extinguisher

brandstation [n.; ~en, ~er] fire station

brandutgång [n.; ~en, ~er] fire exit

brandvarnare [n.; ~n, ~] (automatic) fire alarm

brandvägg [n.; ~en, ~ar] firewall [IT]

brann [v.past; see: **brinna**]

bransch [n.; ~en, ~er] branch, line of business, trade

brant[1] [adj.; ~a] steep; ~ **backe** steep hill, steep descent

brant[2] [n.; ~en, ~er] precipice

brasiliansk [adj.; ~t, ~a] Brazilian

Brasilien [n.] Brazil

brast [v.past; see: **brista**]

braxen [n.] bream, sea bream [fish]

bred [adj.; brett, ~a] broad, wide

breda [v.; breder, bredde, brett] spread; ~ **en smörgås** make a sandwich

bredband [n.; ~et] broadband [IT]

bredbandsmodem [n.; ~et, ~] broadband modem [IT]

bredbandsnät [n.; ~et, ~] broadband network [IT]

bredbandsuppkoppling [n.; ~en, ~ar] broadband connection [IT]

bredd [n.; ~en, ~er] breadth, width

breddare [adj. comp.] wider

breddgrad [n.; ~en, ~er] latitude

bredd/höjdförhållande [n.; ~t, ~n] aspect ratio [IT]

bredvid [prep.] next to, beside

brett [see: **bred, breda**]

brev [n.; ~et, ~] letter [mail]

brevbärare [n.; ~n, ~] mailman

brevfack [n.; ~et, ~] letter slot, letter box

brevhuvud [n.; ~et, ~] letterhead

brevkorg [n.; ~en, ~ar] in-tray, out-tray

brevlåda [n.; ~n,-lådor] mail box

brevpapper [n.; ~et, ~] writing paper, note paper

brevvän [n.; -vännen, -vänner] pen pal

brevväxla [v.; ~r, ~de, ~t] correspond [by letter]

bricka [n.; ~n, brickor] tray; place mat; tag, token, washer

bridge [n.; ~en] bridge [card game]

bringa [v.; bringer, bragte, bragt] bring

brinna [v.; brinner, brann, brunnit] burn, blaze

brinnande [adj.] burning; ardent, fervent

brist [n.; ~en, ~er] lack, shortage; deficit, defect; **i ~ på** for want of, lacking

brista [v.; brister, brast, brustit] burst; lack

bristande [adj.] deficient, inadequate, insufficient; defective

brits [n.; ~en, ~ar] couch, bunk

britt [n.; ~en, ~er] Briton

brittisk [adj.; ~t, ~a] Brittish

bro [n.; ~n, ~ar] bridge

broccoli [n.; ~n] broccoli

broder [see: **bror**]

brodera [v.; ~r, ~de, ~t] embroider

broderi [n.; ~et, ~er] embroidery

broiler [n.; ~n, broilrar] broiler [chicken for broiling]

broms [n.; ~en, ~ar] brake

bromsa [v.; ~r, ~de, ~t] brake

bromsbelägg [n.; ~et, ~] brake pads

bromskrafter [n.pl.] brake horsepower [engineering term]

bromsljus [n.; ~et, ~] brakelight

bromspedal [n.; ~en] brake pedal

bromsvätska [n.; ~n] brake fluid

bronker [n.pl.] bronchial tubes

bronkit [n.; ~en, ~er] bronchitis

brons [n.; ~en] bronze

bronsåldern [n.] bronze age

bror [n.; brodern, bröder] brother

brorsa [n.; colloq.] brother

brorsdotter [n.; ~n, -döttrar] niece

brorson [n.; ~en, -söner] nephew

brosch [n.; ~en, ~er] brooch

broschyr [n.; ~en, ~er] pamphlet

brott [n.; ~et, ~] crime; **begå ett ~** commit a crime

brottare [n.; ~n, ~] wrestler

brottmål [n.; ~et, ~] criminal case

brottning [n.; ~en] wrestling

Brottsförebyggande rådet (BRÅ) [n.] National Council for Crime Prevention

brottslig [adj.; ~t, ~a] criminal; guilty

brottslighet [n.; ~en] criminality

brottsling [n.; ~en, ~ar] criminal

Brottsoffermyndigheten [n.] Crime Victim Compensation and Support Authority

brottsplats [n.; ~en, ~er] scene of the crime

brud [n.; ~en, ~ar] bride

brudgum [n.; -gummen, -gummar] bridegroom

brudklänning [n.; ~en, ~er] wedding dress

brudpar [n.; ~et, ~] bridal couple

bruk [n.; ~et, ~] use

bruka [v.; ~r, ~de, ~t] be in the habit of, do something usually; ~de vara used to be

bruksanvisning [n.; ~en, ~ar] user's instructions

brun [adj.; ~t, ~a] brown; brunette; ~a bönor baked brown beans; ~t kuvert Manila envelope

brunett [n.; ~en, ~er] brunette

brunn [n.; ~en, ~ar] well

brunnit [v.past; see: **brinna**]

brus [n.; ~et] roar, noise

brustit [v.past; see: **brista**]

bruten [adj.; brutet, brutna] broken, fractured; cut off

brutit [v.past; see: **bryta**]

brutto- [prefix] gross

bruttoinkomst [n.; ~en, ~er] gross income

bruttonationalprodukt (BNP) [n.; ~en, ~er] gross national product (GNP)

bry sig om [v.; bryr, brydde, brytt] care about, bother about

brygga¹ [n.; ~n, bryggor] jetty, pier; bridge [ship]

brygga² [v.; brygger, brygde, brygt] brew; ~ kaffe make coffee

brylépudding [n.; ~en, ~ar] crème caramel

bryna [v.; bryner, brynte, brynt] brown

brynt [adj.; ~a] sautéed, browned

Bryssel [n.] Brussels

brysselkål [n.; ~en, ~er] Brussels sprouts

bryta [v.; bryter, bröt, brutit] break, break off, switch off; open [letter]; break [law]

brytare [n.; ~n, ~] toggle switch [IT]

brytarspetsar [n.pl.] points [car engine]

brytbönor [n.pl.] string beans, green beans

brytpunkt [n.; ~en, ~er] breakpoint [IT]

bråck [n.; ~et, ~] hernia

bråddjup [n.; ~et, ~] precipice

brådskande [adj.] urgent

bråk [n.; ~et, ~] fraction; noise; trouble

bråka [v.; ~r, ~de, ~t] fight, argue

bråttom [adv.]: ha ~ be in a hurry; vara ~ be urgent

bräcka [v.; bräcker, bräckte, bräckt] break, crack; fry

bräckkorv [n.; ~en, ~ar] smoked pork sausage

brädsegling [n.; ~en] windsurfing

brädspel [n.; ~et] backgammon

bränder [n.pl.; see: **brand**]

bränna [v.; bränner, brände, bränt] burn [trans.]; distill; ~ sig get burned

brännare [n.; ~n, ~] burner (CD, DVD) [IT]

bränning [n.; ~en, ~ar] breaker [surf]

brännskada [n.; ~n, -skador] burn

brännsår [n.; ~et, ~] burn

brännvin [n.; ~et] schnapps, hard liquor

bränsle [n.; ~t, ~n] fuel

bräserad [adj.; -rat, ~e] broiled, braised

bröd [n.; ~et, ~] bread

bröder [n.pl.; see: **bror**]

brödkniv [n.; ~en, ~ar] bread knife

brödrost [n.; ~en, ~ar] toaster

brödskiva [n.; ~n, -skivor] slice of bread

brödsmulor [n.pl.] bread crumbs

bröllop [n.; ~et, ~] wedding

bröllopsdag [n.; ~en, ~ar] wedding day

bröllopsresa [n.; ~n, -resor] honeymoon trip

bröst [n.; ~et, ~] breast, chest

bröstficka [n.; ~n, -fickor] breast pocket

bröstmjölk [n.; ~en] breast milk

bröstmjölksersättning [n.; ~en] infant formula

bröstvårta [n.; ~n, -vårtor] nipple

bröt [v.past; see: **bryta**]

BSE [abbrev: galna ko-sjukan] mad
cow disease (BSE)

B-skatt [n.;~en, ~er] tax not withheld at the source

bubbelbad [n.; ~et, ~] jacuzzi;
bubble bath

buckla [n.; ~n, bucklor] dent

bud [n.; ~et, ~] command; offer, bid;
message; messenger; availability,
disposal

budbil [n.; ~en, ~ar] delivery van

buddist [n.; ~en, ~er] Buddhist

budget [n.; ~en, ~er] budget

budgetplanen [n.] financial pers-
pectives [EU]

budgetproposition [n.; ~en, ~er]
budget bill

budgetunderskott [n.; ~et, ~]
budget deficit

budgetutgifter [n.pl.] budget
expenditures

budgetår [n.; ~et, ~] budget year

budskap [n.; ~et, ~] message,
announcement

buffé [n.; ~n, ~er] buffet, snack bar

buffert [n.; ~en, ~ar] buffer [IT]

buk [n.; ~en, ~ar] belly, abdomen

Bukarest [n.] Bucharest

bukett [n.; ~en, ~er] bunch of
flowers, bouquet

buksmärta [n.; ~n, -smärtor] abdominal pain

Bulgarien [n.] Bulgaria

bulgarisk [adj.; ~t, ~a] Bulgarian

bulgariska [n.; ~n] Bulgarian
language

buljong [n.; ~en, ~er] consommé,
broth

bulle [n.; ~n, bullar] bun, roll

buller [n.; bullret, ~] noise

bullsam [adj.; ~t, ~a] noisy

bult [n.; ~en, ~ar] bolt, pin

bundit [v.past; see: binda]

bungy-hopp [n.; ~et] bungee-
jumping

bunke [n.; ~n, bunkar] bowl, dish;
pan

bunt [n.; ~en, buntar] bunch

bur [n.; ~en, ~ar] cage

burit [v.past; see: bära]

burk [n.; ~en, burkar] can, jar

burköl [n.; ~et] canned beer

Burma [n.] Burma, Myanmar

burmansk [adj.; ~t, ~a] Burmese

burmanska [n.; ~n] Burmese
language

bus: leva ~ [v.] be a nuisance, be
noisy

busa [v.; ~r, ~de, ~t] make trouble,
be noisy

buske [n.; ~n, buskar] bush

buss [n.; ~en, bussar] bus

bussavgift [n.; ~en, ~er] bus fare

bussbiljett [n.; ~en, ~er] bus ticket

busschaufför [n.; ~en, ~er] bus
driver

bussfil [n.; ~en, ~er] bus lane

bussförare [n.; ~n, ~] bus driver

busshållplats [n.; ~en, ~er] bus
stop

bussig [adj.; ~t, ~a] kind

busskö [n.; ~n, ~ar] line waiting for
the bus

busslinje [n.; ~n, ~r] bus route

busstation [n.; ~en, ~er] bus station

bussterminal [n.; ~en, ~er] bus
station, bus terminal

bussväg [n.; ~en, ~ar] bus route

butangas [n.; ~en] butane gas

butik [n.; ~en, ~er] shop

BVC [abbrev: barnavårdscentral]
childcare center

by [n.; ~n, ~ar] village

byfest [n.; ~en, ~er] village festival

byffé [see: buffé]

bygga [v.; bygger, byggde, byggt]
build; ~ ut expand, develop

byggande [n.; ~t, ~n] building,
construction

byggd [adj.; byggt, ~a] built

bygglov [n.; ~et, ~] building permit

byggmästare [n.; ~n, ~] building
contractor

byggnad [n.; ~en, ~er] building

byggnadsarbetare [n.; ~n, ~] construction worker

byggnadsnämnd [n.; ~en, ~er]
local housing committee

by-passoperation [n.; ~en, ~er]
bypass operation

byracka [n.; ~n, -rackor] mongrel,
mutt

byrå¹ [n.; ~n, ~er] office
byrå² [n.; ~n, ~ar] chest of drawers
byråkrati [n.; ~n, ~er] bureaucracy
byrålåda [n.; ~n, -lådor] drawer
Byrån för tekniskt bistånd och informationsutbyte (Taiex) [n.] Technical Assistance Information Exchange (TAIEX) [EU]
bysthållare [n.; ~n, ~] brassiere, bra
byta [v.; byter, bytte, bytt] change; exchange; ~ **körfält/~ fil** change lanes; ~ **blöjer** change diapers; ~ **namn** rename [IT]; ~ **om kläder** change clothes; ~ **på babyn** change the baby's diapers; ~ **tåg** change trains, transfer; ~ **ut** exchange
byte¹ [n.; ~t, ~n] byte [IT]
byte² [n.; ~t, ~n] exchange; transfer
bytesrätt [n.; ~en] right to exchange
byxor [n.pl.] pants, trousers
båda [pron.] both; **både Anna och Per** both Anna and Per
båge [n.; ~n, bågar] bow, curve, arc
bål [n.; ~en, ~ar] punch; bowl; torso
båt [n.; ~en, ~ar] boat, ship
båtkryssning [n.; ~en, ~ar] cruise, boat trip
båtresa [n.; ~n, -resor] boat trip
båttur [n.; ~en, ~er] boat tour
bäck [n.; ~en, ~ar] stream
bäcken [~et, ~] pelvis; basin, bedpan
bädd [n.; ~en, ~ar] berth
bädda [v.; ~r, ~de, ~t] make a bed; ~ **in** embed [IT]
bäddsoffa [n.; ~n, -soffor] sofabed, daybed
bägge [see: **båda**]
bälte [n.; ~t, ~n] belt; seat belt
bältros [n.; ~en] shingles [disease]
bänk [n.; ~en, ~ar] bench; row
bär [n.; ~et, ~] berry
bära [v.; bär, bar, burit] carry, bear; wear
bärare [n.; ~n, ~] porter; caddie [golf]
bärbar [adj.; ~t, ~a] portable; ~ **dator** laptop computer, notebook computer [IT]
bärga [v.; ~r, ~de, ~t] salvage; tow
bärgningsbil [n.; ~en, ~ar] tow truck

bärgningsservice [n.; ~n, ~] towing service
bärkasse [n.; ~n, -kassar] shopping bag
bärnsten [n.; ~en, ~ar] amber
bärplansbåt [n.; ~en, ~ar] hydrofoil
bärsele [n.; ~n] baby carrier
bärutflykt [n.; ~en, ~er] berrypicking expedition
bärvåg [n.; ~en, ~or] carrier, carrier wave [IT]
bäst [adj./adv. superl.: bra, god] best; **det är ~ att vi** we had better; ~ **före** best before (date)
bästa [n.] best
bästa praxis [n.] best practice
bättre [adj./adv.comp.: bra, god] better
böcker [n.pl.; see: **bok**]
böckling [n.; ~en, ~ar] smoked Baltic herring, kipper
bödel [n.; ~n, bödlar] executioner, hangman; tormentor
böhmisk [adj.; ~t, ~a] Bohemian
böja [v.; böjer, böjde, böjt] bend
böjning [n.; ~en, ~ar] bending; inflection, declension, conjugation [gram]
böla [v.; ~r, ~de, ~t] moo
böld [n.; ~en, ~er] boil, abcess
bön [n.; ~en, ~er] prayer
böna [n.; ~n, bönor] bean
bönder [n.pl.; see: **bonde**]
bönskott [n.pl.] bean sprouts
böra [v.; bör, borde, bort] ought to, should
bördig [adj.; ~t, ~a] fertile
börja [v.; ~r, ~de, ~t] begin, start
börjad [adj.; börjat, ~e] begun
början [n.] beginning; **från ~** from the start; **i ~** in the beginning, at first
börs [n.; ~en, ~er] stock exchange
börsnotering [n.; ~en, ~ar] stock exchange quote
böter [n.pl.] fine
bötefälla (ngn) [v.; ~r, ~de, ~t] fine (someone)
böteslapp [n.; ~en, ~ar] parking ticket

C

c [abbrev: centerpartiet; cirka] Center Party; about
ca [abbrev: cirka] about
cabriolet [n.; ~en, ~er] convertible [car]
cachad [adj.; cachat, ~e] cached, stored in cache memory [IT]
cacheminne [n.; ~t, ~n] cache memory [IT]
café [n.; ~et, ~er] café
cafeteria [n.; ~n, -terior] cafeteria
camcorder [n.; ~n, ~] camcorder
campa [v.; ~r, ~de, ~t] camp
campingplats [n.; ~en, ~er] camp-site
cancer [n.; ~n, cancrar] cancer
cancerframkallande [adj.] carcino-genic
cayennepeppar [n.; ~n, ~] cayenne pepper
CD-brännare [n.; ~n, ~] CD recorder, CD writer [IT]
CD-enhet [n.; ~en, ~er] CD drive [IT]
CD-läsare [n.; ~n, ~] CD reader [IT]
CD-romläsare [n.; ~n, ~] CD-ROM reader, CD-ROM drive [IT]
CD-romskiva [n.; ~n, -skivor] CD-ROM disc [IT]
CD-romspelare [n.; ~n, ~] CD-ROM reader [IT]
CD-skiva [n.; ~n, -skivor] compact disc (CD)
CD-spelare [n.; ~n, ~] CD player
cell [n.; ~en, ~er] cell
cellprov [n.; ~et, ~] cervical smear test, Pap smear test
cellskräck [n.; ~en] claustrophobia
Celsius [n.] Centigrade [-10°C=14°F; 0°C=32°F; 10°C=50°F; 20°C=68°F; 30°C=86°F; 37°C=98.6°F; 100°C=212°F]
CE-märkning [n.; ~en, ~ar] CE marking, CE mark [EU, product safety]
censur [n.; ~en, ~er] censorship
center [n.; ~n, centrer] center
centern [n.; see: Centerpartiet]
Centerns Ungdomsförbund (CUF) [n.; ~et] Center Youth Alliance

Centerpartiet [n.] Center Party
centiliter [n.; ~n, ~] centiliter [⅓ oz.]
centimeter [n.; ~n, ~] centimeter [0.4 in.]
central [adj.; ~t, ~a] central; bo ~t live downtown
Centrala försöksdjursnämnden (CFN) [n.] Central Laboratory Animal Board
Centrala studiestödsnämnden (CSN) [n.] Central Student Aid Board
centralbank [n.; ~en, ~er] central bank
centralenhet [n.; ~en, ~er] central processing unit (CPU) [IT]
centralprocessor [n.; ~n, ~er] cen-tral processing unit (CPU) [IT]
centralstation [n.; ~en, ~er] main station
centralvärme [n.; ~n] central heat-ing
centrerad [adj.; -rat, ~e] centered
centrifug [n.; ~en, ~er] centrifuge; spin dryer
centrum [n.; ~et, ~] downtown area, town center
cerat [n.; ~et, ~] lip balm
ceremoni [n.; ~n, ~er] ceremony
certifikat [n.; ~et, ~] certificate
Chalmers tekniska högskola [n.; ~n] Chalmers University of Tech-nology [Göteborg]
champagne [n.; ~en] champagne
champinjon [n.; ~en, ~er] (button) mushroom
champinjonsoppa [n.; ~n] mush-room soup
chans [n.; ~en, ~er] opportunity, chance
charad [n.; ~en, ~er] charade
charkuteri [n.; ~et, ~er] butcher-delicatessen
charm [n.; ~en] attractiveness, charm
charterresa [n.; ~n, -resor] charter flight
chatta [v.; ~r, ~de, ~t] chat [IT]
chauffö r [n.; ~en, ~er] driver

check [n.; ~en, ~ar] check
checka [v.; ~r, ~de, ~t] check; **~ in** check in [airport, hotel]; **~ ut** check out [hotel]
checkhäfte [n.; ~t, ~n] checkbook
checkkonto [n.; ~t, ~n] checking account
chef [n.; ~en, ~er] manager, head
chefredaktör [n.; ~en, ~er] editor-in-chief
chefsåklagare [n.; ~n, ~] district attorney
Chile [n.] Chile
chilensk [adj.; ~t, ~a] Chilean
chilipeppar [n.; ~n, ~] chili pepper
chips [n.; ~et] potato chips; chip [IT]
chock [n.; ~en, ~er] shock
chocka [v.; ~r, ~de, ~t] shock
choke [n.; ~n] choke
choklad [n.; ~en] chocolate; cocoa
chokladask [n.; ~en, ~ar] box of chocolates
chokladglass [n.; ~en] chocolate ice cream
chokladkaka [n.; ~n, -kakor] chocolate bar; chocolate cake
chokladsås [n.; ~en] chocolate sauce
cigarett [n.; ~en, ~er] cigarette
cigarettfimp [n.; ~en, ~ar] cigarette butt
cigarettändare [n.; ~n, ~] cigarette lighter
cigarr [n.; ~en, ~er] cigar
cikoria [n.; ~n] chicory
cirka [adv.] approximately, about
cirkel [n.; ~n, cirklar] circle
cirkeldiagram [n.; -grammet, ~] pie chart [IT]
cirkelsåg [n.; ~en, ~ar] circular saw
cirkulationsrubbning [n.; ~en, ~ar] circulatory disorder
cirkus [n.; ~en, cirkusar] circus
cirkusartist [n.; ~en, ~er] circus performer
cirkusnummer [n.; -numret, ~] circus act
cirkustält [n.; ~et, ~] circus tent
ciss [n.] C sharp [music]
citat [n.; ~et, ~] quotation, quote; **slut ~** end of quote, unquote
citationstecken [n.; ~et, ~] quotation mark [IT]

citron [n.; ~en, ~er] lemon
citronfromage [n.; ~n, ~r] lemon mousse
citronjuice [n.; ~n] lemon juice
city [n.] city center
civ.ek. [abbrev: civilekonom] graduate in economics or business
civil [adj.; ~t, ~a] civil; civilian; **~a samhället** civil society
civilekonom [n.; ~en, ~er] economist, person with a degree in economics and/or business
civilförsvar [n.; ~et] civil defense
civilisation [n.; ~en, ~er] civilization
civilmål [n.; ~et, ~] civil case
civilrättsligt samarbete [n.; ~t] judicial cooperation in civil matters [EU]
civilstånd [n.; ~et] marital status
civ.ing. [n.; abbrev: civilingenjör] graduate in engineering
cl [abbrev: centiliter; 1/3 fl.oz.] centiliter
clementin [n.; ~en, ~er] clementine
clown [n.; ~en, ~er] clown
cm [abbrev: centimeter; 0.4 in.] centimeter
c/o [abbrev.] care of (c/o)
Co. [abbrev: kompani] Company (Co.)
Connex [n.; ~en] Connex [private mass transport company]
Coreper [n.; abbrev.] Committee of Permanent Representatives (COREPER) [EU Council body]
Coreu [n.; abbrev.] Correspondance européenne (COREU) [EU communications network]
COSAC [abbrev.] Conference of European Affairs Committees (COSAC) [EU inter-parliamentary body]
Cotonouavtalet [n.] Cotonou Agreement [EU & ACP countries]
crawla [v.; ~r, ~de, ~t] swim the crawl [swim stroke], swim freestyle
creme fraiche [n.] sour cream
CSA [abbrev: Centralförbundet för Socialt Arbete] Central Organization of Social Work

CSN [abbrev: Centrala studiestöds-
nämnden] Central Student Aid
Board

Ctrl-tangent [n.; ~en] control key
(Ctrl) [IT]

cup [n.; ~en, ~er] cup, sports championship

cupfinal [n.; ~en, ~er] cup final
[sports]

cupspel [n.; ~et, ~] cup match,
championship game

curling [n.; ~en] curling

curry [n.; ~n] curry

currysoppa [n.; ~n, -soppor] curry
soup, mulligatawny soup

cyberrymd [n.; ~en] cyberspace [IT]

cykel [n.; ~n, cyklar] bicycle;
cycling

cykelbana [n.; ~n, -banor] bicycle
path

cykeldäck [n.; ~et, ~] bicycle tire

cykelhjälm [n.; ~en, ~ar] cycling
helmet

cykelled [n.; ~en, ~er] bicycle path

cykelsport [n.; ~en] cycling

cykelspår [n.; ~et, ~] bicycle path

cykelstyre [n.; ~t, ~n] handlebars

cykelställ [n.; ~et, ~] bicycle stand

cykeltur [n.; ~en, ~er] cycle tour

cykeltävling [n.; ~en, ~ar] bicycle
racing; bicycle race

cykelväg [n.; ~en, ~ar] bicycle path

cykelåkare [n.; ~n, ~] cyclist

cykla [v.; ~r, ~de, ~t] cycle, ride a
bicycle

cykling [n.; ~en] cycling

cyklist [n.; ~en, ~er] cyclist

cyklopöga [n.; ~t, -ögon] diving
mask

Cypern [n.] Cyprus

cypriotisk [adj.; ~t, ~a] Cypriot

D

D [abbrev: damer] ladies' restroom
d. [abbrev: död] dead, died
dacapo [n.; ~t, ~n] encore
dadlar [n.pl.] dates
dag [n.; ~en, ~ar] day; **i ~** today;
~en därpå the next day; **~en efter**
the day after
dagbarnvårdare [n.] day care
provider
dagbok [n.; ~en, -böcker] diary
dagens [adj.] today's; **~ meny**
menu of the day; **Dagens Nyheter**
Dagens Nyheter [major daily
newspaper]; **~ rätt** today's special
[restaurant menu]
daggmask [n.; ~en, ~ar] earthworm
daghem [n.; -hemmet, ~] nursery
school, day care center
dagis [n.; ~et, ~; colloq.] day care
center
dagisplats [n.; ~en, ~er] place in a
day care center
dagkort [n.; ~et, ~] day pass
daglig [adj.; ~t, ~a] daily
dagligen [adv.] daily
dagmamma [n.; ~n, -mammor]
female day care provider, nanny
dagordning [n.; ~en, ~ar] agenda
dags [adv.]: **hur ~?** at what time?;
~ att time to
dagsbesökare [n.; ~n, ~] day guest,
day visitor
dagsböter [n.pl.] fine proportional
to one's daily income
dagsläge [n.; ~t, ~n] current situation
dagsprogram [n.; -grammet, ~]
daily program
dagssyssla [n.; ~n, -sysslor] daily
occupation
dagstidning [n.; ~en, ~ar] daily
paper, newspaper
dagsutflykt [n.; ~en, ~er] day trip
dagtid [n.; ~en] daytime
dakapo [n.; ~t, ~n; see: **dacapo**]
dal [n.; ~en, ~ar] valley
dalahäst [n.; ~en, ~ar] painted
wooden horse [from Dalecarlia]
Dalarna [n.] Dalecarlia [province
in central Sweden]

dalstation [n.; ~en, ~er] ski lift station at bottom of mountain
dam [n.; ~en. ~er] lady; queen;
checkers
Damaskus [n.] Damascus
damavdelning [n.; ~en, ~ar] ladies'
section [clothing store]
dambinda [n.; ~n, -bindor] sanitary
napkin
damdubbel [n.; ~n, -dubblar]
women's doubles [tennis]
damer [n.pl.] ladies; ladies' restroom
damfrisering [n.; ~en, ~ar] ladies'
hairdressers, beauty parlor
damfrisör [n.; ~en, ~er] ladies'
hairdresser
damfrisörska [n.; ~n, -skor]
female hairdresser; ladies' hairdressers salon
damkläder [n.pl.] ladies' wear
damkonfektion [n.; ~en] ladies'
wear
damm [n.; ~en, ~ar] pond
damma [v.; ~r, ~de, ~t] dust
dammig [adj.; ~t, ~a] dusty
dammsugare [n.; ~n, ~] vacuum
cleaner
dammtrasa [n.; ~n, -trasor] dust
rag
damsingel [n.; ~n, -singlar] women's
singles [tennis]
damspel [n.; ~et] checkers
damtidning [n.; ~en, ~ar] women's
magazine
damtoalett [n.; ~en, ~er] ladies'
restroom
dan [colloq.: dagen; see: **dag**]
Danmark [n.] Denmark
dans [n.; ~en, ~er] dance
dansa [v.; ~r, ~de, ~t] dance
dansare [n.; ~n, ~] dancer
dansbana [n.; ~n, -banor] dance
floor
dansband [n.; ~et, ~] dance band
dansgolv [n.; ~et] dance floor
Danshögskolan [n.] College of
Dance
dansk [adj.; ~t, ~a] Danish

danska [n.] Danish language

dansteater [n.; ~n, -teatrar] dance theater

dansös [n.; ~en, ~er] female dancer

Dardanellerna [n.pl.] Dardanelles

darra [v.; ~r, ~de, ~t] shiver, shake, tremble

data- [prefix] data-, computer- [IT]

dataakut [n.; ~en] help desk, computer assistance center [IT]

dataavdelning [n.; ~en, ~ar] data processing department, IT department [IT]

databas [n.; ~en, ~er] database [IT]

databashantering [n.; ~en] database management [IT]

databransch [n.; ~en] data processing sector [IT]

databrott [n.; ~et, ~] computer crime [IT]

databuss [n.; ~en, ~ar] data bus, bus [IT]

datacell [n.; ~en, ~er] data cell [IT]

datafil [n.; ~en, ~ar] data file [IT]

datafångst [n.; ~en] data capture [IT]

dataförråd [n.; ~et, ~] data mart [IT]

datagruvdrift [n.; ~en] data mining [IT]

datainsamling [n.; ~en, ~ar] data acquisition [IT]

Datainspektionen [n.] **(DI)** Data Inspection Board [IT]

datakomprimering [n.; ~en, ~ar] data compression [IT]

datakonsult [n.; ~en, ~er] computer consultant [IT]

datalager [n.; -lagret, ~] data warehouse, data mart [IT]

datalagerhantering [n.; ~en] data warehousing [IT]

datanörd [n.; ~en, ~er] computer nerd, geek [IT]

dataprogram [n.; -grammet, ~] computer program [IT]

dataregister [n.; -registret, ~] database, list of data [IT]

dataskydd [n.; ~et] computer protection [IT]

dataskärm [n.; ~en, -skärmar] computer monitor [IT]

dataspel [n.; ~et, ~] computer game [IT]

datasystem [n.; ~et, ~] computer system, data processing system [IT]

datateknik [n.; ~en] computer science [IT]

dataterminal [n.; ~en, ~er] computer terminal [IT]

datautrustning [n.; ~en] computer equipment, hardware [IT]

datavirus [n.; ~et, ~] computer virus [IT]

dataöverföring [n.; ~en, ~ar] data transfer [IT]

daterad [adj.; -rat, ~e] dated

dativobjekt [n.; ~et, ~] indirect object [gram]

dator [n.; ~n, ~er] computer [IT]

datoranimation [n.; ~en, ~er] computer animation [IT]

datorgrafik [n.; ~en, ~er] computer graphics [IT]

datorhjälp [n.; ~en] computer assistance [IT]

datorjour [n.; ~n, ~er] help desk, computer assistance service [IT]

datorlåda [n.; ~n, -lådor] PC case, PC box [IT]

datormus [n.; ~en, -möss] computer mouse [IT]

datormusik [n.; ~en] computer music, synthesized music [IT]

datorprogram [n.; -grammet, ~] computer program [IT]

datorskärm [n.; ~en, -skärmar] computer screen [IT]

datorspel [n.; ~et, ~] computer game [IT]

datorstödd [adj.]: ~ **konstruktion** computer-aided design [IT]; ~ **utbildning** computer-aided instruction, computer-based training, e-learning [IT]

datortomografi [n.; ~n] computer tomography [IT]

datorutrustning [n.; ~en] hardware [IT]

datum [n.; ~et, ~] date; **vad är det för ~ i dag?** what's the date today?

de[1] [def.art.pl.] the; ~ **där** those; ~ **flesta** most; ~ **här** these

de² [pron.pl.; deras, dem; usually pronounced: dom] they

debatt [n.; ~en, ~er] discussion, debate; opinion

debattartikel [n.; ~n, -artiklar] op-ed piece

debattämne [n.; ~t, ~n] controversial subject

debet [n.] debit

debetkort [n.; ~et, ~] debit card

debut [n.; ~en, ~er] debut

debutera [v.; ~r, ~de, ~t] make one's debut

dec. [abbrev.; see: **december**]

december [n.] December

decennium [n.; decenniet, decennier] decade

decentralisera [v.; ~r, ~de, ~t] decentralize

decentralisering [n.; ~en, ~ar] decentralization

decibel [n.; ~] decibel

deciliter [n.; ~n, ~] deciliter [0.1 liter, approx. 3 fl. oz.]

decimal [n.; ~en, ~er] decimal

decimalbråk [n.; ~et, ~] decimal fraction

decimalkomma [n.; ~n, -kommor] decimal point

deckare [n.; ~en, ~] crime novel, detective story, thriller

dedikerad [adj.; -rat, ~e] dedicated [IT]

defekt [n.; ~en, ~er] defect, fault

definitiv [adj.; ~t, ~a] definitive; final

defragmentering [n.; ~en] defragmentation [IT]

deg [n.; ~en, ~ar] dough

degskrapa [n.; ~n, -skrapor] spatula

dej [pron.obj.; see: **dig**]

dekan [n.; ~en, ~er] dean [university]

deklaration [n.; ~en, ~er] declaration; income tax return

deklarera [v.; ~r, ~de, ~t] declare

deklination [n.; ~en, ~er] declension [gram]

dekompilera [v.; ~r, ~de, ~t] decompile [IT]

dekompilering [n.; ~en] decompilation [IT]

dekor [n.; ~en, ~er] scenery [theater]

dekoration [n.; ~en, ~er] decoration

dekryptering [n.; ~en] deciphering, decryption [IT]

del [n.; ~en, ~ar] part; **en ~ av** some, a part of; **~s A och ~s B** partly A and partly B

dela [v.; ~r, ~de, ~t] divide; distribute; **~ med sig** share; **~ ut** share out, distribute; award; distribute

delad [adj.; delat, ~e] shared; divided; **~ med** divided by; **~ skärm** split screen [IT]

delaktighet [n.; ~en, ~er] participation, involvement; complicity

delas upp [v.; ~, ~des, ~ts] be divided up, be shared out

Delegationen för utländska investeringar i Sverige [n.] Invest in Sweden Agency

delikatessaffär [n.; ~n, ~er] delicatessen

delikatessbutik [n.; ~en, ~er] delicatessen

delikatessdisk [n.; ~en, ~ar] deli counter

delfin [n.; ~en, ~er] dolphin

delning [n.; ~en, ~ar] division, partition; fission; sharing; distribution [IT]

delpension [n.; ~en, ~er] partial pension

dels [see: **del**]

delstat [n.; ~en, ~er] state within a union/federation [e.g. New Jersey]

delta¹ [n.; ~n, deltor] delta

delta² [v.; ~r, -tog, -tagit] take part

deltagande¹ [adj.] sympathetic

deltagande² [n.; ~en] participation; sympathy; participant

deltagare [n.; ~n, ~] participant

deltagit [v.past; see: **delta**]

deltid [n.; ~en, ~er] part-time

delägare [n.; ~n, ~] part-owner, joint owner

dem [pron.obj.; usually pronounced: dom; see: **de**] them

demokrati [n.; ~n, ~er] democracy

demokratisk [adj.; ~t, ~a] democratic

demokratiskt underskott [n.; ~et] democratic deficit [EU]

demon [n.; ~en, ~er] demon

demonstrant [n.; ~en, ~er] demonstrator, participant in demonstration
demonstration [n.; ~en, ~er] demonstration
demonstrativt pronomen [n.] demonstrative pronoun [gram]
demonstrera [v.; ~r, ~de, ~t] demonstrate
den[1] [def.art.; det, de] the
den[2] [pron.; det, dess, de, deras] this; it; ~ **här** that; ~ **här veckan** this week
denim [n.] denim
denne [pron.; denna] this, that; he, she, it; ~**s** of this month
densamme [pron.; detsamma, densamma] the same
deodorant [n.; ~en, ~er] deodorant
departement [n.; ~et, ~] ministry; department
departementschef [n.; ~en, ~er] head of ministry
departementsråd [n.; ~et, ~] director
departementssekreterare [n.; ~n, ~] senior administrative officer, desk officer
Departementsserien (Ds) [n.] Ministry Publications Series
deponens [n.] deponent [gram]
deponera [v.; ~r, ~de, ~t] make a deposit
deponeringsavgift [n.; ~en, ~er] deposit
depression [n.; ~en, ~er] depression
deprimerad [adj.; -rat, ~e] depressed
deras [pron.poss.; see: **de**] their(s)
desinfektionsmedel [n.; -medlet, ~] disinfectant
desinficera [v.; ~r, ~de, ~t] disinfect
deskriptiv [adj.; ~t, ~a] descriptive
desperat [adj.; ~a] desperate
dess [pron.poss.; see: **den**] its
dessa [pron.; see: **den här, den där**] these, those
dessert [n.; ~en, ~er] dessert
dessertvin [n.; ~et, ~er] dessert wine
dessförinnan [adv.] before then, beforehand
dessutom [adv.] besides, apart from that
dessvärre [adv.] unfortunately

destination [n.; ~en, ~er] destination
desto bättre [adv.] all the better, so much the better
det[1] [def.art.; see: **den**] the; ~ **enda** the only thing
det[2] [pron.] it; that; ~ **finns** there is/are; ~ **gör inget** it doesn't matter; ~ **har du rätt i** you're right; ~ **vill säga** that is, I mean; ~ **är bra så** that's fine
detalj [n.; ~en, ~er] detail; retail
detaljerad [adj.; -rat, ~e] detailed
detektiv [n.; ~en, ~er] detective
determinant [n.; ~en, ~er] determiner [gram]
determinativt pronomen [n.; ~et, ~en] determinative pronoun [gram]
detsamma [pron.; see also: **densamme**] the same, the same thing; **det gör mig** ~ it's all the same to me, I don't care; **med** ~ right away; **tack,** ~ the same to you
detta [pron.dem.; see also: **denna**] this, that
devalvering [n.; ~en, ~ar] devaluation
di: ge ~ [v.] suckle; breastfeed
dia [v.; ~r, ~de, ~t] suck; suckle
diabetes [n.; ~en] diabetes
diabetiker [n.; ~n, ~] diabetic
diabild [n.; ~en, ~er] slide [photograph]
diafragma [n.; ~n, -fragmor] diaphragm
diagnos [n.; ~en, ~er] diagnosis
diagnosprogram [n.; -grammet, ~] diagnostic program [IT]
diagonal [adj.; ~t, ~a] diagonal
diagram [n.; -grammet, ~] diagram
diakritiskt tecken [n.; tecknet, ~] diacritical mark, accent mark
dialekt [n.; ~en, ~er] dialect
dialog [n.; ~en, ~er] dialogue
dialogruta [n.; ~n, -rutor] dialogue box [IT]
diamant [n.; ~en, ~er] diamond
diameter [n.; ~n, -metrar] diameter
diapositiv [n.; ~et, ~] transparency, slide
diarieföring [n.; ~en, ~ar] registration
diarré [n.; ~n] diarrhea

dieselolja [n.; ~n] diesel fuel

diet [n.; ~en] diet

difteri [n.; ~n] diphtheria

dig [pron.obj.; du] you, yourself

digital [adj.; ~t, ~a] digital [IT]; ~ **signatur** digital signature [IT]; ~**a pengar** digital cash, e-cash [IT]

digital-analog-omvandlare [n.; ~n, ~] digital-to-analog converter [IT]

digitaliserare [n.; ~n, ~] digitizer [IT]

digitalkamera [n.; ~n, -kameror] digital camera [IT]

digitalpengar [n.pl.] digital cash [IT]

dikt [n.; ~en, ~er] poem; poetry; fiction

diktamen [n.] dictation

diktator [n.; ~n, ~er] dictator

diktatur [n.; ~en, ~er] dictatorship

dilemma [n.; ~t, ~n] dilemma

dill [n.; ~en] dill

dillkött [n.; ~et] stewed lamb or veal with dill sauce

dillpotatis [n.; ~en, ~ar] potatoes boiled with dill

dillsås [n.; ~en] dill sauce

dimension [n.; ~en, ~er] dimension

dimljus [n.; ~et, ~] fog light

dimma [n.; ~n] fog

dimmig [adj.; ~t, ~a] foggy

dimrisk [n.; ~en] risk of fog

din [poss.pron.; ditt, dina; see: **du**] your, yours; **Din/Er tillgivne** Yours sincerely

dir. [abbrev: direktör] director

direkt [adj.; ~a; adv.] direct; directly; online [IT]; ~ **effekt** direct effect [EU]; ~ **fråga** direct question [gram]; ~ **objekt** direct object [gram]

direktansluten [adj.; -tet, -tna] online [IT]

direktflyg [n.; ~et, ~] direct flight, non-stop flight

direkthjälp [n.; ~en] online help [IT]

direktiv [n.; ~en, ~er] terms of reference; instructions; directive [EU]

direktlinje [n.; ~n, ~r] hotline, direct line [IT]

direktlänk [n.; ~en, ~ar] direct link [IT]

direktmeddelande [n.; ~t, ~n] instant messaging [IT]

direktservice [n.; ~n, ~] direct service

direktsändning [n.; ~en, ~ar] live broadcast

direkttjänst [n.; ~en, ~er] online service [IT]

direkttåg [n.; ~et, ~] direct train, express train

direktuppspelad video [n.] streamed video [IT]

direktuppspelning [n.; ~en, ~ar] streaming [IT]

direktör [n.; ~en, ~er] manager

dirigent [n.; ~en, ~er] conductor [orchestra]

dirigera [v.; ~r, ~de, ~t] conduct [orchestra]

disciplin [n.; ~en] discipline; branch of learning

disco [see: **diskotek**]

disk [n.; ~en, ~ar] counter; dish washing; dishes; disk

diska [v.; ~r, ~de, ~t] wash dishes, do the dishes

diskborste [n.; ~n, -borstar] dish brush

diskbråk [n.; ~et, ~] slipped disc

diskbänk [n.; ~en, ~ar] kitchen sink; draining board

diskett [n.; ~en, ~er] diskette [IT]

diskettenhet [n.; ~en, ~er] disk drive [IT]

diskhandduk [n.; ~en, ~ar] dish towel

diskho [n.; ~n, ~ar] sink for washing dishes

diskjockey [n.; ~n, ~er] disc jockey

diskmaskin [n.; ~en, ~er] dishwasher

diskmaskinsfast [adj.; ~a] dishwasher-proof

diskmedel [n.; -medlet, ~] dishwashing soap

diskning [n.; ~en, ~ar] dishwashing

diskonto [n.; ~t, ~n] minimum lending rate, market rate

diskotek [n.; ~et, ~] discotheque

diskret [adj.; ~a] discrete

diskrimin<u>e</u>ra [v.; ~r, ~de, ~t]
discriminate against
diskrimin<u>e</u>rad [adj.; -rat, ~e]
discriminated against
diskrimin<u>e</u>ring [n.; ~en, ~ar]
discrimination
diskrimin<u>e</u>rings<u>o</u>mbudsman (DO)
[n.; -mannen, -män] equal oppor-
tunity ombudsman
d<u>i</u>skst<u>ä</u>ll [n.; ~et, ~] dish rack
d<u>i</u>sktr<u>a</u>sa [n.; ~n, -trasor] dishcloth,
dishrag
diskuss<u>i</u>on [n.; ~en, ~er] discussion
diskuss<u>i</u>onsf<u>o</u>rum [n.; ~et, ~] discussion group, newsgroup [IT]
diskuss<u>i</u>onsfr<u>å</u>ga [n.; ~n, -frågor]
topic of/for discussion
diskuss<u>i</u>onsgr<u>u</u>pp [n.; ~en, ~er]
discussion group, newsgroup [IT]
disk<u>u</u>tera [v.; ~r, ~de, ~t] discuss
disputat<u>i</u>on [n.; ~en, ~er] doctoral
thesis defense
dist<u>a</u>ns¹ [n.; ~en, ~er] distance
dist<u>a</u>ns-² [prefix] remote- [IT]
dist<u>a</u>nsarbete [n.; ~t, ~n] telecommuting, working from home [IT]
distribut<u>i</u>onsl<u>i</u>sta [n.; ~n, -listor]
distribution list, mailing list [IT]
distr<u>i</u>kt [n.; ~en, ~er] district
distr<u>i</u>ktsläkarm<u>o</u>ttagning [n.; ~en,
~ar] district medical center
dit [adv.] to there, thither (motion)
d<u>i</u>to [adv.] ditto, likewise
ditr<u>e</u>ring [n.; ~en] dithering [IT]
ditt [poss.pron.; see: **din**] your [sing.],
yours
div. [see: **diverse**]
div<u>e</u>rse [adj.] various
divid<u>e</u>ra (med) [v.; ~r, ~de, ~t]
divide (by)
divis<u>i</u>on [n.; ~en, ~er] division
divis<u>i</u>onst<u>e</u>cken [n.; -tecknet, ~]
division sign
dj<u>u</u>ngel [n.; ~n, djungler] jungle
djup¹ [adj.; ~t, ~a] deep; ~ **t<u>a</u>llrik**
soup plate, bowl
djup² [n.; ~et, ~] depth
dj<u>u</u>pfr<u>y</u>st [adj.; ~a] frozen; ~ **mat**
frozen food; ~**a v<u>a</u>ror** frozen foods
djur [n.; ~et, ~] animal
dj<u>u</u>rf<u>o</u>der [n.; -fodret] animal feed

dj<u>u</u>rh<u>e</u>m [n.; -hemmet, ~] animal
shelter
dj<u>u</u>rl<u>i</u>v [n.; ~et] wild life
dj<u>u</u>rl<u>ä</u>te [n.; ~t, ~n] animal cry/call
dj<u>u</u>rm<u>a</u>t [n.; ~en] pet food
dj<u>u</u>rp<u>a</u>rk [n.; ~en, ~er] zoo
dj<u>u</u>rsk<u>y</u>dd [n.; ~et] animal welfare
[EU]
Dj<u>u</u>rskyddsm<u>y</u>ndigheten [n.] National Animal Welfare Agency
djärv [adj.; ~t, ~a] daring
dj<u>ä</u>vul [n.; ~n, djävlar] devil;
djävlar! damn!
dj<u>ä</u>vla [vul.; see also: **jävla**] damned
[colloq.]
dl [see: **deciliter**]
DN [see: **Dagens Nyheter**]
DNA [abbrev: deoxiribonukle<u>i</u>n-
s<u>y</u>ra] DNA [abbrev: deoxyribonucleic acid]
dnr [abbrev: di<u>a</u>rien<u>u</u>mmer] register number, record number
DO¹ [see: **diskrimineringsom-
budsman**]
d:o² [abbrev: d<u>i</u>to] ditto, likewise
doc. [see: **docent**]
doc<u>e</u>nt [n.; ~en, ~er] senior lecturer; associate professor
dock [adv.] yet; however
d<u>o</u>cka¹ [n.; ~n, dockor] doll; dock
d<u>o</u>cka² [v.; ~r, ~de, ~t] dock
d<u>o</u>ckningstat<u>i</u>on [n.; ~en, ~er]
docking station [IT]
doft [n.; ~en, ~er] scent, fragrance
dog [v.past; see: **dö**]
d<u>o</u>ktor [n.; ~en, ~er] doctor
doktor<u>a</u>ndanst<u>ä</u>llning [n.; ~en,
~ar] predoctoral fellowship
doktor<u>a</u>ndst<u>u</u>dier [n.pl.] studies
for a doctorate
d<u>o</u>ktorens rum [n.; ~et] doctor's
consultation room
doktor<u>e</u>ra [v.; ~r, ~de, ~t] pursue a
doctoral degree
doktor<u>i</u>nna [n.; ~n] doctor's wife
d<u>o</u>ktors<u>a</u>vhandling [n.; ~en, ~ar]
doctoral dissertation, doctoral thesis
dokum<u>e</u>nt [n.; ~et, ~] document
dokumentat<u>i</u>on [n.; ~en, ~er] documentation
dokum<u>e</u>ntmall [n.; ~en, ~ar] style
sheet [IT]

dokumentär [adj.; ~t, ~a] documentary

dokumentärfilm [n.; ~en, ~er] documentary film

dold [adj.; dolt, ~a] hidden

dolde, dolt [v.past; see: **dölja**]

dolk [n.; ~en, ~ar] sheath knife, hunting knife

dollar [n.; ~en, ~] dollar

dom[1] [n.; ~en, ~ar] judgement, sentence, verdict

dom[2] [n.; ~en, ~er] cathedral

dom[3] [pron.; colloq.; see: **de, dem**] they, them

domare [n.; ~n, ~] judge; referee, umpire

domherre [n.; ~n, -herrar] bullfinch

dominans [n.; ~en] domination

dominera [v.; ~r, ~de, ~t] dominate

dominerande [adj.] dominating

Dominikanska republiken [n.] Dominican Republic

domino [n.; ~t] dominoes

domkraft [n.; ~en, ~er] jack [automobile]

domkyrka [n.; ~n, -kyrkor] cathedral

domptör [n.; ~en, ~er] animal tamer

domstol [n.; ~en, ~ar] court [law]

domstolsbyggnad [n.; ~en, ~er] courthouse

domstolsförhandling [n.; ~en, ~ar] court proceedings

Domstolsverket (DV) [n.] National Court Administration

domänadress [n.; ~en, ~er] domain address [IT]

domännamn [n.; ~et, ~] domain name [IT]

domännamnregistrering [n.; ~en] domain name registration [IT]

don [n.; ~et, ~] tool, implement; gear

donation [n.; ~en, ~er] donation

Donau [n.] Danube

donera [v.; ~r, ~de, ~t] donate; ~ **organ** donate organs

dop [n.; ~et, ~] christening, baptism

dopattest [n.; ~en, ~er] baptism certificate

dopp [n.; ~et, ~] dip, plunge

doppa [v.; ~r, ~de, ~t] dip; ~ **i**

grytan dip bread into the juice from the Christmas ham

dos [n.; ~en, ~er] dose

dosa [n.; ~n, dosor] box

dosering [n.; ~en, ~ar] dosage

doseringsmått [n.] measuring cup

dotter [n.; ~n, döttrar] daughter

dotterbolag [n.; ~et, ~] subsidiary company

dotterdotter [n.; ~n, -döttrar] granddaughter [daughter of one's daughter]

dotterson [n.; ~en, -söner] grandson [son of one's daughter]

dov [adj.; ~t, ~a] dull, muffled; aching

downlink [n.] downlink [IT]

dr [see: **doktor**]

dra [v.; ~r, drog, dragit] pull, drag; ~ **här** pull here, tear here; ~ **igen** close, shut; ~ **sig** lounge in bed; ~ **ut** pull out, extract; ~ **åt en skruv** tighten a screw

drabba [v.; ~r, ~de, ~t] hit, strike; affect; attack; ~**s av** be stricken with; be attacked by

drack [v.past; see: **dricka**]

drag [n.; ~et, ~] pull

draga [see: **dra**]

dragig [adj.; ~t, ~a] draughty

dragit [v.past; see: **dra**]

dragkamp [n.; ~en, ~er] tug-of-war

dragkrok [n.; ~en, ~ar] tow hook

draglift [n.; ~en, ~ar] tow lift

dragon [n.; ~en] tarragon

dragspel [n.; ~et, ~] accordion

drake [n.; ~n, drakar] dragon; kite

drakflygning [n.; ~en] kite flying; hang gliding

drama [n.; ~t, dramer] drama, serious play

Dramaten [n.; colloq: Kungliga Dramatiska Teatern] Royal Dramatic Theater

dramatik [n.; en] drama, dramatics

dramatisk [adj.; ~t, ~a] dramatic

Dramatiska institutet [n.] College of Film, Radio, Television and Theater

draperi [n.; ~et, ~er] curtains, drapery

drastisk [adj.; ~t, ~a] drastic
dressing [n.; ~en, ~ar] dressing
dressyr [n.; ~en] dressage, training
drev [see: **driva**]
dribbla [v.; ~r, ~de, ~t] dribble [sports]
dricka [v.; dricker, drack, druckit] drink; ~ **ur** drink up
dricks [n.; ~en] tip, gratuity, service charge
dricksvatten [n.; ~et] drinking water; **ej** ~ not drinking water
drift [n.; ~en, ~er] urge, impulse; operation, working; **på** ~ adrift
drink [n.; ~en, ~ar] drink [alcoholic]
driva [v.; driver, drev, drivit] drive; operate, run; force; urge; drift; ~ **med ngn** pull someone's leg; ~ **ut** drive out
drivande [adj.] driving
driving-range [n.] driving range
drivrutin [n.; ~en, ~er] driver [IT]
drog[1] [n.; ~en, ~er] drug
drog[2] [v.past; see: **dra**]
droppa [v.; ~r, ~de, ~t] drip
droppe [n.; ~n, droppar] drop
droppstensgrotta [n.; ~n, -grottor] dripstone cave
drott [n.; ~en, ~ar] ruler, sovereign, king
drottning [n.; ~en, ~ar] queen
druckit [v.past; see: **dricka**]
druva [n.; ~n, druvor] grape
druvsocker [n.; -sockret, ~] dextrose [grape sugar]
dryck [n.; ~en, ~er] drink, beverage
dryg [adv.] about, a good, full, solid, just over
dråp [n.; ~et, ~] manslaughter
dräkt [n.; ~en, ~er] suit [woman's]; costume
dröja [v.; dröjer, dröjde, dröjt] be late; take some time; delay; linger, dawdle; **var god dröj!** please wait/hold! [on phone]
dröm [n.; drömmen, drömmar] dream
drömma [v.; drömmer, drömde, drömt] dream
ds. [abbrev: **dennes, densamme**] of this month, the same

dt. [abbrev: **deciton**] tenth of a ton [200 lbs.]
du [pron.; din/ditt/dina, dig] you [sing.]
dubbad [adj.; dubbat, ~e] dubbed [film]
dubbel [adj.; ~t, dubbla] double, dual, twice; doubles; ~ **majoritet** double majority [EU]; ~ **precision** double precision [IT]; ~**t sned-streck** double slash [IT]; ~ **start** dual boot [IT]
dubbeldäckare [n.; ~n, ~] double-decker [bus]
dubbelhytt [n.; ~en, ~er] cabin for two, double cabin
dubbelklicka [v.; ~r, ~de, ~t] double click [IT]
dubbelriktad [adj.; -riktat, ~e] bidirectional, duplex [IT]; ~ **trafik** two-way traffic
dubbelrum [n.; -rummet, ~] double room
dubbelsäng [n.; ~en, ~ar] double bed
dubbelt [adv.] doubly, double
duga [v.; duger, dög, dugt] be acceptable, be good enough
dugg: inte ett ~ [adv.] not a bit
duggregn [n.; ~et, ~] drizzle
duk [n.; ~en, ~ar] canvas; tablecloth
duka [v.; ~r, ~de, ~t] ~ **av** clear the table; ~ **bordet** set the table; ~ **fram** set out food
duktig [adj.; ~t, ~a] clever, bright, good
dum [adj.; dumt, dumma] stupid
dumburken [n.] boob tube [colloq.: TV]
dumhet [n.; ~en, ~er] stupidity, nonsense
dun [n.; ~et] down
dunjacka [n.; ~n, -jackor] down jacket
dunka [v.; ~r, ~de, ~t] pound; thud
duntäcke [n.; ~t, ~n] down quilt, duvet
dur [n.; ~en] major [music]
durkslag [n.; ~et, ~] colander
dusch [n.; ~en, ~ar] shower

duscha [v.; ~r, ~de, ~t] take a shower
duschgelé [n.; ~n] shower gel
duschkabin [n.; ~en, ~er] shower stall
duschrum [n.; -rummet] shower room
duschstol [n.; ~en, ~ar] shower seat
dussin [n.; ~et, ~] dozen
duva [n.; ~n, duvor] pigeon, squab
DVD [n.; abbrev.] DVD [abbrev: Digital Versatile Disc]
DVD-format [n.; ~et] DVD format [IT]
dvs. [abbrev: det vill säga] that is to say (i.e.)
d.y.[1] [abbrev: den yngre] junior, the younger
dy[2] [n.; ~n] mud, sludge
dygn [n.; ~et, ~] day, 24 hours; **~et runt** round the clock, all day long
dygnsrytm [n.]: **rubbad ~ efter längre flygresa** jet lag
dyka [v.; dyker, dök, dykt] dive; **~ upp** emerge, turn up
dykapparat [n.; ~en, ~er] aqualung
dykardräkt [n.; ~en, ~er] diving suit
dykare [n.; ~n, ~] diver
dykarutrustning [n.; ~en] diving equipment/gear
dykning [n.; ~en, ~ar] diving; **~ förbjuden** no diving
dyktrampolin [n.; ~en, ~er] diving board
dylik [adj.; ~t, ~a] of that kind; **eller ~t** or something like that, and that sort of thing
dynamisk [adj.; ~t, ~a] dynamic
dynamit [n.; ~en] dynamite
dynamo [n.; ~n, ~r] generator
dynasti [n.; ~n, ~er] dynasty
dyr [adj.; ~t, ~a] expensive
dysenteri [n.; ~] dysentery
dyslektiker [n.; ~n, ~] dyslexic
dyster [adj.; ~t, dystra] gloomy
då [conj., adv.] then; **~ och då** now and then, sometimes; **~ så** now then; **~ säger vi så** that's settled then
dåd [n.; ~et, ~] outrage, crime; deed

dålig [adj.; ~t, ~a; comp. sämre, sämst or värre, värst] bad; ill; **~ väg** poor road surface; **inte ~t** not bad
d.ä. [abbrev: den äldre] senior, the elder
däck [n.; ~et, ~] tire; deck
däckstol [n.; ~en, ~ar] deck chair
däggdjur [n.; ~et, ~] mammal
där [adv.] there; where [location]; **~ borta** over there; **~ framme** over there in front; **~ uppe** up there
därav [adv.] of that
därefter [adv.] then
däremot [adv.] on the other hand
därför [adv.] therefore, for that reason
därför att [conj./adv.] because
däribland [adv.] including
därifrån [adv.] from there
därigenom [adv.] by that means, thereby, for that reason
därinne [adv.] in there
därmed [adv.] therewith, by that; by those means; consequently
därpå [adv.] following
därtill [adv.] to that, thereto; besides
däruppe [adv.] up there
därute [adv.] out there
därutöver [adv.] in addition, more
dö [v.; dör, dog, dött) die
död[1] [adj.; dött, ~a] dead
död[2] [n.; ~en] death
döda [v.; ~r, ~de, ~t] kill; cancel
Döda havet [n.] Dead Sea
dödande[1] [adj.] fatal, mortal, killing
dödande[2] [n.; ~n] killing
dödsannons [n.; ~en, ~er] obituary
dödsattest [n.; ~en, ~er] death certificate
dödsbo [n.; ~et, ~n] estate [after death], inheritance
dödsfall [n.; ~et, ~] death
dödshjälp [n.; ~en] euthanasia
dödsoffer [n.; -offret, ~] fatal casualty, victim, killed, dead
dödsruna [n.; ~n, -runor] obituary
dödsstraff [n.; ~et, ~] death penalty, capital punishment

döende [adj.] moribund
dög [v.past; see: **duga**]
dölja [v.; döljer, dolde, dolt] hide,
disguise
döma [v.; dömer, dömde, dömt]
judge; sentence; referee [sports]
döpa [v.; döper, döpte, döpt] baptize, christen; ~ **om** rename
döpt [adj.; ~a] baptized
dör [see: **dö**]
dörr [n.; ~en,~ar] door
dörrbredd [n.; ~en, ~er] door width
dörrhandtag [n.; ~et, ~] door
handle

dörrkod [n.; ~en, ~er] door code
dörrmatta [n.; ~n, -mattor] doormat
dörröppning [n.; ~en, ~ar] doorway
dött [see: **dö, död**]
döttrar [see: **dotter**]
döv [adj.; ~t, ~a] deaf; ~ **person**
deaf person
dövstum [adj.; ~t, -stumma] deaf-
mute

E

e- [prefix] e-, electronic [IT]
e-adress [n.; ~en, ~er] e-mail address [IT]
ebb [n.; ~en] low tide
ebba ut [v.; ~r, ~de, ~t] ebb away, peter out
ebenholts [n.; ~en] ebony
e-bok [n.; ~en, -böcker] e-book [IT]
e-bokfil [n.; ~en, ~ar] e-book file [IT]
e-brev [n.; ~et, ~] e-mail [IT]
e-brevlåda [n.; ~n, -lådor] mailbox [IT]
ECB [abbrev: Europeiska centralbanken] European Central Bank (ECB) [EU]
ECBS [abbrev.] European Central Bank System (ECBS) [EU]
ECHO [abbrev: Avdelningen för humanitärt bistånd] European Community Humanitarian Aid Office (ECHO) [EU]
ed.[1] [abbrev: eller dylikt] or the like
ed[2] [n.; ~en ~er] oath; **avlägga en ~** swear an oath
edyl. [abbrev: eller dylikt] or the like
EES [abbrev: Europeiska ekonomiska samarbetsområdet] European Economic Area (EEA)
EESK [abbrev: Europeiska ekonomiska och sociala kommittén] European Economic and Social Committee (EESC) [EU]
eEurope [n.] eEurope [EU]
effekt [n.; ~en, ~er] effect; output; goods, belongings; **kvarglömda ~er** lost and found office
effektförvaring [n.; ~en, ~ar] baggage checkroom
effektiv [adj.; ~t, ~a] efficient; actual
Efta [n.; abbrev: Europeiska frihandelssammanslutningen] European Free Trade Association (EFTA)
efter [prep./adv.] after; for; from; along; according to
efterfrågan [n.] demand; inquiry
efterhand: i ~ [adv.] after everyone else, last, afterwards

efterlysa [v.; -lyser, -lyste, -lyst] search for; have sbdy/sth sought, post as missing/wanted
eftermiddag [n.; ~en, ~ar] afternoon; **i ~** this afternoon; **på ~en** in the afternoon
efternamn [n.; ~et, ~] last name
efterrätt [n.; ~en, ~er] dessert course
efter-solkräm [n.; ~en, ~er] after-sun lotion
eftersom [conj.] as, because
eftersända [v.; -sänder, -sände, -sänt] forward (mail)
eftersändningsadress [n.; ~en, ~er] forwarding address
eftertanke [n.; ~n] consideration, reflection
eftertraktad [adj; -tat, ~e] coveted
efterträda [v.; -träder, -trädde, -trätt] succeed
efterträdare [n.; ~n, ~] successor (company, firm)
eftervärld [n.; ~en] posterity
efteråt [adv.] afterwards
eftr. [abbrev.; see: **efterträdare**]
EG [abbrev: Europeiska gemenskapen/gemenskaperna] European Community/Communities (EC) [EU]
eg. [abbrev: egentligen] actually
EG-domstolen [n.] European Court of Justice (ECJ), Court of Justice of the European Communities [EU]
Egeiska havet [n.] Aegean Sea
egen [adj.; eget, egna] own; **på ~ hand** on one's own; **~ företagare** self-employed person; **egna medel** own resources [EU]
egendom [n.; ~en, ~ar] property
egendomlig [adj.; ~t, ~a] peculiar, strange; characteristic
egennamn [n.; ~et, ~] proper noun [gram]
egenskap [n.; ~en, ~er] feature, quality, property [IT]
egenskapsgenitiv [n.; ~en] genitive of quality [gram]

egentlig [adj.; ~t, ~a] real; **~t sub-jekt** actual subject [gram]
egentligen [adv.] really, actually
eget [see: **egen**]
EG-fördraget [n.] Treaty establish-ing the European Community (TEC), Treaty of Rome [EU 1957]
egna [see: **egen**]
EG-rätten [n.] European Community law [EU]
EGT [abbrev: Europeiska gemenskapernas officiella tidning] Official Journal (OJ) [EU]
Egypten [n.] Egypt
egyptisk [adj.; ~t, ~a] Egyptian
e-handel [n.; ~n; abbrev: elektronisk handel] e-commerce [abbrev: electronic commerce] [IT]
EIB [abbrev: Europeiska investeringsbanken] European Investment Bank (EIB) [EU]
ej [adv.] not, no
ejderdun [n.; ~et, ~] eider down
ek [n.; ~en, ~ar] oak
eker [n.; ~n, ekrar] spoke [wheel]
EKG [n.; abbrev: elektrokardiogram] electrocardiogram (EKG)
eko[1] [n.; ~t, ~n] echo; reaction
eko-[2] [prefix] ecological, environmental; economic
Ekobrottsmyndigheten (EBM) [n.] National Economic Crimes Bureau
Ekofin [n.] Ecofin [EU economics and finance body]
ekollon [n.; ~et, ~] acorn
ekolod [n.; ~et, ~] echo sounder, sonar
ekologisk [adj.; ~t, ~a] environmental; **~t odlade varor** organic foods; **~t område** conservation area
ekon. [abbrev: ekonomi] economics
ekon.dr. [abbrev: ekonomie doktor] doctoral degree in economics
ekon.kand. [abbrev: ekonomie kandidat] graduate in economics
ekon.mag. [abbrev: ekonomie magister] Master's in economics
ekonom [n.; ~en, ~er] economist
ekonomi [n.; ~n, ~er] economy

ekonomisk [adj.; ~t, ~a] economic; economical; **~ brottslighet** white-collar crime [fraud, embezzlement, bribery, forgery, etc.]; **~ politik** economic policy; **~, social och territoriell sammanhållning** economic, social and territorial cohesion [EU]
Ekonomiska och monetära unionen (EMU) [n.] Economic and Monetary Union (EMU)
Ekonomistyrningsverket (ESV) [n.] National Financial Management Administration
ekorre [n.; ~n, ekorrar] squirrel
ekorrhjul [n.; ~et] treadmill, rat race
e.Kr. [abbrev: efter Kristus] Anno Domini (A.D.)
eksem [n.; ~et, ~] eczema
e-kurs [n.; ~en, ~er] e-learning [IT]
ekvation [n.; ~en, ~er] equation
ekvatorn [n.] equator
el [abbrev: elektricitet] electricity; electrical
el. [abbrev: eller] or
elaffär [n.; ~en, ~er] electrical goods store
elak [adj.; ~t, ~a] evil, wicked, malicious; nasty, foul
elartiklar [n.pl.] electrical goods
elastisk binda [n.; ~n, bindor] elastic bandage
eld [n.; ~en, ~ar] fire, flame; light [for a cigarette]; **göra upp ~** light a fire
elda [v.; ~r, ~de, ~t] light a fire
eldfast [adj.; ~a] ovenproof; **~ form** ovenproof dish
Eldsland [n.] Tierra del Fuego
eldvapen [n.; -vapnet, ~] firearm
el.dyl. [abbrev: eller dylikt] or the like
elefant [n.; ~en, ~er] elephant
elegant [adj.; ~a] elegant
elektricitet [n.; ~en] electricity
elektricitetsmätare [n.; ~n, ~] electric meter
elektriker [n.; ~n, ~] electrician
elektrisk [adj.; ~t, ~a] electric(al); **~a varor** electrical goods

elektronik [n.; ~en] electronics [IT]
elektronisk [adj.; ~t, ~a] electronic
[IT]; ~ **almanacka** personal digital assistant [IT]; ~ **blixt** electronic flash; ~ **bok** e-book [IT]; ~
certifikat electronic certificate [IT];
~ **post** e-mail [IT]; ~**a motor-**
vägar digital highway [IT]
element [n.; ~en, ~er] element;
radiator
elev [n.; ~en, ~er] pupil, student
elevkår [n.; ~en, ~er] student body
elevråd [n.; ~et, ~] student council
elfenben [n.; ~et] ivory
Elfenbenkusten [n.] Côte d'Ivoire
[formerly Ivory Coast]
elfte [num.] eleventh
elgitarr [n.; ~en, ~er] electric guitar
elit [n.; ~en, ~er] elite
elitidrott [n.; ~en] top-level sports
elitserien [n.] top-level sports
league [especially ice hockey]
eller [conj.] or; ~ **dylikt** or the like,
and that sort of thing; ~ **hur?** or
what?, is that right?; ~ **också** or
else
elljusspår [n.; ~et] running track
with lighting
elmätare [n.; ~n, ~] electric meter
elnät [n.; ~et, ~] power grid
elreparatör [n.; ~en, ~er] electrician
elrullstol [n.; ~en, -stolar] electric
wheelchair
elräkning [n.; ~en, ~ar] electric bill
Elsass [n.] Alsace
Elsäkerhetsverket [n.] National
Electrical Safety Board
eluttag [n.; ~et, ~] electrical outlet,
socket
elva [num.] eleven
elvahundratalet [n.] **(1100-talet)**
twelfth century
elverk [n.; ~et, ~] power station
elvisp [n.; ~en, ~ar] electric mixer
elände [n.; ~t] misery; bad luck
EM [abbrev: europamästerskap]
European Championship
em. [abbrev: eftermiddagen] afternoon (p.m.) [abbrev: post meridiem]
e-mail [n.] e-mail [abbrev: electronic mail] [IT]

emalj [n.; ~en, ~er] enamel
EMAS [abbrev.] Eco-Management
and Audit Scheme (EMAS) [EU
environmental body]
embarkera [v.; ~r, ~de, ~t] board,
go on board, embark
embarkeringskort [n.; ~et, ~]
boarding card
e-meddelande [n.; ~t, ~n] e-mail
[IT]
emellan [prep., adv.] between, in
between
emellanåt [adv.] occasionally
emellertid [adv.] however
emfas [n.; ~en] emphasis
emfatisk omskrivning [n.; ~en]
clefting [gram]
emigrant [n.; ~en, ~er] emigrant
emigrera [v.; ~r, ~de, ~t] emigrate
emot [prep./adv.] against, towards;
ha något ~ mind, object; **ta** ~
receive, take in, accept
emotikon [n.; ~en, ~er] emoticon,
smiley [IT]
EMS [abbrev: Europeiska monetära systemet] European Monetary
System (EMS) [EU]
em-streck [n.; ~et] em dash [IT]
EMU [abbrev: Ekonomiska och
monetära unionen] Economic and
Monetary Union (EMU) [EU]
en¹ [adv.; usually with num.] about,
approximately
en² [indef. art.; ett] a/an
en³ [n.; ~en, ~ar] juniper
en⁴ [num.; ett] one; **den/det ena** the
one, one of them
en⁵ [pron.obj.; man] one, someone
ena [v.; ~r, ~de, ~t] unite
enarmad bandit [n.] slot machine,
one-armed bandit
enastående [adj.] unique, remarkable
enbart [adv.] merely; exclusively
enbär [n.; ~et, ~] juniper berry
enda [adj.] single; only
endagsbiljett [n.; ~en, ~er] one-
day ticket/pass
endast [adv.] only
endiv [n.; ~en, ~er] endive, chicory
energi [n.; ~n] energy

energisk [adj.; ~t, ~a] energetic
enfamiljsvilla [n.; ~n, -villor] single-family house
enfilig [adj.; ~t, ~a] single file
enfärgad [adj.; -färgat, ~e] plain; monochromatic
engagemang [n.; ~en, ~er] engagement, contract; obligation, commitment
engagera [v.; ~r, ~de, ~t] engage, commit; ~ **sig** commit oneself, be committed
engelsk [adj.; ~t, ~a] English
engelska [n.] English language; Englishwoman
engelsktalande [adj.] English-speaking
engelsman [n.; -mannen, -män] Englishman
England [n.] England
en gros [adv.] wholesale
engångskamera [n.; ~n, -kameror] disposable camera
engångsrakhyvel [n.; -hyveln, -hyvlar] disposable razor
enhet [n.; ~en, ~er] unity: unit; drive [IT]
enhetlig [adj.; ~t, ~a] homogeneous, uniform
enhetsbeteckning [n.; ~en, ~ar] drive specification [IT]
enhällighet [n.; ~en] unanimity
enig [adj.; ~t, ~a] united; unanimous
enighet [n.; ~en, ~er] agreement; unity
enkel [adj.; ~t, enkla] single; plain, simple; easy; ~ **biljett** one-way ticket; ~ **resa** one-way trip
enkelhet [n.; ~en, ~er] simplicity
enkelhytt [n.; ~en, ~er] cabin for one, single cabin
enkelriktad gata [n.; ~n, gator] one-way street
enkelrum [n.; -rummet, ~] single room
enkelt [see: **enkel**]
enkrona [n.; ~n] 1-krona coin
enkät [n.; ~en, ~er] inquiry, investigation, survey
enl. [abbrev.; see: **enligt**]
enlighet [n.]: **i ~ med**.in accordance with

enligt [prep.] according to; ~ **tidtabell** according to the schedule, scheduled
enorm [adj.; ~t, ~a] enormous
enplansvilla [n.; ~n, -villor] one-story house, bungalow
enrisrökt [adj.; ~a] smoked over juniper coals
enrumslägenhet [n.; ~en, ~er] one-room apartment
ens [pron.; see: **en**] one's
ensam [adj.; ~t, ~a] alone, by oneself; lonely
ensamhet [n.; ~en] solitude; loneliness
ensamstående [adj.] single, not married
ense (om) [adj.] agreed (on)
ensemble [n.; ~n, ~r] ensemble
enskild [adj.; -skilt, ~a] separate, private, personal
enstaka [adj.] alone; unique
entré [n.; ~n, ~er] entrance, way in
entrecôte [n.; ~n, ~r] sirloin steak
entreprenör [n.; ~en, ~er] contractor
entusiasm [n.; ~en] enthusiasm
entydig [adj.; ~t, ~a] unequivocal, unambiguous; clear-cut
envis [adj.; ~t, ~a] stubborn, obstinate; persistent
enzym [n.; ~et, ~] enzyme
e.o. [abbrev: extraordinarie] temporary, pro tempore
epilepsi [n.; ~n] epilepsy
epileptiker [n.; ~n, ~] epileptic
epitet [n.; ~et, ~] epithet [gram]
epok [n.; ~en, ~er] epoch
epokgörande [adj.] epoch-making
e-post [n.; ~en] e-mail [IT]
e-posta [v.; ~r, ~de, ~t] e-mail [IT]
e-postadress [n.; ~en, ~er] e-mail address [IT]
e-postansvarig [n.] postmaster [IT]
e-posthantering [n.; ~en] e-mail management, e-mail administration [IT]
e-postkonto [n.; ~t, ~n] e-mail account [IT]
e-postlista [n.; ~n, -listor] mailing list [IT]
e-postmeddelande [n.; ~t, ~n] e-mail message [IT]

e-postmästare [n.; ~n, ~] postmaster [IT]

e-postprogram [n.; -grammet, ~] e-mail program [IT]

e-posttjänst [n.; ~en, ~er] e-mail service [IT]

EPSCO-rådet [n.] Employment, Social Policy, Health and Consumer Affairs Council (EPSCO Council) [EU]

er¹ [pron.obj.pl. & sing. formal; see: ni] you

er² [pron.poss.pl.; ert, era] your, yours

era¹ [n.; ~n, eror] era

era² [see: er)]

Erasmus [n.] ERASMUS [EU scholarship program]

erbjuda [v.; -bjuder, -bjöd, -bjudit] offer

erbjudande [n.; ~t, ~n] offer

erbjuden [adj.; -bjudet, -bjudna] offered; bli ~ be offered

erfara [v.; erfar, erfor, erfarit] learn; get to know; experience

erfaren [adj.; -faret, -farna] experienced; skilled

erfarenhet [n.; ~en, ~er] experience

erfordra [v.; ~r, ~de, ~t] require, demand; ~s be required

Eritrea [n.] Eritrea

erkänd [adj.; -känt, ~a] recognized, approved

erkänna [v.; -känner, -kände, -känt] recognize

erkännande [n.; ~t, ~n] acknowledgment; recognition

ersätta [v.; -sätter, -satte, -satt] replace

ersättare [n.; ~n, ~] substitute, proxy

ersättning [n.; ~en, ~ar] compensation, refund

ersättningstecken [n.; -tecknet, ~] wild card [IT]

ESA [abbrev: Europeiska rymdorganisationen] European Space Agency (ESA) [EU]

escape-tangent [n.; ~en] Escape key (Esc) [IT]

eskimå [n.; ~n, ~er] Eskimo

ess [n.; ~et, ~] ace [cards]

Estland [n.] Estonia

estländsk [adj.; ~t, ~a] Estonian

estländska [n.] Estonian language

estnisk [adj.; ~t, ~a] Estonian

etablera [v.; ~r, ~de, ~t] establish; ~ sig establish o.s., set oneself up as; settle down

etapp [n.; ~en, ~er] stage

etappklippning [n.; ~en] layered cut

etc. [abbrev: et cetera] etc. [abbrev: et cetera]

etik [n.; ~en, ~er] ethics

etikett [n.; ~en, ~er] label; etiquette

etikettsregel [n.; ~n, -regler] rule of etiquette

Etiopien [n.] Ethiopia

etiopisk [adj.; ~t, ~a] Ethiopian

etisk [adj.; ~t, ~a] ethical

etnisk [adj.; ~t, ~a] ethnic

Etnografiska museet [n.] National Museum of Ethnography

etsning [n.; ~en, ~ar] etching

ett [num.; indef.art; see: en] one; a

ettan [n.] first gear; ~s växel first gear

et-tecken [n.; -tecknet, ~] ampersand (&) [IT]

EU¹ [abbrev: Europeiska unionen] European Union (EU)

e.u.² [abbrev: enligt uppdrag] by order of

EU-byråkrat [n.; ~en, ~er] EU bureaucrat

EU-direktiv [n.; ~et, ~] Euro directive

EU-domstolen [n.] European Court of Human Rights

EUF [abbrev: Europeiska utvecklingsfonden] European Development Fund (EDF) [EU]

EU-fördraget [n.] Treaty on European Union, Maastricht Treaty [EU]

EU-institutioner [n.pl.] EU institutions

EU-kommissionen [n.] European Commission

EU-lagstiftning [n.; ~en] EU legislation, EU laws

EU-land [n.; ~et, -länder] EU member country

EU-medborgare [n.; ~n, ~] EU citizen

EU-medborgarskap [n.; ~et] citizenship of the Union [EU]

EU-ordförandeskap [n.; ~et] EU Presidency [EU]

EU-parlamentet [n.] European Parliament

Euratom [abbrev: Europeiska atomenergigemenskapen] European Atomic Energy Community (Euratom) [EU]

euro [n.; ~n, ~] euro [EU currency]

Eurobarometer [n.; ~n] Eurobarometer [EU, attitude surveys]

Eurogruppen [n.] Euro Group [EU, Ecofin]

Eurojust [n.] Eurojust [EU]

eurokrat [n.; ~en, ~er] eurocrat [EU bureaucrat]

euroland [n.; ~et, -länder] euro country [EU, country that has euro as its currency]

Europa [n.] Europe; ~ **à la carte** Europe 'à la carte' [EU]; ~ **med två hastigheter** two-speed Europe [EU]

Europaavtalet [n.] Europe Agreement [EU]

Europabolag [n.; ~et] European company [EU]

Europadagen [n.] Europe Day [EU, May 9]

Europadomstolen [n.] European Court of Human Rights

europamästerskap (EM) [n.; ~et] European championship

Europaparlamentet [n.] European Parliament

Europarådet [n.] Council of Europe

europeisk [adj.; ~t, ~a] European

europeisk säkerhets- och försvarsidentitet [n.; ~en] European security and defence identity [EU]

Europeisk säkerhets- och försvarspolitiken (ESFP) [n.] European Security and Defence Policy (ESDP) [EU]

Europeiska byrån för bedrägeribekämpning (OLAF) [n.] European Anti-fraud Office (OLAF) [EU]

Europeiska centralbanken (ECB) [n.] European Central Bank (ECB) [EU]

Europeiska ekonomiska och sociala kommittén (EESK) [n.] European Economic and Social Committee (EESC) [EU]

Europeiska ekonomiska samarbetsområdet (EES) [n.] European Economic Area (EEA) [EU]

Europeiska enhetsakten [n.] Single European Act [EU 1987]

Europeiska fackliga samorganisation (EFS) [n.; ~en] European Trade Union Confederation (ETUC)

Europeiska gemenskapen (EG) [n.] European Community (EC) [EU]

Europeiska gemenskapernas domstol (EG-domstolen) [n.; ~en] Court of Justice of the European Communities [EU]

Europeiska gemenskapernas officiella tidning (EGT) [n.; ~en] Official Journal (OJ) [EU]

Europeiska investeringsbanken (EIB) [n.] European Investment Bank (EIB) [EU]

Europeiska kommissionen [n.] European Commission (EC) [EU]

Europeiska kommissionens ordförande [n.; ~n] President of the European Commission [EU]

Europeiska konventet om EU:s framtid [n.] European Convention, Convention on the Future of Europe [EU]

Europeiska konventionen om skydd för de mänskliga rättigheterna [n.] European Convention on Human Rights (ECHR) [EU]

Europeiska ombudsmannen [n.] European Ombudsman [EU]

Europeiska området för forskningsverksamhet (ERA) [n.] European Research Area (ERA) [EU]

Europeiska revisionsrätten [n.] European Court of Auditors [EU]

Europeiska rådet [n.] European Council [EU]

Europeiska sammanslutningen av industri- och arbetsgivarorganisationer (UNICE) [n.] Union of Industries of the European Community (UNICE) [EU]

Europeiska sysselsättningsstrategin [n.] European Employment Strategy (EES) [EU]

Europeiska unionen (EU) [n.] European Union (EU) [EU]

Europeiska unionens pelare [n.pl.] pillars of the European Union [EU]

Europeiska unionens råd [n.; ~et] Council of the European Union [EU]

Europeiska utvecklingsfonden (EUF) [n.] European Development Fund (EDF) [EU]

Europeiskt centrum för offentliga företag (CEEP) [n.] European Centre for Public Enterprises (CEEP)

Europeiskt initiativ för demokrati och mänskliga rättigheter [n.] European Initiative for Democracy and Human Rights (EIDHR) [EU]

Europeiskt politiskt samarbete (EPS) [n.] European political cooperation (EPC) [EU]

Europeiskt straffrättsligt nätverk [n.] European Judicial Network in criminal matters (EJN) [EU]

Europol [abbrev: Europeiska polisbyrån] Europol [abbrev: European Police Office] [EU]

euroskeptiker [n.; ~n, ~] Euroskeptic [person who doubts value of EU]

Eurostat [n.] Eurostat [abbrev: Statistical Office of the European Communities] [EU]

EU-rådet [n.] Council of the European Union

EU-rätten [n.] European Union law [EU]

EU-rättsakter [n.pl.] EU legislation

e-utbildning [n.; ~en] e-learning [IT]

EU-toppmöte [n.; ~t, ~n] EU summit meeting

EU-val [n.; ~et, ~] vote connected with EU

ev. [see: eventuellt]

evangelium [n.; -liet, -lier] gospel

evenemang [n.; ~en, ~er] event

evenemangsprogram [n.; -grammet, ~] program of events

eventuell [adj.; ~t, ~a] possible

eventuellt [adv.] possibly, perhaps, if necessary

evig [adj.; ~t, ~a] eternal, everlasting

evighet [n.; ~en, ~er] eternity, ages

ex. [abbrev: exempel; exemplar] example; copy

exakt [adj.; ~a] exact; ~ **belopp** exact amount, exact fare; ~ **växel** exact change

examen [n.; examina] examination; degree

examensfri [adj.; -fritt, ~a] without examination

exekverbar [adj.; ~t, ~a] executable [IT]

exempel [n.; exemplet, ~] example; **till** ~ for example

exempelvis [adv.] for example

exemplar [n.; ~et, ~] copy, specimen

exil [n.; ~en] exile

existens [n.; ~en, ~er] existence

existera [v.; ~r, ~de, ~t] exist

exkl. [see: **exklusive**]

exklusive [prep.] excluding

expanderat minne [n.; ~t] expanded memory [IT]

expansion [n.; ~en, ~er] expansion

expansionskort [n.; ~et, ~] expansion board [IT]

expedit [n.; ~en, ~er] sales clerk, store clerk

expedition [n.; ~en, ~er] sending, mailing; carrying out; service; office, department; expedition

expeditionsavgift [n.; ~en, ~er] commission, service charge

expeditionschef [n.; ~en, ~er] director-general for administrative affairs

expeditionspersonal [n.; ~en] office staff

expeditionsregering [n.; ~en, ~er] caretaker government
expeditionstid [n.; ~en] office hours
experiment [n.; ~en, ~er] experiment, test, trial
expert [n.; ~en, ~er] expert
expertsystem [n.; ~et, ~] expert system [IT]
explodera [v.; ~r, ~de, ~t] explode
exponentiellt skrivsätt [n.; ~et] scientific notation [IT]
exponering [n.; ~en, ~ar] exposure
exponeringsmätare [n.; ~n, ~] exposure meter
export [n.; ~en, ~er] export
exportera [v.; ~r, ~de, ~t] export
Exportkreditnämnden (EKN) [n.] Export Credit Board
Exportrådet [n.] Export Council
exportöl [n.; ~et] strong beer
express [n.; ~en] special delivery, express mail/shipment/transfer/ train
expressionism [n.; ~en] expressionism
expresspost [n.; ~en] special delivery, express mail
expresståg [n.; ~et, ~] express train

exteriör [n.; ~en, ~er] exterior
extern [adj.; ~t, ~a] external
externminne [n.; ~t] external memory [IT]
extra [adj.] extra, spare; ~ **portion** side order
extraarbete [n.; ~t] additional work
extrafönster [n.; -fönstret, ~] popup window [IT]
extralektion [n.; ~en, ~er] private lesson
extranummer [n.; -numret, ~] encore
extraordinarie [adj.] extraordinary; temporary
extrapris [n.; ~et] special discount price, special offer
extrasäng [n.; ~en, ~ar] spare bed, extra bed
extravagant [adj.; ~a] extravagant
extravecka [n.; ~n, -veckor] extra week
extrem [adj.; ~t, ~a] extreme
exv. [abbrev: exempelvis] for example (e.g.), for instance

F

f. [abbrev: förre; och följande (sida); född] former; and following (page); born

fabrik [n.; ~en, ~er] factory

fabrikant [n.; ~en, ~er] manufacturer, producer

fabrikat [n.; ~et] manufacture, product, make; **av svenskt ~** made in Sweden

fabriksarbetare [n.; ~e, ~] factory worker

facit [n.] answer, result

fack [n.; ~et, ~] partition, compartment; department, branch; profession, trade

fackbok [n.; ~en, -böcker] non-fiction; handbook, textbook

fackförbund [n.; ~et, ~] federation of trade unions

fackförening [n.; ~en, ~ar] trade union

fackföreningrörelse [n.; ~n, ~r] trade-union movement

facklig [adj.; ~t, ~a] trade-union; **~a organisationer** trade unions; **~t ansluten** member of a trade union

facklitteratur [n.; ~en] non-fiction [books]

fadder [n.; ~n, faddrar] godfather

fader [n.; formal; see: **far**]; **Fader vår** Our Father [prayer]

fagott [n.; ~en, ~er] bassoon

fakta [n.pl.; see: **faktum**] non-fiction

faktisk [adj.; ~t, ~a] real, actual, factual

faktiskt [adv.] really, actually, in fact

faktor [n.; ~n, ~er] factor

faktum [n.; ~et, fakta] fact

faktura [n.; ~n, fakturor] invoice

fakultativ [adj.; ~t, ~a] optional

fakultet [n.; ~en, ~er] department [university], faculty

falk [n.; ~en, ~ar] hawk, falcon

fall [n.; ~et, ~] fall, decline, collapse; case, instance; **i alla ~** anyway; **i så ~** in that case; **i varje ~** in any case

falla [v.; faller, föll, fallit] fall

fallande sortering [n.; ~en] descending sort [IT]

fallen [adj.; fallet, fallna] fallen, slain; gifted in/at

fallskärm [n.; ~en, ~ar] parachute

fallskärmshoppning [n.; ~en] parachuting

falsk [adj.; ~t, ~a] false; **~t alarm** false alarm

falukorv [n.; ~en, ~ar] spicy smoked sausage

familj [n.; ~en, ~er] family

familjebidrag [n.; ~et, ~] family allowance

familjeföretag [n.; ~et, ~] family business

familjeförsörjare [n.; ~n, ~] family breadwinner

familjehotell [n.; ~et, ~] hotel for families on vacation

familjemedlem [n.; -medlemmen, -medlemmar] family member

familjenöje [n.; ~t] family entertainment

familjeplanering [n.; ~en] family planning

familjerådgivare [n.; ~n, ~] family counselor

familjerätt [n.; ~en] family law

familjesida [n.; ~n, -sidor] social page

familjeskäl [n.; ~et, ~] personal reasons

fan¹ [n.] devil; ~! [vul.] damn! [colloq.]; **fy ~!** damn! [colloq.]; **vad/vem ~ är det?** what/who the devil is that? [colloq.]

fan² [n.; ~, ~s] fan [devotee]

fana [n.; ~n, fanor] flag, banner

fanatiker [n.; ~n, ~] fanatic

fann [v.past; see: **finna**]

fantasi [n.; ~n, ~er] imagination, fantasy

fantast [n.; ~en, ~er] enthusiast; dreamer

fantastisk [adj.; ~t, ~a] fantastic

fantastiskt [adv.] incredibly; fantastic

far [n.; fadern, fäder] father
fara[1] [n.; ~n, faror] danger
fara[2] [v.; farer, for, farit] go, travel, ride
farbror [n.; -brodern, -bröder] uncle [paternal]; gentleman
farfar [n.; -fadern] grandfather [paternal]
farfarsfar [n.; -fadern] greatgrandfather [paternal]
farfarsmor [n.; -modern] greatgrandmother [paternal]
farhåga [n.; ~n, -hågor] apprehension, misgiving, fear
farinsocker [n.; -sockret] brown sugar
farlig [adj.; ~t, ~a] dangerous; serious
farligt [adv.]: **inte ~** not bad, not serious
farm. (abbrev: farmacie) pharmaceutics, pharmacy [science]
farmor [n.; -modern] grandmother [paternal]
farmorsfar [n.; -fadern] greatgrandfather [paternal]
farmorsmor [n.; -modern] greatgrandmother [paternal]
FARR [abbrev: Flyktinggruppernas och Asylkommittéernas Riksråd] National Council of Refugee Groups and Asylum Committees
farsa [n.; ~n; colloq.] dad [colloq.], pa [colloq.], "old man" [colloq.]
farstu [n.; ~n, ~r] vestibule, front hall, landing
fart [n.; ~en] speed, pace; force, energy; **minska ~en** reduce speed; **öka ~en** increase speed
fartbegränsning [n.; ~en, ~ar] speed limit
fartdåre [n.; ~n, -dårar] speeder
fartgräns [n.; ~en, ~er] speed limit
fartgupp [n.; ~et, ~] speed bump
farthinder [n.; -hindret, ~] speed bump
fartkontroll [n.; ~en, ~er] speed check
fartsyndare [n.; ~n, ~] speeder
fartyg [n.; ~et, ~] vessel, ship, craft
farväl [interj.] goodbye

fas [n.; ~en, ~er] phase; aspect
fasad [n.; ~en, ~er] facade, front
fasan [n.; ~en, ~er] pheasant
fascinerande [adj.] fascinating
fascistisk [adj.; ~t, ~a] Fascist
fast[1] [adj.; ~a] fixed, stuck; **~ anslutning** leased line [IT]; **~ anställning** permanent employment; **~ apposition** fixed epithet [gram]; **~ mellanslag** hard space, sticky space [IT]; **~ program** firmware, hard-wired program [IT]
fast[2] [adv.] though
fasta [v.; ~r, ~de, ~t] fast; **på ~nde mage** on an empty stomach
fastan [n.] Lent
faster [n.; ~n, fastrar] aunt [paternal]
fastighet [n.; ~en, ~er] real estate, building
fastighetsmäklare [n.; ~n, ~] real estate agent
fastighetsskatt [n.; ~en, ~er] real estate tax
fastighetsägare [n.; ~n, ~] house owner, property owner
fastlagen [n.] Lent
fastlagsbulle [n.; ~n, -bullar] Lenten bun [filled with almond paste and cream]
fastland [n.; ~et] mainland, dry land
fastna [v.; ~r, ~de, ~t] get caught, get stuck
fastpris [n.; ~et] fixed rate, flat rate
fastskiva [n.; ~n, -skivor] fixed disk [IT]
fastslå [v.; -slår, -slog, -slagit] lay down, establish; fix
fastställa [v.; -ställer, -ställde, -ställt] fix; determine; confirm; establish
fastän [conj.] although
fat [n.; ~et, ~] dish; saucer; bowl; barrel, vat
fatal [adj.; ~t, ~a] fatal; disastrous, regrettable
fatta [v.; ~r, ~de, ~t] understand, grasp; **~s** be missing
fattig [adj.; ~t, ~a] poor; **~a riddare** French toast

fattigdom [n.; ~en] poverty; lack

fatöl [n.; ~et, ~] draft beer, beer on tap

favorit [n.; ~en, ~er] favorite

fax¹ [n.; ~et, ~] fax [IT]

fax² [n.; ~en, ~ar] fax machine [IT]

faxa [v.; ~r, ~de, ~t] fax, send by fax

fd. [abbrev: före detta] formerly

feb. [see: februari]

feber [n.; ~n, febrar] fever; **ha ~** have a temperature

febernedsättande medel [n.; -medlet, ~] antipyretic

febertermometer [n.; ~n, -metrar] fever thermometer

febr. [see: februari]

febrig [adj.; ~t, ~a] feverish

februari [n.] February

federal [adj.; ~t, ~a] federal

federalism [n.; ~en] federalism

fel¹ [adj./adv.] wrong; ~ **nummer** wrong number

fel² [n.; ~et, ~] mistake; fault; defect; **göra ett ~** make a mistake

felaktig [adj.; ~t, ~a] wrong, mistaken; incorrect; defective

felfri [adj.; -fritt, ~a] faultless, correct

felhanterare [n.; ~n, ~] error handler [IT]

felstavad [adj.; -stavat, ~a] misspelled [IT]

felsökning [n.; ~en] debugging [IT]

fem [num.] five

femininum [n.; ~et] feminine [gram]

feminist [n.; ~en, ~er] feminist

feministisk [adj.; ~t, ~a] feminist

femkamp [n.; ~en, ~er] pentathlon

femkrona [n.; ~n, -kronor] 5-krona coin

femma [n.; ~n, femmor] 5-krona coin, # 5, fiver

femte [num.] fifth; May

femtio [num.] fifty

femtiolapp [n.; ~en, ~ar] 50-krona bill

femtionde [num.] fiftieth

femtioöring [n.; ~en, ~ar] 50-öre coin [1/2 krona]

femton [num.] fifteen

femtonde [num.] fifteenth

femtonhundratalet (1500-talet) sixteenth century

femöring med ägg [n.] small steak with fried egg

Fenix [n.] Phoenix

fenomen [n.; ~et, ~] phenomenon

ferier [n.pl.] vacation, holidays

fermenterade mjölkprodukter [n.pl.] cultured milk products

fest [n.; ~en, ~er] party

festival [n.; ~en, ~er] festival

festmiddag [n.; ~en, ~er] banquet

fet [adj.; ~t, ~a] fatty, oily; rich [food]; ~ **hud** oily skin; ~**t hår** greasy hair; ~ **text** bold [IT]

fetma [n.; ~n] corpulence, obesity

fetstil [n.; ~en] bold, boldface [IT]

fett [n.; ~et, ~er] fat; ~**er i kosten** dietary fats

fettersättningar [n.pl.] fat substitutes

fettfri [adj.; ~t, ~a] fat-free

fettinnehåll [n.; ~et] fat content

fettisdagen [n.] Shrove Tuesday [Tuesday before Lent], Mardi Gras

FF¹ [abbrev: fotbollsförening] soccer association, soccer club

ff.² [abbrev: och följande sidor] and following pages

fiberoptisk kabel [n.; ~n, kablar] fiberoptic cable [IT]

fick [v.past; see: få]

ficka [n.; ~n, fickor] pocket

fickdator [n.; ~n, ~er] handheld computer, personal data assistant (PDA), pocket computer [IT]

fickkniv [n.; ~en, ~ar] pocket knife

ficklampa [n.; ~n, -lampor] flashlight

fickminne [n.; ~t, ~n] flash memory, flash drive [IT]

ficktjuv [n.; ~en, ~ar] pickpocket

fiende [n.; ~n, ~r] enemy

fientlig programvara [n.; ~n, -varor] malware, malicious software [IT]

FIFA [abbrev: Fédération Internationale de Football Association] Fédération Internationale de Football Association (FIFA) [international soccer federation]

fig. [see: **figur**]
figur [n.; ~en, ~er] figure
fika [v.; ~r, ~de, ~t] have a coffee
fikapaus [n.; ~en, ~er] coffee break
fikon [n.; ~et, ~] fig
fikonträd [n.; ~et, ~] fig tree
fiktiv variabel [n.; ~n, -abler] dummy variable [IT]
fikus [n.; ~en, ~ar] rubber plant
fil¹ [n.; ~en, ~er] traffic lane; (thin) yogurt; file [IT]
fil² [n.; ~en, ~ar] file [tool]
fil.³ [see: **filosofi**]
filallokeringstabell [n.; ~en, ~er] file allocation table (FAT) [IT]
fil.dr. [abbrev: filosofie doktor] Doctor of Philosophy (PhD)
filé [n.; ~n] filet mignon; ~ **Oscar** veal fillet [with bearnaise sauce, asparagus and lobster]
filformat [n.; ~et, ~] file format [IT]
filhanterare [n.; ~n] file manager [IT]
filial [n.; ~en, ~er] branch [business, store]
Filippinerna [n.pl.] Philippines
filippinsk [adj.; ~t, ~a] Philippine, Filipino
fil.kand. [abbrev: filosofie kandidat] Bachelor of Arts/Science (B.A./B.S.)
fil.lic. [abbrev: filosofie licentiat] Licentiate of Arts/Science
film [n.; ~en, ~er] film, movie
fil.mag. [abbrev: filosofie magister] Master of Arts/Science (M.A./M.S.)
filmcensur [n.; ~en] film censorship
filmduk [n.; ~en, ~ar] movie screen, screen
filmjölk [n.; ~en] sour milk, yogurt
filmmanuskript [n.; ~et, ~] screenplay, script
filmproducent [n.; ~en, ~er] film producer
filmregissör [n.; ~en, ~er] film director
filmrulle [n.; ~n, -rullar] roll of film
filmskådespelare [n.; ~n, ~] film actor, film actress
filmsnutt [n.; ~en, ~ar] film clip [IT]

filmstjärna [n.; ~n, -stjärnor] film star
filnamn [n.; ~et, ~] file name [IT]
filnamnssuffix [n.; et, ~] file name extension [IT]
filnamnstillägg [n.; ~et, ~] file name extension [IT]
filnamnsändelse [n.; ~n, ~r] file name extension [IT]
filosof [n.; ~en, ~er] philosopher
filosofi [n.; ~n, ~er] philosophy
filosofie doktor (fil.dr.) [n.; ~n] Doctor of Philosophy (Ph.D.)
filosofie kandidat (fil.kand.) [n.; ~en] Bachelor of Science/Art (B.S./B.A.)
filosofie licentiat (fil.lic.) [n.; ~en] Licentiate of Science/Art [between M.A. and Ph.D.]
filosofie magister (fil.mag.) [n.; ~n] Master of Science/Art (M.S./M.A.)
filosofiska fakulteterna [n.pl.] departments/faculties of arts and sciences
filstorlek [n.; ~en] file size [IT]
filt [n.; ~en, ~ar] blanket
filter [n.; filtret, ~] filter
filtercigaretter [n.pl.] filter cigarettes
filterpåse [n.; ~n, -påsar] filter [coffee maker]
filtillägg [n.; ~et, ~] file extension [IT]
fimp [n.; ~en, ~ar] cigarette butt
fin [adj.; ~t, ~a] fine, beautiful
final [n.; ~en, ~er] finale, finals [sports]
finalfokus [n.; ~en, ~] end focus [gram]
final konjunktion [n.; ~en, ~er] purpose conjunction [gram]
finaltyngd [adj.; -tyngt, ~a] end weighted [gram]
Finansdepartementet [n.] Ministry of Finance
finansiell [adj.; ~t, ~a] financial
finansiera [v.; ~r, ~de, ~t] finance, fund
finansiering [n.; ~en, ~er] financing
Finansinspektionen [n.] Finance Inspection Board

finansminister [n.; ~n] Minister of Finance

Finansutskottet [n.] Committee on Finance (in Parliament)

finbageri [n.; ~et, ~er] pastry shop

finger [n.; fingret, fingrar] finger

fingeravtryck [n.; ~et, ~] fingerprint

finhackad [adj.; -hackat, ~a] finely chopped

finit [adj.; ~a] finite [gram]

finkornig [adj.; ~t, ~a] fine-grained

Finland [n.] Finland

finländsk [adj.; ~t, ~a] Finnish

finna [v.; finner, fann, funnit] find

finnas [v.; finns, fanns, funnits] exist, be; ~ **kvar** remain, still exist; **det finns** there is/are; **finns det?** is/are there?

finne [n.; ~n, finnar] Finn; pimple

finns [v.; see: **finnas**]

finsk [adj.; ~t, ~a] Finnish

finska [n.] Finnish language; Finnish woman

finsktalande [adj.] Finnish-speaking

fint [adv.] fine

fiol [n.; ~en, ~er] violin, fiddle

FIOS (abbrev: Förenade invandrar-organisationer i Sverige) United Immigrant Organizations of Sweden

fira [v.; ~r, ~de, ~t] celebrate; ~ **jul** celebrate Christmas

firma [n.; ~n, firmor] firm, company

firmabil [n.; ~en, ~ar] company car

firmafest [n.; ~en, ~er] office party

firmamärke [n.; ~t, ~n] trademark

fisk [n.; ~en, ~ar] fish; ~ **och skaldjur** seafood

fiska [v.; ~r, ~de, ~t] fish

fiskaffär [n.; ~en, ~er] fish store

fiskare [n.; ~n, ~] fisherman

Fiskarna [n.pl.] Pisces

fiskben [n.; ~et, ~] fishbone; herringbone

fiskbullar [n.pl.] codfish balls

fiskdisk [n.; ~en, ~ar] fish stall

fiske [n.; ~t] fishing; ~ **ej tillåtet** no fishing; ~ **förbjudet** no fishing; ~ **tillåtet** fishing permitted

fiskeby [n.; ~n, ~ar] fishing village

fiskebåt [n.; ~en, ~ar] fishing boat

fiskedon [n.; ~et] fishing tackle

fiskehamn [n.; ~n, ~er] fishing port

fiskekort [n.; ~et, ~] fishing license

fiskeläge [n.; ~t, ~n] fishing village

fiskeredskap [n.pl.] fishing gear/tackle

Fiskeriverket [n.] National Board of Fisheries

fiskfärs [n.; ~en] fish mousse

fiskhandlare [n.; ~n, ~] fishmonger

fiskmjöl [n.; ~et] fish flour

fiskmås [n.; ~en, ~ar] gull

fisknät [n.; ~et, ~] fish net

fiskodling [n.; ~en] fish farming

fiskpinnar [n.pl.] fish sticks

fiskprodukter [n.pl.] fish products

fiskrätt [n.; ~en, ~er] fish dish

fisksoppa [n.; ~n, -soppor] fish soup

fiskutrustning [n.; ~en] fishing gear

fitta [n.; vul.; ~n, fittor] cunt [vul.]

fixa [v.; ~r, ~de, ~t] fix, mend

fjol [n.]: **i** ~ last year

fjolårets [adj.] last year's

fjor [see: **fjol**]

fjorton [num.] fourteen; **om** ~ **dagar** in 2 weeks time

fjortonde [num.] fourteenth

fjortonhundratalet (1400-talet) [n.] fifteenth century

fjäder [n.; ~n, fjädrar] feather; spring [metal]

fjäderfä [n.; ~t] poultry

fjädring [n.; ~en] suspension [auto]

fjäll [n.; ~et, ~] mountain

fjällripa [n.; ~n, -ripor] ptarmigan, white grouse

fjälltrakt [n.; ~en, ~er] mountain area

fjällvandring [n.; ~en, ~ar] mountain hike/hiking

fjärde [num.] fourth; April

fjärdedel [n.; ~en, ~ar] quarter

fjäril [n.; ~en, ~ar] butterfly; moth

fjärilsim [n.; -simmet] butterfly stroke [swimming]

fjärr- [suffix] remote-

fjärran [adv.] far off, remote, distant; **i** ~ in the distance; ~ **Östern** Far East

fjärr**ansluten** [adj.; -slutet, -slutna] remote(ly) connected [IT]

fjärr**anslutning** [n.; ~en, ~ar] remote connection [IT]

fjärrkontr**oll** [n.; ~en] remote control [IT]

fjärrs**amtal** [n.; ~et, ~] long-distance call

fjärrt**åg** [n.; ~et, ~] long-distance train

fjärr**åtkomst** [n.; ~en] remote access [IT]

fjärt [n.; colloq.; ~en, ~] fart [colloq]

fjärta [v.; colloq.; ~r, ~de, ~t] fart [colloq]

FK [abbrev: Försäkringskassan] National Social Insurance Agency

FK-konto [n.; ~t, ~n] social insurance number

f.Kr. [abbrev: före Kristus] B.C. [abbrev: before Christ]

fladderm**us** [n.; ~en, -möss] bat

flagga [n.; ~n, flaggor] flag

flamberad [adj.; -rat, ~e] flambé

flaml**ändsk** [adj.; ~t, ~a] Flemish

flamsk [adj.; ~t, ~a] Flemish

flanell [n.] flannel

flanera [v.; ~r, ~de, ~t] wander

flashminne [n.; ~t, ~n] flash memory [IT]

flaska [n.; ~n, flaskor] bottle

flaskbank [n.; ~en, ~er] bottle recycling bin

flaskvärmare [n.; ~n, ~] bottle warmer

flasköl [n.; ~et, ~] bottled beer

flasköppnare [n.; ~n, ~] bottle opener

fler- [suffix] multi-, many, poly-; more

flera [adj. comp. of: många] several; more

flerfunktionsskrivare [n.; ~n, ~] multifunctional printer, all-in-one printer [IT]

flerpacketerad [adj.; -rat, ~e] multipack(ed)

flersändning [n.; ~en, ~ar] multicasting [IT]

flertal [n.; ~et] plural; majority; several

flertrådsteknik [n.; ~en] multithreading [IT]

fleruppdragskörning [n.; ~en] multitasking [IT]

flerårig [adj.; ~t, ~a] of several years; perennial

flesta [adj.superl.: många] most; de ~ most, the majority of

flexibilitet [n.; ~en] flexibility

flextid [n.; ~en, ~er] flextime

flicka [n.; ~n, flickor] girl

flicknamn [n.; ~et] maiden name

flickvän [n.; -vännen, -vänner] girlfriend

flight [n.] flight

flik [n.; ~en, ~ar] flap, tab [IT]

flingor [n.pl.] cornflakes, breakfast cereal

flintskallig [adj.; ~t, ~a] bald

flirta [see: flörta]

flitig [adj.; ~t, ~a] diligent, busy, assiduous; ~a Lisa impatiens [flower]

flock [n.; ~en, ~ar] flock, herd

flod [n.; ~en, ~er] river; high tide

flodkryssning [n.; ~en, ~ar] river cruise

flodrand [n.; ~en, -ränder] river bank

flodstrand [n.; ~en, -stränder] river bank

florett [n.; ~en, ~er] foil [fencing]

florsocker [n.; -sockret] icing

flott [adj.; ~a] fancy, splendid

flotta [n.; ~n, flottor] navy, fleet

flotte [n.; ~n, flottar] raft

fluga [n.; ~n, flugor] fly; craze; bow tie

flundra [n.; ~n, flundror] flounder

flutit [v.past; see: flyta]

fly [v.; ~r, ~dde, ~tt] flee, escape from

flyg [n.; ~et, ~] flight; plane; med ~ by air

flyga [v.; flyger, flög, flugit] fly

flygare [n.; ~n, ~] aviator, pilot

flygbiljett [n.; ~en, ~er] plane ticket

flygbolag [n.; ~et, ~] airline

flygbuss [n.; ~en, ~ar] airport bus

flygbåt [n.; ~en, ~ar] hydrofoil

flygel [n.; ~n, flyglar] wing [of a building]; grand piano

flygfrakt [n.; ~en, ~er] air freight
flyginformation [n.; ~en] flight
information
flygkapten [n.; ~en, ~er] captain,
pilot
flygnummer [n.; -numret, ~] flight
number
flygplan [n.; ~et, ~] plane
flygplats [n.; ~en, ~er] airport
flygplatsavgift [n.; ~en, ~er] airport
tax
flygpost [n.; ~en] airmail
flygresa [n.; ~n, -resor] flight
flygsjukpåse [n.; ~n, -påsar] airsickness bag
flygskärm [n.; ~en, ~ar] paraglider
flygsteward [n.; ~en, ~er] flight
attendant [male]
flygterminal [n.; ~en, ~er] air
terminal
flygvärdinna [n.; ~n, -värdinnor]
flight attendant [female]
flykt [n.; ~en] flight; escape
flyktigt minne [n.; ~t] volatile
memory [IT]
flykting [n.; ~en, ~ar] refugee
flyktingförläggning [n.; ~en] im-
immigration center
flyktinginvandring [n.; ~en, ~ar]
immigration of refugees
flyktingkommissariaten [n.] High
Commissioner for Refugees
(UNHCR) [UN]
flyktingläger [n.; -lägret, ~] refugee
camp
flyktingpolitik [n.; ~en] refugee
policy
flyktingstatus [n.; ~en] refugee
status
flyta [v.; flyter, flöt, flutit] float; flow
flytande [adj.] fluent; ~ **kristaller**
liquid crystal (display) [IT]
flytta [v.; ~r, ~de, ~t] move; ~ **ihop**
move in with each other, start living together; ~ **till** move to
flyttalssystem [n.; ~et] floating
point representation [IT]
flyttbar [adj.; ~t, ~a] removable
flyttbil [n.; ~en, ~ar] moving van
flyttfågel [n.; ~n, -fåglar] migratory
bird

flyttkarl [n.; ~en, ~ar] furniture
mover
flyttning [n.; ~en, ~ar] moving
[changing residence]
flyttningsanmälan [n.; -anmäl-
ningar] change of address notice
flytväst [n.; ~en, ~ar] life jacket
fläck [n.; ~en, ~ar] spot, stain
fläkt [n.; ~en, ~ar] fan; breeze
fläktrem [n.; -remmen, -remmar]
fan belt
fläsk [n.; ~et] pork
fläskben [n.; ~et, ~] pork on the
bone
fläskfilé [n.; ~n, ~er] pork fillet
fläskkarré [n.; ~n] pork loin
fläskkorv [n.; ~en, ~ar] pork
sausage
fläskkotlett [n.; ~en, ~er] pork chop
fläskkött [n.; ~et] pork
fläsklägg [n.; ~en, ~ar] pork knuckle
fläskpannkaka [n.; ~n, -kakor]
bacon-stuffed pancake
fläskpastej [n.; ~en, ~er] pork pie
fläskstek [n.; ~en, ~ar] pork roast
flödesplan [n. ~en, ~er] flowchart
[IT]
flög [v.past; see: **flyga**]
flöjt [n.; ~en, ~er] flute
flörta [v.; ~r, ~de, ~t] flirt
flöt [v.past; see: **flyta**]
FM [abbrev: frekvensmodulering]
frequency modulation (FM)
fm. [abbrev: förmiddagen] before
noon, morning
FN [abbrev: Förenta Nationerna]
United Nations (UN)
f.n. [abbrev: för närvarande] at present, for the time being
FN-stadgan [n.] United Nations
Charter
fnuttar [n.pl.; colloq.] quotation
marks [IT]
foajé [n.; ~n, ~er] foyer
fobi [n.; ~n, ~er] phobia
foder [n.; fodret, ~] lining; fodder
fodral [n.; ~et, ~] case, cover
foga [v.; ~r, ~de, ~t] join; merge
fogde [n.; ~n, fogdar] sheriff
fokus [n.; ~en, ~ar] focus
fokusera [v; ~r, ~de, ~t] focus

folie [n.; ~n, ~r] foil
foliepapper [n.; -pappret] aluminum foil
folk [n.; ~et, ~] people; nation; ~ **och Försvar** Society and Defense Federation [defense and security policy organization]
folkbokförd [adj.; -fört, ~a] registered [in civil registry]
folkbokföring [n.; ~en] civil registration
folkdans [n.; ~en, ~er] folk dance
folkdräkt [n.; ~en, ~er] folk costume
folkgrupp [n.; ~en, ~er] national group, minority
folkhem [n.; -hemmet] welfare state
folkhälsa [n.; ~n] public health [EU]
folkhögskola [n.; ~n, -skolor] people's college [institutions for adult and continuing education at the secondary and post-secondary levels]
folkkonst [n.; ~en] folk art
folkliv [n.; ~et] daily life [of ordinary people]
folklore [n.; ~en] folklore
folkmord [n.; ~et] genocide
folkmusik [n.; ~en] folk music
folkomröstning [n.; ~en, ~ar] referendum
Folkpartiet [n.] People's Party, Liberal Party; ~ **liberalerna** Liberal People's Party
folkpension [n.; ~en] national old-age pension
folkrörelse [n.; ~n, ~r] popular movement
folkskola [n.; ~n, -skolor] primary school
folkuniversitet [n.; ~en] people's university [college for adults, continuing education]
folkvisa [n.; ~n, -visor] folk song
folköl [n.; ~et] medium-strong beer [2.25-3.5 % alcohol]
fond [n.; ~en, ~er] background; center [section in theater]; funds, capital; foundation; stock, store
fontän [n.; ~en, ~er] fountain
for [v.past; see: **fara**]

fordon [n.; ~et, ~] vehicle
fordonsförare [n.; ~n, ~] driver
fordonsteknisk utbildning [n.; ~en] automobile technology program [high school]
fordra [v.; ~r, ~de, ~t] demand; ~s be required
forell [n.; ~en, ~er] trout
form[1] [n.; ~en, ~ar] mold; dish, baking pan
form[2] [n.; ~en, ~er] form, shape; **hålla sig i** ~ keep fit; **i ~ av** in the form of
format [n.; ~et, ~] format
formatera [v.; ~r, ~de, ~t] format [IT]
formatering [n.; ~en, ~ar] formatting [IT]
formatmall [n.; ~en, ~ar] style, page style [IT]
formel [n.; ~n, formler] formula
formell [adj.; ~t, ~a] formal; ~ **klädsel** formal wear; **~t subjekt** formal subject, anticipatory subject [gram]
formge [v.; -ger, -gav, -givit] design
formgivning [n.; ~en] design, designing
formulera [v.; ~r, ~de, ~t] formulate, word
formulering [n.; ~en, ~ar] formulation, wording
formulär [n.; ~et, ~] form, blank
forn [adj.; ~t, ~a] former, earlier; ancient
fors [n.; ~en, ~ar] rapids; torrent
forska [v.; ~r, ~de, ~t] search, carry out research, inquire into, investigate
forskarassistent [n.; ~en, ~er] postdoctoral fellow, assistant professor
forskare [n.; ~n, ~] researcher
forskning [n.; ~en, ~ar] research
forskningsassistent [n.; ~en, ~er] research assistant
forskningsresa [n.; ~n, -resor] research trip, scientific expedition
Forskningsrådet för arbetsliv och socialvetenskap (FAS) [n.] Research Council on Working Life and Social Science

Forskningsrådet för miljö, areella näringar och samhällsbyggande (Formas) [n.] Research Council for Environment, Agricultural Sciences and Spatial Planning

forsränning [n.; ~en] rafting, river running

fort [adv.] quickly

fortbildning [n.; ~en] continuing education

fortbildningskurs [n.; ~en, ~er] continuing education course

fortfarande [adv.] still

Fortifikationsverket (FORTV) [n.] National Fortifications Administration

forts. (abbrev: fortsättning) continued (cont.)

fortsatt [adj.; ~a] continued, continuous, further

fortskaffningsmedel [n.; -medlet, ~] means of transportation

fortsätta [v.; -sätter, -satte, -satt] continue

fortsättning [n.; ~en, ~ar] continuation

fortsättningskurs [n.; ~en, ~er] advanced course

forum [n.; ~et, ~] forum

fosfat [n.; ~et, ~] phosphate

foster [n.; fostret, ~] fetus; offspring; creation

fosterbarn [n.; ~et, ~] foster child

fosterföräldrar [n.pl.] foster parents

fot [n.; ~en, fötter] foot

fotboll [n.; ~en, ~ar] soccer

fotbollslag [n.; ~et, ~] soccer team

fotbollsmatch [n. ~en, ~er] soccer game

fotbollsplan [n.; ~en, ~er] soccer field

fotbollsspelare [n.; ~n, ~] soccer player

fotbroms [n.; ~en, ~ar] foot-brake

fotgängare [n.; ~n, ~] pedestrian

fotnot [n.; ~en. ~er] footnote [IT]

foto [n.; ~t, ~n] photograph

fotoaffär [n.; ~en, ~er] camera store, photo shop

fotoartiklar [n.pl.] photographic materials

fotoavtryck [n.; ~et, ~] print, photograph

fotogen [n.; ~en] kerosene

fotogenkök [n.; ~et, ~] kerosene stove

fotogenlampa [n.; ~n, -lampor] kerosene lamp

fotograf [n.; ~en, ~er] photographer

fotografera [v.; ~r, ~de, ~t] take photographs

fotografering [n.; ~en] photographing

fotografi [n.; ~et, ~er] photograph; photography

fotokurs [n.; ~en, ~er] photography course

fotpall [n.; ~en, ~ar] footstool

fots: till ~ [adv.] on foot

fotskrapa [n.; ~n, -skrapor] shoe scraper

fotstig [n.; ~en, ~ar] footpath

fotvandring [n.; ~en, ~ar] walking, hiking; hike

fp [abbrev: Folkpartiet liberalerna] People's Party, Liberal Party

fr. [abbrev: från; fröken; fru] from; Miss; Mrs.

fr.a. [abbrev: framför allt] first and foremost

frack [n.; ~en, ~ar] tails, tailcoat

frakt [n.; ~en, ~er] freight, cargo, goods; shipping cost, postage

fraktur [n.; ~en, ~er] fracture; German type

fralla [n.; ~n, frallor] roll [baked goods]

fram [adv.] forward; further along; later; ~ **till** up to

framben [n.; ~et, ~] foreleg

framdörr [n.; ~en, ~ar] front door

framfall [n.; ~et, ~] prolapse

framfart [n.; ~en] rampaging, ravaging; reckless movement

framför [prep.] in front of, before, ahead of; more than, above, rather than

framföra [v.; -för, -förde, -fört] present; deliver, convey

framgå [v.; -går, -gick, -gått] be clear, be evident

framgång [n.; ~en, ~ar] success

framgångsrik [adj.; ~t, ~a] successful

framhjul [n.; ~et, ~] front wheel

framhjulsdrift [n.; ~en] front wheel drive

framhålla [v.; -håller, -höll, -hållit] emphasize, stress; state

framhäva [v.; -häver, -hävde, -hävt] bring out, show, accentuate

framifrån [adv.] from the front

framkalla [v.; ~r, ~de, ~t] develop [film]

framkallning [n.; ~en] development [film]

framkomlig [adj.; ~t, ~a] accessible, passable

framkomlighet [n.; ~en] accessibility

framljus [n.; ~et, ~] front light, headlight

framme [adv.] in front; arrived, there [at destination]; **vara ~** have arrived

framsida [n.; ~n, -sidor] front, front side

framsteg [n.; ~et, ~] progress, advancement

Framstegspartiet [n.] Progress Party

framstå [v.; -står, -stod, -stått] stand out, appear

framstående [adj.] prominent, eminent

framställa [v.; -ställer, -ställde, -ställt] represent, depict, describe; present; produce

framsäte [n.; ~t] front seat

framtand [n.; ~en -tänder] front tooth

framtid [n.; ~en] future

framtida [adj.] future

framtidsplan [n.; ~en, ~er] future plan(s)

framtill [adv.] in the front

framträda [v.; -träder, -trädde, -trätt] appear before the public; come into view

framträdande[1] [adj.] prominent, outstanding

framträdande[2] [n.; ~t, ~n] appearance

framväxt [n.; ~en] growth, rise

framåt [adv.] forward

framöver [adv.] forward, ahead, onward

frank [adj.; ~t, ~a] frank, open, direct

frankera [v.; ~r, ~de, ~t] stamp, put stamps on

frankering [n.; ~en] stamping, putting postage on

Frankrike [n.] France

fransk [adj.; ~t, ~a] French

franska [n.] French language

franskbröd [n.; ~et, ~] white bread, French bread

fransman [n.; -mannen, -män] Frenchman

fransyska [n.; ~n, -skor] French-woman

fras [n.; ~en, ~er] expression, phrase

frasvåffla [n.; ~n, -våfflor] crisp waffle

fre. [see: fredag]

fred [n.; ~en, ~er] peace; **i ~** in peace, alone

fredag [n.; ~en] Friday

fredlig [adj.; ~t, ~a] peaceful, gentle

fredsavtal [n.; ~et, ~] peace treaty

fredspris [n.; ~et, ~] peace prize

fredsprocess [n.; ~en, ~er] peace process

fredsrörelse [n.; ~n, ~r] peace movement

freestyle [n.; ~en] personal cassette player, personal CD player

freeware [n.] freeware [IT]

frekvens [n.; ~en, ~er] frequency

frescomålning [n.; ~en, ~ar] fresco

frestelse [n.; ~n, ~r] temptation

fri [adj.; fritt, fria] free; without charge; **~ höjd** headroom [height restriction]; **~tt inträde** free admission; **~tt porto** postage paid; **~ rörlighet** free movement; **~ sjukvård** free medical care

fria [v.; ~r, ~de, ~t] acquit; propose marriage

friande dom [n.; ~en, ~ar] verdict of acquittal

friare [n.; ~n, ~] suitor, admirer

frid [n.; ~en] peace, tranquility

fridlyst [adj.; ~a] protected; ~ **område** nature preserve
frieri [n.; ~et, ~er] marriage proposal
frige [v.; -ger, -gav, -gitt] set free, liberate; release; ~ **med borgen** release on bail
frihandel [n.; ~n, ~] free trade
frihandelsområde [n.; ~et, ~] free trade area [EU]
frihet [n.; ~en, ~er] freedom; privilege
frihetshjälte [n.; ~n, -hjältar] champion of liberty
frihöjd [n.; ~en, ~er] clearance
friidrott [n.; ~en] athletics, track and field
frikadeller [n.pl.] boiled veal meatballs
friklättring [n.; ~en] freeclimbing
frikort [n.; ~et, ~] admission pass [to events]; entitlement card for medical expenses
frikyrka [n.; ~n, -kyrkor] church outside State Church system
frilufts- [prefix] open-air
friluftsmuseum [n.; -museet, -museer] open-air museum
friluftsteater [n.; ~n, -teatrar] open-air theater
frimärke [n.; ~t, ~n] stamp
frimärksautomat [n.; ~en, ~er] stamp machine
frisbee [n.; ~n, ~r] frisbee
frisera håret på någon [v.; ~r, ~de, ~t] do someone's hair
frisersalong [n.; ~en, ~er] hairdresser's, beauty parlor
frisim [n.; -simmet] freestyle swimming
frisk [adj.; ~t, ~a] healthy; cool, fresh; ~ **luft** fresh air; ~a **luften** open air; ~t **vind** brisk breeze
frispark [n.; ~en, ~ar] free kick
frissa [n.; colloq.; ~n, frissor] female hairdresser for women
fristående [adj.] free standing, detached, stand-alone [IT]; ~ **artikel** detached article [gram]; ~ **gymnastik** floor exercises; ~ **satsförkortning** clause without a finite verb [gram]; ~ **system** stand-alone system

frisyr [n.; ~en, ~er] hairstyle, haircut
frisyrgelé [n.; ~n, ~er] hairstyling gel
frisör [n.; ~en, ~er] barber, hairdresser
frisörsalong [n.; ~en, ~er] barbershop, hairdresser's
frisörska [n.; ~n, -skor] hairdresser [female]
friterad [adj.; -rat, ~e] deep-fried
fritid [n.; ~en] leisure, spare time; **på** ~ in one's leisure
fritidsaktivitet [n.; ~en] leisure activity, recreation
fritidshus [n.; ~et, ~] weekend cottage, summer house
fritidsintresse [n.; ~t, ~n] hobby
fritidskläder [n.pl.] leisure/casual clothes, sportswear
fritt[1] [adj.; see: **fri**]
fritt[2] [adv.] freely
frivillig [adj.; ~t, ~a] voluntary; optional
frivilligorganisation [n.; ~en, ~er] non-governmental organization (NGO)
friår [n.; ~et, ~] year off, sabbatical year
frk. [abbrev: fröken] miss, young lady
fr.o.m. (abbrev: från och med) as of [date]
fromage [n.; ~n, ~r] cold mousse
front [n.; ~en, ~er] front
frontalkrock [n.; ~en, ~ar] head-on collision
frossa[1] [n.; ~n] shivers
frossa[2] [v.; ~r, ~de, ~t] gorge oneself
frost [n.; ~en] frost
frostskyddsmedel [n.; -medlet, ~] anti-freeze
frottéhandduk [n.; ~en, ~ar] terrycloth towel
fru [n.; ~n, ~ar] Mrs; wife
frukost [n.; ~en, ~ar] breakfast
frukostbord [n.; ~et] breakfast table
frukostbuffé [n.; ~n] breakfast buffet
frukostflingor [n.pl.] breakfast cereal

frukostrum [n.; ~et, ~] breakfast room
frukt [n.; ~en, ~er] fruit
frukta [v.; ~r, ~de, ~t] fear
fruktan [n.] fear
fruktansvärd [adj.; -värt, ~a] terrifying
fruktassiett [n.; ~en, ~er] fruit plate
fruktjos [see: **fruktjuice**]
fruktjuice [n.; ~n, ~r] fruit juice
fruktkompott [n.; ~en, ~er] stewed fruit
fruktpress [n.; ~en, ~ar] fruit press
fruktsallad [n.; ~en, ~er] fruit salad
fruktskål [n.; ~en, ~ar] fruit bowl
fruktsoda [n.; ~n, ~] carbonated fruit drink
frusen [adj.; fruset, frusna] frozen, icy
frusit [v.past; see: **frysa**]
frys [n.; ~en, ~ar] freezer
frysa [v.; fryser, frös, frusit] be cold, feel cold; freeze [food]
frysbox [n.; ~en, ~ar] freezer [chest]
frysfack [n.; ~et, ~] freezer compartment
fryshus [n.; ~et] cold storage
frysskåp [n.; ~et, ~] freezer [upright]
fryst mat [n.; ~en] frozen foods
fråga[1] [n.; ~n, frågor] question; **det kommer inte på ~** that is out of the question
fråga[2] [v.; ~r, ~de, ~t] ask; **~ efter** ask about; **~ om hjälp** ask for assistance; **~ vid receptionen** ask at the front desk
frågebisats [n.; ~en, ~er] interrogative clause [gram]
frågekonjunktion [n.; ~en, ~er] interrogative conjunction [gram]
frågesport [n.; ~en, ~er] quiz
frågespråk [n.; ~et] query language [IT]
frågetecken [n.; -tecknet, ~] question mark [IT]
från [prep.] from; **~ måndag till fredag** from Monday to Friday; **~ och med** as of, starting; **~ senare tid** from more recent times
frånkopplad [adj.; -kopplat, ~e] disconnected, offline [IT]

frånskild [adj.; -skilt, ~a] divorced
frånvaro [n.; ~n] absence; lack
fräck [adj.; ~t, ~a] impudent, shameless; pretty, elegant
frälsare [n.; ~n, ~] savior
frälsning [n.; ~en] salvation
Frälsningsarmén [n.] Salvation Army
främja [v.; ~r, ~de, ~t] promote, encourage, support
främling [n.; ~en, ~ar] stranger, foreigner
främlingsfientlighet [n.; ~en] xenophobia, hostility to foreigners
främlingspass [n.; ~et, ~] alien's passport
främmande [adj.] foreign, alien
främmande språk [n.pl.] foreign languages
främre [adj.] front, forward, on the front side/end
främst [adv.] foremost, leading
fräsa [v.; fräser, fräste, fräst] hiss, fizz, sizzle
fräsch [adj.; ~t, ~a] fresh; new
frö [n.; ~t, ~n] seed
fröken [n.; ~, fröknar] miss; female teacher; waitress
frös [v.past; see: **frysa**]
F-skatt [n.; ~en, ~er] preliminary tax paid by self-employed
FTP [abbrev.] File Transfer Protocol (FTP) [IT]
FTP-klient [n.; ~en ~er] FTP-client (program) [IT]
FU [abbrev: **Folkuniversitet**] People's University
fukt [n.; ~en] damp, moisture
fuktig [adj.; ~t, ~a] humid
ful [adj.; ~t, ~a] ugly
full [adj.; ~t, ~a] full; drunk; **~t med folk** crowded
fullbelagt [adj.] no vacancy
fullblodig [adj.; ~t, ~a] thoroughbred
fullbokad [adj.; -bokat, ~e] no vacancy, fully booked
fullfölja [v.; -följer, följde, -följt] complete; prosecute
fullgjord [adj.; -gjort, ~a] completed

fullgöra [v.; -gör, -gjorde, -gjort] complete

fullkomlig [adj.; ~t, ~a] perfect; complete; utter

fullkornsbröd [n.; ~et] whole wheat bread

fullkornsmjöl [n.; ~et] whole wheat flour

fullmakt [n.; ~en, ~er] power of attorney, proxy

fullmäktig [n.; ~en, ~e] authorized representative

fullständig [adj.; ~t, ~a] complete, entire; total; absolute

fullständigt [adv.] completely

fullt [adv.] completely

fullträff [n.; ~en, ~ar] direct hit, bull's eye

fulregistrering [n.; ~en] typosquatting [IT; registration of typos as domain names]

fult [see: **ful**]

fumlig [adj.; ~t, ~a] fumbling, awkward

fundera [v.; ~r, ~de, ~t] think, ponder; ~ **på** consider, think about

fundering [n.; ~en, ~ar] thoughts, ideas; speculation

fungera [v.; ~r, ~de, ~t] work, function

funka [v.; colloq.; ~r, ~de, ~t] work, function

funktion [n.; ~en, ~er] function

funktionalitet [n.; ~en] functionality [IT]

funktionell [adj.; ~t, ~a] functional

funktionsavbrott [n.; ~et, ~] failure [IT]

funktionshinder [n.; -hindret, ~] physical handicap

funktionshindrad [adj.; -hindrat, ~e] handicapped

funktionstangent [n.; ~en, ~er] function key (Fn) [IT]

funnit [v.past; see: **finna**]

funt [n.; ~en] font [baptism]

fura [n.; ~n, furor] pine [tree]

furubord [n.; ~et, ~] pine table

fusion [n.; ~en, ~er] fusion, merger

Fusionsfördraget [n.] Merger Treaty [EU]

fusk [n.; ~et] cheating, cutting corners

fuska [v.; ~r, ~de, ~t] cheat; do a poor job; dabble in

futurum [n.] future tense [gram]

f.v.b. [abbrev: för vidare befordran] please forward, to be forwarded

fy! [interjection] ugh!; ~ **skam!/ skäms!** shame on you!; ~ **fan!** [vul.] damn! [colloq.], shit! [vul.]

fylla [v.; fyller, fyllde, fyllt] fill; ~ **50 år** have one's 50th birthday; ~ **i** fill in; ~ **på** fill up with

fylld [adj.; fyllt, ~a] stuffed

fyllig [adj.; ~t, ~a] full-bodied

fyllning [n.; ~en, ~ar] filling; stuffing

fyllningshandtag [n.; ~et, ~] fill handle [IT]

fynd [n.; ~et, ~] find; bargain

fyndighet [n.; ~en] inventiveness, ingenuity; deposit (ore)

fyndpris [n.; ~et, ~er] bargain price

fyr [n.; ~en, ~ar] lighthouse; fire, stove

fyra [num.] four

fyrhjulsdrift [n.; ~en] four-wheel drive

fyrkant [n.; ~en, ~er] square, quadrangle; pound sign, hash mark [IT]

fyrkantig [adj.; ~t, ~a] square, quadrangular

fyrtio [num.] forty

fyrtiofem [num.] forty-five

fyrtionde [num.] fortieth

fyrtorn [n.; ~et, ~] lighthouse

fyrverkeri [n.; ~et, ~er] fireworks

fysik [n.; ~en] physics

fysisk [adj.; ~t, ~a] physical; ~**t funktionshinder** physical handicap, disability

få[1] [pron.; comp: färre] few

få[2] [v.; får, fick, fått] get; be able to; be permitted to; have to; ~**r jag betala?** may I pay?; **vi ~r se** we'll see; ~ **barn** have a baby; ~ **syn på** catch sight of; ~ **tag i/på** obtain, get; ~ **upp** open

fågel [n.; ~n, fåglar] bird, poultry

fågelbo [n.; ~t, ~n] bird's nest

fågelhund [n.; ~en, ~ar] bird dog

fågelreservat [n.; ~et, ~] bird reserve
fågelskådning [n.; ~en] bird-watching
fågelvägen [adv.] as the crow flies
fågelägg [n.; ~et, ~] bird's egg
fånga [v.; ~r, ~de, ~t] catch
fångare [n.; ~n, ~] catcher
fånge [n.; ~n, fångar] prisoner
får [n.; ~et, ~] sheep; mutton; ~ i
  kål mutton and cabbage stew
fårfiol [n.; ~en, ~er] dried salted/
  smoked leg of lamb
fårkött [n.; ~et, ~] mutton
fårost [n.; ~en, ~ar] sheep's milk
  cheese
fårskinn [n.; ~et, ~] sheepskin
fårstek [n.; ~en, ~ar] roast mutton
fåtal [n.; ~et] a few, a minority
fått [v.past; see: få]
fåtölj [n.; ~en, ~er] armchair
fäktning [n.; ~en] fencing [sport]
fälg [n.; ~en, ~ar] rim [wheel]
fälla[1] [n.; ~n, fällor] trap
fälla[2] [v.; fäller, fällde, fällt] fell,
  bring down; shed; pronounce,
  express; ~ en brottsling convict a
  criminal
fällande dom [n.; ~en, ~ar] guilty
  verdict, conviction
fällas för [v.passive; fälls, fälldes,
  fällts] be convicted of
fällbord [n.; ~et, ~] folding table
fällkniv [n.; ~en, ~ar] jackknife
fällstol [n.; ~en, ~ar] folding chair
fält [n.; ~et, ~] field; sphere
fältbiolog [n.; ~en, ~er] field biologist
fängelse [n.; ~t, ~r] prison
fängelsestraff [n.; ~et] imprisonment
fänkål [n.; ~en] fennel
färd [n.; ~en, ~er] journey; departure; i ~ med busy with
färdas [v.; färdas, färdades, färdats]
  travel
färdig [adj.; ~t, ~a] ready, complete
färdigkokt [adj.; ~a] cooked, done
färdigstekt [adj.; ~a] roasted, done
färdigställa [v.; -ställer, -ställde,
  -ställt] make ready, prepare
färdtjänst [n.; ~en] transportation
  service [for disabled]
färg [n.; ~en, ~er] color; dye; suit
  [cards]; gå i ~ match

färgad [adj.; färgat, ~e] colored;
  dyed
färgfilm [n.; ~en, ~er] color film
färgglad [adj.; -glatt, ~a] brightly
  colored
färghandel [adj.; ~n, -handlar]
  paint store
färghållbar [adj.; ~t, ~a] colorfast
färgkritor [n.pl.] crayons
färglåda [n.; ~n, -lådor] box of
  paints
färgning [n.; ~en, ~ar] dye
färgnyans [n.; ~en, ~er] shade, tint
färgpenna [n.; ~n, -pennor] colored
  pencil
färgschema [n.; ~n, -schemor]
  color scheme [IT]
färgsköljning [n.; ~en] color rinse
färg-tv [n.; ~n, ~ar] color television
färja [n.; ~n, färjor] ferry
färre [adv.comp.: få] fewer, less
  numerous
färsk [adj.; ~t, ~a] fresh, new
färskost [n.; ~en] cottage cheese;
  cream cheese
färskpotatis [n.; ~en, ~ar] new
  potato(es)
färskrökt lax [n.; ~en] smoked
  salmon
färskvaror [n.pl.] fresh produce,
  perishables
färskvatten [n.; -vattnet] fresh water
färutsättning [n.; ~en, ~ar] possibility, chance, potential
Färöarna [n.pl.] Faroe Islands
fästa [v.; fäster, fäste, fäst] fasten,
  tighten
fäste [n.; ~t, ~n] hold; handle; abut-
  ment; stronghold, fortress
fästing [n.; ~en, ~ar] tick [insect]
fästman [n.; -mannen] fiancé
fästmö [n.; ~n] fiancée
fästning [n.; ~en, ~ar] fortress,
  citadel
Fästning Europa [n.] Fortress Europe [term used by opponents of
  immigration and asylum]
f.ö. [abbrev: för övrigt] besides,
  incidentally, otherwise, by the way
föda[1] [n.; ~n] food, nourishment

föda² [v.; föder, födde, fött] give birth to; nourish

födas [v.passive; födes, föddes, fötts] be born

född [adj.; fött, födda] born; **vara ~** be born

födelse [n.; ~n, ~r] birth

födelseattest [n.; ~en, ~er] birth certificate

födelsedag [n.; ~en, ~ar] birthday

födelsedatum [n.; ~et] date of birth

födelseland [n.; ~et] country of birth

födelseort [n.; ~en] place of birth

födelseår [n.; ~et] year of birth

födsel [n.; ~n, födslar] birth

födslovärkar [n.pl.] labor, labor pains

följ. [see: **följande**]

följa [v.; följer, följde, följt] follow; keep up with; **~ efter någon** follow someone; **~ med** accompany, join

följaktligen [adv.] consequently

följande [adj.] following

följd [n.; ~en, ~er] consequence, result; succession

följdkonjunktion [n.; ~en, ~er] resultative conjunction [gram]

föna håret [v.; ~r, ~de, ~t] blow-dry one's hair

föning [n.; ~en] blow-dry

fönster [n.; fönstret, ~] window

fönsterbord [n.; ~et, ~] table by the window

fönsterbräde [n.; ~t, ~r] windowsill

fönsterkarm [n.; ~en, ~ar] window frame

fönsterlucka [n.; ~n, -luckor] shutter [window]

fönsterplats [n.; ~en, ~et] window seat

fönsterputsare [n.; ~n, ~] window cleaner

fönsterruta [n.; ~n, -rutor] window pane

för¹ [adv.] too; **~ länge** too long; **~ mycket** too much

för² [conj.] because; **~ att** because, in order to

för³ [n.; ~en, ~ar] bow [boat]

för⁴ [prep.] for; **vad är det ~ hund?** what kind of a dog is that?; **~ 2 veckor sedan** 2 weeks ago; **~ all del** don't mention it, you're welcome; by all means; **~ det mesta** mostly; **~ länge sedan** long ago; **~ närvarande** at present

föra [v.; för, förde, fört] carry, take; conduct; **~ dagbok** keep a diary; **~ krig** wage war; **~ samtal** carry on a conversation

förakt [n.; ~et] contempt, disdain, scorn

förankring [n.; ~en, ~ar] anchorage; roots, support

förare [n.; ~n, ~] driver

förarglig [adj.; ~t, ~a] annoying

förargligt [adv.]: **så ~!** what a nuisance!

förarplats [n.; ~en, ~er] driver's seat

förband [n.; ~et, ~] bandage; unit [mil.]

förbandslåda [n.; ~n, -lådor] first-aid kit

förbannad [adj.; -bannat, ~e] angry; cursed, damned

förbehåll [n.]: **med ~** subject to reservations; **utan ~** without reservation

förbereda [v.; -bereder, -beredde, -berett] prepare

förberedelse [n.; ~n, ~r] preparation

förbi [adv.] past; **kan jag få komma ~, tack?** may I come by/through here, please?

förbinda [v.; ~r, ~de, ~t] bandage, dress; attach, combine

förbindelse [n.; ~n, ~r] connection; relations

förbjuda [v.; -bjuder, -bjöd, -bjudit] forbid, prohibit

förbjuden [adj.; -bjudet, -bjudna] prohibited, forbidden; **parkering ~** no parking

förbli [v.; -blir, -blev, -blivit] remain

förbruka [v.; ~r, ~de, ~t] use

förbrytare [n.; ~n, ~] criminal, felon

förbud (mot) [n.; ~et, ~] prohibition (against)

förbund [n.; ~et, ~] compact, alliance; association, league

förbundskapten [n.; ~en, ~er] coach of the national team

Förbundsrepubliken [n.] Federal Republic

förbättra [v.; ~r, ~de, ~t] improve

förbättrad [adj.; -bättrat, ~e] improved, enhanced

förbättring [n.; ~en, ~ar] improvement; recovery

fördel [n.; ~en, ~ar] advantage

fördela [v.; ~r, ~de, ~t] distribute, dispense, allot

fördelaktig [adj.; ~t, ~a] advantageous

fördelare [n.; ~n, ~] distributor

fördelning [n.; ~en, ~ar] distribution

fördjupat samarbete [n.] enhanced cooperation [EU]

fördom [n.; ~en, ~ar] prejudice

fördrag [n.; ~et, ~] treaty, agreement; patience

före [prep.] before; ~ **detta** former, ex-; formerly; ~ **Kristi födelse (f.Kr.)** before Christ (B.C.); ~ **måltiden** before meals

förebild [n.; ~en, ~er] prototype, pattern

förebygga [v.; -bygger, -byggde, -byggt] prevent, preclude, forestall

förebyggande [adj.] preventive

föredra [v.; -drar, -drog, -dragit] prefer; present; ~ **A framför B** prefer A to B

föredrag [n.; ~et, ~] lecture

föredragningslista [n.; ~n, -listor] agenda

förefalla [v.; -faller, -föll, -fallit] occur, pass; seem, appear

föreg. [see: **föregående**]

föregående [adj.] previous

föregångare [n.; ~n, ~] precursor

förekomma [v.; -kommer, -kom, -kommit] happen, occur

förekommande [adj.] occuring

föreligga [v.; -ligger, -låg, -legat] be, exist; be available

föreläsning [n.; ~en, ~ar] lecture

föreläsningslokal [n.; ~en, ~er] lecture room

föreläsningssal [n.; ~en, ~ar] lecture room

föremål [n.; ~et, ~] object

förena [v.; ~r, ~de, ~t] unite

förenad [adj.; -nat, ~e] joined, united [gram]

Förenade arabemiraten [n.pl.] United Arab Emirates

Förenade kungariket [n.] United Kingdom

förening [n.; ~en, ~ar] union, society, club

Föreningen Norden [n.] Norden Association

förenkla [v.; ~r, ~de, ~t] simplify

förenkling [n.; ~en, ~ar] simplification; ~ **av fördragen** revision of the Treaties [EU]

Förenta Nationerna (FN) [n.pl.] United Nations (UN)

Förenta Staterna (USA) [n.pl.] United States (USA)

föreslagen [adj.; -slaget, -slagna] proposed

föreslå [v.; -slår, -slog, -slagit] propose, suggest

förestående [adj.] approaching, imminent

föreställa [v.; -ställer, -ställde, -ställt] represent; introduce; ~ **sig** imagine; introduce oneself

föreställning [n.; ~en, ~ar] performance, show

företag [n.; ~et, ~] firm, company

företagare [n.; ~n, ~] businessman, entrepreneur

företagsekonom [n.; ~en, ~er] business economist

företagsvinst [n.; ~en, ~er] corporate profits

företeelse [n.; ~n, ~r] phenomenon, fact, occurence

företrädare [n.; ~n, ~] predecessor; representative; advocate

företräde [n.; ~t, ~n] precedence, priority; advantage; **lämna** ~ yield priority [in traffic]

förf. [see: **författare**]

förfalla [v.; -faller, -föll, -fallit] fall into decay, deteriorate, degenerate; lapse, expire; be due for payment

förf<u>a</u>llod<u>a</u>g den ... [n.] payment
due on ...

förf<u>a</u>rande [n.; ~t, ~n] procedure;
~ **med <u>e</u>nkelt <u>y</u>ttrande** consultation procedure [EU]; ~**t vid <u>a</u>llt-
för st<u>o</u>ra <u>u</u>ndersk<u>o</u>tt** excessive
deficit procedure [EU]

förf<u>a</u>ttare [n.; ~n, ~] author, writer

författar<u>i</u>nna [n.; ~n, -innor]
authoress

förf<u>a</u>ttarskap [n.; ~et] authorship

förf<u>a</u>ttarv<u>e</u>rktyg [n.; ~et, ~]
authoring tool [IT]

förfl<u>u</u>ten [adj.; -flutet, -flutna] past,
previous, last

förf<u>o</u>gande [n.; ~t] disposal

förfr<u>i</u>skningar [n.pl.] refreshments

förfr<u>å</u>gning [n.; ~en, ~ar] inquiry,
request

förf<u>ä</u>rlig [adj.; ~t, ~a] terrible

förf<u>ö</u>lja [v.; -följer, -följde, -följt]
pursue; persecute

förf<u>ö</u>ljelse [n.; ~n, ~r] persecution,
chase

förg<u>a</u>sare [n.; ~en, ~] carburetor

förg<u>i</u>ftning [n.; ~en, ~ar] poisoning

förg<u>ä</u>tmigej [n.; ~en, ~er] forget-
me-not

förg<u>ä</u>ves [adv.] in vain

förhand: på ~ [adv.] beforehand, in
advance

förh<u>a</u>ndla [v.; ~r, ~de, ~t] negotiate,
discuss, deliberate

förh<u>a</u>ndling [n.; ~en, ~ar] deliberation, proceeding; negotiation

förhandsbest<u>ä</u>llning [n.; ~en, ~ar]
advance booking

förhandsb<u>o</u>kning [n.; ~en, ~ar]
advance reservation

förhandsgr<u>a</u>nska [v.; ~r, ~de, ~t]
preview [IT]

förh<u>i</u>ndra [v.; ~r, ~de, ~t] prevent

förh<u>i</u>ndrad [adj.; -drat, ~e]
prevented

förhist<u>o</u>risk [adj.; ~t, ~a] prehistoric

förh<u>o</u>ppning [n.; ~en, ~ar] hope,
expectation; (pl.) prospects

förh<u>o</u>ppningsvis [adv.] hopefully

förh<u>å</u>llande [n.; ~t, ~n] conditions,
circumstances; relationship

förh<u>å</u>llandevis [adv.] proportion-
ately

förh<u>ö</u>r [n.; ~et, ~] examination,
interrogation, hearing; test

förh<u>ö</u>ra [v.; -hör, -hörde, -hört]
question, interrogate

för<u>i</u>ntelse [n.; ~n] annihilation,
destruction

förkl<u>a</u>ra [v.; ~r, ~de, ~t] explain

förkl<u>a</u>ring [n.; ~en, ~ar] explanation

förkl<u>ä</u>de [n.; ~t, ~n] apron

förkn<u>i</u>ppad [adj.; -knippat, ~e]
associated

förk<u>o</u>rtning [n.; ~en, ~ar]
abbreviation

förk<u>y</u>ld [adj.]: **v<u>a</u>ra ~** have caught
a cold

förk<u>y</u>lning [n.; ~en, ~ar] cold

förk<u>ö</u>p [n.; ~et, ~] advance purchase

förk<u>ö</u>rsrätt [n.; ~en] right of way,
priority

förl<u>a</u>g [n.; ~et, ~] publishing house,
publisher

förl<u>a</u>mning [n.; ~en] paralysis

förl<u>e</u>gad [n.; -legat, ~e] antiquated,
obsolete

Förl<u>i</u>kningskommitt<u>é</u>n [n.]
Conciliation Committee [EU]

förl<u>o</u>pp [n.; ~et] lapse [time];
course [of events]

förl<u>o</u>ra [v.; ~r, ~de, ~t] lose

förl<u>o</u>rad [adj.; -lorat, ~e] lost; ~**e
eff<u>e</u>kter** lost and found office;
förl<u>o</u>rat ägg poached egg

förl<u>o</u>rare [n.; ~n, ~] loser

förl<u>o</u>ssning [n.; ~en, ~] delivery,
childbirth; redemption

förl<u>o</u>ssnings<u>a</u>vdelning [n.; ~en,
~ar] delivery ward

förl<u>o</u>ssningsv<u>ä</u>rkar [n.pl.] labor
pains

förl<u>o</u>va sig [v.; ~r, ~de, ~t] get
engaged

förl<u>o</u>vad [adj.; -lovat, ~e] engaged

förl<u>o</u>vningsann<u>o</u>ns [n.] engagement
announcement

förl<u>o</u>vningsring [n.; ~en, ~ar]
engagement ring

förl<u>u</u>st [n.; ~en, ~er] loss

förl<u>u</u>stfri komprim<u>e</u>ring [n.; ~en]
lossless compression [IT]

förl<u>å</u>t [interj.] sorry, excuse me; ~
mig excuse me, I beg your pardon

förlåta [v.; -låter, -lät, -låtit] forgive

förläggning [n.; ~en, ~ar] center, camp

förlänga [v.; -länger, -längde, -längt] extend

förlängd [adj.; -längt, ~a] extended

förlängning [n.; ~en, ~ar] extension; extra time

förlängningssladd [n.; ~en, ~ar] extension cord

förmedla [v.; ~r, ~de, ~t] mediate; act as intermediary

förmiddag (fm) [n.; ~en, ~ar] morning (a.m.); **i ~s** during the morning

förmiddagskaffe [n.; ~t] morning coffee

förminska [v.; ~r, ~de, ~t] reduce, make smaller

förmodligen [adv.] presumably, probably

förmå [v.; -mår, -mådde, -mått] be able to, be capable of; induce someone to, persuade someone to

förmåga [n.; ~n] powers, capacity, ability; talent, gift; person with abilities

förmån [n.; ~en, ~er] advantage; benefit

förmögenhet [n.; ~en, ~er] wealth

förnamn [n.; ~et, ~] first name

förneka [v.; ~r, ~de, ~t] deny, dispute, disown

förnuft [n.; ~et] reason; sense

förnya [v.; ~r, ~de, ~t] renew

förnyelse [n.; ~n, ~r] renewal

förnäm [adj.; ~t, ~a] stately, aristocratic, dignified; haughty

förordnande [n.; ~t, ~n] appointment [to a post]

förordning [n.; ~en, ~ar] ordinance, regulation

förorena [v,; ~r, ~de, ~t] pollute

förorenad [adj.; -nat, ~e] polluted

förorening [n.; ~en, ~ar] pollution

förort [n.; ~en, ~er] suburb

förpackning [n.; ~en] wrapping, packaging

förpackningsdag [n.; ~en, ~ar] packing day [when moving]

förpliktelse [n.; ~n, ~r] duty, obligation, commitment

förr [adv.] before; sooner; **~ eller senare** sooner or later; **~ i tiden** in the old days

förre [adj.; förra] former, earlier, previous; last, past; **förra måndagen** last Monday

förresten [adv.] by the way, incidentally

förrgår: i ~ [adv.] the day before yesterday

förråd [n.; ~et] store, stock; storeroom

förråda [v.; -råder, -rådde, -rått] betray

förrädare [n.; ~n, ~] traitor; betrayer

förrän [conj.] not until

förrätt [n.; ~en, ~er] appetizer, first course

församling [n.; ~en, ~ar] parish; congregation

förseelse [n.; ~n, ~r] fault, offense

försenad [adj.; -senat, ~e] late, delayed; **2 timmar försenat** delayed 2 hours, 2 hours late

försening [n.; ~en, ~ar] delay

försiktig [adj. ~t, ~a] careful

försiktighetsprincipen [n.] precautionary principle [EU]

förskingring [n.; ~en, ~ar] embezzlement, misappropriation; **i ~en** in the diaspora

förskola [n.; ~n, -skolor] preschool

förskolebarn [n.; ~et, ~en] preschool child

förskolelärare [n.; ~n, ~] preschool teacher

förskräcklig [adj.; ~t, ~a] terrible

förslag [n.; ~et, ~] suggestion, proposal

försprång [n.; ~et] start, lead; headstart

först [adv.] first; **~ till kvarn får ~ mala** first come first serve

förste [adj.; första] first; January; **första april** April Fool's Day; **första hjälpen** first aid; **första klass** first class; **första maj** May Day [May 1]; **första raden** dress

circle [theater seats] ; **första
våning** second floor
första-hjälpenlåda [n.; ~n, -lådor]
first-aid kit
Förstainstansrätten [n.] Court of
First Instance of the European
Communities (CFI) [EU]
förstasida [n.; ~n, -sidor] home
page [IT]
förstavelse [n.; ~n, ~r] prefix [gram]
först-in-först-ut [n.] first-in-first-
out (FIFO) [IT]
förstoppning [n.; ~en] constipation
förstora [v.; ~r, ~de, ~t] enlarge
förstukvist [n.; ~en, ~ar] front
porch, stoop
förstå [v.; -stå, -stod, -stått] understand
förståelse [n.; ~n] understanding,
comprehension
förstående [adj.] sympathetic
förstånd [n.; ~et] intelligence,
wisdom, understanding
förståndshandikappad [adj.; -kap-
pat, ~e] mentally retarded
förstås [adv.] of course
förstärka [v.; -stärker, -stärkte,
-stärkt] strengthen, reinforce
förstärkare [n.; ~n, ~] amplifier
förstärkning [n.; ~en, ~ar] rein-
forcement, strengthening
förstärkt kvalificerad majoritet
[n.] reinforced qualified majority
[EU]
förstöra [v.; -stör, -störde, -stört]
destroy, devastate, damage; ruin,
waste; spoil
förstörande komprimering [n.;
~en] destructive compression,
lossy compression [IT]
förstörd [adj. -stört, ~a] destroyed
försura [v.; ~r, ~de, ~t] acidify
försvann [v.past; see: **försvinna**]
försvar [n.; ~et] defense
försvara [v.; ~r, ~de, ~t] defend
Försvarets forskningsanstalt [FOA]
[n.; ~en] Defense Research
Institute
Försvarets materielverk (FMV)
[n.; ~et] Defense Material Administration

Försvarets radioanstalt (FRA)
[n.; ~en] National Defense Radio
Establishment
forsvarsadvokat [n.; ~en, ~er]
counsel for the defense
Försvarsdepartementet (Fö) [n.]
Ministry of Defense
Försvarshögskolan [n.] National
Defense College
Försvarsmakten [n.] Swedish
Armed Forces
försvarsminister [n.; ~n] Minister
of Defense
Försvarsutskottet [n.] Committee
on Defense [in Parliament]
försvinna [v.; -svinner, -svann,
-svunnit] disappear
försvunnen [adj.; -svunnet,
-svunna] missing
försäkra [v.; ~r, ~de, ~t] insure
försäkring [n.; ~en] insurance
försäkringsbolag [n.; ~et, ~]
insurance company
försäkringsbrev [n.; ~et, ~] insurance card, insurance policy
Försäkringskassan (FK) [n.]
National Social Insurance Agency
försäkringskort [n.; ~et, ~]
insurance card
försäkringspremie [n.; ~n, ~r]
insurance premium
försäljare [n.; ~n, ~] seller, trader
försäljning [n.; ~en] sales
försäljningsdatum [n.; ~et] sell-
before date [latest date when
product can be sold]
försäljningsvillkor [n.; ~et, ~]
terms of sale
försämra [v.; ~r, ~de, ~t] impair;
make worse
försök [n.; ~et, ~] attempt, effort,
test, experiment
försöka [v.; -söker, -sökte, -sökt]
try, attempt
försörja [v.; -sörjer, -sörjde, -sörjt]
provide for
försörjning [n.; ~en] living, support
förteckning [n.; ~en, ~ar] list,
catalog [IT]
förtid: i ~ [adv.] too early,
prematurely

förtidspension [n.; ~en] early retirement pension

förtjusande [adj.] delightful

förtjusning [n.; ~en] delight,
enthusiasm

förtjust (i) [adj.; ~a] delighted
(by), fond (of); in love (with)

förtjäna [v.; ~r, ~de, ~t] deserve;
earn

förtjänst [n.; ~en, ~ar] earnings;
merit

förtjänt [adj.]:: göra sig ~ distinguish oneself

förtroende [n.; ~t] confidence

förtryck [n. ~et] oppression

förtrycka [v.; -trycker, -tryckte,
-tryckt] oppress

förtulla [v.; ~r, ~de, ~t] declare (to
customs); pay duty on

förtvivlad [adj.; -lat, ~e] disconso-
late, in despair

förtvivlan [n.] despair, desperation

förtära [v.; -tär, -tärde, -tärt] consume, eat

förtöjning [n.; ~en, ~ar] mooring

förtöjningsboj [n.; ~en, ~ar] mooring
buoy

förundersökning [n.; ~en, ~ar]
preliminary investigation

förut [adv.] before, previously,
earlier

förutom [prep.] besides

förutsatt att [conj.] provided that

förutsätta [v.; -sätter, -satte, -satt]
assume, suppose; take it for granted

förutsättning [n.; ~en, ~ar] assumption, supposition; prerequi-
site, condition

förval [n.; ~et, ~] default value [IT]

förvalt värde [n.; ~t, ~n] default
value [IT]

förvaltare [n.; ~n, ~] administrator,
trustee

förvaltning [n.; ~en] administration;
management

Förvaltningsavdelningen [n.]
Department of Administration

förvaltningschef [n.; ~en] permanent secretary

förvandla [v.; ~r, ~de, ~t] transform, change

förvara [v.; ~r, ~de, ~t] keep, store

förvaring [n.; ~en] storage, safekeeping

förvaringsbox [n.; ~en, ~ar] baggage locker

förvaringsfack [n.; ~et, ~] baggage
locker

förvaringsskåp [n.; ~et, ~] filing
cabinet

förvaringsvätska [n.; ~n] storage
solution [contact lenses]

förverkliga [v.; ~r, ~de, ~t] realize

förvirrad [adj.; -rat, ~e] bewildered

förvirring [n.; ~en] confusion,
bewilderment

förvisso [adv.] certainly, as is well
known

förvåna [v.; ~r, ~de, ~t] surprise,
amaze

förvånad [adj.; -nat, ~e] surprised

förvånansvärt [adv.] surprisingly

förväg: i ~ [adv.] in advance

förvänta [v.; ~r, ~de, ~t] expect;
look forward to

förväntansfull [adj.; ~t, ~a]
expectant

förväntning [n.; ~en, ~ar] expectation

förvärva [v.; ~r, ~de, ~t] acquire

förvärvsarbete [n.; ~t, ~n] paid
employment

förälder [n.; ~n, föräldrar] parent

föräldraförening [n.; ~en, ~ar]
parents' association

föräldraförsäkring [n.; ~en]
parental insurance

föräldraledighet [n.; ~en, ~er]
parental leave

föräldralön [n.; ~en] supplementary benefit for parents [with newborn children]

föräldralös [adj.; ~t, ~a] orphaned,
without parents; ~t barn orphan

föräldramöte [n.; ~t, ~n] parent-
teacher consultation

föräldrapenning [n.; ~en] allowance for parents [for birth, childcare, sickness of child]

förälska sig (i) [v.; ~r, ~de, ~t] fall
in love (with)

förälskad [adj.; -skat, ~e] in love

förändra [v.; ~r, ~de, ~t] change
förändring [n.; ~en, ~ar] change
förödande [adj.] devastating,
 ravaging
fötter [see: **fot**]

G

g [abbrev: gata; gram; godkänd] street; gram; pass [school grade]

gadd [n.; ~en, ~ar] sting

GAERC [abbrev: Allmänna rådet] General Affairs and External Relations Council (GAERC) [EU]

gaffel [n.; ~n, gafflar] fork

galax [n.; ~en, ~er] galaxy

galen [adj.; galet, galna] crazy, mad

galge [n.; ~n, galgar] clothes hanger; gallows

galleri [n.; ~n, ~er] gallery

galleria [n.; ~n, gallerior] shopping mall

galna ko-sjukan (BSE) [n.] mad cow disease, bovine spongiform encephalopathy (BSE)

galopp [n.; ~en] gallop

galoppbana [n.; ~n, -banor] racetrack

galoppera [v.; ~r, ~de, ~t] gallop

galt [n.; ~en, ~ar] boar

gam [n.; ~en, ~ar] vulture

gammal [adj.; ~t, gamla; comp.: äldre, äldst] old; gamla stan old town; Gamla Testamentet Old Testament; hur ~ är du? how old are you?

gammaldags [adj.] old fashioned

ganska [adv.] rather, fairly, quite

gapa [v.; ~r, ~de, ~t] open one's mouth, gape

garage [n.; ~t, ~] garage

garantera [v.; ~r, ~de, ~t] guarantee

garanti [n.; ~n, ~er] guarantee

garantipension [n.; ~en, ~er] guaranteed minimum pension

garderob [n.; ~en, ~er] wardrobe, clothes closet; checkroom, cloakroom

gardin [n.; ~en, ~er] curtain

garn [n.; ~et, ~er] yarn

garnera [v.; ~r, ~de, ~t] trim, garnish

garnering [n.; ~en, ~ar] garnish, trimming

gas [n.; ~en, ~er] gas; gauze; ~er flatulence

gasbinda [n.; ~n, -bindor] gauze bandage

gascylinder [n.; ~n, -cylindrar] gas bottle, gas cylinder

gasol [n.; ~en] bottled gas, liquefied petroleum gas (LPG)

gasolflaska [n.; ~n, -flaskor] gas bottle, gas canister

gaspatron [n.; ~en, ~er] gas cartridge

gaspedal [n.; ~en] accelerator, gas pedal

gasspis [n.; ~en, -spisar] gas stove

gata [n.; ~n, gator] street

gate [n.] gate (airport)

gathörn [n.; ~et, ~] corner, street corner

gatuadress [n.; ~en, ~er] address

gatukorsning [n.; ~en, ~ar] intersection, junction

gatukök [n.; ~et, ~] street food stand

gatuplan [n.; ~en] ground floor

gav [v.past; see: ge]

gavel [n.; ~n, gavlar] gable

gay [adj.] gay [homosexual]

gayklubb [n.; ~en, ~ar] gay club

Gbg. [abbrev: Göteborg] Gothenburg

Gbyte [n.] gigabyte (GB) [IT]

GD [abbrev: Generaldirektorat] General Directorate [EU]

ge [v.; ger, gav, givit/gett] give; ~ sig av be off; ~ sig iväg depart, leave; ~ ut spend; publish

gehör [n.; ~et] ear [musical]; hearing, respect; absolut ~ perfect pitch

gelé [n.; ~n/et] jelly, gel

gem [n.; ~et, ~] paper clip

gemen [adj.; ~t, ~a] common, ordinary; low, mean; ~er lower-case letters

gemensam [adj.; ~t, ~a] joint, common; ~ beredning joint drafting procedure; ~ marknad common market, single market; ~ strategi common strategy; ~ ståndpunkt common position, joint position; ~ åtgärd joint action [EU]; ~t försvar collective defence; ~t

utt̲a̲lande joint statement, common position

Gem̲e̲nsam fiskeri̲politi̲k [n.; ~en] Common fisheries policy [EU]

Gem̲e̲nsam h̲a̲ndelspoliti̲k [n.; ~en] Common commercial policy [EU]

Gem̲e̲nsam j̲o̲rdbrukspolitik (GJP) [n.; ~en] Common Agricultural Policy (CAP)

Gem̲e̲nsam organisati̲o̲n av j̲o̲rdbruksm̲a̲rknaderna [n.] Common organization of agricultural markets (COM) [EU]

Gem̲e̲nsam transp̲o̲rtpoliti̲k [n.; ~en] Common transport policy [EU]

Gem̲e̲nsam u̲trikes- och s̲ä̲kerhetspoliti̲k (GUSP) [n.; ~en] Common Foreign and Security Policy (CFSP)

gem̲e̲nsamt med [prep.] in common with

gem̲e̲nskap [n.; ~et] community; fellowship

Gem̲e̲nskapen [n.] (European) Community

Gem̲e̲nskapens bef̲o̲genheter [n.pl.] Community powers [EU]

Gem̲e̲nskapens r̲e̲gelv̲e̲rk [n.; ~et, ~] Community legal instruments [EU]

gem̲e̲nskapsfrå̲ga [n.]: **göra till ~** Communitization, make sth. a Community matter [EU]

gem̲e̲nskapsmet̲o̲d [n.; ~en, ~er] Community method [EU decision-making procedure]

gem̲e̲nskapspat̲e̲nt [n.; ~et, ~] Community patent [EU]

gem̲e̲nskapss̲a̲marbete [n.; ~t, ~n] Community cooperation, Communitization [EU procedure]

gen [n.; ~en, ~er] gene

gen̲a̲st [adv.] immediately, at once

gen̲e̲ra [v.; ~r, ~de, ~t] bother, trouble, inconvenience

gen̲e̲rad [adj.; -rat, ~e] embarrassed, self-conscious

gener̲a̲l[1] [n.; ~en, ~er] general

general-[2] [prefix] general, overall, highest level

Gener̲a̲ladvok̲a̲t [n.; ~en, ~er] Advocate General [EU]

gener̲a̲ldirekt̲ö̲r [n.; ~en, ~er] director-general

gener̲a̲lförs̲a̲mling [n.; ~en, ~ar] General Assembly

gener̲a̲lrepetiti̲o̲n [n.; ~en, ~er] dress rehearsal

gener̲a̲lsekret̲e̲rare [n.; ~n, ~] secretary general

Gener̲a̲ltull̲s̲tyrelsen [n.] Board of Customs

generati̲o̲n [n.; ~en, ~er] generation

generati̲o̲nskl̲y̲fta [n.; ~n] generation gap

gener̲a̲tor [n.; ~n, ~er] generator, alternator

gener̲e̲ll [adj.; ~t, ~a] general

gen̲e̲risk [adj.; ~t, ~a] generic

gener̲ö̲s [adj. ~t, ~a] generous

gen̲e̲tik [n.; ~en] genetics

gen̲e̲tisk [adj.; ~t, ~a] genetic

gen̲e̲tiskt modifi̲e̲rade org̲a̲nismer (GMO) [n.pl.] genetically modified organisms (GMO) [EU]

Gen̲è̲ve [n.] Geneva

Gen̲è̲vekonventi̲o̲nerna [n.pl.] Geneva Conventions

gen̲g̲äld: i ~ [adv.] in return, in compensation

geniti̲v [n.; ~en] genitive [gram]

genitivattrib̲u̲t [n.; ~en] genitive of quality, attributive genitive [gram]

genmanipul̲e̲rad [adj.; -rat, ~e] gene-manipulated

genmodifi̲e̲rad [adj.; -rat, ~e] genetically modified

gen̲o̲m [prep.] through, via; ~ **att skr̲i̲va** in writing

genombr̲o̲tt [n.; ~et, ~] breakthrough

genomf̲a̲rt [n.; ~en] passage; ~ **förbj̲u̲den** no thoroughfare

gen̲o̲mfartsv̲ä̲g [n.; ~en, ~ar] through road

genomf̲ö̲ra [v.; -för, -förde, -fört] carry out

genomg̲å̲ [v.; -gå, -gick, -gått] undergo

genomgående [adj.] pervasive; thorough; through; throughout
genomgång [n. ~en, ~er] passage, thoroughfare; screening
genomresa [n.; ~n] transit travel, passing through
genomskinlig [adj.; ~t, ~a] transparent
genomslag [n.; ~et] penetration; breaking through
genomsnitt [n.; ~et, ~] cross section; average
genomsnittlig [adj.; ~t, ~a] average
genomstekt [adj.; ~a] well done [meat]
genomsöka [v.; -söker, -sökte, -sökt] search
genre [n.; ~n, ~er] genre
genrep [abbrev: generalrepetition] dress rehearsal
Gentekniknämnden [n.] National Gene Technology Advisory Board
gentemot [prep.] against; in comparison with
genuin [adj.; ~t, ~a] genuine
genus [n.; ~et, ~] gender [gram]
genusvetenskap [n.; ~et] gender studies
genväg [n.; ~en, ~ar] shortcut [IT]
geografi [n.; ~n] geography
geologi [n.; ~n] geology
Georgien [n.] Georgia [in Caucasus]
gerilla [n.; ~n, gerillor] guerrilla war/warfare
gerillakrig [n.; ~et, ~] guerrilla war/warfare
ges [v.passive; gis, gavs, givits/getts] show, perform, present
gest [n.; ~en, ~er] gesture
gestalt [n.; ~en, ~er] figure, character, image, shape
gestikulera [v.; ~r, ~de, ~t] gesticulate, make gestures
get [n.; ~en, getter] goat
geting [n.; ~en, ~ar] wasp
getingbo [n.; ~et, ~n] wasp's nest
getost [n.; ~en, ~ar] goat cheese [soft, slightly sweet]
gett [v.past.; see: **ge**]
gevär [n.; ~et, ~] rifle, gun
ggr. [abbrev: gånger] times

Gibraltar sund [n.; ~et] Straits of Gibraltar
gick [v.past; see: **gå**]
gift[1] **(med)** [adj.; ~a] married (to)
gift[2] [n.; ~et, ~er] poison
gifta sig (med) [v.refl.; ~r, ~de, ~t] get married (to); ~ **sig borgerligt** have a civil wedding ceremony
giftermål [n.; ~et, ~] marriage
giftig [adj.; ~t, ~a] poisonous
giftinformation [n.; ~en, ~er] poison (information) center
Giftinformationscentralen [n.] National Poison Information Center
gigabyte [n.] gigabyte [IT]
gigantisk [adj.; ~t, ~a] gigantic
gilla [v.; ~r, ~de, ~t] like
gillestuga [n.; ~n, -stugor] recreation room
giltig [adj.; ~t, ~a] valid
giltighet [n.; ~en] validity
gips [n.; ~en, ~er] plaster
gipsa [v.; ~r, ~de, ~t] put a cast on
gipsförband [n.; ~et, ~] (plaster) cast
giraff [n.; ~en, ~er] giraffe
girering [n.; ~en, ~ar] direct bank transfer, giro transfer
gissa [v.; ~r, ~de, ~t] guess
gisslan [n.] hostage
gitarr [n.; ~en, ~er] guitar
gitarrist [n.; ~en, ~er] guitarist
giva [see: **ge**]
givande [adj.] rewarding
given [adj.; givet, givna] given, clear, evident
givetvis [adv.] of course
givit [v.past; see: **ge**]
gjord [adj.; gjort, gjorda; see: **göra**] designed, made; done; ~ **i Sverige** made in Sweden; **gjort är gjort** what's done is done, no use crying over spilt milk
GJP [abbrev: Gemensamma jordbrukspolitiken] Common Agricultural Policy (CAP) [EU]
gjuta [v.; gjuter, göt, gjutit] pour; spread; cast, found, mold
gjutning [n.; ~en, ~ar] molding
glace au four [n.] sponge cake

filled with ice cream, served
flambé

glaciär [n.; ~en, ~er] glacier

glad [adj.; glatt, ~a] happy; ~ **Påsk!**
Happy Easter!

glans [n.; ~en] luster, brilliance,
splendor

glansperiod [n.; ~en] golden age

glas [n.; ~et, ~] glass; glassware;
lens [eyeglasses]

glasbruk [n.; ~et] glassworks

glasmålning [n.; ~en, ~ar] glass
painting, stained glass

glass [n.; ~en] ice cream

glasscoupe [n.] sundae

glassförsäljare [n.; ~n, ~] ice cream
vendor

glasstrut [n.; ~en, ~ar] ice cream
cone

glasögon [n.pl.] eyeglasses, glasses

glasögonbågar [n.pl.] eyeglass
frames

glasögonfodral [n.; ~et, ~] glasses
case

glasögonorm [n.; ~en, ~ar] cobra

glatt[1] [adj.; ~a] smooth

glatt[2] [see: **glad, glädja**]

gled [v.past; see: **glida**]

gles [adj.; ~t, ~a] thin, sparse

glesbefolkad [adj.; -kat, ~a]
sparsely populated

glesbygd [n.; ~en, ~er] thinly settled
area

Glesbygdsverket [n.] National
Rural Development Agency

glida [v.; glider, gled, glidit] glide;
slide, slip

glimt [n.; ~en, ~ar] gleam; twinkle;
glimpse

glitter [n.; glittret, ~] tinsel

glittra [v.; ~r, ~de, ~t] glitter, sparkle

glob [n.; ~en, ~er] globe

global [adj.; ~t, ~a] global; ~ **uppvärmning** global warming

globalisering [n.; ~en] globalization

gloslista [n.; ~n, -listor] word list,
vocabulary

glutenfri [adj.; -fritt, ~a] gluten free

glykol [n.; ~en] antifreeze

glädja [v.; glädjer, gladde, glatt]
make happy

glädje [n.; ~n] joy, pleasure, delight, happiness, satisfaction

glädjedödare [n.; ~n, ~] killjoy,
wet blanket

glänsande [adj.] shining, lustrous;
brilliant

glödlampa [n.; ~n, -lampor] light
bulb

glögg [n.; ~en] mulled wine

glömma [v.; glömmer, glömde,
glömt] forget; **glöm inte att** don't
forget to

gm. [abbrev: **genom**] through, via

gnugga [v.; ~r, ~de, ~t] rub

gnägga [v.; ~r, ~de. ~t] neigh [horse]

gobeläng [n.; ~en, ~er] tapestry

god [adj.; gott, goda; comp.: bättre,
bäst] good; tasty; **ha gott om**
have lots of; ~ **dag!** Hello!, How
do you do! [on first meeting]; ~
fortsättning! Happy New Year!;
~ **Jul!** Merry Christmas!; ~ **kväll!**
good evening!; ~ **middag!** good
afternoon!; ~ **morgon!** good
morning!

Godahoppsudden [n.] Cape of
Good Hope

godis [n.; ~et] candy, sweets

godkänd [adj.] pass(ing) [school
mark]

godkänna [n.; -känner, -kände,
-känt] approve; pass (a student);
agree to; accept

godkännande [n.; ~t, ~n] approval,
acknowledgement

**godkännande av Europeiska
kommissionen** [n.] confirmation
of the European Commission
[EU]

godnatt [interj.] good night

gods [n.; ~et] property; goods,
freight; estate, manor

godsägare [n.; ~n, ~] landowner

golf [n.; ~en] golf

golfbana [n.; ~n, -banor] golf
course; **9/18-håls~** 9/18-hole golf
course

golfklubba [n.; ~n, -klubbor] golf
club

golfrunda [n.; ~n, -rundor] round
of golf

golfspelare [n.; ~n, ~] golf player, golfer
Golfströmmen [n.] Gulf Stream
golv [n.; ~et] floor
golvlampa [n.; ~n, -lampor] floor lamp
gom [n.; gommen, gommar] palate
gonorré [n.; ~n] gonorrhea
googla [v.; ~r, ~de, ~t] Google [IT]
gorilla [n.; ~n, goriller] gorilla
gosse [n.; ~n, gossar] boy
gotik [n.; ~en] Gothic
gott [adj.; see: **god**] **allt ~!** all the best!; **~ Nytt År!** Happy New Year!
grabb [n.; ~en, ~ar] fellow, guy
grabba [v.; ~r, ~de, ~t] grab
grad [n.; ~en, ~er] degree [-10°C= 14°F; 0°C=32°F; 10°C=50°F; 20°C=68°F; 30°C=86°F; 37°C= 98.6°F; 100°C=212°F]
gradadverbial [n.; ~et] adverbial of degree [gram]
gradvis [adv.] by degrees, gradually
grafik [n.; ~en, ~er] graphic art; graphic works
grafiker [n.; ~n, ~] graphic artist
grafikkort [n.; ~et, ~] graphics card, video card [IT]
grafiska användargränssnitt [n.; ~et] graphic(al) user interface (GUI) [IT]
grahamsbröd [n.; ~et, ~] whole wheat bread
gram [n.; grammet, ~] gram [1/25 oz.]
grammatik [n.; ~en, ~er] grammar
grammatiskt genus [n.] grammatical gender [gram]
gran [n.] spruce, Christmas tree
granatäpple [n.; ~t, ~n] pomegranate
grand: litet ~ [adv.] a little bit
granne [n.; ~n, grannar] neighbor
grannhus [n.; ~et, ~] neighboring house
grannland [n.; ~et, -länder] neighboring country
grannskapspolitik [n.; ~en] neighborhood policy [EU]
granska [v.; ~r, ~de, ~t] examine; check; review; scan

granskning [n.; ~en, ~ar] examination, scrutiny, checkup
Granskningsnämnden för radio och TV [n.] Broadcasting Commission
grapefrukt [n.; ~en, ~er] grapefruit
gratinerad [adj.] au gratin
gratis [adv.] free, no charge
gratisprogram [n.; -grammet, ~] freeware, free program [IT]
gratisprov [n.; ~et, ~] free sample
grattis [interj.] congratulations
gratulation [n.; ~en, ~er] congratulation; **varma/hjärtliga ~er!** congratulations!
gratulationskort [n.; ~et, ~] birthday card
gratulera [v.; ~r, ~de, ~t] congratulate; **~r på födelsedagen!** happy birthday!
gratäng [n.; ~en] gratin
grav [n.; ~en, ~ar] grave, tomb
grav accent [n.; ~en] grave accent [gram]
gravad [adj.; gravat, ~e] marinated; **~ lax** marinated salmon
gravera [v.; ~r, ~de, ~t] engrave
gravid [adj.; ~a] pregnant
graviditet [n.; ~en, ~er] pregnancy
gravlax [n.; ~en] marinated salmon
gravplats [n.; ~en, ~er] cemetery
gravsten [n.; ~en, ~ar] gravestone
gravvalv [n.; ~et, ~] crypt
gravvård [n.; ~en, ~ar] memorial stone, monument
gravyr [n.; ~en, ~er] engraving
greenfee [n.] green fee [golf]
grej [n.; ~en, ~er/or] thing
greja [v.; ~r, ~de, ~t] fix, put right
grek [n.; ~en, ~er] Greek
grekinna [n.; ~n, grekinnor] Greek woman
grekisk [n.; ~t, ~a] Greek
grekiska [n.] Greek language
Grekland [n.] Greece
gren [n.; ~en, ~ar] branch, bough
grep [v.past; see: **gripa**]
grepp [n.; ~et, ~] grasp, grip
grevé [n.] semi-hard cheese [like Gouda]

griddteknik [n.; ~en] grid computing, grid technology [IT]

griljera [v.; ~r, ~de, ~t] coat with egg and breadcrumb mix and roast

grill [n.; ~en, ~ar] grill; **från ~en** from the grill, grilled

grilla [v.; ~r, ~de, ~t] grill, barbecue

grillad [adj.; grillat, ~e] grilled, broiled

grillbar [adj.; ~t, ~a] fast-food place

grillfest [n.; ~en, ~er] barbecue party

grillkol [n.; ~et] charcoal

grillkorv [n.; ~en, ~ar] grilled sausage

grillning [n.; ~en] barbecue

grillplats [n.; ~en, ~er] barbecue area

grillspett [n.; ~et, ~] skewer; kebab

grind [n.; ~en, ~ar] gate

grindstolpe [n.; ~n, -stolpar] gatepost

grinig [adj.; ~t, ~a] whining

gripa [v.; griper, grep, gripit] seize, arrest

gripande [adj.] touching, moving

gripen [adj.; gripet, gripna] seized; touched, moved

gris [n.; ~en, ~ar] pig; pork

griskotlett [n.; ~en, ~er] pork chop

grisstek [n.; ~en, ~ar] roast pork

groda [n.; ~n, grodor] frog; blunder

grodman [n.; -mannen, -män] frogman

grodlår [n.pl.] frog's legs

grogg [n.; ~n, ~ar] whisky and soda, cocktail with carbonated mixer

gropig [adj.; ~t, ~a] full of holes; bumpy; rough

grosshandlare [n.; ~n, ~] wholesaler

grossist [n.; ~en, ~er] wholesaler

grotesk [adj.; ~t, ~a] grotesque; ~ **vattenkastare** gargoyle

grotta [n.; ~n, grottor] cave, grotto

grov [adj.; ~t, ~a] coarse

grovkornig [adj.; ~t, ~a] coarse-grained

grubbla [v.; ~r, ~de, ~t] think, meditate

grund[1] [adj.; grunt, ~a] shallow

grund[2] [n.; ~en, ~er] ground, soil; foundation, basis; cause, reason; **på ~ av** because of

grunda [v.; ~r, ~de, ~t] found

grundad [adj.; grundat, ~e] founded

grundare [n.; ~, ~] founder

grundform [n.; ~en, ~er] base form [gram]

grundkasus [n.] base case [gram]

grundlag [n.; ~en, ~ar] fundamental law, constitution

grundlägga [v.; -lägger, -lade, -lagt] lay the foundation of

grundläggande [adj.] fundamental, basic; ~ **rättigheter** fundamental rights

grundläggare [n.; ~n, ~] founder

grundskola [n.; ~n, -skolor] elementary school

grundskoleelev [n.; ~en, ~er] elementary school pupil

grundskolekompetens [n.; ~en] completion of nine year compulsory schooling

grundskolelärare [n.; ~n, ~] elementary school teacher

grundtal [n.; ~et, ~] cardinal number [gram]

grundutbildning [n.; ~en] basic education, basic training

grundvux [abbrev: grundutbildning för vuxna] elementary school for adults

grupp [n.; ~en, ~er] group; **~er välkomna** groups are welcome

gruppbiljett [n.; ~en, ~er] group ticket

gruppledare [n.; ~n, ~] group leader

gruppresa [n,; ~n, -resor] group excursion/tour

grupprogram [n.; -grammet, ~] groupware [IT]

grus [n.; ~et] gravel

grusbana [n.; ~n, -banor] clay court

grusgång [n.; ~en, ~er] gravel walk

grusväg [n.; ~en, ~ar] gravel road

gruva [n.; ~n, gruvor] mine

gruvarbetare [n.; ~n, ~] miner

grym [adj.; ~t, ~a] cruel
gryn [n.; ~et, ~] hulled grain
gryning [n.; ~en, ~ar] dawn
gryta [n.; ~n, grytor] pot, casserole
grytlapp [n.; ~en, ~ar] pot holder
grytlock [n.; ~et, ~] pot lid
grytstek [n.; ~en, ~ar] pot roast
grytvante [n.; ~en, -vantar] oven mitt
grå [adj.; ~tt, ~a] gray
gråhårig [adj.; ~t, ~a] gray-haired
gråskala [n.; ~n, -skalor] gray scale [IT]
gråta [v.; gråter, grät, gråtit] cry, weep
grädda [v. ~r, ~de, ~t] bake; ~ **pannkakor** make pancakes
grädde [n.; ~n] cream
gräddfil [n.; ~en] sour cream
gräddmjölk [n.; ~en] light cream
gräddsås [n.; ~en, ~er] cream sauce
gräddtårta [n.; ~n, -tårtor] sponge cake with cream and jam
gräl [n.; ~et, ~] quarrel
gräll [adj.; ~t, ~a] loud, garish
gränd [n.; ~en, ~er] alley, lane
gräns [n.; ~en, ~er] border
gränssnitt [n.; ~et, ~] interface [IT]
gränssnittskort [n.; ~et, ~] interface card [IT]
gräs [n.; ~et, ~] grass
gräsbana [n.; ~n, -banor] grass court (tennis)
gräshoppa [n.; ~n, -hoppor] grasshopper, locust
gräsklippare [n.; ~n, ~] lawn mower
gräslök [n.; ~en, ~ar] chive
gräsmatta [n.; ~n, -mattor] lawn; ~**n får ej beträdas!** keep off the grass!
grät [v.past; see: **gråta**]
gräva [v.; gräver, grävde, grävt] dig, burrow; rummage
grävling [n.; ~en, ~ar] badger
grön [adj.; ~t, ~a] green; ~ **paprika** green pepper; ~**a bönor** green beans; ~**a vindruvor** white grapes; **i det ~a** outdoors, in the open
Grönbok [n.; ~en, -böcker] Green Paper [EU]
grönkål [n.; ~en] kale

Grönland [n.] Greenland
grönsak [n.; ~en, ~er] vegetable
grönsaksaffär [n.; ~en, ~er] greengrocer
grönsakssoppa [n.; ~n, -soppor] vegetable soup
grönsakstallrik [n.; ~en, ~ar] vegetable plate
grönsallad [n.; ~en, ~er] lettuce; green salad
Grön Ungdom [n.] Green Youth
gröt [n.; ~en] porridge, hot cereal
grövre [adj.comp.; see: **grov**]
Guatemala [n.] Guatemala
guatemalansk [adj.; ~t, ~a] Guatemalan
gubbe [n.; ~n, gubbar] old man
gud[1] [n.; ~en, ~ar] god
Gud[2] [n.; ~en] God
gudbarn [n.; ~et, ~en] godchild
guddotter [n.; ~n, -döttrar] goddaughter
gudfar [n.; -fadern, -fäder] godfather
gudinna [n.; ~n, gudinnor] goddess
gudmor [n.; -modern, -mödrar] godmother
gudson [n.; ~en, -söner] godson
gudstjänst [n.; ~en, ~er] church service
guidad [adj.; guidat, ~e] guided
guide [n.; ~n, ~r] guide; wizard [IT]
guidebok [n.; ~en, -böcker] guide book
guidetur [n.; ~en, ~er] guided tour
gul [adj.; ~t, ~a] yellow; ~**a febern** yellow fever; ~**a sidorna** yellow pages
gula [n.; ~n, gulor] yolk
gulasch [n.; ~en, ~er] goulash
guld [n.; ~et] gold
guldarbete [n.; ~t] gold work
gulddoublé [n.] gold plate
guldmedalj [n.; ~en, ~er] gold medal
guldsmed [n.; ~en, ~er] goldsmith
guldsmide [n.; ~t] goldsmithing
guldstjärna [n.; ~n, -stjärnor] golden star
guldålder [n.; ~n] golden age
gulsot [n.; ~en] jaundice
gult [see: **gul**]

gummi [n.; ~t, ~n] rubber
gummibåt [n.; ~en, ~ar] rubber dinghy
gummiring [n.; ~en, ~ar] rubber tire; rubber ring
gummistövlar [n.pl.] rubber boots
gunga [v.; ~r, ~de, ~t] swing, rock
gungbräde [n.; ~t, ~n] seesaw
gungstol [n.; ~en, ~ar] rocking chair
gurka [n.; ~n, gurkor] cucumber
GUSP [abbrev: Gemensamma utrikes- och säkerhetspolitiken] Common Foreign and Security Policy [EU]
gyllene [adj.] golden, gilded
gylf [n.; ~en, ~ar] fly [pants]
gym [n.; gymmet, gymmen] fitness center, health club, gym
gymnasiekompetens [n.; ~en, ~er] high school (equivalency) diploma
gymnasielärare [n.; ~n, ~e] high school teacher
gymnasieskola [n.; ~n, -skolor] upper secondary school, senior high school
gymnasium [n.; -siet, -sier] upper secondary school, senior high school
gymnastik [n.; ~en, ~er] gymnastics
gymnastiklärare [n.; ~n, ~] physical training/education teacher
gymnastikredskap [n.; ~et, ~] gymnastics apparatus
gymnastiksal [n.; ~en, ~ar] gymnasium, gym
gymnastikskor [n.pl.] gym shoes
gymnastisera [v.; ~r, ~de, ~t] do exercise
Gymnich möte [n.; ~t, ~n] Gymnich meeting [EU, informal meetings of EC foreign ministers near Bonn]
gymping [n.; ~en] aerobics
gynekolog [n.; ~en, ~er] gynecologist
gynna [v.; ~r, ~de, ~t] favor, promote
gå [v.; går, gick, gått] go, walk; happen; ~ **av** get off; ~ **bra** be fine, be OK; ~ **om en klass** repeat a grade; ~ **ombord** go on board; ~

sönder break down; ~ **till** go to; ~ **ut** expire, run out; ~ **vilse** go astray, lose one's way, get lost; ~ **över** cross [street]; pass, get better; ~ **över till** change over to
gående [n.; ~t, ~n] pedestrian
gågata [n.; ~n, -gator] pedestrian street
gång [n.; ~en, ~er] aisle; time, occasion; walk; **5 ~er om dagen** 5 times a day; **en annan** ~ another time; **en** ~ once; sometime; **en** ~ **till** once more; **få i** ~ **något** get sthg going/started; **för en ~s skull** for once; **för första ~en** for the first time; **plats vid ~en** aisle seat; **på samma** ~ at the same time; **sätta i** ~begin, start
gångare [n.; ~n, ~] walker
gångbro [n.; ~n, ~ar] pedestrian overpass, foot bridge
gången [adj.] gånget, gångna] gone, gone by; advanced [sickness]
gånger [n.pl.] times, multiplied by [IT]
gånghjälpmedel [n.; -medlet, ~] walking aid
gångstig [n.; ~en, ~ar] walkway, path
gångtunnel [n.; ~n, -tunnlar] pedestrian underpass
går [n.]: i ~ yesterday; **i** ~ **kväll** last night; **i** ~ **morse** early yesterday, yesterday morning
gård [n.; ~en, ~ar] farm; yard, courtyard
gårdagen [n.] yesterday
gårdvar [n.; ~en, ~ar] watchdog
gås [n.; ~en, gäss] goose
gåslever [n.; ~n] goose liver (paté)
gåva [n.; ~n, gåvor] donation, gift
gädda [n.; ~n, gäddor] pike
gäddfärsbullar [n.pl.] pike dumplings
gälla [v.; gäller, gällde, gällt] be valid, apply; ~ **för** be valid for
gällande [adj.] valid; effective
gäng [n.; ~et, ~] gang
gärna [adv.] willingly, gladly; by all means, really
gärning [n.; ~en, ~ar] deed, act

gärningsman [n.; -mannen, -män] criminal, culprit

gäss [n.pl.; see: **gås**]

gäst [n.; ~en, ~er] guest

gästbok [n.; ~en, -böcker] guest book

gästgivargård [n.; ~en, ~ar] country inn

gästgiveri [n.; ~n, ~er] inn

gästhamn [n.; ~en, ~ar] guest harbor (for private boats)

gästrum [n.; -rummet, ~] guest room

gäststuderande [n.; ~n, ~] foreign student

gäststuga [n.; ~n, -stugor] guest house

gödningsmedel [n.; -medlet, ~] fertilizer

gödsla [v.; ~r, ~de, ~t] fertilize, apply manure

gök [n.; ~en, ~ar] cuckoo

gömma [v.; gömmer, gömde, gömt] hide; keep for oneself

göra [v.; gör, gjorde, gjort] do, make; ~ **om** repeat, re-do; ~ **upp eld** light a (camp) fire

Göran [n.]: **Sankt ~** Saint George

gör-det-själv varuhus [n.; -huset, ~] do-it-yourself store

gös [n.; ~en, ~ar] walleyed pike

göt [v.past; see: **gjuta**]

Götaland [n.; -landet] Gothland [southern third of Sweden]

Göteborg [n.] Gothenburg

H

h¹ [abbrev: Högern, Högerpartiet] Party of the Right

H² [abbrev: herrar] men's restroom

ha [v.; har, hade, haft] have

Haag [n.] The Hague

Haagprogrammet [n.] The Hague Programme [EU]

hack [n.; ~et, ~] scratch

hacka¹ [n.; ~n, hackor] pick(axe), hoe

hacka² [v.; ~r, ~de, ~t] hack [IT]

hackad [adj.; hackat, ~e] minced, chopped; ~ biff hamburger steak

hackare [n.; ~n. ~] hacker [IT]

hackspett [n.; ~en, ~ar] woodpecker

hade [v.past; see: ha]

haft [v.past; see: ha]

hage [n.; ~en, ~ar] meadow

hagel [n.; haglet] hail, hailstones

haj [n.; ~en, ~ar] shark

haka [n.; ~n] chin

haka upp sig [v.; ~r, ~de, ~t] stick, get stuck, get jammed; hang up [IT]

haklapp [n.; ~en, ~ar] bib

hakparenteser [n.pl.] square brackets [IT]

hal [adj.; ~t, ~a] slippery; ~t väglag slippery roads, icy roads

halka [n.; ~n] slipperiness [road condition]

hall [n.: ~en, ~ar] hall

hallon [n.; ~et, ~] raspberry

hallå [interj.] hello [on telephone]

hallåkvinna [n.; ~n, -kvinnor] announcer [f.] [radio]

hallåman [n.; -mannen, -män] announcer [m.] [radio]

halm [n.; ~en] straw

halmtak [n.; ~et, ~] thatched roof

hals [n.; ~en, ~ar] neck; throat; ont i ~en sore throat

halsband [n.; ~et, ~] necklace

halsbränna [n.; ~n] heartburn

halsduk [n.; ~en, ~ar] scarf

halsfluss [n.; ~en] tonsillitis

halsinfektion [n.; ~en, ~er] throat infection

halsont [n.; ~et] sore throat

halstabletter [n.pl.] throat lozenges

halstrad fisk [n.] grilled fish

halt [see: hal]

halta [v.; ~r, ~de, ~t] limp

halv [adj.; ~t, ~a] half; ~ 9 half past 8; ~t kilo half kilo; ~a priset half price

halva [n.; ~n, halvor] half

halvblodig [adj.; ~t, ~a] medium rare

halvera [v.; ~r, ~de, ~t] halve, bisect

halvflaska [n.; ~n, -flaskor] half a bottle

halvförsäkring [n.; ~en] insurance for third party liability, fire and theft [compare: helförsäkring]

halvklot [n.; ~et, ~] hemisphere

halvledare [n.; ~n, ~] semiconductor [IT]

halvlek [n.; ~en] half [sports event]

halvljus [n.; ~et, ~] dimmed headlights, low beam

halvpension [n.; ~en] half board [breakfast and evening meal]

halvt [see: halv]

halvtid [n.; ~en] half time

halvtidstjänst [n.; ~en] part-time work/job

halvtimme [n.; ~n, -timmar] half hour

halvtorr [adj.; ~t, ~a] semi-dry, demi-sec

halvår [n.; ~et, ~] half year

halvö [n.; ~n, ~ar] peninsula

hamburgare [n.; ~en, ~] hamburger

hammare [n.; ~n, ~] hammer

hamn [n.; ~en, ~ar] port, harbor

hamna (i/på) [v.; ~r, ~de, ~t] land (on), end up (in)

hamnkapten [n.; ~en, ~er] harbor master

hamnområde [n.; ~t, ~n] harbor area

hamnstyrelse [n.; ~n] harbor board, port authorities

han [pron.; hans, honom] he

hand [n.; ~en, händer] hand; egen ~ on one's own; ta ~ om take care of

handarbete [n.; ~t] handwork;
needlework, embroidery
handbagage [n.; ~et] carry-on
baggage
handbok [n.; ~en, -böcker] handbook, manual
handboll [n.; ~en] handball
handbroms [n.; ~en] handbrake
handbukett [n.; ~en, ~er] small
bouquet
handcykel [n.; ~n, -cyklar] hand
bike
handdator [n.; ~n, ~er] handheld
computer, palmtop computer, PDA
[IT]
handduk [n.; ~en, ~ar] towel
handel [n.; ~n] trade
handelplats [n.; ~en, ~er] place of
business
handelsbalans [n.; ~en ~er] balance
of trade
handelsbojkott [n.; ~en, ~er] trade
boycott
Handelsdepartementet [n.] Ministry of Trade
handelsfirma [n.; ~n, -firmor]
trading firm
Handelsflottans kultur- och
fritidsråd (HKF) - Sjömansser-
vice [n.] Merchant Marine Culture
and Leisure Council - Seamen's
Service
handelshögskola [n.; ~n, -skolor]
school of economics and business
administration
handelskammare [n.; ~n] chamber
of commerce
handelssida [n.; ~n, -sidor] financial
page
handelsskola [n.; ~n, -skolor]
business school
handfat [n.; ~et, ~] washbasin, sink
handflata [n.; ~n, -flator] palm
handfull [n.] handful
handgas [n.; ~en] hand throttle
handgjord [adj.; -gjort, ~a] handmade
handikapp [n.; ~et, ~] handicap,
disability
handikappad [adj.; -kappat, ~e]
disabled

handikappanpassad [adj.; -passat,
~e] suitable for the disabled
handikappersättning [n.; ~en]
disability benefit
handikappfordon [n.; ~et, ~]
handicap vehicle
handikapptoalett [n.; ~en, ~er]
handicap toilet
Handikappombudsmannen (HO)
[n.] Disability Ombudsman
handikappvård [adj.; ~t, ~a]
services for handicapped
handikappvänlig [adj.; ~t, ~a]
handicapped accessible
handkräm [n.; ~en] hand cream
handla [v.; ~r, ~de, ~t] go shopping, shop; deal, do business; act;
~ om deal with, be about
handlande[1] [n.; ~t] conduct,
dealings
handlande[2] [n.; ~n, ~] shopkeeper,
dealer
handlare [n.; ~n, ~] tradesperson,
dealer
handled [n.; ~en, ~er] wrist
handledare [n.; ~n, ~] instructor;
guide; supervisor
handledning [n.; ~en] instruction,
guidance; supervision; guide
handling [n.; ~en, ~ar] action,
deed; story, plot; document; ~ar
documents, papers
handlägga [v.; -lägger, -lade, -lagt]
deal with, handle
handpenning [n.; ~en] deposit,
down payment
handreglage [n.; ~et] hand controls
handskakning [n.; ~en] handshaking
[IT]
handskar [n.pl.] gloves
handskfack [n.; ~et] glove compartment
handskrift [n.; ~en, ~er] manuscript
handskriven [adj.; -skrivet, -skrivna]
hand written
handsydd [adj.; -sytt, ~a] hand sewn
handtag [n.; ~et, ~] handle; handlebars
handtvätt [n.; ~en] washing by hand
handväska [n.; ~n, -väskor] handbag

handvävd [adj.; -vävt, ~a] hand-
woven
hane [n.; ~n, hanar] male of an
animal; cock, rooster
hankontakt [n.; ~en, ~er] male
connector [IT]
hann [v.past; see: hinna]
hans [pron.poss.] his
Hanseförbundet [n.] Hanseatic
League
hantera [v.; ~r, ~de, ~t] manage
hanterare [n.; ~n, ~] manager,
handler [IT]
hantering [n.; ~en] handling,
management
hantverk [n.; ~et, ~] crafts
hare [n.; ~n, harar] rabbit, hare
haricots verts [n.pl.] green beans
harkla sig [v.; ~r, ~de, ~t] clear
one's throat
harm [n.; ~en] indignation, resent-
ment, vexation
harmoni [n.; ~n, ~er] harmony
harmonisering [n.; ~en, ~ar]
harmonization [EU]
harpa [n.; ~n, harpor] harp
harpun [n.; ~en, ~er] harpoon
harstek [n.; ~en] roast hare
hasardspel [n.; ~et, ~] gambling
hasch [n.; ~en] hashish
hasselbackspotatis [n.; ~en] oven-
baked sliced potatoes in breadcrumbs
hasselnötter [n.pl.] hazelnuts
hastig [adj.; ~t, ~a] rapid
hastighet [n.; ~en, ~er] speed
hastighetsbegränsning [n.; ~en]
speed limit
hastighetskontroll [n.; ~en] speed
trap
hastighetsmätare [n.; ~n] speedometer
hat [n.; ~et] hatred
hata [v.; ~r, ~de, ~t] hate
hatt [n.; ~en, ~ar] hat
hatthylla [n.; ~n, -hyllor] hat rack
hav [n.; ~et,~] ocean, sea
hava [see: ha]
havande [adj.] pregnant
havandeskapspenning [n.; ~en, ~ar]
maternity allowance

havre [n.; ~n] oats
havregrynsgröt [n.; ~en] oatmeal
havsabborre [n.; ~n, -abborrar] sea
bass
havsdjup [n.; ~et] depth of the sea
havsfiske [n.; ~t, ~n] deep-sea
fishing
havskräfta [n.; ~n, -kräftor] sea
crayfish, Norway lobster
havsmålning [n.; ~en, ~ar] seascape
havsutsikt [n.; ~en, ~er] view of
the sea
havsyta [n.; ~n] sea level
Hb [abbrev: hemoglobin] hemoglo-
bin (Hb)
HD [abbrev: Högsta domstolen)
Supreme Court
hebreiska [n.; ~n] Hebrew language
hed [n.; ~en, ~er] moor, heath
heder [n.; ~n] honor
hedersdoktor [n.; ~n, ~er] honorary
doctor
hedersmord [n.; ~et, ~] honor killing, murder motivated by honor
hedersrelaterad [adj.; -terat, ~e]
related to honor
hedersskuld [n.; ~en, ~er] debt of
honor
hedersvåld [n.; ~et] violence based
on honor
hednisk [adj.; ~t, ~a] heathen, pagan
hej! [interj.] hello, hi; ~ då! bye!;
~ så länge! so long!
hejda [v.; ~r, ~de, ~t] stop, put a
stop to
hejsan! [interj.] hi there
hektar [n.; ~et, ~] hectare [2.5 acres]
hekto [see: hektogram]
hektogram [n.; -grammet, ~] hec-
togram [100 grams, about ¼ lb.]
hel [adj.; ~t, ~a] whole, all; ~a
natten all night
heldragen linje [n.; ~n, ~r] contin-
uous/unbroken line
helförsäkring [n.; ~en] comprehensive insurance [compare: halv-
försäkring]
helg [n.; ~en, ~er] holiday, weekend; trevlig ~! have a good weekend!; i ~en during the weekend
helgdag [n.; ~en, ~ar] holiday

helgedom [n.; ~en, ~ar] sanctuary, temple

helgeflundra [see: hälleflundra]

helgon [n.; ~et, ~] saint

helgrabatt [n.; ~en, ~er] holiday discount, weekend discount

helgtariff [n.; ~en, ~er] weekend rate

helhet [n.; ~en] whole, entirety

helig [adj.; ~t, ~a] holy, sacred; Helige Ande Holy Spirit

helikopter [n.; ~n, -koptrar] helicopter

heller [adv.; after neg.] not either, also not; inte jag ~ not me either

helljus [n.; ~et] high-beam headlights

hellre [adv.comp.: gärna] rather; skulle ~ prefer to

helpension [n.; ~en] full board [all meals]

helsiden [n.; ~et] all/pure silk

Helsingfors [n.] Helsinki

helst [adv.superl.: gärna] preferably, most of all; -ever; vad som ~ whatever; när som ~ whenever

helstekt [adj.; ~a] roasted whole

helt [adv.; adj.: see: hel] totally; ~ ny brand new; ~ och hållet entirely

heltal [n.; ~et, ~] whole number, integer

heltid [n.; ~en] full time

heltidsjobb [n.; ~et] full-time job

heltäckningsmatta [n.; ~n] wall-to-wall carpeting

helvete [n.; ~t] hell

helylle [n.; ~t] pure wool, all wool

helår [n.; ~et] whole year

hem¹ [adv.] homeward, to home, home [motion]

hem² [n.; hemmet, ~] home; Riksförbundet ~ och Skola National Parent-Teacher Association

hemadress [n.; ~en, ~er] home address

hembakad [adj.; -bakat, ~e] home-baked

hembesök [n.; ~et, ~] home visit, house call

hemförsäkring [n.; ~en, ~ar] property insurance, home owners insurance

hemgjord [adj.; -gjort, ~a] home-made

hemhjälp [n.; ~en, ~ar] domestic help

hemifrån [adv.] from home

heminredning [n.; ~en, ~ar] home furnishings

hemkatalog [n.; ~en, ~er] home directory [IT]

hemkomst [n.; ~en, ~er] return home, arrival at home

hemkunskap [n.; ~en] home economics

hemlagad [adj.; -lagat, ~e] home-made

hemland [n.; ~et, -länder] home country

hemlig [adj.; ~t, ~a] secret, hidden; ~ kopia blind copy (bcc) [IT]; ~ nyckel private key [IT]; ~t telefonnummer unlisted telephone number

hemlighet [n.; ~en, ~er] secret; secrecy, privacy

hemlighetsfull [adj.; ~t, ~a] secretive

hemlängtan [n.] home sickness

hemlös [adj.; ~t, ~a] homeless

hemlöshet [n.; ~en] homelessness

hemma [adv.] at home; ~ hos Jan at Jan's house

hemmabruk [n.; ~et] home use

hemmafru [n.; ~n, ~ar] housewife

hemmalag [n.; ~et] home team

hemmamatch [n.; ~en, ~ar] home game

hemmaplan [n.; ~en] home field, home ground, home stadium

hemorrojder [n.pl.] hemorrhoids

hemort [n.] legal residence, place of residence

hemsida [n.; ~n, -sidor] home page [IT]

hemsk [adj.; ~t, ~a] terrible

hemskt [adv.] awfully

hemslöjd [n.; ~en] handicraft, home industry

hemspråk [n.; ~et, ~] language spoken at home [by immigrants and minorities]

hemspråkslärare [n.; ~n, ~] teacher for immigrant children in their home language

hemspråksundervisning [n.; ~en] teaching of children in their home language

hemstad [n.; ~en, -städer] home town

hemtjänst [n.; ~en] help at home [for the elderly or sick]

hemtrevlig [adj.; ~t, ~a] cosy, comfortable, snug

hemvist [n.; ~et] domicile, residence

hemväg [n..]: **på ~en** on the way home

Hemvärnet [n.] Home Guard [volunteer territorial defense force]

henne [pron.obj.] her

hennes [pron.poss.] her(s)

Henrik [n.] Henry

herdebrev [n.; ~et, ~] circular [EU]

heroin [n.; ~et] heroin

herr [n.; ~en, ~ar] Mr.; gentleman; lord

herravälde [n.; ~t, ~n] domination, rule, supremacy, control

herrdubbel [n.; ~n; -dubblar] men's doubles [sports]

Herre Gud! Good Lord!

herrfrisör [n.; ~en, ~er] barber

herrgård [n.; ~en, ~ar] manor, mansion

herrgårdsakvavit [n.; ~en] aquavit flavored with caraway

herrgårdsost [n.; ~en] semi-hard cheese with nutty flavor

herrkläder [n.pl.] menswear

herrkostym [n.; ~en, ~er] man's suit

herrsingel [n.; ~n, -singlar] men's singles [sport]

herrtoalett [n.; ~en] men's restroom

hes [adj.; ~t, ~a] hoarse

heshet [n.; ~en] hoarseness

het [adj.; hett, ~a] hot

heta [v.; heter, hette, hetat] be called; **vad heter du?** what's your name?

heterogen [adj.; ~t, ~a] heterogeneous

heterosexuell [adj.; ~t, ~a] heterosexual

hetta [n.; ~n] heat

hette [v.past; see: **heta**]

hexadecimal [adj.; ~t, ~a] hexadecimal [IT]

hg [abbrev: hektogram] hektogram [100 g., about 1/4 lb.]

hicka [v.; ~r, ~de, ~t] hiccup

himmel [n.; himlen, himlar] sky; heaven

hinder [n.; hindret, ~] obstacle, impediment; **utan ~** barrier-free

hinderhoppning [n.; ~en] show jumping

hinderlöpning [n.; ~en] steeplechase

hindra [v.; ~r, ~de, ~t] prevent, deter; hamper

hindu [n.; ~n, ~er] Hindu

hink [n.; ~en, ~ar] bucket, pail

hinna [v.; hinner, hann, hunnit] have time to, be in time, manage; **~ med** catch, have time to

hiss [n.; ~en, ~ar] elevator

hissa [v.; ~r, ~de, ~t] hoist

historia [n.; -rien, -rier] history; story; affair

historiker [n.; ~n, ~] historian

historisk [adj.; ~t, ~a] historical; historic; **~ byggnad** historic building; **~ sevärdhet** historical feature

Historiska museet [n.] Museum of National Antiquities

hit [adv.] to here, hither [motion]

hitta [v.; ~r, ~de, ~t] find; **~ hit** find one's way here; **~ på** think up, come upon

hittegodsexpedition [n.; ~en] lost and found office, lost property office

hittegodsmagasin [n.; ~et] lost and found office

hittills [adv.] so far, up to now

hiv [abbrev: humant immunbristvirus] human immunodeficiency virus (HIV)

hiv-positiv [adj.; ~t, ~a] HIV-positive

hiv-smittad [adj.; -smittat, ~e] HIV-infected

hiv-test [n.; ~et, ~] HIV test

hjort [n.; ~en, ~ar] deer; venison

hjortkött [n.; ~et] venison

hjortron [n.; ~et, ~] cloudberry

hjortronsylt [n.; ~en] cloudberry jam

hjul [n.; ~et, ~] wheel
hjulaxel [n.; ~n, -axlar] axle
hjulbalansering [n.; ~en] wheel balancing
hjulinställning [n.; ~en] wheel alignment
hjullås [n.; ~et, ~] wheel boot [parking enforcement]
hjulnav [n.; ~et, ~] wheel hub
hjälm [n.; ~en, ~ar] helmet
hjälp [n.; ~en] help; **tack för ~en!** thanks for your help!
hjälpa [v.; hjälper, hjälpte, hjälpt] help; **~ till** help with
hjälpcentral [n.; ~en, ~er] help desk [IT]
hjälpfönster [n.; -fönstret, ~] help window [IT]
hjälpknapp [n.; ~en, ~ar] help button [IT]
hjälplinje [n.; ~n, ~r] help line
hjälpmedel [n.; -medlet, ~] aid, helping device
Hjälpmedelsinstitutet (HI) [n.] Swedish Handicap Institute
hjälp-meny [n.; ~n, ~er] help menu [IT]
hjälporganisation [n.; ~en, ~er] aid organization
hjälpprogram [n.; -programmet, ~] utility program [IT]
hjälpsam [adj.; ~t, ~a] helpful
hjälpskärm [n.; ~en, ~ar] help screen [IT]
hjälpstation [n.; ~en, ~er] first-aid station
hjälptangent [n.; ~en] help key [IT]
hjälpverb [n.; ~et, ~] auxiliary verb [gram]
hjälte [n.; ~n, hjältar] hero
hjärna [n.; ~n, hjärnor] brain
hjärnblödning [n.; ~en, ~ar] stroke, cerebral hemorrhage
hjärndöd [adj.; -dött, ~a] brain-dead
hjärnhinneinflammation [n.; ~en] meningitis
hjärnskakning [n.; ~en, ~er] concussion
hjärntumör [n.; ~en, ~er] brain tumor
hjärta [n.; ~t, ~n] heart

hjärtattack [n.; ~en, ~er] heart attack
hjärtbesvär [n.; ~et, ~] heart trouble
hjärter [n.; ~n, ~] hearts [cards]
hjärtfel [n.; ~et, ~] heart condition, heart defect
hjärtinfarkt [n.; ~en, ~er] heart attack
hjärtklappning [n.; ~en, ~ar] palpitation
hjärtlig [adj.; ~t, ~a] sincere, warm; **~a gratulationer!** hearty congratulations!; **~a hälsningar!** warm regards!; **~a lyckönskningar!** hearty congratulations!
hjärtmusslor [n.pl.] cockles
hjärtproblem [n.; ~et, ~] heart condition/problem
hjärtslag [n.; ~et, ~] heartbeat
hjärttransplantation [n.; ~en, ~er] heart transplant
HKH [abbrev: Hans/Hennes Kunglig Höghet] His/Her Royal Highness
hk(r). [abbrev: hästkraft(er)] horsepower
H.M. [abbrev: Hans/Hennes Majestät] His/Her Majesty
hoax [n.; ~en, ~er] hoax [IT]
hobby [n.; ~n, ~er] hobby
hockey [n.; ~n] hockey
Holland [n.] Holland
hollandaisesås [n.; ~en] hollandaise sauce
holländare [n.; ~n, ~] Dutchman
holländsk [adj.; ~t, ~a] Dutch
holländska [n.] Dutch language
holme [n.; ~n, holmar] little island
homosexualitet [n.; ~en] homosexuality
homosexuell [adj.; ~t, ~a] homosexual
hon [pron.; hennes, henne] she
hona [n.; ~n, honor] female of an animal
honkontakt [n.; ~en, ~er] female connector [IT]
honom [pron.obj.] him
honung [n.; ~en] honey
honungsmelon [n.; ~en, ~er] honeydew melon

hopfällbar [adj.; ~t, ~a] folding, collapsible

hopp [n.; ~et, ~] hope; jump; branch, goto instruction [IT]

hoppa [v.; ~r, ~de, ~t] jump; ~ **bock** play leapfrog; ~ **hage** play hopscotch; ~ **rep** jump rope

hoppas [v.passive; hoppas, hoppades, hoppats] hope

hopplös [adj.; ~t, ~a] hopeless

hopprep [n.; ~et, ~] jump rope

horisont [n.; ~en, ~er] horizon

horisontell [adj.; ~t, ~a] horizontal

horn [n.; ~et, ~] horn, antler

hortensia [n.; ~n; -sior] hydrangea

horunge [n.; ~n, -ungar] bastard; widow [IT; at top of page], orphan [IT; at bottom of page]

hos [prep.] at, at sbdy's house; ~ **Jan** at Jan's house

hosta¹ [n.; ~n] cough

hosta² [v.; ~r, ~de, ~t] cough

hostig [adj.; ~t, ~a] plagued with a cough

hostmedicin [n.; ~en, ~er] cough medicine

hot [n.; ~et] threat, menace

hota [v.; ~r, ~de, ~t] threaten

hotad [adj.; hotat, ~e] threatened

hotell [n.; ~et, ~] hotel

hotellbetjäning [n.; ~en] hotel staff

hotelldirektion [n.; ~en, ~er] hotel management

hotellfoajé [n.; ~n, ~er] hotel lounge

hotellkedja [n.; ~n, -djor] hotel chain

hotellrum [n.; -rummet, ~] hotel room

hov¹ [n.; ~et, ~] court [royal]

hov² [n.; ~en, ~ar] hoof

hovdessert [n.; ~en] meringues and whipped cream

hovmästare [n.; ~n, ~] headwaiter

hovmästarsås [n.; ~en] dill sauce [for marinated salmon]

hovrätt [n.; ~en, ~er] court of appeal

hr. [abbrev: herr] Mr. (abbrev: Mister)

HTML [abbrev.] HyperText Markup Language (HTML) [IT]

HTML-editor [n.; ~en] HTML editor [IT]

HTML-kod [n.; ~en] HTML code [IT]

hubb [n.] hub [IT]

hud [n.; ~en, ~ar] skin

hudkräm [n.; ~en] skin moisturizer

hudläkare [n.; ~n, ~] dermatologist

hudsjukdom [n.; ~en, ~ar] skin disease

human [adj.; ~t, ~a] humane; fair, reasonable

humaniora [n.pl.] humanities, arts and letters [group of subjects/ disciplines in education]

humanistiska fakulteten [n.] Faculty of Arts and Letters

humanitär [adj.; ~t, ~a] humanitarian

humanitärt bistånd [n.] humanitarian aid [EU]

humla [n.; ~n, humlor] bumblebee

humle [n.; ~n] hops

hummer [n.; ~n, humrar] lobster

hummerklo [n.; ~n, ~r] lobster claw

humor [n.; ~n] humor

humör [n.; ~et] temperament; mood; **på dåligt** ~ in a bad mood; **på godt** ~ in a good mood

hund [n.; ~en, ~ar] dog

hundkoja [n.; ~n, -kojor] dog kennel

hundras [n.; ~en, ~er] breed of dog

hundskatt [n.; ~en, ~er] dog license

hundskattemärke [n.; ~t, ~n] dog tag

hundvalp [n.; ~en, ~ar] puppy

hundra [num.] hundred

hundrade [num.] hundredth

hundralapp [n.; ~en, ~ar] 100-kronor bill

hundratals [adv.] hundreds (of)

hunger [n.; ~n] starvation, hunger

hungerstrejk [n.; ~en, ~er] hunger strike

hungrig [adj.; ~t, ~a] hungry

hunnit [v.past; see: **hinna**]

hur [adv.] how; **eller ~?** right?; ~ **dags?** at what time?; ~ **länge?** how long?; ~ **mycket?** how much?; ~ **många?** how many?; ~ **ofta?** how often?; ~ **så?** pardon?, say again?, what did you say?; ~

som helst in any way, however possible, anyhow
hurra [interj.] hurray!
huruvida [adv.] whether
hus [n.; ~et, ~] house; **~ets special-itet** speciality of the house; **~ets vin** house wine
husapotek [n.; ~et] medicine cabinet
husbil [n.; ~en, ~ar] mobile home
husbåt [n.; ~en, ~ar] houseboat
husdjur [n.; ~et, ~] pet
husgeråd [n.; ~et, ~] household utensils
hushåll [n.; ~et, ~] housekeeping; household; **sköta ~et själv** do one's own housekeeping
hushållsartiklar [n.pl.] household goods
hushållslinne [n.; ~t, ~n] household linen
hushållsost [n.; ~en, ~ar] farmhouse cheese [tangy]
hushållspapper [n.; ~et] paper towel
husmanskost [n.; ~en] home cooking, plain food
husmor [n.; -modern, -mödrar] housewife
husnummer [n.; -numret, ~] house number
husrannsakan [n.] search of a house
hustru [n.; ~n, ~r] wife
hustrumisshandel [n.; ~n] wife beating/battering
husvagn [n.; ~en, ~ar] trailer, camper
huvud [n.; ~et, ~] head; header [IT]
huvud- [prefix] head, main, central
huvuddel [n.; ~en, ~ar] main part, bulk
huvudform [n.; ~en, ~er] main form [gram]
huvudgata [n.; ~n, -gator] main street
huvudkontor [n.; ~et, ~] main office, head office
huvudled [n.; ~en, ~er] main road
huvudord [n.; ~et, ~] head word [gram]
huvudpostkontor [n.; ~et] main post office

huvudregel [n.; ~n] general rule
huvudroll [n.; ~en, ~er] leading role, lead part
huvudrätt [n.; ~en, ~er] main course
huvudsak [n.; ~en, ~er] main thing
huvudsakligen [adv.] mainly
huvudsats [n.; ~en, ~er] main clause [gram]
huvudstad [n.; ~en, -städer] capital city
huvudverb [n.; ~et, ~] main verb [gram]
huvudvärk [n.; ~et] headache
huvudvärkstabletter [n.pl.] headache pills
Hv [abbrev: Hemvärnet] Home Guard
hyacint [n.; ~en, ~er] hyacinth
hyckla [v.; ~r, ~de, ~t] pretend, feign; be hypocritical
hycklare [n.; ~n, ~] hypocrite
hydda [n.; ~n, hyddor] hut, cabin
hyfsa [v.; ~r, ~de, ~t] tidy up, trim; simplify
hyfsad [adj.; hyfsat, ~e] nice; OK, not so bad
hygglig [adj.; ~t, ~a] reasonable; nice, friendly
hylla [n.; ~n, hyllor] shelf, rack
hyllning [n.; ~en, ~ar] congratulations; homage
hylsnyckel [n.; ~n, -nycklar] box wrench
hyperlänk [n.; ~en, ~ar] hyperlink [IT]
hypertext [n.; ~en, ~er] hypertext [IT]
hypotax [n.] hypotaxis [gram]
hypotekslån [n.] mortgage (loan)
hypotenusa [n.; ~n, -sor] hypotenuse
hypotetisk [adj.; ~t, ~a] hypothetical
hyra¹ [n.; ~n] rent, rental
hyra² [v.; hyr, hyrde, hyrt] rent; **att ~** for rent; **till ~** for rent; **~ i andra hand** sublet; **~ ut** rent out, let
hyrbil [n.; ~en, ~ar] rented car
hyrd [adj.; hyrt, ~a] rented
hyresbidrag [n.; ~et, ~] rent allowance, housing allowance

hyresgäst [n.; ~en, ~er] tenant; **~ i andra hand** subtenant

Hyresgästernas Sparkasse och Byggnadsförenings Riksförbund (HSB:s Riksförbund) [n.] National Housing Cooperative Federation

hyresgästförening [n.; ~en, ~ar] tenants association

hyreshus [n.; ~et, ~] apartment house

hyreskontrakt [n.; ~et, ~] rental agreement

hyreslägenhet [n.; ~en, ~er] rental apartment

hyresnämnd [n.; ~en, ~er] rent court

hyresrättslägenhet [n.] apartment that can be rented out

hyresvärd [n.; ~en, ~ar] landlord

hysa [v.; hyser, hyste, hyst] house; bear [feelings], entertain [emotions]

hytt [n.; ~en, ~er] cabin; booth, cubicle

hyttdäck [n.; ~et] cabin deck

hyvel [n.; ~n, hyvlar] plane [tool]; [see also: **osthyvel, rakhyvel**]

hål [n.; ~et, ~] hole; cavity

hålfot [n.; ~en, -fötter] arch [foot]

hålfotsinlägg [n.; ~et, ~] arch support

håll [n.; ~et, ~] direction; manner, way

hålla [v.; håller, höll, hållit] hold, keep; **~ avstånd** keep one's distance, not tailgate; **~ grinden stängd** keep the gate shut; **~ till höger** stay to the right; **~ till vänster** stay to the left; **~ med någon om** agree with someone about; **~ med om** agree on/about; **~ ner** press down, hold down [IT]; **~ på med** be busy with, go in for

hållbar [adj.; ~t, ~a] durable, lasting; tenable; **~ utveckling** sustainable development [EU]

hållning [n.; ~en, ~ar] carriage, deportment; attitude; firmness

hållplats [n.; ~en, ~er] stop

hålslag [n.; ~et, ~] hole/paper punch

hår [n.; ~et] hair

håravfall [n.; ~et] hair loss

hårbalsam [n.; ~en] hair conditioner

hårband [n.; ~et, ~] hair band

hårborste [n.; ~n, -borstar] hairbrush

hårbotten [n.; -bottnen, -bottnar] scalp

hård [adj.; hårt, ~a] hard; **~ i magen** constipated; **~ kärna** hard core [EU]; **hårt bindestreck** hard hyphen [IT]; **hårt bröd** crispbread; **hårt mellanslag** hard space [IT]

hårddisk [n.; ~en, ~ar] hard disk, hard drive [IT]

hårdkokt [adj.; ~a] hard-boiled

hårdvara [n.; ~n, -varor] hardware [IT]

hårdvarunyckel [n.; ~n, -nycklar] hardware key, dongle [IT]

hårfrisör [n.; ~en, ~er] hairdresser, stylist

hårgelé [n.; ~n] hair gel

hårmousse [n.; ~n] hair mousse

hårnålar [n.pl.] hairpins

hårnålskurva [n.] hairpin curve

hårnät [n.; ~et, ~] hairnet

hårprodukt [n.; ~en, ~er] hair care product

hårschampo [n.; ~t, ~n] hair shampoo

hårsnodd [n.; ~en, ~ar] hairband

hårspray [n. ~en, ~er] hair spray

hårspänne [n.; ~et, ~en] hair clip

hårstreck [n.; ~et] serif [IT]

hårt [see: **hård**]

hårtork [n.; ~en, ~ar] hairdryer

hårvård [n.; ~en] hair care; hair products

häck [n.; ~en, ~ar] rack; hedge; hurdle

häcksax [n.; ~en, ~ar] hedge shears

häftad bok [n.; ~en, böcker] paperback book

häftapparat [n.; ~en, ~er] stapler

häfte [n.; ~t, ~n] booklet [tickets, checks, stamps]

häftig [adj.; ~t, ~a] violent, vehement; acute; impulsive

häftklammer [n.; ~n, -klamrar] staple

häftstift [n.; ~et, ~] thumbtack, drawing pin

häkta [v.; ~r, ~de, ~t] hook; arrest, take into custody

häkte [n.; ~t, ~n] police custody

häktning [n.; ~en, ~ar] detention

häktningsorder [n.; ~n, ~] detention order, arrest warrant

häl [n.; ~en, ~ar] heel

hälft [n.; ~en, ~er] half

hälla [v.; häller, hällde, hällt] pour

hälleflundra [n.; ~n, -flundror] halibut

hälsa¹ [n.; ~n] health

hälsa² [v.; ~r, ~de, ~t] greet; give one's regards to; ~ **Elsa åt mig** give Elsa my regards; ~ **på** visit; greet; ~ **till Erik** give my regards to Erik

hälsning [n.; ~en, ~ar] greeting; **med vänlig ~** sincerely yours

Hälso- och sjukvårdens ansvarsnämnden (HSAN) [n.] Medical Responsibility Board

hälsokontroll [n.; ~en, ~er] health check

hälsokost [n.; ~en] health food

hälsokostaffär [n.; ~en, ~er] health food store

hälsotillstånd [n.; ~et, ~] health condition

hämnd [n.; ~en] revenge

hämta [v.; ~r, ~de, ~t] fetch, go get, pick up, retrieve; ~ **hem** get, download [IT]

hämtas [v.passive; hämtas, hämtades, hämtats] get fetched/picked up

hämtning [n.; ~en, ~ar] retrieval [IT]

hämtservice [n.; ~n] pick-up service

hända [v.; händer, hände, hänt] happen, occur

händelse [n.; ~n, ~r] event

händelsehanterare [n.; ~n, ~] event handler [IT]

hänga [v.; hänger, hängde, hängt] hang; ~ **med** come/go along with someone; keep up with; ~ **upp tvätten** hang up the wash; **spela ~ gubbe** play hangman [game]

hängande indrag [n.; ~et] hanging indent [IT]

hängare [n.; ~n, ~] hanger

hängbro [n.; ~n, ~ar] suspension bridge

hängflygning [n.; ~en] hang gliding

hängig [adj.; ~t, ~a] tired

hängmatta [n.; ~n, -mattor] hammock

hängslen [n.pl.] suspenders

hängsmycke [n.; ~t, ~n] pendant

hänsyn [n.; ~en, ~] consideration; **visa ~ mot** show consideration to

hänvisa (till) [v.; ~r, ~de, ~t] refer (to)

hänvisning [n.; ~en, ~ar] reference

häpen [adj.; häpet, häpna] amazed; startled

häpna [v.; ~r, ~de, ~t] amaze

häpnadsväckande [adj.] amazing

här [adv.] here

härifrån [adv.] from here

härlig [adj.; ~t, ~a] lovely, fine, delicious

härmed [adv.] hereby

härom [adv.] from here; about this

häromdagen [adv.] the other day

häromkvällen [adv.] the other night

härtappning [n.; ~en, ~ar] imported wine bottled in Sweden

häruppe [adv.] up here

häst [n.; ~en, ~ar] horse; knight [chess]

hästkapplöpning [n.; ~en] horse racing

hästkapplöpningsbana [n.; ~n, -banor] racetrack, race course

hästkrafter [n.pl.] horsepower

hästpolo [n.; ~t] polo

hästsvans [n.; ~en, ~ar] ponytail

hävda [v.; ~r, ~de, ~t] maintain, uphold; assert

häxa [n.; ~n, häxor] witch

hö [n.; ~et] hay

höft [n.; ~en, ~er] hip

hög¹ [adj.; ~t, ~a] high, elevated; loud; ~**e representanten** [n.] High Representative [EU]

hög² [n.; ~en, ~ar] heap, pile; hillock

Högaktningsfullt [adv.; complimentary closing] Yours respectfully

höger [adj.; högra] right

högerhänt [adj.; -hänta] right-handed

högerjusterad text [n.] right-justified text [IT]
högerklicka [v.; ~r, ~de, ~t] right
click [IT]
högerkörning [n.; ~en] driving on
the right
Högern [n.] Party of the Right,
Conservatives
Högerpartiet [n.] Party of the
Right, Conservatives
högerställa [v.; -ställer, -ställde,
-ställt] right-justify [IT]
högerstyrd [adj.; -styrt, ~a] right-
hand drive [steering wheel on
right]
högertrafik [n.; ~en] right-hand
traffic [drive on right side]
högfjällshotell [n.; ~et, ~] mountain hotel
höghastighet [n.; ~en] high speed
höghus [n.; ~et, ~] high-rise building
högklackad [adj.; -klackat, ~e]
high-heeled
högkonjunktur [n.; ~en] boom
period, prosperous period
högljudd [adj.; -ljutt, ~a] noisy
högnivåspråk [n.; ~et, ~] high-
level language [IT]
högra [see: **höger**]
högre [adj.comp.: hög] higher;
louder
högsk. [abbrev: högskola] college
högskola [n.; ~n, -skolor] college,
university
Högskoleverket [n.] Higher Education Administration
högspänningsledning [n.; ~en, ~ar]
high voltage line
högst [adj.superl; ~a; see: hög]
highest; highly; at most, no more
than
högstadium [n.; -stadiet, -stadier]
upper level of comprehensive
school, school classes for older
adolescents [13-16 years old]
Högsta domstolen (HD) [n.]
Supreme Court
högstudieskola [n.; ~n, -skolor]
upper level of comprehensive
school, school classes for older

adolescents [13-16 years old]
högsäsong [n.; ~en, ~er] high season
högt[1] [see: **hög**]
högt[2] [adv.] high; loud, out loud
högtalare [n.; ~n, ~] loudspeaker,
speaker
högtid [n.; ~en, ~er] celebration,
festival
högtidlig [adj.; ~t, ~a] solemn
högtrafik [n.; ~en] heavy traffic,
peak traffic
högtryck [n.; ~et] high pressure
högupplösning [n.; ~en] high resolution [IT]
högvatten [n.; -vattnet, ~] high tide
höja [v.; höjer, höjde, höjt] raise,
increase
höjd [n.; ~en, ~er] height; hill; ~
över havet height above sea level
höjdhopp [n.; ~et] high jump
höjning [n.; ~en, ~ar] raising; rise
höjt [v.past; see: **höja**]
hök [n.; ~en, ~ar] hawk; **duvor och
~ar** doves and hawks
hökarpanna [n.; ~n] kidney stew
höll [v.past.; see: **hålla**]
höna [n.; ~n, hönor] chicken, hen
höns [n.; ~et] poultry; chicken [meat]
höra [v.; hörer, hörde, hört] hear;
belong; **låta ~ av sig** call, communicate, stay in touch; **vi hörs**
talk to you later, we'll be in touch;
~ ihop belong together; **~ talas
om** hear about/of
hörlur [n.; ~en, ~ar] receiver [tele-
phone]; **~ar** headphones
hörn [n.; ~et, ~] corner
hörna [n.; ~n] corner kick [soccer]
hörnbord [n.; ~et, ~] corner table
hörnskåp [n.; ~et, ~] corner cupboard
hörnsten [n.; ~en, ~ar] cornerstone
hörntand [n.; ~en, -tänder] canine
tooth
hörs [v.passive; see: **höra**]
hörsel [n.; ~n] hearing
hörselskadad [adj.; -skadat, ~e]
hard of hearing
hörslinga [n.; ~n] hearing loop, in-
duction loop hearing aid system
hösnuva [n.; ~n] hay fever

höst [n.; ~en, ~ar] fall, autumn
höstas: i ~ [adv.] last fall
höstdagjämning [n.; ~en] autumn
  equinox
hösttermin [n.; ~en, ~er] fall semester, fall term
hövlighet [n.; ~en, ~er] politeness,
  courtesy

I

i [prep.] in; at; for; to [before the hour]; **5 gånger ~ timmen** 5 times an hour; **kvart ~ två** quarter to two; **~ 2 timmar** for 2 hours; **~ 5 dagar** for 5 days; **~ allmänhet** usually; **~ dag** today; **~ fjol** last year; **~ måndags** last Monday; **~ stället för** instead of; **~ synnerhet** especially; **~ telefon** on the telephone; **~ år** this year

i2010 [n.] i2010 [EU Information Society initiative]

iakttagelse [n.; ~n, ~r] observation

i allm. [abbrev: i allmänhet] in general, usually

IBF [abbrev: innebandyförening] floorball association

IBK [abbrev: innebandyklubb] floorball club

ibland [adv.] sometimes

ICA [abbrev: Inköpscentralernas aktiebolag] ICA [retail store chain]

ICC [abbrev: Internationella brottmålsdomstolen] International Criminal Court (ICC)

icke [adv.] not, non-; **~ godkänd (IG)** fail [school mark]

icke-flyktigt minne [n.; ~t, ~n] non-volatile memory [IT]

icke-nödvändig [adj.; ~t, ~a] non-essential [gram]

icke-restriktiv [adj.; ~t, ~a] non-restrictive [gram]

icke-rökardel [n.; ~en, ~ar] non-smoking section

icke-rökare [n.; ~n] non-smoker; non-smoking

ID [see: **ID-bricka, identitetshandling**]

idag [adv.; see: **dag**] today

ID-bricka [n.; ~n, -brickor] ID card

ide [n.; ~et] winter lair; **gå i ~** go into hibernation

idé [n.; ~n, ~er] idea; **en bra ~** a good idea; **det är ingen ~ att** there is no point/no use in

ideal [adj.; ~t, ~a] ideal

ideell [adj.; ~t, ~a] idealistic; non-profit; **~ förening** non-profit organization

ideligen [adv.] continually

identifiera [v.; ~r, ~de, ~t] identify

identitet [n.; ~en] identity

identitetshandling [n.; ~en, ~ar] identity documents, papers

identitetskort [n.; ~et, ~] identity card

identitetsnummer [n.; -numret, ~] identity number

ideologi [n.; ~n, ~er] ideology

ideologisk [adj.; ~t, ~a] ideological

idéprocessor [n.; ~n, ~er] outliner [IT]

idiot [n.; ~en, ~er] idiot

idiotsäker [adj.; ~, -säkra] foolproof

ID-kort [n.; ~et, ~] ID card

idrott [n.; ~en] athletics, sports

idrottare [n.; ~n, ~] sportsman, athlete

idrottselit [n.; ~en, ~er] top-level sportsmen/athletes

idrottsförening [n.; ~en, ~ar] sports association

idrottshall [n.; ~en, ~ar] sports center, gymnasium

Idrottshögskolan i Stockholm [n.] Stockholm College for Physical Education and Sports

idrottsklubb [n.; ~n, ~ar] athletics club

idrottskvinna [n.; ~n, -kvinnor] sportswoman

idrottsman [n.; -mannen, -män] sportsman

idrottsplan [n.; ~et, ~] sports field

idrottsplats [n.; ~en, ~er] sports field

IF [abbrev: idrottsförening] sports association, athletics association

ifall [adv.] in case, whether

IFK [abbrev: Idrottsföreningen Kamraterna] IFK [association of sports clubs]

ifrågasätta [v.; -sätter, -satte, -satt] question, call into question

ifrån [prep.] from; **Jan kommer ~ Sverige** Jan comes from Sweden
ifylld [adj.; ifyllt, ~a] filled in, completed
IG [see: **icke godkänd**]
IGC [abbrev: Regeringskonferens] Intergovernmental Conference (IGC) [EU]
igelkott [n.; ~er, ~ar] hedgehog
igen [adv.] again; back, together; remaining; shut; **få ~ något** get something shut
igenkänningstecken [n.] token [IT]
igenom [prep.] through; **Jan gick ~ sina övningar** Jan went through his exercises.
igång [see: **gång**] going, in motion
igår [see: **går**] yesterday
ihjäl [adv.] mortally, to death
ihjälskjuten [adj.; -skjutet, -skjutna] shot to death
ihop [adv.] together
ihåg [adv.]: **komma ~** remember
ihållande [adj.] prolonged, persistent, constant
IK [abbrev: idrottsklubb] sports club
IKC [abbrev: Invandrarnas kulturcentrum] Immigrant Culture Center
IKEA [n.] IKEA [major furniture chain]
ikon [n.; ~en, ~er] icon [IT]
ikväll [see: **kväll**] this evening
i-land [abbrev: industriland] developed country, industrialized country
ilgods [n.; ~et] express shipment [parcel]
ill. [abbrev: illustration; illustrerad] illustration; illustrated
illa [adv.] bad(ly), not well; **göra sig ~** hurt oneself; **må ~** feel sick; **ta ~ upp** take offense, take something badly
illamående [adj.] nauseous, feeling sick
illegal [adj.; ~t, ~a] illegal
iller [n.; ~n, illrar] polecat
illojal [adj.; ~t, ~a] disloyal; **~ konkurrens** unfair competition
illustratör [n.; ~en, ~er] illustrator

ILO [abbrev: Internationella arbetesorganisationen] International Labor Organization (ILO) [UN]
ilpaket [n.; ~et, ~] express parcel
ilska [n.; ~n] anger, rage, fury
imam [n.; ~en, ~er] imam
IMF [abbrev: Internationella Valutafonden] International Monetary Fund (IMF) [UN]
imitation [n.; ~en, ~er] imitation
immateriella rättigheter [n.pl.] intellectual property [EU]
immun (mot) [adj.; ~t, ~a] immune (to, against)
immunförsvar [n.; ~et] immune defense
IMO [abbrev.] International Maritime Organization (IMO) [UN]
imorgon [see: **morgon**] tomorrow
imorse [see: **morse**] this morning
imperativ [n.; ~en, ~er] imperative [gram]
imperfekt [n.; ~et] imperfect [gram]
imponerad [adj.; -rat, ~e] impressed
imponerande [adj.] impressive
importera [v.; ~r, ~de, ~t] import
import- och exportfirma [n.; ~n, -firmor] import/export company
impressionism [n.; ~en] impressionism
in [prep.] into, in [motion]; **~ på** into
inackorderingsrum [n.; -rummet, ~] rented room, furnished room; room with board
inaktuell [adj.; ~t, ~a] out-of-date [IT]
inalles [adv.] in all, altogether
inbjuda [v.; -bjuder, -bjöd, -bjudit] invite
inbjudan [n.] invitation
inbjuden [adj.; -bjudet, -bjudna] invited
inblandad [adj.; -blandat, ~e] involved, implicated, mixed up in
inblandning [n.; ~en, ~ar] interference, meddling
inbollning [n.; ~en] warm-up
inbromsning [n.; ~en] braking
inbrott [n.; ~et, ~] burglary, break-in; **göra ~** break in

inbyggd [adj.; -byggt, ~a] internal, built-in [IT]; **inbyggt system** embedded system [IT]

inbäddad [adj.; -bäddat, ~e] embedded [IT]

inbördes [adj.] mutual, reciprocal

inbördeskrig [n.; ~et, ~] civil war

incheckning [n.; ~en] check-in, check-in desk [airport]

indefinit pronomen [n.] indefinite pronoun [gram]

index [n.; ~et,~] index [IT]

indexerad sökning [n.] indexed search [IT]

indexsida [n.; ~n, -sidor] index page [IT]

indian [n.; ~en, ~er] American Indian

indicier [n.pl.] circumstantial evidence

Indien [n.] India

indier [n.; ~n, ~] Indian [from India]

indikativ [n.; ~en] indicative [gram]

indirekt [adj.; ~a] indirect; ~ **anföring** indirect speech [gram]; ~ **fråga** indirect question [gram]; ~ **objekt** indirect object [gram]

indisk [adj.; ~t, ~a] Indian

Indiska Oceanen [n.] Indian Ocean

individ [n.; ~en, ~er] individual

individuell [adj.; ~t, ~a] individual

indomr [abbrev: industri område] industrial area

Indonesien [n.] Indonesia

indonesisk [adj.; ~t, ~a] Indonesian

indrag [n.; ~et, ~] indent [IT]

industri [n.; ~n, ~er] industry

Industrifonden [n.] National Industrial Development Fund

industriland [n.; ~et, -länder] industrial country

industriområde [n.; ~t, ~n] business district, industrial district

industrisamhälle [n.; ~t, ~n] industrial society

industrisemester [n.; ~n, -semestrar] summer vacation (usually July when most factories close)

industristad [n.; ~en, -städer] industrial city

infart [n.; ~en, ~er] entrance [for vehicles], driveway

infartsparkering [n.; ~en, ~ar] park-and-ride parking lot

infattning [n.; ~en, ~ar] border, edging, frame; setting [jewel]

infektera [v.; ~r, ~de, ~t] infect

infekterad [adj.; -rat, ~e] infected

infektion [n.; ~en, ~er] infection

infinit [adj.; ~a] non-finite [gram]; infinite

infinitiv [n.; ~en, ~er] infinitive [gram]

infinitivmärke [n.; ~t, ~n] infinitive marker [gram]

inflammation [n.; ~en, ~er] inflammation

inflation [n.; ~en, ~er] inflation

influensa [n.; ~n, -ensor] influenza, flu

inflytande [n.; ~t, ~n] influence, effect, leverage; **använda sitt ~** use one's influence, pull strings

infoga [v.; ~r, ~de, ~t] insert, incorporate [IT]

infogningsläge [n.; ~t] insert mode [IT]

information [n.; ~en, ~er] information; ~**en** information desk

informationsbärare [n.; ~n, ~] token [IT]

informationschef [n.; ~en, ~er] director of information

informationsdisk [n.; ~en] information counter

informationskontor [n.; ~et, ~] information office

informations- och kommunikationsteknik (IKT) [n.; ~en] information and communications technology (ICT) [IT]

Informationssamhället [n.] Information Society [EU]

informationstavla [n.; ~n, -tavlor] information board

informationsteknik (IT) [n.; ~en] information technology (IT) [IT]

informationsvetenskap [n.; ~en] information science

informell [adj.; ~t, ~a] informal

informera [v.; ~r, ~de, ~t] inform

infrastruktur [n.; ~en, ~er] infrastructure

infrastrukturminister [n.; ~n] Minister for Communications and Regional Policy

inför [prep.] in front of, before

införa [v.; -för, -förde, -fört] introduce; post (an ad in the paper)

införsel [n.; ~n] import

inga [pron.pl.; see: **ingen**] no, none; ~ **barn under 5 år** no children under 5 years of age; ~ **EU-medborgare** not for EU citizens; ~ **kreditkort** no credit cards

ingalunda [adv.] by no means, not at all

ingefära [n.; ~n] ginger

ingen [pron.; inget, inga] no, none, no one; ~ **ingång** no entry, no admittance; ~ **orsak!** you are welcome!, don't mention it!; ~ **som helst** none whatsoever, no one whosoever

ingenjör [n.; ~en, ~er] engineer

ingenstans [adv.] nowhere

ingenting [pron.] nothing

inget [pron.; see: **ingen**] nothing, none; ~ **särskilt** nothing special; ~ **vidare** not very (good)

ingick [v.past; see: **ingå**]

ingrep [v.past; see: **ingripa**]

ingrepp [n.; ~et, ~] operation [surgery]; encroachment

ingripa [v.; -griper, -grep, -gripit] intervene, interfere

ingå [v.; -går, -gick, -gått] be included

ingående [adj.] thorough, in detail; ~ **saldo** balance brought forward

ingång [n.; ~en, ~ar] access, entry; entrance; ~ **utan trappsteg** stepless access [for disabled]

ingångssida [n.; ~n, -sidor] home page [IT]

inhemsk [adj.; ~t, ~a] domestic, home, internal

inifrån [prep., adv.] from within

initialer [n.pl.] initials

initiativ [n.; ~et, ~] initiative

initiativrätt [n.; ~en] right of initiative [EU]

initiera [v.; ~r, ~de, ~t] initialize [IT]

injektion [n.; ~en, ~er] injection

injektionsnål [n.; ~en, ~ar] injection needle

injektionsspruta [n.; ~n, -sprutor] syringe, hypodermic

inkl [abbrev.; see: **inklusive**]

inkludera [v.; ~r, ~de, ~t] include

inkluderad [adj.; -rat, ~e] included

inklusive [prep.] including; ~ **betjäning** service included; ~ **serveringsavgift** service included

inkokt [adj.; ~a] preserved, cooked and served cold

inkommande [adj.] incoming [IT]

inkomst [n.; ~en, ~er] income

inkomstanmälan [n.] income declaration

inkorg [n.; ~en, ~ar] inbox [IT]

inkrementering [n.; ~en, ~ar] incrementation; increment [IT]

inköp [n.; ~et, ~] purchase

inköpslista [n.; ~n, -listor] shopping list

inlade [v.past; see: **inlägga**]

inlagd [adj.; -lagt, ~a] marinated, pickled; ~ **gurka** pickle; ~ **sill** pickled herring; ~**a rödbetor** pickled beets

inland [n.; ~et] interior [of country]

inlands [adj.] domestic, interior, not-foreign

inleda [v.; -leder, -ledde, -lett] begin, open, initiate; lead into

inledande [adj.] introductory, preliminary

inledning [n.; ~en, ~ar] beginning; introduction

inledningsvis [adv.] by way of introduction

inlett [v.past; see: **inleda**]

inleveranser [n.pl.] incoming deliveries

inlines [n.pl.] inline skates

inloggningsuppgifter [n.pl.] log-in information [IT]

inlåst [adj.; ~a] locked up

inlägg [n.; ~et, ~] contribution; insert

inlägga [v.; -lägger, -lade, -lagt] put in, insert, enter, lodge

inmatning [n.; ~en] input [IT]

innan [adv./ conj.] before

innanför [prep.] inside, within

inne [adv.] in, inside, indoors; at home (location); ~ **i** [prep.] inside

innebandy [n.; ~n] floorball [sport]

innebära [v.; -bär, -bar, -burit] signify, mean, involve

innebörd [n.; ~en, ~er] meaning, significance

innefatta [v.; ~r, ~de, ~t] contain, include, consist of

inneh. [abbrev: innehavare] proprietor

innehav [n.; ~et] possession, ownership

innehavare. [n; ~n, ~] proprietor, owner

innehåll [n.; ~et] contents

innehålla [v.; -håller, -höll, -hållit] contain

innehållsförteckning [n.; ~en] table of contents

innehöll [v.past; see: innehålla]

innergård [n.; ~en, ~ar] inner courtyard

innerlig [adj.; ~t, ~a] intimate, heartfelt

innerslang [n.; ~en, ~ar] inner tube

innersta [adj.superl.: see: inre] innermost

innertak [n.; ~et] ceiling

inom [prep.] within; ~ en vecka within a week, in a week's time; ~ hörhåll within earshot

inomhus [adv.] indoor(s)

inomhusbassäng [n.; ~en, ~er] indoor swimming pool

inpackning [n.; ~en, ~ar] packing, packaging

inre¹ [adj.] inner, interior, internal; inside; ~ marknaden internal market, single market [EU]

inre² [n.] interior

inreda [v.; -reder, -redde, -rett] decorate, furnish

inredning [n.; ~en, ~ar] decoration, equipment, furnishing(s), fixture

inredningsarkitekt [n.; ~en, ~er] interior decorator

inresa [n.; ~n, -resor] entry [into a country]

inrikes [adj.] domestic [not foreign]

Inrikesdepartementet [n.] Ministry of the Interior

inrikesflyg [n.; ~et] domestic flights

inrikeshandel [n.; ~n] domestic trade/commerce

inrikesminister [n.; ~n] Minister of the Interior

inrikesnyheter [n.pl.] domestic news, national news

inrikespolitik [n.; ~en, ~er] domestic policy

inrikessamtal [n.; ~et, ~] long-distance call [inter-city, not international]

inrikesterminal [n.; ~en, ~er] domestic terminal [airport]

inriktad (på) [adj.; -riktat, ~e] concentrating (on), focused (on)

inriktning [n.; ~en] putting into position, adjusting, aiming

inräknad [adj.; -räknat, ~e] included

insats [n.; ~en, ~er] insert; performance, contribution; stake, deposit

insatslägenhet [n.; ~en, ~er] cooperative apartment

insatsstyrka [n.; ~n, -styrkor] rapid reaction force [EU]

inse [v.; -ser, -såg, -sett] see, perceive, realize, be aware of

insekt [n.; ~en, ~er] insect

insektsbett [n.; ~et, ~] insect bite, sting

insektsmedel [n.; -medlet] insect repellant

insett [v.past; see: inse]

insida [n.; ~n, -sidor] inner side, interior, inside; inside page

insikt [n.; ~en, ~er] understanding, insight; knowledge

insjö [n.; ~n, ~ar] lake

insjökräftor [n.pl.] lake crayfish

inskrift [n.; ~en, ~er] inscription

inskrivning [n.; ~en, ~ar] enrollment, registration

inskrivningsblankett [n.; ~en, ~er] registration form

inslag [n.; ~et, ~] element, segment

inslagning [n.; ~en] wrapping

insläpp [n.; ~et, ~] admission; opening

insnöad [adj.; -snöat, ~e] snowbound

Inspektionen för strategiska produkter (ISP) [n.] National Inspectorate for Strategic Products

inspelning [n.; ~en, ~ar] recording; production (film)

inspiration [n.; ~en, ~er] inspiration

inspirera [v.; ~r, ~de, ~t] inspire

installation [n.; ~en, ~er] installation [IT]

installationsfil [n.; ~en, ~er] installation file [IT]

installera [v.; ~r, ~de, ~t] install [IT]

instans [n.; ~en, ~er] instance; authority

insticks- [prefix] plug-in [IT]

instickskort [n.; ~et, ~] plug-in card [IT]

insticksprogram [n.; -grammet, ~] plug-in program [IT]

instifta [v.; ~r, ~de, ~t] establish

institut [n.; ~et, ~] institute

Institutet för framtidsstudier [n.] Institute for Future Studies

Institutet för internationell ekonomi [n.] Institute for International Economic Studies

Institutet för jordbruks- och miljöteknik (JTI) [n.] Institute for Agricultural and Environmental Engineering

Institutet för miljömedicin [n.] Institute of Environmental Medicine

Institutet för psykosocial medicin (IPM) [n.] Institute for Psychosocial Medicine

Institutet för rymdfysik (IRF) [n.] Institute for Space Physics

Institutet för social forskning [n.] Swedish Institute for Social Research

Institutet för tillväxtpolitiska studier (ITPS) [n.] Swedish Institute for Growth Policy Studies

institution [n.; ~en, ~er] institute, university department; institution

instruktion [n.; ~en, ~er] instruction [IT]

instruktionsmängd [n.; ~en, ~er] instruction set [IT]

instruktör [n.; ~n, ~er] instructor

instrument [n.; ~en, ~er] instrument

instrumentbräda [n.; ~n, -brädor] dashboard

inställd [adj.; ~a] cancelled

inställning [n.; ~en, ~ar] installation; setting [IT]

instämma [v.; -stämmer, -stämde, -stämt] agree, concur

insyn [n.; ~en] view; insight

insåg [v.past; see: **inse**]

insändare [n.; ~n, ~] letter to the editor

insättning [n.; ~en, ~ar] deposit

insättningspunkt [n.; ~en, ~er] insertion point [IT]

inta [v.; -tar, -tog, -tagit] take; occupy; consume

inte [adv.] not

inteckningslån [n.; ~et, ~] mortgage

integration [n.; ~en, ~er] integration

integrationsminister [n.; ~n] Minister for Democracy and Integration Issues

integrationspolitik [n.; ~en, ~er] integration policy

Integrationsverket [n.] National Integration Board

integrerad krets [n.; ~en, ~ar] integrated circuit [IT]

integritet [n.; ~en] integrity

intellektuell [adj.; ~t, ~a] intellectual

intelligenskvot [n.; ~en, ~er] intelligence quota (IQ)

intelligent [adj.; ~a] intelligent

intendent [n.; ~en, ~er] manager, steward, supervisor; curator

intensiv [adj.; ~t, ~a] intensive, intense; energetic

intensivvård [n.; ~en] intensive care

interaktioner [n.pl.] interactions

interaktivitet [n.; ~en] interactivity [IT]

interaktiv kommunikation [n.] interactive communication [IT]

intercity tåg [n.; ~et, ~] intercity train

interiör [n. ~en, ~er] interior

interjektion [n.; ~en, ~er] interjection [gram]

intern [adj.; ~t, ~a] internal; ~ **television** closed-circuit television (CCTV)

internationell [adj.; ~t, ~a] international

Internationella programkontoret för utbildningsområdet [n.] International Program Office for Education and Training

internatskola [n.; ~n, -skolor] boarding school

Internet [n.; ~et] Internet [IT]

Internetabonnemang [n.; ~et, ~] Internet subscription [IT]

Internetadress [n.; ~en, ~er] Internet address [IT]

Internetbank [n.; ~en, ~er] online bank [IT]

Internet-café [n.; ~t, ~er] Internet café [IT]

Internetleverantör [n.; ~en, ~er] Internet service provider (ISP) [IT]

Internetserver [n.; ~n, -servrar] Internet server [IT]

Internettelefoni [n.; ~n] Internet phone, Voice over Internet (VOI), Voice over Internet Protocol (VOIP) [IT]

Internetuppkoppling [n.; ~en, ~ar] Internet connection [IT]

internminne [n.; ~t, ~n] internal memory, RAM [IT]

internpost [n.; ~en, ~er] internal mail

interrogativ [adj.; ~t, ~a] interrogative [gram]

intervju [n.; ~n, ~er] interview

intervjuare [n.; ~n, ~] interviewer

intervjuobjekt [n.; ~en, ~er] interviewee

intet [pron.] nothing, nothingness

intill [prep., adv.] next to, up to; until; adjacent

intim [adj.; ~t, ~a] intimate

intog (see: **inta**)

intolerant [adj.; ~a] intolerant

intransitiv [adj.; ~t, ~a] intransitive [gram]

intranät [n.; ~et, ~] intranet [IT]

intravenös [adj.; ~t, ~a] intravenous; **~t dropp** intravenous drip

intressant [adj.; ~a] interesting

intresse [n.; ~t, ~n] interest

intressent [n.; ~en, ~er] interested party, stakeholder

intressera [v.; ~r, ~de, ~t] interest

intresserad (av) [adj.; -rat, ~] interested (in)

introducera [v.; ~r, ~de, ~t] introduce

introduktionskurs (ITK) [n.; ~en, ~er] introductory course

intryck [n.; ~et, ~] impression

intrång [n.; ~et, ~] encroachment, trespassing

inträde [n.; ~t] entrance, admission

inträdesavgift [n.; ~en, ~er] entrance fee, admission fee

inträdesbiljett [n.; ~en, ~er] admission ticket

inträdeskrav [n.; ~et, ~] requirements for admission

inträdesprov [n.; ~et, ~] entrance examination

inträffa [v.; ~r, ~de, ~t] occur

intyg [n.; ~et, ~] certificate

intäkt [n.; ~en, ~er] income, revenue, yield

inuti [prep.] inside

inv (abbrev: invånare) inhabitants

invalid [n.; ~en, ~er] invalid

invandra [v.; ~r, ~de, ~t] immigrate

invandrare [n.; ~n, ~] immigrant

Invandrarnas kulturcentrum (IKC) [n.] Immigrant Culture Center

invandrarpolitik [n.; ~en, ~er] immigration policy

invandring [n.; ~en] immigration

inverkan [n.] effect, influence

inversion [n.; ~en, ~er] inversion [gram]

investera [v.; ~r, ~de, ~t] invest

investering [n.; ~en, ~ar] investment

inviga [v.; -viger, -vigde, -vigt] inaugurate, open; wear for the first time; initiate

invigning [n.; ~en, ~ar] inauguration, opening, dedication

invitation [n.; ~en, ~er] invitation

invånare [n.; ~n, ~] inhabitant

invända [v.; -vänder, -vände, -vänt] raise an objection, protest

invändig [adj.; ~t, ~a] interior, inside, internal

invändning [n.; ~en, ~ar] objection
invärtes [adj.] internal; **för ~ bruk**
for internal use; **~ sjukdom** internal disease
invärtesmedicin [n.; ~en] internal
medicine
inåt [prep., adv.] towards the interior; inwards
Ioannina-kompromissen [n.]
Ioannina compromise [EU]
IOK [abbrev: Internationella
Olympiska Kommittén] International Olympic Committee (IOC)
IP-telefoni [n.; ~n] Voice over
Internet Protocol (VOIP) [IT]
Irak [n.] Iraq
irakier [n.; ~n, ~] Iraqi
irakisk [adj.; ~t, ~a] Iraqi
Iran [n.] Iran
iranier [n.; ~n, ~] Iranian
iransk [adj.; ~t, ~a] Iranian
iris [n.; ~en, ~ar] iris
iriska [n.; ~n] Irish language
Irland [n.] Ireland
irländare [n.; ~n, ~] Irishman
irländsk [adj.; ~t, ~a] Irish
ironi [n.; ~n, ~er] irony
ironisk [adj.; ~t, ~a] ironic
irritera [v.; ~r, ~de, ~t] irritate
irriterad [adj.; -rat, ~e] irritated
irriterande [adj.] irritating
is [n.; ~et] ice
isbana [n.; ~n, -banor] skating rink
isberg [n.; ~et, ~] iceberg
isbit [n.; ~en, ~ar] ice cube
isbjörn [n.; ~en, ~ar] polar bear
ISBN [abbrev: Internationellt stan-
dardboknummer] International
Standard Book Number (ISBN)
ischias [n.; ~en] sciatica
isfri [adj.; ~tt, ~a] ice free
isglass [n.; ~en, ~ar] popsicle
ishall [n.; ~en, ~ar] indoor skating
rink
ishav [n.]: **Norra/Södra Ishavet**
Arctic/Antarctic Ocean

ishockey [n.; ~n] ice hockey
i sht. [abbrev: i synnerhet] particularly, especially
isig [adj.; ~t, ~a] icy
iskaffe [n.; ~t, ~] iced coffee
iskall [adj.; ~t, ~a] ice cold
iskyld [adj.; -kylt, ~a] iced
islam [n.] Islam
islamisk [adj.; ~t, ~a] Islamic
islamist [n.; ~en, ~er] Islamist
islamistisk [adj.; ~t, ~a] Islamist
Island [n.] Iceland
islåda [n.] ice tray
isländsk [adj.; ~t, ~a] Icelandic
isländska [n.] Icelandic language
Israel [n.] Israel
israelier [n.; ~n, ~] Israeli
israelisk [adj.; ~t, ~a] Israeli
iste [n.; ~t, ~er] iced tea
isterband [n.; ~et, ~] smoked
sausage [made with beef, pork
and barley]
i st.f. [abbrev: i stället för] instead
of
istället [see: ställe] instead
isvatten [n.; -vattnet] ice water
isär [adv.] apart, away from each
other
IT [abbrev: informationsteknik]
information technology (IT)
Italien [n.] Italy
italiensk [adj.; ~t, ~a] Italian
italienska [n.] Italian language
IT-bolag [n.; ~et, ~] IT company
IT-bransch [n.; ~en] IT sector
IT-företag [n.; ~et, ~] IT company
ITK [see: introduktionskurs]
itu [adv.]: **ta ~ med** set to work on
iv [abbrev: intravenös] intravenous
(IV)
ivrig [adj.; ~t, ~a] eager, excited
iväg [adv.] away, en route, on the
way, travelling; **ge sig ~** set off

J

ja [interj.] yes; ~ **då!** Yes! [emphatic]; ~ **tack!** yes please!; ~ **visst!** of course!

jacka [n.; ~n, jackor] jacket

jade [n.; ~en] jade

jag [pron.; min/mitt/mina, mig] I

jaga [v.; ~r, ~de, ~t] chase, hunt

jaha [interj.] hmm, I see

jakt [n.; ~en, ~er] hunting; hunt; yacht

jakthund [n.; ~en, ~ar] hunting dog

jaktkort [n.; ~et, ~] hunting license

jaktlag [n.; ~en, ~ar] hunting law

jaktmark [n.; ~en, ~er] hunting ground

jaktplan [n.; ~et, ~] fighter plane

jaktsäsong [n.; ~en, ~er] hunting season

jaktvård [n.; -en] game management

jama [v.; ~r, ~de, ~t] meow

jan. [see: **januari**]

Janssons frestelse [n.; ~n] Jansson's temptation [casserole with potatoes, anchovies and onions]

jantelag [n.; ~en] social pressure not to stand out

januari [n.] January

Japan [n.] Japan

japansk [adj.; ~t, ~a] Japanese

japanska [n.] Japanese language

ja-sidan [n.] "yes" voters in a referendum

jaså [interj.] really, is that so

javisst [interj.] of course

jazz [n.; ~en] jazz

jeans [n.pl.; ~en] jeans

jeep [n.; ~en, ~ar] jeep

Jesus [n.] Jesus

Jesusbarnet [n.] Baby Jesus, Christ Child

jet-ski [n.] jet-ski

jfr. [abbrev: jämför] compare

jiddisch [n.; ~en] Yiddish language

JK [abbrev: justitiekansler] Minister of Justice, Attorney General

JM [abbrev: juniormästerkap] junior championship

JO[1] [abbrev: justitieombudsman] Ombudsman for the Judiciary and Civil Administration

jo[2] [interj.] yes [in answer to negative question]; well, it's like this [introductory phrase]; **Du har inte sett min bok, har du? Jo, det har jag.** You haven't seen my book, have you? Yes, I have.; **Vad gjorde jag i dag? Jo, först gick jag ned till Gamla Stan och sedan ...** What did I do today? Well, first I walked down to the Old Town and then ...

jobb [n.; ~et, ~] job, work; **prata ~** talk shop

jobba [v.; ~r, ~de, ~t] work

jobbig [adj.; ~t, ~a] tough, hard, tiring

jod [n.; ~en] iodine

jodtinktur [n.; ~en] tincture of iodine

jodå [interj.; see: **jo**] yes

jogga [v.; ~r, ~de, ~t] go jogging

jogging [n.; ~en] jogging

joggingbyxor [n.pl.] jogging pants, running pants

joggingoverall [n.; ~en] tracksuit, jogging suit

Johan [n.] John

Johannes [n.] John

joker [n.; ~n, jokrar] joker [cards]

jokertecken [n.; -tecknet, ~] wildcard character [IT]

jolle [n.; ~n, jollar] dinghy

Jon[1] [n.] John

jon[2] [n.; ~en, ~er] ion

jonglör [n.; ~en, ~er] juggler

jord [n.; ~et] earth; ground

Jordanien [n.] Jordan

jordanier [n.; ~n, ~] Jordanian

jordansk [adj.; ~t, ~a] Jordanian

jordbruk [n.; ~et] farming, agriculture

Jordbruksdepartementet (Jo) [n.] Ministry of Agriculture, Food and Consumer Affairs

jordbruksgröda [n.; ~n, -grödor] crop

jordbruksland [n.; ~et, -länder] agricultural country

jordbrukspolitik [n.; ~en, ~er] agricultural policy

jordbruksprodukt [n.; ~en, ~er] farm product

jordbrukssamhälle [n.; ~t, ~n] agricultural society

jordbruksstöd [n.; ~et, ~] farm subsidy

Jordbruksverket [n.] Agriculture Administration

jordbävning [n.; ~en, ~ar] earthquake

jordglob [n.; ~en] globe

jordgubbar [n.pl.] strawberries

jordgubbstårta [n.; ~n, -tårtor] strawberry cake

jordklot [n.; ~et] globe

jordlös [adj.; ~t, ~a] landless

jordnötter [n.pl.] peanuts

jordärtskocka [n.; ~n, -kockor] Jerusalem artichoke

jos [see: **juice**]

jourhavande [adj.] on duty, on call

jourläkare [n.; ~n, ~] doctor on duty

journalist [n.; ~en, ~er] journalist, reporter, newspaper person

journalistik [n.; ~en] journalism

journummer [n.; -nummret] helpline

jourtid [n.; ~en, ~ar] emergency duty (hours)

jourtjänst [n.; ~en] emergency service, on-call service; **ha ~** be on duty, be on call

j-pris [see: **jämförspris**]

jr. [abbrev: **junior**] junior (Jr.)

ju [adv.] of course, as you know; ~ **mer desto bättre** the more the merrier

jubileum [n.; jubileet, jubileer] anniversary

jude [n.; ~n, judar] Jew

judinna [n.; ~n, judinnor] Jewess

judisk [adj.; ~t, ~a] Jewish

judo [n.; ~n] judo

jugendstil [n.; ~en] art nouveau

jugoslav [n.; ~en, ~er] Yugoslav

Jugoslavien [n.] Yugoslavia

jugoslavisk [adj.; ~t, ~a] Yugoslav

juice [n.; ~n, ~r] juice

jul.¹ [see: **juli**]

jul² [n.; ~en, ~ar] Christmas; **God**

Jul! Merry Christmas!

Julafton [n.; ~en, -aftnar] Christmas Eve

julas [n.]: **i ~** last Christmas

julbak [n.; ~et] Christmas baked goods

julbord [n.; ~et] Christmas buffet

Juldagen [n.] Christmas Day

juldekorationer [n.pl.] Christmas decorations

julgotter [n.pl.] Christmas goodies/sweets

julgran [n.; ~en, ~ar] Christmas tree

julgransplundring [n.; ~en] stripping of Christmas tree [children's party]

julhandel [n.; ~n, ~] Christmas shopping

julhelg [n.; ~en] Christmas holiday

julhälsning [n.; ~en, ~ar] Christmas greeting

juli [n.] July

julklapp [n.; ~en, ~ar] Christmas present

julklappspapper [n.; -pappret] Christmas wrapping paper

julklappsstrumpa [n.; ~n, -strumpor] Christmas stocking

julkort [n.; ~et, ~] Christmas card

julkorv [n.; ~en, ~ar] Christmas sausage

julkrubba [n.; ~n, -krubbor] nativity crib

jullov [n.; ~et] Christmas vacation

julmust [n.; ~en] malted Christmas drink

julpynt [n.; ~et] Christmas decorations

julrim [n.; -rimmet] verse on Christmas presents

julskinka [n.; ~n] baked ham

julskyltning [n.; ~en, ~ar] Christmas window display

julstjärna [n.; ~n, -stjärnor] poinsettia

julstämning [n.; ~en] Christmas spirit

julsång [n.; ~en, ~er] Christmas carol

jultomte [n.; ~en] Santa Claus

jumper [n.; ~n, jumprar] sweater
jun. [see: **juni**]
jungfru [n.; ~n, -fruar] maiden, virgin
Jungfrun [n.] Virgo
juni [n.] June
junilistan [n.] June List [political movement for reformed cooperation with Europe]
junior [n.; ~en, ~er] junior; junior member; undergraduate
Jupiter [n.] Jupiter
jur. [abbrev: juris] of laws
jur.dr. [abbrev: juris doktor] Doctor of Laws
jur.kand. [abbrev: juris kandidat] Bachelor of Laws
jur.lic. [abbrev: juris licentiat] Licentiate in Law
juridik [n.; ~en] law (study), jurisprudence
juridisk [adj.; ~t, ~a] legal; ~ **person** legal person
juris doktor [n.] Doctor of Laws
jurist [n.; ~en, ~er] lawyer, legal adviser, jurist
jury [n.; ~n, ~er] jury
just [adv.] precisely; ~ **bakom** just behind; ~ **det** exactly, that's right; ~ **nu** at present, right now
justerad text [n.; ~en] justified text [IT]
Justitiedepartementet (Ju) [n.] Ministry of Justice
Justitiekanslern (JK) [n.] Office of the Chancellor of Justice
justitieminister [n.; ~n] Minister for Justice
Justitieombudsmannen (JO) [n.] Parliamentary Ombudsman, Ombudsman for the Judiciary and Civil Administration
Justitieutskottet [n.] Committee on Justice (in Parliament)
juvel [n.; ~en, ~er] jewel
juvelerare [n.; ~n, ~] jeweler
jägare [n.; ~n, ~] hunter
jägarschnitzel [n.; ~n] veal cutlet with mushrooms
jäkel [n.; ~n, jäklar] devil; **jäklar!** damn!

jäktad [adj.; jäktat, ~e] driven, pushed, pressured, rushed
jämföra [v.; -för, -förde, -fört] compare
jämförbar [adj.; ~t, ~a] comparable
jämförd [adj.; -fört, ~a] compared; ~ **med** compared to
jämförelse [n.; ~n, ~r] comparison
jämförelsekonjunktioner [n.pl.] conjunctions expressing comparison [gram]
jämförelsevis [adv.] comparatively, relatively
jämförspris [n.; ~et, ~] price per unit [kilo, liter, etc.]
jämlik [adj.; ~t, ~a] equal
jämlikhet [n.; ~en] equality
jämlikhetsnät [n.; ~et, ~] peer-to-peer network [IT]
jämn [adj.; ~t, ~a] even; level; flat; ~ **paritet** even parity [IT]; ~**a pengar** exact payment, exact change; ~**a tal** even numbers
jämnt [adv.] exactly; **det är 10 kronor** ~ that will be exactly 10 kronor; **det är** ~**!** keep the change!
jämnårig [adj.; ~t, ~a] of the same age
JämO [abbrev: Jämställdhetsombudsmannen] Ombudsman for Equal Opportunities
jämställa [v.; -ställer, -ställde, -ställt] juxtapose; place on an equal footing
jämställdhet [n.; ~en] gender equality
jämställdhetsminister [n.; ~n] Minister for Women and Equality
Jämställdhetsombudsmannen (JämO) [n.] Equal Opportunities Ombudsman
jämt [adv.] all the time, always, constantly
Jämtland [n.] Jämtland [region in northern Sweden]
jämvikt [n.; ~en] balance; ~ **mellan institutionerna** institutional balance [EU]
järn [n.; ~et] iron
järnhandel [n.; ~n, -handlar] hardware store

järnklubba [n.; ~n, -klubbnor] iron [golf club]
järnmalm [n.; ~en] iron ore
järnsmide [n.; ~t, ~n] forged iron-work
järnväg [n.; ~en, -vägar] railroad
järnvägskorsning [n.; ~en, ~ar] railroad crossing
järnvägsstation [n.; ~en, ~er] railroad station, train station
järnvägsövergång [n.; ~en, ~er] railroad crossing, level crossing
järpe [n.; ~n, järpar] hazel hen/grouse
jäsa [v.; jäser, jäste, jäst] ferment; rise
jäst [n.; ~en] yeast

jätte- [prefix] very big
jättebra [adj.] great, fantastic
jättefin [adj.; ~t, ~a] terrific, lovely
jättelik [adj.; ~t, ~a] gigantic
jättesnygg [adj.; ~t, ~a] stunning, really attractive
jättesnäll [adj.; ~t, ~a] terribly kind
jättestor [adj.; ~t, ~a] very big, huge
jäv [n.; ~et, ~] challenge, objection
jäv- [see: **djäv-**]
jävla [adv.; vul.] damned [colloq.], very
jävligt [adv.] damned, darned
jökel [n.; ~n, jöklar] glacier

K

kabal [n.; ~en, ~er] cabal
kabaré [n.; ~n,~er] cabaret
kabel [n.; ~n, kablar] cable
kabelmodem [n.; ~et, ~] cable modem [IT]
kabel-TV [n.; -TV:n, -TV:ar] cable TV
kabinett [n.; ~et, ~] cabinet
kabinettssekreterare [n.; ~n, ~] State Secretary for Foreign Affairs
kabinlift [n.; ~en, ~ar] cable car
kackerlacka [n.; ~n, -lackor] cockroach
kafé [n.; ~et, ~er] café
kafeteria [n.; ~n, -rior] cafeteria
kafévagn [n.; ~en, ~ar] café car [in train]
kaffe [n.; ~t, ~] coffee; **koka ~** make coffee
kaffeapparat [n.; ~en, ~er] coffee machine
kaffebryggare [n.; ~n, ~] coffee machine
kaffefat [n.; ~en, ~] saucer
kaffekanna [n.; ~n, -nnor] coffee pot
kaffekopp [n.; ~en, ~ar] coffee cup
kaffepanna [n.; ~n, -nnor] coffee pot
kafferast [n.; ~en, ~er] coffee break
kaffeservis [n.; ~en, ~er] coffee set
kaffetermos [n.; ~en, ~ar] coffee thermos
Kairo [n.] Cairo
kaj [n.; ~en, ~er] pier, wharf
kajak [n.; ~en, ~er] kayak
kajennpeppar [n.; ~n] cayenne pepper
KAK [abbrev: Kungliga Automobilklubben] Royal Automobile Club
kaka [n.; ~n, -kor] cake; cookie [IT]
kakel [n.; kaklet, ~] tile
kakelplatta [n.; ~n, plattor] glazed tile
kakelugn [n.; ~en, ~ar] tile oven/ stove
kaktus [n.; ~en, ~ar] cactus
kal [adj.; ~t, ~a] bare, treeless

kalas [n.; ~et, ~] party, feast
kalendarium [n.; -riet, -rier] calendar of events
kalender [n.; ~n, -drar] calendar, almanac; yearbook
kalium [n.; ~et] potassium
kalkerpapper [n.; ~et, ~] tracing paper
kalkon [n.; ~en, ~er] turkey
kalkylblad [n.; ~et, ~] spreadsheet [IT]
kalkylera [v.; ~r, ~de, ~t] calculate
kalkylprogram [n.; ~met, ~] spreadsheet program [IT]
kall [adj.; ~t, ~a] cold, chilled
kalla [v.; ~r, ~de, ~t] call
kallad [adj.; kallat, kallade] called; **så ~** so called
kallas [v.passive; ~, kallades, kallats] be called
Kalle Anka [n.] Donald Duck
kallna [v.; ~r, ~de, ~t] grow cold
kallskuret [n.] cold cuts
kallstart [n.; ~en, ~er] cold boot [IT]
kallvatten [n.; -vattnet, ~] cold water
kalops [n.; ~en, ~er] beef stew
kalorifattig [adj.; ~t, ~a] low calorie
kalsonger [n.pl.] underpants
kalt [adv.; see: **kall**] cold
kalv [n.; ~en, ~ar] calf; veal
kalvbräss [n.; ~en, ~ar] sweetbreads
kalvdans [n.; ~en] curds, cottage cheese
kalvfilé [n.; ~n, ~er] veal fillet
kalvfrikassé [n.; ~n, ~er] veal stew
kalvjärpe [n.; ~n, -par] veal meatball
kalvkotlett [n.; ~en, ~er] veal chop
kalvkött [n.; ~et, ~] veal
kalvlever [n.; ~n, -vrar] calf's liver, veal liver
kalvskinn [n.; ~et] calfskin
kalvstek [n.; ~en, ~ar] roast veal
kalvsylta [n.; ~n, -tor] jellied veal
kam [n.; -mmen, -mmar] comb; crest

kamaxel [n.; ~n, -axlar] camshaft
Kambodja [n.] Cambodia
kambodjansk [adj.] Cambodian
kamel [n.] camel
kamera [n.; ~n, -ror] camera
kamerafodral [n.; ~et, ~] camera case
Kamerun [n.] Cameroon
kamerunsk [adj.] Cameroonian
kamma [v.; ~r, ~de, ~t] comb
Kammarkollegiet [n.] Legal, Financial and Administrative Services Agency
kammarkonsert [n.; ~en, ~er] chamber music concert
kammarmusik [n.; ~en, ~] chamber music
kammarrätt [n.; ~en, ~er] administrative court of appeal
kammussla [n.; ~n, -musslor] scallop
kamomillte [n.; ~et, ~er] camomile tea
kamp [n.; ~en, ~er] struggle, fight, competition; wrestling
kampanj [n.; ~en, ~er] campaign; sales drive/promotion
kampsport [n.; ~en, ~er] martial arts
kamrat [n.; ~en, ~er] friend
kan [v.; see: **kunna**]
Kanada [n.] Canada
kanadensisk [adj.; ~t, ~a] Canadian
kanal [n.; ~en, ~er] channel; canal
kanalbåt [n.; ~en, ~er] river boat
kanariefågel [n.; ~n, -fåglar] canary [bird]
kand. [abbrev: kandidat] bachelor's degree
kanderad frukt [n.; ~en, ~er] candied fruit
kandidat [n.; ~en, ~er] candidate
kandidatland [n.; ~et, -länder] candidate country [EU]
kanel [n.; ~en, ~er] cinnamon
kanelbulle [n.; ~n, ~llar] cinnamon roll
kanin [n.; ~en, ~er] rabbit
kanot [n.; ~en, ~er] canoe
kanoting [n.; ~en] canoeing
kanotpaddling [n.; ~en] canoe paddling

kanske [adv.] perhaps, maybe
kansliråd [n.; ~et, ~] deputy director
kant [n.; ~en, ~er] edge, corner
kantareller [n.pl.] chanterelle mushrooms
kantlinje [n.; ~n, ~r] border line [IT]
kaos [n.; ~et] chaos
kaotisk [adj.; ~t, ~a] chaotic
kap. [abbrev: kapitel] chapter
kapa [v.; ~r, ~de, ~t] hijack
kapacitet [n.; ~en, ~er] capacity; able person
kapell [n.; ~et, ~] chapel
kapital [n.; ~et, ~] capital
kapitel [n.; -tlet, ~] chapter
kapitäler [n.pl.] capital letters [IT]
kapning [n.; ~en, ~ar] hijacking
kapp [n.]: **i ~** in a race
kappa [n.; ~n, kappor] coat [woman's]
kapplöpning [n.; ~en, ~ar] race, competition
kapplöpningsbana [n.; ~n, -nor] racetrack
kapprustning [n.; ~en, ~ar] arms race
kappsegling [n.; ~en, ~ar] sailing race, regatta
kappsäk [n.; ~en, ~ar] bag, clothes bag
kaprifol [n.; ~en] honeysuckle
kapris [n. ~en, ~er] caprice, whim; capers
kapsel [n.; ~n, kapslar] capsule, ampule
Kapstaden [n.] Capetown
kapsyl [n.; ~en, ~er] bottle top
kapsylöppnare [n.; ~n, ~] bottle opener
kapten [n.; ~en, ~er] captain
karaff [n.; ~en, ~er] carafe [about 2 glassfuls]
karakterisera [v.; ~r, ~de, ~t] characterize
karakteristisk [adj.; ~t, ~a] characteristic
karaktär [n.; ~en, ~er] character, quality, nature
karameller [n.pl.] candy, sweets
karaoke [n.; ~n] karaoke

karat [n.; ~en/~et, ~] carat
karate [n.; ~n] karate
karburator [n.; ~n] carburettor
kardborrband [n.; ~et, ~] Velcro fastening
kardborrknäppning [n.; ~en, ~ar] Velcro fastening
kardemumma [n.; ~n] cardamom
Karibiska havet [n.] Caribbean Sea
karies [n.] tooth decay
Karl[1] [n.] Charles
karl[2] [n.; ~en, ~ar] man
Karlavagnen [n.] Big Dipper
karljohanssvamp [n.; ~en, ~ar] boletus mushroom
karneval [n.; ~en] carnival
karosseri [n.; ~t, ~er] car body
karott [n.; ~en, ~er] deep dish
karottunderlägg [n.; ~et, ~] table mat
karp [n.; ~en, ~ar] carp
karpaltunnelsyndrom [n.; ~et] carpal tunnel syndrome [IT]
karré [n.; ~n, ~er] loin of pork
karriär [n.; ~en, ~er] career
karriärjakt [n.; ~en] rat race
karriärkvinna [n.; ~n, -nnor] career woman
karta (över) [n.; ~n, -tor] map (of); **på ~n** on the map
kartlägga [v.; -lägger, -lade, -lagt] map, chart; survey
kartläggning [n.; ~en, ~ar] map, chart; survey
kartong [n.; ~en, ~er] carton, cardboard box; cartoon
kartotek [n.; ~et, ~] card file/index
KAS [abbrev: kontant arbetsmarknadsstöd] cash unemployment benefits
kasino [n.; ~t, ~n] casino
kassa [n.; ~n, -ssor] checkout counter, cashier's desk; fund
kassaapparat [n.; ~en, ~er] cash register
kassaskåp [n.; ~et, ~] safe
kasse [n.; ~n, -ssar] paper bag, plastic bag, shopping bag
kassera [v.; ~r, ~de, ~t] reject; discard, scrap; ~ **in** collect, cash

kassett [n.; ~en, ~er] cassette
kassettbandspelare [n.; ~n, ~] cassette player
kassler [n.; ~n] smoked pork loin
kassör [n.; ~en, ~er] cashier
kassörska [n.; ~n, ~skor] cashier [female]
kast [n.; ~et, ~] throw, toss; cast; jerk
kasta [v.; ~r, ~de, ~t] throw; ~ **boll** play catch; ~ **en blick** glance; ~ **vatten** urinate
kastanj [n.; ~en, ~er] chestnut
kastanjefärgad [adj.; -gat, ~e] auburn-colored
kastrull [n.; ~en, ~er] saucepan
kasus [n.; ~et, ~] case [gram]
katakomber [n.pl.] catacombs
katalog [n.; ~en, ~er] directory, catalogue; folder [IT]
katastrof [n.; ~en, ~er] catastrophe, disaster
kateder [n.; ~n] teacher's desk
katedral [n.; ~en, ~er] cathedral
kategori [n.; ~n, ~er] category
katolik [n.; ~en, ~er] Catholic
katolsk [adj.; ~t, ~a] Catholic
katrinplommon [n.; ~et, ~] prune
katrinplommonkompott [n.; ~en, ~er] stewed prunes
katt [n.; ~en, ~er] cat
Kattegatt [n.] Kattegat [strait between Sweden and Denmark]
katthem [n.; -hemmet, ~] cat shelter
kattmat [n.; ~en] cat food
kattunge [n.; ~n, -ungar] kitten
kausal [adj.; ~t, ~a] causal [gram]
kavaj [n.; ~en, ~er] jacket; informal dress
kavla [v.; ~r, ~de, ~t] roll; ~ **upp ärmarna** roll up one's sleeves
kavring [n.; ~en, ~ar] rye bread [dark, sweetened]
KBV [abbrev: Kustbevakningen] Coast Guard
kbyte [n.; abbrev: kilobyte] kilobyte (KB) [IT]
kd [n.; abbrev: Kristdemokraterna] Christian Democrats
kedja [n.; ~n, -djor] chain
kedjebrev [n.; ~et, ~] chain letter

kedjehus [n.; ~et, ~] row house
kedjeskydd [n.; ~et, ~] chain guard
kejsare [n.; ~n, ~] emperor
kejsarinna [n.; ~n, ~nnor] empress
kejsarsnitt [n.; ~et, ~] Cesarean section
keltisk [adj.; ~t, ~a] Celtic
kemi [n.; ~n] chemistry
Kemikalieinspektionen [n.] National Chemical Inspectorate
kemikalier [n.pl.] chemicals
kemisk [adj.; ~t, ~a] chemical
kemtvätt [n.; ~en, ~ar] dry-cleaning, dry-cleaners
kemtvättad [adj.; -ttat, ~e] dry-cleaned
Kenya [n.] Kenya
kenyansk [adj.; ~t, ~a] Kenyan
keramik [n.; ~en] pottery, ceramics
keso [n.; ~n] cottage cheese
ketchup [n.; ~en] ketchup
kex [n.; ~et, ~] cracker, biscuit; cookie
KF [abbrev: Kooperativa förbundet] Consumers' Cooperative Organization
KFUK [abbrev: Kristliga Föreningen (av) Unga Kvinnor] Young Women's Christian Association (YWCA)
KFUM [abbrev: Kristliga Föreningen (av) Unga Män] Young Men's Christian Association (YMCA)
kg [abbrev.; see: **kilogram**]
kidnappa [v.; ~r, ~de, ~t] kidnap
kidnappning [n.; ~en, ~ar] kidnapping
kikare [n.; ~n, ~] binoculars
kikhosta [n.; ~n] whooping cough
kikärter [n.pl.] chickpeas
kil [n.; ~en, ~ar] wedge
kila [v.; ~r, ~de, ~t] scamper, hurry
killa [see: **kittla**]
kille [n.; ~n, -llar] boy; boy friend
kilo [n.; ~t, ~; see: **kilogram**]
kilobyte [n.] kilobyte [IT]
kilogram (kg) [n.; -grammet, ~] kilogram [2.2 lbs.]
kilometer (km) [n.; ~n, ~] kilometer [0.6 miles]; **100 ~ i timmen** 60 miles an hour

kilometerpris [n.; ~et, ~] charge per kilometer
Kina [n.] China
kinarestaurang [n.; ~en, ~er] Chinese restaurant
kinaschack [n.; ~et] Chinese checkers
kind [n.; ~en, ~er] cheek
kinesisk [adj.; ~t, ~a] Chinese
kinesiska [n.; ~n] Chinese language
kiosk [n.; ~en, ~er] kiosk, stand, booth
kirgizisk [adj.; ~t, ~a] Kyrgyz
Kirgizistan [n.] Kyrgyzstan
kiropraktiker [n.; ~n, ~] chiropractor
kirurg [n.; ~en, ~er] surgeon
kirurgi [n.; ~n] surgery
kirurgiskt ingrepp [n.; ~et, ~] operation [surgery]
kissa [v.; ~r, ~de, ~t] pee, urinate
kista [n.; ~n, -tor] chest, box; coffin
kittel [n.; ~n, kittlar] cooking pot; kettle
kittla [v.; ~r, ~de, ~t] tickle
kivas (om) [v.passive; kivas, kivades, kivats] argue (about)
kiwifrukt [n.; ~en, ~er] kiwi
kjol [n.; ~en, ~ar] skirt
kjollängd [n.; ~en] skirt-length
kl. [abbrev: klockan; klass] o'clock; class
klack [n.; ~en, ~ar] heel
klaffbord [n.; ~et, ~] drop-leaf table
klaga (över) [v.; ~r, ~de, ~t] complain (about), grumble; **~ på** find fault with
klagomål (på, över) [n.; ~et, ~] complaint (against)
klammerparenteser [n.pl.] curly brackets [IT]
klar [adj.; ~t, ~a] clear; light; definite; ready; **vara ~ med** be ready with, have finished
klara [v.; ~r, ~de, ~t] clear up; settle; manage; **~ provet** pass the exam; **~ sig** manage, get by
klarblå [adj.] light blue
klarhet [n.; ~en] clarity, light
klarinett [n.; ~en, ~er] clarinet

klarna (upp) [v.; ~r, ~de, ~t] clear (up) [weather]

klart [adv.; also see: **klar**] clearly

klartecken [n.; -cknet, ~] clear sign, OK signal

klartext [n.; ~en] plain text, non-encrypted text [IT]

klase [n.; ~n, -sar] bunch, cluster

klass [n.; ~en, ~er] class

klassföreståndare [n.; ~n, ~] head teacher for a class

klassicism [n.; ~en] classicism

klassificering [n.; ~en, ~ar] classification

klassifikation [n.; ~en, ~er] classification

klassiker [n.; ~n, ~] classic; classics scholar

klassisk [adj.; ~t, ~a] classical

klasskamp [n.; ~en, ~er] class struggle

klasskamrat [n.; ~en, ~er] classmate

klasskonferens [n.; ~en, ~er] class evaluation meeting

klassmöte [n.; ~t, ~n] class meeting

klassrum [n.; -rummet, ~] classroom

klaviatur [n.; ~en, ~er] keyboard [music]

klenät [n.; ~en, ~er] cruller

klev [v.past; see: **kliva**]

klia [v.; ~r, ~de, ~t] itch; **det ~r i örat på mig** my ear itches; **~ sig** scratch an itch

klick [n.; ~en, ~ar] clique

klicka [v.; ~r, ~de, ~t] click; misfire; **~ på** click on [IT]

klient [n.; ~en, ~er] client

klientprogram [n.; -programmet, ~] client program [IT]

klient-server [n.; ~n, -servrar] client/server [IT]

klient-serverteknik [n.; ~en, ~er] client/server technology [IT]

klimat [n.; ~et, ~] climate

klimp [n.; ~en, -par] dumpling; lump

klinik [n.; ~en, ~er] clinic

klippa[1] [v.; klipper, klipte, klipt] cut; **~ gräset** mow the lawn; **~ håret** get a haircut; **~ ut** cut out; **~ sig** get a haircut

klippa[2] [n.; ~n, klippor] cliff

klippbestigning [n.; ~en, ~ar] rock climbing

klippklättring [n.; ~en, ~ar] rock climbing

klippning [n.; ~en, ~ar] cut, haircut; **~ av topparna** trim

klister [n.; klistret] paste

klistra [v.; ~r, ~de, ~t] paste; **~ igen** seal; **~ in** paste in [IT]

kliva [v.; kliver, klev, klivit] stride, step; climb; **~ av** get off; **~ på** get on, step in

klo [n.; ~n, ~r] claw; talon; clutch

klocka [n.; ~n, ~ckor] clock; bell; **Hur mycket är ~n?** What time is it?; **~n är 7** It's 7 o'clock

klockspel [n.; ~et] bell chimes

klok [adj.; ~t, ~a] wise, sensible, intelligent; **inte ~** crazy, not all there

kloster [n.; ~tret, ~] monastery, convent, nunnery

klosterkyrka [n.; ~n, -kor] abbey

klubb [n.; ~en, ~ar] club

klubba [n.; ~n, klubbor] club, bat, hockey stick

klubbhus [n.; ~et, ~] clubhouse

klubbmedlem [n.; -lemmen, -lemmar] club member

kluven [adj.; kluvet, kluvna] split; diced; **~ sats** cleft sentence [gram]

klyfta [n.; ~n, klyftor] gorge, ravine; segment [citrus fruit]

klyftpotatis [n.] potato wedges

klåda [n.; ~n, -dor] itch

klä [v.; ~r, ~dde, ~tt] dress, clothe; upholster; **~ av sig** get undressed; **~ julgranen** decorate the Christmas tree; **~ majstången** decorate the maypole; **~ någon** suit someone; **~ om sig** change one's clothes; **~ på sig** get dressed; **~ sig** dress

klädaffär [n.; ~en, ~er] clothing store

klädd i [adj.] dressed in, wearing

kläder [n.pl.] clothes, clothing

klädesplagg [n.; ~et, ~] piece of clothing

klädhängare [n.; ~n, ~] hanger, clothes hanger

klädkammare [n.; ~n, ~] clothes closet

klädnypa [n.; ~n, -nypor] clothespin

klädsam [adj.; ~t, ~a] becoming, suited

klädsel [n.; ~n, klädslar] clothing

klädskåp [n.; ~et, ~] clothes wardrobe, clothes locker

klädstreck [n.; ~et, ~] clothes line

klämma [v.; klämmer, klämde, klämt] squeeze, hug; pinch

klämta [v.; ~r, ~de, ~t] toll; ~ i klockan toll the bell

klängväxt [n.; ~en, ~er] climbing plant, creeper

klänning [n.; ~en, ~ar] dress

klätterområde [n.; ~t, ~n] climbing region

klättra [v.; ~r, ~de, ~t] climb

klättring [n.; ~en, ~ar] climbing, mountaineering

klöver [n.; ~n, ~] clover; clubs [cards]; [colloq.] money

km [abbrev: kilometer] kilometer [0.6 miles]

km/h [abbrev: kilometer i timmen] kilometers per hour [40 km/h = 24 MPH, 100 km/h = 60 MPH]

K.M:t¹ [abbrev: Kunglig majestät] Royal Majesty

km/t² [see: **km/h**]

KN [abbrev: Kombinerade nomenklaturen] Combined Nomenclature (CN)

knacka [v.; ~r, ~de, ~t] knock, tap

knapp¹ [adj.; ~t, ~a] scarce, scanty, short, meager

knapp² [n.; ~en, ~ar] button; knob

knappast [adv.superl.] hardly

knappt [adv.] hardly

knark [n.; ~t] drugs, dope

knarkbegär [n.; ~et] drug addiction

knarklangare [n.; ~en, ~] pusher, peddler [drugs]

knekt [n.; ~en, ~ar] jack [cards]

knep [v.past; see: **knipa**]

knipa [v.; kniper, knep, knipit] pinch

kniv [n.; ~en, ~ar] knife

knoge [n.; ~n, knogar] knuckle

knop [n.; ~en, ~ar] knot [nautical speed]

knopp [n.; ~en, ~ar] bud

knulla [v.; vul.; ~r, ~de, ~t] fuck [vul.]

knut [n.; ~en, ~ar] knot; kilometers per hour

knyta [v.; knyter, knöt, knutit] tie, fasten; clench; knot

knyte [n.; ~t, ~n] bundle; turnover [pastry]

knytkalas [n.; ~et, ~] potluck supper/party, bring your own (BYO)

knytnäve [n.; ~en, -nävar] fist

knä [n.; ~et, ~n] knee

knäcka [v.; ~r, ~de, ~t] crack; break; ruin

knäckebröd [n.; ~et, ~] crispbread

knäppa [v.; knäpper, knäppte, knäppt] click, tick; take a photograph; snap [fingers]; crack [nut]; button (up); ~ upp unbutton

knäskydd [n.; ~et, ~] kneepad

knästrumpor [n.pl.] knee socks

knöl [n.; ~en, ~ar] bump, lump, knob; son of a bitch [vul.]

KO¹ [abbrev: konsumentombudsmannen] ombudsman for consumer affairs

ko² [n.; ~n, ~r] cow

koalition [n.; ~en, ~er] coalition

kock [n.; ~en, ~ar] cook

kod [n.; ~en, ~er] code

kodifiering [n.; ~en, ~ar] codification

koffeinfri [n.; -tt, -a] caffeine free, decaffeinated

kofta [n.; ~n, koftor] sweater

kofångare [n.; ~n, ~] bumper

koj [n.; ~en, ~ar] bunk

koja [n.; ~n, kojor] cabin, hut, little house

koka [v.; ~r, ~de, ~t] cook

kokbok [n.; ~en, -böker] cookbook

kokmöjligheter [n.pl.] cooking facilities

kokosnöt [n.; ~en, ~ter] coconut

kokplatta [n.; ~n, ~ttor] hot plate

kokt [adj.] boiled, stewed; ~ ägg boiled egg

kokvrå [n.; ~n, ~r] kitchenette
kol [n.; ~et/~en, ~] coal; charcoal
kola [n.; ~n, kolor] caramel, fudge
kolasås [n.; ~en, ~er] caramel sauce
koldioxid [n.; ~en] carbon dioxide
kolera [n.; ~n] cholera
kolgrillad [adj.; -llat, ~e] charcoal-grilled
kolhydrat [n.; ~en, ~er] carbohydrate
kolik [n.; ~en] colic
kolja [n.; ~n, -jor] haddock [fish]
koll [n.; ~en, ~ar] check, verification
kolla [v.; ~r, ~de, ~t] check, make sure
kollega [n.; ~n, ~er/-gor] colleague
kollegieblock [n.; ~et, ~] note pad
kollegium [n.; -giet, -gier] teaching staff
kollektiv [adv., ~t, ~a] collective
kollektivtrafik [n.; ~en] public transport
kolli [n.; ~t, ~] package; piece of luggage
kollidera [v.; ~r, ~de, ~t] collide
kolon [n.; ~et, ~] colon
koloni [n.; ~n, ~er] colony; settlement; summer camp
kolonilott [n.; ~en, ~er] rented garden plot, allotment
kolsyra [n.; ~n]: **med ~** carbonated; **utan ~** uncarbonated
kolsyrad [adj.; -syrat, ~e] carbonated
koltrast [n.; ~en, ~er] blackbird
kolumn [n.; ~en, ~er] column
kolumnhuvud [n.; ~et, ~] column header [IT]
kom- [suffix] communications [IT]
kombination [n.; ~en, ~er] combination
kombinera [v.; ~r, ~de, ~t] combine
komedi [n.; ~n, ~er] comedy
komma[1] [n.; ~t, ~n] comma; decimal point; **3,5% (tre ~ fem procent)** 3.5% (three point five percent)
komma[2] [v.; kommer, kom, kommit] come; **Hur kommer det?** Why is that?; **~ att** [+ inf] will, be going to; **~ bort** be missing; **~ emellan** get in the way; **~ fel** dial the wrong number; **~ fram** arrive;

~ fram till go up to; **~ ihåg** remember; **~ in på** access [IT]; **~ till** get to; **~ vilse** get lost; **~ överens om** agree on; **~ sig** happen; be due to
kommande [adj.] coming, forthcoming, future
kommando [n.; ~t, ~n] command [IT]
kommandoprompt [n.] command prompt, prompt [IT]
kommentar [n.; ~en, ~er] comment, commentary
kommentera [v.; ~r, ~de, ~t] comment on, annotate
kommers [n.; ~en, ~er] trade, business
kommersiell [adj.; ~t, ~a] commercial
Kommerskollegium [n.; ~et] National Board of Trade
kommissarie [n.; ~n, ~r] superintendent; inspector; commissioner
kommission [n.; ~en, ~er] commission
kommitté [n.; ~n, ~er] committee
kommittébetänkande [n.; ~t, ~n] committee report
kommittéförfaranden [n.] committee procedure, "comitology" [EU procedure]
Kommittén för utrikes- och säkerhetspolitik (KUSP) [n.] Political and Security Committee (PSC) [EU]
kommittéordförande [n.; ~n, ~] committee chairman
kommun [n.; ~en, ~er] municipality, local authority
kommunal [adj.; ~t, ~a] municipal; **~a myndigheter** local authorities; **~ självstyrelse** local self-government; **~ vuxenutbildning (komvux)** adult education
kommunalråd [n.; ~et, ~] municipal commissioner
kommunalval [n.; ~et, ~] local election
kommunfullmäktige [n.pl.] municipal council; city council

kommunförbund [n.; ~et, ~]
federation of local authorities

kommunicera [v.; ~r, ~de, ~t]
communicate [IT]

kommunikation [n.; ~en, ~er]
communication(s); transportation

Kommunikationsforsknings-
beredningen (KFB) [n.] Communication Research Committee

kommunikationsmedel [n.; -medlet,
~] means of communication, means
of transportation

kommunikationsminister [n.; ~n,
-ministrar] Minister of Transport
and Communication

kommunikativ [adj.; ~t, ~a]
communicative

kommuniké [n.; ~en, ~er] commu-
niqué, press release, statement

kommunist [n.; ~en, ~er]
Communist

kommunistisk [adj.; ~t, ~a]
Communist

Kommunistiska Partiet Marxist-
Leninisterna (revolutionärerna)
(KPML(r)) [n.] Communist Party
Marxist-Leninists (revolutionaries)

kommunstyrelse [n.; ~n, ~r]
municipal council

kompakt [adj.; ~a] compact

kompaktskiva (CD) [n.; ~n, -skivor]
compact disc

kompani [n.; ~et, ~er] company

komparation [n.; ~en, ~er] comparison [gram]

komparativ [adj.; ~t, ~a]
comparative

kompass [n.; ~en, ~er] compass

kompensation [n.; ~en, ~er]
compensation

kompensera [v.; ~r, ~de, ~t]
compensate

kompetens [n.; ~en, ~er] competence; qualifications

kompetent [adj.; ~a] competent

kompilator [n.] compiler [IT]

kompis [n.; colloq.; ~en, ~ar]
friend, buddy [colloq.]

kompledighet [n.; ~en, ~er] com-
pensatory leave

komplement [n.; ~et, ~] complement

komplett [adj.; ~a] complete;
absolute

komplettera [v.; ~r, ~de, ~t]
complete

kompletterande befogenheter
[n.pl.] subsidiary powers [EU]

komplicerad [adj.; ~rat, ~e] complex, complicated

komplimang [n.; ~en, ~er]
compliment

komplott [n.; ~en, ~er] plot

komponent [n.; ~en, ~er]
component

kompositör [n.; ~en, ~er] composer

kompott [n.; ~en, ~er] stewed fruit

kompression [n.; ~en, ~er]
compression

komprimera [v.; ~r, ~de, ~t]
compress

komprimerad [adj.; -rat, ~e]
compressed

kompromiss [n.; ~en, ~er]
compromise

kompromissa (om) [v.; ~r, ~de, ~t]
compromise (on)

Komsumentombudsman (KO)
[n.] Consumer Ombudsman

komvux [n.; abbrev: kommunal
vuxenutbildning] secondary
school for adults

koncentration [n.; ~en, ~er]
concentration

koncentrationssvårigheter [n.pl.]
difficulties in concentrating

koncentrera [v.; ~r, ~de, ~t]
concentrate

koncentriska cirklar [n.pl.]
concentric circles [EU]

koncept [n.; ~et, ~er] draft

koncern [n.; ~en, ~er] group of
companies

koncernchef [n.; ~en, ~er] president and chief executive officer
(CEO)

koncessiv [adj.; ~t, ~a] concessive
[gram]

kondition [n.; ~en, ~er] condition,
physical fitness; i dålig ~ out of
shape, unfit

konditional [adj.; ~t, ~a] conditional [gram]

konditionalis [n.] conditional mood [gram]

konditionsträning [n.; ~en, ~ar] fitness training

konditori [n.; ~et, ~er] coffee shop, pastry shop

kondom [n.; ~en, ~er] condom

konduktör [n.; ~en, ~er] conductor, ticket collector

konfektion [n.; ~en, ~er] ready-to-wear clothing

konfektionsstorlek [n.; ~en, ~ar] clothing size

konferens [n.; ~en, ~er] conference

konferensrum [n.; -rummet, ~] conference room

konfigurera [v.; ~r, ~de, ~t] set up [IT]

konflikt [n.; ~en, ~er] conflict; ~ **med annan medicin** interference with other drugs

Kongo [n.] Congo

kongress [n.; ~en, ~er] congress, conference

kongresshall [n.; ~en, ~ar] convention hall

kongruens [n.; ~en, ~er] agreement [gram]

konjak [n.; ~en] cognac

konjugation [n.; ~en, ~er] conjugation [gram]

konjunktion [n.; ~en, ~er] conjunction [gram]

konjunktiv [n.; ~en, ~er] subjunctive [gram]

konjunktur [n.; ~en, ~er] economic situation, business cycle; business conditions

Konjunkturinstitutet (KI) [n.] National Institute for Economic Research

konkret [adj.; ~a] concrete, tangible, specific

konkurrens [n.; ~en] competition

konkurrenskraft [n.; ~en] competitiveness

Konkurrensverket [n.] National Competition Authority

konkurrent [n.; ~en, ~er] competitor, rival

konkurrera [v.; ~r, ~de, ~t] compete

konkurs [n.; ~en, ~er] bankruptcy

konsekutiv [adj.; ~t, ~a] consecutive [gram]

konsekvens [n.; ~en, ~er] consequence; consistency

konsekvent [adj.; ~a] consistent

Konseljen [n.] Council of State, Cabinet

konsert [n.; ~en, ~er] concert

konserthus [n.; ~et, ~] concert hall

konserv [n.; ~en, ~er] canned food, preserves

konservativ [adj.; ~t, ~a] conservative

Konservativa Partiet (KP) [n.] Conservative Party

konservburk [n.; ~en, ~ar] can, preserving jar

konservera [v.; ~r, ~de, ~t] preserve

konserverad frukt [n.; ~en, ~er] preserved fruit

konserveringsmedel [n.; -medlet, ~] food preservative

konservöppnare [n.; ~n, ~] can opener

konsolidering [n.; ~en] consolidation

konsonant [n.; ~en, ~er] consonant

konspiration [n.; ~en, ~er] conspiracy, plot

konst [n.; ~en, ~er] art

Konstakademien [see: **Kungliga Akademien för de fria konsterna**]

konstans [n.; ~en] constancy

konstant [adj.; ~a] constant, fixed, invariable

konstapel [n.; ~n, -staplar] police officer

konstatera [v.; ~r, ~de, ~t] point out; notice; ascertain

konstfiber [n.; ~n, -fibrer] synthetic/manmade/artificial fiber

konstföremål [n.; ~et, ~] art object

konstgalleri [n.; ~et, ~er] art gallery

konstgjord [adj.; -gjort, ~a] artificial; ~ **andning** artificial respiration

konstgödsel [n.; ~n] (artificial) fertilizer

konsthandlare [n.; ~n, ~] art dealer

konsthantverk [n.; ~et, ~] arts and crafts

konstig [adj.; ~t, ~a] strange

konstituera [v.; ~r, ~de, ~t] constitute

konstitution [n.; ~en, ~er] constitution

Konstitutionsutskottet (KU) [n.] Committee on the Constitution

konstmuseum [n.; -museet, -museer] art museum

konstnär [n.; ~en, ~er] artist, painter, designer

konstnärlig [adj.; ~t, ~a] artistic

Konstnärsnämnden [n.] Artists' Board

konstruera [v.; ~r, ~de, ~t] construct

konstruktion [n.; ~en, ~er] construction

konstruktiv röstnedläggelse [n.; ~en] constructive abstention, positive abstention

konstsiden [n.; ~et] artificial silk, rayon

konstverk [n.; ~et, ~] work of art

konståkning [n.; ~en] figure skating

konsul [n.; ~n, ~er] consul

konsulat [n.; ~et, ~] consulate

konsulent [n.; ~en, ~er] adviser

konsult [n.; ~en, ~er] consultant, adviser

konsultfirma [n.; ~n, -firmor] consulting company

konsument [n.; ~en, ~er] consumer

konsumentombudsmannen (KO) [n.] ombudsman for consumer affairs

konsumentprisindex (KPI) [n.; ~et, ~] consumer price index (CPI)

konsumentskydd [n.; ~et] consumer protection [EU]

Konsumentverket [n.] National Consumer Agency

konsumentvägledare [n.; ~n, ~] consumer guide

konsumtion [n.; ~en, ~er] consumption

kontakt [n.; ~en, ~er] contact; outlet (electrical), plug; **ta ~ med** get in touch with

kontakta [v.; ~r, ~de, ~t] contact, get in touch with; consult

kontaktinformation [n.; ~en, ~er] contact information

kontaktlins [n.; ~en, ~er] contact lens; **hårda ~er** hard contact lenses; **mjuka ~er** soft contact lenses

kontaktperson [n.; ~en, ~er] contact person

kontant [adj./adv.] cash; **betala ~** pay cash; **köpa ~** pay cash; **~ arbetsmarknadsstöd (KAS)** unemployment assistance in cash

kontanter [n.pl.] cash

kontantkort [n.; ~et, ~] debit card, cash card [IT]

kontinent [n.; ~en, ~er] continent

konto [n.; ~t, ~n] account

kontohavare [n.; ~n, ~] account holder

kontokort [n.; ~et, ~] debit card

kontonamn [n.; ~et, ~] account name, user ID [IT]

kontonummer [n.; -numret, ~] account number

kontor [n.; ~et, ~] office

kontorist [n.; ~en, ~er] clerk

kontorsautomatisering [n.; ~en] office automation [IT]

kontorschef [n.; ~en, ~er] office manager

kontorsnätverk [n.; ~et, ~] office network [IT]

kontorsstädning [n.; ~en] office cleaning

kontorstid [n.; ~en, ~er] office hours

kontoutdrag [n.; ~et, ~] bank statement, statement of account

kontraindikationer [n.pl.] counter-indications

kontrakt [n.; ~et, ~] contract

kontraktsbrott [n.; ~et, ~] breach of contract

kontrast [n.; ~en, ~er] contrast

kontrastiv [adj.; ~t, ~a] contrastive [gram]

kontroll [n.; ~en, ~er] control, check, inspection, surveillance; **~ av EG-rättens tillämpning** monitoring the application of Community law [EU]

kontrollant [n.; ~en, ~er] supervisor, inspector

kontrollbesiktning [n.; ~en, ~ar] technical inspection [car]; veterinary inspection

kontrollera [v.; ~r, ~de, ~t] check, verify

kontrollerkort [n.; ~et, ~] controller card [IT]

kontrollpanel [n.; ~n, ~er] control panel [IT]

kontrollsumma [n.; ~n, -summor] check sum [IT]

kontroversiell [adj.; ~t, ~a] controversial

kontusion [n.; ~en, ~er] contusion

konung [n.; ~en, ~ar] king

Konvention [n.; ~en] Convention [EU; meetings/bodies convened to draw up important documents]

konvergens [n. ~en] convergence [EU]

konvergenskriterier [n.pl.] convergence criteria [EU]

konversation [n.; ~en, ~er] conversation

konvertera [v.; ~r, ~de, ~t] convert

kooperativ [adj.; ~t, ~a] cooperative

Kooperativa förbundet (KF) [n.] Swedish Cooperative Union (KF)

kopia [n.; ~n, kopior] copy, cc; **göra kopior** make copies

kopiator [n.; ~n, ~er] photocopier

kopiera [v.; ~r, ~de, ~t] copy

kopiering [n.; ~en] copying

kopieringsskydd [n.; ~et, ~] copy protection [IT]

kopp [n.; ~en, ~ar] cup

koppar [n.; ~n] copper

kopparstick [n.; ~et, ~] etching

koppel [n.; kopplet, ~] leash

koppla [v.; ~r, ~de, ~t] connect; put on the leash; ~ **av** relax; ~ **in** switch on; ~ **till** connect to; ~ **upp** connect up, make a connection [IT]

kopplad [adj.; kopplat, ~e] connected; ~ **utskrift** merge printing [IT]

koppling [n.; ~en, ~ar] connection,

coupling; clutch; switch

kopplingspedal [n.; ~en, ~er] clutch pedal

kopplington [n.; ~en, ~er] dial tone

kopula [n.; ~n, kopulor] copula, linking verb [gram]

kor [n.; ~et, ~] choir

korall [n.; ~en, ~er] coral

Koranen [n.] the Koran

Korea [n.] Korea

koreansk [adj.; ~t, ~a] Korean

koreanska [n.] Korean language

korg [n.; ~en, ~ar] basket

korint [n.; ~en, ~er] currant

kork [n.; ~en, ~ar] cork, stopper

korkskruv [n.; ~en, ~ar] corkscrew

korksmak [n.; ~en] corked wine taste

korn [n.; ~et, ~] grain; barley

korp [n.; ~en, ~ar] crow; pickaxe

korrekt [adj.; ~a] correct

korrekturläsning [n.; ~en] proof reading

korrelat [n.; ~et, ~] antecedent, correlate [gram]

korrespondent [n.; ~en, ~er] correspondent

korridor [n.; ~en, ~er] corridor, hall; lobby (political)

korrumperad [adj.; -rat, ~e] corrupted [IT]

korruption [n.; ~en, ~er] corruption

kors [n.; ~et, ~] cross; sharp sign (music)

korsa [v.; ~r, ~de, ~t] cross, intersect; go across

korsad kabel [n.; ~en, kablar] crosslinked cable, crossover cable [IT]

korsande [adj.] crossing; merging; ~ **huvudled** major road ahead

korsförhör [n.; ~et, ~] cross examination

Korsika [n.] Corsica

korsning [n.; ~en, ~ar] intersection, junction

korsord [n.; ~et, ~] crossword

korsrygg [n.; ~en] small of the back

korsvirkeshus [n.; ~et, ~] half-timbered house

kort[1] [adj.; ~a] short
kort[2] [n.; ~et, ~] card; photograph
kortfilm [n.; ~en, ~er] short film
korthet [n.; ~en] shortness, brevity
kortkommando [n.; ~t, ~n] short-cut key [IT]
kortlek [n.; ~en, ~ar] deck/pack of cards
kortslutning [n.; ~en, ~ar] short circuit
korttidsparkering [n.; ~en] short-term parking
korv [n.; ~en, ~ar] sausage; ~ **och mos** sausage and mashed potatoes; **varm** ~ hot dog
korvkiosk [n.; ~en, ~er] hot-dog stand
korvstånd [n.; ~et, ~] hot-dog stand
ko-sjukan [see: **galna ko-sjukan**]
kosmetika [n.; ~n] cosmetics, make-up
Kosovo [n.] Kosovo
kosovoalbansk [adj.; ~t, ~a] Kosovar
kosta [v.; ~r, ~de, ~t] cost
kostfibrer [n.pl.] dietary fiber, roughage
kostnad [n.; ~en, ~er] cost, expense
kosttillskott [n.; ~et, ~] dietary supplements
kostym [n.; ~en, ~er] suit [man's]
kota [n.; ~n, kotor] vertebra
kotförskjutning [n.; ~en] slipped disc
kotlett [n.; ~en, ~er] cutlet, chop
kotpelare [n.; ~n, ~] spinal column; backbone
kotte [n.; ~n, kottar] pine cone
kp [abbrev: Kommunistiska partiet] Communist Party
KPI [abbrev: konsumentprisindex] consumer price index (CPI)
kr [abbrev: kronor] kronor, crowns
krabba [n.; ~n, krabbor] crab
kraft [n.; ~en, ~er] force, power, strength
kraftfull [adj.; ~t, ~a] powerful
kraftig [adj.; ~t, ~a] powerful; substantial; sturdy
kraftverk [n.; ~et, ~] power station
krage [n.; ~en, kragar] collar

kragmått [n.; ~et, ~] collar size
kram [n.; ~en, kramar] hug
krama [v.; ~r, ~de, ~t] squeeze; hug, cuddle
kramp [n.; ~en, ~er] cramp
kran [n.; ~en, kranar] faucet
krans [n.; ~en, ~ar] wreath
krasse [n.; ~en] garden cress
krav [n.; ~et, ~] demand, claim
kravaller [n.pl.] riots, disturbances
kreativ [adj.; ~t, ~a] creative
kreativitet [n.; ~en] creativity
kredit [n.; ~en, ~er] credit; **på** ~ on credit
kreditkort [n.; ~et, ~] credit card; **vi tar** ~ we accept credit cards
Kreml [n.] Kremlin
Kreta [n.] Crete
krets [n.; ~en, ~ar] circle, ring; district
kretsa [v.; ~r, ~de, ~t] circle, move in circles
krfm. [abbrev: kronofogdemyndigheten] enforcement service
krig [n.; ~et, ~] war
kriga [v.; ~r, ~de, ~t] wage war
krigare [n.; ~en, ~] soldier, warrior
krigarkung [n.; ~en, ~ar] warrior king
krigförande [adj.] belligerent
krigsfartyg [n.; ~et, ~] naval vessel, warship
krigsfånge [n.; ~n, -fångar] prisoner of war
krigsförbrytare [n.; ~n, ~] war criminal
krigshandling [n.; ~en, ~ar] act of war
krigsherre [n.; ~n, -herrar] warlord
krigsmonument [n.; ~et, ~] war memorial
krigsskepp [n.; ~et, ~] warship
kriminalare [n.; ~n, ~] detective, plain-clothes police officer
kriminalfilm [n.; ~en, ~er] thriller, mystery
kriminalitet [n.; ~en] criminality
kriminalpolisen [n.] criminal investigation department
kriminalvård [n.; ~en] correctional treatment of offenders

Kriminalvårdsnämnden [n.]
National Parole Board
Kriminalvårdsstyrelsen (KVS)
[n.] National Prison and Probation
Administration
kriminell [adj.; ~t, ~a] criminal; ~
verksamhet criminal activity
kring [prep./adv.] around
kringfartsled [n.; ~en, ~er] ring
road, bypass, beltway
kris [n.; ~en, ~er] crisis
Krisberedskapsmyndigheten [n.]
Swedish Emergency Management
Agency
kristall [n.; ~en, ~er] crystal; cut
glass
kristallglas [n.; ~et, ~] crystal
[glass]
Kristdemokraterna (kd) [n.pl.]
Christian Democrats, Christian
Democrat party
**Kristdemokratiska Ungdomsför-
bundet (KDU)** [n.] Christian-
Democratic Youth Alliance
kristen [adj.; kristna] Christian;
kristna tron Christian faith
kristendom [n.; ~en] Christianity
Kristi himmelfärdsdag [n.; ~en]
Ascension Day [Thursday 40 days
after Easter]
Kristus [n.] Christ
krita [n.; ~n, kritor] chalk, crayon
kriterium [n.; -riet, -rier] criterion
[pl.: criteria]
kritik [n.; ~en] criticism, critique
kritiker [n.; ~n, ~] critic
kritisera [v.; ~r, ~de, ~t] criticize,
find fault with; review
kritisk [adj.; ~t, ~a] critical
kritstreckrandig [adj.; ~t, ~a] pinstriped
krm. [abbrev: kryddmått) pinch [of
spice]
Kroatien [n.] Croatia
kroatisk [adj.; ~t, ~a] Croatian
kroatiska [n.; ~n] Croatian language
krock [n.; ~en, ~ar] collision, crash
krocket [n.; ~en] croquet
krog [n.; ~en, ~ar] restaurant, inn,
pub; **på ~en** at the restaurant
krok [n.; ~en, ~ar] hook

kroki [n.; ~n, ~er] sketch, life
drawing
krokig [adj.; ~t, ~a] crooked,
winding
krokodil [n.; ~en, ~er] crocodile
kromosom [n.; ~en, ~er] chromosome
krona [n.; ~n, kronor] krona [unit
of currency]; crown
Kronans egendom [n.; ~en] State
property
kronjuveler [n.pl.] crown jewels
kronofogde [n.; ~n, -fogdar]
senior enforcement officer [debt
collection]
kronofogdemyndighet [n.; ~en,
~er] enforcement office; enforcement officer [debt collection]
kronprins [n.; ~en, ~ar] crown
prince
kronprinsessa [n.; ~n, -sessor]
crown princess
kronärtskockor [n.pl.] artichokes
kronärtskocksbotten [n.; -botten,
-bottnar] artichoke hearts
kropp [n.; ~en, ~ar] body
kroppkakor [n.pl. potato dumplings
with bacon and onion
kroppsdel [n.; ~en, ~ar] part of the
body
kroppsvård [n.; ~en] toiletries
krossa [v.; ~r, ~de, ~t] crush, smash;
wreck
krucifix [n.; ~et, ~] crucifix
kruka [n.; ~n, krukor] pot, jar;
pitcher; coward
krukmakare [n.; ~n, ~] potter
krukmakeri [n.; ~et, ~er] pottery,
potter's workshop
krukväxt [n.; ~en, ~er] potted plant
krullalfa (@) [n.; ~n, -alfor; see:
snabel-a] [IT]
krupit [v.past; see: **krypa**]
krusbär [n.pl.] gooseberries
kry [adj.; ~tt, ~a] in good health
krya på dig! [phrase] get well!
krycka [n.; ~n, kryckor] crutch
krydda[1] [n.; ~n, kryddor] spice,
seasoning
krydda[2] [v.; ~r, ~de, ~t] season,
flavor

kryddad [adj.; -ddat, ~e] spicy
kryddnejlika [n.; ~n, -kor] clove
kryddost [n.; ~en, ~ar] sharp
cheese with caraway seeds
kryddpeppar [n.; ~n] allspice
kryddsmör [n.; ~et] herb butter
kryddstark [adj.; ~t, ~a] spicy
krympa [v.; krymper, krympte,
krympt] shrink
krympfri [adj.; ~tt, ~a] shrinkproof
krypa [v.; kryper, kröp, krupit]
creep
kryptering med öppen nyckel [n.;
-ringen] public key encryption [IT]
krypteringsnyckel [n.; ~n, -nyck-
lar] encryption key [IT]
kryss [n.; ~et, ~] cross
kryssa [v.; ~r, ~de, ~t] cruise; beat,
tack; zigzag; mark with a cross
kryssning [n.; ~en, ~ar] cruise
kryssningsfartyg [n.; ~et, ~] cruise
liner
kryssningsrobot [n.; ~en, ~ar]
cruise missile
kryssruta [n.; ~n, -rutor] check box
[IT]
kråka [n.; ~n, -kor] crow; check
mark
krånglig [adj.; ~t, ~a] difficult,
troublesome, complicated
kräfta [n.; ~n, kräftor] crayfish;
cancer
Kräftan [n.] Cancer; **~s vändkrets**
Tropic of Cancer
kräkas [v.passive; kräkes, kräktes,
kräkts] vomit, throw up
kräkning [n.; ~en] vomiting
kräm [n.; ~en, ~er] cream; com-
pote; polish; [colloq.] electricity
krämpa [n.; ~n, krämpor] ailment
kränka [v.; kränker, kränkte, kränkt]
violate, infringe; hurt, wrong
kräsen [adj.; kräset, kräsna] particular, discriminating
kräva [v.; kräver, krävde, krävt]
demand
krävande [adj.] demanding, exact-
ing, trying
krönika [n.; ~n, -kor] chronicle,
annals, survey of events
kröp [v.past; see: **krypa**]

KSSS [abbrev: Kungliga Svenska
Segelsällskapet] Royal Swedish
Sailboat Association
KU [see: **Konstitutionsutskottet**]
Kuba [n.] Cuba
kubansk [adj.; ~t, ~a] Cuban
kubikmeter [n.; ~n, ~] cubic meter
[about 1.3 cubic yards, 35.3 cubic
feet]
kubism [n.; ~en] cubism
kudde [n.; ~n, kuddar] pillow
kugga [v.; ~r, ~de, ~t] fail, flunk
[exam]
kuk [n.; colloq.; ~en, ~ar] dick
[vul.], prick [vul.], cock [vul.]
kul [adj.; ~] fun, cool; **ha ~** have
fun
kula [n.; ~n, kulor] ball, bullet;
marble; scoop [ice cream]
kuling [n.; ~en] gale, high wind
kulle [n.; ~n, kullar] hill
kullerbytta [n.; ~n, -byttor]
somersault
kulspetspenna [n.; ~n, -pennor]
ballpoint pen, pen
kultur [n.; ~en, ~er] culture
Kulturdepartementet (Ku) [n.]
Ministry of Culture
kulturell [adj.; ~t, ~a] cultural
kulturförening [n.; ~en, ~ar] culture society
kulturhus [n.; ~et, ~] cultural arts
center, community center
kulturhuvudstad [n.; ~en, -städer]
cultural capital
kulturminnesmärke [n.;~t, ~n]
historical monument
kulturråd [n.; ~et,~] council for
cultural affairs
kultursida [n.; ~n, -sidor] arts page
Kulturutskottet [n.] Committee on
Cultural Affairs
kummel [n.; ~n, kumlar] hake [fish]
kummin [n.; ~et] caraway, cumin
kund [n.; ~en, ~er] customer, client
kunde [v.past; see: **kunna**]
kundinformation [n.; ~en, ~er]
customer information
kundparkering [n.; ~en, ~ar]
customer parking
kundservice [n.; ~en] customer
service

kundtjänst [n.; ~en] customer
service
kundvagn [n.; ~en, ~ar] shopping
basket
kung [n.; ~en, ~ar] king
kungafamiljen [n.] royal family
kungapar [n.; ~et, ~] royal couple,
King and Queen
kunglig [adj.; ~t, ~a] royal
Kunglig Majestät [n.; ~et, ~er]
His/Her Royal Majesty; the gov-
ernment
Kungliga Akademien för de fria
konsterna (Konstakademien)
[n.] Royal Academy of Fine Arts
Kungliga Automobilklubben [n.]
Royal Automobile Club
Kungliga Biblioteket (Sveriges
nationalbibliotek) [n.] Royal
Library (National Library of
Sweden)
Kungliga Dramatiska Teatern
(Dramaten] [n.] Royal Dramatic
Theater
Kungliga Hovstaterna [n.pl.]
Royal Court
Kungliga Ingenjörsvetenskaps-
akademien (IVA) [n.] Royal
Academy of Engineering Sciences
Kungliga Konsthögskolan [n.]
Royal College of Fine Arts
Kungliga Krigsvetenskaps-
akademien [n.] Royal Academy
of War Sciences
Kungliga Musikaliska
Akademien [n.] Royal Academy
of Music
Kungliga Musikhögskolan i
Stockholm [n.] Royal College of
Music in Stockholm
Kungliga Operan [n.] Royal Opera
Kungliga Skogs- och Lantbruks-
akademien [n.] Royal Academy
of Agriculture and Forestry
Kungliga Slottet [n.] Royal Palace
Kungliga Tekniska högskolan
(KTH) [n.] Royal Institute of
Technology
Kungliga Vetenskapsakademien
[n.] Royal Academy of Sciences
Kungliga Vitterhets Historie och

Antikvitets Akademien [n.]
Royal Academy of Letters, History and Antiquities
kungliga våningen [n.] royal apartments
Kungl. Maj:t [abbrev: Kunglig
Majestät] Royal Majesty
Kungsträdgården [n.] Royal Garden
kunna [v.; kan, kunde, kunnat] can,
be able to; know how
kunnande [n.; ~t] skill, ability,
know-how
kunskap [n.; ~en, ~er] knowledge
kupé [n.; ~n, ~er] compartment
[train]
kupol [n.; ~en, ~er] dome
kupp [n.; ~en, ~er] coup; robbery
kur [n.; ~en, ~er] cure
kurator [n.; ~n, ~er] social welfare
officer; counselor; curator
kurd [n.; ~en, ~er] Kurd
kurdisk [adj.; ~t, ~a] Kurdish
kurdiska [n.] Kurdish language
kurragömma: leka ~ play hide-
and-seek
kurs [n.; ~en, ~er] course, class
kursiv [n.; ~en] italics
kursplan [n.; ~en, ~er] curriculum
kursverksamhet [n.; ~en, ~er]
training courses
kurva [n.; ~n, kurvor] bend, curve
kurvritare [n.; ~en, ~] plotter, x-y
plotter [IT]
kusin [n.; ~en, ~er] cousin
kusinbarn [n.; ~et, ~] first cousin
once removed; second cousin
kust [n.; ~en, ~er] coast
Kustbevakningen [n.] National
Coast Guard
kuvert [n.; ~et, ~] envelope; cover
[plate & silverware, place setting]
kuvertavgift [n.; ~en, ~er] cover
charge
kuvertbröd [n.; ~et, ~] (small)
French roll
kvadrat [n.; ~en, ~er] square;
squared
kvadratmeter [n.; ~n, ~] square
meter [1.2 sq. yards or 10.8 sq. ft.]
kval [n.; ~et, ~] pain, suffering,
anguish

kvalific**e**rad [adj.; -rat, ~e] qualified; ~ **majorit**e**t** qualified majority [EU]

kvalit**e**t [n.; ~en, ~er] quality

kvalit**e**tsst**a**ndard [n.; ~en, ~er] quality standard

kv**a**ntmekan**i**k [n.; ~en] quantum mechanics

kvar [adv.] left over, remaining

kvark [n.; ~en] fresh curd cheese

kvarn [n.; ~en, ~ar] mill

kv**a**rs**i**ttare [n.; ~n, ~] student who has not been promoted

kv**a**rsk**a**tt [n.; ~en, ~er] back taxes, tax arrears

kv**a**rst**å** [v.; ~r, -stod, ~tt] be left over, remain

kvart [n.; ~en, ~] quarter; fifteen minutes; ~ **i** **å**tta quarter to eight; ~ **över sju** quarter past seven

kvart**a**l [n.; ~et, ~] quarter (of a year)

kvart**e**r [n.; ~et, ~] quarter, neighborhood, part of town; block

kvart**e**rskr**o**g [n.; ~en, ~ar] neighborhood restaurant, pub

kv**a**rtsfin**a**l [n.; ~en, ~er] quarter finals

kvartsk**i**lo [n.; ~t, ~] quarter of a kilo [about 1/2 lb.]

kv**a**rv**a**rande [adj.] remaining

kvast [n.; ~en, ~ar] broom

kvav [n.; ~t, ~a] stuffy, sultry, close, muggy

kv**i**cks**a**nd [n.; ~en] quicksand

kv**i**cks**i**lver [n.; -silvret] mercury

kv**i**ga [n.; ~n, kvigor] heifer

kv**i**nna [n.; ~n, kvinnor] woman

kv**i**nnlig [adj.; ~t, ~a] female; ~ **o**msk**ä**relse female circumcision

kv**i**nnoför**e**ning [n.; ~en, ~ar] women's organization

kv**i**nnoförtr**y**ck [n.; ~et] oppression of women

kv**i**nnoj**o**ur [n.; ~en, ~er] crisis center for women

kv**i**nnol**ä**kare [n.; ~n, ~] gynecologist

kv**i**nnorör**e**lse [n.; ~n, ~r] women's movement, women's liberation

kvist [n.; ~en, ~ar] branch, twig

kvitt**e**ra [v.; ~r, ~de, ~t] acknowledge receipt, sign for; settle a debt, repay

kv**i**tto [n.; ~t, ~n] receipt

kvot [n.; ~en, ~er] quotient; quota

kv**o**tfl**y**kting [n.; ~en, ~ar] refugee brought in under UN quota

kv**ä**ljning [n.; ~en, ~ar] nausea, feeling sick

kväll [n.; ~en, ~ar] evening; **i** ~ this evening; **i** **m**o**rgon** ~ tomorrow evening; **på** ~**en** in the evening

kv**ä**llskurs [n.; ~en, ~er] evening course

kv**ä**llsl**i**v [n.; ~et] nightlife

kv**ä**llsm**a**t [n.; ~en] supper

kv**ä**llst**i**dning [n.; ~en, ~ar] evening newspaper

kv**ä**llsöppen [adj.; ~t, -öppna] open in the evening

kv**ä**ve [n.; ~t] nitrogen

k**y**ckling [n.; ~n, ~ar] chicken

k**y**cklingl**å**r [n.; ~et, ~] chicken leg

k**y**cklings**a**llad [n.; ~en, ~er] chicken salad

k**y**cklings**o**ppa [n.; ~n, -soppor] chicken soup

k**y**la[1] [n.; ~n] cold

k**y**la[2] [v.; kyler, kylde, kylt] chill (trans.)

k**y**lare [n.; ~n, ~] radiator

k**y**larsl**a**ng [n.; ~en, ~ar] radiator hose

k**y**larsyst**e**m [n.; ~et, ~] cooling system

k**y**larv**a**tten [n.; -vattnet] cooling water

k**y**larv**ä**tska [n.; ~n] cooling fluid, coolant

kyld [adj.; kylt, ~a] chilled, cold

k**y**ld**i**sk [n.; ~en, ~ar] refrigerated display case, frozen food counter

k**y**lfl**ä**ns [n.; ~en, ~ar] cooling fin, heat sink [IT]

k**y**lig [adj.; ~t, ~a] chilly

k**y**lkl**a**mp [n.; ~en, ~ar] ice pack

k**y**lsk**å**p [n.; ~et, ~] refrigerator

k**y**lsystem [n.; ~et, ~] cooling system

k**y**lv**ä**ska [n.; ~n, -väskor] cooler

K**y**otoprotok**o**llet [n.] Kyoto Protocol

k**y**pare [n.; ~n, ~] waiter

k**y**rka [n.; ~n, kyrkor] church

kyrkbröllop [n.; ~et, ~] church
wedding
kyrklig vigsel [n.; ~n, vigslar]
church wedding
kyrkobokförd [adj.; ~a] registered
in the parish registry
kyrkobokföring [n.; ~en, ~ar]
parish registration
kyrkogård [n.; ~en, ~ar] cemetery,
churchyard
kyrkoherde [n.; ~n, -herdar] rector,
vicar, pastor, priest
kyrktorn [n.; ~et, ~] steeple, church
tower
kyssa [v.; kysser, kysste, kysst] kiss
kål [n.; ~en] cabbage
kåldomar [n.pl.] stuffed cabbage
kålrot [n.; ~en, -rötter] turnip,
rutabaga
kålsoppa [n.; ~n, -soppor] cabbage
soup
kår [n.; ~en, ~er] corps, body, union
kårhus [n.; ~et, ~] student union
building
kåseri [n.; ~et, ~er] informal talk;
light conversational article/column
käk [n.; ~et; colloq.] food, chow,
grub
käka [v.; ~r, ~de, ~t; colloq.] eat
käke [n.; ~n, käkar] jaw
kälke [n.; ~n, kälkar] sled; åka ~
go sledding
källa [n.; ~n, källor] source, spring
källare [n.; ~n, ~] basement, cellar
källarvåning [n.; ~en, ~ar] basement
källbeskattning [n.; ~en] taxation
at the source, pay-as-you-go plan
källkod [n.; ~en, ~er] source code
[IT]
källkrasse [n.; ~n] watercress
kämpa [v.; ~r, ~de, ~t] fight
känd [adj.; ~t, ~a] famous, known
känguru [n.; ~n, ~er] kangaroo
känna [v.; känner, kände, känt]
feel; know; ~ igen recognize; ~
till be familiar with, know; ~ sig
feel; ~ sig nere be out of sorts
kännas [v.passive; kännes, kändes,
känts] feel; ~ vid acknowledge
kännedom [n.; ~en] knowledge,
information; familiarity

känsla [n.; ~n, känslor] feeling
känslig (för) [adj.; ~t, ~a] sensitive
(to); sympathetic; moving
känt [see: känna, känd]
käpp [n.; ~en, käppar] cane, stick
kär [adj.; ~t, ~a] dear; bli ~ i fall in
love with
Kära/Käre [opening greeting in
letter] Dear [f./m.]
kärande [n.; ~n, ~] plaintiff
käring [n.; ~en, ~ar] witch; bitch
[vul.]
kärlek [n.; ~en, ~ar] love
kärlkramp [n.; ~en] angina, vascu-
lar spasm
kärna [n.; ~n, kärnor] seed, grain;
kernel, nucleus; core
kärnkraft [n.; ~en] nuclear power
Kärnkraftinspektionen [n.] Nuclear Power Inspectorate
kärnkraftsavfall [n.; ~et] nuclear
waste
kärnkraftverk [n.; ~et, ~] nuclear
power station
kärnmjölk [n.; ~en] buttermilk
kärnvapen [n.; -vapnet, ~] nuclear
weapons
kärnvapenprov [n.; ~et, ~] nuclear
weapon test
kärr [n.; ~et, ~] swamp
kärra [n.; ~n, kärror] cart, waggon
käx [see: kex]
kö [n.; ~n, ~er] line; queue, first-in-
first-out list [IT]; stå i ~ stand in
line
kök [n.; ~et, ~] kitchen
köksbord [n.; ~et, ~] kitchen table
köksbänk [n.;~en, ~ar] kitchen
counter
köksinredning [n.; ~en, ~ar]
kitchen fixtures
köksmaskin [n.; ~en, ~er] kitchen
appliance
köksmästare [n.; ~en, ~] chef, cook
köksredskap [n.pl.] kitchen utensils
köksskåp [n.; ~et, ~] kitchen cabinet
kölapp [n.; ~en, ~ar] number ticket
[in a line at store]
Köln [n.] Cologne
kön [n.; ~et, ~] sex; gender [gram]
könsdelar [n.pl.] genitals

könsorgan [n.; ~et, ~] sexual organ, genitals

könssjukdom [n.; ~en, ~ar] venereal disease

könsstympning [n.; ~en] genital mutilation

köp [n.; ~et, ~] purchase

köpa [v.; köper, köpte, köpt] buy; köpes wanted, need to buy [ad, sign]

köpare [n.; ~en, ~] buyer

köpcentrum [n.; ~et, ~] shopping center

Köpenhamn [n.] Copenhagen

Köpenhamnskriterierna [n.pl.] Copenhagen criteria [EU, accession criteria]

köpes [v.passive; see: köpa] be bought

köpman [n.; ~nen, -män] merchant

köpvillkor [n.; ~et, ~] terms of sale

kör [n.; ~en, ~er] chorus, choir; sjunga i ~ sing in a chorus

köra [v.; kör, körde, kört] drive; ~ på höger sida drive on the right; ~ av vägen drive off the road; ~ bil drive a car; ~ igång start up [IT]; ~ om pass (a car); ~ på drive into, run into

körbana [n.; ~n, -banor] roadway

körbar [adj.; ~t, ~a] fit for driving; executable [IT]

körfil [n.; ~en, ~er] traffic lane

körfält [n.; ~et, ~] traffic lane

körförbud [n.; ~et, ~] driving ban

körkort [n.; ~et, ~] driver's license

körlektion [n.; ~en, ~er] driving lesson

körning [n.; ~en, ~ar] driving

körningsmodul [n.; ~en, ~er] run-time module [IT]

körsbär [n.; ~et, ~] cherry

körsnär [n.; ~en, ~er] furrier

körtel [n.; ~, körtlar] gland

körvel [n.; ~n] chervil

kött [n.; ~et] meat

köttaffär [n.; ~en, ~er] butcher shop

köttbuljong [n.; ~en, ~er] meat stock, consommé

köttbulle [n.; ~n, -bullar] meatball

köttdisk [n.; ~en, ~ar] meat counter

köttfärs [n.; ~en, ~er] minced meat

köttgryta [n.; ~n, -grytor] stew pot; meat casserole

kötträtt [n.; ~en, ~er] meat dish

köttsoppa [n.; ~n, -soppor] hearty beef soup with vegetables and dumplings

köttsås [n.; ~en] bolognese sauce

köttvara [n.; ~n, -varor] meat product

L

L [abbrev: Lilla] Lesser, Little [in place names]
laboratorium [n.; -toriet, -torier] laboratory
lack [n.; ~et] varnish
lada [n.; ~n, lador] hay barn
ladda [v.; ~r, ~de, ~t] load; charge [battery]; ~ ned/ner download [IT]
lade [v.past; see: lägga]
ladusvala [n.; ~n, -svalor] barn swallow
Laekenförklaringen [n.] Laeken Declaration [EU]
lag[1] [n.; ~en, ~ar] law
lag[2] [n.; ~et, ~] layer; team; set, company
laga [v.; ~r, ~de, ~t] repair; patch; cook, prepare; ~ kläder mend clothes; ~ mat cook food
lager [n.; lagret, ~] layer; warehouse; store, stock; bearing
lagerarbetare [n.; ~n, ~] stockroom worker
lagerblad [n.; ~et, ~] bay leaf
lageröl [n.; ~et, ~] lager beer
lagförslag [n.; ~et, ~] proposed law
laglig [adj.; ~t, ~a] lawful, legitimate, legal
lagom [adv.] enough, just right; medium
lagra [v.; ~r, ~de, ~t] save, store [IT]
lagringsmedium [n.; -mediet, -medier] storage medium [IT]
lagringsplats [n.; ~en, ~er] storage space [IT]
lagringsutrymme [n.; ~t, ~n] storage space [IT]
Lagrådet [n.] Council on Legislation
lagstiftning [n.; ~en, ~ar] legislation
lagt [v.past; see: lägga]
Lagutskottet [n.] Committee on Civil-Law Legislation [in Parliament]
lajv [adj./adv.] live [performance]
lakan [n.; ~et, ~] sheet, bed sheet
lake [n.; ~n, lakar] burbot [freshwater fish]
lamm [n.; ~et, ~] lamb

lammbog [n.; ~en] lamb shoulder
lammbringa [n.; ~n] lamb brisket
lammgryta [n.; ~n] lamb stew
lammkött [n.; ~et] lamb [meat]
lampa [n.; ~n, lampor] lamp
lamphållare [n.; ~n, ~] lamp socket
lampkontakt [n.; ~en, ~er] light switch
lampskärm [n.; ~en, -skärmar] lamp shades
land [n.; ~et, länder] land, country; countryside; i ~ ashore [motion]; på ~et in the countryside
landa [v.; ~r, ~de, ~t] land
landgång [n.; ~en, ~ar] gangway; long open sandwich
landhockey [n.; ~n] field hockey
landmärke [n.; ~t, ~n] landmark
landning [n.; ~en, ~ar] landing
landningsbana [n.; ~n, -banor] landing field, runway
landområde [n.; ~t, ~n] territory
landsarkiv [n.; ~et, ~] regional archives
landsbygd [n.; ~en] countryside, rural parts
landsbygdsutveckling [n.; ~en] rural development [EU]
landsdel [n.; ~en, ~ar] part of the country
landsförräderi [n.; ~et, ~er] treason
landshövding [n.; ~en, ~ar] county governor
landskamp [n.; ~en, ~er] international game [sports]
landskap [n.; ~et, ~] landscape; province
landslag[1] [n.; ~en, ~ar] national law code
landslag[2] [n.; ~et, ~] national team
landsnummer [n.; -numret, ~] country code [telephone]
Landsorganisationen (LO) [n.] Confederation of Trade Unions
Landsrådet för Sveriges Ungdomsorganisationer (LSU) [n.] National Council of Swedish Youth Organizations

landsting [n.; ~et, ~] county council
Landstingsförbundet [n.] Association of County Councils
landsväg [n.; ~en, ~ar] main road, country road
landsvägsbuss [n.; ~en, ~ar] rural bus; intercity bus
landsvägscykel [n.; ~n, -cyklar] touring bike
lankesisk [adj.; ~t, ~a] Sri Lankan
lansera [v.; ~r, ~de, ~t] market, launch
lantarbetare [n.; ~n, ~] agricultural worker, farm hand
lantbrukare [n.; ~n, ~] farmer
Lantbrukarnas Riksförbund (LRF) [n.] National Federation of Farmers
lantbruksuniversitet [n.; ~et, ~] university of agricultural sciences
lantegendom [n.; ~en, ~ar] estate, large property
lanthandel [n.; ~n, -handlar] country store
Lantmäteriet [n.] National Land Survey
Lantmäteriverket [n.] National Land Survey
lapp [n.; ~en, ~ar] patch; label, tag; piece of paper; Laplander, Sami
lappa [v.; ~r, ~de, ~t] patch
Lappland [n.] Lapland [northernmost part of Sweden, Norway and Finland]
lapplisa [n.; ~n, -lisor] meter maid
lappländsk [adj.; ~t, ~a] Laplandish, Sami
lapplänning [n.; ~en, ~ar] Laplander, Sami
lappning [n.; ~en, ~ar] patch, quick fix [IT]
lappsk [adj.; ~t, ~a] Sami, Lappish
lapskojs [n.; ~en] casserole of potatoes, meat and vegetables
larm [n.; ~et] noise; alarm
larv [n.; ~en, ~er] larva, caterpillar, grub
larvig [adj.; ~t, ~a] silly, stupid
LAS [abbrev: Lagen om anställningssäkerhet] Employment Security Act

lasarett [n.; ~et, ~] hospital
laserskrivare [n.; ~n, ~] laser printer [IT]
last [n.; ~en, ~er] cargo, freight; burden
lastbil [n.; ~en, ~ar] truck
lastbilschaufför [n.; ~en, ~er] truck driver
lastbilssläp [n.; ~et, ~] truck trailer
lastning [n.; ~en] loading
lat [adj.; ~, ~a] lazy
lata sig [v.; ~r, ~de, ~t] take it easy, be lazy
latin [n.; ~et] Latin language
Latinamerika [n.] Latin America
latinamerikansk [adj.; ~t, ~a] Latin American
latinsk [adj.; ~t, ~a] Latin
latitud [n.; ~en, ~er] latitude
lava [n.; ~n] lava
lavemang [n.; ~et, ~] enema
lavin [n.; ~en, ~er] avalanche
lavinfara [n.; ~n] threat/danger of avalanche
lax [n.; ~en, ~ar] salmon
laxativ [n.; ~et] laxative
laxermedel [n.; -medlet, ~] laxative
laxpudding [n.; ~en] baked layers of flaked salmon, potatoes, onions
laxöring [n.; ~en, ~ar] salmon trout
layout [n.; ~en, ~er] layout [IT]
layoutprogram [n.; -grammet, ~] desktop publishing (DTP) [IT]
le [v.; ler, log, lett] smile
led[1] [n.; ~en, ~er] way, route, trail; joint; ur ~ out of joint, dislocated
led[2] [v.past; see: lida]
leda [v.; leder, ledde, lett] lead
ledamot [n.; ~en, ledamöter] member
ledande [adj.] leading; conductive [electricity]
ledare [n.; ~n, ~] leader; editorial
ledarhund [n.; ~en, ~ar] seeing-eye dog, guide dog
ledarskap [n.; ~et] leadership
ledbandskada [n.; ~n, -skador] torn ligament
ledig [adj.; ~t, ~a] free, available, vacant; Är det ~t här? Is this seat free?; ~ dag day off; ~t rum

vacancy; ~a platser job openings, help wanted ads

ledinflammation [n.; ~en] arthritis

ledning [n.; ~en, ~ar] guidance, management; clue, lead; the managers; wire, lead

ledsaga [v.; ~r, ~de, ~t] accompany, escort, attend

ledsen [adj.; ledset, ledsna] sad, sorry

ledstång [n.; ~en, -stänger] handrail

leende [n.; ~t, ~n] smile

leg [abbrev; see: legitimation, legitimerad]

legalitetsprincipen [n.] legality principle [EU]

legat¹ [n.; ~et] legacy, bequest

legat² [v.past; see: ligga]

leggings [n.pl.] leggings

legitimation [n.; ~en, ~er] proof of identity

legitimera [v.; ~r, ~de, ~t] prove one's identity

legitimerad [adj.; -rat, ~e] registered, certified, qualified; ~ läkare registered doctor

legymsallad [n.; ~en, ~er] salad of blanched vegetables, Russian salad

lejon [n.; ~et, ~] lion

Lejonet [n.] Leo [zodiac sign]

lejongap [n.; ~et, ~] snapdragon

lek [n.; ~en, ~ar] game, play; playing

leka [v.; leker, lekte, lekt] play

lekande lätt [adv.] as easy as pie

lekgrupp [n.; ~en, ~er] play group

lekkamrat [n.; ~en, ~er] playmate

lekplats [n.; ~en, ~er] playground

leksak [n.; ~en, ~er] toy

leksaksaffär [n.; ~en, ~er] toy store

lektion [n.; ~en, ~er] lesson, class

lektor [n.; ~n, ~er] teacher [senior high school]; lecturer [university]

lemonad [n.; ~en, ~er] lemonade

lenrimmad [adj.; -rimmat, ~e] lightly salted

lera [n.; ~n, leror] clay

lergods [n.; ~et] pottery

lesbisk [adj.; ~t, ~a] Lesbian

leta (efter) [v.; ~r, ~de, ~t] look (for), seek, search (for)

lett [v.; see: le, leda]

lettisk [adj.; ~t, ~a] Latvian

lettiska [n.] Latvian language

Lettland [n.] Latvia

leva [v.; lever, levde, levt] live

levande [adj.] living, growing; animate; ~ ljus candlelight; ~ musik live music

leve [interj.] hurray for ..., long live ..., 3 cheers for ...

lever [n.; ~n] liver

leverans [n.; ~en, ~er] delivery

leveranskostnad [n.; ~en, ~er] delivery charge

leveranstid [n.; ~en, ~er] delivery time

leveransvillkor [n.pl.] terms of delivery

leverantör [n.; ~n, ~er] supplier, provider [IT]

leverera [v.; ~r, ~de, ~t] deliver

leverkorv [n.; ~en, ~ar] liverwurst

leverpastej [n.; ~en, ~er] liver paté

levnad [n.; ~en] life

levnadsbeskrivning [n.; ~en, ~ar] curriculum vitae

levnadsförhållanden [n.pl.] living conditions

levnadsstandard [n.; ~en] living standard

levt [v.past; see: leva] lived

lexikon [n.; ~et, ~] dictionary

libanesisk [adj.; ~t, ~a] Lebanese

Libanon [n.] Lebanon

liberal [adj.; ~t, ~a] liberal

Liberala Ungdomsförbundet (LUF) [n.] Liberal Youth Alliance

liberalism [n.; ~en] liberalism

Libyen [n.] Libya

libysk [adj.; ~t, ~a] Libyan

lic. [see: licentiat]

licens [n.; ~en, ~er] license

licensavtal [n.; ~et, ~] license agreement [IT]

licenstagare [n.; ~n, ~] licensee [IT]

licentiat [n.] licentiate [degree between Master's and PhD]

lida (av) [v.; lider, led, lidit] suffer (from)

lidande¹ [adj.] suffering
lidande² [n.; ~t, ~n] suffering
lie [n.; ~n, liar] scythe
lift [n.; ~en ~ar] lift [ski, hitchhiking]
lifta [v.; ~r, ~de, ~t] hitchhike
liftkort [n.; ~et, ~] lift pass, lift ticket
liftning [n.; ~en] hitchhiking
liga [n.; ~n, ligor] league; gang
ligament [n.; ~en, ~er] ligament
ligga [v.; ligger, låg, legat] lie; be situated; **~ med** sleep with; **~ ner** lie down
liggande [adj.] lying, reclining; **~ utskrift** landscape mode [IT]
liggplats [n.; ~en, ~er] couchette berth [in train]
liggvagn [n.; ~en, ~ar] couchette car [6 berths per compartment]
lik [adj.; ~t, ~a] alike; like, similar; **~a möjligheter** equal opportunities [EU]
lika [adv.] equal; equally, as; deuce [tennis]; **~ dyr som** as expensive as; **~ långt** as far
likabehandling av kvinnor och män [n.; ~en] equal treatment for men and women [EU]
likadan [adj.; ~t, ~a] alike, similar, of the same sort
likaså [adv.] also; similarly
like [n.; ~n, likar] equal
likhet [n.; ~en, ~er] resemblance, likeness; similarity; identity, equality
likhetstecken [n.; -tecknet, ~] equals sign (=) [IT]
likkista [n.; ~n, -kistor] coffin
likna [v.; ~r, ~de, ~t] be like, be similar to; compare
liknande [adj.] similar, of same sort
liksom [adv.] like, sort of; as it were
likström [n.; -strömmen] direct current (D.C.)
likväl [adv.] nevertheless, all the same
likör [n.; ~n, ~er] liqueur
lila [adj.] mauve, purple
lilja [n.; ~n, liljor] lily
liljekonvalj [n.] lily of the valley
lilla [adj. def.; see: **liten**] little,

small; **~ julafton** December 23rd; **~ Björnen** Little Dipper
lillasyster [n.; ~n] little sister
lillebror [n.; ~] little brother
lim [n.; limmet] glue
limabönor [n.pl.] lima beans
lime [n.; ~n, ~r] lime
limpa [n.; ~n, limpor] loaf; rye bread: carton [cigarettes]
lin [n.; ~et] flax
lina [n.; ~n, linor] rope, cord; wire
lind [n.; ~en, ~ar] linden [tree]
linda¹ [n.; ~n, lindor] swaddling clothes; infancy
linda² [v.; ~r, ~de, ~t] tie, wind
lindrigt [adv.] slightly
lingon [n.; ~et, ~] wild cranberries
linjal [n.; ~en, ~er] ruler, straight-edge
linje [n.; ~en, ~er] line; band; program in school
linjärer [n.pl.] sans serif [IT]
linne [n.; ~t] linen; slip, camisole, undershirt
lins [n.; ~en, ~er] lens
linser [n.pl.] lentils
linsskydd [n.;~et, ~] lens cap
linssoppa [n.; ~n] lentil soup
Lissabon [n.] Lisbon
Lissabonstrategin [n.] Lisbon Strategy [EU]
lista [n.; ~n, listor] list
listpil [n.; ~en, ~ar] list arrow [IT]
listruta [n.; ~n, -rutor] list box [IT]
lita (på) [v.; ~r, ~de, ~t] trust
Litauen [n.] Lithuania
litauisk [adj.; ~t, ~a] Lithuanian
litauiska [n.; ~n] Lithuanian language
lite [adv.; comp.: mindre, minst] a little; **~ av varje** a bit of everything, a bit of each, this and that; **~ grann** a little bit; **~ mer** a little more; **~ över 5** a little past 5 o'clock
liten [adj.; litet, lilla, små; comp.: mindre, minst] little, small; **~ väg** alley; **litet torn** turret
liter [n.; ~n, ~] liter [1.1 quarts]
literpris [n.; ~et] price per liter
litet [adj.; see: **liten**]

litiumjonbatteri [n.; ~n, ~er] lithium ion battery [IT]

litografi [n.; ~n, ~er] lithography; lithograph

litteratur [n.; ~en, ~er] literature

litteraturförteckning [n.; ~en, ~ar] bibliography, list of references

litterär [adj.; ~t, ~a] literary

liv [n.; ~et, ~] life; waist

livbåt [n.; ~en, ~ar] lifeboat

livbälte [n.; ~t, ~n] life preserver, life belt

livemusik [n.; ~en] live music

livlig [adj.; ~t, ~a] lively

livmoder [n.; ~n] womb, uterus

Livrustkammaren [n.] Royal Armory

livräddare [n.; ~n, ~] life guard

livsfara [n.; ~n] mortal danger

livsfarlig [adj.; ~t, ~a] extremely dangerous

livshotande [adj.] life threatening

livsmedel [n.; -medlet, ~] food

livsmedelsaffär [n.; ~en, ~er] grocery store

livsmedelsbutik [n.; ~en, ~er] grocery store

Livsmedelsekonomiska institutet (SLI) [n.] Food Economics Institute

livsmedelstillsatser [n.pl.] food additives

Livsmedelsverket [n.] National Food Administration

livsstil [n.; ~en, ~ar] lifestyle, way of life

livsstycke [n.; ~t, ~n] underbodice, camisole

livstidsstraff [n.; ~et] life imprisonment

livvakt [n.; ~en, ~er] lifeguard

livväst [n.; ~en, ~ar] life jacket

ljud [n.; ~et, ~] sound

ljudbok [n.; ~en, -böcker] recorded book, book on tape [IT]

ljuddämpare [n.; ~n] muffler

ljudkort [n.; ~et, ~] sound card [IT]

ljudstyrka [n.; ~n] volume [sound]

ljuga [v.; ljuger, ljög, ljugit] lie, tell lies

ljung [n.; ~en] heather

ljus¹ [adj.; ~t, ~a] light, fair; **~t öl** light beer [color], pale ale

ljus² [n.; et, ~] light; candle

ljusblå [adj.; -blått, ~a] light blue

ljushårig [adj.; ~t, ~a] fair-haired, blond

ljuskänslighet [n.; ~en] light sensitivity; sensitivity (film)

ljusmätare [n.; ~n, ~] light meter

ljuspenna [n.; ~n, -pennor] light pen [IT]

ljusstake [n.; ~n, -stakar] candle-stick

ljög [v.past; see: **ljuga**]

LO¹ [abbrev: Landsorganisationen i Sverige] Swedish Trade Union Organization

lo² [n.; ~n, ~ar] lynx

lock¹ [n.; ~et, ~] lid, cover

lock² [n.; ~en, ~ar] curl, lock

locka [v.; ~r, ~de, ~t] attract

lockande [adj.] attractive, enticing

lodjur [n.; ~et, ~] lynx

lodrät [adj.; -rätt, ~a] vertical; down [crosswords]

lodstreck [n.; ~et, ~] vertical bar [IT]

log [v.past; see: **le**]

loge [n.; ~n, ~r] box [theater]

logga (in/ut) [v.; ~r, ~de, ~t] log (in/on; out/off) [IT]

logi [n.; ~t, ~er] accommodation

logik [n.; ~en] logic

logisk [adj.; ~t, ~a] logical

logoped [n.; ~en, ~er] speech therapist

lojalitetsprincipen [n.] loyalty principle [EU]

lokal¹ [adj.; ~t, ~a] local; **~t skattekontor** local tax office

lokal² [n.; ~en, ~er] premises

lokalnätverk [n.; ~et, ~] local network [IT]

lokalsamtal [n.; ~et, ~] local call

lokaltrafik [n.; ~en] local traffic

lokaltåg [n.; ~et, ~] local train

lokalvårdare [n.; ~n, ~] cleaner, janitor

lom [n.; lommen, lommar] loon [water bird]

longitud [n.; ~en, ~er] longitude

lopp [n.; ~et, ~] race; course, run

loppmarknad [n.; ~en, ~er] flea market

loss [adv.] loose, away

lossa [v.; ~r, ~de, ~t] loosen, slacken; ~ **en skruv** unscrew, loosen a screw

lossna [v.; ~r, ~de, ~t] get loose

lossnad [adj.; lossnat, ~e] disconnected

lott [n.; ~en, ~er] lot, share; allotment; lottery ticket

lotta [n.; ~n, lottor] member of women's voluntary defense service

lotteri [n.; ~et, ~er] lottery

Lotteriinspektionen [n.] Lottery Inspectorate

lottning [n.; ~en, ~ar] drawing of lots

lotto [n.; ~t] sports lottery, betting pool, numbers game

lov [n.; ~et, ~] permission; vacation; praise; **få ~ att** be allowed to; have to

lova [v.; ~r, ~de, ~t] promise

lovdag [n.; ~en, ~ar] holiday, day off

LRF [see: **Lantbrukarnas Riksförbund**]

Luciadagen [n.] Lucia Day [December 13]

luciafirande [n.; ~t] Lucia Day celebrations

lucka [n.; ~n, luckor] window [bank, post office, box office]; gap, blank

lucktest [n.; ~et, ~] fill-in-the-blank test

luddig [adj.; ~t, ~a] fluffy, downy

Ludvig [n.] Louis

luffa [v.; ~r, ~de, ~t] tramp around; lope, lumber

luffarschack [n.; ~et] tic-tac-toe

luft [n.; ~en] air

Luftfartsverket (LFV) [n.] Civil Aviation Administration

luftfilter [n.; -filtret, ~] air filter

luftförorening [n.; ~en] air pollution

luftig [adj.; ~t, ~a] airy

luftkonditionerad [adj.; -rat, ~e] air-conditioned

luftkonditionering [n.; ~en] air conditioning

luftmadrass [n.; ~en, ~er] air mattress

luftpost [n.; ~en] airmail

luftstrupe [n.; ~n, -strupar] windpipe, trachea

lufttryck [n.; ~et] air pressure

luftväxling [n.; ~en] ventilation

lugg [n.; ~en, ~ar] bangs/fringe [hair]

lugn [adj.; ~t, ~a] calm, quiet

lugna sig [v.; ~r, ~de, ~t] calm down

lugnande medel [n.; medlet, ~] sedative

lugnt [adv.] calmly; **ta det ~** take it easy

Lukas [n.] Luke

lukt [n.; ~en] smell, odor

lukta [v.; ~r, ~de, ~t] smell of, have an odor of

luktärt [n.; ~en, ~er] sweet peas

lumpen [n.]: **göra ~** do one's military service

Lunarstorm [n.; ~en] Lunarstorm [Sweden's biggest Internet community/site for young people]

lunch [n.; ~en, ~er] lunch

lunchrast [n.; ~en, ~er] lunch break/hour

lunchtid [n.]: **vid ~** around lunchtime

lund [n.; ~en, ~ar] grove

lunga [n.; ~n, lungor] lung

lungcancer [n.; ~n] lung cancer

lunginflammation [n.; ~en] pneumonia

lungsjukdom [n.; ~en, ~ar] lung disease

lur [n.; ~en, ~ar] telephone receiver

lura [v.; ~r, ~de, ~t] lie in wait; deceive, trick; entice

lus [n.; ~en, löss] bug [IT]

lussekatt [n.; ~en, ~er] saffron bun served on Lucia Day

lust [n.; ~en] inclination, urge; pleasure; **ha ~ att** feel like (doing); **jag har ingen ~ med det** I don't feel like it

lustig [adj.; ~t, ~a] funny; odd; **göra sig ~ över** make fun of

lustspel [n.; ~et, ~] comedy

luta (mot) [v.; ~r, ~de, ~t] lean

(against); incline; ~ **ut** lean out
lutersk [adj.; ~t, ~a] Lutheran
lutfisk [n.; ~en] boiled ling cod
[preserved in lye solution]
lutning [n.; ~en] incline, gradient
luva [n.; ~n, luvor] knitted wool cap
Luxemburg [n.] Luxembourg
Luxemburg-kompromissen [n.]
Luxembourg compromise [EU]
luxuös [adj.; ~t, ~a] luxurious
lya [n.; ~n, lyor] lair, den, pad
[colloq.]
lycka [n.; ~n] happiness; luck; ~
till! good luck!
lyckas [v.passive; lyckas, lyckades,
lyckats] succeed
lycklig [adj.; ~t, ~a] happy
lyckligtvis [adv.] fortunately, luckily
lyckönskning [n.; ~en, ~ar] congratulations; **varma ~ar** best
wishes
lyda [v.; lyder, lydde/löd, lytt] listen
to, obey; be subject to; state, read
lyft [n.; ~et, ~] lift; boost
lyfta [v.; lyfter, lyfte, lyft] lift, raise
lyftkran [n.; ~en, ~er] lifting crane
lykta [n.; ~n, lyktor] headlight
lymfkörtel [n.; ~n, -körtlar] lymph
gland
lyrik [n.; ~en] poetry; lyric poetry
lysa [v.; lyser, lyste. lyst] shine; ~
upp brighten; illuminate
lysande [adj.] shining, bright,
brilliant
lysdiod [n.; ~en, ~er] light emitting
diode (LED) [IT]
lyse [n.; ~t, ~n] light, lighting
lysning [n.; ~en, ~ar] banns [formal
engagement announcement]
lyssna (på) [v.; ~r, ~de, ~t] listen (to)
lyssnare [n.; ~n, ~] listener
lyxig [adj.; ~t, ~a] luxurious
lyxrestaurang [n.; ~en, ~er] luxury
restaurant
låda [n.; ~n, lådor] box, case; desk
drawer; casserole
låg[1] [adj.; ~t, ~a; comp.:lägre, lägst]
low; ~ **bro** low bridge
låg[2] [v.past; see: **ligga**]
låggolvsbuss [n.; ~en, ~ar] low-
floor bus

låghus [n.; ~et, ~] low-rise apartment house
lågklackad [adj.; -klackat, ~e]
low-heeled
lågkonjunktur [n.; ~en, ~er]
depression, slump
lågpris [n.; ~et, ~] low price
lågsäsong [n.; ~en] low season
lågtryck [n.; ~et] low pressure
lågvatten [n.; -vattnet, ~] low tide
lån [n.; ~et, ~] loan
låna [v.; ~r, ~de, ~t] borrow; lend;
~ **om** renew a loan; ~ **ut** lend
låneansökan [n.; ~, -ansökningar]
loan application
lånekort [n. ~et, ~] library card
lånevillkor [n.; ~et, ~] loan terms
lång [adj.; ~t, ~a; comp.: längre]
long, tall; distant; **~t fordon** long
vehicle; **i det ~a löppet** in the long
run; **på ~ sikt** in the long term
långbyxor [n.pl.] trousers, long
pants
långfilm [n.; ~en, ~er] full-length
film, feature film
långfredag [n.; ~en] Good Friday
långfärdsbuss [n.; ~en, ~ar] long-
distance bus
långfärdsåkning [n.; ~en] cross-
country skiing
långhårig [adj.; ~t, ~a] long-haired
långsam [adj.; ~t, -samma] slow; ~
trafik slow traffic
långsammare [adv.comp.] more
slowly
långsamt [adv.] slowly
långsiktig [adj.; ~t, ~a] long-term
långsynt [adj.; ~a] far-sighted
långt [adj./adv.; see: **lång**] far
långtgående [adj.] far-reaching,
extensive
långtidsparkering [n.; ~en] long-
term parking
långtradare [n.; ~n, ~] long-haul
truck
långtråkig [adj.; ~t, ~a] boring
långvård [n.; ~en] long-term care
långåkning [n.; ~en] cross-country
skiing
långärmad [adj.; -mat, ~e] long-
sleeved

låns [n.]: **till ~** on loan
lår [n.; ~et, ~] thigh
lårben [n.; ~et, ~] thigh bone, femur
lås [n.; ~et, ~] lock
låsa [v.; låser, låste, låst] lock; **~ ut** lock out
låssmed [n.; ~en, ~er] locksmith
låt [n.; ~en, ~ar] melody, tune
låta [v.; låter, lät, låtit] allow, let; sound; **det låter bra** that sounds good; **låt bli!** Stop!; Cut it out!
låtsas [v.passive; låtsas, låtsades, låtsats] pretend; **~ inte om** ignore
läcka [v.; läcker, läckte, läckt] leak
läcker [adj.; ~t, läckra] delicious
läder [n.; lädret] leather
läderaffär [n.; ~en, ~er] leather goods store
lädersula [n.; ~n, -sulor] leather sole
lädervaror [n.pl.] leather goods
läge [n.; ~t, ~n] situation, location; state, view [IT]; **hur är ~t?** what's up? how's it going?
lägenhet [n.; ~en, ~er] apartment
läger [n.; lägret, ~] camp; group, party; lair
lägesrapport [n.; ~en, ~er] progress report
lägg [n.; ~en, ~ar] shank [meat cut]
lägga [v.; lägger, lade, lagt] lay; put; set [hair]; **~ av** stop, lay off; **~ ihop tvätten** fold the wash; **~ in** preserve, can; insert; install [IT]; **~ in backen** get into reverse gear; **~ in ettan** get into first gear; **~ ned** lay down; pack; discontinue; spend; **~ på** lay on, apply; hang up; **~ sig** go to bed; **~ till** add [IT]; **~ till vid** land at, reach; **~ upp** upload [IT]; **~ ut** spend
läggning [n.; ~en, ~ar] disposition; set (hair); **sexuell ~** sexual preference
läggningsvätska [n.; ~n] setting lotion
lägre [adj.comp.: låg] lower
lägsta [adj.superl.: låg] lowest
läkarbesök [n.; ~et, ~] visit to the doctor
läkare [n.; ~n, ~] doctor
Läkare utan gränser [n.] Médecins sans frontières (MSF), Doctors Without Borders

läkargrupp [n.; ~en, ~er] medical center
läkarintyg [n.; ~et, ~] medical certificate
läkarmottagning [n.; ~en] doctor's office
läkarundersökning [n.; ~en, ~ar] medical examination
läkemedel [n. -medlet, ~] medication
Läkemedelsförmånsnämnden [n.] Pharmaceutical Benefits Board
Läkemedelsverket [n.] Medical Products Administration
läktare [n.; ~n, ~] viewing gallery, platform, bleachers
lämna [v.; ~r, ~de, ~t] leave; give, hand; **~ företräde** yield priority [in traffic]; **~ in** hand in; **~ någon i fred** leave someone in peace; **~ något tillbaka** return sthg
lämning [n.; ~en, ~ar] remains
lämplig [adj.; ~t, ~a] suitable, adequate, appropriate
län [n.; ~et, ~] administrative district, county
länder [see: **land**]
längd [n.; ~en] length; height; **i ~en** in the long run/term
längdgrad [n.; ~en, ~er] longitude
längdhopp [n.; ~et] broad jump
längdskidsåkning [n.; ~en] cross-country skiing
länge [adv.] long time
längre [adj./adv.comp.: lång, länge] longer; further; **~ bak** further back; **~ fram** further forward
längs [prep.] along
längst [adv.superl.: länge] longest, furthest; **~ bak** at the very back, all the way back; **~ fram** at the very front
längta (efter) [v.; ~r, ~de, ~t] long (to); long (for)
längtan [n.] longing
länk [n.; ~en, ~ar] link [IT]
länka [v.; ~r, ~de, ~t] link, create a link [IT]
länsarbetsnämnd [n.; ~en, ~er] county labor board
länsrätt [n.; ~en, ~er] county administrative court

länsskattekontor [n.; ~et, ~] county tax office

länsstyrelse [n.; ~n, ~r] county administration

läpp [n.; ~en, ~ar] lip

läppstift [n.; ~et] lipstick

lära [v.; lär, lärde, lärt] teach; ~ **känna** get to know; ~ **sig** learn

lärare [n.; ~n, ~] teacher

lärarhögskola [n.; ~n, -skolor] teacher-training college

Lärarhögskolan i Stockholm (HSL) [n.] Stockholm Institute of Education

lärarinna [n.; ~n, -rinnor] teacher [female]

lärarkår [n.; ~en, ~er] teaching staff

lärarvikarie [n.; ~n, ~r] substitute teacher

lärjunge [n.; ~n, -jungar] disciple

lärka [n.; ~n, lärkor] lark

lärkträd [n.; ~et, ~] larch [tree]

lärobok [n.; ~en, -böcker] textbook

läromedel [n.; -medlet, ~] teaching aid

läsa [v.; läser, läsde, läst] read; study; ~ **igenom** read through; ~ **läxor** do homework

läsare [n.; ~n, ~] reader

läsbar [adj.; ~t, ~a] readable

läsförståelse [n.; ~n] reading comprehension

läsk [n.; ~en] carbonated soft drink

läskedryck [n.; ~en, ~er] carbonated soft drink

läslampa [n.; ~n, -lampor] reading light

läsning [n.; ~en] reading; reading matter

läspenna [n.; ~n, -pennor] pen reader, wand [IT]

läsplatta [n.; ~n, -plattor] e-book disc [IT]

läst [adj.; ~a] read [IT]

läsår [n.; ~et, ~] school year

lät [v.past; see: **låta**]

lätt [adj.; ~a] light; easy; light-bodied [wine]; ~ **att laga** fast-cooking, easy to cook

lättläst [adj.; ~a] easy-to-read, easily read

lättmjölk [n.; ~en] low-fat milk, skim milk

lättnad [n.; ~en] relief, alleviation, simplification

lättrökt [adj.; ~a] lightly smoked

lättsam [adj.; ~t, ~a] light, easy-going

lättstekt [adj.; ~a] medium-rare [meat]

lättviktare [n.; ~n, ~] lightweight

lättöl [n.; ~et] light beer, low-alcohol beer [under 2.25 % alcohol]

läxa [n.; ~n, läxor] lesson, homework; **göra ~n** do homework; **läsa läxor** do homework

löd [v.past; see: **lyda**]

lödder [n.; löddret] soapsuds, lather

lödkolv [n.; ~en, ~ar] soldering iron

löfte [n.; ~t, ~] promise

lögn [n.; ~en, ~er] lie, falsehood

löjlig [adj.; ~t, ~a] ridiculous, funny, absurd

löjrom [n.; -rommen] bleak roe

löjtnant [n.; ~en, ~er] lieutenant

lök [n.; ~en, ~ar] onion

löksoppa [n.; ~n] onion soup

lön [n.; ~en, ~er] wage, salary, pay

löna sig [v.; ~r, ~de, ~t] be worthwhile, be profitable

löneförhandlingar [n.pl] wage negotiations

lönestopp [n.; ~et] wage freeze

lönesänkning [n.; ~en, ~ar] fall in wages, salary decrease

löneökning [n.; ~en, ~ar] rise in wages, salary increase

lönn [n.; ~en, ~ar] maple

lönsam [adj.; ~t, ~a] profitable

lönsamhet [n.; ~en] profitability

löpa [v.; löper, löpte, löpt] run; ~ **ut** expire

löpande [adj.] running; current; ~ **text** running text [IT]

löpare [n.; ~n, ~] runner; bishop [chess]

löparskidor [n.pl.] cross-country skis

löparskor [n.pl.] running shoes

löpning [n.; ~en, ~ar] running; race

lör. [abbrev.; see: **lördag**]

lördag [n.; ~en] Saturday; **i ~s** last Saturday

lös [adj.; ~t, ~a] loose; **~ i magen** have diarrhea

lösa [v.; löser, löste, löst] dissolve; solve; cash; **~ i vatten** dissolve in water; **~ in** cash [a check]; **~ korsord** do a crossword puzzle

lösblad [n.; ~et, ~] loose page

lösenord [n.; ~et, ~] password [IT]

löskokt [adj.; ~a] soft-boiled [egg]

lösning [n.; ~en, ~ar] solution; settlement

lösnummer [n.; -numret, ~] single copy

löstagbar disk [n.] removable disk [IT]

löständer [n.pl.] false teeth

löv [n.; ~et, ~] leaf

lövbiff [n.; ~en, ~ar] sliced beef fried in onions

lövverk [n.; ~et] foliage

M

m¹ [abbrev: meter; Moderata samlingspartiet] meter [3.3 feet]; Moderate Party

m.² [abbrev: med] with

Maastrichtfördraget [n.] Maastricht Treaty [EU]

Maastrichtkriterier [n.pl.] Maastricht criteria [EU]

mack [n.; ~en, ~ar; colloq.] gas station, garage

madrass [n.; ~en, ~er] mattress

maffia [n.; ~n, maffior] mafia

mag. [abbrev: magisterexamen] master's degree

magasin [n.; ~et, ~] storehouse; magazine

magbesvär [n.; ~et, ~] indigestion, upset stomach

mage [n.; ~n, magar] stomach; **dålig ~** upset stomach; **vara hård i ~n** be constipated; **vara lös i ~n** have diarrhea; **ha ont i ~n** have a stomachache/upset stomach

mager [adj.; ~t, magra] thin [person, animal]; lean [meat]; low-fat

magi [n.; ~n] magic

magiker [n.; ~n, ~] magician

maginfluensa [n.; ~n] stomach flu

magisk [adj.; ~t, ~a] magical

magister [n.; ~n, magistrar] person with a master's degree

magkatarr [n.; ~en, ~er] gastritis

magknip [n.; ~et] stomachache

magnet [n.; ~en, ~er] magnet

magnetisk [adj.; ~t, ~a] magnetic

magplåga [n.; ~n, -plågor] stomach pain

magpumpning [n.;~en, ~ar] stomach pumping

magsmärtor [n.pl.] stomachache

magsår [n.; ~et, ~] stomach ulcer

magsäck [n.; ~en] stomach

mail [n.; ~et, ~] e-mail [message] [IT]

maila [v.; ~r, ~de, ~t] e-mail [IT]

maj [n.] May

majonnäs [n.; ~en] mayonnaise

major [n.; ~en, ~er] major

majoritet [n.; ~en] majority

majs [n.;~en] sweet corn

majskolv [n.; ~en, ~ar] corncob; corn on the cob

majsolja [n.; ~n] corn oil

majstång [n.; ~en, ~er] maypole

maka [n.; ~n, makor] wife, spouse

makalös [adj.; ~t, ~a] without match, unique

makaroner [n.pl.] macaroni

make [n.; ~n, makar] husband, spouse; equal, like, match

Makedonien [n.] Macedonia

makedonsk [adj.; ~t, ~a] Macedonian

makedonska [n.] Macedonian language

makrill [n.; ~en, ~ar] mackerel

makro [n.; ~t] macro [IT]

makt [n.; ~en, ~er] power

makthavare [n.; ~n, ~] ruler, the one in power

maktlös [adj.; ~t, ~a] powerless

mal [n.; ~en, ~ar] freshwater catfish; moth

malaria [n.; ~n] malaria

Malaysia [n.] Malaysia

mald [adj.; malt, ~a] minced, ground

malkula [n.; ~n, -kulor] mothball

mall [n.; ~en, ~ar] template [IT]

mallig [adj.; ~t, ~a] snooty, stuck-up

malm [n.; ~en, ~er] ore, rock

malmbrytning [n.; ~en] ore mining

mamma [n.; ~n, mammor] mama

mammaklänning [n.; ~en, ~ar] maternity dress

mammaledighet [n.; ~en, ~er] maternity leave

man¹ [n.; mannen, män] man; husband

man² [pron.; ens, en] one; you; people, they

manchester [n.; ~n] corduroy

mandarin [n.; ~en, ~er] tangerine

mandat [n.; ~et, ~] commission; authorization; seat in parliament; term of office

mandatsperiod [n.; ~en, ~er] term of office

mandel [n.; ~n, mandlar] almond; tonsil
mandelbiskvi [n.; ~n, ~er] macaroon
mandelmassa [n.; ~n] almond paste
mandelpotatis [n.; ~en, ~ar] almond potato [oval, yellowish]
mandeltårta [n.; ~n] almond cake
mandlar [n.pl.] almonds
manet [n.; ~en, ~er] jellyfish
mangelfri [adj.; ~tt, ~a] non-iron
mango [n.; ~n, ~er] mango
manierism [n.; ~en] mannerism
manifestation [n.; ~en, ~er] manifestation
manikyr [n.; ~en, ~er] manicure
manlig [adj.; ~t, ~a] male, manly, virile
mannagryn [n.pl.] semolina
mannekäng [n.; ~en, ~er] fashion model
manschettknappar [n.pl.] cuff links
manschettyrke [n.; ~t, ~n] white-collar job
manssamhälle [n.; ~t] male-dominated society
mantalsskrivning [n.; ~en, ~ar] census registration
manuell [adj.; ~t, ~a] manual [IT]; ~ **växel** manual transmission
manuskript [n.; ~et, ~] manuscript
manöver [n.;~n, ~er] maneuver
m.a.o. [abbrev: med andra ord] in other words, i.e.
mapp [n.; ~en, ~ar] folder, directory, catalogue [IT]
mapplista [n.; ~n, -listor] directory list [IT]
mappstruktur [n.; ~en] folder/directory structure [IT]
mardröm [n.; -drömmen, -drömmar] nightmare
margarin [n.; ~et] margarine
marginal [n.; ~en, ~er] margin [page]
Maria [n.] Mary
marijuana [n.; ~n] marijuana
Marinen [n.] Swedish Naval Forces
marinerad [adj.; -rat, ~e] marinated
Marinmuseum [n.; -museet] Naval Museum
marionetteater [n.; ~n, -teatrar] puppet theater

mark [n.; ~en, ~er] ground, land; field
markant [adj.; ~a] striking, conspicuous
markera [v.; ~r, ~de, ~t] mark, check off, select, highlight [IT]
markerad [adj.; -rat, ~e] marked, selected [IT]
markering [n.; ~en] selecting, selection, highlighting [IT]
marklägenhet [n.; ~en, ~er] garden apartment
marknad [n.; ~en, ~er] market
marknadsavdelning [n.; ~en, ~ar] marketing department
marknadschef [n.; ~en, ~er] marketing director
Marknadsdomstolen [n.] Market Court
marknadsekonomi [n.; ~n] market economy
marknadsföra [v.; -för, -förde, -fört] market, launch
marknadsföring [n.; ~en] marketing
marknivå [n.; ~n, ~er] ground level
Markus [n.] Mark
markägare [n.; ~n, ~] landowner
markör [n.; ~en, ~er] marker; cursor [IT]
marmelad [n.; ~en, ~er] jam, marmalade
marmor [n.; ~n] marble
marockansk [adj.; ~t, ~a] Moroccan
Marocko [n.] Morocco
mars[1] [n.] March
Mars[2] [n.] Mars
marschera [v.; ~r, ~de, ~t] march
marsipan [n.; ~en] marzipan
marsipanlimpa [n.; ~n, -limpor] bar of marzipan
martyr [n.; ~en, ~er] martyr
marulk [n.; ~en, ~ar] monkfish, angler fish
marxistisk [adj.; ~t, ~a] Marxist
maräng [n.; ~en, ~er] meringue
marängsviss [n.; ~en, ~er] meringues with whipped cream
mascara [n.; ~n] mascara
mask[1] [n.; ~en, ~ar] worm
mask[2] [n.; ~en, ~er] mask [IT]
maskera [v.; ~r, ~de, ~t] mask; disguise

maskin [n.; ~en, ~er] machine
maskininstruktion [n.; ~en, ~er]
  machine instruction [IT]
maskinist [n.; ~en, ~er] mechanic;
  engineer; projectionist; stage
  mechanic
maskinkod [n.; ~en, ~er] machine
  code [IT]
maskintekniker [n.; ~n, ~er]
  mechanical engineer
maskintvätta [v.; ~r, ~de, ~t] wash
  by machine
maskinvara [n.; ~n] hardware [IT]
maskros [n.; ~en, ~or] dandelion
maskulin [adj.; ~t, ~a] masculine,
  male
maskulinum [n.; maskulinet]
  masculine [gram]
massa [n.; ~n, massor] mass; substance; crowd; a lot of
massage [n.; ~n] massage
massaker [n.; ~n, massakrer]
  massacre
massförstörelsesvapen [n.pl.]
  weapons of mass destruction
  (WMD)
massmedium [n.; -mediet, -medier/
  media] mass media
massminne [n.; ~t, ~n] bulk storage,
  mass storage [IT]
massord [n.; ~et, ~] mass noun
  [gram]
masssport [n.; ~en, ~er] popular
  sport
massör [n.; ~en, ~er] masseur
massös [n.; ~en, ~er] masseuse
mast [n.; ~en, ~er] pylon, pole, mast
mat [n.; ~en] food
mata [v.; ~r, ~de, ~t] feed
matavdelning [n.; ~en] food
  department
matberedare [n.; ~n, ~] food
  processor
matbestick [n.; ~et, ~] utensils,
  cutlery
matbutik [n.; ~en, ~er] grocery
  store, general store
match [n.; ~en, ~er] match, game
matcha [v.; ~r, ~de, ~t] match [IT]
matematik [n.; ~en] mathematics
matematisk [adj.; ~t, ~a]
  mathematical

materia [n.; materien, materier]
  matter, substance
material [n.; ~en, ~er] material
materiel [n.; ~en] tools, equipment
materiell [adj.; ~t, ~a] material,
  financial
matförgiftning [n.; ~en] food
  poisoning
matiné [n.; ~n, ~er] matinée
matjesill [n.; ~en] pickled herring
matkasse [n.; ~n, -kassar] food
  shopping bag
matlagning [n.; ~en] cooking
matlust [n.; ~en, ~ar] appetite
matrester [n.pl.] leftovers
matris [n.; ~en, ~er] matrix, array
  [IT]
matrisskrivare [n.; ~n, ~] dot matrix printer [IT]
matrum [n.; -rummet] dining room
maträtt [n.; ~en, ~er] dish; course
matsal [n.; ~en] dining room
matsedel [n.; ~n, -sedlar] menu
matservering [n.; ~en, ~ar] eating
  establishment
matsked [n.; ~en, ~ar] tablespoon
matsmältning [n.; ~en] digestion;
  dålig ~ indigestion
matställe [n.; ~t, ~n] place to eat
matsäck [n.; ~en, -säckar] packed
  lunch, box lunch
matt[1] [adj.; ~a] faint; dull, lacklus-
  ter, matte
matt[2] [n; ~en] checkmate, mate
matta [n.; ~n, mattor] carpet, rug, mat
matte [n.; colloq.] math
Matteus [n.] Matthew
Mattias [n.] Matthew
matvara [n.; ~n, -varor] foodstuff
matvrå [n.; ~n, ~r] dining nook
max. [abbrev: maximum] maximum
maximal [adj.; ~t, ~a] maximum,
  maximal
maximum [n.; ~et, ~] maximum
maxtaxa [n.; ~n, -taxor] maximum
  rate, maximum charge
m.b.a. [abbrev: med begränsad
  ansvarighet] with limited responsibility
MBL [see: medbestämmandelagen]
Mbyte [abbrev.] megabyte (Mb)
  [IT]

mc. [abbrev: motorcykel] motorcycle
md. [abbrev: miljard(er)] billion
  [US = thousand million]
mdkr. [abbrev: miljard(er) kronor]
  billion crowns
Mecka [n.] Mecca
med[1] [adv.] together; with; also;
  vara ~ i agree; **vara ~ om** live
  through, experience; **vara ~ på**
  take part in, join in
med[2] [prep.] with; **ha ~ sig** bring,
  have with one; **inte ha råd ~** not
  be able to afford
med.[3] [abbrev: medicin] medicine
  [study]
medalj [n.; ~en, ~er] medal
medaljong [n.; ~en, ~er] medallion;
  small fillet
medan [conj.] while; **~ ni väntar**
  while you wait
medarbetare [n.; ~n, ~] co-worker
medbeslutandeförfarandet [n.]
  codecision procedure [EU]
medbestämmandelagen (MBL)
  [n.] law on right of participation
  in decision-making
medborgare [n.; ~n, ~] citizen
medborgarrättsrörelse [n.; ~n]
  civil rights movement
medborgarskap [n.; ~et] citizenship
medborgerlig [adj.; ~t, ~a] civic,
  civil
meddela [v.; ~r, ~de, ~t] inform;
  communicate; instruct
meddelande [n.; ~t, ~n] message
  [IT]
meddelandefält [n.; ~et] system
  tray [IT]
meddelanderuta [n.; ~n, -rutor]
  message box [IT]
meddelandeverifiering [n.; ~en]
  message verification [IT]
med.dr. [abbrev: medicine doktor]
  Doctor of Medicine
medel [n.; medlet, ~] means, remedy; funds, resources
Medelhavet [n.] Mediterranean Sea
Medelhavsmuseet [n.] National
  Museum of Mediterranean and
  Near Eastern Antiquities [in
  Stockholm]

medellivslängd [n.; ~en] average
  length of life
medelmåttig [adj.; ~t, ~a] mediocre
medelstor [adj.; ~t, ~a] medium-
  sized
medelsvensson [n.] average, boring, conservative middle-class
  Swede
medeltal [n.]: **i ~** on average
medeltida [adj.] medieval
medeltiden [n.pl.] Middle Ages
medelålders [adj.] middle-aged
medföljande person [n.; ~en, ~er]
  accompanying person
medföra [v.; -för, -förde, -fört]
  carry with one, bring; bring about,
  cause
medgav [v.past; see: **medge**]
medge [v.; -ger, -gav, -givit] admit,
  concede; allow, permit
medgivande [adj.] concessive [gram]
media [n.pl.] media [IT]
medicin [n.; ~en] medicine; medication; **receptbelagd ~** prescription drug; **receptfri ~** over-the-
  counter drug
medicinsk [adj.; ~t, ~a] medical;
  ~a fakulteten medical school
medicinskåp [n.; ~et, ~] medicine
  cabinet
medier [n.pl.] media
meditation [n.; ~en] meditation
meditera [v.; ~r, ~de, ~t] meditate
medium [n.; mediet, medier]
  medium; mean
med.kand. [abbrev: medicine kan-
  didat] Bachelor of Medicine
medl. [abbrev: medlem(mar)]
  member(s)
medlem [n.; -lemmen, -lemmar]
  member
medlemskap [n.; ~et] membership
medlemsland [n.; ~et, -länder]
  member country
medlemsstat [n.;~en, ~er] member
  state
medlemsstaternas parlament
  [n.pl.] national parliaments [EU]
med.lic. [abbrev: medicine licen-
  tiat] Licentiate of Medicine
medlidande [n.; ~t, ~n] compassion,
  sympathy

Medlingsinstitutet [n.] National Mediation Office

medurs [adv.] clockwise

medverka [v.; ~r, ~de, ~t] contribute; take part; perform

medverkan [n.] cooperation; assistance, support

medverkande [n.pl.] performers, cast

medvetande [n.; ~t] consciousness

medveten [adj.; -vetet, -vetna] conscious; deliberate

medvetet [adv.] consciously, deliberately

medvetslös [adj.; ~t, ~a] unconscious

medvind [n.; ~en, ~ar] tail wind

megabyte (MB) [n.] megabyte (MB) [IT]

megahertz (MHz) [n.] megahertz (MHz)

megaton [n.] megaton

megawatt (MW) [n.] megawatt (MW)

mej [pron.obj; see: **mig**]

mejeri [n.; ~et, ~er] dairy

mejeriprodukt [n.; ~en, ~er] dairy product

mejerivara [n.; ~n, -varor] dairy product

mejl [n.; ~et, ~en] e-mail [IT]

mejla [v.; ~r, ~de, ~t] e-mail [IT]

mejram [n.; ~en] majoram

mejsel [n.; ~n, mejslar] chisel

meka [v.; ~r, ~de, ~t; colloq.] repair cars

mekanik [n.; ~en] mechanics

mekaniker [n.; ~n, ~] mechanic

mekanisk [adj.; ~t, ~a] mechanical

mekanism [n.; ~en, ~er] mechanism

melankolisk [adj.; ~t, ~a] melancholy, sad

melittafilter [n.; -filtret, ~] coffee filter

mellan [prep.] between

mellanakt [n.; ~en, ~er] intermission

Mellanamerika [n.] Central America

mellandag [n.; ~en, ~ar] day between Christmas and New Year's

Mellaneuropa [n.] Central Europe

mellangärde [n.; ~t, ~] diaphragm [membrane]

mellankopplingskabel [n.; ~n, -kablar] patch cable [IT]

mellanlagrare [n.; ~n, ~] spooler [IT]

mellanlandning [n.; ~en, ~ar] stopover

mellanmål [n.; ~et, ~] snack

mellannivå [n.; ~n] intermediate level

mellanprogram [n.; -grammet, ~] middleware [IT]

mellanrum [n.; -rummet, ~] space, interval

mellanserver [n.; ~n, -servrar] proxy server [IT]

mellanslag [n.; ~et, ~] space character [IT]

mellanstadium [n.; -stadiet] middle school [10-13 year olds]

mellanstatlig [adj.; ~t, ~a] intergovernmental [EU]

mellansvår [adj.; ~t, ~a] of average difficulty

mellantid [n.; ~en, ~er] intermission [sports events]

mellanvara [n.; ~n, -varor] middleware [IT]

mellanöl [n.; ~et, ~] medium-strong beer [2.25-3.5 % alcohol]

Mellanöstern [n.] Middle East

mellersta [adj.] central, middle

melodi [n.; ~n, ~er] tune, melody

melodifestival [n.; ~en, ~er] regional song contest

melodramatisk [adj.; ~t, ~a] melodramatic

melon [n.; ~en, ~er] melon

memoarer [n.pl.] memoirs

men [conj.] but

mena [v.; ~r, ~de, ~t] mean

mened [n.; ~en, ~er] perjury

mening [n.; ~en, ~ar] opinion; meaning; intention; sentence [gram]; **det var inte ~en att** it was not my/our intention that/to

meningsfull [adj.; ~t, ~a] meaningful

meningslös [adj.; ~t, ~a] meaningless

meningsutbyte [n.; ~t, ~n] exchange of views, debate

mens [n.; ~en, ~ar; colloq.] period,

menstruation; **ha** ~ have one's period

menssmärtor [n.pl.] period pains, menstrual cramps

mentalitet [n.; ~en, ~er] mentality

mentalsjukdom [n.; ~en, ~ar] mental illness

meny [n.; ~n, ~er] menu; ~ **för 100 kronor** set menu for 100 krona; ~ **för bantare** diet menu; ~ **till fast pris** set menu, pris fixe menu

menyalternativ [n.; ~et, ~] menu choice, option [IT]

menyrad [n.; ~en] menu bar [IT]

MEP [abbrev: ledamot i Europaparlamentet] member of the European Parliament (MEP) [EU]

mer[1] [adj.comp.: många] more; ~ **tid** more time

mer[2] [adv.comp.: mycket] more; **inte** ~ **än 5 saker** 5 items or less; ~ **anpassad** more suited

merit [n.; ~en, ~er] qualification, merit

meritförteckning [n.; ~en] list of qualifications

Merkurius [n.] Mercury [planet]

merpart [n.; ~en] greater part

Mertensgruppen [n.] Mertens Group [EU, COREPER]

mervärdesskatt (moms) [n.; ~en] value-added tax (VAT)

mes [n.; ~en, ~ar] titmouse [bird]

mesost [n.; ~en] whey cheese [soft, sweet]

Messias [n.; ~en] Messiah

messmör [n.; ~et] whey cheese

mest [adv.superl.: mycket] most, mostly; **tycka om** ~ like the most, prefer

mesta [adv.]: **det** ~ most; **för det** ~ mostly

mestadels [adv.] mostly

meta [v.; ~r, ~de, ~t] fish, catch fish

metadata [n.pl.] metadata [IT]

metall [n.; ~en, ~er] metal

metallindustri [n.; ~n] metal industry

metalltråd [n.; ~en, ~ar] wire

metatagg [n.; ~en, ~ar] metatag [IT]

meteorolog [n.; ~en, ~er] meteorologist, weatherman

meter [n.; ~n,~] meter [39.4 in., 3.3 feet, 1.1 yards]

metkrok [n.; ~en, ~ar] fish hook

metning [n.; ~en] fishing, angling

metod [n.; ~en, ~er] method

metspö [n.; ~t, ~n] fishing rod

mexikansk [adj.; ~t, ~a] Mexican

Mexiko [n.] Mexico

MFF [abbrev: Malmö fotbollsförening] MFF [Malmö soccer club/team]

m fl [abbrev: med flera] and others, inter alia

mg [abbrev: milligram] milligram [1/1000 of a gram]

miau [interj.] meow [cat]

middag [n.; ~en, ~ar] noon, midday; dinner; **god** ~! good afternoon!; **äta** ~ **kl 7** have dinner at 7

midja [n.; ~n] waist, waistline

midnatt [n.; ~en] midnight

midnattssol [n.; ~en] midnight sun

midsommar [n.; ~(e)n] midsummer

Midsommardagen [n.] Midsummer Day [celebrated on first Saturday after June 19]

midsommarfirande [n.; ~t] Midsummer celebration

midsommarstång [n.; ~en, -stänger] maypole

midvinter [n.; ~n] midwinter

MIF [abbrev: Malmö ishockeyförening, Malmö Redhawks] Malmö Redhawks [ice hockey team]

mig [pron.obj.; see: **jag**] me; myself

Migrationsverket [n.] National Migration Administration

migrän [n.; ~en] migraine

mikro- [prefix] micro-

mikrofilmkort [n.; ~et, ~] microfiche [IT]

mikrofon [n.; ~en, ~er] microphone

mikrokredit [n.; ~en, ~er] microcredit

mikroprocessor [n.; ~n, ~er] microprocessor [IT]

mikrougn [n.; ~en, ~ar] microwave oven

mikrovågsugn [n.; ~en, ~ar] microwave oven

mil [n.; ~en, ~] Swedish mile [10 km, 6 US miles]

Milano [n.] Milan
mild [adj.; milt, ~a] mild
milis [n.; ~en, ~er] militia
militant [adj.; ~a] militant
militaristisk [adj.; ~t, ~a]
  militaristic
militär¹ [adj.; ~t, ~a] military
militär² [n.; ~en, ~er] military man;
  military forces
militärallians [n.; ~en, ~er] military alliance
militärtjänst [n.; ~en] military
  service
milj. [see: **miljon**]
miljard [n.; ~en, ~er] billion [thou-
  sand million]
miljon [n.; ~en, ~er] million
miljö [n.; ~n, ~er] environment
miljöansvar [n.; ~et] environmental liability [EU]
Miljödepartementet (M) [n.]
  Ministry of the Environment
miljöfarlig [adj.; ~t, ~a] harmful to
  the environment
miljöförstöring [n.; ~en, ~ar]
  environmental pollution
miljögaranti [n.] environmental
  guarantee [EU]
**miljökonsekvensbeskrivning
  (MKB)** [n.; ~en, ~ar] environmental impact statement
Miljö- och jordbruksutskottet [n.]
  Committee on Agriculture and the
  Environment (in Parliament)
**Miljö- och samhällsbyggnadsde-
  partementet** [n.] Ministry of Sustainable Development
Miljöpartiet (de Gröna) [n.] Party
  for the Environment, Green Party
miljörörelsen [n.] environmental
  movement
miljöskydd [n.; ~et] environmental
  protection
miljövård [n.; ~en] environmental
  protection
Miljövårdsberedningen [n.] Environmental Advisory Council
miljövän [n.; -vännen, -vänner]
  environmentalist
miljövänlig [adj.; ~t, ~a] environment friendly

Miljööverdomstolen [n.] Environmental Court of Appeal
milkshake [n.; ~en] milk shake
millimeter (mm) [n.; ~n, ~] millimeter (mm) [1/25 inch]
milt [adv./adj.; see: **mild**] mild(ly)
min¹ [pron.poss.; mitt, mina] my,
  mine
min.² [abbrev: minut; minimum]
  minute; minimum
mindervärdeskomplex [n.; ~et, ~]
  inferiority complex
mindervärdig [adj.; ~t, ~a] inferior
mindre¹ [adj.comp.: liten) lesser,
  smaller; **ett ~ problem** a smaller
  problem
mindre² [adv.comp.; litet] less; **på
  ~ än 5 minuter** in less than 5
  minutes
mindre-än-tecken (<) [n.; -tecknet,
  ~] less-than sign, left-hand angle
  bracket [IT]
mineral [n.; ~et, ~] mineral
mineralfyndighet [n.; ~en, ~er]
  mineral deposit
mineralvatten [n.; -vattnet] mineral
  water
miniatyrbild [n.; ~en, ~er] thumbnail image [IT]
minibar [n.; ~en, ~er] minibar
minibild [n.; ~en, ~er] thumbnail
  image [IT]
minigolf [n.; ~en] minigolf
minimera [v.; ~r, ~de, ~t] minimize [IT]
minimilagstiftning [n.; ~en, ~ar]
  minimum common legislation [EU]
minimilön [n.; ~en, ~er] minimum
  wage
minimipris [n.; ~et, ~er] minimum
  charge
minimiålder [n.; ~n] minimum age
minimum [n.; ~et, ~] minimum
miniprogram [n.; -grammet, ~]
  applet [IT]
miniräknare [n.; ~n, ~] pocket
  calculator
minister [n.; ~n, ministrar] minister
  [govt.]
ministerpresident [n.; ~en, ~er]
  prime minister

Ministerrådet [n.] Council of Ministers, Council of the EU [EU]

minnas [v.passive; minns, mindes, mints] remember

minne [n.; ~t, ~n] memory, reminder; souvenir; memory [IT]; **till ~ av** in memory of

minnesdump [n.; ~en] memory dump [IT]

minnesförlust [n.; ~en, ~er] amnesia, loss of memory

minneskort [n.; ~et, ~] memory card [IT]

minnesmärke [n.; ~t, ~n] memorial, monument

minnesruna [n.; ~n, -runor] obituary

minnestilldelning [n.; ~en] memory allocation [IT]

minnesvärd [adj.; -värt, ~a] memorable

minoritet [n.; ~en, ~er] minority

minoritetsregering [n.; ~en, ~ar] minority government

minsann [adv.] certainly

minska (med) [v.; ~r, ~de, ~t] reduce (by), make smaller; **~ farten** reduce speed

minskning [n.; ~en, ~ar] reduction, decrease

minst¹ [adj.superl.: liten] least, slightest; **~a gemensamma nämnare** lowest common denominator

minst² [adv.superl.: litet] least, at least

minus¹ [adv.] minus

minus² [n.; ~et, ~] minus

minustecken [n.; -tecknet, ~] minus sign

minut [n.; ~en, ~er] minute

missa [v.; ~r, ~de, ~t] miss, fail to reach/accomplish

missbruk [n.; ~et, ~] addiction; abuse

missbruka [v.; ~r, ~de, ~t] abuse, misuse

missbrukare [n.; ~n, ~] addict

missfall [n.; ~et, ~] miscarriage

missförstå [v.; -står, -stod, -stått] misunderstand

missförstånd [n.; ~et, ~] misunderstanding

misshandel [n.; ~n] maltreatment; assault

misshandla [v.; ~r, ~de, ~t] maltreat, ill-treat; assault, batter

mission [n.; ~en, ~er] mission

misslyckad [adj.; -lyckat, ~e] unsuccessful

misslyckande [n.; ~t, ~n] failure

misslyckas [v.passive; -lyckas, -lyckades, -lyckats] fail, prove unsuccessful

missnöjd [adj.; -nöjt , ~a] displeased, dissatisfied

missnöje [n.; ~t] dissatisfaction, discontent

misstag [n.; ~et, ~] mistake

misstanke [n.; ~n, -tänkar] suspicion

missta sig [v.; -tar, -tog, -tagit] make a mistake, be mistaken

misstro [v.; -tror, trodde, -trott] distrust, have no faith in

misstroendeförklaring [n.; ~en, ~ar] declaration of no confidence

misstroendevotum [n.; ~et, ~] vote of no confidence

misstänka [v.; -tänker, -tänkte, -tänkt] suspect

misstänksamhet [n.; ~en, ~er] suspicion

misstänkt [adj.; ~a] suspected

missväxtår [n.; ~et, ~] bad harvest year

miste: gå ~ om miss out on

mistel [n.; ~n] mistletoe

mistlur [n.; ~en, ~ar] foghorn

mitella [n.; ~n, -llor] sling, triangular bandage

mitt¹ [adv.] in the middle; deep; **~ emot** opposite; **~ i** in the middle of; **~ på dagen** noon, at noon

mitt² [n.; ~en] middle

mitt³ [poss.pron.; see: min] my

mittemellan [prep.] between

mittemot [prep.] opposite

Mittenparti [n.; ~et, ~er] Center Party

mittfältare [n.; ~n, ~] midfielder [soccer]

mittgång [n.; ~en, ~er] aisle

mittskepp [n.; ~et] nave

mjuk [adj.; ~t, ~a] soft

mjukost [n.; ~en] soft white cheese
mjukt bindestreck [n.; ~et, ~] soft hyphen [IT]
mjäll [n.; ~et] dandruff
mjöl [n.; ~et] flour
mjölk [n.; ~en] milk
mjölkaffär [n.; ~en, ~er] dairy products store
mjölkersättningar [n.pl.] milk substitutes
mjölkprodukter [n.pl.] dairy products
MKB [abbrev: miljökonsekvensbeskrivning] environmental impact statement
Mkr. [abbrev: miljoner kronor] million crowns
mm [abbrev: med mera; millimeter] et cetera, and so forth; millimeter
mn [abbrev: miljoner] million
mnkr [abbrev: miljoner kronor] million crowns
mobba [v.; ~r, ~de, ~t] bully, gang up on
mobbning [n.; ~en] bullying, ganging up on, harassment
mobil [n.; ~t, ~a] mobile
mobiltelefon [n.; ~en, ~er] cell phone, mobile telephone [IT]
mocka [n.; ~n] suede
mod [n.; ~et] courage; mood, spirits; fashion, style
modalt hjälpverb [n.; ~et, ~] modal auxiliary verb [e.g. can, should, might] [gram]
mode [n.; ~t, ~n] fashion
modell [n.; ~en, ~er] model
modem [n.; ~et, ~] modem [IT]
modemkabel [n.; ~n, -kablar] modem cable [IT]
modemkapning [n.; ~en] modem hijacking [IT]
moder [n.; see: **mor**] mother
moderat [adj; ~a] moderate
Moderata Samlingspartiet [n.] Moderate Rally Party
Moderata Ungdomsförbundet (MUF) [n.] Moderate Youth Alliance
moderaterna [n.pl.; see: **Moderata Samlingspartiet**] the moderates

moderkort [n.; ~et, ~] mother board [IT]
modern [adj.; ~t, ~a] modern; ~ konst modern art
modernisera [v.; ~r, ~de, ~t] modernize
modersmål [n.; ~et, ~] mother tongue
modersmålsundervisning [n.; ~en] instruction in mother tongue
modetecknare [n.; ~n, ~] fashion designer
modevisning [n.; ~en, ~ar] fashion show
modig [adj.; ~t, ~a] courageous, brave
modist [n.; ~en, ~er] hat shop, milliner
modulär programmering [n.; ~en] modular programming [IT]
modus [n.] mood [gram]
mogen [adj.; moget, mogna] ripe, mature
Moldavien [n.] Moldavia
molekyl [n.; ~en, ~er] molecule
moll [n.] minor [music keys]
moln [n.; ~et, ~] cloud
molnig [adj.; ~t, ~a] cloudy
moms [abbrev: mervärdesskatt] value-added tax (VAT); ~ inräknad value-added tax included
moms-kvitto [n.; ~t, ~n] value-added tax receipt [for reimbursement on exiting country]
monarki [n.; ~n, ~er] monarchy
monetär [adj.; ~t, ~a] monetary; ~ politik monetary policy [EU]
Mongoliet [n.] Mongolia
mongolisk [adj.; ~t, ~a] Mongolian
monolog [n.; ~en, ~er] monolog
monopol [n.; ~et, ~] monopoly
monoton [adj.; ~t, ~a] monotonous
monster [n.; monstret, ~] monster
monter [n.; ~n, montrar] display case, showcase, exhibition stand
montering [n.; ~en, ~ar] mounting; assembly
monteringsfärdig [adj.; ~t, ~a] prefabricated
monument [n.; ~et, ~] monument

moped [n.; ~en, ~er] moped [motorbike]
mor [n.; modern, mödrar] mother
moral [n.; ~en] ethics; morale
moralisk [adj.; ~t, ~a] moral, ethical
morbror [n.; -brodern, -bröder] maternal uncle, mother's brother
mord [n.; ~et, ~] murder
mordbrand [n.; ~en, -bränder] arson
morfar [n.; -fadern] maternal grandfather, mother's father
morfologi [n.; ~n] morphology [gram]
morgon [n.; ~en, morgnar] morning; **god** ~! good morning!; **i** ~ tomorrow; **i** ~ **bitti** tomorrow morning, early tomorrow; **på** ~**en** in the morning; ~**en därpå** the next morning
morgondagens [adj.] tomorrow's
morgongymnastik [n.; ~en] early morning exercises
morgonrock [n.; ~en, ~ar] dressing gown
morgontidning [n.; ~en, ~ar] morning newspaper
morkulla [n.; ~n, -kullor] woodcock
mormor [n.; -modern] maternal grandmother, mother's mother
morot [n.; ~en, morötter] carrot
morotssoppa [n.; ~n, -soppor] carrot soup
morsa [n.; ~n, morsor; colloq.] mom
Morsdagen [n.] Mother's Day [usually last Sunday in May]
morse [n.]: **i** ~ this morning
morötter [n.pl.] carrots
mos [n.; ~et] mash, pulp
mosaik [n.; ~en, ~er] mosaic
moské [n.; ~n, ~er] mosque
Moskva [n.] Moscow
mossmark [n.; ~en, ~er] bog
moster [n.; ~n, mostrar] maternal aunt, mother's sister
mot[1] [n.; ~et, ~] highway junction, interchange
mot[2] [prep.] to, toward; facing, against; **vägen går** ~ **söder** the road runs southwards

motell [n.; ~et, ~] motel
motion [n.; ~en, ~er] exercise; motion
motionscykel [n.; ~n; -cyklar] exercise bike
motionsgymnastik [n.; ~en] exercise(s), physical training
motionsrum [n.; -rummet, ~] exercise room
motionsspår [n.; ~et, ~] running track; cross-country skiing track
motiv [n.; ~et, ~] motif, subject
motivera [v.; ~r, ~de, ~t] motivate
motivering [n.; ~en] motivation
motocross [n.; ~en] motocross
motor [n.; ~n, ~er] motor, engine
motorbåt [n.; ~en, ~ar] motor boat
motorcykel [n.; ~n, -cyklar] motorcycle
motorfel [n.; ~et, ~] engine trouble
motorfordon [n.; ~et, ~] vehicle, motor vehicle
motorhuv [n.; ~en, ~ar] hood [auto]
motorolja [n.; ~n, -oljor] motor oil
motorsport [n.; ~en] motor sports, car racing
motorstopp [n.; ~et] breakdown [motor vehicle]; **få** ~ have a breakdown [motor vehicle]
motorsåg [n.; ~en, ~ar] chain saw
motortrafik [n.; ~en] vehicle traffic
motorväg [n.; ~en, -vägar] highway
motorvägsavgift [n.; ~en, ~er] highway toll
motorvägskorsning [n.; ~en, ~ar] highway junction
motorvägspolis [n.; ~en, ~er] highway police(man)
motorvärmare [n.; ~n, ~] engine warmer/pre-heater
motsade [v.past; see: **motsäga**]
motsagt [v.past; see: **motsäga**]
motsats [n.; ~en, ~er] contrast, opposite
motsatskonjunktion [n.; ~en, ~er] adversative conjunction [gram]
motsatt [adj.; ~a] opposite, contrary
motstånd [n.; ~et] resistance; resistor (electricity)
motståndare [n.; ~n, ~] opponent, adversary

motsv. [abbrev: motsvarande] corresponding, analogous
motsvara [v.; ~r, ~de, ~t] correspond
motsvarande [adj.] corresponding
motsvarighet [n.; ~en, ~er] equivalent
motsäga [v.; -säger, -sade, -sagt] contradict
motsättning [n.; ~en, ~ar] opposition; antagonism
mottagaranpassning av dokument/brev [n.] mail merge [IT]
mottagare [n.; ~n, ~] receiver; addressee; ~**n betalar samtalet** collect call, reverse-charges call
mottagning [n.; ~en] reception; consultation; doctor's office, consultation room
moturs [adv.] counterclockwise
motverka [v.; ~r, ~de, ~t] counteract
motvikt [n.; ~en, ~er] counterweight, counterbalance
motvillig [adj.; ~t, ~a] reluctant, averse
motvind [n.; ~en, ~ar] headwind
mountainbike [n.] mountain bike
mousserande [adj.] sparkling, bubbling
mp [abbrev: Miljöpartiet] Green Party
MP3-spelare [n.; ~n, ~] MP3 player [IT]
MR [abbrev: mänskliga rättigheter] human rights
msk [abbrev: matsked] tablespoon
MTG [abbrev: Modern Times Group] MTG [big media company: radio, TV, film]
mugg [n.; ~en, ~ar] mug
Muhammed [n.] Mohammed
mulen [adj.; mulet, mulna] overcast, cloudy
mulla [n.; ~n] mulla [Muslim cleric]
mullbär [n.; ~et, ~] mulberry
mullvad [n.; ~en, ~ar] mole
multe [n.; ~n] mullet [fish]
multifunktionsskrivare [n.; ~n] multifunctional printer, all-in-one printer [IT]
multikörning [n.; ~en] multitasking [IT]

multimedia [n.pl.] multimedia [IT]
multipel skleros (MS) [n.] multiple sclerosis (MS)
multiplicera (med) [v.; ~r, ~de, ~t] multiply (by)
multiplikation [n.; ~en] multiplication [IT]
mumla [v.; ~r, ~de, ~t] mumble
mumsa [v.; ~r, ~de, ~t] nibble, chew
mun [n.; munnen, munnar] mouth
München [n.] Munich
munk [n.; ~en, ~ar] monk; doughnut
munspel [n.; ~et, ~] harmonica
munter [adj.; ~t, muntra] cheerful, merry
muntlig [adj.; ~t, ~a] oral; ~ **tentamen** oral examination [school]
munvatten [n.; -vattnet] mouthwash
mur [n.; ~en, ~ar] wall
murare [n.; ~n, ~] bricklayer, mason
murgröna [n.; ~n] ivy
murkelstuvning [n.; ~en] creamed morel mushrooms
murkelsås [n.; ~en] morel mushroom sauce
murken [adj.; ~t, murkna] decayed, rotted
murkla [n.; ~n, murklor] morel mushroom
mus [n.; ~en, möss] mouse
museiby [n.; ~n, ~ar] museum village
museum [n.; museet, museer] museum
musicera [v.; ~r, ~de, ~t] make music
musik [n.; ~en] music
musikaffär [n.; ~en, ~er] music store
musikal [n.] musical
musikalisk [adj.; ~t, ~a] musical
musiker [n.; ~n, ~] musician
musikfil [n.; ~en, ~er] music file [IT]
musikhandel [n.; ~n, ~] music store
musiklärare [n.; ~n, ~] music teacher
Musikmuseet [n.] Museum of Music [in Stockholm]
musikprogram [n.; -grammet, ~] music program

muskel [n.; ~n, muskler] muscle
muskelsträckning [n.; ~en, ~ar] strained muscle
musknapp [n.; ~en] mouse button [IT]
muskot [n.; ~en] nutmeg
muskotnöt [n.; ~en, -nötter] nutmeg
müsli [n.; ~n] muesli
muslim [n.; ~en, ~er] Muslim
muslimsk [adj.; ~t, ~a] Muslim
musmatta [n.; ~n] mouse pad [IT]
muspekare [n.; ~n] mouse pointer [IT]
Musse Pigg [n.] Mickey Mouse
mussla [n.; ~n, musslor] mussel, clam
mustasch [n.; ~en, ~er] moustache
mustig [adj.; ~t, ~a] full-bodied [beverage]
muta¹ [n.; ~n, mutor] bribe; **ta mutor** take bribes
muta² [v.; ~r, ~de, ~t] bribe
mutter [n.; ~n, muttrar] nut [hardware]
muttra [v.; ~r, ~de, ~t] mutter
MW [abbrev: megawatt] megawatt
MVG [abbrev: mycket väl godkänt] passed with great distinction [highest grade/mark in school]
mycket [adv.] very, much, a lot; ~ **gärna** willingly, gladly
mygga [n.; ~n, myggor] mosquito
myggbett [n.; ~et, ~] mosquito bite
myggmedel [n.; -medlet, ~] mosquito repellant
myggnät [n.; ~et, ~] mosquito net
myndig [adj.; ~t, ~a] of age, major; **vara** ~ be of age
myndighet [n.; ~en, ~er] agency, authority
Myndigheten för internationella adoptionsfrågor (MIA) [n.] Swedish Intercountry Adoption Authority
Myndigheten för kvalificerad yrkesutbildning [n.] Swedish Agency for Advanced Vocational Education
Myndigheten för skolutveckling [n.] Swedish National Agency for School Improvement

Myndigheten för Sveriges nätuniversitet [n.] Swedish Net University Agency
mynna [v.; ~r, ~de, ~t] flow into; lead to, result in
mynt [n.; ~et, ~] coin
mynta [v.; ~r, ~de, ~t] mint
mynttelefon [n.; ~en, ~er] pay phone
myr [n.; ~en, ~ar] marsh
myra [n.; ~n, myror] ant
mysig [adj.; ~t, ~a] cosy, charming
mysteriös [adj.; ~t, ~a] mysterious
mystisk [adj.; ~t, ~a] mysterious
myt [n.; ~en, ~er] myth
mytisk [adj.; ~t, ~a] mythical
mytologi [n.; ~n, ~er] mythology
må¹ [v.; mår, mådde, mått] feel; may; **han ~r inte bra** he's not feeling well; **Hur ~r du?** How are you? How do you feel?; ~ **illa** feel sick
må² [v.modal; måtte] may, let; must (not) [in neg.]; **ja, ~ han/hon leva!** Happy Birthday to him/her!
måg [n.; ~en, ~ar] son-in-law
måhända [adv.] maybe
mål [n.; ~et, ~] speech, dialect; case, lawsuit; meal; goal, objective; mark; **göra** ~ score a goal
måla [v.; ~r, ~de, ~t] paint; ~ **om** repaint
målad [adj.; målat, ~e] painted; **målat glas** stained glass
målarbok [n.; ~en, -böcker] coloring book
målarfärg [n.; ~en, ~er] paint [artistic]
målare [n.; ~n, ~] painter
målarprogram [n.; -grammet, ~] paint program [IT]
måleri [n.; ~et, ~er] painting
målerifirma [n.; ~n, -firmor] decorating company
mållinje [n.; ~n, ~r] finish line [sports]
målning [n.; ~en, ~ar] painting
målsman [n.; -mannen, -män] guardian; accompanying adult
målstolpe [n.; ~n, -stolpar] goalpost
målsättning [n.; ~en, ~ar] aim, purpose, goal

måltid [n.; ~en, ~er] meal; **efter** ~ after meals [medicines]; **smaklig** ~ enjoy your meal, bon appetit; ~ **till fast pris** pris fixe meal, set menu

målvakt [n.; ~en, ~er] goalkeeper

mån¹ (om) [adj.; ~a] anxious (about), careful (of), particular (about)

mån² [n.] degree, measure, extent

mån.³ [see: **månad**; **måndag**]

månad [n.; ~en, ~er] month

månadsavgift [n.; ~en, ~er] monthly charge

månadskort [n.; ~et, ~] monthly ticket

månadslön [n.; ~en, ~er] monthly wages/salary

månatlig [adj.; ~t, ~a] monthly

måndag [n.] Monday

måne [n.; ~n, månar] moon

många [adj.pl.; comp.: fler, flest] many

mångbiograf [n.; ~en, ~er] multiplex cinema

mångfaldig [adj.; ~t, ~a] many, multiple

mångkulturell [adj.; ~t, ~a] multicultural

mångsidig [adj.; ~t, ~a] many-sided, diverse

mångtydig [adj.; ~t, ~a] ambiguous

månsten [n.; ~en, ~ar] moonstone

mås [n.; ~en, ~ar] gull

måste [v.modal; måste, måst] must, have to

mått [n.; ~et, ~] measure

måtta [n.; ~n] moderation, limit

måttband [n.; ~et, ~] tape measure

måtte [v.past; see: **må (modal)**] may [wish]; must [conviction]

måttsadverbial [n.; ~et, ~] adverbial of quantity/degree [gram]

måttsattribut [n.; ~et, ~] quantifier [gram]

måttsgenitiv [n.; ~en] genitive of measure [gram]

mäklare [n.; ~n, ~] broker; real estate agent

mäktig [adj.; ~t, ~a] rich

män [n.pl.; see: **man**]

mängd [n.; ~en, ~er] amount, quantity

människa [n.; ~n, -skor] person, human being; [pl.] people

människofientlig [adj.; ~t, ~a] misanthropic

människohandel [n.; ~n] trafficking in persons

människovänlig [adj.; ~t, ~a] humanitarian, humane; philanthropic

mänsklig [adj.; ~t, ~a] human; humane; reasonable; **~a rättigheter** human rights [EU]

mänsklighet [n.; ~en] humanness; humanity

märg [n.; ~en] marrow

märka [v.; märker, märkte, märkt] mark; notice

märke [n.; ~t, ~n] mark, label; brand; **lägga ~ till** notice

märklig [adj.; ~t, ~a] remarkable, notable; strange, odd

märkning [n.; ~en, ~ar] marking, labeling

märkvärdig [adj.; ~t, ~a] strange, curious; remarkable

märr [n.; ~en, ~ar] mare

mässa [n.; ~n, mässor] mass, worship service; trade fair, exhibition

mässing [n.; ~en] brass

mässling [n.; ~en] measles

mästare [n.; ~n, ~] master; champion

mästerskap [n.; ~et, ~] championship

mästerstycke [n.; ~t, ~n] masterpiece

mästerverk [n.; ~et, ~] masterpiece

mäta [v.; mäter, mätte, mätt] measure

mätare [n.; ~n, ~] meter, measuring device

mätning [n.; ~en, ~ar] measuring; measurement

mätt [adj.; ~a] satisfied, full up

möbel [n.; ~n, möbler] furniture, piece of furniture

möbelaffär [n.; ~en, ~er] furniture store

möblera [v.; ~r, ~de, ~t] furnish

möblerad [adj.; -rat, ~e] furnished

möda [n.; ~n, mödor] pains, trouble, toil

mödragymnastik [n.; ~en] prenatal and postnatal exercises

mödrar [n.pl.; see: **mor**] mothers
mödravård [n.; ~en] prenatal and postnatal care
möglig [adj.; ~t, ~a] moldy
möjl. [see: **möjligen**]
möjlig [adj.; ~t, ~a] possible; ~ **försening** possible delay
möjligen [adv.] possibly
möjlighet [n.;~en, ~er] possibility
möjligtvis [adv.] possibly
mönster [v.; mönstret, ~] pattern; regular expression [IT]
mönsteridentifiering [n.; ~en] pattern recognition [IT]
mör [adj.; ~t, ~a] tender [food]
mörda [v.; ~r, ~de, ~t] murder
mördad [adj.; mördat, ~e] murdered
mördare [n.; ~n, ~] murderer
mördas [v.passive; mördas, mördades, mördats] be murdered
mördegskaka [n.; ~n, -kakor] shortbread

mörk [adj.; ~t, ~a] dark; ~**t öl** dark beer
mörkbrun [adj.; ~t, ~a] dark brown
mörker [n.; mörkret] darkness, dark
mört [n.; ~en, ~ar] roach [freshwater fish]
mössa [n.; ~n, mössor] cap
möta [v.; möter, mötte, mött] meet [trans.]
mötande [adj.] oncoming; ~ **trafik** oncoming traffic, two-way traffic
mötas [v.passive; möts, möttes, mötts] meet [intrans.]
möte [n.; ~t, ~n] meeting
mötesfrihet [n.; ~en] right of public meeting, right of assembly
mötesplats [n.; ~en, ~er] meeting place

N

n.¹ [abbrev: norr, norra] north, northern

N² [abbrev: norr, norra] north, northern

nackdel [n.; ~en, ~ar] disadvantage

nacke [n.; ~n, nackar] back of the head and neck, nape of the neck

nackspärr [n.; ~en, ~ar] wryneck, torticollis

nafsa [v.; ~r, ~de, ~t] snap, grab

nagel [n.; ~n, naglar] nail

nagelborste [n.;] nailbrush

nagelfil [n.; ~en, ~ar] nail file

nagelklippare [n.; ~n, ~] nail clipper

nagellack [n.; ~et, ~] nail polish

nagellackborttagningsmedel [n.; -medlet] nail polish remover

nagelsax [n.; ~en, ~ar] nail scissors

nageltrång [n.; ~et, ~] ingrown toe nail

naken [adj.; ~t, nakna] naked, nude

nakenstudie [n.; ~n, ~r] nude [art work]

nalle [n.; ~n, nallar] teddy bear; ~ Puh Winnie the Pooh

namn [n.; ~et, ~] name; **Hur var ~et?** What is your name? What did you say your name is?

namnsdag [n.; ~en, ~ar] name's day, saint's day [each name has its day in the church calendar and almanac]

namnskylt [n.; ~en, ~ar] name plate

namnteckning [n.; ~en, ~ar] signature

namnunderskrift [n.; ~en, ~er] signature

namnupplösning [n.; ~en] name resolution [IT]

nanoteknologi [n.; ~n, ~er] nano-technology [IT]

Napoleonbakelse [n.; ~n, ~r] Napoleon cream cake

napp [n.; ~en, ~ar] teat, nipple; baby's pacifier

nappa [n.; ~r, ~de, ~t] bite [fishing]

nappflaska [n.; ~n, -flaskor] baby bottle, feeding bottle

narkoman [n.; ~en, ~er] drug addict

narkos [n.; ~en, ~er] anesthetic

narkosläkare [n.; ~n, ~] anesthesiologist

narkotika [n.; ~n] narcotics, drugs

narkotikaberoende [n.; ~t] drug addiction, drug dependence

narkotikabrott [n.; ~et, ~] drug crime

narkotikahandel [n.; ~n] drug traffic

narkotikalangare [n.; ~n, ~] drug peddler, drug trafficker

narrativ [n.; ~en, ~er] narrative [gram]

nation [n.; ~en, ~er] nation

nationaldräkt [n.; ~en, ~er] national costume

nationalekonom [n.; ~en, ~er] political economist

Nationalföreningen för trafik-säkerhetens främjande (NTF) [n.] National Association for Road Safety

nationalist [n.; ~en, ~er] nationalist

nationalistisk [adj.; ~t. ~a] nationalistic

nationalitet [n.; ~en, ~er] nationality

Nationalmuseet [n.] National Museum of Fine Arts

nationalpark [n.; ~en, ~er] national park

nationalstat [n.; ~en. ~er] nation state

nationalsång [n.; ~en, ~er] national anthem

nationell [adj.; ~t, ~a] national

Nato [abbrev; Atlantpaktsorganisationen] North Atlantic Treaty Organization (NATO); **Det nya ~** New-look NATO

natrium [n.] sodium

natt [n.; ~en, nätter] night; **god ~!** good night!; **i ~** tonight; **på ~en** at night

nattapotek [n.; ~et, ~] all-night pharmacy

nattduksbord [n.; ~et, ~] bedside table

nattetid [adv.] at night, in the nighttime

nattklocka [n.; ~n] night bell

nattklubb [n.; ~en, ~er] night club

nattkräm [n.; ~en, ~er] night cream

nattlig [adj.; ~t, ~a] nocturnal; nightly

nattlinne [n.; ~t, ~] nightgown, nightie

nattliv [n.; ~et, ~] night life

nattportier [n.; ~en, ~er] night receptionist, night clerk, night doorman

nattsköterska [n.; ~n, -skor] night nurse

nattuggla [n.; ~n, -ugglor] night-owl

nattvandra [v.; ~r, ~de, ~t] go out on community night patrol [volunteer community service by parents to mix with young people at night]

nattvandrare [n.; ~n, ~] night patroller [see: **nattvandra**]

nattvarden [n.] Holy Communion, Lord's Supper

nattöppen [adj.; -öppet, -öppna] open all-night

natur [n.; ~en] nature, scenery

Natura 2000 [n.] Natura 2000 [EU]

naturbehov [n.; ~et, ~] "call" of nature

naturhistoria [n.; ~n] natural history

naturhistoriskt museum [n.; museet, museer] natural history museum

Naturhistoriska riksmuseet [n.] Museum of Natural History

naturkatastrof [n.; ~en, ~er] natural disaster

naturlig [adj.; ~t, ~a] natural; ~t **genus** natural gender [gram]

naturligtvis [adv.] naturally, of course

naturorienterande ämnen (NO) [n.pl.] science subjects [school program]

naturreservat [n.; ~et, ~] nature reserve

naturskyddsförening [n.; ~en, ~ar] nature conservation society

naturtillgång [n.; ~en, ~ar] natural resource

naturvetenskap [n.; ~en, ~er] science

naturvetenskaplig [adj.; ~t, ~a] scientific; ~ **linje** science program [upper secondary school]

Naturvårdsverket [n.] Environmental Protection Administration

navel [n.; ~n, navlar] navel

navigera [v.; ~r, ~de, ~t] navigate

navigeringsknapp [n.; ~en, ~ar] navigation button [IT]

navkapsel [n.; ~n, -kapslar] hubcap

nazist [n.; ~en, ~er] Nazi

nazistisk [adj.; ~t, ~a] Nazi

nb¹ [abbrev: nedre botten] ground floor

NB² [abbrev: nota bene] note

NCC [abbrev: Nordic Construction Company] NCC [major construction company]

nd [abbrev: Nationaldemokraterna] National Democrats [political party]

Neapel [n.] Naples

ned [adv.; formal, often replaced by **ner**] downward(s), down [motion]; fully, extremely; **en trappa** ~ one flight down, the floor below

ned- [prefix; see also **ner-**] extremely, fully, thoroughly

nedanför [adv./prep.] below, at the bottom of; to the south of

nedanstående [adj.] below, stated below

nedbäddad [adj.; -bäddat, ~e] inset [IT]

nederbörd [n.; ~en] precipitation

nederkant [n.; ~en, ~er] lower edge [IT]

nederlag [n.; ~et, ~] defeat

nederländare [n.; ~n, ~] Dutchman

Nederländerna [n.pl.] Netherlands

nederländsk [adj.; ~t, ~a] Dutch

nederländska [n.] Dutch language

nederst [adj.superl.; ~a] furthest down, lowest

nedför [prep.] down, downwards; ~ **trappan** down the stairs

nedförsbacke [n.; ~n, -backar] downhill slope, descent

nedgång [n.; ~en, ~ar] way down; descent, setting; drop, decrease

nedifrån [adv.] from below

nedkomst [n.; ~en, ~er] delivery, birth

nedkopplad [adj.; -kopplat, ~e] offline [IT]

nedladdning [n.; ~en] downloading [IT]

nedlagd [adj.; -lagt, ~a] no longer in use, closed down

nedläggning [n.; ~en] discontinuation; shutdown

nedre [adj.comp.] lower [IT]; ~ **botten** ground floor

nedsatt [adj.; ~a] lowered, reduced; ~ **hörsel** hearing defect; deaf person [warning sign]; ~ **pris** reduced price; ~ **syn** impaired vision; blind person [roadside warning sign]

nedskärning [n.; ~en, ~ar] cutting back, reduction, cut

nedslag [n.; ~et, ~] downbeat [music]; keystroke [IT]

nedslagen [adj.; ~t, -slagna] depressed, dejected

nedslående [adj.] disappointing

nedströms [adv.] downstream

nedsänkt text [n.; ~en] subscript [IT]

nedsättande [adj.] disparaging, deprecatory

nedåt [adv.] downward

nedåtväxling [n.; ~en] fallback [IT]

negation [n.; ~en] negation [gram]

negativ [adj.; ~t, ~a] negative

nej [interj.] no; ~, **tack** no, thanks

nejlikor [n.pl.] cloves

nej-sidan [n.] opponents to a particular idea, nay-sayers

neka [v.; ~r, ~de, ~t] deny, refuse, prevent [IT]

nekrolog [n.; ~en, ~er] obituary

nektarin [n.; ~en, ~er] nectarine

neonljus [n.; ~et, ~] neon light

Neptunus [n.] Neptune

ner-[1] [prefix; see: **ned-**] extemely, fully, thoroughly

ner[2] [adv.; colloq.; see also: **ned**] downward; fully, extremely

nere[1] [adj.] depressed

nere[2] [adv.] down below, downstairs [location]

nerför [adv.; see: **nedför**]

nerifrån [adv.; see: **nedifrån**]

nerladdning [n.; see: **nedladdning**]

nerv [n.; ~en, ~er] nerve

nervsammanbrott [n.; ~et, ~] nervous breakdown

nervsystem [n.; ~et] nervous system

nervös [adj.; ~t, ~a] nervous

neråt [adv.; see: **nedåt**]

netto [n.; ~t] net [weight, finance]

nettoinkomst [n.; ~en, ~er] net income

nettovikt [n.; ~en, ~er] net weight

net-zine [n.; see: **nätzine**]

neuronnät [n.; ~et, ~] neural network [IT]

neurotisk [adj.; ~t, ~a] neurotic

neutral [adj.; ~t, ~a] neutral

neutralitet [n.; ~en] neutrality

neutrum [n.] neuter gender [gram]

news-grupp [n.; ~en, ~er] newsgroup [IT]

ngn. [abbrev: någon] someone

ngt. [abbrev: något] something

ni [pron.; er/ert/era, er] you [pl. & obsolete formal sing.]

Nicefördraget [n.] Treaty of Nice [EU]

nicka [v.; ~r, ~de, ~t] nod; head [soccer]

nikotin [n.; ~et] nicotine

Nilen [n.] Nile

nio [num.] nine

nionde [num.] ninth; September

nittio [num.] ninety

nittionde [num.] ninetieth

nitton [num.] nineteen

nittonde [num.] nineteenth

nittonhundratalet (1900-talet) [n.] twentieth century

nivå [n.; ~n ~er] level; standard

nivåskillnad [n.; ~en, ~er] difference in level

nja [interj.] well ...

njurbälte [n.; ~t, ~n] kidney belt [off-road motorcycling]

njure [n.; ~n, njurar] kidney

njurinflammation [n.; ~en]

nephritis, inflammation of the kidney

njursten [n.; ~en, ~ar] kidney stone

njuta (av) [v.; njuter, njöt, njutit] enjoy

NK [abbrev: Nordiska kompanjet] Nordic Company [large department store in Stockholm]

NM [abbrev: nordiskt mästerkap] Nordic Championship

NO [abbrev: Näringsfrihetsombudsmannen] Ombudsman for Freedom of Trade

Nobeldagen [n.] Nobel Prize day [December 10 - day that prizes are awarded]

Nobelpris [n.; ~et, ~] Nobel Prize

nobelpristagare [n.; ~n, ~] Nobel Prize winner

Nobelstiftelsen [n.] Nobel Foundation

nod [n.;~en, ~er] node [IT]

nog [adv.] enough; probably; I guess; ~ **för idag** enough for today; **det blir ~ regn i morgon** it will probably rain tomorrow

noga[1] [adj.] careful, exact; scrupulous; particular, meticulous; **vara ~ med** be careful with; **det är inte så ~** it's not very important

noga[2] [adv.] carefully, exactly

noggrann [adj.; ~t, ~a] careful

noll [num.] zero; love [tennis]

nollsummespel [n.; ~et, ~] zero-sum game

nomad [n.; ~en, ~er] nomad

nomen [n.] noun [gram]

nominalfras [n.; ~en, ~er] noun phrase [gram]

nominativ [n.; ~en] nominative [gram]

nonstop [adv.] nonstop

nord[1] [adv.] north; ~ **om** north of

nord[2] [n.; ~en] north

nord-[3] [prefix] northern

Nordafrika [n.] North Africa

nordafrikansk [adj.; ~t, ~a] North African

Nordamerika [n.] North America

Norden [n.] Nordic countries [Scandinavia, incl. Finland]

Nordirland [n.] Northern Ireland

nordisk [adj.; ~t, ~a] Nordic, Scandinavian

Nordiska Afrikainstitutet [n.] Nordic Africa Institute

Nordiska Investeringsbanken [n.] Nordic Investment Bank

Nordiska kulturfonden [n.] Nordic Cultural Fund

Nordiska ministerrådet [n.] Nordic Council of Ministers

Nordiska rådet [n.] Nordic Council

Nordkalotten [n.] arctic Scandinavia

Nordkappet [n.] North Cape

Nordkorea [n.] North Korea

nordlig [adj.; ~t, ~a] northern

nordost [n.; ~en] northeast

nordpolen [n.] North Pole

nordpolsområdet [n.] the Arctic

Nordsjön [n.] North Sea

nordväst [n.; ~en] northwest

nordöst [see: **nordost**] northeast

Norge [n.] Norway

normal [adj.; ~t, ~a] normal; ~ **hud** normal skin

normaltid [n.; ~en] standard time

norr [n.; adv.] north; ~ **om** north of

norra [adj.] northern

Norra ishavet [n.] Arctic Ocean

norra polcirkeln [n.] Arctic Circle

Norrland [n.] Norrland [northern half of Sweden]

norrländsk [adj.; ~t, ~a] from Norrland

norrman [n.; -mannen, -män] Norwegian

norrut [adv.] northwards

norsk [adj.; ~t, ~a] Norwegian

norska [n.] Norwegian language; Norwegian woman

nos [n.; ~en, ~ar] muzzle, nose [animal]

noshörning [n.; ~en, ~ar] rhinoceros

nostalgisk [adj.; ~t, ~a] nostalgic

not [n.; ~en, ~er] note [music]; annotation, footnote

nota [n.; ~n, notor] bill, check

notarie [n.; ~n, ~r] recording clerk, law clerk

noter [n.pl.; see: **not**] sheet music

notera [v.; ~r, ~de, ~t] note

noterad byggnad [n.; ~en, ~er] listed building

notis [n.; ~en, ~er] notice, short account in press

nov. [see: **november**]

novell [n.; ~en, ~er] short story, novella

november [n.] November

nr. [abbrev: **nummer**] number

NTF [abbrev: Nationalförengningen för trafiksäkerhetens främjande] National Association for Traffic Safety

nu [adv.] now; **~ i kväll** this evening; **~ på morgonen** this morning

nubb [n.; ~en, ~ar] tack

nubbe [n.; ~n, ~ar] glass of brandy, schnapps

nudiststrand [n.; ~en, -stränder] nudist beach

nudlar [n.pl.] noodles

nuförtiden [adv.] nowadays

nukleär [adj.; ~t, ~a] nuclear; **~a vapen** nuclear weapons

numera [adv.] nowadays, at present

numerisk [adj.; ~t, ~a] numerical; **~t tangentbord** numeric keypad [IT]

numerus [n.] number [gram]

nummer [n.; numret, ~] number; size

nummerbricka [n.; ~n, -brickor] cloakroom ticket/token

nummerbyrå [n.; ~n] telephone information, directory assistance

nummerlapp [n.; ~en, -lappar] number ticket [in line at store]

nummerplåt [n.; ~en, ~ar] license plate

nummerskiva [n.; ~n, -skivor] telephone dial

nummerskylt [n.; ~en, ~ar] license plate

nummertecken (#) [n.; -tecknet, ~] number sign (#), pound sign (#) [IT]

nummerupplysning [n.; ~en, ~ar] information [telephone]

numrera [v.; ~r, ~de, ~t] number

numret [n.; see: **nummer**]

nunnekloster [n.; -klostret, ~] nunnery, convent

nupit [v.past; see: **nypa**]

nutid [adv.] present day, present times

nutida [adj.] contemporary, of today

nuvarande [adj.] present, existing, current

ny [adj.; nytt, nya] new; **~a titlar** new titles; **~a utgåvor** new releases

Ny Framtid [n.] New Future [political party, pro-EU]

nyans [n.; ~en, ~er] shade, nuance

Nya Testamentet [n.] New Testament

Nya Zeeland [n.] New Zealand

nybakad [adj.; -bakat, ~e] freshly baked

nybörjarbacke [n.; ~n, -backar] beginner's slope

nybörjare [n.; ~n, ~] beginner

nybörjarkurs [n.; ~en, ~er] beginner's course

nyckel [n.; ~n, nycklar] key

nyckelben [n.; ~et, ~] collar bone

nyckelfärdig [adj.; ~t, ~a] turnkey [IT]

nyckelhål [n.; ~et, ~] keyhole

nyckelindustri [n.; ~n, ~er] key industry

nyckelord [n.; ~et, ~] keyword [IT]

nyckelpiga [n.; ~n, -pigor] ladybug

nyckelring [n.; ~en, ~ar] key ring

nyfiken [adj.; nyfiket, nyfikna] curious

nyfikenhet [n.; ~en] curiosity, inquisitiveness

nyfödd [adj.; -fött, ~a] newborn

nygift [adj.; ~a] newly married

nyhet [n.; ~en, ~er] piece of news, news; **~er** [n.pl.] news

nyhetsbrev [n.; ~et, ~] newsletter; e-zine [IT]

nyhetsbyrå [n.; ~n, ~er] news agency

nyhetssändning [n.; ~en, ~ar] news broadcast

nykter [adj.; ~t, nyktra] sober

nykterhet [n.; ~en] sobriety; temperance

nykterhetsrörelse [n.; ~n] temperance movement

nyligen [adv.] recently

nylonstrumpor [n.pl.] nylon stockings

nymalen [adj.; -malet, -malna]
freshly ground

nymålad [adj.; -målat, ~e] wet paint

nypa [v.; nyper, nöp, nupit] pinch

nyponsoppa [n.; ~n, -soppor] rose-
hip compote/soup

nysa [v.; nyser, nyste/nös, nyst/nysit]
sneeze

nysilver [n.; -silvret] silver plate

nysnö [n.; ~n] fresh snow, powder
snow

nyss [adv.] just, a short time earlier

nytta [n.; ~n] use, benefit, advantage, utility

nyttig [adj.; ~t, ~a] useful

nyttja [v.; ~r, ~de, ~t] use; partake
of

nyutbildad [adj.; -bildat, ~e] newly
trained, recently graduated trainees

nyval [n.; ~et, ~] new election

nyzeeländsk [adj.; ~t, ~a] of New
Zealand

Nyår [n.; ~et] New Year

nyårsafton [n.; ~en] New Year's
Eve

nyårsdagen [n.] New Year's Day

nyårshelg [n.; ~en] New Year

nyårslöfte [n.; ~t, ~n] New Year's
resolution

nyårsvaka: hålla ~ celebrate New
Year's Eve

nå [v.; når, nådde, nått] reach, get
to, attain

nåd [n.; ~en] grace, mercy; pardon

någon [pron.; något, några] some,
any; someone, anyone; ~ **annan**
somebody else; ~ **annans** somebody else's; ~ **som helst** anybody

någonsin [adv.] ever

någonstans [adv.] somewhere,
anywhere

någonting [pron.] something.
anything

någorlunda [adv.] fairly, reasonably, moderately

något [pron.; see: **någon**] something, anything; ~ **annat** something else

några [pron.pl.; see: **någon**] a few,
several

nåja [interj.] well, oh well

nål [n.; ~en, ~ar] needle, pin

nålsöga [n.; ~t] eye of a needle

nån [pron.; colloq.; see: **någon**]
some, someone

nånting [pron.; colloq.; see:
någonting] something

nånsin [adv.; colloq.; see: **någonsin**] ever

nånstans [pron.; colloq.; see:
någonstans] somewhere

näbb [n.; ~en, ~ar] bill, beak

näckros [n.; ~en, ~or] water lily

näktergal [n.; ~en, ~ar] nightingale

nämen! [interj.] well!, what do you
know! [expressing surprise]

näml. [see: **nämligen**]

nämligen [adv.] you see, namely

nämna [v.; nämner, nämnde,
nämnt] name

nämnd [n.; ~en, ~er] panel, committee, board

nämndeman [n.; -mannen, -män]
lay judge [elected]

**Nämnden för Europeiska
unionen (EU-nämnden)** [n.]
Committee on European Union
Affairs

**Nämnden för offentlig upphand-
ling (NOU)** [n.] National Board
for Public Procurement

när¹ [adv.] when; near; ~ **som helst**
at any time, whenever

när² [conj.] when

nära¹ [adj.; comp.: närmare, när-
mast] near

nära² [adv./prep.] near, nearly,
almost, next to; ~ **affär** close to
shops; ~ **havet** near the sea

närbutik [n.; ~en, ~er] convenience store, minimart

närhet [n.; ~en] vicinity; **i ~en**
nearby; **i ~ av** in the vicinity of

närhetsprincipen [n.] principle of
closeness [to citizens] [EU]

näring [n.; ~en] nourishment;
livelihood; industry

Näringsdepartementet (N) [n.]
Ministry of Industry, Employment
and Communications

näringsfrihetsombudsmannen
[n.] Commissioner for freedom of
trade

näringsliv [n.; ~et] economy,
business

näringslivspolitik [n.; ~en, ~er]
economic policy [EU]

näringsmedel [n.; -medlet, ~]
foodstuff

näringsminister [n.; ~n] Minister
for Industry and Trade

**Närings- och teknikutvecklings-
verket (NUTEK)** [n.] Industrial
and Technical Development
Administration

näringsrik [adj.; ~t, ~a] nutritious

Näringsutskottet [n.] Committee on
Industry and Trade (in Parliament)

näringsvärde [n.; ~t, ~n] nutritional value

närliggande [adj.] related [IT]

närmare [adj.comp.: nära] nearer;
~ **samarbete** enhanced cooperation

närma sig [v.; ~r, ~de, ~t] approach,
get near

närmast [adj.superl.: nära] nearest;
i det ~e nearly, almost

närmiljö [n.; ~n, ~er] local environment, surroundings

närsynt [adj.; ~a] near-sighted

närvarande [adj.] present

närvaro [n.]: **i ~ av** in the presence
of

närvarolista [n.; ~n] attendance list

näröppet [n.] corner shop

näsa [n.; ~n, näsor] nose; **~n rinner
på henne** her nose is running

näsblod [n.; ~et] nosebleed

näsborre [n.; ~n, -borrar] nostril

näsduk [n.; ~en, ~ar] handkerchief

nässelfeber [n.; ~n] hives

nässelsoppa [n.; ~n] nettle soup

näst [adv.] next

nästa [adj.; n.] next; neighbor; **~ år**
next year

nästan [adv.] almost

nästkommande [adv.] next; ~
måndag next Monday

nästkusin [n.; ~en, ~er] second
cousin

nästlad [adj.; -lat, ~e] nested [IT]

nät [n.; ~et, ~] net

nätbaserad [adj.; -rat, ~e] web-
based [IT]

nätbrygga [n.; ~n, -bryggor] gateway [IT]

nätdator [n.; ~n, ~er] network
computer [IT]

nätfiske [n.; ~t] phishing [IT]

näthandel [n.; ~n] e-commerce,
online shopping [IT]

nätikett [n.; ~en] netiquette [IT]

nätnav [n.; ~et, ~] hub [IT]

nätsurfare [n.; ~n, ~] web surfer
[IT]

nätter [n.pl.; see: natt] nights

nättjänstleverantör [n.; ~en, ~er]
network service provider [IT]

nätuttag [n.; ~et, ~] electrical
outlet

nätverk [n.; ~et, ~] network [IT]

nätverksanslutning [n.; ~en, ~ar]
network connection [IT]

nätverksföretag [n.; ~et, ~] network company

nätverkskabel [n.; ~n, -kablar]
network cable [IT]

nätverkskort [n.; ~et, ~] network
card [IT]

nätvett [n.; ~et] netiquette [IT]

nätzine [n.; ~t] netzine, webzine
[IT]

näve [n.; ~en, nävar] fist; fistful

nöd [n.; ~en] need, distress, want; **i
~ och lust** for better or for worse

nödbroms [n.; ~en, ~ar] emergency
brake

nödfall [n.] necessity, emergency

nödlandning [n.; ~en, ~ar] emergency landing

nödläge [n.; ~t, ~n] emergency

nödsignal [n.; ~en, ~er] distress
signal

nödsituation [n.; ~en, ~er]
emergency

nödutgång [n.; ~en, ~ar] emergency exit

nödvändig [adj.; ~t, ~a] essential,
necessary

nödvändigtvis [adv.] necessarily

nöja sig [v.; nöjer, nöjde, nöjt] be
satisfied with, content oneself with

nöjd (med) [adj.; nöjt, nöjda]
pleased (with), enjoying, satisfied
with
nöje [n.; ~t, ~n] pleasure; amusement, entertainment
nöjesfält [n.; ~et, ~] amusement
park, fair ground
nöjesresa [n.; ~n, -resor] pleasure
trip

nöp [v.past; see: **nypa**]
nörd [n.; ~en, ~er] nerd
nös [v.past; see: **nysa**]
nöt [n.; nötten, nötter] nut
nötknäckare [n.; ~n, ~] nutcracker
nötkött [n.; ~et] beef
nötter [n.pl.] nuts

O

o¹ [interj.] oh
o-² [prefix] un-, in-, im-, not
o.³ [abbrev: omkring; och] about; and
O⁴ [abbrev: ostlig] eastern
o.a. [abbrev: och annat, och andra] and others
oacceptabel [adj.; ~t, -tabla] unacceptable
oartig [adj.; ~t, ~a] impolite
oavbruten [adj.; -brutet, -brutna] uninterrupted
oavgjord [adj.; -gjort, ~a] tied game, draw [sports]
oavsedd [adj.; -sett, ~a] unintended
oavsett att [conj.] despite the fact that
oavsiktligen [adv.] unintentionally
obegriplig [adj.; ~t, ~a] incomprehensible
obegränsad [adj.; -sat, ~e] unlimited; ~ självständighet unlimited independence [gram]
obehaglig [adj.; ~t, ~a] unpleasant
obehörig [adj.; ~t, ~a] unauthorized; tillträde förbjudet för ~a no entry unless authorized
obekväm [adj.; ~t, ~a] uncomfortable
obelisk [n.; ~en, ~er] obelisk
oberoende¹ (av) [adj.] independent (of)
oberoende² [n.; ~t] independence
obestämd [adj.; -stämt, ~a] indefinite; ~ artikel indefinite article; ~ form indefinite form [gram]; ~ pronomen [n.] indefinite pronoun [gram]
obesökt [adj.; ~a] unvisited [IT]
obetonad stavelse [n.; ~n, ~r] unstressed syllable
objekt [n.; ~et, ~] object; ~ med infinitiv object with infinitive [gram]
objektiv¹ [adj.; ~t, ~a] objective, unbiased; ~ genitiv objective genitive [gram]; ~ predikatsfyllnad objective complement [gram]
objektiv² [n.; ~en, ~er] objective; lens

objektorienterad programmering [n.; ~en] object-oriented programming [IT]
objektsbisats [n.; ~en, ~er] object clause [gram]
objektsform [n.; ~en] object form [gram]
obl. [see: obligatorisk]
obligatorisk [adj.; ~t, ~a] required, compulsory, mandatory; ~t ämne compulsory subject [school]
obs! [abbrev: observera!] caution!, careful!, watch out!; nota bene!
observation [n.; ~en, ~er] observation
observatorium [n.; -toriet, -torier] observatory
observera [v.; ~r, ~de, ~t] note, observe
ocean [n.; ~en, ~er] ocean
och [conj.; pron.: ock] and; ~ dylikt (o.d.) etc.; ~ så vidare (o.s.v.) and so forth
och/eller [conj.] and/or
och-tecken [n.; -tecknet, ~] ampersand (&) [IT]
också [adv.] also; too
ockupant [n.; ~en, ~er] occupier, occupant; squatter
ockupation [n.; ~en, ~er] occupation
ockupera [v.; ~r, ~de, ~t] occupy
ockuperad [adj.; -rat, ~e] occupied
o.d. [abbrev: och dylikt] etc.
odds [n.pl.; ~en] odds
odemokratisk [adj.; ~t, ~a] undemocratic
odla [v.; ~r, ~de, ~t] cultivate, grow
odlad [adj. odlat, ~e] cultivated
odling [n.; ~en, ~ar] cultivation; plantation
odlingslott [n.; ~en, ~er] rented garden plot
odont. [abbrev: odontologie] dentistry
odont.dr. [abbrev: odontologie doktor] Doctor of Dentistry
odont.kand. [abbrev: odontologie kandidat] Bachelor of Dentistry
odont.lic. [abbrev: odontologie licentiat] Licentiate of Dentistry

odräglig [adj.; ~t, ~a] unbearable; ~**t dyr** unreasonably expensive, rip-off
o.dyl. [abbrev: och dylikt] and the like
odåga [n.; ~n, -gor] good-for-nothing
OECD [abbrev.] Organization for Economic Cooperation and Development (OECD)
oerhörd [adj.; ~t, ~a] unprecedented; enormous
offensiv [adj.; ~t, ~a] offensive; aggressive
offentlig [adj.; ~t, ~a] public; ~ **försvarare** public defender, legal aid lawyer; ~ **upphandling** public procurement [EU]; ~**a tjänster** public services [EU]
offentlighetsprincipen [n.] freedom of information principle
offer [n.; offret, ~] sacrifice; victim, casualty
offert [n.; ~en, ~er] offer, bid, quote
officerare [n.; ~n, ~] officer
officiell [adj.; ~t, ~a] official
offren [n.pl.def; see: offer]
ofreda [v.; ~r, ~de, ~t] molest
ofredande: sexuellt ~ sexual harassment
ofta [adv.] often, frequently
oftast [adv.superl.] in most cases
ofullständig [adj.; ~t, ~a] incomplete, imperfect, defective
oförmåga [n.; ~n] inability, incapacity
oförändrad [adj.; ~t, ~e] unchanged
ogift [adj.; ~a] unmarried
ogräs [n.; ~et] weeds
ogärna [adv.] reluctantly, unwillingly
oheroisk [adj.; ~t, ~a] unheroic
oj! [interj.] oh!, oh dear!, oh my!
ojdå! [interj.] gosh!
ojämförbar [adj.; ~t, ~a] incomparable
ojämn [adj.; ~t, ~a] odd; uneven, irregular, unequal; ~ **väg** uneven road surface
ojäst [adj.; ~a] unleavened
OK [interj.] OK
okej [interj.] okay

oklanderlig [adj.; ~t, ~a] faultless, impeccable
oklar [adj.; ~t, ~a] unclear
okt. [see: oktober]
oktanvärde [n.; ~t, ~] octane rating
oktober [n.] October
okänd [adj.; okänt, ~a] unknown
OLAF [abbrev: Europeiska byrån för bedrägeribekämpning] European Anti-fraud Office (OLAF) [EU]
olaga [adj.] unlawful, illegal
olaglig [adj.; ~t, ~a] unlawful, illegal, illicit
olik [adj.; ~t, ~a] different (from), unlike; ~**a** various
olika [adv.] differently, unequally
oliver [n.pl.] olives
olivolja [n.; ~n] olive oil
olja [n.; ~n] oil
oljebyte [n.; ~t] oil change
oljefilter [n.; -filtret, ~] oil filter
oljefält [n.; ~et, ~] oil field
oljemålning [n.; ~en, ~ar] oil painting
oljemätare [n.; ~n] oil gauge
oljemätsticka [n.; ~n, -stickor] dipstick
oljenivå [n.; ~n, ~er] oil level
oljerigg [n.; ~en, ~ar] oil rig
oljud [n.; ~et] noise
olle [n.; ~n, ollar] thick sweater
olycka [n.; ~n, olyckor] accident
olycklig [adj.; ~t, ~a] unhappy, distressed, unfortunate, ill-fated
olycksbådande [adj.] sinister
olycksfall [n.; ~et, ~] accident
olycksfallsavdelning [n.; ~en] emergency medical service
olycksförsäkring [n.; ~en] accident insurance
olyckshändelse [n.; ~n, ~r] accident, mishap
Olympiska sommarspelen [n.pl.] Summer Olympic Games
Olympiska spelen (OS) [n.pl.] Olympic Games
Olympiska vinterspelen [n.pl.] Winter Olympic Games
olämplig [adj.; ~t, ~a] inappropriate, unwanted [IT]

oläst [adj.; ~a] unread [IT]

om[1] [adv.] around; back; past; again, anew

om[2] [conj.] if; whether; ~ **än** [conj.] even if

om[3] [prep.] around; about; in [time]; ~ **20 minuter** in 20 minutes; ~ **en timma** in an hour; ~ **året** per year

omarbetning av lagstiftning [n.] recasting of legislation [EU]

ombokning [n.; ~en, ~ar] change in reservation

ombord [adv.] on board

ombordstigningskort [n.; ~et, ~] boarding card

ombrytning [n.; ~en] makeup, formatting, layout [IT]

ombud [n.; ~et, ~] representative; deputy; agent

ombudsman [n.; -mannen, -män] ombudsman [official who investigates complaints by citizens against government decisions]

Ombudsmannen mot diskriminering på grund av sexuellläggning (HomO) [n.] Office of the Ombudsman against Discrimination because of Sexual Orientation

Ombudsmannen mot etnisk diskriminering (DO) [n.] Ombudsman against Ethnic Discrimination

ombyggd [adj.; -byggt, ~a] rebuilt

ombyggnad [n.; ~en] refurbishing

omdöme [n.; ~t, ~n] judgment, discrimination; opinion

omedelbar [adj.; ~t, ~a] immediate; natural, spontaneous

omedelbart [adv.] immediately

omelett [n.; ~en, ~er] omelet

omfartsled [n.; ~en] bypass [road]

omfatta [v.; ~r, ~de, ~t] comprise, apply to

omfattande [adj.] comprehensive, extensive

omfattning [n.; ~en] extent, scope, scale

omfördelning [n.; ~en, ~ar] redistribution, reallocation

omg. [see: **omgående**]

omge [v.; -ger, -gav, -givit] surround, encircle

omgivning [n.; ~en, ~ar] environs, surroundings

omgående [adj.] immediately

omgång [n.; ~en, ~ar] round, turn

omklädd [adj.; -klätt, ~a] reupholstered

omklädningsrum [n.; ~et] changing room

omkomma [v.; -kommer, -kom, -kommit] be killed, die

omkopplare [n.; ~n, ~] toggle, switch [A/B] [IT]

omkr. [see: **omkring**]

omkring [adv./prep.] around; about

omkull [adv.] down, over [fall]

omkörning [n.; ~en] passing; ~ **förbjuden** no passing

omläggning [n.; ~en] rearrangement, change; repaving; bandaging, dressing

omm. [abbrev: om och endast om] if and only if (iff)

ommålad [adj.; -målat, ~e] repainted

omodern [adj.; ~t, ~a] out of date

omogen [adj.; -moget, -mogna] unripe, immature

område [n.; ~t, ~n] area, district, land; ~ **med frihet, säkerhet och rättvisa** area of freedom, security and justice [EU]

omröstning [n.; ~en] voting, poll; **sluten** ~ secret ballot

omskaka [v.; ~r, ~de, ~t] shake

omskrivbar [adj.; ~t, ~a] rewritable [IT]

omskärelse [n.; ~n] circumcision

omslag [n.; ~et, ~] wrapping; dust jacket [book]; change [weather]; compress

omslagspapper [n.; -papperet] wrapping paper

omsorg [n.; ~en] care, trouble, pains

omsorgsfull [adj.; ~t, ~a] careful

omstarta [v.; ~r, ~de, ~t] reboot [IT]

omständighet [n.; ~en, ~er] circumstance

omsätta [v.; -sätter, -satt, -sätt] convert, transform; turn over, sell; renew

omsättning [n.; ~en] renewal, prolongation; turnover, business volume

omtumlad [adj.; -tumlat, ~e] shaken up

omval [n.; ~et, ~] new election; re-election

omvandlare [n.; ~n, ~] converter [IT]

omvårdnad [n.; ~en] care, nursing

omväg [n.; ~en, ~ar] detour

omvänd [adj.; ~t, ~a] reverse, opposite; converted; ~ **ordföljd** inverted word order [gram]; **omvänt snedstreck (\)** [n.] backslash [IT]

omvärld [n.; ~en] milieu, environment, surrounding world

omväxlande [adj.] alternating, varied, diversified; changeable

omyndig [adj.; ~t, ~a] underage, minor

omänsklig [adj.; ~t, ~a] inhuman

omättat fett [n.] unsaturated fat

omöjlig [adj.; ~t, ~a] impossible

ond [adj.; ont, onda] bad, evil; angry; aching

onekligen [adv.] undeniably

ons. [see: onsdag]

onsdag [n.; ~en] Wednesday

ont [n.] pain, ache; **göra ~** be painful, hurt; **ha ~ om** be short of; ~ **i halsen** sore throat; ~ **i huvudet** headache; ~ **i magen** stomachache; ~ **i ryggen** backache; ~ **i öronen** earache

onyx [n.; ~en, ~ar] onyx

onödan: i ~ [adv.] unnecessarily, without cause

onödig [adj.; ~t, ~a] unnecessary

oordnad lista [n.] unordered list [IT]

op. [abbev: opus] opus, work

opak [adj.; ~t, ~a] opaque

opal [n.; ~en, ~er] opal

opartisk [adj.; ~t, ~a] impartial, unbiased; non-party

OPEC [abbrev.] Organization of Petroleum Exporting Countries (OPEC)

opera [n.; ~n, operor] opera; opera house

operahus [n.; ~et] opera house

Operahögskolan i Stockholm [n.] College of Opera in Stockholm

operation [n.; ~en, ~er] operation; campaign

operationsanalys [n.; ~en] operations research [IT]

operationssal [n.; ~en, ~ar] operating room

operativsystem [n.; ~et] operating system [IT]

operatör [n.; ~en, ~er] operator [IT]

operera [v.; ~r, ~de, ~t] operate, perform operation

operett [n.; ~en, ~er] operetta

opersonlig [adj.; ~t, ~a] impersonal [gram]

opinion [n.; ~en, ~er] opinion, public opinion

opinionsbildning [n.; ~en] formation of public opinion

opinionssiffror [n.pl.] poll ratings

opinionsundersökning [n.; ~en, ~ar] opinion poll, opinion research

oplacerad [adj.; -rat, ~e] unplaced [sports]

opp [see: **upp**] up

opposition [n.; ~en, ~er] opposition

oppositionsparti [n.; ~et, ~er] party in the opposition

optiker [n.; ~n, ~] optician

optimering [n.; ~en, ~ar] optimization [IT]

optimism [n.; ~en] optimism

optimistisk [adj.; ~t, ~a] optimistic

optisk [adj.; ~t, ~a] optical; ~ **fiber** fiber-optic cable [IT]; ~ **klartextläsning** optical character recognition (OCR) [IT]

oralt [adv.] orally

orange [adj.] orange [color]

ord [n.; ~et, ~] word

ordbehandlare [n.; ~n] word processor [IT]

ordbehandlingsprogram [n.; -grammet, ~] word-processing program [IT]

ordbok [n.; ~en, -böcker] dictionary

ordentlig [adj.; ~t, ~a] proper

ordentligt [adv.] properly

ordf. [abbrev: ordförande] chairman

ordföljd [n.; ~en] word order [gram]

ordförande [n.; ~n, ~] president, chairman

ordförandeskap [n.; ~et] chairmanship, presidency

Ordförandeskapet i Europeiska unionens råd [n.] Presidency of the Council of the European Union [EU]

ordförråd [n.; ~et, ~] vocabulary

ordinarie [adj.] ordinary, regular, established; ~ professor full professor

ordination [n.; ~en, ~er] prescription

ordinera [v.; ~r, ~de. ~t] prescribe

ordklass [n.; ~en, ~er] word class [gram]

ordlista [n.; ~n, -listor] glossary

ordna [v.; ~r, ~de, ~t] arrange; get, obtain; organize, arrange [IT]

ordnad lista [n.; ~n, listor] ordered list [IT]

ordning [n.; ~en, ~ar] order; göra i ~ prepare, fill a prescription

ordningsregel [n.; ~n, -regler] regulation, rule

ordningstal [n.; ~et, ~] ordinal number [gram]

ordspråk [n.; ~et, ~] saying, proverb

ordval [n.; ~et, ~] choice of words

oregano [n.; ~n] oregano

oregelbunden [adj.; -bundet, -bundna] irregular

oregelbundet verb [n.; ~et, ~] irregular verb [gram]

organ [n.; ~et, ~] organ; body, agency

organdonator [n.; ~n, ~er] organ donor

organisation [n.; ~en, ~er] organization

organisera [v.; ~r, ~de, ~t] organize

organiserad [adj.; -rat, ~e] organized; ~ brottslighet organized crime

organisk [adj.; ~t, ~a] organic

organism [n.; ~en, ~er] organism

organist [n.; ~en, ~er] organist

organtransplantation [n.; ~en, ~er] organ transplant

orgel [n.; ~n, orglar] organ [musical instrument]

Orienten [n.] Orient

orientering [n.; ~en] orientation; orienteering

orienteringstavla [n.; ~n, -tavlor] information board; route map

orienteringsämne (OÄ) [n.] general subjects [primary school]

original [n.; ~et, ~] original

originell [adj.; ~t, ~a] unusual

orimlig [adj.; ~t, ~a] unreasonable, preposterous

ork [n.; ~en] energy, strength, stamina

orka [v.; ~r, ~de, ~t] have the energy to

orkan [n.; ~en, ~er] hurricane

orkester [n.; ~n, orkestrar] orchestra

orkesterdike [n.; ~t, ~n] orchestra pit

orkidé [n.; ~n, ~er] orchid

orm [n.; ~en, ~ar] snake, serpent

ormbunke [n.; ~n, -bunkar] fern

ornament [n.; ~et, ~] ornament

ornitologi [n.; ~n] ornithology

oro [n.; ~n] worry

oroa sig [v.; ~r, ~de, ~t] worry [intrans.]

orolig [adj.; ~t, ~a] worried

orre [n.; ~n, orrar] black grouse

orsak [n.; ~en, ~er] cause, reason; ingen ~ don't mention it

orsaka [v.; ~r, ~de, ~t] cause

orsaksadverbial [n.; ~et, ~] causal adverbial [gram]

orsaksbisats [n.; ~en, ~er] causal clause [gram]

orsakskonjunktion [n.; ~en, ~er] causal conjunction [gram]

ort [n.; ~en, ~er] place

ortoped [n.; ~en, ~er] orthopedist

ortopedi [n.; ~n] orthopedics

oräknebart substantiv [n.] noncount noun, uncountable noun [gram]

orättvis [adj.; ~t, ~a] unfair

OS [abbrev: Olympiska spelen] Olympic Games

o.s.a.[1] [abbrev: om svar anhålles] reply requested, R.S.V.P.

osa[2] [v.; ~r, ~de, ~t] smell of smoke, reek

osagd [adj.; osagt, osagda] unsaid

osannolik [adj.; ~t, ~a] unlikely, improbable

oskarp logik [n.; ~en] fuzzy logic [IT]

oskriven [adj.; -vet, -vna] unwritten

oskummad mjölk [n.; ~et] whole milk

oskyldig [adj.; ~t, ~a] innocent, not guilty; inoffensive

OSS[1] [abbrev: Oberoende staters samvälde] Commonwealth of Independent States (CIS)

oss[2] [pron.pl.obj.: vi] us; ourselves

ost [n.; ~en, ~ar] cheese

ostadig [adj.; ~t, ~a] unstable; ~ vägren soft shoulder [road]

osthyvel [n.; ~n, -hyvlar] cheese knife/slicer

ostkaka [n.; ~n, -kakor] curd cake, cheese cake

ostkex [n.; ~et, ~] crackers

ostlig [adj.; ~t, ~a] easterly, from the east

ostron [n.pl.] oysters

ostsmörgås [n.; ~en, ~ar] cheese sandwich

osv. [abbrev: och så vidare] etc., and so forth

osynlig [adj.; ~t, ~a] invisible

osäker [adj.; ~t, -säkra] uncertain

osäkerhet [n.; ~en] uncertainty

otalig [adj.; ~t, ~a] innumerable

otrevlig [adj.; ~t, ~a] unpleasant

otrolig [adj.; ~t, ~a] incredible

otur: vilken ~! [adv.] what bad luck!, what a shame!

otålig [adj.; ~t, ~a] impatient

otäck [adj.; ~t, ~a] nasty, mean

otänkbar [adj.; ~t, ~a] inconceivable, unthinkable

oval [adj.; ~t, ~a] oval

ovanför [adv./prep.] above, higher than; to the north of

ovanlig [adj.; ~t, ~a] unusual

ovanpå [adv.] above, on top, upstairs

oviss [adj.; ~t, ~a] uncertain

oväntad [adj.; -tat, ~e] unexpected

oxbringa [n.; ~n, -bringor] brisket of beef

oxe [n.; ~n, oxar] ox

Oxen [n.] Taurus

oxfilé [n.; ~n, ~er] fillet of beef, tenderloin

oxjärpe [n.; ~n, -järpar] beef meatball

oxkött [n.; ~et] beef

oxrulad [n.; ~en] braised rolled beef

oxsvanssoppa [n.; ~n] ox-tail soup

oxtunga [n.; ~n] beef tongue

oåtkomlig [adj.; ~t, ~a] inaccessible, out of reach

OÄ [abbrev: orienteringsämnen] general subjects [school program]

oäkta [adj.] fake, imitation, not genuine, false

oändlig [adj.; ~t, ~a] endless, infinite, limitless; ~ slinga infinite loop [IT]

oärlig [adj.; ~t, ~a] dishonest

P

P [abbrev: parkering] parking
pacemaker [n.; ~n, -makrar] pacemaker
packa [v.; ~r, ~de, ~t] pack; **~ in** pack up; **~ ner** pack; **~ upp** unpack; **~ ur** unpack
packning [n.; ~en] packing, packaging, wrapping; gasket, washer
paddel [n. ~n, paddlar] paddle
paddla [v.; ~r, ~de, ~t] paddle
pagefrisyr [n.] pageboy [hairstyle]
pain riche [n.; ~n] French bread, baguette
paj [n.; ~en, ~er] pie
paket [n.; ~et, ~] pack, package, parcel; packet, suite (of programs) [IT]
paketförmedling [n.; ~en] packet switching [IT]
paketinlämning [n.; ~en] package counter, package drop-off center
paketpris [n.; ~et, ~] package price
paketresa [n.; ~n, -resor] package tour
Pakistan [n.] Pakistan
pakistansk [adj.; ~t, ~a] Pakistani
palats [n.; ~en, ~er] palace, castle
Palestina [n.] Palestine
palestinier [n.] Palestinian
palestinsk [adj.; ~t, ~a] Palestinian
pall [n.; ~en, ~ar] stool, footstool; pallet
palm [n.; ~en, ~er] palm(tree)
palmsöndagen [n.] Palm Sunday
palsternacka [n.; ~n, -nackor] parsnips
pampuscher [n.pl.] overshoes, galoshes
Panamakanalen [n.] Panama Canal
panel [n.; ~en, ~ar] panel; paneling
panerad [adj.; -rat, ~e] breaded
panik [n.; ~en] panic
panna [n.; ~n, pannor] forehead; pan; boiler, furnace
pannbiff [n.; ~en] hamburger
pannhåla [n.; ~n, -hålor] sinus (frontalis)
pannkaka [n.; ~n, -kakor] pancake
pannkakssmet [n.; ~en] pancake batter

panorama [n.; ~n, -ramor] panorama
pant [n.; ~en, ~er] pledge, security; returnable deposit [glass bottles]
papegoja [n.; ~n, -gojor] parrot
papiljotter [n.pl.] curlers [hair care]
pappa [n.; ~n, pappor] dad, father
pappaledighet [n.; ~en, ~er] paternity leave
papper [n.; papperet, ~] paper, piece of paper
pappersark [n.; ~et, ~] sheet of paper
pappershandel [n.; ~n, ~] stationer
pappersklämma [n.; ~n, -klämmor] paper clip [IT]
papperskorg [n.; ~en, ~ar] wastebasket; recycle bin [IT]
papperslös [adj.; ~t, ~a] paperless; lacking documents, undocumented
pappersnäsduk [n.; ~en, ~ar] paper tissue
pappersservetter [n.pl.] paper napkins
pappersvaror [n.pl.] paper goods; stationers
paprika [n.; ~n, paprikor] pepper [green, red, yellow]; paprika
Papua Nya Guinea [n.] Papua New Guinea
par [n.; ~et, ~] pair, couple; par [golf]
parabel [n.; ~en, ~er] parabola; parable
parabolantenn [n.; ~en, ~er] satellite dish
parad [n.; ~en, ~er] parade; parry
paradigmskifte [n.; ~t, ~n] paradigm shift
paradis [n.; ~et, ~] paradise
paraffin [n.; ~et] paraffin wax
paragraf [n.; ~en, ~er] section, paragraph, article
parallell [adj.; ~t, ~a] parallel
parallellbearbetning [n.; ~en] multiprocessing [IT]
parallellkörning [n.; ~en] multiprocessing, parallel processing [IT]

parameter [n.; ~n, -metrar] parameter [IT]

paraply [n.; ~et, ~er] umbrella; sunshade

parasoll [n.; ~et, ~] parasol, sun umbrella

paratax [n.] parataxis [gram]

parentes [n.; ~en, ~er] parenthesis

parentestecken [n.; -tecknet, ~] parenthesis [IT]

parfym [n.; ~en, ~er] perfume

parfymeri [n.; ~et, ~er] perfume shop, toiletry shop

parhus [n.; ~et, ~] semi-detached house

parisare [n.; ~n, ~] minced beef with capers, onions and fried egg

paritet [n.; ~en] parity [IT]

park [n.; ~en, ~er] park

parkera [v.; ~r, ~de, ~t] park

parkering [n.; ~en, ~ar] parking; parking lot; ~ **förbjuden** no parking; ~ **tillåten** parking permitted

parkeringsautomat [n.; ~en, ~er] parking meter

parkeringsavgift [n.; ~en, ~er] parking fee

parkeringsböter [n.pl.] parking tickets, parking fines

parkeringshus [n.; ~et, ~] multi-storied parking garage

parkeringsmätare [n.; ~n, ~] parking meter

parkeringsplats [n.; ~en, ~er] parking space; parking lot

parkeringsplatsnummer [n.; -numret, ~] parking space number

parkeringsruta [n.; ~n, -rutor] parking space

parkeringsvakt [n.; ~en, ~er] parking lot attendant

parkett [n.; ~en, ~er] orchestra seats [concert hall, theater]

parkettgolv [n.; ~et] parquet floor(ing)

parlament [n.; ~et, ~] parliament

parlamentsutskott [n.; ~et, ~] parliamentary committee

part [n.; ~en, ~er] part; party [legal]

parti [n.; ~et, ~er] party [political]

particip [n.; ~et, ~] participle [gram]

partikel [n.; ~n, partiklar] particle

partikelverb [n.; ~et, ~] phrasal verb [gram]

partiledare [n.; ~n, ~] party leader

partiledardebatt [n.; ~en, ~er] debate among party leaders

partiledning [n.; ~en] party leadership

partisekreterare [n.; ~n] party secretary

partistyrelse [n.; ~n] party leadership, party executive committee

partitionering [n.; ~en, ~ar] partitioning [IT]

partitur [n.; ~et, ~] music score

partner [n.; ~n, ~s] partner

Partnerskap för fred (PFF) [n.; ~et] Partnership For Peace (PFP)

partnerskap inför anslutningen [n.] accession partnership [EU]

party [n.; ~t, ~n] party [recreation]

pass [n.; ~et, ~] passport; gorge, pass; pass, no bid [cards]

passa [v.; ~r, ~de, ~t] adapt; wait for; look after, mind; pass; fit, be suited; take advantage of; ~ **barn** look after children; ~ **in i** fit into; ~ **på** watch out, take care; ~ **till** be suitable (for), go with

passagerare [n.; ~n, ~] passenger

passande [adj.] appropriate, suitable

passare [n.; ~n, ~] compass [drawing instrument]

passera [v.; ~r, ~de, ~t] pass, go by

passfoto [n.; ~t, ~n] passport photo

passiv [adj.; ~t, ~a] passive [gram]; ~ **form** passive voice

passkontroll [n.; ~en, ~er] passport control

passkontrollör [n.; ~en] passport control official

passning [n.; ~en] tending, nursing, looking after; fit, alignment; pass [ball sports]

passnummer [n.; -nummret] passport number

pasta [n.; ~n] pasta; paste

pastej [n.; ~en, ~er] paté; pie

pastor [n.; ~n, ~er] pastor

pastorsexpedition [n.; ~en, ~er] parish office

Patentbesvärsrätten [n.] Court of Patent Appeals
Patent- och registreringsverket (PRV) [n.] National Patent and Registration Office
patient [n.; ~en, ~er] patient
patientavgift [n.; ~en, ~er] fee paid by patient
patientbricka [n.; ~n, -brickor] patient card
patientkort [n.; ~et, ~] patient card
patriot [n.; ~en, ~er] patriot
patron [n.; ~en, ~er] cartridge [rifle, ink, film]
Paulus [n.] Paul
paus [n.; ~en, ~er] intermission, break; rest [music]
paviljong [n.; ~en, ~er] pavilion
PC [abbrev.] personal computer (PC)
pedagog [n.; ~en, ~er] education specialist
pedagogik [n.; ~en] pedagogy, education, teaching methods
pedal [n.; ~en, ~er] pedal
pedikyr [n.; ~en, ~er] pedicure
peka (på) [v.; ~r, ~de, ~t] point (to)
pekande hand [n.; ~en, händer] pointing hand [IT]
pekskärm [n.; ~en, ~ar] touch screen [IT]
pelare [n.; ~n, ~] pillar, column; **EU:s tre ~** EU's three pillars [1: economic, social and environmental policies; 2: foreign policy and military matters; 3: cooperation in the fight against crime]
pelargång [n.; ~en, ~ar] colonnade; cloister
pendeltåg [n.; ~et, ~] commuter train
pendla [v.; ~r, ~de, ~t] swing, vacillate; commute
pendlare [n.; ~n, ~] commuter
pengar [n.pl.] money
penicillin [n.; ~et] penicillin
penis [n.; ~en, ~ar] penis
penna [n.; ~n, pennor] pen
penning[1] [n.; ~en, ~ar] money, coin
penning-[2] [prefix] financial, money
penninglotteri [n.; ~et, ~er] state lottery

penningtvätt [n.; ~en] money laundering
pennkniv [n.; ~en, ~ar] penknife
pennvässare [n.; ~n, ~] pencil sharpener
pensel [n.; ~n, penslar] paint brush [artistic]
pension [n.; ~en, ~er] old age pension; **få ~** get a pension; **gå i ~** retire
pensionat [n.; ~et, ~] guesthouse, boardinghouse
pensionerad [adj.; -rat, ~e] retired
pensionering [n.; ~en, ~ar] retirement, pensioning
pensionsförsäkring [n.; ~en, ~ar] retirement annuity
pensionsålder [n.; ~n] retirement age
pensionär [n.; ~en, ~er] pensioner, senior citizen, retired
Pensionärernas riksorganisation (PRO) [n.; ~en] National Pensioners Organization
pensionärsförening [n.; ~en, ~ar] pensioners' association
pensionärshem [n.; ~et, ~] retirement home
pentry [n.; ~t, ~n] kitchenette; galley [airplane]
peppar [n.; ~n] pepper [spice]
pepparkaka [n.; ~n, -kakor] gingerbread cake/cookie
pepparkaksgubbe [n.; ~n, -gubbar] gingerbread man
pepparkakshus [n.; ~et, ~] gingerbread house
pepparkvarn [n.; ~en, ~ar] pepper grinder, pepper mill
pepparrot [n.; ~en] horseradish
pepparrotskött [n.; ~et] boiled beef with horseradish sauce
pepparrotssås [n.; ~en] horseradish sauce
pepparströare [n.; ~n, ~] pepper shaker
peppra [v.; ~r, ~de, ~t] pepper
per [prep.] per; **~ dag** per day; **~ kilo** per kilo; **~ natt** per night; **~ post** by mail; **~ vecka** per week
perenn [adj.; ~t, ~a] perennial

perf_e_kt¹ [adj.: ~a; adv.] perfect; perfectly

perf_e_kt² [n.; ~et] perfect (tense) [gram]; ~ **partic_i_p** past participle [gram]

periferi_e_nhet [n.; ~en, ~er] peripheral device [IT]

peri_o_d [n.; ~en, ~er] period

perman_e_nt [adj.; ~a] permanent [also hair care]

perman_e_ntad [adj.] permed [hair care]

perman_e_nt upp_e_hållst_i_llstånd (PUT) [n.; ~et] permanent residence permit

permissi_o_n [n.; ~en, ~er] leave, furlough

perr_o_ng [n.; ~en, ~er] platform [train]

pers. [see: **person**]

P_e_rsien [n.] Persia

persi_e_nn [n.; ~en, ~er] Venetian blind

p_e_rsika [n.; ~n, persikor] peach

pers_i_lja [n.; ~n] parsley

pers_i_ljesm_ö_r [n.; ~et] parsley butter

p_e_rsisk [adj.; ~t, ~a] Persian

P_e_rsiska V_i_ken [n.] Persian Gulf

pers_o_n [n.; ~en, ~er] person

person_a_l [n.; ~en] staff, personnel

personal_a_vdelning [n.; ~en] human resources department

personalr_u_m [n.; ~et] staff room

personb_e_vis [n.; ~et] civil status certificate, birth certificate

personb_i_l [n.; ~en, ~ar] private car

pers_o_nd_a_tor [n.; ~n, ~er] personal computer (PC) [IT]

pers_o_nlig [adj.; ~t, ~a] personal; ~ **bruk** personal use; **~a pron_o_men** personal pronoun [gram]; **~t telef_o_nsamtal** person-to-person call

pers_o_nligen [adv.] in person, personally

pers_o_nlighet [n.; ~en, ~er] personality; personage

pers_o_nn_u_mmer [n.; -numret, ~] personal identity number

pers_o_ns_ö_kare [n.; ~n, ~] beeper, pager [IT]

pers_o_nuppgift [n.; ~en, ~er] personal information

person_ä_ndelse [n.; ~n, ~r] ending indicating person [gram]

perspekt_i_v [n.; ~et, ~] perspective; prospect; outlook

Per_u_ [n.] Peru

peru_a_nsk [adj.; ~t, ~a] Peruvian

per_u_k [n.; ~en, ~er] wig

pess_a_r [n.; ~et, ~er] diaphragm [contraceptive], pessary

pessim_i_stisk [adj.; ~t, ~a] pessimistic

pest [n.; ~en, ~er] pest, plague

p_e_ta [v.; ~r, ~de, ~t] pick, poke

P_e_tersberguppdragen [n.pl.] Petersberg tasks [EU]

petit-ch_o_u [n.; ~en, ~er] cream puff

P-förb_u_d [n.; ~et] parking prohibited

pg. [abbrev: p_o_stgiro] postal giro savings service

pga. [abbrev: på grund av] because of, owing to

Phare [abbrev: Progr_a_m för gem_e_nskapsst_ö_d till l_ä_nderna i Centr_a_l- och _Ö_steur_o_pa) Programme of Community aid to the countries of Central and Eastern Europe (Phare) [EU]

pi [n.] pi [math.]

pian_i_st [n.; ~en, ~er] pianist, piano player

pi_a_no [n.; ~t, ~n] piano

pi_a_nost_ä_mmare [n.; ~n, ~] piano tuner

p_i_cknick [n.; ~en, ~ar/~er] picnic

p_i_cknickk_o_rg [n.; ~en, ~ar] picnic basket

p_i_cknick_o_mråde [n.; ~t, ~n] picnic area

p_i_ckolafl_ö_jt [n.; ~en, ~er] piccolo

p_i_ckolo [n.; ~n, ~r] bellhop, page; porter

pigg [adj.; ~t, ~a] fit, alert

p_i_ggvar [n.; ~en, ~ar] turbot [fish]

pil [n.; ~en, ~ar] arrow; willow

p_i_lgrimsk_y_rka [n.; ~n, -kyrkor] pilgrimage church

p_i_lgrimsm_u_sslor [n.pl.] scallops

p_i_ller [n.; pillret, ~] pill

p_i_llerb_u_rk [n.; ~en, -burkar] pillbox

pil_o_t [n.; ~en, ~er] pilot

pil_o_tst_u_die [n.; ~n, ~r] pilot study

piltangent [n.; ~en, ~er] arrow key, cursor movement key [IT]

pincett [n.; ~en, ~er] tweezers

Pingstdagen [n.] Pentecost [seventh Sunday after Easter]

pingstlilja [n.; ~n, -liljor] (white) narcissus

pingströrelsen [n.] Pentecostal movement

pingvin [n.; ~en, ~er] penguin

PIN-kod [n.; ~en, ~er] PIN code, PIN number

pinne [n.; ~n, pinnar] peg, stick, rung

pinnmat [n.; ~en] small snacks, appetizers, munchies

pinsam [adj.; ~t, ~a] painful; embarrassing, awkward

pion [n.; ~en, ~er] peony

pipa¹ [n.; ~n, pipor] pipe

pipa² [v.; piper, pep, pipit] chirp, squeak, wheeze

pirat [n.; ~en, ~er] pirate

piratkopiering [n.; ~en] pirate copying, pirating [IT]

piska [v.; ~r, ~de, ~t] whip, flog; beat; ~ **mattor** beat carpets

piss [n.; colloq.; ~et] piss [vul.]

pissa [v.; colloq.; ~r, ~de, ~t] piss [vul.]

pist [n.; ~en, ~er] slope, ski trail

pistachglass [n.; ~en] pistachio ice cream

pistmaskin [n.; ~en, ~er] snow-grooming machine [ski slope]

pistol [n.; ~en, ~er] pistol

pitabröd [n.; ~et] pita bread

pittoresk [adj.; ~t, ~a] picturesque

pivottabell [n.; ~en, ~er] pivot table [IT]

pixel [n.; ~n, pixlar] pixel [IT]

pizza [n.; ~n, pizzor] pizza

pjäs [n.; ~en, ~er] play [theater]

pjäxor [n.pl.] ski boots

placera [v.; ~r, ~de, ~t] place; invest

placering [n.; ~en, ~ar] placing; investment; rank [in competition]

plagg [n.; ~et, ~] piece of clothing

plakat [n.; ~en, ~er] placard, poster

plan¹ [n.; ~et, ~] open area, field; plan, scheme; map

plan² [n.; ~en, ~er] plane; level, floor; airplane

planera [v.; ~r, ~de, ~t] plan

planering [n.; ~en, ~ar] planning

planeringskalender [n.; ~n, -kalendrar] personal organizer, planner

planet [n.; ~en, ~er] planet

planetarium [n.; -tariet, -tarier] planetarium

plankstek [n.; ~en, ~ar] plank(ed) steak [steak on a board]

plankurvritare [n.; ~n, ~] flatbed plotter [IT]

planmässig [adj.; ~t, ~a] proceeding according to plan

planskild korsning [n.; ~en] highway interchange; overpass/underpass

planta [n.; ~n, plantor] young plant, seedling

plantera [v.; ~r, ~de, ~t] plant

plantering [n.; ~en, ~ar] small park, garden

planteringsspade [n.; ~n, -spadar] trowel

plantskola [n.; ~n, -skolor] garden center

plaskdamm [n.; ~en, ~ar] wading pool

plasmabildskärm [n.; ~en, ~ar] plasma display [IT]

plast [n.; ~en, ~er] plastic

plastfolie [n.; ~n, ~r] plastic wrap

plastpåse [n.; ~n, -påsar] plastic bag

platan [n.; ~en, ~er] plane (tree), buttonwood, sycamore

platina [n.; ~n] platinum

Platon [n.] Platon

plats [n.; ~en, ~er] place; room; seat; square

platsannons [n.; ~en, ~er] employment ad, help-wanted ad

platsansökan [n.; pl. -ansökningar] job application

platsbiljett [n.; ~en, ~er] seat reservation [in addition to ticket]

Platsjournalen [n.] weekly paper listing jobs available

platshållare [n.; ~n, ~] place holder [IT]

platskarta [n.; ~n, -kartor] site map [IT]

platsmarkering [n.; ~en, ~ar] place holder [IT]

platsnummer [n.; -numret, ~] seat number

platssökande [n.; ~n, ~] job applicant

platt [adj.; ~a] flat; ~ fil flat file [IT]

platta[1] [n.; ~n, plattor] hotplate; tile; phonograph record

platta[2] (till) [v.; ~r, ~de, ~t] flatten, squash; smooth down

plattform [n.; ~en, ~ar] platform

plattformsoberoende [adj.] cross-platform, platform independent [IT]

plikt [n.; ~en, ~er] duty; fine

Pliktverket [n.] Military Service Administration

plocka [v.; ~r, ~de, ~t] pick, gather; ~ blommor/bär/svamp pick flowers/berries/mushrooms

plockepinn [n.; ~et] pick-up sticks

ploga [v.; ~r, ~de, ~t] clear of snow, plow

plomb [n.; ~en, ~er] filling [tooth]

plommon [n.; ~et, ~] plum

plommonträd [n.; ~et, ~] plum tree

plugga [v.; ~r, ~de, ~t] plug, stop up; study hard, cram

plural [n.; ~en] plural [gram]

plus[1] [adv.] plus

plus[2] [n.; ~et, ~] advantage, asset

pluskvamperfekt [n.; ~et] pluperfect [gram]

plustecken (+) [n.; -tecknet, ~] plus sign (+) [IT]

Pluto [n.] Pluto

plåga [v.; ~r, ~de, ~t] pain, torment; plague, bother

plånbok [n.; ~en, -böcker] wallet

plåster [n.; plåstret, ~] adhesive bandage

plåstra om [v.; ~r, ~de, ~t] patch up, tend to someone's wounds

plättar [n.pl.] small pancakes

plötslig [adj.; ~t, ~a] sudden

PM [abbrev: promemoria] memo

PO [abbrev: Pressombudsmannen] Press Ombudsman

pocherad [adj.; -rat, ~e] poached [egg, fish]

pocketbok [n.; ~en, -böcker] paperback, pocket book

podium [n.; podiet, podier] podium, platform; catwalk [fashion]

poem [n.; ~et, ~] poem

poesi [n.; ~n] poetry

poet [n.; ~en, ~er] poet

pojke [n.; ~n, pojkar] boy

pojkvän [n.; -vännen, -vänner] boyfriend

pol[1] [n.; ~en, ~er] pole

pol.[2] [abbrev: politices] political science [study, degree]

polack [n.; ~en, ~er] Pole

Polarforskningssekretariatet [n.] Polar Research Secretariat

polcirkeln [n.] Arctic/Antarctic Circle

Polen [n.] Poland

poliklinik [n.; ~en, ~er] outpatient clinic

polio [n.; ~n] polio

poliovaccin [n.; ~et, ~er] polio vaccine

polis [n.; ~en] police; policeman

polisanmäla [v.; -anmäler, -anmälde, -anmält] report something to the police

polisanmälan [n.] report/complaint to the police

polisbil [n.; ~en, -bilar] police car

polishögskola [n.; ~n, -skolor] police academy

poliskontroll [n.; ~en, ~er] police check, police check-point

polisman [n.; -mannen, -män] policeman

polismyndighet [n.; ~en, ~er] police authority

polismästare [n.; ~n, ~] police commissioner

polisonger [n.pl.] sideburns

polisrapport [n.; ~en, ~er] police report

polissamarbete och straffrättsligt samarbete [n.] police and judicial cooperation in criminal matters [EU]

polisstation [n.; ~en, ~er] police station

politik [n.; ~en] politics; policy

politiker [n.; ~n, ~] politician

politisk [adj.; ~t, ~a] political; ~
fånge political prisoner; ~ **kupp**
political coup; ~ **sakkunnig** political adviser

polka [n.; ~n, polkor] polka

pollenhalt [n.; ~en, ~er] pollen count

pollett [n.; ~en, ~er] check, token

pollettera bagaget [v.] check (in)
one's baggage [on train]

pol.mag. [abbrev: politices magis-
ter] master's degree in economics
and political science

polokrage [n.; ~n, -kragar] turtleneck

polsk [adj.; ~t, ~a] Polish

polska [n.; ~] Polish woman; Polish language; reel dance

Polstjärnan [n.] North Star

pommes frites [n.pl.] french fries

pop [n.; ~en] pop [music]

popcorn [n.] popcorn

popgrupp [n.; ~en, ~er] pop group

popkonsert [n.; ~en, ~er] pop
concert

popmusik [n.; ~en] pop music

poppel [n.; ~n, popplar] poplar

POP-server [n.; ~n, -servrar] POP
server [for incoming e-mail] [IT]

populär [adj.; ~t, ~a] popular

popup-fönster [n.; -fönstret, ~]
pop-up window [IT]

popup-meny [n.; ~n, ~er] pop-up
menu, shortcut menu [IT]

pornografisk [adj.; ~t, ~a] porno-
graphic

porr [n.; ~en] pornography, porn

porslin [n.; ~et] dishes, crockery;
porcelain

port [n.; ~en, ~ar] front door,
entrance gate

portabel [adj.; ~t, portabla] portable

portabilitet [n.; ~en] portability [IT]

portal [n.; ~en, ~er] portal

porter [n.; ~n, ~] stout, porter [beer]

portfölj [n.; ~en, ~er] briefcase

portföljdator [n.; ~n, ~er] laptop
computer [IT]

portier [n.; ~en, ~er] reception
clerk, desk clerk

portion [n.; ~en, ~er] portion;
extra ~ side order; **barn-~** children's portion

portmonnä [n.; ~n, ~er] purse

porto [n.; ~t, ~n] shipping charge,
postage

portofritt [adv.] postpaid

portotabell [n.; ~en, ~er] list of
postage rates

porträtt [n.; ~et, ~] portrait

Portugal [n.] Portugal

portugisisk [adj.; ~t, ~a] Portuguese

portugisiska [n.] Portuguese
language

portvakt [n.; ~en, ~er] doorman;
janitor

portvin [n.; ~et, ~er] port

position [n.; ~en, ~er] position

positiv [adj.; ~t, ~a] positive

possessiv [adj.; ~t, ~a] possessive;
~ **genitiv** possessive genitive
[gram]; **~t pronomen** possessive
pronoun [gram]

post [n.; ~en, ~er] mail; post office;
record [database] [IT]

posta [v.; ~r, ~de, ~t] mail, send by
mail/e-mail

postadress [n.; ~en, ~er] mailing
address

postanvisning [n.; ~en, ~ar] money
order

posten [n.] post office

poste restante [n.] general delivery
[post office holds mail]

postförskott [n.; ~et] cash on
delivery

postgiro [n.; ~t, ~n] postal bank
account [for paying bills through
transfers]

postkontor [n.; ~et, ~] post office

postlucka [n.; ~n, -luckor] window
at post office

postlåda [n.; ~n, -lådor] mailbox

postlåsning [n.; ~en] record locking [IT]

postnummer [n.; -numret, ~]
postal code, zip code

Post- och telestyrelsen (PTS) [n.]
National Postal and Telecommunications Agency

postorder [n.; ~n, ~] mail order

postorderfirma [n.; ~n, -firmor]
mail order company

poströsta [v.; ~r, ~de, ~t] vote by
mail

postsparbank [n.; ~en] post-office savings bank

poststämpel [n.; ~n, -stämplar] postmark

potatis [n.; ~en, ~ar] potato

potatischips [n.; ~et, ~] potato chips

potatisgratäng [n.; ~en] potatoes au gratin

potatismos [n.; ~et] mashed potatoes

potatisskalare [n.; ~n, ~] potato peeler

potatissoppa [n.; ~n, -soppor] potato soup

potential [n.; ~en, ~er] potential

potentiell [adj.; ~t, ~a] potential, possible

poäng [n.; ~en, ~er] point

poängs: fempoängskurs [n.] 5-credit course

p-piller [n.; -pillret, ~] contraceptive pill

p-plats [abbrev: parkeringsplats] parking place

PR [abbrev.] public relations (PR)

Prag [n.] Prague

pragmatisk [adj.; ~t, ~a] pragmatic

praktik [n.; ~en] practice

praktikant [n.; ~en, ~er] trainee

praktisk [adj.; ~t, ~a] practical; ~ **arbetslivsorientering i skolan (prao)** practical work experience in school

praktiskt taget [adv.] practically, nearly

pralin [n.; ~en, ~er] (cream-filled) chocolate confection

prao [see: praktisk arbetslivsorientering i skolan]

prata (om) [v.; ~r, ~de, ~t] talk (about); speak (about); ~ **i telefon** be on the phone

pratshow [n.; ~n, ~er] talk show

praxis [n.; ~en] practice, custom

precis [adv.] just, precisely, exactly, quite; **inte** ~ not exactly

precisera [v.; ~r, ~de, ~t] specify, define, clarify

predika [v.; ~r, ~de, ~t] preach

predikat [n.; ~et, ~] predicate [gram]

predikativ [adj.; ~t, ~a] predicative [gram]; **~t attribut** predicative attribute [gram]

predikatsdel [n.; ~en, ~ar] predicate component [gram]

predikatsfyllnad [n.; ~en, ~er] predicative complement [gram]

predikstol [n.; ~en, ~ar] pulpit

prefix [n.; ~en, ~er] prefix

preliminär [adj.; ~t, ~a] preliminary; provisional

preliminärskatt [n.; ~en, ~er] withholding tax

premie [n.; ~n, ~r] premium, bonus

Premiepensionsmyndigheten (PPM) [n.] Premium Pension Authority

premium [n.] premium [gasoline]

premiär [n.; ~en, ~er] premiere, opening night

premiärminister [n.; ~n, -ministrar] prime minister

prenumeration [n.; ~en, ~er] subscription

prenumerera (på) [v.; ~r, ~de, ~t] subscribe (to)

preparat [n.; ~et, ~] preparation; specimen, slide

preposition [n.; ~en, ~er] preposition [gram]

prepositionsattribut [n.; ~et, ~] prepositional attribute [gram]

prepositionsverb [n.; ~et, ~] phrasal verb [gram]

presens [n.] present [gram]; ~ **particip** present participle [gram]

present [n.; ~en, ~er] present, gift

presentaffär [n.; ~en, ~er] gift shop

presentation [n.; ~en, ~er] introduction, presentation

presentera [v.; ~r, ~de, ~t] introduce; **jag vill ~ dig för min fru** I want to introduce you to my wife; ~ **sig** introduce oneself

presentkort [n.; ~et, ~] gift certificate

presentshop [n.; -shoppen, -shopper] gift shop

president [n.; ~en, ~er] president

presidentkandidat [n.; ~en, ~er] presidential candidate

presidentval [n.; ~et, ~] presidential election

preskriptiv [adj.; ~t, ~a] prescriptive [gram]

press [n.; ~en, ~ar] press; pressure; crease

pressa [v.; ~r, ~de, ~t] press, iron; squeeze

pressbyrå [n.; ~n, ~er] press agency

pressekreterare [n.; ~n, ~] press secretary

Pressens Opinionsnämnd [n.] National Press Council

pressfoder [n.; -fodret] silage

presskonferens [n.; ~en, ~er] press conference

pressmeddelande [n.; ~t, ~n] press release

Presstödsnämnden [n.] Press Subsidies Board

pressylta [n.; ~n] headcheese

prestation [n.; ~en, ~er] performance, achievement

preteritum [n.] simple past tense, preterite, imperfect [gram]

preventivmedel [n.; -medlet, ~] contraceptive

prick [n.; ~en, ~ar] dot; **~ar** dotted line [IT]

primula [n.] primrose

primuskök [n.; ~et, ~] kerosene stove

primärnyckel [n.; ~n, -nycklar] primary key [IT]

primärrätt [n.; ~en] primary law [EU: treaties and accession agreements]

princip [n.; ~en, ~er] principle; **~en om förbud mot diskriminering** non-discrimination principle [EU]

prins [n.; ~en, ~ar] prince

prinsessa [n.; ~n, prinsessor] princess

prinsesstårta [n.; ~n, -tårtor] sponge cake with custard and almond paste

prinskorv [n.; ~en, ~ar] small sausage

prioritet [n.; ~en] priority

pris [n.; ~en, ~ar] price; prize; **~ per förpackning** price per package; **~ per liter** price per liter; **~ per rum** rate per room

prisklass [n.; ~en, ~er] price category

prislapp [n.; ~en, ~ar] price tag

prisutdelning [n.; ~en] distribution/awarding of prizes

privat [adj.; ~a] private; **~ område** private property

privatbilism [n.; ~en] private automobile use/traffic

privatdetektiv [n.; ~en, ~er] private detective

privatisera [v.; ~r, ~de, ~t] privatize

privatisering [n.; ~en, ~ar] privatization

privatrum [n.; -rummet, ~] private room

privatskola [n.; ~n, -skolor] private school

PRO [abbrev: Pensionärernas riksorganisation] National Pensioners Organization

problem [n.; ~et, ~] problem

procent [n.; ~en, ~] percent [IT]

procentandel [n.; ~en, ~ar] percentage [IT]

procentenhet [n.; ~en, ~er] percentage point

process [n.; ~en, ~er] lawsuit, proceedings; process, procedure

processor [n.; ~n, ~er] processor [IT]

producent [n.; ~en, ~er] producer [film, TV]

producera [v.; ~r, ~de, ~t] produce, manufacture

produkt [n.; ~en, ~er] product

produktion [n.; ~en, ~er] production

produktiv [adv.; ~t, ~a] productive

prof. [abbrev: professor] professor

profan [adj.; ~t, ~a] profane

professionell [adj.; ~t, ~a] professional

professor [n.; ~n, ~er] professor, full professor

profet [n.; ~en, ~er] prophet

proffs [n.; colloq.] pro, professional player [sports]

profil [n.; ~en, ~er] profile

profitera [v.; ~r, ~de, ~t] profit

prognos [n.; ~en, ~er] prognosis, forecast

program [n.; -grammet, ~] program, software [IT]

programbibliotek [n.; ~et, ~] program library, download site [IT]

programfil [n.; ~en, ~er] program
file [IT]

programfix [n.; ~en, ~er] patch [IT]

programkrasch [n.; ~en, ~er] fatal
error [IT]

programledare [n.; ~n] master of
ceremonies (MC); chairman
[debate]

programmerare [n.; ~n, ~]
programmer [IT]

programmeringsspråk [n.; ~et, ~]
programming language [IT]

programmodul [n.; ~en, ~er] program module [IT]

programspråk [n.; ~et, ~] programming language [IT]

programvara [n.; ~n, -varor]
software [IT]

progressiv [adj.; ~t, ~a] progressive

projekt [n.; ~et, ~] project, plan,
scheme

projektledare [n.; ~n, ~] project
leader

promemoria [n.; ~n, -memorior]
memo

promenad [n.; ~en, ~er] walk, stroll

promenera [v.; ~r, ~de, ~t] walk

promillegräns [n.; ~en, ~er] legal
blood alcohol limit

promillehalt [n.; ~en, ~er] blood
alcohol level

promotion [n.; ~en, ~er] conferral
of doctoral degrees; promotion

prompt [n.; ~en] prompt [IT]

pronomen [n.; ~et, ~] pronoun
[gram]

pronominaladverb [n.; ~et, ~]
pronominal adverb [gram]

propagera [v.; ~r, ~de, ~t] advocate

proportionalitetsprincipen [n.]
proportionality principle [EU]

proposition [n.; ~en, ~er] proposal,
bill [government]; proposition

propp [n.; ~en, ~ar] stopper; clot;
fuse

prostatbesvär [n.; ~et, ~] prostate
problem

prostituerad [n.] prostitute

protest [n.; ~en, ~er] protest; ~
godkännes objection sustained; ~
ogillas objection overruled

protestantisk [adj.; ~t, ~a]
Protestant

protestera [v.; ~r, ~de, ~t] protest,
object

protokoll [n.; ~et, ~] minutes, record;
protocol [IT]

prov [n.; ~et, ~] test; sample,
specimen

prova [v.; ~r, ~de, ~t] try out, test;
try on

provanställd [adj.; -ställt, ~a] on
probationary employment status

provanställning [n.; ~en, ~ar]
probationary employment

provhytt [n.; ~en, ~er] fitting room

provins [n.; ~en, ~er] province

provisorisk [adj.; ~t, ~a] provisional, temporary

provocera [v.; ~r, ~de, ~t] provoke,
incite

provokatorisk [adj.; ~t, ~a]
provocative

provrum [n.; -rummet, ~] fitting
room

provsmaka [v.; ~r, ~de, ~t] taste
[food]

provtagning [n.; ~en, ~ar] taking
of samples for testing [blood,
urine, etc.]

provversion [n.; ~en, ~er] trial version [IT]

proxyserver [n.; ~n, -servrar] proxy
server [IT]

pruta [v.; ~r, ~de, ~t] bargain,
haggle

prutt [n.; colloq.; ~en, ~ar] fart
[colloq.]

prutta [v.; colloq.; ~r, ~de, ~t] fart
[colloq.]

pryda [v.; pryder, prydde, prytt]
adorn, decorate

prydnadssaker [n.pl.] knickknacks,
bric-a-brac, trinkets

pryo [abbrev.; ~n, ~r] practical introduction to working life [school
program]

prägla [v.; ~r, ~de, ~t] coin, mint;
characterize

präst [n.; ~en, ~er] priest, clergyman

prästgård [n.; ~en, ~ar] parsonage,
vicarage

prästost [n.; ~en, ~ar] granular hard cheese [cows milk]

pröva [v.; ~r, ~de, ~t] try

prövning [n.; ~en, ~ar] test, trial; inquiry; ordeal

PS [abbrev: postskriptum] PS [abbrev: post script]

psalm [n.; ~en, ~er] psalm; hymn

psalmbok [n.; ~en, -böcker] hymnal

Psaltaren [n.] Book of Psalms

psykiatriker [n.; ~n, ~] psychiatrist

psykiatrisk [adj.; ~t, ~a] psychiatric

psykisk [adj.; ~t, ~a] psychic, mental; ~ sjukdom mental illness

psykiskt funktionshindrad [adj.] mentally handicapped

psykolog [n.; ~en, ~er] psychologist

psykologi [n.; ~n] psychology

psykologisk [n.; ~t, ~a] psychological

PTS [abbrev: Post- och telestyrelsen] National Postal and Telecommunications Agency

pub [n.; pubben, pubbar] pub

publicera [v.; ~r, ~de, ~t] publish [IT]

publicering [n.; ~en, ~ar] publication [IT]

publik¹ [adj.; ~t, ~a] public; ~a nycklar public keys [encryption] [IT]

publik² [n.; ~en] audience, crowd, the public

puckelpist [n.; ~en, ~er] mogul slope

pudding [n.; ~en, ~ar] baked casserole

pudel [n.; ~n, pudlar] poodle

puder [n.; pudret] powder

puderdosa [n.; ~n, -dosor] powder compact

pudersnö [n.; ~n] powder snow

puderunderlag [n.; ~et] foundation cream, powder base

pudervippa [n.; ~n, -vippor] powder puff

puka [n.; ~n, pukor] kettle drum

pull-teknik [n.; ~en] pull technology [IT]

pulpet [n.; ~en, ~er] pulpit; desk

puls [n.; ~en, ~ar] pulse; ta ~en på ngn take/feel someone's pulse

pulserande [adj.] throbbing, pulsating

pulver [n.; pulvret, ~] powder

pump [n.; ~en, ~ar] pump

pumpa¹ [n.; ~n, pumpor] pumpkin

pumpa² [v.; ~r, ~de, ~t] pump

pund [n.; ~et, ~] pound

punkt [n.; ~en, ~er] dot; period; point [font size] [IT]

punktering [n.; ~en, ~ar] flat tire, puncture

punkteringssats [n.; ~en, ~er] puncture repair kit

punktlig [adj.; ~t, ~a] punctual; accurate

punktskatt [n.; ~en, ~er] selective/specific sales tax

punktskrift [n.; ~en, ~er] braille

punsch [n.; ~en] sweet after-dinner liqueur flavored with arrack

puppa [n.; ~n, puppor] pupa, chrysalis

purjolök [n.; ~en] leek

push-teknik [n.; ~en] push technology, webcasting [IT]

pussel [n.; pusslet, ~] puzzle

PUT [abbrev: permanent uppehållstillstånd] permanent residence permit

putsa [v.; ~r, ~de, ~t] clean, polish; trim [hair]

putsning [n.; ~en, ~er] cleaning, trimming; improvement

putter [n.; ~n] putter [golf]

pyjamas [n.; ~en, ~er] pajamas

pyramidspel [n.; ~et, ~] pyramid scheme

pyssla [v.; ~r, ~de, ~t] putter around

pyttipanna [n.] hash [chopped meat, potatoes, onions and fried egg]

på [prep.] in, at; on; into; vi sitter ~ vår plats we are sitting in our seats; ~ eftermiddagen in the afternoon; ~ grund av (pga.) because of; ~ hotellet at the hotel; ~ hösten in the fall; ~ Internet online [IT]; ~ kartan on the map; ~ kontoret at the office; ~ krogen at the restaurant; ~ kvällarna in the evenings; ~ landet in the country; ~ morgonen in the

morning; ~ **recept** by prescription;
~ **rummet** in the room; ~ **svenska**
in Swedish; ~ **söndag** on Sunday;
~ **tåget** on the train
påannonsera [v.; ~r, ~de, ~t] announce, present [TV, radio]
påbudsmärke [n.; ~t, ~n] mandatory sign [traffic sign indicating
mandatory action]
påfallande [adj.] striking, remarkable
påfågel [n.; ~n, -fåglar] peacock
pågå [v.; -går, -gick, -gått] be going
on, be in progress
pågående [adj.] in progress, current,
present
påhopp [n.; ~et, ~] attack
pålitlig [adj.; ~t, ~a] reliable
pålägg [n.; ~et, ~] toppings, spreads
[meat, cheese, etc. for sandwiches]
påminna (om) [v.; ~minner,
~minde, ~mint] remind (of)
påpeka [v.; ~r, ~de, ~t] point out,
observe
påse [n.; ~n, påsar] bag
Påsk [n.; ~en] Easter; Passover;
Glad Påsk! Happy Easter!
påskalamm [n.; ~et, ~] Easter lamb
Påskdagen [n.] Easter Sunday
påskhare [n.; ~n, -harar] Easter
bunny
påskhelg [n.; ~en, ~er] Easter
holiday
påsklilja [n.; ~n, -liljor] daffodil;
Easter lily
påsklov [n.; ~et, ~] Easter vacation
påskägg [n.; ~et, ~] Easter egg
påssjuka [n.; ~n] mumps
påstigning [n.; ~en] boarding [train,
bus]

påstigningshjälp [n.; ~en] boarding assistance
påstå [v.; -står, -stod, -stått]
maintain
påstående [n.; ~t, ~n] statement,
assertion
påståendesats [n.; ~en, ~er] declar-
ative clause [gram]
påtaglig [adj.; ~t, ~a] obvious,
evident; tangible
påtryckning [n.; ~en, ~ar] pressure
påtryckningsgrupp [n.; ~en, ~er]
pressure group, lobby
påträffa [v.; ~r, ~de, ~t] find, come
across
påve [n.; ~n] Pope
påverka [v.; ~r, ~de, ~t] influence,
affect
påverkan [n.; pl. påverkningar]
influence, effect
päls [n.; ~en, ~ar] fur coat
pälsaffär [n.; ~en, ~er] fur dealer
pälsfodrad [adj.; -fodrat, ~e]
fur-lined
pälsindustri [n.; ~n, ~er] fur industry
pärla [n.; ~n, pärlor] pearl; bead
pärlande [adj.] sparkling
pärlemor [n.; ~n] mother of pearl
pärlhalsband [n.; ~et, ~] pearl
necklace
pärlhöns [n.; ~et, ~] guinea fowl
pärm [n.; ~en, ~ar] folder
päron [n.; ~et, ~] pear
päronträd [n.; ~et, ~] pear tree
pöbel [n.; ~n] riff-raff, mob
pölsa [n.; ~n] hash of boiled pork
(offal) and barley

Q

quenell [n.; ~en, ~er] quenelle
    [fish/chicken paste dumpling]
quiche [n.; ~n, ~r] quiche

R

rabarber [n.; ~n, ~] rhubarb

rabarberkompott [n.; ~en] stewed rhubarb

rabatt [n.; ~en, ~er] reduction, discount

rabatthäfte [n.; ~t, ~n] booklet of tickets

rabattvaruhus [n.; ~et, ~] discount store

rabbin [n.; ~en, ~er] rabbi

racerbil [n.; ~en, ~ar] racing car

racket [n.; ~en, ~ar] racket

rad [n.; ~en, ~er] row, series; line; **i ~ running**, one after another, in a row

radarkontroll [n.; ~en, ~er] radar speed check

radbrytning [n.; ~en, ~ar] line break; text wrap [IT]

radera [v.; ~r, ~de, ~t] delete [IT]

radergummi [n.; ~t, ~n] eraser

radframmåtning [n.; ~en, ~ar] line feed [IT]

radhus [n.; ~et, ~] row house

radhuvud [n.; ~et, ~] row header [IT]

radie [n.; ~n, ~r] radius

radikal [adj.; ~t, ~a] radical

radio [n.; ~n, ~r] radio; **Sveriges Radio** Swedish Broadcasting Corporation

radioaktiv [adj.; ~t, ~a] radioactive

radioaktivitet [n.; ~en] radioactivity

radioapparat [n.; ~en, ~er] radio set

radiolyssnare [n.; ~n, ~] radio listener

Radio- och TV-verket (RTV) [n.] Radio and Television Administration

radioprogram [n.; -grammet, ~] radio program

radioreportage [n.; ~t, ~] radio reporting/commentary

radmatning [n.; ~en, ~ar] line feed [IT]

raffig [adj.; ~t, ~a; colloq.] stunning

raggare [n.; ~n, ~; colloq.] teenage hot-rodder

raggmunk med fläsk [n.] potato pancake with bacon

ragu [n.; ~n, ~er] beef stew

rak [adj.; ~t, ~a] straight; **~ kabel** straight cable [IT]; **~ ordföljd** normal word order [gram]

rakapparat [n.; ~en, ~er] razor, shaver

raka sig [v.; ~r, ~de, ~t] shave (oneself)

rakblad [n.; ~et, ~] razor blade

rakborste [n.; ~n, -borstar] shaving brush

raket [n.; ~en, ~er] rocket, missile

rakhyvel [n.; ~n, -hyvlar] safety razor

rakkniv [n.; ~en, ~ar] straight razor

rakkräm [n.; ~en] shaving cream

rakning [n.; ~en, ~ar] shave

rakt [adv.] straight; **~ fram** straight ahead

raktvål [n.; ~en, ~ar] shaving soap

rakvatten [n.; -vattnet] aftershave lotion

ram[1] [n.; ~en, ~ar] frame

RAM[2] [n.] random access memory (RAM) [IT]

rambeslut [n.; ~et. ~] framework decision [EU]

ramla [v.; ~r, ~de, ~t] fall

ramp [n.; ~en, ~er] ramp

rampfeber [n.; ~n] stage fright

ramteknik [n.; ~en] use of frames, frames technique [IT]

rand [n.; ~en, ränder] stripe

randig [adj.; ~t, ~a] striped

rangordning mellan gemenskaps-rättsakter [n.] hierarchy of Community acts, hierarchy of norms [EU]

rann [v.past; see: **rinna**]

ranson [n.; ~en, ~er] ration, portion, allowance

rapning [n.; ~en, ~ar] belch, burp

rapp [n.] rap [music]

rapphöna [n.; ~n, -hönor] partridge

rapport [n.; ~en, ~er] report, account

rapportera [v.; ~r, ~de, ~t] make a report, make a statement

rar [adj.; ~t, ~a] rare; nice, sweet

ras[1] [n.; ~en, ~er] race, breed

ras[2] [n.; ~et, ~] landslide; collapse

rasa [v.; ~r, ~de, ~t] give way, collapse; rampage, rage

rasande [adj.] raging; furious

rasism [n.; ~en] racism

rasistisk [adj.; ~t, ~a] racist

rask [adj.; ~t, ~a] brisk

rast [n.; ~en, ~er] rest; break, recess

rasterfont [n.; ~en, ~er] bit-mapped font [IT]

rastlös [adj.; ~t, ~a] restless

rastplats [n.; ~en, ~er] rest area, picnic area [on highway]

raststuga [n.; ~n, -stugor] rest hostel [in mountains]

ratt [n.; ~en] steering wheel

rattfylleri [n.; ~et] drunken driving, driving under the influence (of alcohol) (DUI)

ravin [n.; ~en, ~er] ravine

razzia [n.; ~n, razzior] police raid

rea [abbrev: realisation] sale

Reach [abbrev.] Registration, Evaluation and Authorization of Chemicals (REACH) [EU, regulatory framework for chemicals]

reagera [v.; ~r, ~de, ~t] react

reaktion [n.; ~en, ~er] reaction; response

reaktionsmotor [n.; ~n, ~er] jet engine

reaktionär [adj.; ~t, ~a] reactionary

reaktor [n.; ~n, ~er] reactor

real [adj.; ~t, ~a] real, actual, factual

realgenus [n.] real gender, common gender [not neuter] [gram]

realia [n.pl.] facts, realities; exact sciences

realisation (rea) [n.; ~en, ~er] sale

realistisk [adj.; ~t, ~a] realistic

realitet [n.; ~en] reality

realtid [n.; ~en] real time [IT]

reavara [n.; ~n, -varor] discounted article, sale item; **reavaror bytes ej** sale items cannot be exchanged

rebell [n.; ~en, ~er] rebel, insurgent

rebus [n.; ~en, ~ar] rebus, picture puzzle

recensent [n.; ~en, ~er] critic, reviewer

recensera [v.; ~r, ~de, ~t] review, do a critique

recension [n.; ~en, ~er] review, critique

recept [n.; ~et, ~] recipe; prescription; **på ~** by/on prescription; **~ på** prescription for

receptbelagd [adj.; -belagt, ~a] available only on prescription

receptfri [adj.; -fritt, ~a] available without prescription

reception [n.; ~en, ~er] reception; **~en** front desk

reciprok pronomen [n.] reciprocal pronoun [gram]

red [see: **rida**]

reda [n.; ~n] order; knowledge, account; **få ~ på** learn about; **hålla ~ på** look after

reda [v.; reder, redde, rett] prepare, put in order; **~ sig** manage; come out all right

redaktion [n.; ~en, ~er] editorial office, editorial staff

redaktionschef [n.; ~en, ~er] editor-in-chief, managing editor

redaktör [n.; ~en, ~er] editor

redan [adv.] already, as early as

redd [adj.; rett, ~a] thickened, creamy [soup]; **~ champinjonsoppa** cream of mushroom soup; **~ kycklingsoppa** cream of chicken soup; **~ sparrissoppa** cream of asparagus soup; **~ tomatsoppa** cream of tomato soup

rederi [n.; ~et, ~er] shipping company, shipping office

redigera [v.; ~r, ~de, ~t] edit

redo [adj.] ready, prepared

redogöra (för) [v.; -gör, -gjorde, -gjort] give an account (of)

redogörelse [n.; ~n, ~r] account, report; description

redovisa [v.; ~r, ~de, ~t] record; give an account of

redovisning [n.; ~en, ~ar] account; statement of accounts

redovisningsprogram [n.; -grammet, ~] accounting program [IT]

redskap [n.; ~et, ~] tool, instrument; equipment; apparatus

redskapsgymnastik [n.] apparatus gymnastics
reducera [v.; ~r, ~de, ~t] reduce
ref. [abbrev: referens(er)] reference(s)
referat [n.; ~et, ~] report, account, review
referenser [n.pl.] references
reflex [n.; ~en, ~er] reflection; reflector; reflex
reflexiv pronomen [n.] reflexive pronoun [gram]
reflexkamera [n.; ~n, -kameror] single-lens reflex camera
reform [n.; ~en, ~er] reform
reformation [n.; ~en, ~er] reformation
refug [n.; ~en. ~er] traffic island
regatta [n.; ~n, regattor] regatta
regel [n.; ~n, reglar] rule, regulation
regelbrott [n.; ~et, ~] breach of the rules, contravention, foul
regelbunden [adj.; -bundet, -bundna] regular
regelverk [n.; ~et] set of rules and regulations
regent [n.; ~en, ~er] monarch
regera [v.; ~r, ~de, ~t] reign, rule
regerande [adj.] reigning
regering [n.; ~en, ~ar] government; ~en the government
regeringsform [n.;~en, ~er] form of government; constitution; instrument of government
regeringsförklaring [n.; ~en, ~ar] statement of government policy
Regeringskansliet [n.] Government Offices
Regeringskansliets förvaltnings-avdelning [n.] Government Offices' Office for Administrative Affairs
Regeringskonferens [n.] Intergovernmental Conference (IGC) [EU]
regeringsparti [n.; ~et, ~er] party in the government
Regeringsrätten [n.] Supreme Administrative Court
regeringssammanträde [n.; ~t, ~n] Cabinet meeting
regeringsskrivelse [n.; ~n, ~r] written communication from the government

regeringstid [n.; ~en, ~er] reign
reggae [n.] reggae
regi [n.; ~n] direction, production [theater, film]; management, arrangement
regim [n.; ~en, ~er] regime; management
region [n.; ~en, ~er] region
regional [adj.; ~t, ~a] regional
regionerna i gemenskapens ytter-sta randområden [n.pl.] outermost regions [EU]
Regionkommittén [n.] Committee of the Regions [EU]
regionsjukhus [n.; ~et, ~] regional hospital
regissör [n.; ~en, ~er] director [film]
register [n.; ~et, ~] register; index
registrator [n.; ~n, ~er] senior registry clerk
registrera [v.; ~r, ~de, ~t] register
registrerad [adj.; -rat, ~e] registered
registrering [n.; ~en, ~ar] registration
registreringsbevis [n.; ~et, ~] car registration documents
registreringsnummer [n.; -numret, ~] license plate number
registreringspapper [n.; -papperet, ~] car registration documents
registreringsskylt [n.; ~en, ~ar] license plate
reglerad [adj.; -rat, ~e] regulated
regleringsbrev [n.; ~et, ~] budget appropriation directives
regn [n.; ~et] rain
regna [v.; ~r, ~de, ~t] rain
regnig [adj.; ~t, ~a] rainy
regnkappa [n.; ~n, -kappor] raincoat [woman's]
regnrock [n.; ~en, ~ar] raincoat [man's]
regnskog [n.; ~en, ~ar] rain forest
regnskur [n.; ~en, ~ar] rain shower; downpour
reguljärflyg [n.; ~et, ~] regular flight, scheduled flight
rejäl [adj.; ~t, ~a] reliable, honest; full-blown, serious
Rek [abbrev: rekommenderas] Special Delivery

reklam [n.; ~en] advertising, commercial

reklambanner [n.; ~n, ~er] advertising banner [IT]

reklambroschyr [n.; ~n, ~er] publicity brochure

reklamfilm [n.; ~en, ~er] advertising film, commercial

reklam-tv [n.] commercial television

rekommendation [n.; ~en, ~er] recommendation

rekommendationsbrev [n.; ~et, ~] letter of recommendation

rekommendera [n.; ~r, ~de, ~t] recommend

rekommenderad [adj.; -rat, ~e] recommended; ~ **tillagning** cooking instructions; **rekommenderat brev** registered letter

rekonstruera [v.; ~r, ~de, ~t] reconstruct

rekord [n.; ~et, ~] record

rekrytera [v.; ~r, ~de, ~t] recruit

rekrytering [n.; ~en] recruitment

rekryteringsbidrag [n.; ~et, ~] enlistment bonus

rektangel [n.; ~n, -anglar] rectangle

rektangulär [adj.; ~t, ~a] rectangular

rektor [n.; ~n, ~er] principal [school], president [university]

rekursiv [adj.; ~t, ~a] recursive [IT]

relation [n.; ~en, ~er] relation, connection, relationship

relationsdatabas [n.; ~en, ~er] relational database [IT]

relativ [adj.; ~t, ~a] relative; ~ **bisats** relative clause [gram]; ~ **pronomen** relative pronoun [gram]

religion [n.; ~en, ~er] religion

religionsfrihet [n.; ~en] religious freedom

religiös [adj.; ~t, ~a] religious

rem [n.; remmen, remmar] strap

remi [n.; ~n, ~er] draw [game]

remiss [n.; ~en, ~er] referral [to doctor]; **sända på ~ (till)** refer back for consideration (to)

ren[1] [adj.; ~t, ~a] clean, pure; straight [no ice]; ~ **bomull** pure cotton; ~ **infinitiv** pure infinitive [without marker] [gram]; ~ **ull** pure wool

ren[2] [n.; ~en, ~ar] reindeer

rena [v.; ~r, ~de, ~t] clean, purify

renad [adj.; renat, ~e] purified

renat [n.] unflavored aquavit

renbog [n.; ~en] shoulder of reindeer

rengöra [v.; -gör, -gjorde, -gjort] clean

rengöringskräm [n.; ~en, ~er] cleansing cream

rengöringsmedel [n.; -medlet, ~] cleaning agent, detergent

rengöringsvätska [n.; ~n, -vätskor] cleaning solution

renhorn [n.; ~et, ~] reindeer antler

reningsverk [n.; ~et, ~] sewage works

renkött [n.; ~et] reindeer meat

renommé [n.; ~et] reputation, repute

renovera [v.; ~r, ~de, ~t] renovate, redecorate

renoverad [adj.; -rat, ~e] renovated

renovering [n.; ~en, ~ar] renovation

renoveringsarbete [n.; ~t, ~n] renovation, repair work

renrasig [adj.; ~t, ~a] thoroughbred, purebred

rensa [v.; ~r, ~de, ~t] clean; gut [fish]; clear; ~ **ogräs** weed (the garden)

rensadel [n.; ~n] saddle of reindeer [cut of meat]

renskav [n.; ~et] sliced leg of reindeer

renskötare [n.; ~n, ~] reindeer farmer

renskötsel [n.; ~n] reindeer farming

renstek [n.; ~en, ~ar] reindeer roast

rent [adv./adj.: see: **ren**] quite, completely

rentav [adv.] actually, simply, downright

renässans [n.; ~en, ~er] renaissance

rep [n.; ~et, ~] rope

repa [v.; ~r, ~de, ~t] scratch; pick off in bunches/handfuls

reparation [n.; ~en, ~er] repair

reparationsdiskett [n.; ~en] emergency repair disk [IT]

reparationsverkstad [n.; ~en, -städer] repair shop, garage

reparera [v.; ~r, ~de, ~t] repair
repetera [v.; ~r, ~de, ~t] repeat; rehearse
repetition [n.; ~en, ~er] repetition; rehearsal
replik [n.; ~en, ~er] rejoinder
replikering [n.; ~en, ~ar] replication [IT]
reportage [n.; ~et, ~] report, story, commentary
reporter [n.; ~n, reportrar] reporter
representant [n.; ~en, ~er] representative
representation [n.; ~en, ~er] representation; selection; entertainment
representera [v.; ~r, ~de, ~t] represent
repris [n.; ~en, ~er] repeat, revival, rerun; replay
republik [n.; ~en, ~er] republic
republikansk [adj.; ~t, ~a] republican
resa[1] [n.; ~n, resor] journey, trip; **trevlig ~!** have a good trip! bon voyage!
resa[2] [v.; reser, reste, rest] travel; erect, raise; **~ sig** stand up
resande [n.; ~n, ~] travel, traveling; traveler; traveling salesman
resanderum [n.; ~et, ~] rooms for travelers
reseannons [n.; ~en, ~er] travel ad
resebevis [n.; ~et, ~] voucher for prepaid travel bookings
resebyrå [n.; ~n, ~er] travel agency
resecheck [n.; ~en, ~ar] traveler's check
resedokument [n.; ~et, ~] travel document [refugees, asylum seekers]
reseföretag [n.; ~et, ~] travel agency
Resegarantinämnden [n.] Travel Guarantees Board
reseguide [n.; ~n] travel guide
reseledare [n.; ~n, ~] guide
resenär [n.; ~en, ~er] traveler, passenger
reserv [n.; ~en, ~er] reserve; substitute
reservat [n.; ~et, ~] reserve [dedicated land]
reservation [n.; ~en, ~er] reservation

reservdel [n.; ~en, ~ar] spare part, replacement part
reservdunk [n.; ~en, ~ar] reserve/spare tank
reservdäck [n.; ~et, ~] spare tire
reservera [v.; ~r, ~de, ~t] reserve
reserverad [adj.; -rat, ~e] reserved; **~ fil** reserved lane
reservhjul [n.; ~et] spare wheel
reservkopia [n.; ~n, -kopior] backup copy [IT]
reservoar [n.; ~en, ~er] reservoir
reservoarpenna [n.; ~n, -pennor] fountain pen
reservutgång [n.; ~en, ~ar] emergency exit
reseskildring [n.; ~en, ~ar] travel account
reseur [n.; ~et, ~] travel clock
resgods [n.; ~et] baggage
resgodsexpedition [n.; ~en] baggage counter
resgodsinlämning [n.; ~en] baggage checkroom
resklar [adj.; ~t, ~a] ready to leave
reslustkort [n.; ~et, ~] train discount card
resmål [n.; ~et, ~] travel destination
resonemang [n.; ~et, ~] discussion, conversation; reasoning, line of argument
resonera [v.; ~r, ~de, ~t] discuss; argue, reason
resp. [see: **respektive**]
respekt [n.; ~en] respect, esteem
respektera [v.; ~r, ~de, ~t] respect; abide by
respektive [adj./adv.] respective(ly)
rest[1] [v.past; see: **resa**]
rest[2] [n.; ~en, ~er] remainder, rest
restaurang [n.; ~en, ~er] restaurant
restaurangvagn [n.; ~en, ~ar] dining car
restaurera [v.; ~r, ~de, ~t] restore
restaurerad [adj.; -rat, ~e] restored
restera (med) [v.; ~r, ~de, ~t] be in arrears (with)
resterande [adj.] remaining; due, in arrears
rest sten [n.; ~en, ~ar] standing stone

restsumma [n.; ~n] balance due
resultat [n.; ~et, ~] result
resultattavla [n.; ~n, -tavlor]
scoreboard
resultera i [v.; ~r, ~de, ~t] result in
resurs [n.; ~en, ~er] resource; ~er
means, assets
resurstilldelning [n.; ~en] resource
quota [IT]
resväska [n.; ~n, -väskor] suitcase,
piece of luggage
resårband [n.; ~et, ~] elastic
retur¹ [n.; ~en, ~er] return; returned
goods; returnable articles [bottles];
round-trip; ej ~ non-returnable
[no deposit]
Retur² [n.] Return, Enter [key] [IT]
returbiljett [n.; ~en, ~er] round-
trip ticket
returglas [n.; ~et, ~] returnable
bottle
reumatisk sjukdom [n.; ~en, ~ar]
rheumatic disease
reumatism [n.; ~en] rheumatism
rev [v.past; see: riva]
revansch [n.; ~en] vengeance,
revenge
revben [n.; ~et, ~] rib
revbensspjäll [n.; ~et, ~] spareribs
revision [n.; ~en, ~er] audit; revision
Revisionsrätten [n.] European
Court of Auditors [EU]
revisor [n.; ~n, ~er] accountant;
auditor
revolution [n.; ~en, ~er] revolution
revolutionär [adj.; ~t, ~a]
revolutionary
revy [n.; ~n, ~er] revue, light theater
RFoD [abbrev: Riksföreningen för
Folkmusik och Dans] Swedish
Association for Folk Music and
Dance
RFSL [abbrev: Riksförbundet för
sexuellt likaberättigande] Swedish
Federation for Lesbian, Gay, Bisexual and Transgender Rights
RFSU [abbrev: Riksförbundet för
sexuell upplysning] National Association for Sex Education
RGB-värde [n.; ~t, ~n] RGB value
[red-green-blue] [IT]

Rhen [n.] Rhine
rida [v.; rider, red, ridit] ride [horse]
ridbana [n.; ~n, -banor] riding
track
riddare [n.; ~n, ~] knight
Riddarhuset [n.] House of the Nobility [building in Stockholm]
ridhus [n.; ~et] indoor riding school
ridning [n.; ~en] horseback riding
ridskola [n.; ~n, -skolor] riding
school
ridstövlar [n.pl.] riding boots
ridtur [n.; ~en, ~er] horseback ride
ridväg [n.; ~en, ~ar] bridle path
ridå [n.; ~n, ~er] curtain [theater]
RIF-rådet [abbrev: Ministerrådet
för rättsliga och inrikes frågor]
Justice and Home Affairs Council
(JHA) [EU]
rik [adj.; ~t, ~a] rich
rike [n.; ~t, ~n] kingdom, realm;
sphere
rikedom [n.; ~en, ~ar] riches
Riksantikvarieämbetet [n.]
National Heritage Board
Riksarkivet [n.] National Archive
Riksbanken [n.] Swedish Central
Bank
Riksdagen [n.] Parliament
Riksdagens ombudsmän (JO)
[n.pl.] Parliamentary Ombudsmen
riksdagsförhandlingar [n.pl.]
Parliament proceedings
Riksdagshuset [n.] Parliament
building
riksdagsledamot [n.; ~en, -ledamöter]
member of Parliament
riksdagsordning [n.; ~en, ~ar] act
of Parliament
riksdagsval [n.; ~et, ~] general
election
Riksförbundet för sexuellt likabe-
rättigande (RFSL) [n.] Swedish
Federation for Lesbian, Gay, Bi-
sexual and Transgender Rights
Riksförbundet Sveriges lot-
takårer [n.] Swedish Women's
Voluntary Defence Service
Riksförsäkringsverket [n.]
National Social Insurance
Administration

Riksgäldskontoret [n.] National Debt Office

Riksidrottsförbundet [n.] Swedish Sports Confederation

Rikskriminalpolisen [n.] National Criminal Police

Riksmarskalksämbetet [n.] Office of the Marshal of the Realm

rikspolischef [n.; ~en] national police commissioner

Rikspolisstyrelsen (RPS) [n.] National Police Administration

Riksrevisionen [n.] National Audit Administration

Riksrevisionsverket (RRV) [n.] National Audit Administration

rikssamtal [n.; ~et, ~] long-distance call [not international]

Riksskatteverket (RSV) [n.] National Tax Administration

Riksteatern [n.] National Touring Theater

rikstest [n.; ~et] national test [in Swedish for foreigners wishing to enter a university]

Rikstrafiken [n.] National Public Transport Agency

Riksutställningar [n.pl.] National Traveling Exhibitions Agency

riksväg [n.; ~en, ~ar] major road

Riksåklagaren (RÅ) [n.] Office of the Prosecutor-General

rikt [see: rik]

rikta [v.; ~r, ~de, ~t] direct, aim, point

riktig [adj.; ~t, ~a] real, true, right, correct

riktigt [adv.] really, properly

riktlinje [n.; ~n, ~r] guideline

riktmärkning [n.; ~en, ~ar] benchmarking [EU]

riktning [n.; ~en, ~ar] direction

riktnummer [n.; -numret, ~] area code [telephone]

rim [n.; ~et, ~] rhyme

rimfrost [n.; ~en] hoarfrost, rime

rimlig [adj.; ~t, ~a] reasonable

rimmad [adj.; rimmat, ~e] cured, lightly salted; ~ lax cured salmon

ring [n.; ~en, ~ar] ring, circle

ringa [v.; ringer, ringde, ringt] ring;

call [telephone]; ~ av hang up [phone]; ~ efter call for; ~ ett samtal make a phone call; ~ fel dial a wrong number; ~ upp call

ringblomma [n.; ~n, -blommor] marigold

ringled [n.; ~en, ~er] ring road

ringmur [n.; ~en, ~ar] city walls

ringnät [n.; ~et, ~] ring network [IT]

rinna [v.; rinner, rann, runnit] run, flow

rinnande vatten [n.; vattnet] running water

ripa [n.; ~n, ripor] ptarmigan, grouse

ris [n.; ~et] rice; ~ a la Malta rice pudding with whipped cream

risgrynsgröt [n.; ~en] rice pudding

risig [adj.; ~t, ~a] tattered, battered

risk [n.; ~en, ~er] risk, danger

riskera [v.; ~r, ~de, ~t] risk, hazard; jeopardize

riskfri [adj.; -fritt, ~a] without danger

rispa [v.; ~r, ~de, ~t] scratch

rispudding [n.; ~en] rice pudding

rita [v.; ~r, ~de, ~t] draw, design

ritprogram [n.; -grammet, ~] drawing program [IT]

RITS [abbrev: Räddnings insatser till sjöss] maritime fire and rescue operations

riva [v.; river, rev, rivit] grate, scratch

riven [adj.; rivet, rivna] grated

Rivieran [n.] Riviera

rivjärn [n.; ~et, ~] grater

rivstart [n.; ~en, ~er] flying start, quick start [IT]

ro[1] [n.; ~n] rest, peace, quiet

ro[2] [v.; ror, rodde, rott] row

roa (sig) [v.; ~r, ~de, ~t] amuse (oneself)

rock [n.; ~en, ~ar] coat [man's]; rock [music]

rocka [n.; ~n, rockor] ray, skate

rockmusik [n.; ~en] rock music

rodd [n.; ~en] rowing

roddarlag [n.; ~et, ~] rowing team, crew

roddbåt [n.; ~en, ~ar] rowing boat

roddtävling [n.; ~en, ~ar] rowing regatta, boat race

roder [n.; rodret, ~] rudder

rodnad [n.; ~en, ~er] redness, blush; rash

rododendron [n.; ~en, ~] rhododendron

rokoko [n.; ~n] rococo

rolig [adj.; ~t, ~a] amusing, funny; interesting; **ha det ~t** have fun, enjoy oneself

roll [n.; ~en, ~er] role, part

rom[1] [n.; rommen] roe; rum

ROM[2] [n.] read-only memory (ROM) [IT]

Rom[3] [n.] Rome

roman [n.; ~en, ~er] novel; **~er** fiction [books]

romani [n.; ~n] Roma(ny) [Gypsy language]

romansk [adj.; ~t, ~a] Romanesque

romantiken [n.] romanticism

romantisk [adj.; ~t, ~a] romantic

romersk [adj.; ~t, ~a] Roman

Romfördraget [n.] Treaty of Rome [EU 1957]

rond [n.; ~en, ~er] round; rounds, beat

rondell [n.; ~en, ~er] traffic circle, rotary

rop [n.; ~et, ~] call, cry; **i ~et** in fashion

ropa [v.; ~r, ~de, ~t] call, shout

ros [n.; ~en, ~or] rose

rosa [adj.] pink

rosenbönor [n.pl.] runner beans

rosévin [n.; ~et] rosé, blush [wine]

rosmarin [n.; ~en] rosemary

rostad [adj.; rostat, ~e] toasted

rostat bröd [n.] toast

rostbiff [n.; ~en] roast beef

rostfritt stål [n.; ~et] stainless steel

rostig [adj.; ~t, ~a] rusty

rot [n.; ~en, rötter] root

rotera [v.; ~r, ~de, ~t] rotate [IT]

rotfyllning [n.; ~en, ~ar] root canal

rotmos [n.; ~et] mashed turnips

rotselleri [n.; ~et] celery root, celeriac

rouge [n.; ~et] rouge

router [n.; ~n] router [IT]

rov [n.; ~et] prey; robbery; booty

rova [n.; ~n, rovor] turnip

rovdjur [n.; ~et, ~] predator

rubba [v.; ~r, ~de, ~t] move; disturb, upset

rubbad [adj.] disturbed, somewhat deranged, crazy; **~ dygnsrytm** jet lag

rubbning [n.; ~en, ~ar] disturbance, disorder

rubin [n.; ~en, ~er] ruby

rubrik [n.; ~en, ~er] headline; heading, header, title

rubrikcell [n.; ~en, ~er] header cell [IT]

rufsig [adj.; ~t, ~a] unkempt, ruffled

rugby [n.] rugby

ruin [n.; ~en, ~er] ruin

rulla [n.; ~n, rullor] roll; scroll [IT]

rullande text [n.; ~en, ~er] rolling text, marquee [IT]

rullband [n.; ~et, ~] conveyer belt

rullbord [n.; ~et, ~] tea cart

rullgardin [n.; ~en, ~er] shade, blind [window]

rullgardinsmeny [n.; ~n, ~er] scroll-down menu, drop-down menu [IT]

rullningslist [n.; ~en, ~er] scroll bar [IT]

rullskridskobana [n.; ~n, -banor] roller skating rink

rullskridskor [n.pl.] roller skates

rullstol [n.; ~en, ~ar] wheelchair

rullstolsanpassad [adj.; -anpassat, ~e] wheelchair accessible, wheelchair suitable

rullstolsbunden [adj.; -bundet, -bundna] wheelchair-bound, confined to a wheelchair

rullstolsburen person [n.; ~en, ~er] wheelchair user

rullstolslyft [n.; ~et, ~] wheelchair lifting platform

rullstolsramp [n.; ~en, ~er] wheelchair ramp

rullstolsvandring [n.; ~en, ~ar] wheelchair hike

rulltrappa [n.; ~n, -trappor] escalator

rulltrottoar [n.; ~en, ~er] moving walkway

rulltårta [n.; ~n, -tårtor] jelly roll, chocolate roll
rum [n.; rummet, ~] room; ~ inklusive frukost bed and breakfast
rumpstek [n.; ~en] rump steak
rumsadverbial [n.; ~et, ~] adverbial of place [gram]
rumsbetjäning [n.; ~en] room service
rumservice [n.; ~n] room service
rumstemperatur [n.; ~en] room temperature
Rumänien [n.] Romania
rumänsk [adj.; ~t, ~a] Romanian
rumänska [n.] Romanian language, Romanian woman
runa [n.; ~n, runor] rune
rund [adj.; runt, ~a] round
runda[1] [n.; ~n, rundor] round; gå en ~ go for a walk; play a round [golf]
runda[2] [v.; ~r, ~de, ~t] round; ~ av round off; ~ nedåt round down; ~ uppåt round up [number]
rundbågestil [n.; ~en] Romanesque style [arch.]
rundresa [n.; ~n, -resor] tour
rundstycke [n.; ~t, ~n] roll [bread]
rundsändning [n.; ~en, ~ar] broadcast [IT]
rundtur [n.; ~en, ~er] tour, excursion; round trip
rundvandring [n.; ~en, ~ar] tour
runsten [n.; ~en, ~ar] stone with runes, rune stone
runt [adv./prep.; adj.: see: rund] around; ~ omkring around
rusa [v.; ~r, ~de, ~t] rush
rusningstid [n.; ~en] rush hour
russin [n.; ~et, ~] raisins
rustkammare [n.; ~n] armory
rustning [n.; ~en, ~ar] armament; armor
rustningsindustri [n.; ~n, ~er] arms industry
ruta [n.; ~n, rutor] square, box
rutad [adj.; rutat, ~e] checkered
ruter [n.; ~n, ~] diamonds [cards]
rutig [adj.; ~t, ~a] checkered, plaid; ~t papper graph paper
rutin [n.; ~en, ~er] routine

rutinerad [adj.; -rat, ~e] experienced, skilled
rutschbana [n.; ~n, -banor] slide
rutt [n.; ~en, ~er] route
rutten [adj.; ruttet, ruttna] rotten, decayed
Rwanda [n.] Rwanda
ryamatta [n.; ~n, -mattor] long-pile rug, hooked rug
ryck [n.; ~et, ~] jerk, wrench; burst
rycka [v.; rycker, ryckte, ryckt] pull, jerk, snatch, wrench
rygg [n.; ~en, ~ar] back; ont i ~en pain in the back, backache
ryggkota [n.; ~n, -kotor] vertebra
ryggmärg [n.; ~en] spinal cord
ryggmärgsbedövning [n.; ~en, ~ar] spinal anesthesia
ryggmärgsskadad [adj.; -skadat, ~e] paraplegic
ryggrad [n.; ~en, ~er] spine
ryggradsdjur [n.pl.] vertebrates
ryggradslösa djur [n.pl.] invertebrates
ryggradsnät [see: stamnät] backbone network [IT]
ryggsim [n.; -simmet] backstroke
ryggskott [n.; ~et] lumbago
ryggsmärta [n.; ~n, -smärtor] back pain
ryggstöd [n.; ~et, ~] back support; back [of a chair]
ryggsäck [n.; ~en, ~ar] knapsack, rucksack, backpack
rykta [v.; ~r, ~de, ~t] groom, dress [horse]
rykte [n.; ~t, ~n] reputation; rumor
ryktning [n.; ~en, ~ar] direction
rymd [n.; ~en] volume, capacity; space
Rymdstyrelsen [n.] National Space Agency
rymlig [adj.; ~t, ~a] roomy, spacious
rymma [v.; rymmer, rymde, rymt] contain, hold; flee, escape; elope
rymmare och fasttagare [n.pl.] cops and robbers
ryms: den ~ i fickan it fits in the pocket, the pocket can hold it
rysa [v.; ryser, rös/ryste, ryst] shiver, shake, tremble

rysk [adj.; ~t, ~a] Russian
ryska [n.] Russian language
ryss [n.; ~en, ~ar] Russian
Ryssland [n.] Russia
RÅ[1] [abbrev: Riksåklagare] Attorney General
rå[2] [adj.; rått, råa] raw
rå[3] (med) [v.; rår, rådde, rått] handle, manage, deal (with) [IT]
råbiff [n.; ~en] steak tartare
råd [n.; ~et, ~] advice, counsel; council; councilor; means; **ha ~ med** be able to afford
råda [v.; råder, rådde, rått] advise; be in charge; prevail
rådande [adj.] prevailing, current
Rådet för forsknings- och utvecklingssamarbete inom EU [n.] Swedish EU Research and Development Council
rådfrågning [n.; ~en] consultation, asking for advice
rådgivande [adj.] advisory
rådgivare [n.; ~n, ~] advisor, guide, counselor
rådgivning [n.; ~en, ~ar] advice, consultation
rådhus [n.; ~et] city hall
rådjur [n.; ~et] venison
rådjurstek [n.; ~en] venison roast
rådsarbetsgrupp [n.; ~en, ~er] Council working party [EU]
råg [n.; ~en] rye
rågbröd [n.; ~et] rye bread
rågummisula [n.; ~n, -sulor] crepe (rubber) sole [shoes]
råka[1] [n.; ~n, råkor] rook [bird]
råka[2] [v.; ~r, ~de, ~t] happen to (do); **~ ut för** be involved in; meet with
råkost [n.; ~en] raw vegetables
råma [v.; ~r, ~de, ~t] moo, low [cow]
råmaterial [n.; ~et, ~] raw material
rån [n.; ~et, ~] robbery, mugging
rånad [adj.; rånat, ~e] robbed
rånare [n.; ~n, ~] robber
råolja [n.; ~n] crude oil
rårörd [adj.; -rört, ~a] preserved raw
råsiden [n.; ~et] raw silk
råtta [n.; ~n, råttor] rat
råvara [n.; ~n, -varor] raw material

räcka [v.; räcker, räckte, räckt] reach; pass [salt]; offer [one's hand]; be enough, suffice; **det räcker** that's enough; **~ över** hand over, pass
räcke [n.; ~t, ~n] banister
rädd [adj.; ~a] afraid; careful; **vara ~ för** be afraid of; **vara ~ om** be careful with, take care of
rädda [v.; ~r, ~de, ~t] save
Rädda Barnen [n.] Save the Children [non-governmental organization]
räddning [n.; ~en, ~ar] save
räddningsbåt [n.; ~en, ~ar] lifeboat
räddningshelikopter [n.; ~n, -koptrar] rescue helicopter
räddningskår [n.; ~en, ~er] breakdown service; salvage/rescue corps
räddningstjänst [n.; ~en, ~er] rescue service
Räddningsverket [n.] Rescue Services Administration
räddningsväst [n.; ~en, ~ar] life jacket
rädisa [n.; ~n, rädisor] radish
rädsla [n.; ~n] fear, dread
räfsa [n.; ~n, räfsor] rake [garden]
räkcocktail [n.; ~en, ~er] shrimp cocktail
räkna [v.; ~r, ~de, ~t] count; **~ med** take into account
räknare [n.; ~n, ~] counter, web counter [IT]
räknebart substantiv [n.; et, ~] count noun [gram]
räknedosa [n.; ~n, -dosor] minicalculator
räknefel [n.; ~et, ~] mathematical error, miscalculation
räkneord [n.; ~et, ~] numeral, number
räkning [n.; ~en, ~ar] bill, account; counting, calculation
räkor [n.pl.] shrimps, prawns
räksmörgås [n.; ~en, ~ar] shrimp sandwich
räksoppa [n.; ~n, -soppor] shrimp soup/bisque
rälsbuss [n.; ~en, ~ar] railbus, light-rail train

rännsten [n.; ~en] gutter

ränta [n.; ~n, räntor] interest; ~ på ~ compound interest

räntabel [adj.; ~t, räntabla] profitable

räntefri [adj.; ~tt, ~a] interest free

räntehöjning [n.; ~en, ~ar] increase in the interest rate

räntesats [n.; ~en, ~er] interest rate

räntesänkning [n.; ~en, ~ar] reduction in the interest rate

rätt¹ [adj.; ~a] correct, right

rätt² [adv.] really

rätt³ [n.; ~en, ~er] right, justice; law, court; dish, course; ha ~ i be right about; ha ~ till have the right to; ~ till framställning right of petition [EU]

rätta¹: inför ~ before the court, to court

rätta²: finna sig till ~ adapt oneself, get used to; med ~ rightly, justly

rätta³ [v.; ~r, ~de, ~t] straighten out/up, put straight; correct, set right; adjust, accommodate; ~ till correct, fix [IT]

rättare [n.; ~n] foreman [on farm]

rättegång [n.; ~en, ~ar] trial, legal proceedings

rättegångsbalk [n.; ~en] Code of Judicial Procedure

rättighet [n.; ~en, ~er] right, entitlement

rättika [n.; ~n, rättikor] black radish

rättsakt [n.; ~en, ~er] legal act; legislative act, law [EU regulations, directives and decisions]

rättschef [n.; ~en] Director-General for Legal Affairs

Rättshjälpsmyndigheten [n.] National Legal Aid Authority

rättslig [adj.; ~t, ~a] legal, judicial

Rättsmedicinalverket (RMV) [n.] National Forensic Medicine Administration

rättvis [adj.; ~t, ~a] just, fair, impartial

rättvisa [n.; ~n] justice

Rättvisepartiet Socialisterna (RS) [n.] Socialist Justice Party

räv [n.; ~en, ~ar] fox

röd [adj.; rött, ~a] red; ~ avgång discount train [marked red in timetable]; ~ paprika red pepper; röda hund German measles; röda vinbär red currants

Röda Havet [n.] Red Sea

Röda Korset [n.] Red Cross

rödbeta [n.; ~n, -betor] beet

rödbetssallad [n.; ~en, ~er] beetroot salad

rödbetslag [n.; ~en] liquid from pickled beets

rödhake [n.; ~n, -hakar] robin, redbreast

rödgröna [n.pl.] Red-Green coalition [center-left coalition of Social Democrats and environmentalists]

rödhårig [adj.; ~t, ~a] red-headed

röding [n.; ~en, ~ar] char [fish]

rödkål [n.; ~en] red cabbage

rödsprit [n.; ~en] methylated spirits [colored red]

rödspätta [n.; ~n, -spättor] plaice [fish]

rödtunga [n.; ~n, -tungor] lemon sole [fish]

rödvin [n.; ~et] red wine

rök [n.; ~en, ~ar] smoke, fumes

röka [v.; röker, rökte, rökt] smoke; får jag ~? may I smoke?

rökare [n.; ~n, ~] smoker, smoking; icke-rökare non-smoking

rökfri [adj.; ~tt, ~a] smoke-free

rökning [n.; ~en] smoking

rökt [adj.; ~a] smoked; ~ lax smoked salmon; ~ sill kipper; ~ ål smoked eel

rölleka [n.; ~n, -ekor] yarrow, milfoil

rönn [n.; ~en, ~ar] mountain ash, rowan

rönnbär [n.pl.] rowanberries [tart red berries]

rönnbärsgelé [n.; ~et, ~er] rowanberry jelly

röntga [v.; ~r, ~de, ~t] x-ray

röntgenbehandling [n.; ~en, ~er] x-ray treatment, radiotherapy

röntgenbild [n.; ~en, ~er] x-ray image

röntgenundersökning [n.; ~en, ~er] x-ray examination
röntgenolog [n.; ~en, ~er] radiologist
röntgenplåt [n.; ~en, ~ar] x-ray plate
rör [n.; ~et, ~] pipe, tube; reed, cane
röra [v.; rör, rörde, rört] touch, mix, move [trans.]; ~ **sig** move [intrans.], keep moving
rörande[1] [adj.] touching, moving
rörande[2] [prep.] concerning, regarding
rörd [adj.; rört, ~a] moved, touched; stirred; ~ **soppa** [n.] cream soup
rörelse [n.; ~n, ~r] movement
rörelsehindrad [adj.; -hindrat, ~e] disabled, handicapped
rörlig [adj.; ~t, ~a] mobile; flexible; agile
rörlighet [n.; ~en] mobility

rörläggare [n.; ~n, ~] plumber
rörmokare [n.; ~n, ~] plumber
rörmontör [n.; ~en, ~er] plumber
rört [adj.; see: **rörd**]
röst [n.; ~en, ~er] vote; voice
rösta [v.; ~r, ~de, ~t] vote; ~ **borgerligt** vote non-Socialist; ~ **genom fullmakt** vote by proxy; ~ **socialistiskt** vote Socialist
röstbrevlåda [n.; ~n] voice-mailbox [IT]
röstigenkänning [n.; ~en] voice recognition, speech recognition [IT]
röstlängd [n.; ~en, ~er] electoral roll/register
rösträtt [n.; ~en] right to vote
röstvärvning [n.; ~en, ~ar] canvassing
rött [see: **röd**] ~ **ljus** red light; ~ **pris** discount price [trains]; ~ **vin** red wine

S

s¹ [abbrev: socialdemokraterna] Social Democrats

s.² [abbrev: sida, sidor] page(s)

S³ [abbrev: söder, södra] southern

sa¹ [v.past; see: **säga**] said

sa.² [abbrev: summa] total, amount

Saab [originally abbrev: Svenska Aeroplan AB] Saab [Swedish automobile and aircraft manufacturer]

sabbat [n.; ~en] Sabbath

sabotör [n.; ~en, ~er] saboteur

SAC [abbrev: Sveriges Arbetares Centralorganisation] Central Organization of the Workers of Sweden

SACO [abbrev: Sveriges Akademikers Centralorganisation] Swedish Confederation of Professional Associations

sade [v.past; pronounced: sa; see: **säga**]

sadel [n.; sadeln, sadlar] saddle; bicycle seat

SAF [abbrev: Svenska Arbetsgivarförening] Swedish Employers Confederation

safflorolja [n.; ~n] safflower oil

saffran [n.; ~en] saffron

saffransbulle [n.; ~n, -bullar] saffron bun

safir [n.; ~en, ~er] sapphire

saft [n.; ~en, ~er] fruit drink, syrup

saftig [adj.; ~t, ~a] juicy

saga [n.; ~n, sagor] fairytale, story

sagt [v.past; see: **säga**]

sajt [n.; ~en, ~er] (web)site [IT]

sak [n.; ~en, ~er] thing, matter

sakna [v.; ~r, ~de, ~t] lack; miss, not have

saknas [v.passive; ~, ~des, ~ts] be missing

sakregister [n.; -registret, ~] index, subject index

sakta¹ [adv.] slow; slowly

sakta² (in) [v.; ~r, ~de, ~t] slow (down)

SAL¹ [abbrev: Svenska Amerika Linien AB] Swedish American Line

sal² [n.; ~en, ~ar] room, hall

salami [n.; ~n, ~er] salami

saldo [n.; ~t, ~n] balance [bank]

sallad [n.; ~en, ~er] salad; lettuce

salladsbestick [n.; ~et, ~] salad serving set

salladsbuffé [n.; ~n, ~er] salad bar

salladshuvud [n.; ~et, ~] lettuce

salladssås [n.; ~en, ~er] salad dressing

salong [n.; ~en, ~er] lounge; hairdressers

salt¹ [adj.; ~, ~a] salty; **~a biten** salted boiled beef

salt² [n.; ~et] salt

salta [v.; ~r, ~de, ~t] salt, add salt, put salt on

saltad [adj.; saltat, ~e] salted

saltgurka [n.; ~n, -gurkor] salt-pickled gherkins

saltströare [n.; ~n, ~] saltshaker

salu: till ~ for sale

saluföra [v.; -för, -förde, -fört] offer for sale

saluhall [n.; -hallen, -hallar] indoor market

salva [n.; ~n, salvor] ointment, salve; **~ mot brännskador** ointment for burns

salvia [n.; ~n] sage

sam¹ [v.past; see: **simma**]

sam-² [prefix] together, co-, joint

samarbeta [v.; ~r, ~de, ~t] cooperate

samarbete [n.; ~t, ~n] cooperation

samarbetsförfarande [n.; ~t, ~n] cooperation procedure [EU]

samband [n.;] conjunction; **i ~ med** in connection with

sambo [n.; ~n, ~r] cohabiting partner, common-law spouse

same [n.; ~n, ~r] Sami [native of Lappland]

sameby [n.; ~n, ~ar] Sami village

sameslöjd [n.; ~en, ~er] Sami crafts

Sametinget [n.] Sami Parliament

samhälle [n.; ~t, ~n] society; community; village

samhällskunskap [n.; ~en, ~er] civics

samhällsomfattande tjänster
[n.pl.] universal service [EU]
**samhällsorienterande ämnen
(SO)** [n.pl.] social sciences, civics
samhällsvetenskap [n.; ~en, ~er]
social science
samiska [n.; ~n] Sami language,
Lappish [avoid this term]
samkörningsmöjlighet [n.; ~en,
~er] interoperability [IT]
samla [v.; ~r, ~de, ~t] gather, collect; ~ **på** collect
samlad [adj.; samlat, ~e] gathered,
collected
samlas [v.passive; ~, samlades,
samlats] gather [intrans.]; meet
samling [n.; ~en, ~ar] collection
samlingsplats [n.; ~en, ~er] gathering place
samlingsregering [n.; ~en, ~ar]
coalition government
samma [adj.] same
samman [adv.] together
sammanbo [v.; -bor, -bodde, -bott]
live together [as a couple], cohabit
sammandragna former [n.pl.]
contracted forms [gram]
sammanfatta [v.; ~r, ~de, ~t]
summarize, sum up
sammanflätad [adj.; -flätat, ~e]
interlaced [IT]
sammanfoga [v.; ~r, ~de, ~t] join,
merge
sammanhang [n.; ~et, ~] context,
connection, relation
sammanhangsberoende hjälp [n.;
~en] context-sensitive help [IT]
Sammanhållningsfonden [n.]
Cohesion Fund [EU]
sammankalla [v.; ~r, ~de, ~t]
summon
sammankoppla [v.; ~r, ~de, ~t]
connect [IT]
sammanlagd [adj.; -lagt, ~a] total,
combined
sammansatt [adj.; ~, ~a] compound
sammanslagning [n.; ~en, ~ar]
merger, fusion
sammanställa [v.; -ställer, -ställde,
-ställt] put together, compile
sammanställning [n.; ~en, ~ar]
putting together, compilation, list

sammansättning [n.; ~en, ~ar]
composition, mixture; compound
sammanträde [n.; ~t, ~n] meeting,
conference
sammet [n.; ~en] velvet
samnordisk [adj.; ~t, ~a] joint
Scandinavian, joint Nordic
samordna [v.; ~r, ~de, ~t]
coordinate
samordnande konjunktion [n.;
~en, ~er] coordinating conjunction [gram]
samordning [n.; ~en, ~ar] coordination [gram]
sampling [n.; ~en, ~ar] sampling
[IT]
samråd [n.; ~et, ~] consultation,
conference
samråda [v.; -råder, -rådde, -rått]
consult
samrådsförfarande [n.; ~t, ~n]
consultation procedure [EU]
samspel [n.; ~et] teamwork,
ensemble
samt [conj.; formal] and, together
with
samtal [n.; ~et, ~] conversation;
phone call; ~ **som mottageren
betalar** collect call
samtala [v.; ~r, ~de, ~t] converse,
talk
samtalsavgift [n.; ~en, ~er] charge
for phone call
samtalsmarkering [n.; ~en, ~er]
beep [marking units of phone
charges]
samtida [adj.] contemporary
samtidig [adj.; ~t, ~a] contempora-
neous; simultaneous
samtidigt [adv.] at the same time
samtliga [adj.] all
samtyckesförfarande [n.; ~t]
assent procedure [EU]
samvaro [n.; ~n] being together,
relations
samverkan [n.; ~] cooperation,
collaboration
samvete [n.; ~t, ~n] conscience
samvälde [n.; ~t, ~n] commonwealth
samåka [v.; -åker, -åkte, -åkt]
carpool

sand [n.; ~en] sand
sandaler [n.pl.] sandals
sandig [adj.; ~t, ~a] sandy
sandlåda [n.; ~n, -lådor] sand box
sandslott [n.; ~et, ~er] sand castle
sandstrand [n.; ~en, -stränder] sandy beach
sanitära bekvämligheter [n.pl.] sanitary facilities
Sankt/Sankta (S:t/S:ta) [n.] Saint (St.) [m./f.]
sanktion [n.; ~en, ~er] sanction; assent
sann [adj.; sant, ~a] true, real; inte sant? Isn't that right?
sannerligen [adv.] really, truly
sanning [n.; ~en] truth
sanningstabell [n.; ~en, ~er] truth table [IT]
sannolik [adj.; ~t, ~a] probable, likely
sannolikhet [n.; ~en] likelihood
sanserif [n.] sanserif [type style] [IT]
sant [adv.; see also: sann] truly, sincerely
SAP [abbrev: Socialdemokratiska Arbetarepartiet] Social Democratic Workers Party
sardeller [n.pl.] anchovies
sardiner [n.pl.] sardines
Sardinien [n.] Sardinia
sarkofag [n.; ~en, ~er] sarcophagus
SAS [abbrev: Scandinavian Airlines Sverige] Scandinavian Airlines Sweden (SAS) [formerly: Scandinavian Airlines System]
satellit [n.; ~en, ~er] satellite
satellitbild [n.; ~en, ~er] satellite image
satellitsändning [n.; ~en, ~ar] satellite transmission
satellit-TV [n.] satellite TV
sats [n.; ~en, ~er] clause, sentence; movement (music); dose, batch; running start, take-off [sports]
satsa [v.; ~r, ~de, ~t] stake, wager; invest
satsbyggnad [n.; ~en, ~er] sentence structure [gram]
satsdel [n.; ~en, ~ar] sentence/ clause component [gram]

satsförkortning [n.; ~en, ~ar] incomplete sentence [gram]
satsklyvning [n.; ~en, ~ar] clefting, periphrasis [gram]
satslösning [n.; ~en, ~ar] parsing, sentence analysis [gram]
satsning [n.; ~en, ~ar] wager; investment; concentration [school program]
satsvis bearbetning [n.; ~en] batch processing [IT]
satt [v.past; see: sitta, sätta]
satte [v.past; see: sätta]
Saturnus [n.] Saturn
Saudiarabien [n.] Saudi Arabia
sauterad [adj.; -rat, ~e] sautéed
sax [n.; ~en, ~ar] scissors [pl.]
saxofon [n.; ~en, ~er] saxophone
scarf [n.; ~en, ~ar] scarf
SCB [abbrev: Statistiska centralbyrån] Statistics Sweden
scen [n.; ~en, ~er] stage
scenograf [n.; ~en, ~er] set designer
scenunderhållning [n.; ~en, ~ar] floor show
schablonavdrag [n.] standard deduction
schack [n.; ~et] chess; schack! check!
schackbräde [n.; ~t, ~] chessboard
schackdrag [n.; ~et, ~] chess move
schackmatt [adj.] checkmate
schackspel [n.; ~et] chess set
schalotenlök [n.; ~en, ~ar] shallots, spring onions
schampo [n.; ~t, ~n] shampoo
scharlakansfeber [n.; ~n] scarlet fever
schema [n.; ~t, ~n] timetable, schedule
schemalagd arbetstid [n.] scheduled working hours
Schengenavtalet [n.] Schengen Agreement [EU]
Schengen konventionen [n.] Schengen Convention [EU]
Schengensamarbetet [n.] Schengen cooperation [EU, border controls]
schimpans [n.; ~en, ~er] chimpanzee
schlager [n.; ~n, schlagrar] pop song, hit song

schnitzel [n.; ~n, schnitzlar] escalope, fillet

Schweiz [n.] Switzerland

schweizerschnitzel [n.; ~n, -schnitzlar] veal escalope with ham and cheese

schweizisk [adj.; ~t, ~a] Swiss

schäfer [n.; ~n, schäfrar] German shepherd [dog]

screentryck [n.; ~et, ~] silk-screen print

sd [abbrev: Sverigedemokraterna] Swedish Democrats

SDN [abbrev: stadsdelsnämnden] [n.] city district board

se [v.; ser, såg, sett; see also: **ses**] see; **vi ~s snart** see you soon; **~ sig omkring** look around; **~ på TV** watch TV; **~ upp för** watch out for; **~ upp** be careful, be cautious; **~ ut** look, look like, seem; **~ ut som** look like; **~ även** see also

SEB [abbrev: Stockholms Enskilda Bank] SEB [major Swedish bank]

SE Banken [see: **SEB**]

second hand-affär [n.; ~en, ~er] secondhand store

sed [n.; ~en, ~er] custom, habit, manner, moral(s)

sedan [adv.] then, afterward, when; since; **för 10 minuter ~** 10 minutes ago; **för 2 år ~** two years ago; **~ dess** since then; **~ en halvtimme** for half an hour now; **~ kl 8 i morse** since 8 this morning

sedel [n.; ~n, sedlar] bill [currency], banknote

sedelautomat [n.; ~en, ~er] automatic dispenser [gas, tickets, snacks]

sedermera [see: **sedan**]

seg [adj.; ~t, ~a] tough; hard to chew; viscous

segel [n.; ~et, ~] sail

segelbåt [n.; ~en, ~ar] sailboat

segelflyg [n.; ~et] gliding, sailplaning

segelflygplan [n.; ~et, ~] glider, sailplane

segelklubb [n.; ~en, ~ar] sailing club

seger [n.; ~n, segrar] victory, win

segla [v.; ~r, ~de, ~t] sail

segling [n.; ~en] sailing

seglingsinstruktör [n.; ~en, ~er] sailing instructor

segra [v.; ~r, ~de, ~t] win, prevail

segrare [n.; ~n, ~] winner, victor

sej [pron.refl.; see: **sig**]

SEK¹ [abbrev: svenska kronor] Swedish kronor/crowns

sek.² [see: **sekund**] second [1/60 minute]

sekatör [n.; ~en, ~er] pruning shears

sekel [n.; seklet, ~] century

sekelskifte [n.; ~t, ~n] turn of the century

sekr. [see: **sekreterare**]

sekreterare [n.; ~n, ~] secretary

sekretess [n.; ~en] secrecy; privacy

sekretesslag [n.; ~en] Official Secrets Act

sekretesspolicy [n.; ~n] privacy policy [IT]

sekt [n.; ~en, ~er] sect; sparkling wine [German]

sektor [n.; ~n, ~er] sector

sekund [n.; ~en, ~er] second [1/60 of minute]

sekunda [adj.] second-rate

sekundärrätt [n.; ~en] secondary law [EU]

sekventiell åtkomst [n.; ~en, ~er] serial access [IT]

selleri [n.; ~n] celery, celery root

semantik [n.; ~en] semantics [gram]

semester [n.; ~n, semestrar] vacation

semesterby [n.; ~n, ~ar] vacation campground

semesterort [n.; ~en, ~er] vacation resort

semesterschema [n.; ~t, ~n] vacation timetable

semesterstuga [n.; ~n, -stugor] vacation cottage, weekend cottage

semesterstängd [adj.; -stängt, ~a] closed for vacation

semestra [v.; ~r, ~de, ~t] go on vacation

semifinal [n.; ~en, ~er] semifinals [sports]

semikolon (;) [n.; ~t, ~] semicolon (;)

seminarium [n.; -nariet, -narier] seminar

semla [n.; ~n, semlor] Lenten cream-stuffed bun

sen¹ [adj. ; ~t, ~a] late

sen² [adv.; see: **sedan**]

sena [n.; ~n, senor] tendon

senap [n.; ~en] mustard

senapsväxt [n.; ~en, ~er] mustard plant

senare [adj./adv.comp.; see: **sen**] later; **en stund ~** a little later

senast [adj./adv.superl.] latest; recent; at the latest; **tack för ~!** thanks for last time!; **~ när** by when, when at the latest; **~e tillträde kl 23** night entry no later than 11 p.m.

senhöst [n.; ~en] late autumn

sensommar [n.; ~en] Indian summer

sent [adv./adj.; see: **sen**] late

separerad [adj.; -rerat, ~e] separated

september [n.] September

Serafimerorden [n.] Order of the Seraphim

serb [n.; ~en, ~er] Serb

Serbien [n.] Serbia

serbisk [adj.] Serbian

serie [n.; ~n, ~r] series; league [sports]; comic strip, cartoon drawing

seriefigur [n.; ~en, ~er] character in a comic strip

seriekrock [n.; ~en, ~ar] multiple collision

seriell [adj.; ~t, ~a] serial [IT]

serieport [n.; ~en, ~ar] serial port [IT]

serietidning [n.; ~en, ~ar] comic book

seriös [adj.; ~t, ~a] serious

serve [n.; ~n, servar] serve [tennis]

server [n.; ~n, ~] server [IT]

servera [v.; ~r, ~de, ~t] serve; **hur maten ~s** serving suggestions; **~s med** to be served with

serverdator [n.; ~n, ~er] server [IT]

servering [n.; ~en, ~ar] service; eating establishment; serving, sitting [dining car]

serveringsavgift [n.; ~en, ~er] service charge, tip

serveringsfat [n.; ~et, ~] serving dish

serveringspersonal [n.; ~en] wait staff, servers

serverprogram [n.; ~et, ~] server program [IT]

servett [n.; ~en, ~er] napkin

service [n.; ~n] service

serviceavgift [n.; ~en, ~er] service charge

servicehus [n.; ~et, ~] assisted-living apartments

serviceinriktad [adj.; -riktat, ~e] service-oriented

servicemedveten [adj.; -vetet, -vetna] conscientious

servicepaket [n.; ~et, ~] service pack [IT]

serviceuppdatering [n.; ~en, ~ar] service update [IT]

servitris [n.; ~en, ~er] waitress

servitör [n.; ~en, ~er] waiter

servobromsar [n.pl.] power brakes

servostyrning [n.; ~en] power steering

ses [v.refl.; ses, sågs, setts] meet, see one another; **vi ~** see you later

sesamolja [n.; ~n] sesame oil

sett [v.past; see: **se**]

sevärdhet [n.; ~en, ~er] sight, something worth seeing

sex¹ [n.; ~et] sex

sex² [num.] six

sextio [num.] sixty

sextionde [adj.] sixtieth

sexton [num.] sixteen

sextonde [adj.] sixteenth

sextonhundratalet (1600-talet) [n.] seventeenth century

sexualundervisning [n.; ~en] sex education

sexuell [adj.; ~t, ~a] sexual

sexuellt ofredande [n.] sexual harassment, molestation

SF [abbrev: Svenska filmindustri AB] Swedish Film Industry Corp.

sfi [abbrev: svenska för invandrare] Swedish for immigrants

sg. [see: **singularis**]

shareware [n.] shareware [IT]

shobresvenska [n.; ~n] slang used

by youth [with many foreign words]

shoppa [v.; ~r, ~de, ~t] shop

shoppingcenter [n.; ~et, -centrer] shopping center, shopping mall

shoppingkorg [n.; ~en, ~ar] shopping basket

shoppingvagn [n.; ~en, ~ar] shopping cart

shoppingväska [n.; ~n, -väskor] shopping bag

shorts [n.; ~en] shorts [pl.] [clothing]

show [n.; ~en, ~er] show [entertainment]

Sibirien [n.] Siberia

Sicilien [n.] Sicily

sicksack: i ~ in a zigzag

sid. [abbrev: sidan] page (p.)

SIDA¹ [abbrev: Swedish International Development Agency] Swedish International Development Agency (SIDA)

sida² [n.; ~n, sidor] side; page; **på vänster/höger ~** on the left/right side

sidbrytning [n.; ~en, ~ar] page break [IT]

siden [n.; ~et] silk

sidenmåleri [n.; ~et, ~er] silk painting

sidfot [n.; ~en, -fötter] footer [IT]

sidnumrering [n.; ~en] pagination [IT]

sidogata [n.; ~n, -gator] side street

sidoljus [n.; ~et, ~] sidelight

sidospegel [n.; ~n; -speglar] side mirror

siffra [n.; ~n, siffror] figure, numeral

SIFO [abbrev: Svenska institutet för opinionsundersökning] Swedish Institute for Opinion Research

sig [pron.refl.] oneself (himself, herself, itself, themselves)

sightseeingtur [n.; ~en, ~er] sightseeing tour

sign. [abbrev: signatur; signum] signature; signed

signal [n.; ~en, ~er] signal; car horn

signalhorn [n.; ~et, ~] car horn

signatur [n.; ~en, ~er] signature

sik [n.; ~en, ~ar] whitefish

siklöja [n.; ~n, -löjor] small whitefish

sikrom [n.; ~en, ~] whitefish roe

sikt [n.; ~en, ~er] visibility, view; presentation; term, run

sikta [v.; ~r, ~de, ~t] aim, take aim; point; sight

sikte [n.; ~t, ~n] sight [gun]; sight, view

sil [n.; ~en, ~ar] sieve, collander, strainer

silke [n.; ~t] silk

silkespapper [n.; -pappret] tissue paper

sill [n.; ~en, ~ar] herring

sillbricka [n.; ~n, -brickor] plate of assorted herring

sillsallad [n.; ~en] beet and herring salad

silltallrik [n.; ~en, ~ar] plate of assorted herring

silver [n.; silvret] silver

silversaker [n.pl.] silverware

silverskål [n.; ~en, ~ar] silver bowl

simbassäng [n.; ~en, ~er] swimming pool

simborgarmärke [n.; ~t, ~n] swimming badge [national 200 meter swim test]

simdyna [n.; ~n, -dynor] swimming belt, swimming float; water wing

simfötter [n.pl.] swim fins, flippers

simhall [n.; ~en, ~ar] indoor swimming pool

SIM-kort [n.; ~et; ~] SIM card [IT]

simkunnig [adj.; ~t, ~a] able to swim

simlärare [n.; ~n, ~] swimming coach

simma [v.; simmar, sam, summit] swim; **~ bröstsim/crawl/fjärilsim/ryggsim** do the breaststroke/crawl/butterfly/backstroke

simmare [n.; ~n, ~] swimmer

simning [n.; ~en] swimming

simskola [n.; ~n, -skolor] swimming school, swimming lessons

simtävling [n.; ~en, ~ar] swimming race, swim meet

sin [adj.poss.; sitt, ~a] his/her/its/their own

sing. [see: **singularis**]

singel [n.; ~n, singlar] singles

singularis [n.; singularen] singular [gram]

sinne [n.; ~t, ~n] sense; ~ **för humor** sense of humor

sirap [n.; ~en] syrup, molasses

SIS [abbrev: Swedish Standards Institute] Swedish Standards Institute (SIS)

sist [adv.] last, at the end; last time; **till** ~ at the end

sista [adj.] last; **i** ~ **minuten** at the last minute

sistnämnd [adj.; -nämnt, ~a] latter, just mentioned

sistone: på ~ lately, of late

sitt [adj.poss.; see: **sin**]

sitta [v.; sitter, satt, suttit] sit; ~ **barnvakt** babysit; ~ **bra** fit; ~ **fast** be stuck, be jammed; ~ **ihop** be stuck together; ~ **kvar** be kept after school; not be promoted

sittande [adj.] sitting, seated; in office; in session

sittplatsbiljett [n.; ~en, ~er] seat reservation ticket

sittvagn [n.; ~en, ~ar] stroller [baby]; ordinary train car [not sleeper]

situation [n.; ~en, ~er] situation

SJ [abbrev: Statens Järnvägar] State Railroad System

sjal [n.; ~en, ~ar] shawl

sju [num.] seven

sjuk [adj.; ~t, ~a] ill, sick

sjukanmäla sig [v.; ~r ~de, ~t] call in sick

sjukdom [n.; ~en, ~ar] illness, disease

sjukersättning [n.; ~en, ~er] sickness benefit

sjukförsäkring [n.; ~en] health insurance, medical insurance

sjukförsäkringsintyg [n.; ~et, ~] medical insurance certificate

sjukgymnast [n.; ~en, ~er] physiotherapist

sjukgymnastik [n.; ~en] physiotherapy

sjukhem [n.; ~et, ~] nursing home

sjukhus [n.; ~et, ~] hospital, infirmary

sjukhusakuten [n.] emergency room

sjukintyg [n.; ~et, ~] doctor's certificate

sjukkassa [n.; ~n, -kassor] health insurance office

sjukledig [adj.; ~t, ~a] on sick leave, off sick

sjuklön [n.; ~en, ~er] sickness allowance, sick pay

sjukpenning [n.; ~en, ~ar] sickness allowance

sjukpension [n.; ~en, ~er] disability pension

sjukskriva [v.; -skriver, -skrev, -skrivit] put on sick/medical leave

sjukskriven [adj.; -skrivet, -skrivna] out sick, on sick leave

sjuksköterska [n.; ~n, -sköterskor] nurse

sjuksköterskaskola [n.; ~n, -skolor] nursing school

sjukvård [n.; ~en] medical care, medical treatment

sjukvårdsbiträde [n.; ~t, ~n] hospital orderly/assistant

sjukvårdsystem [n.; ~et] medical care system

sjunde [adj.] seventh; July

sjunga [v.; sjunger, sjöng, sjungit] sing; ~ **falskt** sing off key/out of tune; ~ **rent** sing in tune

sjunka [v.; sjunker, sjönk, sjunkit] sink

sjuställig [adj.; ~t, ~a] seven-bit [IT]

sjuttio [num.] seventy

sjuttionde [adj.] seventieth

sjutton [num.] seventeen; ~**!** darn! [colloq.], damn! [colloq.]

sjuttonde [adj.] seventeenth

sjuttonhundratalet (1700-talet) [n.] eighteenth century

själ [n.; ~en, ~ar] soul; mind, spirit

Själland [n.] Zealand [in Denmark]

själv [adj.] self, oneself, yourself, himself, etc.

självbetjäning [n.; ~en] self-service

självfallen [adj.; -fallet, -fallna] obvious

självförsvar [n.; ~et] self-defense

självförtroende [n.; ~t, ~n] self-confidence, self-reliance

självhushåll [n.; ~et] housekeeping by tenant

självklar [adj.; ~t, ~a] obvious; natural

självklarhet [n.; ~en] obviousness

självkännedom [n.; ~en] self-awareness

självmord [n.; ~et, ~] suicide; **begå ~** commit suicide

självmordsbombare [n.; ~n, ~] suicide bomber

självservering [n.; ~en] self-service

självservice [n.; ~en] self-service; **~ restaurang** [n.] self-service restaurant

självstyrelse [n.; ~n] self-government

självständig [adj.; ~t, ~a] independent, stand-alone

självständighet [n.; ~en] independence

självsäker [adj.; ~t, -säkra] self-confident

självutlösare [n.; ~n] self-timer [camera]

sjätte [adj.] sixth; June

sjö [n.; ~n, ~ar] lake; sea; **till sjöss** to sea, at sea, by sea

sjöborre [n.; ~n, -borrar] sea urchin

Sjöfartsverket (SjöV) [n.] National Shipping Administration

sjögång [n.; ~n] rough seas

Sjöhistoriska museet [n.] Maritime Museum

sjökapten [n.; ~en, ~er] sea captain

sjöman [n.; -mannen, -män] sailor

sjömansbiff [n.; ~en] beef casserole with vegetables in beer

sjömil [n.; ~en, ~] nautical mile

sjöresa [n.; ~n, -resor] voyage

sjöräddningstjänst [n.; ~en, ~er] sea rescue service

sjösjuk [adj.; ~t, ~a] seasick

sjösjuka [n.; ~n] seasickness

sjötunga [n.; ~n, -tungor] sole [fish]

sjöutsikt [n.; ~en, ~er] view of the sea

SjöV [abbrev: Sjöfartsverket] Swedish Maritime Administration

sk. [abbrev: så kallad] so called

ska [v.; see: **skola**]

skada¹ [n.; ~n, skador] damage, injury

skada² [v.; ~r, ~de, ~t] injure, hurt; damage

skadad [adj.; skadat, ~e] hurt, damaged

skadas [v.passive; ~, skadades, skadats] get damaged, be damaged

skadegörelse [n.; ~n, ~r] damage

skadestånd [n.; ~et, ~] damages

skaffa [v.; ~r, ~de, ~t] order; obtain, get; **~ sig** get, acquire, get hold of

skagenröra [n.; ~n] shrimp mix [see: **toast skagen**]

Skagerack [n.] Skagerrak [strait between Norway, Denmark and Sweden]

skaka [v.; ~r, ~de, ~t] shake, agitate

skal [n.; ~et, ~] shell; peel; cover

skala¹ [n.; ~n, skalor] scale; spectrum

skala² [v.; ~r, ~de, ~t] peel; shell

skalbagge [n.; ~n, -baggar] beetle

skalbar font [n.; ~en, ~er] scalable font [IT]

skaldjur [n.; ~et, ~] shellfish

skall [v.; see: **skola**]

skalle [n.; ~, skallar] skull; head

skallig [adj.; ~t, ~a] balding

skam [n.; ~en] shame

skandal [n.; ~en, ~er] scandal

Skandinavien [n.] Scandinavia

skandinavisk [adj.; ~t, ~a] Scandinavian

skanna [v.; ~r, ~de, ~t] scan [IT]

skanner [n.; ~n, ~s] scanner [IT]

skanning [n.; ~en, ~ar] scanning [IT]

skans [n.; ~en, ~ar] redoubt, little fort

Skansen [n.] Skansen [park in Stockholm with zoo and museum of village life]

skapa [v.; ~r, ~de, ~t] create

skaplig [adj.; ~t, ~a] pretty good

skar [v.past; see: **skära**]

skara [n.; ~n, skaror] crowd, group, band

skare [n.; ~n] crust [on snow]

skarp [adj.; ~t, ~a] sharp; piercing; piquant

skarpsill [n.; ~en, ~ar] herring, sprat

skarvfri [adj.; ~tt, ~a] seamless

skata [n.; ~n, skator] magpie [bird]

skatt [n.; ~en, ~er] tax

skattebetalare [n.; ~n, ~] taxpayer

skatteflykt [n.; ~en] tax evasion

skattefri [adj.; ~tt, ~a] tax free

skattefrågor [n.pl.] taxation

skatteharmonisering [n.; ~n] tax harmonization [EU]

skattehöjning [n.; ~en, ~ar] tax increase

skattemyndighet [n.; ~en, ~er] tax authority

skattepliktig [adj.; ~t, ~a] taxable

skattesmitare [n.; ~n, ~] tax evader

skattesänkning [n.; ~en] tax reduction

Skatteutskottet [n.] Committee on Taxation [in Parliament]

Skatteverket [n.] Tax Administration [like US Internal Revenue Service]

skattkammare [n.; ~en] treasury

skavsår [n.; ~et, ~] blister

ske [v.; ~r. ~dde, ~tt] happen, occur

sked [n.; ~en, ~ar] spoon

skelögd [adj.; -ögt, ~a] squint-eyed, cross-eyed, walleyed

sken [n.; ~et, ~] light; appearance

skenben [n.; ~et, ~] shinbone

skepp [n.; ~et, ~] ship

skeppskaj [n.; ~en, ~er] pier

skeptisk [adj. ~t, ~a] skeptical

sketch [n.; ~en, ~er] sketch

SKF [abbrev: Svenska kullagerfabriken] Swedish Ball Bearing Company

skick [n.; ~et, ~] condition, state; good order; custom; manners

skicka [v.; ~r, ~de, ~t] send

skickad [adj.; skickat, ~e] sent

skicklig [adj.; ~t, ~a] skillful, capable

skidbacke [n.; ~n, -backar] ski slope

skidbindningar [n.pl.] ski bindings

skidbyxor [n.pl.] ski pants

skidföre [n.; ~t] skiing surface, skiing conditions

skidglasögon [n.pl.] skiing goggles

skidlektion [n.; ~en, ~er] ski lesson

skidlift [n.; ~en, ~ar] ski lift

skidlov [n.; ~et] skiing vacation

skidlöpare [n.; ~n, ~] skier

skidlärare [n.; ~n, ~] ski instructor

skidor [n.pl.] skis; åka ~ go skiing, ski

skidort [n.; ~en, ~er] ski area, ski resort

skidpjäxor [n.pl.] ski boots

skidskola [n.; ~n, -skolor] ski school

skidskytte [n.; ~t] biathlon

skidspår [n.; ~et, ~] ski trail, ski run

skidstavar [n.pl.] ski poles

skidställ [n.; ~et, ~] ski rack

skidsäsong [n.; ~en] skiing season

skidtävling [n.; ~en, ~ar] skiing competition

skidutrustning [n.; ~en] skiing equipment

skidvalla [n.; ~n, -vallor] ski wax

skidåkare [n.; ~n, ~] skier

skidåkning [n.; ~en] skiing

skifta [v.; ~r, ~de, ~t] shift

skiftande [adj.] changing, varied

skiftläge [n.; ~t, ~n] case [letters, i.e. uppercase, lowercase] [IT]

skiftnyckel [n.; ~n, -nycklar] wrench

skifttangent [n.; ~en] shift key [IT]

skild [adj.; skilt, ~a] separate, differing; divorced

skildra [n.; ~r, ~de. ~t] depict

skildring [n.; ~en ~ar] description, account

skilja [v.; skiljer, skilde, skilt] separate; ~ sig divorce

skiljetecken [n.; -tecknet, ~] punctuation marks

skillnad [n.; ~en, ~er] difference; göra någon ~ make a difference

skils [v.passive; skils, skildes, skilts] part; divorce, get divorced

skilsmässa [n.; ~n, -mässor] divorce

skina [v.; skiner, sken, skinit] shine

skinka [n.; ~n, skinkor] ham

skinklåda [n.; ~n] ham and egg casserole

skinksmörgås [n.; ~en, ~ar] ham sandwich

skinn [n.; ~et, ~] fur, leather
skinnbyxor [n.pl.] leather pants
skinnjacka [n.; ~n, -jackor] leather jacket
skinnrock [n.; ~en, ~ar] leather coat
skinnstövlar [n.pl.] leather boots
skirat smör [n.; ~et] melted butter
skissblock [n.; ~et, ~] sketching block
skit [n.; colloq.; ~en] dirt, filth; junk; shit [vul.], crap [colloq.]
skita [v.; vul.; ~r, sket, skitit] shit [vul.]; ~ **i** not give a damn about [colloq.]
skitig [adj.; ~t, ~a] dirty
skitprat [n.; colloq.; ~et] bullshit [vul.], bull [colloq.]
skitsnack [n.; colloq.; ~et] bullshit [vul.], bull [colloq.]
skiva [n.; ~n, skivor] slice; record, CD; party
skivaffär [n.; ~en, ~er] record shop
skivbroms [n.; ~en, ~ar] disc brake
skivenhet [n.; ~en, ~er] disk drive [IT]
skivminne [n.; ~t, ~n] disk drive, hard disk
skivpratare [n.; ~n, ~] disk jockey (DJ)
skivstånge [n.~en, -stänger] barbell
skivtallrik [n.; ~en, ~ar] turntable
skjorta [n.; ~n, skjortor] shirt
skjortblus [n.; ~en, ~ar] shirt blouse
skjul [n.; ~et] shed
skjuta [v.; skjuter, sköt, skjutit] shoot; push; bud
skjutdörr [n.; ~en, ~ar] sliding door
skjutfönster [n.; -fönstret, ~] sash window
skjuten [adj.; skjutet, skjutna] shot
skjuts [n.; ~en, ~ar] lift, ride
sko [n.; ~n, ~r] shoe
skoaffär [n.; ~en, ~er] shoe store
skoborste [n.; ~n, -borstar] shoe brush
skog [n.; ~en, ~ar] forest, wood(s)
skogsarbetare [n.; ~n, ~] woodsman, forestry worker
skogsbrand [n.; ~en, -bränder] forest fire

skogsland [n.; ~et, -länder] forested land
Skogs- och jordbrukets forskningsrådet (SJFR) [n.] Forestry and Agriculture Research Council
Skogsstyrelsen [n.] National Forestry Board
skogssvamp [n.; ~en, ~ar] field mushrooms
skojig [adj.; ~t, ~a] fun
skokräm [n.; ~en, ~er] shoe polish
skola¹ [n.; ~n, skolor] school; **gå i ~n** go to school
skola² [v.; skall/ska, skulle, skolat] will, shall
skolbarn [n.; ~et, ~] school child
skolbetyg [n.; ~et, ~] school marks
skolgång [n.; ~en] schooling
skolgård [n.; ~en, ~ar] school yard
skolhälsovård [n.; ~en] school health service
skolk [n.; ~et] truancy
skolkamrat [n.; ~en, ~er] schoolmate
skollov [n.; ~et, ~] school vacation
skolmat [n.; ~en] school meals
skolmaterial [n.; ~en] school supplies
skolmåltid [n.; ~en, ~er] school lunch
skolplikt [n.; ~en] compulsory schooling
skolpliktig [adj.; ~t, ~a] of school age
skolresa [n.; ~n, -resor] school trip
skolsköterska [n.; ~n, -sköterskor] school nurse
skolstyrelse [n.; ~n, ~r] local school authority
skolsystem [n.; ~et, ~] school system
skoltrött [adj.; ~, ~a] tired of school
skolunderbyggnad [n.; ~en, ~er] educational background
skolungdom [n.; ~en, ~ar] school children
skolvaktmästare [n.; ~n, ~] school caretaker
Skolverket [n.] National Education Administration
skolväska [n.; ~n, -väskor] school bag

skolår [n.; ~et, ~] school year

skomakare [n.; ~n, ~] cobbler; shoe repair shop

skonummer [n.; -numret] shoe size

skorpa [n.; ~n, skorpor] rusk; crust, scab

Skorpionen [n.] Scorpio

skorpsmulor [n.pl.] breadcrumbs

skosnören [n.pl.] shoe laces

skoter [n.; ~n, skotrar] scooter [motorized]

skotsk [adj.; ~t, ~a] Scottish; ~whisky Scotch whisky

skott [n.; ~et, ~] shot; sprout, shoot

skotte [n.; ~n, skottar] Scot

skottkärra [n.; ~n; -kärror] wheelbarrow

Skottland [n.] Scotland

skottår [n.; ~et] leap year

SKR [abbrev: svenska kronor] Swedish crowns (SEK)

skramla [v.; ~r, ~de, ~t] rattle

skrapning [n.; ~en, ~ar] curettage

skratt [n.; ~et, ~] laugh, laughter

skratta [v.; ~r, ~de, ~t] laugh

skrek [v.past; see: **skrika**]

skridskobana [n.; ~n, -banor] skating rink

skridskor [n.pl.] skates; åka ~ skate

skridskoåkning [n.; ~en] skating

skrift [n.; ~en, ~er] publication

skriftlig [adj.; ~t, ~a] written; ~ tentamen written exam

skriftspråk [n.; ~et, ~] written language

skrika [v.; skriker, skrek, skrikit] shout, scream, yell

skript [n.; ~en, ~er] script [IT]

skriptspråk [n.; ~et, ~] script language [IT]

skriva [v.; skriver, skrev, skrivit] write; ~ in sig register; ~ under sign; ~ ut prescribe; print [IT]

skrivare [n.; ~n, ~] printer [IT]

skrivblock [n.; ~et, ~] writing pad

skrivbord [n.; ~et, ~] desk; desktop

skrivbordsunderlägg [n.; ~et] background [PC screen], wallpaper [IT]

skrivelse [n.; ~n, ~r] writing, letter; writ

skriven [adj.; skrivet, skrivna] written

skrivmaskin [n.; ~en, ~er] typewriter

skrivskydda [v.; ~r, ~de, ~t] write protect [file] [IT]

skrot [n.; ~et] scrap, junk

skrotbilstävling [n.; ~en, ~ar] stock-car racing

skrubbsår [n.; ~et, ~] graze, scrape

skruv [n.; ~en, ~ar] screw; spin

skruva [v.; ~r, ~de, ~t] screw, turn; ~ ned turn down [volume]

skruvmejsel [n.; ~n, ~ar] screwdriver

skrynkelfri [adj.; ~tt, ~a] crease-resistant

skryta [v.; skryter, skröt, skrutit] boast

skråma [n.; ~n, skråmor] scratch, cut

skräck [n.; ~en] terror, fright

skräckfilm [n.;] horror movie

skräddare [n.; ~n, ~] tailor

skräddarsydd [adj.; -sytt, ~a] made to measure, tailor-made

skrädderi [n.; ~et, ~er] tailors, dressmakers

skrämma [v.; skrämmer, skrämde, skrämt] frighten

skrämmande [adj.] terrifying

skräp [n.; ~et] junk, trash, rubbish

skräpa ner [v.; ~r, ~de, ~t] litter

skräpmat [n.; ~en] junk food

skräppost [n.; ~en] junk mail, spam [IT]

skräppostfilter [n.; -filtret, ~] junk-mail filter, spam filter [IT]

skugga [n.; ~n, skuggor] shadow

skuggig [adj.; ~t, ~a] shady

skuld [n.; ~en, ~er] blame; guilt; debt

skuldränta [n.; ~n, -räntor] interest on debt

skull [n.] sake; **för Jans ~** for Jan's sake

skulle [v.past; see: **skola**]; ~ vilja would like to

skulptur [n.; ~en, ~r] sculpture

skulptör [n.; ~en, ~er] sculptor
skulptris [n.; ~en, ~er] sculptress
skum [n.; skummet] foam
skumma [v.; ~r, ~de, ~t] skim, read through
skummad mjölk [n.; ~et] skim milk
skurborste [n.; ~n, -borstar] scouring/scrub brush
skurpulver [n.; -pulvret, ~] scouring powder
skutbana [n.; ~n, -banor] shooting range
sky[1] [n.; ~n, ~ar] cloud, sky; gravy
sky[2] [v.; ~r, ~dde, ~tt] avoid, shun, shrink back from
skydd [n.; ~et] protection
skydda [v.; ~r, ~de, ~t] protect; ~ **sig** protect oneself
skyddshelgon [n.; ~et, ~] patron saint
skyfall [n.; ~et, ~] cloudburst
skyffel [n.; ~n, skyfflar] shovel; dustpan
skyldig [adj.; ~t, ~a] in debt; guilty; **vad är jag ~?** how much do I owe?
skyldighet [n.; ~en, ~er] obligation, responsibility
skylla sig själv [v.; skyller, skylde, skylt] have oneself to blame
skylt [n.; ~en, ~ar] sign
skyltfönster [n.; -fönstret, ~] store window
skyltning [n.; ~en, ~ar] display
skyltskåp [n.; ~et, ~] display case
skymning [n.; ~en] dusk, twilight
skymt [n.; ~en, ~ar] glimpse, idea; trace
skynda (sig) [v.; ~r, ~de, ~t] hurry; ~ **på** hurry, speed up
skyttelservice [n.; ~n] shuttle service
Skytten [n.] Sagittarius
skyttetävling [n.; ~en, ~ar] shooting competition
skådespel [n.; ~et, ~] play (theater)
skådespelare [n.; ~n, ~] actor
skådespelerska [n.; ~n, -spelerskor] actress
skål[1] [n.; en, ~ar] bowl
skål![2] [exp] to your health!, cheers!

Skåne [n.] Skåne, Scania [southern tip of Sweden]; aquavit flavored with aniseed
skånsk [adj.; ~t, ~a] of Skåne
skåp [n.; ~et, ~] cupboard
skåpbil [n.; ~en, ~ar] van
skåpmat [n.; ~en] leftovers
skåra [n.; ~n, skåror] cut, notch
skägg [n.; ~et, ~] beard
skäl [n.; ~et, ~] reason
skälla [v.; skäller, skälde, skält] bark [dog]; scold
skämd [adj.; skämt, ~a] rotten, bad, spoiled
skämma [v.; skämmer, skämde, skämt] spoil
skämmas [v.passive; skäms, skämdes, skämts] be ashamed
skämt [n.; ~et, ~] joke
skämta [v.; ~r, ~de, ~t] joke
skämtteckning [n.; ~en, ~ar] cartoon
skänka [v.; skänker, skänkte, skänkt] donate, give
skär[1] [adj.; ~t, ~a] pure; pink
skär[2] [n.; ~et, ~] (cutting) edge; small rocky island
skära [v.; skär, skar, skurit] cut
skärbräda [n.; ~n, -brädor] cutting board
skärgård [n.; ~en, ~ar] archipelago
skärm [n.; ~en, ~ar] screen, display [IT]
skärmaskin [n.; ~en, ~er] slicer
skärmflyging [n.; ~en] paragliding
skärp [n.; ~et, ~] belt
skärpa[1] [n.; ~n] sharpness, keenness
skärpa[2] [v.; skärper, skärpte, skärpt] sharpen; intensify
skärsår [n.; ~et, ~] cut [wound]
skärtorsdagen [n.] Maundy/Holy Thursday [Thursday before Easter]
sköldkörtel [n.; ~n, -körtlar] thyroid gland
sköldpadda [n.; ~n, -paddor] turtle [generic], tortoise [land]
sköldpaddssoppa [n.; ~n, -soppor] turtle soup
skölja [v.; sköljer, sköljde, sköljt] rinse, wash off
skön [adj.; ~t, ~a] nice, comfortable; lovely; ~**a konsterna** fine arts

skönhet [n.; ~en] beauty
skönhetsbehandling [n.; ~en] beauty care
skönhetsmedel [n.; -medlet, ~] beauty product
skönhetssalong [n.; ~en, ~er] beauty parlor, beauty salon
skönlitteratur [n.; ~en] literary works, belles lettres [pl.], fiction and drama and poetry
sköta [v.; sköter, skötte, skött] take care of, deal with; ~ **hushållet själv** cook and clean house for oneself; ~ **om sig** look after oneself
skötas [v.passive; sköts, sköttes, skötts] be looked after
skötbord [n.; ~et, ~] changing table
sköterska [n.; ~n, sköterskor] nurse
skötrum [n.; -rummet, ~] nursery room; changing room for babies
skötsel [n.; ~n] care
skötselråd [n.; ~et, ~] instructions for maintenance/care
SL [abbrev: Storstockholms Lokaltrafik] Stockholm Transport
sladd [n.; ~en, ~ar] cable; skid
slag [n.; ~et, ~] sort, kind; battle; lapel, cuff [pants]; **ett ~s** a kind of
slaganfall [n.; ~et, ~] stroke
slagbord [n.; ~et, ~] drop-leaf table
slagsmål [n.; ~et, ~] fight
slagverk [n.; ~et] percussion instruments
slak [adj.; ~t, ~a] slack, loose
slaktare [n.; ~n, ~] butcher
slalombacke [n.; ~n, ~ar] slalom slope
slalomport [n.; ~en, ~ar] slalom gate
slalomtävling [n.; ~en, ~ar] slalom race
slalomåkare [n.; ~n, ~] slalom skier
slapp [v.past; see: **slippa**]
slappna av [v.; ~r, ~de, ~t] relax
slarva [v.; ~r, ~de, ~t] be careless with/about, neglect
slarvig [adj.; ~t, ~a] careless
slav [n.; ~en, ~ar] slave
slet [v.past; see: **slita**]
slickepinne [n.; ~n, -pinnar] lollipop

slinga [n.; ~n, slingor] coil; wreath; loop; lock [hair]
slingra [v.; ~r, ~de, ~t] wind, twine; ~ **sig** wind, wreathe; be evasive
slipa [v.; ~r, ~de, ~t] grind, polish
slipat glas [n.] cut glass
slippa [v.; slipper, slapp, sluppit] get out of, be excused from, escape, avoid, not have to; slip, sneak
slips [n.; ~en, ~ar] tie
slipsklämma [n.; ~n, -klämmor] tie clip
slira [v. ~r, ~de, ~t] slip, skid
slirig [adj.; ~t, ~a] slippery; ~ **körbana** slippery road surface
slita [v.; sliter, slet, slutit] wear out; tear, pull; work hard, toil; ~ **sig ifrån** tear oneself away; ~ **ut** wear out
sliten [adj.; slitet, slitna] worn
slott [n.; ~et, ~] castle, palace
slottsstek [n.; ~en] pot roast [with brandy, molasses, sprats]
slottstappning [n.; ~en] bottling at the chateau
Slovakien [n.] Slovakia
slovakisk [adj.; ~t, ~a] Slovak
slovakiska [n.] Slovak language
Slovenien [n.] Slovenia
slovensk [adj.; ~t, ~a] Slovene
slovenska [n.] Slovene language
slump [n.; ~en, ~ar] chance, coincidence; remnant
slumpmässig [adj.; ~t, ~a] random
slumpmässiga användaradresser [n.pl.] IP-spoof addresses [IT]
slumptalsgenerator [n.; ~en, ~er] random number generator [IT]
sluss [n.; ~en, ~ar] lock, sluice
slut¹ [adj.] finished, exhausted, empty, all gone
slut² [n.; ~et, ~] end; **till ~** in the end; ~ **på** no more of, out of, end of; ~ **på vägarbete** end of construction [road sign]
sluta [v.; ~r, ~de, ~t] finish, end; quit [studies, job]; stop; ~ **med** finish, stop; ~ **ett avtal** conclude an agreement
slutare [n.; ~n, ~] shutter [photo]

slutbetyg [n.; ~et, ~] diploma, course completion certificate

sluten [adj.; slutet, slutna] closed; secret; reserved; ~ **klass** closed class [gram]; ~ **omröstning** secret ballot

slutföra [v.; -för, -förde, -fört] finish

slutgiltig [adj.; ~t, ~a] definitive, final

slutligen [adv.] finally, in the end

slutsats [n.; ~en, ~er] conclusion, inference; **dra ~en att** draw the conclusion that

slutspel [n.; ~et, ~] endgame; finals

slutstation [n.; ~en, ~er] final station, last stop, terminal

slutsåld [adj.; -sålt, -sålda] sold out

sluttagg [n.; ~en, ~er] end tag, closing tag [IT]

slå [v.; slår, slog, slagit] hit, strike; dial; chime; ~ **0 till receptionen** dial 0 for the front desk; ~ **12** ring 12 o'clock; ~ **9 till linjen** dial 9 for an outside line; ~ **in** wrap; ~ **in PIN numret** enter your PIN; ~ **nummer 345** dial number 345; ~ **sig ner** sit down; ~ **sönder** break; ~ **upp ett tält** pitch a tent; ~ **upp** look up [in a book]; ~ **ut** bloom

slåss [v.; slåss, slogs, slagits] fight

släcka [v.; släcker, släckte, släckt] put out/turn off [light]

släde [n.; ~n, slädar] sleigh

släkt [n.; ~en, ~er] family; relative; related; ~ **på långt håll** distant relatives; **vara ~ med** be related to

släkting [n.; ~en, ~ar] relative

slänga [v.; slänger, slängde, slängt] dump, throw away; swing; ~ **ut** throw out

släp [n.; ~et, ~] trailer

släpa [v.; ~r, ~de, ~t] trail, drag

släplift [n.; ~en, ~er] ski tow

släppa [v.; släpper, släppte, släppt] let go, let drop; relax; ~ **av** drop off

släpvagn [n.; ~en, ~ar] trailer

slät [adj.; slätt, släta] smooth, even; plain

släthårig [adj.; ~t, ~a] smooth-haired

slätt [n.; ~en, ~er] plain

slätvar [n.; ~en, ~ar] brill [fish]

slö [adj.; ~tt, ~a] dull, blunt; slow, sluggish

slöja [n.; ~n, slöjor] veil

slöjd [n.; ~en, ~er] handicraft

slösa [v.; ~r, ~de, ~t] squander, waste; be wasteful

SM [abbrev: svenskt mästerskap] Swedish championship

smak [n.; ~en, ~er] taste, flavor

smaka [v.; ~r, ~de, ~t] taste

smaklig måltid [n.] bon appetit

smaksätta [v.; -sätter, -satte, -satt] season

smaksättning [n.; ~en, ~ar] flavoring

smaktillsatser [n.pl.] condiments

smakämnen [n.pl.] flavoring agents

smal [adj.; ~t, ~a] narrow; ~ **väg** narrow road

smalben [n.; ~et, ~] shin

smalrandig [adj.; ~t, ~a] narrow-striped, pinstriped

smaragd [n.; ~en, ~er] emerald

smart [adj.; ~, ~a] smart

smartkort [n.; ~et, ~] smart card [IT]

smekmånad [n.; ~en, ~er] honeymoon

SMHI [abbrev: Sveriges Meteorologiska och Hydrologiska Institut] Swedish Meteorological and Hydrological Institute [Swedish weather service]

smickra [v.; ~e, ~de, ~t] flatter

smida [v.; smider, smidde, smitt] forge; devise

smide [n.; ~t, ~en] smithwork, forging

sminka [v.; ~r, ~de, ~t] make up, apply cosmetics; ~ **sig** make oneself up

sminkning [n.; ~en, ~ar] makeup

smita [v.; smiter, smet, smitit] avoid, get out of

smitare [n.; ~n, ~] hit-and-run driver

smitta [v.; ~r, ~de, ~t] infect, communicate

smittad [adj.; smittat, ~e] infected, contaminated

smittkoppor [n.pl.] smallpox

smittsam [adj.; ~t, -samma] contagious

Smittskyddsinstitutet (SMI) [n.] National Swedish Institute for Infectious Disease Control

SMK [abbrev: Svenska motor-klubben] Swedish Motor Club

smoking [n.; ~en, ~ar] tuxedo

sms [abbrev: short message service] short message service (SMS)

SMTP-server [n.; ~n, ~] SMTP server [for outgoing e-mail] [IT]

smuggla [v.; ~r, ~de, ~t] smuggle

smugit [v.past; see: **smyga**]

smula [n.; ~n, smulor] crumb, scraps, fragment

smultron [n.; ~et, ~] wild strawberry

smutsig [adj.; ~t, ~a] dirty

smutstvätt [n.; ~en] dirty linen, dirty washing

smycke [n.; ~t, ~n] piece of jewelry

smycken [n.pl.] jewelry

smyga [v.; smyger, smög, smugit] slip; sneak, steal, creep

små [adj.pl; see: **liten**] little, small

småbarn [n.; ~et, ~] toddler

småbröd [n.; ~en] roll

småbåtshamn [n.; ~en, ~ar] small-boat harbor, marina

småfranska [n.; ~n, -franskor] French roll

småföretag [n.; ~et, ~] small business

småkaka [n.; ~n, -kakor] cookie

Småland [n.] Småland [region in southern Sweden]

småningom [adv.] gradually, little by little

små och medelstora företag [n.pl.] small and medium enterprises

småpengar [n.pl.] small change

smårutig [adj.; ~t, ~a] with small check pattern

smårätter [n.pl.] hors d'oeuvres [pl.]

småsill [n.; ~en, ~ar] whitebait

smått [adv.] small; **ha ~ om** be short of

småvarmt [n.] hot snack

smäll [n.; ~en, ~ar] bang

smällare [n.; ~n, ~] firecracker

smälta [v.; smälter, smalt, smält] melt

smältost [n.; ~en] mild cheese [soft, runny]

smärta [n.; ~n, smärtor] pain

smärtsam [adj.; ~t, ~a] painful

smärtstillande medel [n.; medlet, ~] painkiller

smög [v.past; see: **smyga**]

smör [n.; ~et] butter

smöra [v.; ~r, ~de, ~t] butter

smörblomma [n.; ~n, -blommor] buttercup

smördeg [n.; ~en] (puff) pastry

smörfräst [adj.; ~, ~a] sautéed

smörgås [n.; ~en, ~ar] (open) sandwich

smörgåsbord [n.; ~et] cold buffet

smörja [n.; ~n, smörjor] grease

smörjning [n.; ~en, ~ar] lubrication

smörsås [n.; ~en, ~er] butter sauce

snabb [adj.; ~t, ~a] fast, quick; **~ uppkoppling** fast connection [IT]

snabbkaffe [n.; ~t] instant coffee

snabbkassa [n.; ~n] express checkout

snabbknapp [n.; ~en, ~ar] hot key, keyboard shortcut [IT]

snabbköp [n.; ~et, ~] self-service shop, supermarket

snabbmat [n.; ~en] fast food

snabbmatställe [n.; ~t, ~n] fast-food place

snabbmeddelande [n.; ~t, ~n] instant messaging/message [IT}

snabbmeny [n.; ~n, ~er] pop-up menu, shortcut menu [IT]

snabbsökning [n.; ~en, ~ar] quick search [IT]

snabbt [adv.] quickly

snabbtangent [n.; ~en, ~er] hot key, quick key [IT]

snabbtvätt [n.; ~en, ~ar] laundromat

snabbvalsmeny [n.; ~n, ~er] pop-up menu, shortcut menu [IT]

snabel [n.; ~n, snablar] trunk [of an elephant]

snabel-a (@) [n.] at-sign, commercial at (@) [IT]

snack: det är inget ~ om saken there's no question about it, that's that

snacka [v.; ~r, ~de, ~t] chat; chatter
snacks [n.pl.] snacks
snagg [n.; ~en] crew cut
snaps [n.; ~en, ~ar] aquavit, spirits, schnapps
snar [adj.; ~t, ~a] speedy, quick
snart [adv.] soon; så ~ som möjligt as soon as possible
snattare [n.; ~n, ~] shoplifter
snatteri [n.; ~et, ~er] shoplifting
snedstreck [n.; ~et, ~] slash [IT]
snett [adv.] diagonally; awry, wrong; ~ mittemot diagonally opposite
SNF [abbrev: Svenska naturskydds-föreningen] Swedish Society for Nature Conservation
snickarbyxor [n.pl.] overalls
snickare [n.; ~n, ~] carpenter
snickeriverkstad [n.; ~en, -städer] carpentry workshop
snideri [n.; ~et, ~er] carving
snigelfart [n.:] med ~ at a snail's pace
snigelpost [n.; ~en] snail mail [IT]
sniglar [n.pl.] snails
snille [n.; ~t, ~n] genius
snilleblixt [n.; ~en, ~ar] brainwave, stroke of genius
snitt [n.; ~et, ~] cut; section
snok [n.; ~en, ~ar] grass snake
snorkel [n.; ~n, snorklar] snorkel
snorkig [adj.; ~t, ~a] snooty, haughty
snorkla [v.; ~r, ~de, ~t] snorkel
snowboard [n.; ~en, ~er] snowboard
snowrafting [n.; ~en] snowrafting
snuva [n.; ~n] cold, sniffles; ha ~ have a runny nose
snuvig [adj.; ~t, ~a] with a runny nose
snyftreportage [n.; ~t, ~] sob story
snygg [adj.; ~t, ~a] attractive
snyta sig [v.; snyter, snöt, snutit] blow one's nose
snäll [adj.; ~t, ~a] kind; well-behaved; vill du vara ~ och komma nu please come now
snälltåg [n.; ~et, ~] long-distance express train
snäv [adj.; ~t, ~a] tight, narrow; ~ kjol tight skirt

snö [n.; ~n] snow
snöa [v.; ~r, ~ade, ~t] snow
snödroppe [n.; ~n, -droppar] snowdrop
snöglopp [n.; ~et] sleet
snökedjor [n.pl.] snow chains
snöplog [n.; ~en, ~ar] snowplow
snöre [n.; ~t, ~n] string, lace
snöripa [n.; ~n, -ripor] ptarmigan
snöskoter [n.; ~n, -skotrar] snowmobile, ski-doo, snowcat
snöslask [n.; ~et] slush
snöstorm [n.; ~en, ~ar] blizzard
social [adj.; ~t, ~a] social; ~a dimensionen social dimension [EU]
socialarbetare [n.; ~n, ~] social worker
Sociala stadgan [abbrev: Stadga om arbetstagarnas grundläggande sociala rättigheter] Charter of the Fundamental Social Rights of Workers (Social Charter) [EU]
socialavgift [n.; ~en, ~er] payroll tax
socialbidrag [n.; ~et] public assistance
socialdemokrat [n.; ~en, ~er] Social Democrat; Socialdemokraterna Social Democrats
Socialdemokratiska Arbetarepartiet (SAP) [n.] Social Democratic Workers Party
Socialdepartementet (S) [n.] Ministry of Health and Social Affairs
Socialförsäkringsutskottet [n.] Committee on Social Insurance (in Parliament)
socialförvaltning [n.; ~en, ~ar] social welfare administration
socialhjälp [n.; ~en] public assistance
socialist [n.; ~en, ~er] socialist (n)
socialistisk [adj.; ~t, ~a] socialist (adj)
Socialistiska Partiet (SP) [n.] Socialist Party
socialistiskt block [n.; ~et] left-wing coalition
socialminister [n.; ~n] Minister for Health and Social Affairs
socialpolitik [n.; ~en] social policy [EU]

socialsekreterare [n.; ~n] social welfare secretary
Socialstyrelsen [n.] National Board of Health and Welfare
socialtjänst [n.; ~en, ~er] social services
Socialutskottet [n.] Committee on Health and Welfare (in Parliament)
socialvård [n.; ~en] social welfare
socialvårdare [n.; ~n, ~] social welfare worker
sociolog [n.; ~en, ~er] sociologist
socionom [n.; ~en, ~er] trained social worker
socka [n.; ~n, sockor] sock
sockel [n.; ~n, socklar] socket
socken [n.; socknen, socknar] parish
socker [n.; sockret] sugar
sockerdricka [n.; ~n, -drickor] lemonade
sockerfri [adj.; ~tt, ~a] sugar-free
sockerkaka [n.; ~n, -kakor] sponge cake
sockersjuk [adj.; ~t, ~a] diabetic
sockersjuka [n.; ~n] diabetes
sockerskål [n.; ~en, ~ar] sugar bowl
sockerärtor [n.pl.] sugar snap peas
sockor [n.pl.; see: socka] socks
sockra [v.; ~r, ~de, ~t] sugar, sweeten
sodavatten [n.; -vattnet] soda water
soffa [n.; ~n, soffor] sofa
soffbord [n.; ~et, ~] coffee table
Sofia [n.] Sophia
sojabönor [n.pl.] soybeans
sojabönsolja [n.; ~n] soybean oil
sojalivsmedel [n.; -medlet, ~] soy foods
sojamjölk [n.; ~et] soy milk
SOK [abbrev: Sveriges Olympiska Kommitté] Swedish Olympic Committee
sol [n.; ~en, ~ar] sun
solarium [n.; solariet, solarier] solarium
sola sig [v.; ~r, ~de, ~t] sunbathe
solbada [v.; ~r, ~de, ~t] sunbathe
solblockkräm [n.; ~en, ~er] sunblock cream
solbränd [adj.; -bränt, ~a] sunburned, tanned

solbränna [n.; ~n] suntan
solcell [n.; ~en, ~er] solar cell
soldat [n.; ~en, ~er] soldier
soldyrkare [n.; ~n, ~] sun worshipper
soldäck [n.; ~et, ~] sun deck
solglasögon [n.pl.] sunglasses
solhatt [n.; ~en, ~ar] sun hat
solidarisk [adj.; ~t, ~a] loyal, solidary
solidaritet [n.; ~en] solidarity
solig [adj.; ~t, ~a] sunny
solist [n.; ~en, ~er] soloist
solkiga varor [n.pl.] soiled goods
solkräm [n.; ~en, ~er] suntan lotion; ~ med extra skydd sunblock
solljus [n.; ~et] sunlight
solnedgång [n.; ~en ~ar] sunset
sololja [n.; ~n] suntan oil
solparasoll [n.; ~et, ~] parasol
solros [n.; ~en, ~or] sunflower
solsken [n.; ~et] sunshine
solskydd [n.; ~et] sunshade, sunblock
solskyddsfaktor [n.; ~n, ~er] sunblock factor
solskyddskräm [n.; ~en, ~er] sun cream
solsting [n.; ~et] sunstroke
solstol [n.; ~en, ~ar] deck chair, sun chair
solsveda [n.; ~n] sunburn
soltak [n.; ~et] sunroof
soluppgång [n.; ~en, ~ar] sunrise
solöga [n.; ~t] marinated sprats [with onions, beetroot, egg yolk]
som[1] [conj.] as; inte så stor ~ not as big as; ~ vanligt as usual
som[2] [rel.pron.] who, which, that
Somalia [n.] Somalia
somalisk [adj.; ~t, ~a] Somali
somlig [pron./adj.; ~t, ~a] some
sommar [n.; ~en, somrar] summer
sommarhotell [n.; ~et, ~] tourist hostel
sommarlov [n.; ~et, ~] summer vacation
sommarolympiaden [n.] Summer Olympics
sommarsemester [n.; ~n, -semestrar] summer vacation
sommarsolstånd [n.; ~et] summer solstice

sommarställe [n.; ~t, ~n] country place, summer cottage

sommartid [n.; ~en] daylight savings time, summer time

sommartidtabell [n.; ~en, ~er] summer timetable

somna [v.; ~r, ~de, ~t] fall asleep

somras: i ~ last summer

son [n.; ~en, söner] son

sond [n.; ~en, ~er] probe, sound

sondotter [n.; ~n, -döttrar] granddaughter [daughter of son]

sonson [n.; ~en, -söner] grandson [son of son]

sopa [v.; ~r, ~de, ~t] sweep

sopbil [n.; ~en, ~ar] garbage truck

sopborste [n.; ~n, -borstar] dust brush

sophink [n.; ~en, ~ar] garbage can

sopkvast [n.; ~en, ~ar] broom

sopor [n.pl.] garbage, rubbish, trash

soppa [n.; ~n, soppor] soup

soppskål [n.; ~en, ~ar] soup tureen

soppslev [n.; ~en, ~ar] soup ladle

sopptallrik [n.; ~en, ~ar] soup plate

soppåse [n.; ~n, ~påsar] garbage bag

sopran [n.; ~en, ~er] soprano

sopskyffel [n.; ~n, -skyfflar] dustpan

sopsäck [n.; ~en, ~ar] trash bag

soptunna [n.; ~n, -tunnor] trash can

sorbet [n.; ~en] sherbet

sorg [n.; ~en, ~er] sorrow, distress; mourning

sorglig [adj.; ~t, ~a] sad, deplorable, pitiful

sort [n.; ~en, ~er] sort, kind

sortera [v.; ~r, ~de, ~t] sort [IT]

sortiment [n.; ~et, ~] assortment

sos[1] [abbrev: smör, ost och sill] marinated herring, butter and cheese with bread

SOS[2] [abbrev: Sveriges officiella statistik] Statistics Sweden

SOS[3] [abbrev: internationella nödsignalen] SOS [abbrev: save our ship/souls (emergency appeal for help)]

SOS-tjänst [abbrev: Samhällets olycksfalls- och säkerhetstjänst] local emergency service center

sotare [n.; ~n, ~] chimney sweep

SOU [abbrev: Statens offentliga utredningar] Swedish Government Official Reports

soul [n.] soul music

souvenir [n.; ~en, ~er] souvenir

souvenirbutik [n.; ~en, ~er] souvenir shop

sova [v.; sover, sov, sovit] sleep; ~ **middag** take a nap

Sovjetunion [n.; ~en] Soviet Union

sovplats [n.; ~en, ~er] sleeper berth

sovrum [n.; ~et, ~] bedroom

sovsäck [n.; ~en, ~ar] sleeping bag

sovvagn [n.; ~en, ~ar] sleeping car, sleeper

soyaproteiner [n.pl.] soybean proteins

spad [n.; ~et, ~] stock, broth

spade [n.; ~n, spadar] shovel

spader [n.; ~n, ~] spades [cards]

spagetti [n.; ~n] spaghetti

spalt [n.; ~en, ~er] column [IT]

Spanien [n.] Spain

spanjor [n.; ~en, ~er] Spaniard

spann [n.; ~en, ~ar] pail

spansk [adj.; ~t, ~a] Spanish

spanska [n.] Spanish language

spara [v.; ~r, ~de, ~t] save; ~ **som** save as [IT]

sparande [n.; ~t] saving, thrift

sparbank [n.; ~en, ~er] savings bank

sparbanksbok [n.; ~en, -böcker] savings book

sparka [v.; ~r, ~de, ~t] kick

sparkcykel [n.; ~n, -cyklar] (child's) scooter

sparkstötting [n.; ~en, ~ar] kick sled

sparris [n.; ~en] asparagus

sparrisknopp [n.; ~en, ~ar] asparagus tip

sparrissoppa [n.; ~n, -soppor] asparagus soup

sparv [n.; ~en, ~ar] sparrow

spec. [abbrev: speciell] special

speceriaffär [n.; ~en, ~er] grocery store

specialeffekter [n.pl.] special effects

specialerbjudande [n.; ~t, ~n]
special offer
specialfröken [n.; ~, -fröknar] remedial education teacher [female]
specialist [n.; ~en, ~er] specialist
specialitet [n.; ~en, ~er] specialty;
~ för landsdelen local specialty
specialklass [n.; ~en, ~er] remedial
class
specialkost [n.; ~en] specialized
foods
speciell [adj.; ~t, ~a] special;
peculiar
speciellt [adv.] especially
specificerad [adj.; -cerat, ~e]
itemized
specifik betydelse [n.; ~n, ~r]
particularized meaning, restrictive
meaning [gram]
spektakulär [adj.; ~t, ~a] spectacular, sensational
spekulation [n.; ~en, ~er] speculation, venture
spegel [n.; ~n, speglar] mirror
spegla [v.; ~r, ~de, ~t] reflect, mirror
spegling [n.; ~en, ~ar] mirroring
[IT]
spel [n.; ~et, ~] game, play
spela [v.; ~r, ~de, ~t] play; perform;
det ~r ingen roll never mind; ~ in
record; ~ kort play cards; ~ tennis play tennis
speladapter [n.;] game control
adapter [IT]
spelare [n.; ~n, ~] player
spelarkad [n.; ~en, ~er] games
arcade
spelautomat [n.; ~en, ~er] arcade
game
spelkort [n.pl.] playing cards
spelman [n.; ~nen, -männ] folk
musician
spelport [n.; ~en, ~ar] game port [IT]
spelrum [n.; ~et, ~] game room
spenat [n.; ~en] spinach
spermie [n.; ~n, ~r] spermatozoid
spets [n.; ~en, ~ar] point, tip, end;
lace
spetsig [adj.; ~t, ~a] pointed
spetsparenteser [n.pl.] curly
brackets [IT]

spettekaka [n.; ~n, -kakor] cone-
shaped cake
spicken sill [n.] salted herring
spindel [n.; ~n, spindlar] spider
spindelväv [n.; ~en, ~ar] cobweb
spinna [v.; spinner, span, spunnit]
spin; purr
spion [n.; ~en, ~er] spy
spionprogramvara [n.; ~n, -varor]
spyware [IT]
spira [n.; ~n, spiror] spire; spar;
scepter
spis [n.; ~en, ~ar] fireplace; stove,
range
spjäla [n.; ~n, spjälor] lath; splint
spola [v.; ~r, ~de, ~t] flush, rinse,
flood; wind, reel; ~ i/på toaletten
flush the toilet; ~ fram fast forward; ~ tillbaka rewind
spolarvätska [n.; ~n] windshield
cleaning fluid
sponsor [n.; ~n, ~er] sponsor
sponsra [v.; ~r, ~de, ~t] sponsor
spontan [adj.; ~t, ~a] spontaneous
sport [n.; ~en, ~er] sport; games; ~
och idrott games and athletics
sporta [v.; ~r, ~de, ~t] pursue a
sport
sportaffär [n.; ~en, ~er] sporting
goods store
sportbil [n.; ~en, ~ar] sports car
sportdykning [n.; ~en] skin diving
sportevenemang [n.; ~en, ~er]
sports event
sportfiske [n.; ~et] angling, fishing
sporthall [n.; ~en, ~ar] sports hall
sportklubb [n.; ~en, ~ar] sports
club
sportlov [n.; ~et, ~] winter vacation
sportsida [n.; ~n, -sidor] sports
page
sportskor [n.pl.] running shoes
sprack [v.past; see: spricka]
sprang [v.past; see: springa]
spred [v.past; see: sprida]
sprej [n.; ~en, ~er] spray, hairspray
spricka [v.; spricker, sprack,
spruckit] crack, split, burst
sprida [v.; sprider, spred, spridit]
circulate, disseminate, spread; ~
sig spread out

spridd [adj.; spritt, ~a] spread, scattered, dispersed, isolated

spridning [n.; ~en] spreading

spridprogram [n.; ~et, ~] shareware [IT]

springa [v.; springer, sprang, sprungit] run

springare [n.; ~n, ~] knight [chess]

sprit [n.; ~en] spirits, hard liquor

spritärter [n.pl.] green peas

sprucken [adj.; sprucket, spruckna] cracked, split

spruckit [v.past; see: **spricka**]

sprungit [v.past; see: **springa**]

spruta [n.; ~, sprutor] injection, shot; **få en ~** get a shot

språk [n.; ~et, ~] language

språkcenter [n.; -centret, -centrer] language center [community center with study materials, interpretation services, etc.]

språklärare [n.; ~n, ~] language teacher

Språk- och folkminnesinstitutet (SOFI) [n.] Language and Folklore Research Institute

språkrådgivning [n.; ~en] language advice, language consulting

spränga [v.; spränger, sprängde, sprängt] burst, blow up

spunnet socker [n.; sockret] cotton candy

spy [v.; ~r, ~dde, ~tt] vomit

spår [n.; ~et, ~] track; trace

spåra [v.; ~r, ~de, ~t] track, trace

spårbarhet [n.; ~en] accountability

spårvagn [n.; ~en, ~ar] trolley, streetcar

spårvagnshållplats [n.; ~en, ~er] trolley stop

spårväg [n.; ~en, ~ar] trolley line, streetcar line

späda [v.; späder, spädde, spätt] dilute

spädbarn [n.; ~et, ~] baby, infant

spädbarnskläder [n.pl.] babywear

spädgris [n.; ~en, ~ar] suckling pig

spänd [adj.; spänt, ~a] tense

spänn [n.; ~en, ~; colloq.] Swedish crown coin

spänna [v.; spänner, spände, spänt] tighten, fasten

spännande [adj.] exciting

spänning [n.; ~en] tension, suspense, mystery; voltage

spärr [n.; ~en, ~ar] barrier; **4% ~en** "4% hurdle" [parties must get at least 4% of the vote to get into Parliament]

spärra [v.; ~r, ~de, ~t] block, bar, obstruct; spread out, stretch open

spärrfunktion [n.; ~en] parental control, content filter [IT]

spärrlinje [n.; ~n, ~r] road divider line

spätta [n.; ~n, spättor] plaice [fish]

spöka [v.; ~r, ~de, ~t] haunt

spöke [n.; ~t, ~n] ghost, specter

squash [n.; ~en, ~er] squash

SR[1] [abbrev: Sveriges Radio] Swedish Broadcasting Corporation

sr.[2] [abbrev: senior] senior

SRK [abbrev: Svenska Röda korset] Swedish Red Cross

ss [abbrev: såsom] as; like

SSRS [abbrev: Sjöräddningssällskapet] Swedish Sea Rescue Society

SSU [abbrev: Sveriges Socialdemokratiska Ungdomsförbund] Swedish Social Democratic Youth League

S:t[1] [abbrev: Sankt] Saint [male]

ST[2] [abbrev: Stockholms-Tidningen] Stockholms-Tidningen [weekly newspaper]

St.[3] [abbrev: Stora] Great(er) [in place names]

st.[4] [abbrev: styck, stycke] piece; each

S:ta (abbrev: Sankta) Saint [female]

STAB [abbrev: Svenska tändsticks AB] Swedish Match Co.

stabil [adj.; ~t, ~a] stable

Stabiliserings- och associeringsprocess [n.; ~en] Stabilization and Association Process [EU]

stabilitet [n.; ~en] stability

Stabilitets- och tillväxtpakten [n.] Stability and Growth Pact [EU]

stack [n.; ~en, ~ar] stack, pushdown list [IT]

stackars han/hun! [exp.] poor thing/guy/girl!

stad [n.; ~en (also: **stan**), städer] town, city

stadig [adj.; ~t, ~a] steady, regular

stadion [n.; ~en, ~er] stadium

stadium [n.; stadiet, stadier] stage, phase, degree

stadjeep [n.; ~en, ~er] sport utility vehicle (SUV)

stadsbibliotek [n.; ~et, ~] municipal library

stadsbo [n.; ~n, ~r] town dweller

stadsbuss [n.; ~en, ~er] city bus

stadscentrum [n.; -centret] downtown, city center

stadsdel [n.; ~en, ~ar] quarter, district, part of town

stadshus [n.; ~et, ~] town hall

stadskarta [n.; ~n, -kartor] town map

stadsmur [n.; ~en, ~ar] city wall

stadspark [n.; ~en, ~er] public garden, city park

stadsrundtur [n.; ~en, ~er] tour of the city

stafett [n.; ~en, ~er] token [IT]

stafettlöppning [n.; ~en, ~ar] relay race

staket [n.; ~et, ~] fence

stal [v.past; see: **stjäla**]

stall [n.; ~et, ~] stable, barn

stam [n.; stammen, stammar] trunk [tree]; family, lineage

stamnät [n.; ~et, ~] backbone [IT]

stamtavla [n.; ~n, -tavlor] pedigree chart

stan [short form for: staden; see: **stad**]

standard [n.; ~en, ~er] standard; default

standardalternativ [n.; ~et, ~] default [IT]

standardanslutning [n.; ~en, ~ar] default connection [IT]

standardavvikelse [n.; ~n, ~r] standard deviation

standardinställning [n.; ~en, ~ar] default setting [IT]

standardpris [n.; ~et, ~] standard charge, regular price

standardprogram [n.; ~et, ~] default program [IT]

standardtext [n.; ~en, ~er] boilerplate [IT]

standardvärde [n.; ~t, ~n] default, default value [IT]

stanna [v.; ~r, ~de, ~t] stop; stay [at hotel]; ~ **kvar** remain; ~ **motorn** turn off the motor; ~ **vid** stop at

stapeldiagram [n.; -grammet, ~] bar chart [IT]

stare [n.; ~n, starar] starling

stark [adj.; ~t, ~a] strong; hard, alcoholic; hot, spicy; ~t **verb** irregular verb, strong verb [gram]

starksprit [n.; ~en] hard liquor

starköl [n.; ~et] strong beer [over 3.5 % alcohol]

starr [n.; ~en]: grå ~ cataract; grön ~ glaucoma

start [n.; ~en, ~er] start; takeoff

starta [v.; ~r, ~de, ~t] start; boot; ~ **motorn** start the motor

startbana [n.; ~n, -banor] takeoff runway

startkablar [n.pl.] jumper cables

startknapp [n.;] start button [IT]

startmeny [n.; ~n, ~er] start menu [IT]

startmotor [n.; ~n, ~er] starter motor

startplats [n.; ~en, ~er] takeoff area

startsida [n.; ~n, -sidor] start page, home page [IT]

starttagg [n.; ~en, ~ar] start tag, opening tag [IT]

stat [n.; ~en, ~er] state; staff; style; establishment; budget estimates

Statens biografbyrå [n.; ~n] National Board of Film Classification

Statens bostadskreditnämnd (BKN) [n.; ~en] National Housing Credit Guarantee Board

Statens energimyndighet [n.; ~en] National Energy Authority

Statens fastighetsverk (SFV) [n.; ~et] National Property Administration

Statens folkhälsoinstitut (FHI) [n.; ~et] National Institute of Public Health

Statens geotekniska institut (SGI)

[n.; ~et] National Geotechnical Institute

Statens haverikommission (SHK) [n.; ~en] National Accident Investigation Commission

Statens historiska museer [n.pl.] National Historical Museums

Statens institut för handikappfrågor i skolan (SIH) [n.] National Institute for the Handicapped in Schools

Statens institut för kommunikationsanalys (SIKA) [n.] National Institute for Communications Analysis

Statens institut för särskilt utbildningsstöd (SISUS) [n.] National Institute for Special Educational Support

Statens institutionsstyrelse (SiS) [n.; ~n] National Board of Institutional Care

Statens jordbruksverk (SJV) [n.; ~et] National Agricultural Administration

Statens Järnvägar (SJ) [n.pl.] State Railroad System

Statens konstråd (SK) [n.; ~et] National Council for the Arts

Statens kriminaltekniska laboratorium (SKL) [n.; -toriet] National Laboratory of Forensic Science

Statens kulturråd [n.; ~et] National Council for Cultural Affairs

Statens kvalitets- och kompetensråd [n.; ~et] National Council for Quality and Development

Statens kärnkraftinspektion (SKI) [n.; ~en] National Nuclear Power Inspectorate

Statens livsmedelsverk (SLV) [n.; ~et] National Food Administration

Statens ljud- och bildarkiv [n.; ~et] National Archive of Recorded Sound and Moving Images

Statens maritima museer (SMM) [n.pl.] National Maritime Museums

Statens offentliga utredningar (SOU) [n.pl.] Swedish Government Official Reports

Statens pensionsverk (SPV) [n.; ~et] National Pensions Administration

Statens personadressregisternämnd (SPAR-nämnden) [n.; ~en] Swedish Population Address Registry Board

Statens Provningsanstalt [n.; ~en] National Testing Institute

Statens räddningsverk [n.; ~et] Swedish Rescue Services Agency

Statens skaderegleringsnämnd (SSRN) [n.; ~en] National Claims Adjustment Board

Statens skolverk [n.; ~et] National Agency for Education

Statens strålskyddsinstitut (SSI) [n.; ~et] National Radiation Protection Institute

Statens va-nämnd [n.; ~en] National Water Supply and Sewage Tribunal

Statens veterinärmedicinska anstalt (SVA) [n.; ~en] National Veterinary Institute

Statens väg- och transportforskningsinstitut (VTI) [n.; ~et] National Road and Transport Research Institute

Statens vägverk [n.; ~et] National Road Administration

Stadga för de europeiska politiska partierna [n.] Regulation governing European political parties

Stadga för offentliga tjänster [n.; Stadgan] Public service charter [EU]

Stadgan om de grundläggande rättigheterna [n.] Charter of Fundamental Rights [EU]

station [n.; ~en, ~er] station

stationsansvarig [n.; ~, ~a] station manager, station chief

stationsvagn [n.; ~en, ~ar] station wagon [car]

stationär [adj.; ~t, ~a] stationary

statistik [n.; ~en, ~er] statistics [sing.]

Statistiska centralbyrån (SCB) [n.] Statistics Sweden

stativ [n.; ~et, ~] tripod, stand, rack [IT]

statlig [adj.; ~t, ~a] state-run, national, government; **~t företag** state-owned company; **~t stöd** state subsidy, state aid

stats- [prefix] government, state, public

statsanställd [n.; ~a] civil servant

statsbidrag [n; ~et,] government subsidy

statsbudget [n.; ~en, ~er] government budget

statschef [n.; ~en, ~er] head of state

statsegendom [n.; ~en, ~er] state property

statsfinanser [n.pl.] government finances

statshemlighet [n.; ~en, ~er] state secret

Statskontoret [n.] Office of Public Management

statskupp [n.; ~en, ~er] coup d'etat

statslös [adj.; ~t, ~a] stateless

statsman [n.; -mannen, -män] statesman

statsminister [n.; ~n, -ministrar] prime minister

statsmonopol [n.; ~et, ~] government monopoly

statsråd [n.; ~et, ~] cabinet minister

Statsrådsberedningen (SB) [n.] Prime Minister's Office

statssekreterare [n.; ~n, ~] State Secretary

statsskuld [n.; ~en, ~er] national debt

statstjänsteman [n.; -mannen, -män] civil servant

statsunderstöd [n.; ~et, ~] government subsidy/support

statsöverhuvud [n.; ~et, ~] head of state

status [n.; ~en] status

statusfält [n.; ~et, ~] status bar [IT]

statusrad [n.; ~en, ~er] status bar [IT]

staty [n.; ~n, ~er] statue

stav [n.; ~en, ~ar] pole

stava [v.; ~r, ~de, ~t] spell

stavelse [n.; ~n, r] syllable

stavfel [n.; ~et, ~r] spelling mistake [IT]

stavhopp [n.; ~et, ~] pole vault

stavning [n.; ~en, ~ar] spelling [IT]

stavningskontroll [n.; ~en, ~er] spell-check [IT]

stearinljus [n.; ~et, ~] candle

steg¹ [n.; ~et, ~] step

steg² [v.past; see: **stiga**]

stek [n.; ~en, ~ar] roast

steka [v.; steker, stekte, stekt] fry; **~ i ugn** roast

stekpanna [n.; ~n, -pannor] frying pan

stekt [adj.; ~, ~a] fried, sautéed; **~ i panna** fried; **~ i ugn** roasted; **~ på spett** spit-roasted; **~ ägg** fried egg

stel [adj.; ~t, ~a] stiff; **vara ~ i ryggen** have a stiff back

stelkramp [n.; ~en] tetanus

sten [n.; ~en, ~ar] rock, stone

stenbitssoppa [n.; ~n] lumpfish soup

stenblock [n.; ~et, ~] boulder

Stenbocken [n.] Capricorn; **~s vändkrets** Tropic of Capricorn

stendöv [adj.; ~t, ~a] stone deaf

stenig [adj.; ~t, ~a] pebbly, stoney

stenläggning [n.; ~en] paving, pavement

stenografi [n.; ~n] shorthand

stenåldern [n.] Stone Age

stereoanläggning [n.; ~en, ~ar] stereo equipment

steril [adj.; ~t, ~a] sterile

steriliseringsvätska [n.; ~n] sterilizing solution

stetoskop [n.; ~et, ~] stethoscope

steward [n.; ~en, ~er] steward

STF [abbrev: Svenska Turistföreningen] Swedish Tourist Association

Sth. [abbrev: Stockholm] Stockholm

Sthlm [abbrev: Stockholm] Stockholm

stick! [interj.] get lost!, go away!

sticka¹ [n.; ~n, stickor] splinter; knitting needle

sticka² [v.; sticker, stack, stuckit] prick, sting; knit; go off, disappear

stickad [adj.; stickat, ~e] knitted
stickkontakt [n.; ~en, ~er] plug, electric plug
stickning [n.; ~en] knitting
stickpropp [n.; ~en, ~ar] plug
stickylle [n.; ~t, ~n] knitting wool
stift [n.; ~et, ~] pin, tack; diocese
stiftelse [n.; ~n, ~r] foundation
stig [n.; ~en, ~ar] footpath, path
stiga [v.; stiger, steg, stigit] step; come; rise; ~ av get off; ~ in come inside, step inside, enter; ~ på step in; get on; ~ upp get up
stigande ordning [n.] ascending order [IT]
stigning [n.; ~en, ~ar] rise, climb, ascent
stil [n.; ~en, ~ar] style
stilig [adj.; ~t, ~a] handsome
still [adv.] still
stilla¹ [adj.] still, quiet; sitta ~ sit still; Stilla havet Pacific Ocean
stilla² [v.; ~r, ~de, ~t] soothe, appease; quench
stilleben [n.; ~et, ~] still life
stillestånd [n.; ~et] armistice
stilmall [n.; ~en, ~ar] style sheet [IT]
stiltje [n.; ~n, ~] calm, lull
stimulera [v.; ~r, ~de, ~t] stimulate
stimulerande [adj.] stimulating; ~ medel stimulant
stinka [v.; stinker, stank] smell
stins [n.; ~en, ~ar] stationmaster
stipendium [n.; stipendiet, stipendier] grant, scholarship
stirra [v.; ~r, ~de, ~t] stare, gaze
stjäla [v.; stjäl, stal, stulit] steal
stjälk [n.; ~en, ~ar] stalk, stem
stjärna [n.; ~n, stjärnor] star
stjärnbild [n.; ~en, ~er] constellation
stjärntecken [n.; -tecknet, ~] star sign, Zodiac sign; asterisk (*)
stjärt [n.; ~en, ~ar] bottom, butt; tail
sto [n.; ~et, ~n] mare, filly
stockholmare [n.; ~n, ~] Stockholmer
Stockholms internationella fredsforskningsinstitut (SIPRI) [n.] Stockholm International Peace Research Institute (SIPRI)

stod [v.past; see: stå]
stokastisk [adj.; ~t, ~a] stochastic [IT]
stol [n.; ~en, ~ar] chair
stollift [n.; ~en, ~ar] chair lift
stolpiller [n.; ~] suppository
stolsits [n.; ~en, ~ar] seat
stolt [adj.; ~, ~a] proud
stolthet [n.; ~en] pride; arrogance
stopp [n.; ~et, ~] blockage, plug; stop
stoppa [v.; ~r, ~de, ~t] stop, prevent; stuff; darn [socks]
stoppförbud [n.] no stopping, no standing
stopplikt [n.; ~en] obligation to stop and yield [traffic]
stoppskylt [n.; ~en, ~ar] stop sign
stopptecken [n.; -tecknet, ~] stop sign
stor [adj.; ~t, ~a] big; Stora Björnen Big Dipper; ~a kroppspulsådern aorta
storartad [adj.; -artat, ~e] superb
storasyster [n.; ~n, -systrar] big sister
Storbritannien [n.] Great Britain
storebror [n.; -brodern] big brother
storebrorsfasoner [n.pl.] big brother attitude
storlek [n.; ~en, ~ar] size
storm [n.; ~en, ~ar] storm, gale
storma [v.; ~r, ~de, ~t] storm, be stormy; rage
stormakt [n.; ~en, ~er] great power
stormarknad [n.; en, ~er] factory outlet, super store
stormig [adj.; ~t, ~a] stormy
stormvarning [n.; ~en, ~ar] gale warning, storm warning
stormvind [n.; ~en, ~ar] gale
storslagen [adj.; -slaget, -slagna] magnificent
storslalom [n.; ~en] giant slalom
storstad [n.; ~en, -städer] big city
Storstadsdelegationen [n.] Commission on Metropolitan Areas
stort [adj.; see: stor]
stortå [n.; ~n, ~r] big toe
STP [abbrev: särskild tilläggspension] special supplementary pension

straff [n.; ~et, ~] punishment; penalty
straffa [v.; ~r, ~de, ~t] punish
straffarbete [n.; ~t, ~t] hard labor
strafflindring [n.; ~en, ~ar] reduction of sentence
straffregister [n.; -registret, ~] criminal record
straffspark [n.; ~en, ~ar] penalty kick [sports]
strand [n.; ~en, stränder] beach, shore
strandskor [n.pl.] beach shoes
strategi [n.; ~n, ~er] strategy
strategi inför anslutningen [n.] pre-accession strategy [EU]
strategisk [adj.; ~t, ~a] strategic
strax [adv.] soon, in a moment; ~ efter soon after; ~ intill next door, right beside; ~ utanför just outside
streck [n.; ~et, ~] stroke; line
streckad linje [n.] dotted line, dashes [IT]
streckkod [n.; ~en, ~er] bar code
strejk [n.; ~en, ~er] strike
strejka [v.; ~r, ~de, ~t] strike, go on strike
stress [n.; ~en] stress
stressa [v.; ~r, ~de, ~t] get agitated
stressad [adj.; stressat, ~e] agitated, stressed
stressig [adj.; ~t, ~a] stressful
strid [adj.; stritt, ~a] rapid, violent, torrential
strid [n.; ~en, ~er] struggle, fight, combat; dispute
strida [v.; strider, stred, stridit] fight
stridande [adj.] opposing; adverse, contrary; combatant
strikt [adj.; ~, ~a] strict, severe
stroke [n.] stroke [golf]
struken[1] [adj.; struket, strukna] level
struken[2] [v.past; see: **stryka**]
strukit [v.past; see: **stryka**]
strukturfonder [n.pl.] structural funds [EU: regions, social, agriculture, fish]
strumpbyxor [n.pl.] panty hose, tights

strumpor [n.pl.] stockings
strunta (i) [v.; ~r, ~de, ~t] not care (about)
strupe [n.; ~en, ~ar] throat
strut [n.; ~en, ~ar] cone [ice cream, sweet]
struts [n.; ~en, ~ar] ostrich
stryk [n.; ~et] beating, thrashing
stryka [v.; strycker, strök, strukit] stroke; press, iron; smear; cross out, delete; ~ under underline
strykbräde [n.; ~t, ~n] ironing board
strykfri [adj.; -fritt, ~a] wash-and-wear, drip-dry
strykjärn [n.; ~et, ~] iron [appliance]
strå [n.; ~et, ~n] straw
stråke [n.; ~n, stråkar] bow [musical instrument]; **stråkar** strings [musical instruments]
strålande [adj.] beaming, radiant, brilliant
strålföljning [n.; ~en] ray tracing [IT]
strålgång [n.; ~en] ray tracing [IT]
strålkastare [n.; ~en, ~] headlight; floodlight
strålning [n.; ~en, ~ar] radiation
sträcka[1] [n.; ~n, sträckor] distance, stretch
sträcka[2] [v.; sträcker, sträckte, sträckt] reach
sträckning [n.; ~en, ~ar] pulled muscle, pulled ligament
sträng[1] [adj.; ~t, ~a] strict
sträng[2] [n.; ~en, ~ar] string
sträv [adj.; ~t, ~a] rough, harsh, grating
strävan [n.; ~, strävanden] striving, effort, endeavor
strö [v.; strör, strödde, strött] sprinkle
strök [v.past; see: **stryka**]
ström [n.; strömmen, strömmar] stream; current
strömavbrott [n.; ~et, ~] power failure
strömbrytare [n.; ~n, ~] switch
strömförsörjning [n.; ~en, ~ar] power supply [IT]
strömma [v.; ~r, ~de, ~t] stream, flow, gush
strömmande media [n.pl.] streaming media [pl.] [IT]

strömming [n.; ~en, ~ar] Baltic herring, sprat [fish]

strömmingsflundror [n.pl.] fried pairs of sprats

strömmingslåda [n.; ~n] herring and potato casserole

strömstyrka [n.; ~n, -styrkor] voltage

strösocker [n.; -sockret] powdered sugar

stubbe [n.; ~n, stubbar] stump

stucken [adj.; see: **sticka**] bitten, stung

stud. [abbrev: studerande, student] student

student [n.; ~en, ~er] student

studentbostad [n.; ~en, -städer] student housing

studenten [n.; see: **studentexamen**]: **ta ~** pass the national (upper) secondary school completion exam

studentexamen [n.; ~, -examina] diploma from (upper) secondary school

studentkort [n.; ~et, ~] student card

studentkår [n.; ~en, ~er] student union

studentlegitimation [n.; ~en, ~er] student ID

studentrum [n.; ~et, ~] student room

studentska [n.; ~n, studentskor] female student

studera [v.; ~r, ~de, ~t] study; consider, wonder

studerande [n.; ~n, ~] student

studeranderabatt [n.; ~en, ~er] student discount

studie [n.; ~n, ~er] study; sketch; essay

studiebidrag [n.; ~et, ~] study grant

studiecirkel [n.; ~n, -cirklar] adult education class

studieförbund [n.; ~et, ~] adult education association

studiekamrat [n.; ~en, ~er] fellow student

studielån [n.; ~et, ~] education loan

studiemedel [n.; -medlet, ~] financing for students

studier [n.pl.; see: **studium**] studies

studiestöd [n.; ~et, ~] educational assistance, study grant/support

studietid [n.; ~en, ~er] period of study

studieväg [n.; ~en, ~ar] course of study

studio [n.; ~n, ~r] studio

studium [n.; studiet, studier] study

studs [n.; ~en, ~ar] bounce, rebound

studsmatta [n.; ~n, -mattor] trampoline

stuga [n.; ~n, stugor] cottage

stugby [n.; ~n, ~ar] cluster of summer rental cottages

stukad [adj.; stukat, ~e] sprained

stukning [n.; ~en, ~ar] sprain; knocking out of shape

stulen [adj.; stulet, stulna] stolen

stulit [v.past; see **stjäla**]

stum [adj.; ~t, stumma] mute, dumb, speechless

stund [n.; ~en, ~er] period of time, while; **efter en ~** after a while; **en ~ senare** a little later

stundtals [adv.] now and then

stuss [n.; ~en, ~ar] behind, bottom, butt

stuvad [adj.; stuvat, ~a] cooked in white sauce; **~ aborre** poached perch; **~ potatis** creamed potatoes

styck [n.] each, apiece

stycke [n.; ~t, ~n] piece, item; paragraph

stycktryckning [n.; ~en] print on demand [IT]

stygn [n.; ~et, ~] stitch [sewing]

styr [n.] control; **hålla ~ på** keep in order/check

styra [v.; styr, styrde, styrt] steer

styrande [adj.] governing; **de ~** the powers that be, those in charge

styrelse [n.; ~n, ~r] administration; board of directors, executive committee

styrelseformer [n.pl.] governance [EU]

Styrelsen för ackreditering och teknisk kontroll (SWEDAC) [n.] Swedish Board for Accreditation and Conformity Assessment

Styrelsen för internationellt
utvecklingssamarbete (SIDA)
[n.] Swedish International Development Cooperation Agency
(SIDA)
Styrelsen för psykologiskt försvar
[n.] National Board for Psychological Defense
styrelseordförande [n.; ~n, ~]
chairman of the board
styrka¹ [n.; ~n, styrkor] strength,
force
styrka² [v.; styrker, styrkte, styrkt]
strengthen; attest, give proof of
styrketräning [n.; ~en] weight
training
styrkod [n.; ~en, ~er] HTML tag
[IT]
styrkort [n.; ~et. ~] controller card
[IT]
styrkula [n.; ~n, -kulor] trackball
[IT]
styrning [n.; ~en, ~ar] steering;
management; government [gram]
styrplatta [n.; ~n, -plattor] trackpad [IT]
styrrutin [n.; ~en, ~er] device driver
[IT]
styrspak [n.; ~en, ~ar] joystick [IT]
styrstång [n.; ~en, -stänger]
handlebars
styv [adj.; ~t, ~a] stiff
styvbarn [n.; ~et, ~] stepchild
styvdotter [n.; ~n, -döttrar] stepdaughter
styvfar [n.; -fadern, -fäder]
stepfather
styvmor [n.; -modern, -mödrar]
stepmother
styvson [n.; ~en, -soner] stepson
stå [v.; ~r, stod, ~tt] stand; be [loca-
tion]; be written; Hur ~r det till?
How is it going?
stående [adj.; standing; ~ utskrift
portrait mode [IT]
stål [n.; ~et] steel
stånd [n.; ~et, ~] status, state; stand,
stall
ståndpunkt [n.; ~en, ~er] standpoint, position, point of view
stång [n.; ~en, stänger] peg, pole

ståplats [n.; ~en, ~er] standing
room
stått [v.past; see: stå]
städa [v.; ~r, ~de, ~t] clean up, tidy
up
städare [n.; ~n, ~] cleaning person
städer [n.pl.; see: stad] towns
städerska [n.; ~n, städerskor]
cleaning woman, maid
städfirma [n.; ~n, -firmor] cleaning
company
städning [n.; ~en] cleaning
städpersonal [n.; ~en] cleaning
staff
ställa [v.; ställer, ställde, ställt] put;
~ en fråga ask a question; ~ sig
place o.s., stand; ~ till cause; ~
upp put up, arrange; ~ ut put out
ställe [n.; ~t] place; i ~t för instead
of
ställning [n.; ~en, ~ar] position,
employment, job; score
ställningstagande [n.; ~t, ~n] attitude; decision; standpoint
stämband [n.pl.] vocal cords
stämjärn [n.; ~et, ~] chisel
stämma¹ [n.; ~n, stämmor] voice,
part [singing]
stämma² [v.; stämmer, stämde,
stämt] tune; correspond, be correct; bring a suit against; det
stämmer! that's right!
stämning [n.; ~en] atmosphere,
feeling
stämningsfull [adj.; ~t, ~a] moving
stämpla [v.; ~r, ~de, ~t] clock
in/out, stamp; ~ biljetten validate
a ticket, stamp a ticket
ständig [adj.; ~t, ~a] permanent,
constant, perpetual
stänga [v.; stänger, stängde, stängt]
close, shut; ~ av turn off, shut off;
~ i shut in
stängd [adj.; stängt, ~a] closed; ~
för reparation closed for repairs,
closed for renovations; ~ för
trafik closed to traffic
stängningsdags [n.] closing time
stängsel [n.; ~et, ~] enclosure, fence
stänka [v.; stänker, stänkte, stänkt]
sprinkle

stänkskärm [n.; ~en, ~ar] fender, mud guard

stärka [v.; stärker, stärkte, stärkt] strengthen; starch

stärkande [adj.] invigorating

stöd [n.; ~et, ~] support, aid; ~ inför anslutningen pre-accession assistance [EU]

stöda [v.; stöder, stödde, stött] support; rest, lean

stödja [v.; see: stöda]

stödstrumpor [n.pl.] support stockings

stödundervisning [n.; ~en] supplementary instruction

stökig [adj.; ~t, ~a] untidy, messy

stöld [n.; ~en, ~er] theft, larceny

stöldförsäkring [n.; ~en, ~ar] theft insurance

stöldmärkning [n.; ~en, ~ar] anti-theft marking

stöldskydd [n.; ~et, ~] burglar alarm

störa [v.; stör, störde, stört] disturb

störande [adj.] disturbing; noisy

störning [n.; ~en, ~ar] disturbance; interference, noise

större [adj.comp.; see: stor] bigger; större-än-tecken (>) greater-than sign (>) [IT]

störst [adj.superl.; see: stor] biggest

störta [v.; ~r, ~de, ~t] overthrow

störthjälm [n.; ~en, ~ar] crash helmet

störtlopp [n.; ~et, ~] downhill race

stötdämpare [n.; ~n, ~] shock absorber

stötfångare [n.; ~n, ~] bumper

stötsäker [adj.; ~t, -säkra] shock-proof, shock-resistant

stött [v.past; see: stödja]

stöttepelare [n.; ~n, ~] buttress

stövlar [n.pl.] boots

subjekt [n.; ~et, ~] subject; ~ med infinitiv subject with infinitive [gram]

subjektiv [adj.; ~t, ~a] subjective; ~ genitiv subjective genitive [gram]; ~ predikatsfyllnad subjective complement [gram]

subjektsdel [n.; ~en, ~ar] subject component [gram]

subsidiaritet [n.; ~en, ~er] subsidiarity [EU]

subsidiaritetsprincipen [n.] principle of subsidiarity [EU]

substantiv [n.] noun

substantivering [n.; ~en, ~ar] nominalization [gram]

substantivisk [adj.; ~t, ~a] nominal [gram]

subtil [adj.; ~t, ~a] subtle

subtrahera [v.; ~r, ~de, ~t] subtract

subtraktion [n.; ~en, ~er] subtraction

subtraktionstecken (-) [n.; ~en, ~er] subtraction sign (-)

subvention [n.; ~en, ~er] subvention, subsidy

succé [n.; ~n, ~er] success

successiv [adj.; ~t, ~a] successive, gradual

successivt [adv.] gradually

suck [n.; ~en, ~ar] sigh

sucka [v.; ~r, ~de, ~t] sigh

sudda (ut) [v.; ~r, ~de, ~t] erase

suddig [adj.; ~t, ~a] blurred, fuzzy

Suezkanalen [n.] Suez Canal

sufflé [n.; ~n, ~er] soufflé

suga [v.; suger, sög, sugit] suck

sugrör [n.; ~et, ~] straw

sula [n.; ~n, sulor] sole [shoe]

summa [n.; ~n, summor] amount, sum

summera [v.; ~r, ~de, ~t] sum, add up

sump [n.; ~en] grounds [coffee], swamp

sumpmark [n.; ~en, ~er] marsh

sund¹ [adj.; sunt, ~a] healthy; sunt förnuft common sense

sund² [n.; ~en] strait, sound

sundae [n.] sundae

sup [n.; ~en, ~ar] drink [hard liquor]

supa [v.; super, söp, supit] have some drinks [alcoholic]

supé [n.; ~n, ~er] supper

superanvändare [n.; ~n, ~] power user [IT]

superlativ [n.; ~en, ~er] superlative [gram]

supermakt [n.; ~en, ~er] superpower

supertanker [n.; ~n, -tankrar] supertanker

supinum [n.; supinet, supiner] supine, past participle [gram]

supporter [n.; ~n, supportrar] supporter

sur [adj.; ~t, ~a] sour, acid; cross

surdeg [n.; ~en, ~ar] leaven

surfa [v.; ~r, ~de, ~t] surf [IT]

surfing [n.; ~en] surfing

surfingbräda [n.; ~n, -brädor] surfboard; web browser [IT]

surkål [n.; ~en] sauerkraut

surmjölk [n.; ~en] sour milk

surrealism [n.; ~en] surrealism

surstek [n.; ~en, ~ar] marinated roast beef

surströmming [n.; ~en] fermented herring

suttit [v.past; see: sitta]

suverän [adj.; ~t, ~a] sovereign; superb

SVA [abbrev: Statens Veterinärmedicinska Anstalt] National Veterinary Institute

svag [adj.; ~t, ~a] weak

sval [adj.; ~t, ~a] cool

svala [n.; ~n, svalor] swallow

svalg [n.; ~et, ~] throat, pharynx; abyss, chasm

svamp [n.; ~en, ~ar] mushroom, fungus

svampinfektion [n.; ~en, ~er] fungus infection

svampsås [n.; ~en] mushroom sauce

svan [n.; ~en, ~ar] swan

svans [n.; ~en, ~ar] tail; hunden viftar på ~en the dog is wagging its tail

svar [n.; ~et, ~] answer

svara [v.; ~r, ~de, ~t] answer, reply; ~ alla reply (to) all [IT]

svarande [n.; ~n, ~] defendant

svarsblankett [n.; ~en, ~er] answer form

svarstid [n.; ~en, ~er] response time [IT]

svarston [n.; ~en, ~er] dial tone

svart¹ [adj.; ~, ~a] black; ~a börsen black market; Svarta havet Black Sea; ~a tavlan blackboard; ~a vinbär black currants

svart² [adv.] illegally

svartpeppar [n.; ~n] black pepper

svartsjuk [adj.; ~t, ~a] jealous

svartsoppa [n.; ~n] goose blood soup

svartvit film [n.; ~en, ~er] black-and-white film

svavel [n.; svavlet] sulfur

SvD [abbrev: Svenska Dagbladet] Svenska Dagbladet [big daily newspaper]

Svealand [n.; ~et] Svealand [central Sweden, incl. Stockholm]

sveciaost [n.; ~en] Svecia cheese [pungent semi-hard]

sveda [n.; ~n] burning pain

svek¹ [n.; ~et, ~] deceit, treachery, guile; fraud

svek² [v.past; see: svika]

SVEMA [abbrev: Sveriges motorfederation] Swedish Motor Vehicle Federation

svenne [n.; colloq.] ethnic Swede [not an immigrant]; average (conservative) middle-class Swede

svensk¹ [adj.; ~t, ~a] Swedish

svensk² [n.; ~en, ~ar] Swede

svenska [n.; ~n] Swedish language; Swedish woman

Svenska Akademien [n.] Swedish Academy

Svenska Bankföreningen [n.] Swedish Bankers Association

Svenska ESF-rådet [n.] Swedish ESF Council [European Science Foundation]

Svenska Filminstitutet [n.] Swedish Film Institute

svenska för invandrare (sfi) [n.] Swedish for immigrants

Svenska institutet (SI) [n.] Swedish Institute

Svenska Kommunförbundet [n.] Swedish Association of Local Authorities

Svenska kyrkan [n.] Church of Sweden

Svenska miljöinstitutet (IVL) [n.] Swedish Environmental Research Institute

Svenska Naturskyddsföreningen (SNF) [n.] Swedish Society for Nature Conservation

Svenska rikskonserter [n.pl.] Concerts Sweden

Svenska Röda Korset [n.] Swedish Red Cross

Svenska Samernas Riksförbund [n.; ~et] National Union of the Swedish Sami People

Svenska språknämnden [n.] Swedish Language Council

Svenska Tonsättares Internationella Musikbyrå (STIM) [n.; -n] Swedish Performing Rights Society

Svenska Turistföreningen (STF) [n.] Swedish Touring Club

Svensk författningssamling (SFS) [n.; ~en] Swedish Code of Statutes

Svensk Handel [n.; ~n] Swedish Trade Federation

svenskkunskaper [n.pl.] knowledge of Swedish

svensktoppen [n.] Swedish hit songs list

Sverige [n.] Sweden

Sverigedemokraterna (SD) [n.pl.] Sweden Democrats [conservative nationalistic political party]

Sverigedemokraternas Ungdomsförbund (SDU) [n.; ~et] Sweden Democrats Youth Alliance

Sveriges advokatsamfund [n.; ~et] Swedish Bar Association

Sveriges Akademikers Centralorganisation (SACO) [n.; ~en] Swedish Confederation of Professional Associations (SACO)

Sveriges allmänna exportförening [n.] General Export Association of Sweden

Sveriges Allmännyttiga Bostadsföretag (SABO) [n.; ~et] Swedish Association of Municipal Housing Companies

Sveriges Arbetares Centralorganisation (SAC) [n.; ~en] Central Organization of the Workers of Sweden

Sveriges Förenade Studentkårer

(SFS) [n.pl.] Swedish National Union of Students

Sveriges Försäkringsförbund [n.; ~et] Swedish Insurance Federation

Sveriges geologiska undersökning (SGU) [n.; ~en] Geological Survey of Sweden

Sveriges Kommunistiska Parti (SKP) [n.; ~et] Communist Party of Sweden

Sveriges Kommunistiska Ungdomsförbund (SKU) [n.; ~et] Communist Youth Alliance of Sweden

Sveriges lantbruksuniversitet (SLU) [n.; ~et] Swedish University of Agricultural Sciences

Sveriges meteorologiska och hydrologiska institut (SMHI) [n.; ~et] Swedish Meteorological and Hydrological Institute

Sveriges nationalbibliotek (Kungliga Biblioteket) [n.; ~et] National Library of Sweden

Sveriges nätuniversitet [n.; ~et] Swedish Net University

Sveriges Provnings- och Forskningsinstitut (SP) [n.; ~et] Swedish Testing and Research Institute

Sveriges Radio AB (SR) [n.] Swedish Broadcasting Corporation

Sveriges Rese- och Turistråd [n.; ~et] Travel and Tourism Council of Sweden

Sveriges Riksbank [n.; ~en] National Bank of Sweden

Sveriges Riksdag [n.; ~en] Parliament, the Swedish Parliament, the Riksdag

Sveriges Riksidrottsförbund [n.; ~et] Swedish Sports Confederation

Sveriges Socialdemokratiska Arbetareparti (SAP) [n.; ~et] Swedish Social Democratic Workers Party

Sveriges Socialdemokratiska Ungdomsförbund (SSU) [n.; ~et] Social Democratic Youth Alliance of Sweden

Sveriges teknisk-vetenskapliga

attachéverksamhet (Sveriges
tekniska attachéer) [n.; ~en]
Swedish Office of Science and
Technology

Sveriges Television (SVT) [n.;
~en] Swedish Television

Sveriges Utbildningsradio AB [n.;
-radion] Swedish Educational
Broadcasting Company

svetsare [n.; ~n, ~] welder

svettas [v.passive; ~, svettades,
svettats] sweat

svettning [n.; ~en] sweating

svida [v.; svider, sved, svidit] sting,
ache

svika [v.; sviker, svek, svikit] fail,
desert; give out

sviktbräde [n.; ~et] diving board

svimfärdig [adj.; ~t, ~a] feeling
faint

svimma [v.; ~r, ~de, ~t] faint

svimning [n.; ~en, ~ar] faint, faint-
ing spell

svin [n.; ~et, ~] hog

svindel [n.; ~n] dizziness, vertigo;
swindle, fraud, imposture; få ~
feel dizzy

svit [n.; ~en, ~er] suite

svordom [n.; ~en, ~ar] oath, swearword

SVT [abbrev: Sveriges Television]
Swedish Television

svullen [adj.; svullet, svullna]
swollen

svullnad [n.; ~en, ~er] swelling

svåger [n.; ~n, svågrar] brother-in-
law

svår [adj.; ~t, ~a] difficult

svårighet [n.; ~en, ~er] difficulty

svägerska [n.; ~n, svägerskor]
sister-in-law

svälja [v.; sväljer, svälde, svält]
swallow

sväng [n.; ~en, ~ar] turn, curve

svänga [v.; svänger, svängde,
svängt] turn; ~ till vänster/höger
turn left/right

svängdörr [n.; ~en, ~ar] revolving
door

svärd [n.; ~et, ~] sword

svärdfisk [n.; ~en, ~ar] swordfish

svärdotter [n.; ~n, -döttrar] daughter-in-law

svärfar [n.; -fadern, -fädrar] father-
in-law

svärföräldrar [n.pl.] parents-in-law

svärma [v.; ~r, ~de, ~t] swarm; ~
för ngn have a crush on someone

svärmor [n.; -modern, -mödrar]
mother-in-law

svärson [n.; ~en, -söner] son-in-law

sväva [v.; ~r, ~de, ~t] float, hover

svävare [n.; ~n, ~] hovercraft

sy [v.; syr, sydde, sytt] sew; ~ ihop
stitch together

sybehör [n.pl.] sewing materials

syd[1] [n.; ~en] south

syd-[2] [prefix] southern, south

Sydafrika [n.] South Africa

Sydamerika [n.] South America

sydamerikansk [adj.; ~t, ~a] South
American

Sydkorea [n.] South Korea

sydlig [adj.; ~t, ~a] southerly,
southern

sydligaste [adj.superl.] southernmost

sydost [n.; ~en] southeast

Sydostasien [n.] South-East Asia

Sydpolen [n.] South Pole

sydväst [n.; ~en] southwest

syfta (på) [v.; ~r, ~de, ~t] refer to,
aim at

syfte (med) [n.; ~t, ~n] purpose (of,
for), intention

sylt [n.; ~en, ~er] jam

syltad [adj.; syltat, ~e] preserved;
pickled

syltburk [n.; ~en, ~ar] jar of jam

syltomelett [n.; ~en, ~er] omelet
with jam

symaskin [n.; ~en, ~er] sewing
machine

symbol [n.; ~en, ~er] symbol, icon

sympati [n.; ~n, ~er] sympathy

symtom [n.; ~en, ~er] symptom

syn [n.; ~en, ~er] sight, vision; få ~
på catch sight of

syna [v.; ~r, ~de, ~t] inspect, examine, survey

synagoga [n.; ~n, synagogor]
synagogue

synas [v.passive; ~, synades, synats] be seen, be visible; appear

synd [n.; ~en, ~er] sin; pity, shame, too bad

syndrom [n.; ~et, ~] syndrome

synnerhet: i ~ [adv.] in particular, especially

synnerligen [adv.] most, extremely

synonym [n.; ~en, ~er] synonym

synpunkt [n.; ~en, ~er] viewpoint, point of view

synskadad [adj.; -skadat, ~e] partially sighted, visually impaired

synskärpa [n.; ~n] visual acuity, sharpness of vision

syntax [n.; ~en] syntax [gram]

syntaxanalys [n.; ~en] parsing [gram/IT]

syntes [n.; ~en, ~er] synthesis

syntetisk [adj.; ~t, ~a] synthetic, formulated

synvinkel [n.; ~n, -vinklar] visual angle, angle of approach

synål [n.; ~en, ~ar] sewing needle

syo [abbrev: studie- och yrkesorientering] educational and vocational counseling

syo-konsulent [n.; ~en, ~er] adviser on educational and vocational matters

syra [n.; ~n, syror] acid

syre [n.; ~t] oxygen

syrebrist [n.; ~en, ~er] lack of oxygen

syretillförsel [n.; ~en, ~] oxygen supply

syrgasapparat [n.; ~en, ~er] oxygen apparatus

syren [n.; ~en, ~er] lilac

Syrien [n.] Syria

syrsa [n.; ~n, syrsor] cricket

syskon [n.pl.] siblings, brothers and sisters

sysselsättning [n.; ~en, ~ar] employment, occupation

Sysselsättningskommittén [n.] Employment Committee [EU]

syssla med [v.; ~r, ~de, ~t] do for a living; be busy with

syssling [n.; ~en, ~ar] second cousin

system [n.; ~et, ~] system

systematisk [adj.; ~t, ~a] systematic

Systembolaget AB [n.] National Retail Alcohol Monopoly

systembutik [n.; ~en, ~er] state liquor store

systemet [see: **Systembolaget**]

systemfil [n.; ~en, ~er] system file [IT]

systemkrasch [n.; ~en, ~er] system crash [IT]

systemomarbetning [n.; ~en] system reengineering, software reengineering [IT]

systemprogram [n.; -programmet, ~] system program [IT]

syster [n.; ~n, systrar] sister

systerdotter [n.; ~n, -döttrar] niece [sister's daughter]

systerson [n.; ~en, -söner] nephew [sister's son]

sytråd [n.; ~en, ~ar] sewing thread

så¹ [adv.] so; how; **inte ~ stor som** not as big as; **~ här** like this; **~ kallad** so-called; **~ pass att** so that, in such a way that; **~ skönt** how nice; **~ småningom** eventually, after some time; **~ snart som möjligt** as soon as possible; **~ synd** what a shame

så² [v.; sår, sådde, sått] sow

sådan [adj./pron.] such; **två ~a** two like that, two of those

såg¹ [n.; ~en, ~ar] saw

såg² [v.past; see: **se**]

sågverk [n.; ~et, ~] sawmill

såld¹ [adj.; sålt, ~a] sold

såld² [v.past; see: **sälja**]

således [adv.] consequently; thus

såll [n.; ~et, ~] sieve

sålt [v.past; see: **sälja**]

sålunda [adv.] thus, in this manner

sån [adv.; see **sådan**]

sång [n.; ~en, ~er] song

sångare [n.; ~n, ~] singer, vocalist

sångerska [n.; ~n, sångerskor] female singer

sångkår [n.; ~en, ~er] choir, chorus

såpopera [n.; ~n, -operor] soap opera

sår [n.; ~et, ~] wound

sårad [adj.; sårat, ~e] wounded

sårsalva [n.; ~n, -salvor] ointment for cuts

sås [n.; ~en, ~er] sauce

såsom [conj.] as

såvitt [conj.] as far as

såväl [conj.] as well; **A ~ som B** A as well as B, both A and B

säd [n.; ~en, ~er] grain; seed; sperm, semen

sädesslag [n.; ~et, ~] cereals

säga [v.; säger, sade, sagt] say, tell; **~ om** repeat, say again; **~ till någon** let someone know, inform

säker [adj.; ~t, säkra] sure, certain

säkerhet [n.; ~en] security

säkerhetsbälte [n.; ~t, ~n] seatbelt

säkerhetskod [n.; ~en, ~er] access code, PIN code [IT]

säkerhetskontroll [n.; ~en, ~er] security check

säkerhetskopia [n.; ~n, -kopior] backup copy [IT]

säkerhetsnät [n.; ~en, ~ar] safety net

säkerhetsnål [n.; ~en, ~ar] safety pin

Säkerhetspolisen (Säpo) [n.] State Security Service

säkerhetsrep [n.; ~et, ~] security rope

Säkerhetsrådet [n.] Security Council [UN]

säkerhetsventil [n.; ~en, ~er] safety valve

säkerligen [adv.] undoubtedly, certainly

säkert [adv.] certainly, surely, for sure

säkra[1] [v.; ~r, ~de, ~t] safeguard, secure; ensure; fasten

säkra[2] [see: **säker**]; **~ livsmedel** safe foods, food safety [EU]

säkring [n.; ~en, ~ar] fuse; safety catch

säl [n.; ~en, ~ar] seal [sea mammal]

sälja [v.; säljer, sålde, sålt] sell

sällan [adv.] seldom, rarely

sällskap [n.; ~et, ~] company; **göra/hålla ~ med någon** keep someone company, join someone

sällskapsdans [n.; ~en, ~er] ballroom dancing

sällskapsdjur [n.; ~et, ~] pet

sällsynt [adj.; ~, ~a] rare, uncommon, unusual

sämre [adj./adv.comp.; see: **dålig, illa**] worse

sämst [adj./adv.superl.; see: **dålig, illa**] worst

sända [v.; sänder, sände, sänt] send; **~ (med/via) e-post** send (by) e-mail [IT]

sändlista [n.; ~n, -listor] mailing list [IT]

säng [n.; ~en, ~ar] bed

sängbord [n.; ~et, ~] bedside table

sängkläder [n.pl.] bedding

sänglampa [n.; ~n, -lampor] bedside lamp

sängs: gå till ~ go to bed

sängskåp [n.; ~et, ~] Murphy bed [folds up into wall]

sänka[1] [n.; ~n, sänkor] hollow, depression; sedimentation rate [blood test]

sänka[2] [v.; sänker, sänkte, sänkt] lower, reduce, drop; **~a hastigheten** reduce speed

Säpo [abbrev: Säkerhetspolis] security police

särklass [n.; ~en] class of its own

särsk. [see: **särskilt**]

särskild [adj.; särskilt, ~a] special

särskilt [adv.] especially; **inte ~** not very

säsong [n.; ~en, ~er] season

säsongbiljett [n.; ~en, ~er] season ticket

säsongsbetonad [adj.; -betonat, ~e] seasonal

sätt [n.; ~et, ~] way, manner

sätta [v.; sätter, satte, satt] put, place; **~ fast** fasten; **~ i** insert; **~ igång** start, get going; **~ in** deposit; **~ på** turn on; **~ sig** sit down

sättsadverbial [n.; ~et, ~] manner adverbial [gram]

sättskonjunktion [n.; ~en, ~er] conjunction of manner [gram]

söder [n.; ~n] south

Söderhavet [n.] South Pacific, South Seas

söderut [adv.] southwards, to the south

södra [adj.] southern

Södra ishavet [n.] Antarctic Ocean
södra polcirkeln [n.] Antarctic
  Circle
sög [v.; see: **suga**]
söka [v.; söker, sökte, sökt] seek,
  look for; attempt; apply; **sök och
  ersätt** search and replace [IT]; ~
  in på apply for entrance to
sökande[1] [adj.] searching, inquiring
sökande[2] [n.] search; applicant,
  candidate
sökare [n.; ~n, ~] viewfinder
sökmotor [n.; ~n, ~er] search engine [IT]
sökord [n.; ~et, ~] search word [IT]
sökresultat [n.; ~et, ~] search hit,
  search results [IT]
sökruta [n.; ~n, -rutor] search box
  [IT]
söksträng [n.; ~en, ~ar] search
  string [IT]
sökverktyg [n.; ~et, ~] search tool,
  search engine [IT]
sökväg [n.; ~en, ~ar] path [IT]
söm [n.; sömmen, sömmar] seam;
  suture

sömmerska [n.; ~n, sömmerskor]
  seamstress, dressmaker
sömn [n.; ~en] sleep
sömnlös [adj.; ~t, ~a] sleepless
sömnlöshet [n.; ~en] sleeplessness,
  insomnia
sömnmedel [n.; -medlet, ~] sopo-
  rific, sleeping pill
sömnsvårighet [n.; ~en] insomnia
sömntablett [n.; ~en, ~er] sleeping
  pill
sön. [abbrev.; see: **söndag**]
söndag [n.; ~en, ~ar] Sunday
söndagsgudstjänst [n.; ~en, ~er]
  Sunday church service
sönder [adj.] broken
söner [n.pl.; see: **son**] sons
sörja [v.; sörjer, sörjde, sörjd] mourn
söt [adj.; ~, ~a] sweet; pretty
sötningsmedel [n.; -medlet, ~]
  artificial sweetener
sötpotatis [n.; ~en, ~ar] sweet potato
sötsaker [n.pl.] sweets, candy
sötsur sås [n.; ~en] sweet and sour
  sauce
Söul [n.] Seoul

T

t. [abbrev: till] to, till
ta [v.; tar, tog, tagit] take; **hur långt tid ~r det?** how long does it take?; **~ av** take off; turn (off to one side); **~ av sig** undress; take off; **~ bort** delete [IT]; **~ det lugnt** take it easy; **~ emot** accept, receive; **~ hand om** take care of; **~ hem** download [IT]; **~ in på hotellet** stay at the hotel; **~ kontakt med** get in touch with; **~ med** bring; **~ med sig** bring; take out; **~ någon i hand** shake hands with someone; **~ plats** sit down; **~ på sig** put on [clothing]; **~ på sig skulden** take the blame on oneself; **~ reda på** find out; **~ sig** recover, rest; **~ sig in** get in [IT]; **~ till vänster/höger** turn left/right; **~ ut** withdraw, take out
tab. [abbrev.; see: tabell]
tabell [n.; ~en, ~er] table [of numbers]
tablett [n.; ~en, ~er] pill, tablet
tablå [n.; ~n, ~er] tableau
Tacis [abbrev.] Technical Aid to the Commonwealth of Independent States (TACIS) [EU]
tack [n.; ~et] thanks, thank you; please; **~ för hjälpen** thanks for your help; **~ för i kväll** thanks for a nice evening; **~ för senast** thanks for a nice time [said when meeting your host again]; **~ ska du ha** thank you; **~ så mycket** thank you very much; **~ vare** thanks to; **~, detsamma** thanks and the same to you
tacka[1] [n.; ~n, tackor] ewe; ingot
tacka[2] [v.; ~r, ~de, ~t] thank; **tacka ja** I/we accept [an offer]; **tacka nej** I/we decline [with thanks]
tacksam [adj.; ~t, ~a] grateful
tadzjikisk [adj.; ~t, ~a] Tajik
Tadzjikistan [n.] Tajikistan
tag[1] [n.; ~et, ~] grip, grasp; **få ~ på/i** get hold of
tag[2] [n.; ~et, ~] a while, a bit
taga [v.; see: ta]

tagen [adj.; taget, tagna] taken, affected
tagg [n.; ~en, ~er] tag [IT]
taggtråd [n.; ~et] barbed wire
tagit [v.past; see: ta]
tak [n.; ~et, ~] ceiling; roof
take-away mat [n.] take-away food
takfönster [n.; -fönstret, ~] skylight
taklampa [n.; ~n, -lampor] ceiling light
takräcke [n.] roof rack
takt [n.; ~en, ~er] pace
takterrass [n.; ~en, ~er] roof terrace
taktik [n.; ~en, ~er] tactic
takvåning [n.; ~en, ~ar] penthouse
tal [n.; ~et, ~] speech; number; times [repetitions]; **1800-talet** the 19th century; **1900-talet** the 20th century; **1990-talet** the 1990s
tala [v.; ~r, ~de, ~t] speak; **vi ~r engelska** we speak English, English spoken; **~ med** speak to; **~ om** tell
talang [n.; ~en, ~er] talent
talbok [n.; ~en, -böcker] book on tape
talesman [n.; -mannen, -män] spokesman
talesätt [n.; ~et, ~] manner of speaking, figure of speech, phrase
tall [n.; ~en, ~ar] pine, Scotch pine
tallrik [n.; ~en, ~ar] plate; **djup ~** soup plate
Talmud [n.] Talmud
talong [n.; ~en, ~er] ticket stub
talspråk [n.; ~et, ~] spoken language
talsyntes [n.; ~en, ~er] voice synthesis [IT]
taltrast [n.; ~en, ~ar] song thrush
tam [adj.; ~t, ~a] tame, domestic(ated)
tamilsk [adj.; ~t, ~a] Tamil
tampong [n.; ~en, ~er] tampon
tand [n.; ~en, tänder] tooth
tandborste [n.; ~n, -borstar] toothbrush
tandhygienist [n.; ~en, ~er] dental hygienist
tandkräm [n.; ~en, ~er] toothpaste

tandkött [n.; ~et, ~] gum
tandläkare [n.; ~n, ~] dentist
tandpetare [n.; ~n, ~] toothpick
tandprotes [n.; ~en, ~er] denture
tandröta [n.] tooth decay, caries
tandsten [n.; ~en, ~ar] tartar
tandställning [n.; ~en, ~ar] braces [dental]
tandtråd [n.; ~en, ~ar] dental floss
tandutdragning [n.; ~en, ~ar] tooth extraction
tandvård [n.; ~en] dental care
tandvärk [n.; ~en, ~ar] toothache
tangent [n.; ~en, ~er] key [IT]
tangentbord [n.; ~et, ~] keyboard [IT]
tank [n.; ~en, ~ar] tank
tanka [v.; ~r, ~de, ~t] put gas in car
tanke [n.; ~n. tankar] thought, idea
tankfartyg [n.; ~et, ~] tanker
tanklock [n.;] gas cap
tant [n.; ~en, ~er] aunt; lady, elderly woman
tantiem [n.; ~et, ~] bonus, commission on profits
tapet [n.; ~en, ~er] wallpaper; tapestry
tapetsera [v.; ~r, ~de, ~t] paper a wall, put up wallpaper
tappa [v.; ~r, ~de, ~t] lose; drop; **~r inte formen** will not lose its shape
Target [abbrev.] Trans-European Automated Real-time Gross Settlement Express Transfer System (TARGET) [EU]
tarm [n.; ~en, ~ar] intestine
tarmkatarr [n.; ~en, ~er] intestinal inflammation
tass [n.; ~en, ~ar] paw
tavelram [n.; ~en, ~ar] picture frame
tavla [n.; ~n, tavlor] bulletin board, blackboard; picture, painting
tax [n.; ~en, ~ar] dachshund
taxa [n.; ~n, taxor] rate, charge, fee
taxering [n.; ~en, ~er] tax assessment/evaluation
tax-free-butik [n.; ~en, ~er] duty-free shop
tax-fri [adj.; ~tt, ~a] duty-free; **~ affär** duty-free shop; **~a varor** duty-free goods

taxi [n.; ~n, ~] taxi; taxi stand
taxichaufför [n.; ~en, ~er] taxi driver
taxifil [n.; ~en, ~er] taxi lane
taxikort [n.; ~et, ~] taxi driving license
taxistation [n.; ~en, ~er] taxi stand
T-bana [abbrev: tunnelbana] subway
tbc [abbrev: tuberkulos] tuberculosis (TB)
T-benstek [n.; ~en, ~ar] T-bone steak
T-centralen [n.] T-centralen [central hub station of Stockholm's subway]
Tchad [n.] Chad
TCO [abbrev: Tjänstemännens centralorganisation] Central Organization of Salaried Employees
te [n.; ~et, ~er] tea
teater [n.; ~n, teatrar] theater
Teaterhögskolan i Stockholm [n.] College of Drama in Stockholm
teaterkikare [n.; ~n, ~] opera glasses
teaterpjäs [n.; ~en, ~er] play
teaterverkstad [n.; ~en, -städer] theater workshop
tecken [n.; tecknet, ~] sign, mark, symbol
teckensnitt [n.; ~et] font [IT]
teckensnittshantare [n.; ~n] font manager [IT]
teckenspråk [n.; ~et] sign language
teckenstorlek [n.;] font size [IT]
teckna [v.; ~r, ~de, ~t] draw
tecknad film [n.; ~en, ~er] cartoon
tecknare [n.; ~n, ~] draftsman
teckning [n.; ~en, ~ar] drawing
tee [n.] tee [golf]
tefat [n.; ~et, ~] saucer; **flygande ~** flying saucer
teg [v.past; see: **tiga**]
tegel [n.; teglet, ~] brick; tile
tegelhus [n.; ~et, ~] brick house
tegelpanna [n.; ~n, -pannor] roofing tile
tegeltak [n.; ~et, ~] tile roof
tejp [n.; ~en, ~er] tape, sticky tape
tekanna [n.; ~n, -kannor] teapot
tekn. [abbrev: teknologi] technology, engineering

tekn.dr [abbrev: teknologie doktor] doctorate in engineering

teknik [n.; ~en, ~er] technology, engineering

tekniker [n.; ~n, ~] technician, engineer

tekn.lic. [abbrev: teknologie licentiat] licentiate in engineering

teknisk [adj.; ~t, ~a] technological; technical; ~ högskola college/university of technology

Tekniska museet [n.] National Museum of Science and Technology

teknologi [n.; ~n, ~er] technology

tekopp [n.; ~en, ~ar] tea cup

tel. [abbrev.; see: **telefon**]

telefax[1] [n.; ~et, ~] fax

telefax[2] [n.; ~en, ~ar] fax machine

telefon [n.; ~en, ~er] telephone; i ~ on the telephone

telefonabonnemang [n.; ~en, ~er] telephone subscription [IT]

telefonautomat [n.; ~en, ~er] payphone [IT]

telefonavlyssning [n.; ~en, ~er] telephone tapping

telefonbolag [n.; ~et, ~] telephone company [IT]

telefonhytt [n.; ~en, ~er] telephone booth [IT]

telefonist [n.; ~en, ~er] telephone operator [IT]

telefonjack [n.; ~en, ~er] telephone jack/socket [IT]

telefonkatalog [n.; ~en, ~er] telephone directory, telephone book

telefonkiosk [n.; ~en, ~er] telephone booth [IT]

telefonkort [n.; ~et, ~] telephone card [IT]

telefonledning [n.; ~en, ~ar] telephone line [IT]

telefonlinje [n.; ~n, ~er] telephone line [IT]

telefonlur [n.; ~en, ~ar] telephone receiver [IT]

telefonnummer [n.; -numret, ~] telephone number [IT]

telefonsamtal [n.; ~et, ~] telephone call [IT]

telefonsvarare [n.; ~n, ~] answering machine [IT]

telefonväckning [n.; ~en, ~ar] wake-up call

telegrafera [v.; ~r, ~de, ~t] wire, send a telegram

telegram [n.; -grammet, ~] telegram

telekommunikationer [n.pl.] telecommunications

telekort [n.; ~et, ~] telephone card

Telenor [n.] Telenor [major telecommunications and digital services provider]

teleobjektiv [n.; ~et, ~] telephoto lens

teleräkning [n.; ~en, ~ar] telephone bill

teleskop [n.; ~et, ~] telescope

teletjänst [n.; ~en, ~er] telephone service

teletjänstcentral [n.; ~en, ~er] call center [IT]

Televerket [n.] Televerket [government telecommunications monopoly; see: **Telia & Telenor**]

television [n.; ~en, ~er] television; ~ utan gränser television without frontiers [EU]

Telia [n.] Telia [major telecommunications and digital services provider]

tema [n.; ~t, ~n] theme, topic; principal parts of verb [gram]

temp. [abbrev: temperatur] temperature

tempel [n.; templet, ~] temple

tempen [abbrev: temperaturen] the temperature

temperatur [n.; ~en, ~er] temperature [-10°C=14°F; 0°C=32°F; 10°C=50°F; 20°C=68°F; 30°C=86°F; 37°C=98.6°F; 100°C=212°F]; **vad är det för ~ i dag?** what's the temperature today?

tempo [n.; ~t, ~n] tempo, pace, speed

temporal bisats [n.; ~en, ~er] temporal clause [gram]

temporal konjunktion [n.; ~en, ~er] temporal conjunction [gram]

temporalt hjälpverb [n.; ~et, ~] tense-building auxiliary verb [e.g. will, have, be going to] [gram]

tempus [n.; ~] verb tense [gram]
TEN [abbrev: Transeuropeiska nät] Trans-European Networks (TEN) [EU: transport, telecommunications, energy]
tendens [n.; ~en, ~er] tendency, trend; habit
tenn [n.; ~et] pewter
tennis [n.; ~en] tennis
tennisbana [n.; ~n, -banor] tennis court
tennisboll [n.; ~en, ~ar] tennis ball
tennishall [n.; ~en, ~ar] indoor tennis court
tennisracket [n.; ~en, ~ar] tennis racket
tennisspelare [n.; ~n, ~] tennis player
tennisstadion [n.; ~en, ~er] tennis stadium
tennistävling [n.; ~en, ~ar] tennis tournament
tenta¹ [n.; ~n, tentor; abbrev: tentamen] university examination
tenta² [v.; ~r, ~de, ~t] take an exam
tentamen [n.; ~, tentamina] university examination
teol. [abbrev: teologi] theology
teol.dr. [abbrev: teologie doktor] doctorate in theology
teol.kand. [abbrev: teologie kandidat] bachelor's degree in theology
teol.lic. [abbrev: teologie licentiat] licentiate in theology
teologi [n.; ~n, ~er] theology
teoretisk [adj.; ~t, ~a] theoretical
teori [n.; ~n, ~er] theory
tepåse [n.; ~n, -påsar] tea bag
terapeut [n.; ~en, ~er] therapist
termer [n.pl.] hot springs/baths
termin [n.; ~en, ~er] term, semester; deadline, due date
terminal [n.; ~en, ~er] terminal
Terminologicentrum (TNC) [n.; -centret] Swedish Center for Terminology (TNC)
termit [n.; ~en, ~er] termite
termometer [n.; ~n, -metrar] thermometer
termos [n.; ~en, ~ar] thermos
termosflaska [n.; ~n, -flaskor] thermos bottle

termtjänst [n.; ~en, ~er] terminology advice, terminology consulting [IT]
terrakotta [n.; ~n] terra-cotta
terrass [n.; ~en, ~er] terrace
territorialvatten [n.; -vatnet, ~] territorial waters
terror [n.; ~n] terror, terrorism
terrorism [n.; ~en] terrorism
terrorist [n.; ~en, ~er] terrorist
terräng [n.; ~en, ~er] terrain, country; area
terrängcykel [n.; ~n, -cyklar] mountain bike
terränglöpning [n.; ~en, ~ar] cross-country running
terylen [n.; ~en] dacron
tesil [n.; ~en, ~ar] tea strainer
tesked [n.;] teaspoon
test [n.;] test, check
testa [v.; ~r, ~de, ~t] try out, test
testamente [n.; ~t, ~n] testament, will
testamentera [v.; ~r, ~de, ~t] bequeath
testcykel [n.; ~n, -cyklar] exercise bike
testikel [n.; ~n, testiklar] testicle
teve [abbrev.; ~n] TV, television
tevärmare [n.; ~n, ~] tea cosy
t.ex. [abbrev: till exempel] for example (e.g.)
text [n.; ~n, ~er] text
texta [v.; ~r, ~de, ~t] write in block letters; add subtitles
textad film [n.] subtitled film
textanalysator [n.; ~n, ~er] parser [IT]
textbok [n.; ~en, -böcker] textbook
texteditor [n.; ~n, ~er] text editor [IT]
texthantering [n.; ~en] text processing [IT]
textilslöjd [n.; ~en] textile handicrafts
textilvaror [n.pl.] textiles
textredigerare [n.; ~n, ~] text editor [IT]
textremsa [n.; ~n, -remsor] subtitles
textstorlek [n.; ~en, ~ar] text size, print size, font size [IT]

tf. [abbrev: tillförordnad] acting, pro tempore

TFA [abbrev: trygghetsförsäkring vid arbetsskada] workman's compensation [for injury]

tfn. [abbrev: telefon] telephone

t.h. [abbrev: till höger] to the right, on the right

Thailand [n.] Thailand

thailändsk [adj.; ~t, ~a] Thai

thriller [n.; ~n, ~] thriller

tia [n; ~n, tior] 10-kronor bill

Tibet [n.] Tibet

tid [n.; ~en, ~er] time; appointment; **beställa en ~** make an appointment; **i god ~** in good time; **i ~** on time; **~en går fort** time goes fast

tidig [adj.; ~t, ~a] early

tidigare [adj./adv.] earlier

tidigt [adv.] early; **för ~** too early

tidning [n.; ~en, ~ar] magazine, newspaper

Tidningarnas Telegrambyrå (TT) [n.] Swedish News Agency

tidningsbärare [n.; ~n, ~] newspaper deliverer

tidningskiosk [n.; ~en, ~er] newsstand

tidningsnotis [n.; ~en, ~er] news item

tidningsurklipp [n.; ~et, ~] press clipping

tidpunkt [n.; ~en, ~er] point in time

tidsadverbial [n.; ~et, ~] temporal adverbial, time adverbial [gram]

tidsbeställning [n.; ~en, ~ar] appointment

tidsbisats [n.; ~en, ~er] temporal clause, time clause [gram]

tidschema [n.; ~n, -schemor] timetable

tidsdelning [n.; ~en] time sharing [IT]

tidskonjunktion [n.; ~en, ~er] temporal conjunction [gram]

tidskrift [n.; ~en, ~er] periodical, magazine

tidsperiod [n.; ~en, ~er] era

tidtabell [n.; ~en, ~er] schedule, timetable

tidtabellsenligt [adv.] on schedule

tidur [n.; ~et, ~] timer

tidvatten [n.; -vattnet] tide

tidvis [adv.] periodically

tiga [v.; tiger, teg, tegat] be silent

tiger [n.; ~n, tigrar] tiger

tigga [v.; tigger, tiggde, tiggt] beg

tik [n.; ~en, ~ar] bitch, female dog

tilde [n.] tilde [IT]

till[1] [prep.] to; for; **~ dess** until; **~ exempel** for example; **~ följd av** as a result of; **~ höger** on the right; **~ hösten** next fall; **~ ikväll** for tonight; **~ kl 5** till 5 o'clock; **~ och med (t o m)** even, to, until; **~ slut** finally; **~ vänster** on the left

till[2] [adv.] more, extra; **en ~** one more; **en vecka ~** another week

tillade [v.past; see: **tillägga**]

tillaga [v.; ~r, ~de, ~t] cook; **~ från fruset** cook while still frozen

tillagning [n.; ~en] cooking

tillagt [v.past; see: **tillägga**]

tillbaka [adv.] back; return; **komma ~** return, come back

tillbaks [adv.; see: **tillbaka**]

tillbehör [n.; ~et, ~] accessories; side dish

tillbringa tid med [v.; ~r, ~de, ~t] spend time with

tillbringare [n.; ~n, ~] pitcher, jug

tilldela [v.; ~r, ~de, ~t] allot; award, confer

tilldelning [n.; ~en, ~ar] allocation, allotment, assignment, award; mapping; quota

tillfredsställande [adj.] satisfactory, gratifying

tillfriskna [v.; ~r, ~de, ~t] recover, get better

tillfråga [v.; ~r, ~de, ~t] ask, prompt [IT]

tillfälle [n.; ~t, ~n] occasion; **ta ~t i akt** take/seize the opportunity

tillfällig [adj.; ~t, ~a] temporary, occasional; **~t ersätta** override [IT]; **~t utställningsföremål** temporary exhibit

tillfällighet [n.; ~en, ~er] accidental occurrence, coincidence

tillförordnad [adj.; -förordnat, ~e] acting, temporary

tillgodohavande [n.; ~t, ~n] credit

tillgodokvitto [n.;] credit note

tillgång [n.; ~en, ~er] access, availability; asset

tillgänglig [adj.; ~t, ~a] accessible, available

tillgänglighet [n.; ~en] availability; accessibility

tillhöra [v.; -hörer, -hörde, -hört] belong to

tillika [adv.] as well, also

tillit [n.; ~en] trust, confidence, reliance

tillkalla [v.; ~r, ~de, ~t] send for

tillkomma [v.; -kommer, -kom, -kommit] be extra, be added on; be one's due, be one's duty

tillkomst [n.; ~en, ~er] origin; coming into being

tillräcklig [adj.; ~t, ~a] sufficient; ha ~t med pengar have enough money

tillrätta [adv.]; finna seg väl ~ get on well, do well; komma ~ turn up, get found; komma ~ med manage to do, cope with

tills [prep.] until; ~ vidare [adv.] for the time being, until further notice

tillsammans [adv.] together

tillskott [n.; ~et, ~] contribution; increase

tillstånd [n.; ~et, ~] permission, permit; state, condition; ~ behövs permit required, permit-holders only

tillsvidareanställning [n.; ~en, ~ar] permanent employment

tillsynslärare [n.; ~n, ~] assistant principal

tillsätta [v.; -sätter, -satt, -sätt] add

tilltа [v.; -tar, -tog, -tagit] increase

tilltagande[1] [adj.] increasing

tilltagande[2] [n.] increase, growth

tilltro [n.; ~n] credit; credence; confidence

tillträda [v.; -träder, -trädde, -trätt] take up [duties]; take over [property]

tillträde [n.; ~et] access, entrance, admittance, entry; ~ förbjudet keep out, no trespassing

tillträdesdag [n.; ~en, ~ar] date of taking possession, date of beginning work

tillvalsämne [n.; ~t, ~n] elective subject [school]

tillvaro [n.; ~n] existence, life

tillverka [v.; ~r, ~de, ~t] manufacture, produce

tillverkning [n.; ~en, ~ar] production

tillvägagångssätt [n.; ~et, ~] procedure, course of action [IT]

tillväxa [v.; -växer, -växte, -växt/ -vuxit] grow, increase in number

tillväxt [n.; ~en] growth; increase

tillåta [v.; -låter, -lät, -låtit] permit, allow

tillåten [adj.; -låtet, -låtna] permitted, authorized; tillåtet bagage luggage allowance

tillägg [n.; ~et, ~] supplement; extra charge; attachment [IT]

tillägga [v.; -lägger, -lade, -lagt] add

tilläggsavgift [n.; ~en, ~er] supplementary charge

tilläggspension [n.; ~en, ~er] supplementary pension

tilläggsenhet [n.; ~en, ~er] add-on [IT]

tillämpningsprogram [n.; -programmet, ~] application (program) [IT]

tilsammans med [prep.] together with

tim. [abbrev: timme] hour

timjan [n.; ~en] thyme

timlön [n.; ~en, ~er] hourly wage

timma [n.; see: timme]

timme [n.; ~n, timmar] hour

timmer [n.; timret] timber

timmerväg [n.; ~en, ~ar] lumber track

ting [n.; ~et, ~] thing; district court session

tingsrätt [n.; ~en, ~er] district court, city court

tinne [n.; ~n, tinnar] pinnacle, battlement

tinning [n.; ~en, ~ar] temple [head]

tio [num.] ten

tiohundratalet (1000-talet) [n.] eleventh century

tiokamp [n.; ~en, ~er] decathlon
tiokrona [n.; ~n, -kronor] 10-kronor coin
tionde [adj.] tenth; October
tiotal [n.; ~et, ~] ten(s)
tiotusen [num.] ten thousand
tips [n.; ~et, ~] tip, tip-off, advice; soccer betting pool
tipsa [v.; ~r, ~de, ~t] inform, give someone a tip, notify
tis. [abbrev.; see: **tisdag**]
tisdag [n.; ~en, ~ar] Tuesday
tistel [n.; ~n, tistlar] thistle
titel [n.; ~n, titlar] title; **lägga bort titlarna** start saying "du" to one another [set aside formalities]
titta [v.; ~r, ~de, ~t] look; ~ **på** look at, see, watch; ~ **runt** look around
tittare [n.; ~n, ~] viewer [TV]
tivoli [n.; ~t, ~n] amusement park, carnival
tja [expr.] well!
tjattrum [n.; ~et, ~] chat room [IT]
Tjeckien [n.] Czech Republic
tjeckisk [adj.; ~t, ~a] Czech
tjeckiska [n.; ~n] Czech language
Tjeckiska republiken [n.] Czech Republic
tjej [n.; ~en, ~er; colloq] girl
Tjernobylolykan [n.] accident at Chernobyl
Tjetjenien [n.] Chechnya
tjf. [abbrev.; see: **tjänsteförrättare**]
tjl. [abbrev.; see: **tjänstledig**]
tjock [adj.; ~t, ~a] thick, fat; ~ **klient** fat client [IT]
tjocklek [n.; ~en, ~ar] thickness
tjocktarm [n.; ~en, ~ar] large intestine
tjuga [n.; ~n, tjugor] 20-kronor bill
tjugo [num.] twenty
tjugofem [num.] twenty-five
tjugohundratalet (2000-talet) [n.] twenty-first century
tjugondagen [n.] 20 days after Christmas
tjugonde [adj.] twentieth
tjugotal [n.; ~et] about twenty; **i ~et** in the twenties
tjur [n.; ~en, ~ar] bull

tjusig [adj.; ~t, ~a] gorgeous, lovely
tjuta [v.; tjuter, tjöt, tjutit] howl, roar
tjuv [n.; ~en, ~ar] thief
tjuvgods [n.; ~et] stolen property
tjuvlarm [n.; ~et, ~] burglar alarm
tjuvstarta [v.; ~r, ~de, ~t] jump the gun
tjuvåka [v.; -åker, -åkte, -åkt]] ride without paying
tjäder [n.; ~n, tjädrar] wood grouse
tjälskott [n.; ~et, ~] pothole
tjäna [v.; ~r, ~de, ~t] earn
tjänare [n.; ~n, ~] servant; hi!; bye!
tjänst [n.; ~en, ~er] service; **~er av allmänt ekonomiskt intresse** services of general economic interest [EU]; **~er i allmänhetens intresse** general-interest services [EU]
tjänstebil [n.; ~en, ~ar] company car
tjänsteflicka [n.; ~n, -flickor] servant girl, maid
tjänsteförrättare [n.; ~n, ~] acting, officer in charge
tjänsteman [n.; ~n, -män] civil servant
Tjänstemännens Centralorganisation (TCO) [n.; ~en] Confederation of Professional Employees
tjänsteresa [n.; ~n, -resor] business trip
tjänstgöra [v.; -gör, -gjorde, -gjort] work, hold a position/job
tjänstledig [adj.; ~t, ~a] on leave
tjära [n.; ~n] tar
T-korsning [n.; ~en, ~ar] T-intersection
tkr. [abbrev: tusen kronor] thousand crowns
toa [n.; ~n; colloq.] toilet
toalett [n.; ~en, ~er] toilet
toalettartiklar [n.pl.] toiletries
toalettpapper [n.; -pappret] toilet paper
toast skagen [n.] toast with chopped shrimp, mayonnaise, roe
tobak [n.; ~en] tobacco
tobaksaffär [n.; ~en, ~er] tobacconist

tobakshandlare [n.; ~n, ~] tobacconist

tofflor [n.pl.] slippers

tokig [adj.; ~t, ~a] crazy, wild, funny

tolfte [adj.] twelfth; December

tolk [n.; ~en, ~er] interpreter

tolka [n.; ~r, ~de, ~t] interpret; decipher; express

tolkning [n.; ~en, ~ar] interpretation

tolv [num.] twelve

tolvhundratalet (1200-talet) [n.] thirteenth century

tom[1] [adj.; ~t, tomma] vacant, empty

t.o.m.[2] [abbrev: till och med] up to and including, even

tomat [n.; ~en, ~er] tomato

tomatjuice [n.; ~en, ~er] tomato juice

tomatsallad [n.; ~en] tomato salad

tomatsås [n.; ~en, ~er] tomato sauce

tomglas [n.; ~et, ~] empty bottle [deposit refundable glass]

tomma [adj.pl.; see: **tom**]

tomt [n.; ~en, ~er] piece of land, lot; [adj.; see: **tom**]

tomte [n.; ~n, tomtar] brownie, goblin, dwarf; [see also: **jultomte**]

ton[1] [n.; ~en, ~er] tone; hue

ton[2] [n.; ~et, ~] metric ton [ca. 1.1 US tons]

tona [v.; ~r, ~de, ~t] sound, ring; tint; ~ **ned** turn down volume, fade

tonande ljud [n.; ~et, ~] voiced sound [gram.]

tonart [n.; ~en, ~er] key [music]

tonfall [n.; ~et. ~] intonation, accent

tonfisk [n.; ~en, ~ar] tuna

toning [n.; ~en, ~ar] tint, tinting

tonlöst ljud [n.; ~et, ~] voiceless/ unvoiced sound [gram.]

tonsiller [n.pl.] tonsils

tonsillit [n.; ~en] tonsillitis

tonåring [n.; ~en, ~ar] teenager

topp [n.; ~en, ~ar] top, summit, peak

toppdomän [n.; ~en, ~er] top-level domain (TLD) [IT]

toppen [adv.; colloq.] the greatest, the best, super

toppmöte [n.; ~et, ~] summit meeting

toppstation [n.; ~en, ~er] summit station [ski resort]

Tor [n.] Thor

Torah [n.; ~n] Torah

tordes [v.; see **törs**]

torg [n.; ~et, ~] square, market-place, market

torghandel [n.; ~n] market trade

torgstånd [n.; ~et, ~] market stall

torka [v.; ~r, ~de, ~t] dry; ~ **disk** wipe the dishes

torkad [adj.; torkat, ~e] dried; ~ **frukt** dried fruit

torktumlare [n.; ~n, ~] spin/tumble dryer

torn [n.; ~et, ~] tower; castle [chess]

torr [adj.; ~t, ~a] dry; ~ **hud** dry skin

tors. [abbrev.; see: **torsdag**]

torsdag [n.; ~en, ~ar] Thursday

torsk [n.; ~en, ~ar] cod

torskrom [n.; -rommen] cod roe

torso [n.; ~n, torser] torso

tortera [v.; ~r, ~de, ~t] torture

tortyr [n.; ~en] torture

torv [n.; ~en] peat

toscatårta [n.; ~n, -tårtor] cake with caramel glaze

total [adj.; ~t, ~a] entire

Totalförsvarets pliktverk (Pliktverket) [n.] National Service Administration

totalt [adv.] totally, altogether

toto [n.; ~n] off-track betting

tr. [abbrev: trappa; tryckt] floor, stairs; printed

tradition [n.; ~en, ~er] tradition

traditionell [adj.; ~t, ~a] traditional

trafik [n.; ~en] traffic, transport; **ej i ~** not in service; ~ **från motsatt riktning** traffic from the opposite direction

trafikfri zon [n.; ~en, ~er] traffic-free zone

trafikförsäkring [n.; ~en, ~ar] third-party/liability insurance [car]

trafikled [n.; ~en, ~er] traffic route

trafikljus [n.; ~et, ~] traffic light

trafikolycka [n.; ~n, -olyckor] traffic accident

trafikomläggning [n.; ~en, ~ar] detour

trafikpolis [n.; ~en] traffic police

trafikskola [n.; ~n, -skolor] driving school

trafikstockning [n.; ~en, ~ar] traffic jam

trafiksvårigheter [n.pl.] traffic problems

Trafiksäkerhetsverket [n.] National Road Safety Office

Trafikutskottet [n.] Committee on Transport and Communications [in Parliament]

trafikövervakning [n.; ~en, ~ar] traffic control

tragedi [n.; ~n, ~er] tragedy

tragisk [adj.; ~t, ~a] tragic

trakassera [v.; ~r, ~de, ~t] harass

trakasseri [n.; ~n, ~er] pestering; harassment

trakt [n.; ~en, ~er] area

traktamente [n.; ~t, ~n] expense allowance

traktor [n.; ~n, ~er] tractor

trampa [v.; ~r, ~de, ~t] step; ~ **vatten** tread water

trampbåt [n.; ~en, ~ar] pedal boat

trana [n.; ~n, tranor] crane [bird]

tranbär [n.pl.] cranberries

Transeuropeiska nät (TEN) [n.; ~et, ~] Trans-European Networks (TEN) [EU]

transferbuss [n.; ~en, ~ar] transfer bus

transformator [n.; ~n, ~er] transformer

transitiv [adj.; ~t, ~a] transitive [gram]

transport [n.; ~en, ~er] transportation; transfer, carrying forward [balance]

transportband [n.; ~et, ~] conveyor belt

transportmedel [n.; -medlet, ~] means of transportation

trapets [n.; ~et, ~] trapeze

trappa [n.; ~n, trappor] staircase, flight of stairs; doorsteps; **tre trappor upp** three flights up

trapphus [n.; ~et, ~] stairwell

trappor [n.pl.; see: **trappa**] stairs

trappsteg [n.; ~et, ~] step

trappstege [n.; ~n, -stegar] stepladder

trappuppgång [n.; ~en, ~ar] stairs

trasig [n.; ~t, ~a] tattered; broken, damaged, out of order

trasmatta [n.; ~n, -mattor] rag rug

trast [n.; ~en, ~ar] thrush

tratt [n.; ~en, ~ar] funnel

trav [n.; ~et] trot

travbana [n.; ~n, -banor] trotting track

trave [n.; ~n, travar] pile

travtävling [n.; ~en, ~ar] trotting race, harness race

tre [num.] three

trea [n.; ~n, treor] number three [bus, race]; three-room apartment; third gear

tredje [adj.] third; March

tredjedel [n.; ~en, ~ar] one third

tredjepart [n.; ~en, ~er] third party

trefaldighet [n.; ~en] trinity

trehjuling [n.; ~en, ~ar] tricycle

trekant [n.; ~en, ~er] triangle

trekvarts timme [n.] three quarters of an hour

trend [n.; ~en, ~er] trend

trerummare [n.; ~n, ~] three-room apartment

trettio [num.] thirty

trettionde [adj.] thirtieth

trettiotal [n.; ~et] about thirty

tretton [num.] thirteen

Trettondagen [n.] Epiphany [January 6]

trettondag jul [n.] Epiphany [January 6]

trettonde [adj.] thirteenth

trettonhundratalet (1300-talet) [n.] fourteenth century

treva efter [v.; ~r, ~de, ~t] grope for

trevlig [adj.; ~t, ~a] nice, pleasant; **vad ~t** how nice; ~ **helg!** have a nice weekend!; ~ **resa!** bon voyage!, have a good trip!; ~**t att träffas!** nice to meet you!

triangel [n.; ~n, trianglar] triangle

tribunal [n.; ~en, ~er] tribunal

trio [n.; ~n, ~r] trio

triolog [n.; ~en] trialogue [EU]

trist [adj. ~, ~a] gloomy, sad; miserable; tedious

triumf [n.; ~en, ~er] triumph

triumfbåge [n.; ~en, ~ar] triumphal arch

trivas [v.passive; ~, trivades, trivats] get on well, be happy

tro [v.; ~r, ~dde, ~tt] believe, think

trogen [adj.; troget, trogna] faithful

trojansk häst [n.; ~en] Trojan horse [IT]

Trojkan [n.] Troika [EU]

trol. [abbrev: troligen; trolovad] probably; betrothed

troligen [adv.] probably

troligtvis [adv.] probably

troll [n.; ~en, ~ar] troll, elf, goblin

trolla [v.; ~r, ~de, ~t] conjure; do magic tricks

trollkonstnär [n.; ~en, ~er] magician

trollslända [n.; ~n, -ländor] dragonfly

trombon [n.; ~en, ~er] trombone

tron [n.; ~en, ~er] throne; royal power

trosor [n.pl.] panties, briefs

trosskydd [n.; ~et, ~] panty liners

trots [prep.] despite, in spite of

trots att [conj.] although

trottoar [n.; ~en, ~er] sidewalk

trottoarkant [n.; ~en, ~er] curb

trovärdighet [n.; ~en, ~er] credibility

trpt. [abbrev: transport] transportation, freight

truckkort [n.; ~et, ~] truck license

truckkörning [n.; ~en] truck driving

trumma[1] [n.; ~n, trummor] drum

trumma[2] [v.; ~r, ~de, ~t] drum

trumpet [n.; ~en, ~er] trumpet

trumslagare [n.; ~n, ~] drummer

trunkering [n.; ~en, ~ar] truncation [IT]

trupp [n.; ~en, ~er] troop, contingent, team, troupe

trut [n.; ~en, ~ar] gull

tryck [n.; ~et, ~] pressure, weight, stress; print, impression

trycka [v.; ~r, tryckte, tryckt] press, push; print; ~ på press on

tryckfel [n.; ~et, ~] misprint

tryckfrihet [n.; ~en] freedom of the press

tryckfrihetsförordningen (TF) [n.] Freedom of the Press Act

tryckkokare [n.; ~n, ~] pressure cooker

tryckkänslig [n.; ~t, ~a] touch-sensitive [IT]

tryckning på begäran [n.] printing on demand [IT]

tryffel [n.; ~n, tryfflar] truffle

trygg [adj.; ~t, ~a] safe, secure

trygghet [n.; ~en] security

tråd [n.; ~t, ~] thread

trådbuss [n.; ~en, ~ar] trolley bus

tråkig [adj.; ~t, ~a] boring, dull; too bad, unfortunate

trång [adj.; ~t, ~a] tight, narrow

trä [n.; ~et, ~n] wood; **i** ~ wooden, of wood

träd [n.; ~et, ~] tree

träda [v.; träder, trädde, trätt] step, tread; enter; thread; put on [glove]

trädgräns [n.; ~en, ~er] tree line

trädgård [n.; ~en, ~ar] garden

trädgårdsfest [n.; ~en, ~er] garden party

trädgårdsmästare [n.; ~n, ~] gardener

trädgårdsmöbel [n.; ~n, -möbler] garden furniture

trädgårdsredskap [n.; ~et, ~] garden tools

trädgårdsskötsel [n.; ~n] gardening

trädstam [n.; -stammen, -stammar] tree trunk

träff [n.; ~en, ~ar] date, meeting; hit [good shot]

träffa [v.; ~r, ~de, ~t] meet; hit [target]; ~ **mitt i prick** hit the bull's eye

träffas [v.reciprocal; ~, träffades, träffats] meet one another

träfigur [n.; ~en, ~er] wood carving

trähus [n.; ~et, ~] wooden house

träindustri [n.; ~n, ~er] wood products industry

träkniv [n.; ~en, ~ar] wooden knife

träkol [n.; ~et] charcoal

träkyrka [n.; ~n, -kyrkor] wooden church

träna [v.; ~r, ~de, ~t] train, practice; coach

tränare [n.; ~n, ~] trainer, coach

tränga [v.; tränger, trängde, trängt]
feel tight; drive, push, press; force
one's way
trängre [adj.comp.; see: **trång**]
narrower, tighter
trängsel [n.; ~n] crowding,
congestion
trängselskatt [n.; ~en, ~er] congestion tax [charge for driving on
congested roads at peak hours]
träning [n.; ~en, ~ar] training,
practice
träningskor [n.pl.] running shoes
träningsoverall [n.; ~en, ~er]
tracksuit
träningsvärk [n.; ~en]: **ha ~** be
stiff from exercise
träsk [n.; ~et, ~] marsh
träsked [n.; ~en, ~ar] wooden spoon
träskor [n.pl.] clogs
träslöjd [n.; ~en] woodworking,
carpentry
träsnideri [n.; ~et, ~er] wood
carving
träsnitt [n.; ~et, ~] woodcut
trög [adj.; ~t, ~a] stiff
tröja [n.; ~n, tröjor] sweater, jersey
tröskel [n.; ~n, trösklar] threshold,
doorstep
tröst [n.; ~en] consolation, solace
trösta [n.; ~r, ~de, ~t] console;
comfort
trött [adj.; ~, ~a] tired
trötta [v.; ~r, ~de, ~t] tire [trans.]
trötthet [n.; ~en] tiredness, fatigue
tröttna [v.; ~r, ~de, ~t] grow tired
tröttsam [adj.; ~t, ~a] tiring
tsk. [abbrev: tesked] teaspoon
T-skjorta [n.; ~n, -skjortor] T-shirt
TT [abbrev: Tidningarnas Tele-
grambyrå] [n.] Swedish Press
Agency
T-tröja [n.; ~n, - tröjor] T-shirt
tub [n.; ~en, ~er] tube
tuberkulos (tbc) [n.; ~en] tuberculosis (TB)
tuff [adj.; ~t, ~a] tough, hard;
sharp-looking
tugga [v.; ~r, ~de, ~t] chew; **kan ~s**
chewable [tablets]
tuggummi [n.; ~t, ~n] chewing gum

tull [n.; ~en, ~ar] customs; duty;
betala ~ pay duty
tullavgift [n.; ~en, ~er] customs
duty
tulldeklaration [n.; ~en, ~er]
customs declaration
tullfri [adj.; ~tt, ~a] duty free
tullfrihet [n.; ~en] free trade
tullkontroll [n.; ~en] customs
control
tullpliktig [adj.; ~t, ~a] subject to a
duty, dutiable [customs]
tulltjänsteman [n.; -mannen, -män]
customs officer
tullunion [n.; ~en, ~er] customs
union [EU]
Tullverket [n.] National Customs
Administration
tulpan [n.; ~en, ~er] tulip
tumme [n.; ~n, ~ar] thumb
tumvantar [n.pl.] mittens
tumör [n.; ~en, ~er] tumor
tung [adj.; ~t, ~a; tyngre, tyngst]
heavy; **~t snöfall** heavy snow
tunga [n.; ~n, tungor] tongue
tungvikt [n.; ~en] heavyweight
Tunisien [n.] Tunisia
tunisisk [adj.; ~t, ~a] Tunisian
tunn [adj.; tunt, ~a] thin; **~ klient**
thin client [IT]; **~ sås** light sauce
tunna [n.; ~n, tunnor] barrel
tunnbröd [n.; ~et, ~] flat bread
tunnel [n.; ~n, tunnlar] tunnel,
underpass
tunnelbana [n.; ~n, -banor] subway, metro
tunnelbanekarta [n.; ~n, -kartor]
subway map
tunnelbanetåg [n.; ~et, ~] subway
train
tunntarm [n.; ~en, ~ar] small
intestine
tunt [adj.; see: **tunn**]
tupé [n.; ~n, ~er] hairpiece, toupee
tupp [n.; ~en, ~ar] rooster
tur [n.; ~en, ~er] trip, tour; luck;
turn; **ha ~** be lucky; **vilken ~!**
what (good) luck!; **~ och retur**
round-trip
turist [n.; ~en, ~er] tourist
turistattraktion [n.; ~en, ~er]
tourist attraction

turistbok [n.; ~en, -böcker] guide book

turistbroschyr [n.; ~en, ~er] tourist pamphlet

turistbyrå [n.; ~n, ~ar] tourist office

Turistdelegationen [n.] National Tourist Authority

turistgrupp [n.; ~en, ~er] tourist group

turisthotell [n.; ~et, ~] guest house at vacation spots

turistinformation [n.; ~en, ~er] tourist information

turistklass [n.; ~en, ~er] economy class

turistort [n.;] tourist resort

turistsouvenir [n.; ~en, ~er] souvenir

turistsäng [n.; ~en, ~ar] folding bed, camp bed

turistsäsong [n.; ~en, ~er] tourist season

turk [n.; ~en, ~ar] Turk

Turkiet [n.] Turkey

turkisk [adj.; ~t, ~a] Turkish; **~t bad** Turkish bath

turkiska [n.] Turkish language

turkos [adj.; ~t, ~a] turquoise

turlista [n.; ~n, -listor] timetable

turné [n.; ~n, ~er] tour [performance]

turnering [n.; ~en, ~ar] tournament

tusch [n.; ~en] India ink

tuschpenna [n.; ~n, -pennor] felt-tip pen

tusen [num.] thousand

tusende [adj.] thousandth

tusenfoting [n.; ~en, ~ar] centipede, millipede

tusenlapp [n.; ~en, ~ar] 1000-kronor bill

tusensköna [n.; ~n, -skönor] daisy

tusentals [n.pl.] thousands

tuta [v.; ~r, ~de, ~t] honk the horn [auto]

tv[1] [abbrev: television] television (TV)

t.v.[2] [abbrev: tills vidare; till vänster] until further notice; to the left

tv-antenn [n.; ~en, ~er] TV antenna

tv-apparat [n.; ~en, ~er] television set

tv-bild [n.; ~en, ~er] TV picture

tveka [v.; ~r, ~de, ~t] hesitate

tvekan [n.; ~] hesitation, uncertainty, indecision, doubt

tveksam [adj.; ~t, -samma] doubtful, hesitating

tvilling [n.; ~en, ~ar] twin

Tvillingarna [n.pl.] Gemini

tvinga [v.; tvinger, tvang, tvungit] force, constrain; subdue

tvingad [adj.; tvingat, ~e] forced

tvingas [v.passive; tvingas, tvangs, tvungits] be forced

tvivel [n.; tvivlet, ~] doubt

tv-kanal [n.; ~en, ~er] TV channel

tv-licens [n.; ~en, ~er] television viewing license

tv-program [n.; ~met, ~] TV program

tv-rum [n.; ~met, ~] television lounge

tv-ruta [n.; ~n, -rutor] TV screen

tv-skärm [n.; ~en, ~ar] TV screen

tv-station [n.; ~en, ~er] TV station

tv-tittare [n.; ~n, ~] TV viewer

tvungen [adj.; tvunget, tvungna] forced

tv-uttag [n.; ~et, ~] TV socket, TV jack [IT]

två [num.] two

tvåa [n.; ~n] deuce; number 2 [bus, train]; two-room apartment

tvåbäddsrum [n.; ~rummet, ~] double room, room with twin beds

två-filig väg [n.; ~en, ~ar] two-lane highway

tvål [n.; ~en, ~ar] soap

tvålopera [n.; ~n, -operor] soap opera

tvång [n.; ~et] compulsion, coercion, duress

tvärflöjt [n.; ~en, ~er] flute

tvärgata [n.; ~n, -gator] cross street

tvärs över [prep.] right across, straight across

tvärtom [adv.] on the contrary, just the opposite, vice versa

tvårumslägenhet [n.; ~en, ~er] two-room apartment

tvärvetenskaplig [adj.; ~t, ~a] interdisciplinary

tvåtaktsblandning [n.; ~en, ~ar]
two-cycle engine mix
tvätt [n.; ~en, ~ar] laundry, washing; shampoo [hair]
tvätta [v.; ~r, ~de, ~t] wash, do the
laundry; ~ separat wash separately
tvätteri [n.; ~et, ~er] laundry, wash
tvättfat [n.; ~et, ~] wash basin
tvättinrättning [n.; ~en, ~ar] laundry [facilities]
tvättkläder [n.pl.] washing, laundry, wash
tvättklämma [n.; ~n, -klämmor]
clothespin
tvättlapp [n.; ~en, ~ar] wash cloth,
wash rag
tvättmaskin [n.; ~en, ~er] washing
machine
tvättmedel [n.; -medlet, ~] detergent
tvättmöjligheter [n.pl.] laundry
facilities
tvättning [n.; ~en, ~ar] washing
tvättomat [n.; ~en, ~er] laundromat
tvättrum [n.; ~et, ~] washroom
tvättservice [n.; ~n] laundry service
tvättställ [n.; ~et, ~] washstand,
washbasin
tvättäkt [adj.; ~, ~a] colorfast;
genuine
tv-övervakning [n.; ~en] TV
monitoring
ty [conj.] for
tycka [v.; tycker, tyckte, tyckt]
think, consider; ~ om [stress on:
om] like; ~ om [stress on: tycka]
think about, think of
tycke [n.; ~t, ~n] opinion; liking,
fancy
tyda [v.; tyder, tydde, tytt] explain,
interpret; ~ på indicate, show
tydlig [adj.; ~t, ~a] clear
tydligen [adv.] evidently
tyfus [n.; ~en] typhoid fever; typhus
tyg [n.; ~et, ~] fabric, material
tyglar [n.pl.] reins
tynga [v.; tynger, tyngde, tyngt]
weigh down; weigh upon; burden
tyngd [n.; ~en, ~er] weight, load;
gravity
tyngdlyftare [n.; ~n, ~] weight
lifter

tyngre [adj.comp.; see: tung] heavier
tyngst [adj.superl.; see: tung]
heaviest
typ [n.; ~en, ~er] type
typisk [adj.; ~t, ~a] typical
typsnitt [n.; ~et, ~] typeface
tysk [adj.; ~t, ~a] German
tyska [n.] German language; German woman
Tyskland [n.] Germany
tyst [adj.; ~, ~a] quiet
tysta [v.; ~r, ~de, ~t] silence
tystlåten [adj.; -låtet, -låtna] quiet
tystnad [n.; ~en] silence
tystnadsplikt [n.; ~en] professional
secrecy
tyvärr [adv.] unfortunately
tå [n.; ~n, ~r] toe
tåg [n.; ~et, ~] train; procession,
march
tågluffa [v.; ~r, ~de, ~t] travel
around on an Interrail card
tågresenär [n.; ~en, ~er] train
traveler
tågstation [n.; ~en, ~er] train station
tågtider [n.pl.] train timetable
tål [v.; see: tåla]
tåla [v.; tål, tålde, tålt] bear, endure,
be able to take; jag tål inte mjölk
milk doesn't agree with me
tålamod [n.; ~et] patience
tålig [adj.; ~t, ~a] patient
tång [n.; ~en, tänger] tongs, pliers
tår [n.; ~en, ~ar] tear; drop
tårgas [n.; ~en] tear gas
tårpil [n.; ~en, ~ar] weeping willow
tårta [n.; ~n, tårtor] cake [layered
with fruit or cream]
täcka [v.; täcker, täckte, täckt]
cover
täcke [n.; ~t, ~n] cover, covering;
bedcover, quilt
täckjacka [n.; ~n, -jackor] quilted
jacket
tält [n.; ~et, ~] tent
tälta [v.; ~r, ~de, ~t] put up a tent,
pitch a tent, camp
tältlina [n.; ~n, -linor] guy rope
tältning [n.; ~en] camping
tältpinne [n.; ~n, -pinnar] tent peg
tältstake [n.; ~n, -stakar] tent pole

tältsäng [n.; ~en, ~ar] camp bed
tältunderlag [n.; ~et, ~] ground cloth
tältutrustning [n.; ~en] camping equipment
tämligen [adv.] moderately, rather, fairly
tända [v.; tänder, tände, tänt] light, turn on (a light)
tändare [n.; ~n, ~] lighter
tänder [n.pl.; see: **tand**]
tändning [n.; ~en] ignition
tändningsnyckel [n.; ~n, -nycklar] ignition key
tändsticka [n.; ~n, -stickor] match
tändstift [n.; ~et, ~] sparkplug
tänja [v.; tänjer, tänjde, tänjt] stretch
tänka [v.; tänker, tänkte, tänkt] think; imagine; intend; ~ **om** reassess; ~ **på** think of; ~ **ut** work out, think through; ~ **över** consider
tänkbar [adj.; ~t, ~a] thinkable, imaginable
tärna [n.; ~n, tärnor] tern; (brides)-maid, attendant

tärning [n.; ~en, ~ar] dice; cube; **kasta** ~ throw dice
tätort [n.; ~en, ~er] settled area [more than 200 inhabitants]
tätt [adj.; ~, ~a] tight, dense
tättbebyggd [adj.; -byggt, ~a] densely settled
tävla [v.; ~r, ~de, ~t] compete
tävlande [n.] competitor, rival
tävling [n.; ~en, ~ar] competition, contest, match
tävlingscykel [n.; ~n, -cyklar] racing bike
töa [v.; ~r, ~de, ~t] thaw
tömma [v.; tömmer, tömde, tömt] empty; clear
tömning [n.; ~en, ~ar] emptying; collection
tör [v.; ~, torde]: **det ~ inte vara helt sant** it's probably not entirely true
töras [v.passive; törs, tordes, torts] dare
törstig [adj.; ~t, ~a] thirsty

U

ubåt [n.; ~en, ~ar] submarine
UD [abbrev: Utrikesdepartementet]
Ministry of Foreign Affairs
udda [adj.] odd, not even; peculiar;
~ paritet odd parity [IT]; ~ tal
odd numbers
uggla [n.; ~n, ugglor] owl
ugn [n.; ~en, ~ar] oven
ugnsbakad adj.; -bakat, ~e] oven-
baked
ugnsbrynt [adj.; ~, ~a] oven-
browned
ugnstekt [adj.; ~, ~a] roasted
u-hjälp [n.; ~en] aid to developing
countries
Ukraina [n.] Ukraine
ukrainsk [adj.; ~t, ~a] Ukrainian
ukrainska [n.] Ukrainian language
UKV [abbrev: ultrakortvåg] ultra-
shortwave
u-land [abbrev: utvecklingsland;
~et, -länder] developing country
u-landsbistånd [n.; ~et] aid to
developing countries
u-landshjälp [n.; ~en] aid to developing countries
ull [n.; ~en] wool
ultraviolett [adj.; ~, ~a] ultraviolet
ulv [n.; ~en ~ar] wolf
umgås [v.passive; ~, ~gicks, ~gåtts]
spend time together, socialize with;
handle, deal with
umgänge [n.; ~t, ~n] relations;
circle of friends
umgängesliv [n.; ~et] social life
undan [adv.] away, out of the way
undantag [n.; ~et, ~] exception
undantagsfel [n.; ~et, ~] exception
error [IT]
undantagsklausul [n.; ~en] opting-
out clause [EU]
under [prep.] below, beneath, under;
during; ~ 2 timmar for 2 hours;
~ byggnad under construction;
~ dagen during the day; ~ det att
while; ~ kriget during the war
underbar [adj.; ~t, ~a] wonderful,
marvelous
underbädd [n.; ~en, ~ar] lower
berth

underdomän [n.; ~en, ~er] subdomain [IT]
undergång [n.; ~en, ~ar] ruin, fall,
destruction
underhåll [n.; ~et, ~] maintenance
underhållande [adj.] entertaining
underhållning [n.; ~en, ~ar]
entertainment
underhållsbidrag [n.; ~et, ~]
maintenance allowance
underjordsgarage [n.; ~en, ~er]
underground garage
underkjol [n.; ~en, ~ar] petticoat,
slip
underkläder [n.pl.] underwear,
lingerie
underklänning [n.; ~en, ~ar] slip
underkänd [adj.; -känt, ~a] foundation, basis
underlag [n.; ~et, ~] foundation,
basis
underlakan [n.; ~et, ~] bottom
sheet
underlig [n.; ~t, ~a] curious, strange
underliv [n.; ~et] lower belly, genitals; bib
underläge [n.; ~t, ~n] weak position, disadvantage
underlägg [n.; ~et, ~] placemat,
table mat
underlätta [v.; ~r, ~de, ~t] facilitate;
simplify
undermapp [n.; ~en, ~ar] subfolder
[IT]
undermeny [n.; ~n, ~er] submenu
[IT]
underordnad [adj.; -ordnat, ~e]
subordinate [gram]
underordnande konjunktion [n.;
~en, ~er] subordinating conjunction [gram]
underrubrik [n.; ~en, ~er] subtitle
[IT]
underrätta [v.; ~r, ~de, ~t] inform
underskott [n.; ~et, ~] deficit, loss;
deficiency
underskrift [n.; ~en, ~er] signature
understreck [n.; ~et, ~] underscore
[IT]

understruken [adj.; -struket, -strukna] underlined, underscored [IT]

understryka [v.; -stryker, -strök, -strukit] emphasize, stress

understrykning [n.; ~en, ~ar] underlining [IT]

understöd [n.; ~et, ~] support, allowance, subsidy

undersöka [v.; -söker, -sökte, -sökt] study, investigate, examine

undersökning [n.; ~en, ~ar] examination, inquiry

undersökningsrum [n.; ~et, ~] examining room

underteckna [v.; ~r, ~de, ~t] sign

undertröja [n.; ~n, -tröjor] undershirt

undervisa [v.; ~r, ~de, ~t] teach

undervisning [n.; ~en] teaching, instruction

undgå [v.; -går, -gick, -gått] escape

undra [v.; ~r, ~de, ~t] wonder

undvika [v.; -viker, -vek, -vikit] avoid

ung[1] [adj.; ~t, ~a; comp: yngre, yngst] young; **Ung Vänster** Young Left

ung.[2] [abbrev: ungefär] about

ungdom [n.; ~en, ~ar] youth, young person; young people

Ungdomsdelegationen [n.] Commission on Youth

ungdomsfront [n.; ~en] youth front

ungdomsfrågor [n.pl.] youth affairs [EU]

ungdomsförbund [n.; ~et, ~] youth association, youth league

ungdomsrabatt [n.; ~en, ~er] youth discount

Ungdomsstyrelsen [n.] National Board for Youth Affairs

unge [n.; ~n, ungar] young, little ones; child, kid

ungefär [adv.] about, approximately

ungefärlig [adj.; ~t, ~a] approximate

Ungern [n.] Hungary

ungersk [adj.; ~t, ~a] Hungarian

ungerska [n.] Hungarian language; Hungarian woman

ungkarl [n.; ~en, ~ar] bachelor

ungmö [n.; ~n, ~r] maiden, maid

Ungsocialisterna (US) [n.pl.] Young Socialists

ungt [adj.; see: ung]

UNHCR [abbrev: Förenta nationernas flyktingkommissariat] United Nations High Commissioner for Refugees (UNHCR)

unik [adj.; ~t, ~a] unique

union [n.; ~en, ~er] union

Unionsfördraget [see: **EU-fördraget**]

unionsmedborgarskap [n.; ~et] EU citizenship [EU]

universal [adj.; ~t, ~a] universal

universitet [n.; ~et, ~] university

universitetsadjunkt [n.; ~en, ~er] lecturer [no PhD]

universitetslektor [n.; ~n, ~er] senior lecturer [has PhD]

universitetsort [n.; ~en, ~er] university town

universum [n.; ~et] universe

unna [v.; ~r, ~de, ~t] not begrudge, let s.o. have

uplink [n.; ~en, ~er] uplink [IT]

upp [adv.] upward, up [motion]; ~ **och ned** upside-down

uppdatera [v.; ~r, ~de, ~t] update, refresh

uppdaterad [adj.; -daterat, ~e] updated

uppdatering [n.; ~en, ~ar] update

uppdelning [n.; ~en, ~ar] division

uppdrag [n.; ~et, ~] commission, task, assignment; **på ~ av** commissioned by

uppe [adv.] up [location]; upstairs; not in bed; **vara ~** have gotten up

uppehåll [n.; ~et, ~] break, interruption; end, ceasing; sojourn; stop; **utan ~** continuous(ly), without interruption

uppehållstillstånd (UT) [n.; ~et, ~] residence permit

uppemot [adv.] nearly, almost

uppenbar [adj.; ~t, ~a] obvious, evident

uppenbarelse [n.; ~n, ~r] revelation

uppenbarligen [adv.] clearly

uppfatta [v.; ~r, ~de, ~t] perceive, understand, grasp

uppfattning [n.; ~en, ~ar] opinion, point of view

uppfinna [v.; -finner, -fann, -funnit] invent

uppfinnare [n.; ~n, ~] inventor

uppfinning [n.; ~en, ~ar] invention

uppfylla [v.; -fyller, -fyllde, -fyllt] fulfill; carry out; comply with

uppfödning [n.; ~en, ~ar] breeding

uppföljning [n.; ~en, ~ar] follow-up

uppför [prep.] up; ~ **trappan** up the stairs

uppförd [adj.; -fört, ~a] erected, built

uppförsbacke [n.; ~n, -backar] upwards/uphill slope

uppge [v.; -ger, -gav, -givit/-gett] state, say

uppgift [n.; ~en, ~er] information, detail; instructions

uppgradering [n.; ~en, ~ar] upgrade [IT]

uppgång [n.; ~en, ~ar] rise; stairs, entrance

uppgå till [v.; -går, -gick, -gått] amount to, total

uppgörelse [n.; ~n, ~r] agreement, arrangement; settlement [accounts]; dispute, controversy

upphandling [n.; ~en, ~ar] purchase, buying

upphov [n.; ~et, ~] origin, source; beginning; cause; **ge** ~ give rise to

upphovsrätt [n.; ~en] copyright

upphävandeklausul [n.; ~en, ~er] suspension clause [EU]

upphöjd text [n.; ~en] superscript [IT]

upphöra [v.; -hör, - hörde, -hört] cease; close down, go out of business

uppifrån [adv.] from above

uppkallad efter [adj.; -kallat, -kallade] named after

uppklippt [adj.] layered [haircut]

uppkopplad [adj.; -kopplat, ~e] connected

uppkoppling [n.; ~en, ~ar] connection

uppkopplingshastighet [n.; ~en, ~er] connection speed [IT]

uppl. [abbrev.; see: **upplaga**]

uppladda [v.; ~r, ~de, ~t] upload [IT]

upplaga [n.; ~n, -lagor] edition

uppleva [v.; -lever, -levde, -levt] experience

upplevelse [n.; ~n, ~r] experience

upplopp [n.; ~et, ~] riot, tumult; finish [race]

upplysa [v.; -lyser, -lyste, -lyst] inform

upplysning [n.; ~en, ~ar] information, report

upplysningsbyrå [n.; ~n, ~ar] information center/desk

upplyst [adj.; ~, ~a] illuminated

uppläggning [n.; ~en, ~ar] layout, arrangement

upplösning [n.; ~en, ~ar] resolution; disbandment

uppmana [v.; ~r, ~de, ~t] request, encourage; prompt, elicit

uppmaning [n.; ~en, ~ar] request, command; prompt

uppmärksam [adj.; ~t, ~a] attentive, observant

uppmärksamhet [n.; ~en] attention

uppnå [v.; ~r, ~dde, ~tt] reach, attain, achieve

upprepa [v.; ~r, ~de, ~t] repeat

uppriktig [adj.; ~t, ~a] sincere, honest, frank

uppringare [n.; ~n, ~] dialer [IT]

uppringd anslutning [n.; ~en, ~ar] dial-up connection [IT]

uppringd förbindelse [n.; ~n, ~r] dial-up connection [IT]

uppringningsprogram [n.; -programmet, ~] dialer [IT]

upprop [n.; ~et, ~] call, appeal; roll call; **sista ~et** last call

uppror [n.; ~et, ~] revolt

upprustning [n.; ~en] rearmament

upprätt [adj.; ~, ~a] upright

upprätta [v.; ~r, ~de, ~t] found, establish; draw up [document]; rehabilitate, restore

upprätthålla [v.; -håller, -höll, -hållit] maintain, keep up, keep going

uppröra [v.; ~rör, -rörde, -rört] upset

upprörd [adj.; upprört, ~a] upset, indignant
uppsats [n.; ~en, ~er] essay
uppseende [n.; ~t] sensation, attention
uppsikt [n.; ~en] surveillance, supervision
uppskatta [v.; ~r, ~de, ~t] appreciate, value
uppskattning [n.; ~en, ~ar] appreciation, valuation
uppslagsverk [n.; ~et, ~] reference book
uppspelning [n.; ~en, ~ar] playback [IT]
uppstå [v.; - står, -stod, - stått] emerge
uppställning [n.; ~en, ~ar] arrangement, format; table [IT]
uppsägning [n.; ~en, ~ar] notice, notification
uppsägningstid [n.; ~en] period of notice
uppsättning [n.; ~en, ~ar] production [theater]
upptagen [adj.; -taget, -tagna] busy, occupied, taken
upptagetton [n.; ~er, ~en] busy signal
uppträda [v.; -träder, -trädde, -trätt] appear; perform, act; behave; act; occur
uppträdande[1] [adj.] performing; **de ~** the performers
uppträdande[2] [n.; ~t, ~n] appearance, performance; behavior; occurrence
upptäcka [v.; -täcker, -täckte, -täckt] discover, detect
upptäckt [adj.; ~, ~a] discovered, detected
uppvuxen [adj.; -vuxet, -vuxna] raised, grown
uppvärmning [n.; ~en] heating
uppväxt [n.; ~en] growth, growing up
uppåt [adv./prep.] up, upward
uppåtström [adv.] upstream [IT]
ur[1] [n.; ~et, ~] clock
ur-[2] [prefix] from ancient times; [colloq.] extremely

ur[3] [prep./adv.] out of, away; **~ funktion** out of order; **~ led** out of joint, dislocated
uraffär [n.; ~en, ~er] watchmaker's
uran [n.; ~et] uranium
Uranus [n.] Uranus
urban [adj.; ~t, ~a] urbane, affable; urban
urbefolkning [n.; ~en, ~ar] indigenous population
urgammal [adj.; ~t, -gamla] ancient
urin [n.; ~en] urine
urinblåsa [n.; ~n, -blåsor] bladder
urinnevånare [n.; ~n, ~] aboriginal inhabitant
urinprov [n.; ~et, ~] urine test
urinvägsinfektion [n.; ~en, ~er] urinary tract infection, cystitis
urkund [n.; ~en, ~er] document, record
urmakare [n.; ~n, ~] watchmaker
urminnes tider [n.pl.] time immemorial
urolog [n.; ~en, ~er] urologist
urringad [adj.; -ringat, ~e] low-cut
urspr. [adv.; see: **ursprungligen**]
ursprung [n.; ~et, ~] origin
ursprunglig [adj.; ~t, ~a] original, primordial; natural, simple
ursprungligen [adv.] originally
ursäkta [v.; ~r, ~de, ~t] forgive; **ursäkta!** pardon me!, excuse me!
urtiden [n.] prehistoric times
urval [n.; ~et, ~] choice, selection; assortment
USA [abbrev: Förenta Staterna] United States of America (USA)
USB-port [n.; ~en, ~ar] USB port [IT]
usch! [interj.] ugh!
USD [abbrev: US dollars] US dollars
u-sväng [n.; ~en, ~ar] u-turn
ut[1] [adv.] out [motion]; **~ ur** out of
UT[2] [abbrev: uppehållstillstånd] residence permit
utan[1] [conj.] but; **inte A ~ B** not A but B; **~ att** without
utan[2] [prep.] without; **~ kaffein** decaffeinated; **~ måltider** meals not included
utanför [adv./prep.] outside; off

utanförskap [n.; ~et] exclusion, marginalization, alienation
utanpå [adv.] on the outside
utantill [adv.] by heart
utbetalning [n.; ~en, ~ar] payment
utbilda [v.; ~r, ~de, ~t] educate, train; ~ **sig** educate oneself, train, get training
utbildad [adj.; -bildat, ~e] trained
utbildning [n.; ~en] education, training
utbildningslinje [n.; ~n, ~r] study program [university]
Utbildnings- och kulturdepartementet (U) [n.] Ministry of Education, Research and Culture
utbildningssystem [n.; ~et] tutorial [IT]
Utbildningsutskottet [n.] Committee on Education [in Parliament]
utbrott [n.; ~et, ~] outburst, eruption; outbreak
utbryta [v.; -bryter, -bröt, -brutit] remove; break out
utbränna [v.; -bränner, -brände, -bränt] burn out
utbud [n.; ~et, ~] offer [for sale]; supply
utbyggnad [n.; ~en, ~er] extension, enlargement; annex
utbyggnadskort [n.; ~et, ~] expansion board [IT]
utbyte [n.; ~t] exchange; return, yield, profit
utbytesstudent [n.; ~en, ~er] exchange student
utbärning [n.; ~en, ~ar] delivery, distribution
utdelning [n.; ~en, ~ar] distribution
ute[1] [adv.] out [location]; outdoors, outside; not at home; ~ **på havet** out at sea
ute-[2] [prefix] open air
utebassäng [n.; ~en, ~er] outdoor swimming pool
utefter [prep.] along
utekafé [n.; ~n, ~er] pavement cafe
uteservering [n.; ~en, ~ar] open-air café, service outside
utesluta [v.; -sluter, -slöt, -slutit] exclude, eliminate

uteslutande [adj.] exclusive; exclusion
uteslutet [adv.] excluded; no way!
utfart [n.; ~en, ~er] exit for vehicles; ~ **lastbil** truck exit
utflykt [n.; ~en, ~er] excursion
utflyttning [n.; ~en, ~ar] outsourcing
utforma [v.; ~r, ~de, ~t] design
utformad av [adj.; -format, ~e] designed by
utformning [n.; ~en, ~ar] design
utforska [v.; ~r, ~de, ~t] explore, investigate, search
Utforskare [n.; ~n] Explorer [IT]
utföra [v.; -för, -förde, -fört] perform, execute, carry out
utförande [n.; ~t, ~n] execution [IT]
utförandehastighet [n.; ~en, ~er] throughput [IT]
utförd [adj.; utfört, ~a] executed, completed
utförlig [adj.; ~t, ~a] detailed, full
utförsåkning [n.; ~en] downhill skiing, alpine skiing
utförsäljning [n.; ~en] going-out-of-business sale, clearance sale
utg. [abbrev: utgåva; utgiven; utgivare] edition; published; editor, publisher
utgift [n.; ~en, ~er] expense
utgiftsområde [n.; ~, ~n] expenditure area
utgjord [v.past; see: utgöra]
utgrävning [n.; ~en, ~ar] excavation
utgå [v.; -går, -gick, -gått] go out, come out; depart; start
utgående [adj.] outgoing
utgång [n.; ~en, ~ar] exit, way out; end, close; outcome
utgångspunkt [n.; ~en, ~er] point of departure, starting point
utgåva [n.; ~n, utgåvor] edition
utgöra [v.; -gör, -gjorde, -gjort] constitute, represent, be
uthyrd [adj.; uthyrt, ~a] rented
uthyres [phrase] for rent
utifrån [adv.] from outside
utkast [n.; ~et, ~] draft
utkorg [n.; ~en, ~ar] outbox [IT]
utkörning [n.; ~en] delivery
utlandet [n.] abroad

utlandsresa [n.; ~n, -resor] trip abroad

utlandssamtal [n.; ~et, ~] international call

utlandsvistelse [n.; ~n, ~r] stay abroad

utleverans [n.; ~en, ~er] delivery

utlova [v. ~r, ~de, ~t] promise

utlånad [adj.; -lånat, ~e] loaned out, lent

utlåning [n.; ~en, ~ar] lending

utlämna [v.; ~r, ~de, ~t] hand out, issue; give up, surrender; extradite

utlämning [n.; ~en, ~ar] distribution, delivery; extradition

utländsk [adj.; ~t, ~a] foreign; ~ **språk** foreign language; ~ **valuta** foreign currency

utlänning [n.; ~en, ~ar] foreigner

utlöpande datum [n.; ~et] expiration date

utmana [v.; ~r, ~de, ~t] challenge, defy

utmanande [adj.] challenging; defiant; provocative, arrogant

utmaning [n.; ~en, ~ar] challenge

utmatning [n.; ~en, ~ar] output [IT]

utmattad [adj.; ~mattat, ~e] exhausted

utmed [prep.] along

utmärkande [adj.] significant

utmärkelse [n.; ~n, ~er] distinction, honor

utmärkt [adj.; ~, ~a] excellent

utnyttja [v.; ~r, ~de, ~t] use, take advantage of, exploit

utnämna [v.; -nämner, -nämnde, -nämnt] appoint

utom [prep.] except for; outside of; ~ **hörhåll** out of earshot; ~ **protokollet** off the record

utomhus [adv.] outdoors

utomhusbassäng [n.; ~en, ~er] outdoor swimming pool

utomlands [adv.] abroad

utomordentlig [adj.; ~t, ~a] extraordinary

utomnordisk [adj.; ~t, ~a] non-Nordic [not Danish, Finnish, Norwegian or Swedish]

utomstående [adj.] outsider; uninitiated

utopisk [adj.; ~t, ~a] utopian

utpressning [n.; ~en] blackmail

utreda [v.; -reder, -redde, -rett] investigate, analyze

utredning [n.; ~en, ~ar] inquiry, investigation

utresa [n.; ~n, -resor] exit [from country], leaving the country

utrikes- [prefix] foreign, international

Utrikesdepartementet (UD) [n.] Ministry of Foreign Affairs

utrikesflyg [n.; ~et, ~] international flight

utrikeshandel [n.; ~n] foreign trade

utrikeskorrespondent [n.; ~en, ~er] foreign correspondent

utrikesminister [n.; ~n, -ministrar] Minister for Foreign Affairs

utrikesnyheter [n.pl.] foreign news

Utrikesnämnden [n.] Advisory Council on Foreign Affairs

utrikespolitik [n.; ~en] foreign policy

Utrikespolitiska institutet (UI) [n.] Foreign Policy Institute

utrikespostanvisning [n.; ~en, ~ar] international money order

utrikessamtal [n.; ~et, ~] international call

utrikesterminal [n.; ~en, ~er] international terminal

Utrikesutskottet [n.] Committee on Foreign Affairs [in Parliament]

utrop [n.; ~et, ~] call, exclamation, cry; **sista** ~ last call [airport, auction]

utropstecken (!) [n.; -tecknet, ~] exclamation point (!) [gram]

utrumgenus [n.] common gender [see: **realgenus**] [gram]

utrustning [n.; ~en, ~ar] equipment

utrymme [n.; ~et, ~en] space, room

utsatt [adj.; ~, ~a; see also: **utsätta**] allowed, set; exposed, vulnerable

utse [v.; -ser, -såg, -sett] choose, designate

utseende [n.; ~t, ~n] appearance, looks

utsida [n.; ~n, -sidor] exterior, outside

utsikt [n.; ~en, ~er] view

utsiktspunkt [n.; ~en, ~er] viewpoint, point of view

utskott [n.; ~et, ~] rejection; committee

utskrift [n.; ~en, ~er] printout, print [IT]

utskuren biff [n.; ~en] sirloin steak

utslag [n.; ~et, ~] rash, eruption

utslagen [n.; -slagna] outcast, dropout

utsläpp [n.; ~et, ~] outlet; discharging, emission

utspel [n.; ~et, ~] move, play; initiative

utsträckning [n.; ~en] extent

utställning [n.; ~en, ~ar] display, exhibition

utställningsföremål [n.; ~et, ~] exhibit, object on exhibition

utställningskatalog [n.; ~en, ~er] exhibition catalogue

utsåld [adj.; utsålt, ~a] sold out

utsätta för [v.; -sätter, -satte, -satt] expose to

utsökt [adj.; ~, ~a] exquisite

uttag [n.; ~et, ~] withdrawal

uttagsautomat [n.; ~en, ~er] cash machine, automated teller machine (ATM)

uttala [v.; ~r, ~de, ~t] pronounce; ~ sig express one's views

uttalande [n.; ~t, ~n] utterance, statement

utter [n.; ~n, uttrar] otter

uttryck [n.; ~et, ~] expression, phrase

uttrycka sig [v.; -trycker, -tryckte, -tryckt] express oneself

uttröttad [adj.; -tröttat, ~e] exhausted

utvald [adj.; -valt, ~a; see also: **utvälja**] chosen, select, picked

utvandra [v.; ~r, ~de, ~t] emigrate

utvandrare [n.; ~n, ~] emigrant

utvandring [n.; ~en, ~ar] emigration

utveckla [v.; ~r, ~de, ~t] develop

utveckling [n.; ~en, ~ar] development; evolution

utvecklingsbistånd [n.; ~et, ~] development aid

utvecklingslära [n.; ~n, -läror] theory of evolution

utvecklingsprogram [n.; -programmet, ~] development program [IT]

utvidga [v.; ~r, ~de, ~t] widen, expand, broaden

utvidgning [n.; ~en, ~ar] expansion, widening, extension, dilation

utvisa [v.; ~r, ~de, ~t] send out; expel, deport; show

utvisning [n.; ~en, ~ar] deportation, expulsion; penalty [hockey]

utvälja [v.; -väljer, -valde, -valt] select, choose

utvändigt [adv.] externally, on the outside

utvärdera [v.; ~r, ~de, ~t] evaluate

utvärtes [adj.] external

utåt [adv.] out into, out towards

utåtriktad [adj.; -riktat, ~e] outgoing, extrovert

utökad [adj.; -ökat, ~e] enhanced, expanded, enlarged

utöver [prep.] besides, in addition to, beyond

uv [n.; ~en, ~ar] great horned owl

V

V[1] [abbrev: volt] volt

v[2] [abbrev: Vänsterpartiet] Party of the Left

v.[3] [abbrev: vägen; vecka; vice; väster] street; week; vice; western

VA[1] [abbrev: vatten och avlopp] water and sewage [part of public works]

va[2] [pron. colloq., see: **vad**]

vaccin [n.; ~et] vaccine

vaccinationskort [n.; ~et] vaccination card

vaccinering [n.; ~en, ~ar] vaccination

vaccinera (mot) [v.; ~r, ~de, ~t] vaccinate (against)

vaccinerad [n.; vaccinerat, ~e] vaccinated

vacker [adj.; ~t, vackra] beautiful, handsome

vad[1] [n.; ~en, ~er] calf [leg]

vad[2] [n.; ~et, ~] bet, wager; **slå ~** make a bet

vad[3] [pron.] what; **~ kul** what fun; **~ sa du?** what did you say?; **~ som helst** anything, whatever; **~ trevligt** how nice; **~ är klockan?** what time is it?

vadderad [adj.; -derat, ~e] quilted

vagga [n.; ~n, vaggor] cradle

vagn [n.; ~en, ~er] cart; car [in a train]; carriage

vagnsnummer [n.; -numret, ~] car number [train]

vaken [adj.; vaket, vakna] awake, alert, attentive

vakna [v.; ~r, ~de, ~t] wake up, awaken [intrans]

vakt [n.; ~en, ~er] watch; guard

vakta [v.; ~r, ~de, ~t] guard, keep guard, watch over

vaktavlösning [n.; ~en, ~ar] changing of the guard

vaktel [n.; ~n, vaktlar] quail

vakthavande [adj.] on duty

vaktmästare [n.; ~n, ~] messenger; caretaker; attendant, usher

vaktombyte [n.; ~t, ~n] changing of the guard

val[1] [n.; ~en, ~ar] whale

val[2] [n.; ~et, ~] election, choice, selection

valaffisch [n.; ~en, ~er] election poster

Valborgsmässoafton [n.; ~en] Walpurgis Eve [April 30th]

valborgsmässoeldar [n.pl.] Walpurgis Eve bonfires

vald [adj.; valt, ~a] elected; selected; [see: **välja**]

valdag [n.; ~en, ~ar] election day

valdeltagande [n.; ~t, ~n] turnout, participation in election

valdistrikt [n.; ~en, ~er] constituency, voting district

valfisk [n.; ~en, ~ar] whale

valfläsk [n.; ~et] election promises

valfri [adj.; ~tt, ~a] optional, elective; **~a tillbehör** choice of side dishes; **~tt ämne** elective subject [school]

valfrihet [n.; ~en, ~er] freedom of choice

valfusk [n.; ~et] ballot rigging

valfångst [n.; ~en] whaling

valförlust [n.; ~en] defeat at the polls, election defeat

valhemlighet [n.; ~en] confidentiality of voting, ballot secrecy

validering [n.; ~en] validation [IT]

valkampanj [n.; ~en, ~er] election campaign

vall [n.; ~en, ~ar] bank, rampart; pasture, grazing area

vallfartsort [n.; ~en, ~er] pilgrimage site

vallgrav [n.; ~en, ~ar] moat

vallokal [n.; ~en, ~er] polling station

vallonsk [adj.; ~t, ~a] Walloon

vallöfte [n.; ~t, ~n] election promise/pledge

Valmyndigheten [n.] Election Authority

valnöt [n.; ~en, -nötter] walnut

valresultat [n.; ~en, ~er] election result

valrörelse [n.; ~n, ~r] election campaign, electioneering

vals [n.; ~en, ~er] waltz
valsedel [n.; ~n, -sedlar] ballot
valseger [n.; ~n, -segrar] election victory
valspråk [n.; ~et, ~] campaign slogan
valsystem [n.; ~et] electoral procedure
valthorn [n.; ~et, ~] French horn [music]
valurna [n.; ~n, -urnor] ballot box
valuta [n.; ~n, valutor] currency; value
valutakurs [n.; ~en, ~er] exchange rate
valutamarknad [n.; ~en, ~er] foreign exchange market
valutanotering [n.; ~en, ~ar] exchange rate
valutareserv [n.; ~en, ~er] foreign exchange reserve
valutaunion [n.; ~en, ~er] currency union
valutaväxel [n.; ~n, - växlar] currency exchange
valutaväxling [n.; ~en, ~ar] currency exchange
valutgång [n.; ~en, ~er] election result
valv [n.; ~et, ~] vault, arch
vampyr [n.; ~en, ~er] vampire
van (vid) [adj.; ~t, ~a] used (to), accustomed (to)
vana [n.; ~n, vanor] habit, custom; experience
vandalism [n.; ~en] vandalism
vandra [v.; ~r, ~de, ~t] wander, hike, walk; ~ **omkring** wander around
vandrare [n.; ~n, ~] hiker
vandrarhem [n.; -hemmet, ~] youth hostel
vandrarkängor [n.pl.] hiking boots
vandring [n.; ~en, ~ar] walk
vandringskarta [n.; ~n, -kartor] hiking map
vandringsled [n.; ~en, ~er] walking route, hiking trail
vanilj [n.; ~en] vanilla
vaniljsås [n.; ~en] vanilla custard
vanl. [abbrev: vanligen] usually
vanlig [adj.; ~t, ~a] normal, common, usual; ~ **post** surface mail;

~**a frågor** frequently asked questions (FAQ) [IT]
vanligast [adj.superl.] most common
vanligen [adv.] usually
vanligtvis [adv.] usually
vann [v.past; see: vinna]
vansinnig [adj.; ~t, ~a] crazy
vant [adj.; see: van]
vapen [n.; vapnet, ~] weapon
vapenexport [n.; ~en, ~er] arms exports
vapenvila [n.; ~n, -vilor] ceasefire
vapenvägrare [n.; ~n, ~] conscientious objector
var[1] [adv./conj.] where [location]; ~ **finns matsalen?** where is the dining room?; ~ **ligger järnvägsstationen?** where is the train station?; ~ **som helst** anywhere, wherever
var[2] [pron.; ~t] each, every; ~ **och en för sig** separately, each for himself; ~ **sin/sitt/sina** each his own; ~ **tredje** every third
var[3] [v.past; see: vara]
vara[1] [n.; ~n, varor] good, article, product; **tullfria varor** duty-free goods; **varor bytes ej, inga pengar tillbaka** goods cannot be refunded or exchanged; **ta ~ på** take care of; **ta till ~** make use of
vara[2] [v.; är, var, varit] be; **var god vänta** please wait; **var så god** here you are, help yourself, please; you're welcome; naturally, by all means; ~ **med** join in, take part; ~ **rädd om** be careful with, take care of; **vare därmed hur som helst** be that as it may
vara[3] [v.; ~r, ~de, ~t] last, endure
varaktighet [n.; ~en] duration
varandra [pron.] each other, one another
varannan [adj.; vartannat] every other; ~ **dag** every other day
varav [adv.] of which, whereof
vard. [see: vardag]
vardag [n.; ~en, ~ar] weekday, working day
vardaglig [adj.; ~t, ~a] everyday, commonplace

vardagsrum [n.; -rummet, ~] living room

vardera [pron.] each, per person

vare [v.; see: **vara**]: tack ~ Gud! Thank God!, Thanks be to God!

varelse [n.; ~n, ~r] creature; being

varenda [pron.; vartenda] every

varför [adv.] why

varg [n.; ~en, ~ar] wolf

variabel [adj.; ~t, variabla] variable

variant [n.; ~en, ~er] variant, variety

variera [v.; ~r, ~de, ~t] vary

varierande [adj.] varying

varieté [n.; ~n, ~er] music hall, variety theater

varifrån [adv.] from where, whence

varje [pron./adj.] every, each; ~ **månad** monthly; ~ **vecka** weekly

varken [conj.] neither; ~ **igår eller idag** neither yesterday nor today

varm [adj.; ~t, ~a] warm, hot; **gå ~** run hot, get overheated [machinery]; ~ **korv** hot dog

varmrätt [n.; ~en, ~er] main course

varmstart [n.; ~en, ~er] hot boot [IT]

varmvatten [n.; -vattnet, ~] hot water

varmvattenberedare [n.; ~n, ~] water heater

varna [v.; ~r, ~de, ~t] warn

varning [n.; ~en, ~ar] warning; caution; ~ **för hunden** beware of dog

varningsblinkers [n.pl.] hazard warning lights

varningsljus [n.; ~et, ~] warning light

varningsmärke [n.; ~t, ~n] warning sign

varningstriangel [n.; ~n, -trianglar] warning triangle [car]

varpå [adv.] whereupon; on which; on what

vars [pron.; see: **vilken**] whose

varsel [n.; varslet, ~] forewarning; notice, warning

varstans: lite ~ [adv.] here and there

varsågod! [phrase] here you are!, please help yourself!; by all means!, be my guest!; you're welcome! [in response to thank you]; ~ **och kom in!** please come in!

vart[1] [adv.] where to, whither [motion]

vart[2] [pron.; see: **var**] each, every

vartannat [adj.; see: **varannan**] every other

varubeställning [n.; ~en, ~ar] ordering of goods

varuhus [n.; -huset, ~] department store

varuhusinformation [n.; ~en, ~er] store directory

varukorg [n.; ~en, ~ar] shopping basket

varumärke [n.; ~t, ~n] trademark

varusortiment [n.; ~et] range of goods, assortment

varv [n.; ~et, ~] shipyard; turn, revolution; ~ **i minuten** revolutions per minute (rpm)

vas [n.; ~en, ~er] vase

Vasaloppet [n.] Vasa cross-country ski race [in March]

Vasamuseet [n.] Vasa Museum

vass [adj.; ~t, ~a] sharp, sharp-edged

Vatikanstaten [n.] Vatican State, Holy See

vatten [n.; vattnet, ~] water

vattendrag [n.; ~et, ~] water course

vattendunk [n.; ~en, ~ar] water can

vattenfall [n.; ~et, ~] waterfall

vattenflaska [n.; ~n, -flaskor] water bottle

vattenfärg [n.; ~en, ~er] watercolor

vattenförbrukning [n.; ~en] water consumption

vattenglas [n.; ~et, ~] water glass, tumbler

vattenkanna [n.; ~n, -kannor] watering can

vattenkastare [n.; ~n] gargoyle [see: **grotesk**]

vattenkokare [n.; ~n, ~] kettle

vattenkoppor [n.pl.] chickenpox

vattenkraft [n.; ~en, ~er] hydro-electric power

vattenkran [n.; ~en, ~ar] water faucet

vattenkvarn [n.; ~en, ~ar] water mill

vattenledning [n.; ~en, ~ar] water main; water pipe
vattenmelon [n.; ~en, ~er] water-melon
vattenskidor [n.pl.] water skis; åka ~ go water skiing
vattenskidåkning [n.; ~en] water skiing
vattenskoter [n.; ~n, -skotrar] jet ski
vattensport [n.; ~en, ~er] water sports
vattentorn [n.; ~et, ~] water tower
vattentvätt [n.; ~en] washing with water, laundry
vattentät [adj.; -tätt, ~a] waterproof
vattna [v.; ~r, ~de, ~t] water; ~ blommorna water the flowers
Vattumannen [n.] Aquarius
vaxbönor [n.pl.] butter beans
vaxmodell [n.; ~en, ~er] waxwork, wax model
vaxpropp [n.; ~en, ~ar] wax earplug
vd. [abbrev: verkställande direktör] managing director, president
vecka [n.; ~n, veckor] week
veckoavlöning [n.; ~en, ~ar] weekly salary
veckobiljett [n.; ~en, ~er] weekly ticket
veckodag [n.; ~en, ~ar] weekday
veckokort [n.; ~et, ~] week pass
veckolön [n.; ~en, ~er] weekly wages
veckoslut [n.; ~et, ~] weekend
veckotidning [n.; ~en, ~ar] weekly, magazine
ved [n.; ~en] firewood, wood
vedbod [n.; ~en, ~ar] woodshed
vederhäftig [n.; ~t, ~a] reliable
vegan [n.; ~en, ~er] vegan
vegetarian [n.; ~en, ~er] vegetarian
vegetarisk [adj.; ~t, ~a] vegetarian; ~ mat vegetarian food
vegetation [n.; ~en] vegetation
vek¹ [adj.; ~t, ~a] soft, pliant, weak
vek² [v.past; see: vika]
vektor [n.; ~n, ~er] vector
vektorbaserad [n.; -baserat, ~e] vector-based [IT]
vektorfont [n.; ~en, ~er] outline font [IT]

velat [v.past; see: vilja]
velig [adj.; ~t, ~a] vacillating
vem [pron.] who; ~ som helst anybody, whoever
ven [n.; ~en, ~er] vein
Venedig [n.] Venice
venerisk sjukdom [n.; ~en, ~ar] venereal disease
ventil [n.; ~en, ~er] valve; ventilator; porthole
Venus [n.] Venus
veranda [n.; ~n, verandor] veranda
verb [n.; ~et, ~] verb [gram]
verbpartikel [n.; ~n, -partiklar] verb particle [gram]
verifiera [v.; ~r, ~de, ~t] verify
verifiering [n.; ~en, ~ar] authentication
verk [n.; ~et, ~] work; agency; works
verka [v.; ~r, ~de, ~t] seem
verkan [n.; ~, verkningar] effect, result, action; effectiveness
Verket för högskoleservice (VHS) [n.] Administration for Higher Education Services
Verket för innovationssystem (VINNOVA) [n.] Swedish Agency for Innovation Systems
Verket för näringslivsutveckling (NUTEK) [n.] Swedish Business Development Agency
verklig [adj.; ~t, ~a] real
verkligen [adv.] really
verklighet [n.; ~en, ~er] reality
verkligt [adv.] really
verkmästare [n.; ~n, ~] supervisor
verksam [adj.; ~t, ~a] effective; active
verksamhet [n.; ~en, ~er] activity
verkstad [n.; ~en, -städer] workshop, repair shop; garage
verkställa [v.; -ställer, -ställde, -ställt] carry out; apply [IT]
verkställande direktör (vd) [n.; ~en, ~er] managing director
verktyg [n.; ~et, ~] tool
verktygsfält [n.; ~et, ~er] toolbar [IT]
verktygslåda [n.; ~n, -lådor] toolbox
verktygsmeny [n.; ~n, ~er] tools menu [IT]

verktygstips [n.; ~et, ~] tool tip [IT]

vers [n.; ~en, ~er] verse; poem; poetry

versaler [n.pl.] upper-case letters [IT]

version [n.; ~en, ~er] version; build [IT]

vessla [n.; ~n, vesslor] weasel, ferret

veta [v.; vet, visste, vetat] know

vete [n.; ~t] wheat

vetemjöl [n.; ~et] wheat flour [ordinary flour]

vetenskap [n.; ~en, ~er] science; theory

vetenskaplig [adj.; ~t, ~a] scientific, scholarly

vetenskapsman [n.; -mannen, -män] scientist

vetenskapsmuseum [n.; -museet, -museer] science museum

Vetenskapsrådet [n.] National Research Council

veterinär [n.; ~en, ~er] veterinarian

vetorätt [n.; ~en, ~er] veto power [EU]

vettig [adj.; ~t, ~a] sensible, judicious

VG[1] [abbrev: väl godkänd] passed with distinction [2nd highest school mark]

v.g.[2] [abbrev: var god] please; ~ **ring på klockan** please ring the bell; ~ **torka av fötterna** please wipe your feet; ~ **vänta** please wait

vgv [abbrev: var god vänd] please turn over

vi [pron.; vår, oss] we; ~ **hörs** let's keep in touch, talk to you later; ~ **ses** see you later

vice- [prefix] vice-

vid[1] [adj.; vitt, vida] wide

vid[2] [prep.] at, by; around; next to; ~ **behov** if necessary; ~ **fara** in case of danger; ~ **frukostbordet** at the breakfast table; ~ **gången** by the aisle; ~ **halv 9-tiden** around half past eight; ~ **smärta** if you feel pain

vidare [adj./adv.] further

vidarebefordra [v.; ~r, ~de, ~t] forward

vidareutbilda sig [v.; ~r, ~de, ~t] continue one's education/training

vidd [n.; ~en, ~er] vast expanse, wide open space

videoband [n.; ~et, ~] videotape

videobandspelare [n.; ~n, ~] video recorder

videofilm [n.; ~en, ~er] videocassette

videokamera [n.; ~n, -kameror] video camera

videokort [n.; ~et, ~] video card [IT]

videosnutt [n.; ~en, ~ar] video clip [IT]

vidimera [v.; ~r, ~de, ~t] attest, certify

vidimerad [adj.; vidimerat, ~e] certified

vidta [v.; -tar, -tog, -tagit] take, make; continue, begin

viga [v.; viger, vigde, vigt] consecrate; marry a couple

vigda [n.pl.] married, marriages [newspaper notice]

vigsel [n.; ~n, vigslar] wedding, marriage ceremony; **borgerlig** ~ civil wedding; **kyrklig** ~ church wedding

vigselannons [n.; ~en, ~er] wedding announcement

vigselbevis [n.; ~et, ~] marriage certificate

vigselring [n.; ~en, ~ar] wedding ring

vik [n.; ~en, ~ar] bay

vika [v.; viker, vek, vikit] fold; yield; move; turn

vikariat [n.; ~et, ~] substitute, temporary work/post

vikarie [n.; ~n, ~r] deputy, substitute worker, locum tenens

vikariera [v.; ~r, ~de, ~t] substitute, stand in for someone, work as a temp

vikarierande [adj.] deputy, acting

viking [n.; ~en, ~ar] Viking

Vikingapartiet [n.] Viking Party

vikt [n.; ~en, ~er] weight

viktig [adj.; ~t, ~a] important

viktigaste [adj.superl.] most important, very important

vila [v.; ~r, ~de, ~t] rest

vild [adj.; vilt, ~a] wild; **~a champinjoner** field mushrooms

Vilda Västern [n.] Wild West; Western [film]

vildand [n.; ~en, -änder] wild duck

vildjur [n.; ~et, ~] wild beast

vildmark [n.; ~en, ~er] wilderness

vildsvin [n.; ~et, ~] wild boar

Vilhelm [n.] William

vilja¹ [n.; ~n] will, desire, intention

vilja² [v.; vill, ville, velat] want (to); **ja skulle ~ ha** I'd like, please give me; **~ gärna** would like to

vilken [adj.; vilket, vilka] which; what; **~ härlig dag!** what a gorgeous day!

vill [v.; see: **vilja**]

villa [n.; ~n, villor] illusion, delusion; house, cottage

ville [v.past; see: **vilja**]

villkor [n.; ~et, ~] condition

Villkor för Europaparlamentets ledamöter [n.] Statute for Members of the European Parliament [EU]

villkorlig [adj.; ~t, ~a] conditional; **~ dom** suspended sentence; **~ frigivning** release on probation

villkorsbisats [n.; ~en, ~er] conditional clause [gram]

villkorskonjunktion [n.; ~en, ~er] conditional conjunction [gram]

vilse [adj.] lost, astray; **gå ~** lose one's way, get lost

vilstol [n.; ~en, ~ar] easy chair; folding chair

vilt [n.; ~et] game; wild animal(s)

viltpaté [n.; ~n, ~er] game paté

vilträtt [n.; ~en, ~er] game [venison, boar, pheasant, etc.]

vin [n.; ~et, ~er] wine

vinbär [n.; ~et, ~] currants

vind [n.; ~en, ~ar] wind

vindbrygga [n.; ~n, -bryggor] drawbridge

vindby [n.; ~n, ~ar] gust of wind

vindflöjel [n.; ~n, -flöjlar] weathervane

vindförhållanden [n.pl.] wind conditions

vindruta [n.; ~n, -rutor] windshield

vindrutespolare [n.; ~n, ~] windshield washer

vindrutetorkare [n.; ~n, ~] windshield wiper

vindruvor [n.pl.] grapes

vindskydd [n.; ~et, ~] windbreak

vindstilla [n.; ~n, -stillor] calm in storm, lull

vindstyrka [n.; ~n, -styrkor] wind strength, wind force

vindsurfa [v.; ~r, ~de, ~t] windsurf

vindsurfingbräda [n.; ~n, -brädor] windsurfing board

vindtät jacka [n.; ~n, jackor] windbreaker

vinge [n.; ~n, vingar] wing, blade [fan]

vinglas [n.; ~et, ~] wineglass

vinka [v.; ~r, ~de, ~t] wave

vinkel [n.; ~n, vinklar] angle; nook

vinkelparenteser [n.pl.] angle brackets (< >) [IT]

vinkälare [n.; ~n, ~] wine cellar

vinlista [n.; ~n, -listor] wine list

vinna [v.; vinner, vann, vunnit] win

vinnare [n.; ~n, ~] winner

vinn-vinn situation [n.; ~en, ~er] win-win situation

vin- och spriträttigheter [n.pl.] alcohol license

vinsch [n.; ~en, ~ar] winch

vinst [n.; ~en, ~er] gain, profits, yield, proceeds, earnings, winnings; prize

vinstchans [n.; ~en, ~er] odds of winning

vinter [n.; ~n, vintrar] winter

vinterdäck [n.; ~et, ~] snow tire

vinterlov [n.; ~et, ~] winter vacation

vintermörker [n.; -mörkret, ~] winter darkness

vinterolympiaden [n.] Winter Olympics

vinter-OS [n.] Winter Olympic Games

vintersallad [n.; ~en, ~er] "winter" salad with grated carrots, apples, cabbage

vi**ntersem**e**ster** [n.; ~n, -semestrar] winter vacation

vi**ntersolstånd** [n.; ~et, ~] winter solstice

vi**ntersportort** [n.; ~en, ~er] winter sports resort

vi**ntersäsong** [n.; ~en, ~er] winter season

vi**nter t**i**dtabell** [n.; ~en, ~er] winter timetable

vi**ntras** [n.]: **i ~** last winter

vinä**ger** [n.; ~n] vinegar, wine vinegar

vinä**grettsås** [n.; ~en] vinaigrette [dressing]

vio**l** [n.; ~en, ~er] violet [flower]

viole**tt** [adj.; ~, ~a] violet

violonce**ll** [n.; ~en, ~er] cello

vi**rka** [v.; ~r, ~de, ~t] crochet

vi**rke** [n.; ~t] timber, lumber

vi**rrvarr** [n.; ~et] muddle, confusion

virtue**ll v**e**rklighet** [n.; ~en] virtual reality [IT]

vi**rus** [n.; ~et, ~] virus

vi**rusangrepp** [n.; ~et, ~] virus attack [IT]

vi**rusprogr**a**m** [n.; -grammet, ~] virus program [IT]

vi**russkydd** [n.; ~et, ~] virus protection [IT]

vis[1] [adj.; ~t, ~a] wise

vis[2] [n.; ~et, ~] way, manner

vi**sa**[1] [n.; ~n, visor] song, ballad

vi**sa**[2] [v.; ~r, ~de, ~t] show, view; **~ sig** appear

vi**sare** [n.; ~n, ~] turn signal; viewer [IT]

vi**sdom** [n.; ~en] wisdom

vi**sdomstand** [n.; ~en, -tänder] wisdom tooth

visi**tkort** [n.; ~et, ~] visiting card, business card

vi**ska**[1] [n.; ~n, viskor] whisk

vi**ska**[2] [v.; ~r, ~de, ~t] whisper

vi**sning** [n.; ~en, ~ar] showing, demonstration, exhibition; tour

vi**sningsläge** [n.; ~t, ~n] display mode [IT]

visp [n.; ~en, ~ar] beater, whisk

vi**spa** [v.; ~r, ~de, ~t] beat, whip; **~ gr**ä**dde** whip cream; **~ ägg** beat eggs

vi**spgrädde** [n.; ~n] whipped cream, whipping cream

viss [adj.; visst, vissa] certain; some

vi**sselpipa** [n.; ~n, -pipor] whistle

vi**ssen** [adj.; visset, vissna] wilted, spoiled

vi**sserligen** [adv.] admittedly

vi**sst** [adv.] of course, certainly

vi**sste** [v.; see: **veta**]

vi**sstidsanställning** [n.; ~en, ~ar] fixed-term contract

vist [adj.; see: **vis**]

vi**stas** [v.passive; ~, vistades, vistats] stay; live

vi**stelse** [n.; ~n, ~r] stay, residence

vi**sum** [n.; ~et, ~] visa

vit [adj.; vitt, vita] white; **~a b**ö**nor** white beans; **~a s**i**dorna** white pages

vitami**n** [n.; ~et, ~er] vitamin

vitami**nbrist** [n.;] vitamin deficiency

Vi**tbok** [n.; ~en, -böcker] White Paper [EU]

vi**te** [n.; ~t, ~n] fine, penalty

vi**tk**å**l** [n.; ~en] white cabbage

vi**tkålsallad** [n.; ~en] coleslaw

vi**tling** [n.; ~en, ~ar] whiting [fish]

vi**tlök** [n.; ~en, ~ar] garlic

vi**tlökmajonn**ä**s** [n.; ~en] garlic mayonnaise, aioli

vi**tpeppar** [n.; ~n] white pepper

vitri**n** [n.; ~en, ~er] display case, store window

vi**trysk** [adj.; ~t, ~a] White Russian; Belarusian

Vi**tryssland** [n.] White Russia, Belarus

vi**tsippa** [n.; ~n, -sippor] wood anemone

vi**tsås** [n.; ~en, ~er] white sauce

vitt [adj.; see: **vid**, **vit**]; **~ bröd** white bread; **~ vin** white wine

vi**ttna** [v.; ~r, ~de, ~t] bear witness, give evidence, testify

vi**ttne** [n.; ~t, ~n] witness

vi**ttnesm**å**l** [n.; ~et, ~] witness, testimony

VM [abbrev: världsmästerskap] World Championship

voka**l** [n.; ~en, ~er] vowel

vo**l au v**e**nt** [n.] vol au vent [pastry stuffed with meat or fish]

volleyboll [n.; ~en] volleyball
volt [n.; ~en, ~] volt
volym [n.; ~en, ~er] volume; loud-
ness
volymkontroll [n.; ~en, ~er] volume
control
vore [v.past; obsolete; see: vara]
would be, were
vov [interj.] bow-wow
vpk [abbrev: Vänsterpartiet kom-
munisterna] Party of the Left,
Communist Party
vrakpris [n.; ~et, ~] bargain price
vrede [n.; ~n] wrath, fury, rage
vricka [v.; ~r, ~de, ~t] sprain
vrickning [n.; ~er, ~en] sprain
vrida [v.; vrider, vred, vridit] twist,
turn
v-ringad i halsen [adj.] V-necked
vrist [n.; ~en, ~er] ankle
vråla [v.; ~r, ~de, ~t] roar, bellow
vulkan [n.; ~en, ~er] volcano
vunnit [v.past; see: vinna]
vuxen [adj.; vuxet, vuxna] grown-
up, adult
vuxenutbildning [n.; ~en] adult
education
vvd. [abbrev: vice verkställande di-
rektör] deputy director, vice-president
vy [n.; ~n, ~er] view, sight
vykort [n.; ~et, ~] picture postcard
våffla [n.; ~n, våfflor] waffle
våg¹ [n.; ~en, ~ar] scales
våg² [n.; ~en, ~or] wave
våga [v.; ~r, ~de, ~t] dare
Vågen [n.] Libra
vågig [adj.; ~t, ~a] wavy, wiggly
våld [n.; ~et] violence
våldsam [adj.; ~t, ~a] violent, vehement, furious
våldtagen [adj.; -taget, -tagna]
raped, assaulted
våldtäkt [n.; ~en, ~er] rape
våldtäktsman [n.; -mannen, -män]
rapist
vån. [abbrev.; see: våning]
våning [n.; ~en, ~ar] floor, story;
apartment
våningshus [n.; ~et, ~] apartment
building

våningssäng [n.; ~en, ~ar] bunk
bed
vår¹ [adj./pron.poss.; ~t, ~a; see:
vi] our(s)
vår² [n.; ~en, ~ar] spring; i ~ this
spring; i ~as last spring; om/på
~en in spring
vård [n.; ~en, ~ar] care
vårdagjämning [n.; ~en, ~ar]
spring equinox (March 21)
vårdbehövande [adj.] in need of
care
vårdbidrag [n.; ~et, ~] support
subsidy [for minors]
vårdbiträde [n.; ~t, ~n] home
nursing help
vårdcentral [n.; ~en, ~er] clinic,
medical center
vårdnad [n.; ~en] custody,
guardianship [of minors]
vårdnadsbidrag [n.; ~et, ~] child
maintenance allowance
vårdnadshavare [n.; ~n, ~] person
with custody (of children)
vårdskola [n.; ~n, -skolor] school
for training in social care
vårlök [n.; ~en, ~ar] spring onion
vårproposition [n.; ~en] spring fiscal policy bill
vårstädning [n.; ~en] spring cleaning
vårta [n.; ~n, vårtor] wart; nipple
vårtermin [n.; ~en, ~er] spring
semester
våt [adj.; ~t, ~a] wet
våtdräkt [n.; ~en, ~er] wet suit
våtservetter för barn [n.pl.] baby
wipes
väcka [v.; väcker, väckte, väckt]
rouse, awaken [trans.]
väckarklocka [n.; ~n, -klockor]
alarm clock
väckning [n.; ~en, ~ar] wake-up
call
väder [n.; vädret] weather
väderkvarn [n.; ~en, ~ar] windmill
väderleksrapport [n.; ~en, ~er]
weather forecast, weather report
väderleksutsikt [n.; ~en, ~er]
weather forecast
väderprognos [n.; ~en, ~er]
weather forecast

vädra [v.; ~r, ~de, ~t] air
Väduren [n.] Aries
väg [n.; ~en, ~ar] road, way; **den ~en!** this way, please!; **~ med skilda körbanor** divided highway; **~ under byggnad** road under construction; **~en stängd** road closed
väga [v.; väger, vägde, vägt] weigh
vägarbete [n.; ~t, ~n] road work, road under repair
vägavgift [n.; ~en, ~er] road toll
vägbeskrivning [n.; ~en, ~ar] directions [how to get someplace]
vägg [n.; ~en, ~ar] wall
väggmålning [n.; ~en, ~ar] mural, frieze
vägguttag [n.; ~et, ~] wall socket, electric outlet
vägkarta (över) [n.; ~n, -kartor] road map (of)
vägkorsning [n.; ~en, ~ar] road intersection
vägkrog [n.; ~en, ~ar] roadside restaurant
väglag [n. ~et] road conditions
vägmärken [n.pl.] road signs
vägmätare [n.; ~n, ~] odometer
vägning [n.; ~en, ~ar] weighting; **~ av röster i rådet** weighting of votes in the Council [EU]
vägra [v.; ~r, ~de, ~t] refuse, reject, deny
vägran [n.] refusal, declining
vägren [n.; ~en, ~ar] shoulder [road]
vägskäl [n.; ~et, ~] fork in road
vägsträcka [n.; ~n, -sträckor] stretch of road
vägtelefon [n.; ~en, ~er] roadside emergency phone
Vägverket (VV) [n.] National Road Administration
vägvisare [n.; ~n, ~] guide; signpost; wizard [IT]
väja [v.; väjer, väjde, väjt] swerve aside
väjningsplikt [n.; ~en] obligation to yield (traffic)
väl [adv.] well; probably, surely, I suppose; **~ godkänd (VG)** pass with distinction [second highest mark in school]

välbefinnande [n.; ~t] well-being
välbetald [adj.; -betalt, ~a] well-paid
väldig [adj.; ~t, ~a] enormous, mighty, vast
väldigt [adv.] tremendously, really, very
välfärd [n.; ~en] welfare, well-being
välja [v.; väljer, valde, valt] choose, select
väljare [n.; ~n, ~] elector, voter; switch; option [IT]; selector [IT]
väljarkår [n.; ~en, ~er] electorate
välkommen [adj.; -kommet, -komna] welcome; **~ igen** hope you'll come back, hope to see you here again
välkänd [adj.; -känt, ~a] well-known
välling [n.; ~en] gruel
välsmakande [adj.] pleasant tasting
välstekt [adj.; ~, ~a] well-done
välstånd [n.; ~et] prosperity
välutrustad [adj.; -utrustat, ~e] well-equipped
vän [n.; vännen, vänner] friend
vända [v.; vänder, vände, vänt] turn; **~ sig om** turn around
vändbar [adj.; ~t, ~a] reversible
vändkrets [n.; ~en, ~ar] tropic, tropical circle
väninna [n.; ~n, väninnor] female friend
vänja sig [v.; vänjer, vande, vant] get used to
vänlig [adj.; ~t, ~a] friendly, kind; **var ~** please
vänskap [n.; ~en] friendship
vänster [adj.; ~, vänstra] left; **till ~ om** to the left of
vänsterhänt [adj.; ~, ~a] left-handed
vänsterjusterad text [n.] left-justified text [IT]
vänsterklicka [v.; ~r, ~de, ~t] left click [IT]
vänstern [n.; see: **Vänsterpartiet**] the Left
Vänsterpartiet (vp) [n.] Party of the Left
vänsterstyrd [adj.; -styrt, ~a] left-hand drive [car]
vänsterställa [v.; -ställer, -ställde, -ställt] left-justify [IT]

vänstertrafik [n.; ~en] left-hand traffic

vänta [v.; ~r, ~de, ~t] wait; ~ barn expect a baby; ~ på wait for; ~ på ton wait for the tone

väntan [n.] wait, waiting

väntrum [n.; ~et, ~] waiting room

väntsal [n.; ~en, ~ar] waiting room

väpna [v.; ~r, ~de, ~t] arm

väpnad rån [n.;] armed robbery

värd¹ [adj.; värt, ~a] worth, worthy of; esteemed

värd² [n.; ~en, ~ar] landlord; host

värddator [n.; ~n, ~er] host computer [IT]

värde [n.; ~t, ~n] value, worth

värdedeklaration [n.; ~en, ~er] declaration of value

värdefull [adj.; ~t, ~a] valuable

värdera [v.; ~r, ~de, ~t] value, esteem; assess, evaluate

värdering [n.; ~en, ~ar] valuation, appraisal, assessment

värderingar [n.pl.] values

värdesak [n.; ~en, ~er] valuable article; ~er valuables

värdig [adj.; ~t, ~a] worthy, seemly; dignified

värdighet [n.; ~en, ~er] dignity, worthiness

värdinna [n.; ~n, värdinnor] hostess

värdshus [n.; ~et, ~] country inn; pub

värk [n.; ~en, ~ar] pain, ache; labor

värka [v.; värker, värkte, värkt] ache, hurt

värktablett [n.; ~en, ~er] painkiller

värld [n.; ~en, ~ar] world

Världsbanken [n.] World Bank

världsberömd [adj.; -berömt, ~a] world-famous

världscup [n.; ~en, ~er] World Cup

världsdel [n.; ~en, ~ar] continent

Världshandelsorganisationen (WTO) [n.] World Trade Organization (WTO)

världskrig [n.; ~et, ~] world war

världsmedborgare [n.; ~n, ~] world citizen

världsmästare [n.; ~n, ~] world champion

världsnaturfonden [n.] World Wildlife Fund

världsrekord [n.; ~et, ~] world record

värma [v.; värmer, värmde, värmt] warm, heat

värme [n.; ~n] heat, heating

värmebölja [n.; ~n, -böljor] heat wave

värmeelement [n.; ~en, ~er] radiator, electric heater

värmefilt [n.; ~en, ~ar] electric blanket

värmeflaska [n.; ~n, -flaskor] hot-water bottle

värmeplatta [n.; ~n, -plattor] hot plate

värmeslag [n.; ~et] heat stroke

värmeslingor [n.pl.] heating coils

värmeutslag [n.; ~et] hot rash

värna (om) [v.; ~r, ~de, ~t] defend, protect

värnplikt [n.; ~en] compulsory military service

värnpliktig [adj.; ~t, ~a] liable for military service

värnpliktsförhållande [n.; ~t] military service status

värnpliktstid [n.; ~en, ~er] time spent in military service

värnpliktstjänstgöring [n.; ~en] military service

värpa [v.; värper, värpte, värpt] lay [eggs]

värre [adj.comp.: dålig] worse

värst [adj.superl.: dålig] worst

värv [n.; ~et, ~] task, mission, duty, function, work

väsa [v.; väser, väste, väst] hiss

väsen¹ [n.; väsendet] being; nature, character; noise, fuss

-väsen² [suffix] organization; activity

väsentlig [adj.; ~t, ~a] essential; main, important

väska [n.; ~n, väskor] bag, suitcase

väskryckare [n.; ~n, ~] bag-snatcher

väst¹ [n.;] vest, waistcoat

väst-² [prefix] western

Västbanken [n.] West Bank

väster [n.] west

västerbottenost [n.; ~en] Västerbotten cheese [sharp, hard]

Västerlandet [n.] the West

västerländsk [adj.; ~t, ~a] Western

västern [n.] Western [film]

Västeuropeiska unionen (VEU) [n.] Western European Union (WEU) [EU]

västgötaost [n.; ~en] West Göta-land cheese [semi-hard, aromatic, sharp]

Västindien [n.] West Indies

västkust [n.; ~en] west coast

västkustsallad [n.; ~en] West Coast salad [seafood]

västlig [adj.; ~t, ~a] western

västmakterna [n.pl.] the Western powers

västra [adj.] western

Västvärlden [n.] Western world

vätdräkt [n.; ~en, ~er] wetsuit

väte [n.; ~t] hydrogen

vätska [n.; ~n, vätskor] liquid

vätskeersättning [n.; ~en] electrolyte solution, rehydration fluid

väva [v.; väver, vävde, vävt] weave

vävnad [n.; ~en, ~er] tissue; textile

växa [v.; växer, växde, växt] grow [intrans.]

växande [adj.] growing, cumulative

växel [n.; ~n, växlar] change; small change, coins; gear; switch; **behålla ~n** keep the change; **ge ~**

give change

växelkontor [n.; ~et, ~] currency exchange office

växelkurs [n.; ~en, ~er] exchange rate

växellåda [n.; ~n, -lådor] transmission, gearbox

växelspak [n.; ~en] gearshift lever

växelström [n.; - strömmen] alternating current [IT]

växla [v.; ~r, ~de, ~t] change, switch; change gears; ~ **till** switch to

växlande molnighet [n.] varying cloud cover

växlingsavgift [n.; ~en, ~er] commission, service charge

växlingsfil [n.; ~en, ~er] swap file [IT]

växlingskontor [n.; ~et, ~] currency exchange office

växt [n.; ~en, ~er] plant

växtart [n.; ~en ~er] species of plant

växtgift [n.; ~et, ~er] weed killer

växthus [n.; ~et, ~] greenhouse

växtriket [n.] plant kingdom

vörtbröd [n.; ~et, ~] Christmas beer bread

W

W [abbrev: watt] watt
Wallenbergare [n.; ~n] grilled minced veal with egg yolk and cream
Warszawa [n.] Warsaw
WC [abbrev: water closet] toilet, lavatory
wc-borste [n.; ~n, -borstar] toilet brush
webb [n.; ~en] web [IT]
webbadress [n.; ~en, ~er] URL [IT]
webbansvarig [n.] webmaster [IT]
webbaserad [adj.; -baserat, ~e] web-based [IT]; ~ **datalagring** web storage [IT]; ~ **utbildning** e-learning [IT]
webbfönster [n.; -fönstret, ~] browser window [IT]
webbhotell [n.; ~et, ~] web host [IT]
webbkanal [n.; ~en, ~er] web channel [IT]
webbkurs [n.; ~en, ~er] e-learning [IT]
webblagring [n.; ~en, ~ar] web storage [IT]
webbläsare [n.; ~n, ~] browser, web browser [IT]
webbmästare [n.; ~n, ~] webmaster [IT]
webbplats [n.; ~en, ~er] web site [IT]

webbräknare [n.; ~n, ~] counter, web counter, web page counter, tracker [IT]
webbshop [n.; ~en, ~ar] web shop [IT]
webbsida [n.; ~n, -sidor] web page [IT]
webbutbildning [n.; ~en] e-learning [IT]
webbutik [n.; ~en, ~er] web shop [IT]
webbutsändning [n.; ~en, ~ar] webcasting [IT]
webbvaruhus [n.; ~et, ~] web shop [IT]
web-zine [n.] webzine [IT]
WHO [abbrev: Världshälsoorganisationen] World Health Organization (WHO)
Wien [n.] Vienna
wienerbröd [n.; ~et, ~] Danish pastry
wienerkorv [n.; ~en, ~ar] frankfurter
Wilhelm [n.] William
WTO [abbrev: Världshandelsorganisationen] World Trade Organization (WTO)

Y

y-axel [n.; ~n, -axlar] y-axis
YK [abbrev: Yrkeskvinnors klubb] Professional Women's Club
ylle [n.; ~et] wool
yllestrumpor [n.pl.] wool stockings
ylletröja [n.; ~n, -tröjor] wool sweater
yngre [adj.comp.: ung] younger
yngst [adj.superl.: ung] youngest
ynklig [adj.; ~t, ~a] pitiful; puny
yoga [n.; ~n] yoga
yoghurt [n.; ~en] yogurt
yppa [v.; ~r, ~de, ~t] reveal, disclose
ypperlig [adj.; ~t, ~a] excellent, superb
yr [adj.; ~t, ~a] dizzy, giddy
yra [v.; ~r, ~de, ~t] be delirious, rave; whirl
yrka [v.; ~r, ~de, ~t] demand; insist
yrkande [n.; ~t, ~n] claim
yrke [n.; ~t, ~n] occupation, profession
yrkeskurs [n.; ~en, ~er] vocational training course
yrkeskvinna [n.; ~n, -kvinnor] professional woman
yrkeslärare [n.; ~n, ~] vocational teacher
yrkesliv [n.; ~et] world of work
yrkesorienterad [adj.; -orienterat, ~e] skill-oriented
yrkesriktad linje [n.; ~n, ~r] vocational program in school

yrkesskada [n.; ~n, -skador] occupational injury
yrkestrafik [n.; ~en] commercial traffic
yrkesundervisning [n.; ~en] vocational training
yrkesutbildning [n.; ~en] vocational training
yrkesvägledning [n.; ~en] vocational guidance
yrsel [n.; ~n] dizziness
yrväder [n.; -vädret] blizzard, snowstorm
yta [n.; ~n, ytor] area, surface
ytterdörr [n.; ~en, ~ar] outer door
ytterkläder [n.pl.] outdoor clothes
ytterlig [adj.; ~t, ~a] additional
ytterligare [adv.] further
ytterrock [n.; ~en, ~ar] overcoat
yttertak [n.; ~et, ~] roof
yttrande [n.; ~t, ~n] utterance, statement
yttrandefrihet [n.; ~en] freedom of expression/speech
Yttrandefrihetsgrundlagen (YGL) [n.] Fundamental Law on Freedom of Expression
yttre[1] [adj.] outer, exterior, external, outside
yttre[2] [n.; ~] exterior; appearance
yuppienalle [n.; ~n, -nallar] cellphone, mobile phone
yxa [n.; ~n, yxor] axe

Z

zappa [v.; ~r, ~de, ~t] zap [TV]
zebra [n.; ~n, zebror] zebra
zenbuddism [n.; ~en] Zen Buddhism
zigenare [n.; ~n, ~] gypsy, Roma
zodiaken [n.] the zodiac
zodiaktecken [n.; -tecknet, ~] sign
  of the zodiac
zon [n.;~en, ~er] zone
zoo [n. ~t, ~n] zoo
zooaffär [n.; ~en, ~er] pet shop
zoolog [n.; ~en, ~er] zoologist
zoologi [n.; ~n] zoology
zooma [v.; ~r, ~de, ~t] zoom; ~ **in**
  zoom in [IT]; ~ **ut** zoom out [IT]
zucchini [n.; ~n, ~er] zucchini

Å

å!¹ [interj.] oh!

å² [n.; ~n, ~ar] stream, creek

åberopa [v.; ~r, ~de, ~t] refer to, cite

åder [n.; ~n, ådror] vein; artery

åderbråck [n.; ~et] varicose vein(s)

åhörare [n.; ~n, ~] listener, member of the audience

åk [abbrev.; see: årskurs]

åka [v.; åker, åkte, åkt] go, travel, ride; leave; ~ **bort** go away; ~ **buss** ride the bus; ~ **skidor** go skiing, ski; ~ **skridskor** skate; ~ **taxi** take a taxi; ~ **vattenskidor** waterski

åkare [n.; ~n, ~] carrier, hauler

åker [n.; ~n, åkrar] (tilled) field

åklagare [n.; ~n, ~] prosecutor

åklagarkammare [n.; ~n, ~] local public prosecutor's office

åklagarmyndighet [n.; ~en, ~er] regional public prosecutor's office

åkning [n.; ~en, ~ar] going; skiing

åksjuka [n.; ~n] motion sickness

ål [n.; ~en, ålar] eel

Åland [n.] Åland Islands [in Baltic]

ålder [n.; ~n, åldrar] age

ålderdom [n.; ~en] old age

ålderdomshem [n.; -hemmet, ~] old people's home

ålderspension [n.; ~en, ~er] old age pension

ångare [n.; ~n, ~] steamer

ångbåt [n.; ~en, ~ar] steamboat

ångervecka [n.; ~n, -veckor] week for reconsidering a purchase

ångest [n.; ~en, ~ar] anxiety, anguish; dread

ångkokt [adj.; ~, ~a] steamed

ångra [v.; ~r, ~de, ~t] regret; undo [IT]; ~ **sig** change one's mind, reconsider

år [n.; ~et, ~] year; **gott nytt ~!** Happy New Year!; **hela ~et** all year; **i ~** this year; **nästa ~** next year; **förra ~et** last year

åra [n.; ~n, åror] oar

åratal [n.]: **i ~** for years

årgång [n.; ~en, ~ar] annual volume (in a series); age group; vintage

århundrade [n.; ~t, ~n] century

årig [adj.; ~t, ~a] year(s) old; **10-~** 10-year old

årlig [adj.; ~t, ~a] annual, yearly

årligen [adv.] annually

årsinkomst [n.; ~en, ~er] annual income

årskifte [n.; ~t, ~n] turn of the year

årskurs (ak) [n.; ~en, ~er] grade, class [students of a given year]; curriculum

årstid [n.; ~en, ~er] season

årtal [n.; ~et] year [in date]

årtionde [n.; ~t, ~n] decade

ås [n.; ~en, ~ar] ridge

åsidosätta [v.; -sätter, -satte, -satt] override [IT]

åsikt [n.; ~en, ~er] opinion

åska [v.; ~r, ~de, ~t] thunder

åskväder [n.; åskvädret] thunderstorm

åskådare [n.; ~n, ~] spectator

åskådarläktare [n.; ~n, ~] viewing stand, spectators gallery, bleachers

åsna [n.; ~n, åsnor] donkey

åstadkomma [v.; -kommer, -kom, -kommit] produce, bring about, cause, accomplish

åt [prep.] for, to; ~ **mig** for me, for my benefit

åtal [n.; ~et, ~] prosecution, indictment; legal action, legal proceedings

åtala [v.; ~r, ~de, ~t] prosecute, indict, bring legal action

åter [adv.] back; again; **välkommen ~!** come again!

återbetalning [n.; ~en, ~ar] refund

återfinna [v.; -finner, -fann, -funnit] find again, recover

återigen [adv.] again; on the other hand

återkomma [v.; -kommer, -kom, -kommit] come back, come again

återkommande [adj.] recurrent; further to, with reference again to

återkoppling [n.; ~en] feedback [IT]

återlämna [v.; ~r, ~de, ~t] return, give back

återlösa [v.; -löser, -löste, -löst] redeem

återstå [v.; -står, -stod, -stått] remain

återstående [adj.] remaining

återställa [v.; -ställer, -stälde, -städ] reset, restore [IT]

återuppbygga [v.; -bygger, -byggde, -byggd] rebuilt, reconstruct

återvända [v.; -vänder, -vände, -vänt] return, come back, turn back

återvändsgata [n.; ~n, -gator] dead-end street

åtgång [n.; ~en] consumption, usage [IT]

åtgärd [n.; ~en, ~er] measure, step, action

åtgärdsfönster [n.; -fönstret, ~] task pane [IT]

åtkomst [n.; ~en, ~er] possession, acquisition; entry [IT]

åtminstone [adv.] at least

åtskild [adj.; ~t, ~a] separated

åtskillig [adj.; ~t, ~a] considerable, much; several, many

åtta [num.] eight

åttaställig [adj.; ~t, ~a] eight-bit [IT]

åttio [num.] eighty

åttionde [adj.] eightieth

åttonde [adj.] eighth; August

Ä

äcklig [adj.; ~t, ~a] revolting
ädelost [n.; ~en, ~ar] blue cheese
ädelsten [n.; ~et, ~] gemstone
äga [v.; äger, ägde, ägt] own; ~
  rum take place
ägande [n.; ~t] ownership
ägare [n.; ~n, ~] owner
ägg [n.; ~et, ~] egg
äggkopp [n.; ~en, ~ar] egg cup
ägglift [n.; ~en, ~ar] gondola, cable
  car
äggplanta [n.; ~n, -plantor] eggplant
äggrätt [n.; ~en, ~er] egg dish
äggröra [n.; ~n, -röror] scrambled
  eggs
äggsked [n.; ~en, ~ar] egg spoon
äggsmörgås [n.; ~en, ~ar] egg
  sandwich
äggstock [n.; ~en, ~ar] ovary
äggula [n.; ~n, -gulor] egg yolk
äggvita [n.; ~n, -vitor] egg white
ägna [v.; ~r, ~de, ~t] devote, dedicate; ~ sig åt devote oneself to,
  make a living from
ägo [n.] ownership
äkta [adj.] genuine, real; married;
  ~ hustru wedded wife; ~ man
  wedded husband; ~ par married
  couple
äktenskap [n.; ~et, ~] marriage
äkthetsbevis [n.; ~et, ~] certificate
  of authenticity
äldre [adj.comp.; see: gammal]
  older
äldreomsorg [n.; ~en] old-age care
äldst [adj.superl.; see: gammal]
  oldest
älg [n.; ~en, ~ar] elk
älgjakt [n.; ~en, ~er] elk hunt
älgko [n.; ~n, ~r] elk cow
älgkött [n.; ~et] elk meat
älgstek [n.; ~en, ~ar] elk roast
älska [v.; ~r, ~de, ~t] love
älskad [adj.; älskat, ~e] loved,
  beloved
älskling [n.; ~en, ~ar] darling
älsklingsställe [n.; ~t, ~n] favorite
  place
älv [n.; ~en, ~ar] river

älva [n.; ~n, älvor] fairy, elf [female]
älvstrand [n.; ~en, -stränder] river-
  bank
ämbete [n.; ~t, ~n] office, position,
  function
ämne [n.; ~t, ~n] material; subject
  [academic]
ämnesindex [n.; ~en, ~er] subject
  index
ämneslärare [n.; ~n, ~] specialist/
  subject teacher [art, music, etc.]
ämnesregister [n.; -registret, ~]
  subject index
ämnesråd [n.; ~et, ~] senior
  adviser
än[1] [adv.] still; however (much)
än[2] [conj.] than [in comparisons]
ända[1] [adv.] until; as far as; ~ in i
  vår tid right up to our time; ~ till
  until
ända[2] [n.; ~n, ändar] end
ända[3] [n.; ~n, ändor] behind, bottom
ändamål [n.; ~et, ~] purpose, aim,
  end
ände [n.; see: ända]
ändelse [n.; ~n, ~r] ending, suffix
  [gram.]
ändhållplats [n.; ~en, ~er] last stop
ändtarm [n.; ~en, ~ar] rectum
ändra [v.; ~r, ~de, ~t] change; ~ på
  change
ändring [n.; ~en, ~ar] change, alteration; ~ av fördragen revision
  of the Treaties [EU]
ändstation [n.; ~en] last stop
ändtarm [n.; ~en] rectum
ändå [adv.] nevertheless, anyway
äng [n.; ~en, ~ar] meadow
ängel [n.; ~n, änglar] angel
ängslan [n.] anxiety
änka [n.; ~n, änkor] widow
änkling [n.; ~en, ~ar] widower
ännu [adv.] yet, still; inte ~ not yet
äntligen [adv.] at last, finally
äppelkaka [n.; ~n. -kakor] apple
  cake
äppelmos [n.; ~et] apple sauce
äppelmust [n.; ~en, ~er] apple
  juice

äppelpaj [n.; ~en, ~er] apple pie
äppelringar [n.pl.] apple fritters
äpple [n.; ~t, ~n] apple
äppleträd [n.; ~et] apple tree
är [v.; see: vara] am/is/are
ära¹ [n.; ~n] honor, glory; credit
ära² [v.; ~r, ~de, ~t] honor
ärekränkning [n.; ~en] libel,
  defamation
ärende [n.; ~t, ~n] matter; errand
ärkebiskop [n.; ~en, ~ar] archbishop
ärlig [adj.; ~t, ~a] honest, truthful
ärm [n.; ~en, ~ar] sleeve
ärter [n.pl.] peas; ~ och fläsk
  yellow pea soup with diced pork

ärtsoppa [n.; ~n, -soppor] pea soup
ärva [v.; ärver, ärvde, ärvt] inherit
äsch! [interj.] oh!
äta [v.; äter, åt, ätit] eat; ~ frukost
  have breakfast; ~ färdigt finish
  eating; ~ inne eat at home; ~ ute
  eat out
ättika [n.; ~n] vinegar, white vinegar
ättiksgurkor [n.pl.] pickled gherkins
ättling [n.; ~en, ~ar] descendant
äv. (abbrev: även) also
även [adv.] also, as well, too; even;
  ~ om even if
äventyr [n.; ~en, ~ar] adventure
äventyrsfilm [n.; ~en, ~er] thriller,
  adventure movie

Ö

ö[1] [n.; ~n, ~ar] island
ö./Ö.[2] [abbrev: öster, östra; adj.] eastern
ÖB (abbrev: Överbefälhavaren) [n.] Commander-in-Chief
öde[1] [adj.] deserted; desolate
öde[2] [n.; ~t, ~n] fate, destiny
ödemark [n.; ~en, ~er] wilderness
ö.g. [abbrev: över gården] in the back, across the courtyard
öga [n.; ~t, ögon] eye; blått ~ black eye
ögonblick [n.; ~et, ~] moment; ett ~ just a minute
ögonbryn [n.; ~et, ~] eyebrow
ögonbrynspenna [n.; ~n, -pennor] eyebrow pencil
ögondroppar [n.pl.] eye drops
ögonfrans [n.; ~en, ~ar] eyelash
ögonlock [n.; ~et, ~] eyelid
ögonläkare [n.; ~n, ~] eye doctor, ophthalmologist
ögonskugga [n.; ~n] eye shadow
ögonsjukdom [n.; ~en, ~ar] disease of the eye
ö.h. [abbrev: över havet] above sea level
öka [v.; ~r, ~de, ~t] increase, grow; ~ farten accelerate
ökad [adj.; ökat, ~e] increased, added, additional
ökande [adj.] increasing, growing, rising
öken [n.; öknen, öknar] desert, wilderness
ökning [n.; ~en, ~ar] increase
öl [n.; ~et] beer; ljust ~ pale ale; mörkt ~ dark beer; ~ på fat draft beer
öm [adj.; ~t, ömma] sore, tender
ömsom [adv.] sometimes, at times; ~ glad, ~ ledsen sometimes happy, sometimes sad
önska [v.; ~r, ~de, ~t] wish, would like
önskad [adj.; önskat, ~e] desired
önskan [n.; ~, önskningar] wish, desire
önskas [v.passive; önskas, önskades, önskats] be wanted

önskelista [n.; ~n, -listor] wish list
önskemål [n.; ~et, ~] wish, requirement
önskvärd [adj.; -värt, ~a] desirable
öppen [adj.; öppet, öppna] open; ~ klass open class [gram]; ~ källkod open source [IT]; ~ nyckel public key [IT]; ~ nyckel-kryptering public key encryption [IT]; ~ spis (open) fireplace; ~ uppbyggnad open architecture [IT]; öppet 24 timmar open 24 hours a day; öppet köp purchase on approval; öppna samordningsmetoden open method of coordination [EU]
öppenhet [n.; ~en] openness, frankness, candor, transparency
öppet [adj.; see: öppen]
öppettider [n.pl.] business hours, opening hours
öppna[1] [adj.; see: öppen]
öppna[2] [v.; ~r, ~de, ~t] open; ~ här open here
öppning [n.; ~en, ~ar] opening
öra [n.; örat, öron] ear; ont i ~t earache
öre [n.; ~t, ~n] öre [1/100th of a krona]
Öresund [n.; ~et] the Sound [between Sweden and Denmark, site of new bridge]
Öresundsbron [n.] Öresund bridge [between Sweden and Denmark, near Malmö]
örhänge [n.; ~t, ~n] earring
öring [n.; ~en, ~ar] salmon trout
örn [n.; ~en, ~ar] eagle
örngott [n.; ~et, ~] pillow case
örondroppar [n.pl.] ear drops
öroninflammation [n.; ~en, ~er] ear inflammation
öron-, näs- och halsläkare [n.; ~n, ~] ear, nose and throat (ENT) specialist
öronvärk [n.; ~en, ~ar] earache
örsnibb [n.; ~en, ~ar] earlobe
örsprång [n.; ~et] earache
örter [n.pl.] herbs
örtte [n.; ~et, ~er] herbal tea

örundtur [n.; ~en, ~er] tour around the island(s)

ösa [v.; öser, öste, öst] scoop, bail; baste; pour down

ösregna [v.; ~r, ~de, ~t] rain heavily, pour down

öst-[1] [adj.] eastern

öst[2] [n.] east

Östasiatiska museet [n.] Museum of Far Eastern Antiquities

Östasien [n.] East Asia

öster [n.] east; eastern

Österlandet [n.] Orient, the East

Österrike [n.] Austria

österrikisk [adj.; ~t, ~a] Austrian

Östersjön [n.] Baltic Sea

Östeuropa [n.] Eastern Europe

östlig [adj.; ~~t, ~a] easterly

östra [adj.] eastern

Östtimor [n.] East Timor, Timor Leste

öva [v.; ~r, ~de, ~t] practice, train

över[1] [adv.] over, finished

över[2] [prep.] over; across; via, through; past [clock]; **10 ~ 5** 10 past 5 o'clock

överallt [adv.] everywhere

överansträngd [adj.; -ansträngt, ~a] over-tired

överbalans [n.; ~en]: **ta ~en** lose one's balance

Överbefälhavaren (ÖB) [n.] Commander-in-Chief

överbord [adv.] overboard

överbädd [n.; ~en, ~ar] upper berth

överdos [n.; ~en, ~er] overdose

överdrag [n.; ~et, ~] overdraft

överdriva [v.; -driver, -drev, -drivit] exaggerate

överdriven [adj.; -drivet, -drivna] exaggerated

överens (om) [adv.] in agreement (about)

överenskommelse [n.; ~n, ~r] agreement

överfall [n.; ~et, ~] mugging

överfallad [adj.; -fallat, ~e] mugged

överfart [n.; ~en, ~er] crossing

överflödig [adj.; ~t, ~a] redundant, superfluous

överfull [adj.; ~t, ~a] crowded, crammed

överföra [v.; -för, -förde, -fört] transfer; upload [IT]

överföring [n.; ~en, ~ar] transfer; **~ mellan pelarna** Community 'bridge' [EU]

överföringstid [n.; ~en, ~er] transfer time [IT]

överge [v.; -ge, -gav, -givit] abandon, leave; give up (on)

övergiva [v.; see: **överge**]

övergrepp [n.; ~et, ~] unfair treatment, injustice, wrong; assault

övergripande [adj.] overarching

övergå (i) [v.; -går, -gick, -gått] convert (to)

övergång [n.; ~en, ~ar] crossing, changeover, transition; crosswalk; **~ för fotgängare** pedestrian crossing

övergångsbiljett [n.; ~en, ~er] transfer ticket

övergångsregering [n.; ~en, ~ar] transitional government

övergångsställe [n.; ~t, ~n] pedestrian crossing

överhuvud taget [adv.] on the whole, in general

överhängande [adj.] overhanging

överkast [n.; ~et, ~] bedspread

överklaga [v.; ~r, ~de, ~t] appeal against

överklagande [n.; ~t, ~n] appeal

överkropp [n.; ~en] upper body

överlagt mord [n.; ~et, ~en] premeditated murder

överlakan [n.; ~et, ~] top sheet

överleva [v.; -lever, -levde, -levt] survive

överlevande [adj./n.] surviving; survivor

överlevnad [n.; ~en] survival

överlägga [v.; -lägger, -lade, -lagt] confer; discuss, debate

överläggning [n.; ~en; ~ar] discussion, debate

överlägsen [adj.; -lägset, -lägsna] superior

överläkare [n.; ~n, ~] senior doctor, doctor in charge

överläpp [n.; ~en, ~ar] upper lip

övermorgon [n.]: **i ~** the day after tomorrow

övernatta [v.; ~r, ~de, ~t] stay the night, spend the night

övernattningsrum [n.; ~et, ~] pied-à-terre, mini-apartment

övernattningsstuga [n.; ~n -stugor] shelter, refuge, hut

överordnad [adj.; -ordnat, ~e] superordinate [gram]

överraska [v.; ~r, ~de, ~t] surprise

överraskad [adj.; -raskat, ~e] surprised

överraskande [adj.] surprising

överraskning [n.; ~en, ~ar] surprise

överrock [n.; ~en, ~ar] overcoat

övers.[1] [abbrev: översättare, översättning] translator, translation

övers[2] [n.] spare, left over

översikt [n.; ~en, ~er] survey, overview; site map [IT]

överskott [n.; ~et, ~] surplus; overhead

överskrida [v.; -skrider, -skred, -skridit] exceed

överskrivningsläge [n.; ~t] over-write mode [IT]

överst [adv.superl.] on top

översta [adj.superl.] top; ~ **våning** top floor

överstatlighet [n.; ~en ~er] supra-nationality [EU]

överste [n.; ~n, överstar] colonel

överstruken [adj.; -struken, -strukna] struck through [IT]

Överstyrelsen för civil beredskap (ÖCB) [n.] Agency for Civil Emergency Planning

översvämning [n.; ~en, ~ar] flood; flooding, inundation

översyn [n.; ~en, ~er] inspection, overhaul

översätta [v.; -sätter, -satte, -sätt] translate; ~ **till engelska** translate into English

översättare [n.; ~n, ~] translator

översättning [n.; ~en, ~ar] translation

överta [v.; -tar, -tog, -tagit] take over, succeed to

övertag [n.]: **ha/få ~ över** have/get the advantage over

övertala [v.; ~r, ~de, ~t] persuade

övertid [n.; ~en, ~er] overtime

övertrassera [v.; ~r, ~de, ~t] over-draw [banking]

överträdelse [n.; ~n, ~r] infraction, violation, breach

övertyga [v.; ~r, ~de, ~t] convince

övertygad [adj.; -tygat, ~e] convinced

övertäckt marknad [n.] covered market [with roof]

övervaka [v.; ~r, ~de, ~t] supervise; see to it (that ...)

övervakning [n.; ~en] probation

övervikt [n.; ~en] overweight, excess baggage

överviktsbagage [n.; ~t] excess baggage

övervåning: på ~ [adv.] upstairs

överväga [v.; -väger, -vägde, -vägt] consider, reflect, contemplate; outweigh, be in the majority

övervägande[1] [adj.] predominant, greater

övervägande[2] [n.; ~t, ~n] consideration, deliberation

överväldigande [adj.] overwhelming

övning [n.; ~en, ~ar] exercise; practice, training

övre [adj.comp.] upper

övrig [adj.; ~t, ~a] other, remaining

ÖÅ [abbrev: Överståthållarämbetet] Office of the Governor of Stockholm

ENGLISH-SWEDISH
DICTIONARY

' [abbrev: foot; minute (geogr.
  co-ord.)] fot; minut
" [abbrev: inch; ditto; second
  (geogr.coord.)] tum; dito; sekund
@ [abbrev: at] snabel-a; per styck;
  hos
[abbrev: number] nummer

A

A¹ [abbrev: top mark; ampere]
högsta betyg; ampere
a/an² [indef.art.] en/ett
AA [abbrev: Associate of Arts;
Alcoholics Anonymous]
högskolediplom [efter 2 års
studier]; anonyma alkoholister
AAA [abbrev: American Automobile Association] AAA [förening i
USA som framförar upplysningar
och hjälp til bilresenärer]
AB [abbrev: Alberta] Alberta
abandon [v.] ge upp, frångå; överge,
lämna
abbreviation [n.] förkortning
ABC [abbrev: American Broadcasting Company] ABC [tv-bolag i
USA]
abcess [n.; ~es] böld
abdication [n.] abdikation
abdominal pain [n.] buksmärta
ability [n.; -ties] begåvning, förmåga
able [adj.] skicklig, duglig, duktig,
kompetent; ~ **to swim** simkunnig;
be ~ to kunna
abnormal [adj.] abnorm, onormal
aboard [adv./prep.] ombord
abolish [v.; ~es, ~ed] avskaffa,
upphäva
abolition [n.] avskaffande,
upphävande
aboriginal inhabitant [n.]
urinnevånare
abortion [n.] abort
about¹ [adv.] omkring; **be ~** handla
om
about² [prep.] omkring; cirka,
ungefär; om, angående
above¹ [adj.] ovanstående
above² [adv.] ovan, ovanför, däröver
above³ [prep.] över; framför; mer än
abroad [adv.] utlandet, utomlands;
stay ~ utlandsvistelse
abrupt [adj.] abrupt, plötslig, tvärt
avbruten, rumphuggen
ABS [abbrev: antilock braking sys-
tem] ABS-bromsar
absence [n.] bortovaro, frånvaro;
brist

absent [adj.] frånvarande; obefintlig;
tankspridd
absolute [adj.] absolut, fullständig,
fullkomlig
absolutely [adv.] absolut, alldeles,
helt; ~ **not** absolut inte
absorb [v.] absorbera, suga upp;
engagera
absorbent cotton [n.] bomullsvadd
absorption [n.] absorbering,
uppsugning
abstract [adj.] abstrakt, svårfattlig,
teoretisk
absurd [adj.] absurd, orimlig,
befängd, löjlig
abundant [adj.] riklig, överflödande
abuse¹ [n.] missbruk, missförhål-
lande
abuse² [v.] missbruka; skymfa
A/C¹ [abbrev: air conditioning; ac-
count] luftkonditionering; konto
AC² [abbrev: alternating current;
air conditioning] växelström;
luftkonditionering
AC/DC [abbrev.] allström; bisexuell
academic¹ [adj.] akademisk; teoretisk;
~ **year** läsår
academic² [n.] akademiker;
teoretiker
academy [n.; -mies] akademi,
högskola
accelerate [v.] accelerera; påskynda
accelerator [n.] gaspedal; accelerator
accent [n.] accent, uttal; tonfall;
tonvikt; ~ **mark** accenttecken;
diakritiskt tecken
accentuate [v.] framhäva, accen-
tuera, betona
accept [v.] ta emot, acceptera; godta;
anta
acceptable [adj.] godtagbar, accep-
tabel; tillfredsställande
acceptance [n.] erkännande, godkännande, antagande
accepted [adj.] allmänt erkänd,
vedertagen; sedvanlig
access¹ [n.] tillgång, åtkomst, tillträde, ingång; ~ **code** säkerhetskod
access² [v.; ~es, ~ed] komma in

accessibility [n.] framkomlighet, tillgänglighet
accessible [adj.] tillgänglig; framkomlig; handicapped ~ handikapvänlig
accessories [n.pl.] tillbehör
accident [n.] olycka; olycksfall; ~ insurance olycksförsäkring
accidental [adj.] tillfällig; olycks-
accidentally [adv.] oavsiktligt; oförhappandes
accommodate [v.] anpassa sig; förena; hysa
accommodation [n.] bostad, logi
accompany [v.; -nies, -nied] följa med, göra sällskap; ackompanjera
accompanying person [n.] medföljande person
accomplish [v.; ~es, ~ed] uppnå, slutföra
accord¹ [n.] fördrag, överenskommelse; samstämmighet
accord² [v.] ge; stämma överens med
accordance [n.] överenstämmelse; in ~ with i överenstämmelse med
accordingly [adv.] alltså, följaktligen, således, därför
according to [prep.] enligt
accordion [n.] dragspel
account [n.] konto; beräkning; beskrivning, redogörelse, grund; ~ holder kontohavare; ~ name kontonamn; ~ number kontonummer; ~s payable skulder; ~s receivable fordringar; give an ~ of redogöra för; take into ~ ta med i beräkningen
account for [v.] förklara
accountability [n.; -ties] ansvarighet
accountable [adj.] ansvarig
accountant [n.] bokförare, revisor
accounting [n.] bokföring; ~ program redovisningsprogram, affärssystem
accrue [v.] uppkomma, tillfalla
acct. [abbrev: account] konto
accumulate [v.] hopa (sig), samla(s), ackumulera
accumulation [n.] hopande; anhopning
accuracy [n.; -cies] exakthet, noggrannhet

accurate [adj.] exakt, precis, noggrann
accurately [adv.] noggrannt
accusation [n.] anklagelse, beskyllning
accuse [v.] anklaga, beskylla
accused [adj./n.] anklagad; den anklagade
accustomed to [adj.] van vid
ace [n.] ess, äss; baddare
ache¹ [n.] värk, ont
ache² [v.] värka, svida
achieve [v.] utföra; uppnå
achievement [n.] utförande; prestation
aching [adj.] mörbultad
acid¹ [adj.] sur
acid² [n.] syra
acidify [v.; -fies, -fied] försura
acknowledge [v.] erkänna; bekräfta; ~ receipt kvittera
acquaintance [n.]bekantskap; bekant
acquire [v.] skaffa sig
acquisition [n.] förvärv
acre [n.] acre [0,4 hektar]
across¹ [adv.] över, på andra sidan; vågrätt [crossword]; go ~ korsa
across² [prep.] över; ~ the courtyard över gården; right ~ tvärs över
acrylic [n.] akryl
act¹ [n.] handling, gärning; akt [theater]
act² [v.] agera, uppträda som; spela [theater]; fungera, verka
acting¹ [adj.] tillförordnad
acting² [n.] spel
action [n.] åtgärd; ~ film actionfilm
activate [v.] aktivera
active [adj.] aktiv, verksam
actively [adv.] aktivt
activity [n.; -ties] aktivitet, verksamhet
actor [n.] skådespelare
actress [n.; ~es] skådespelerska
actual [adj.] faktisk, egentlig, verklig
actually [adv.] egentligen, faktiskt
acute [adj.] akut; skarp, spetsig; ~ accent (´) akut accent

A.D. [1] [abbrev: A̲nno D̲omini: year of the Lord] efter Kristus (e.Kr.)

ad [2] [abbrev: adv̲ertisement] annons

ada̲pt [v.] anpassa (sig), adaptera

adapta̲tion [n.] anpassning; omarbetning

ada̲pted (to) [adj.] anpassad (till)

ada̲pter [n.] adapter

add [v.] addera; lägga till, tillsätta, tillägga; ~ **up** summera

a̲dded [adj.] ökad, extra; tillagt; **be ~ on** tillkomma

addi̲tion [n.] addition, tillägg

addi̲tional [adj.] ytterlig; ~ **work** extraarbete

a̲dd-on [n.] tillägsenhet

a̲ddress [1] [n.; ~es] adress; bostadsadress; ~ **bar** adressfält; ~ **book** adressbok; ~ **box** adressruta; ~ **he̲ader** adresshuvud; ~ **la̲bel** adresslapp

addre̲ss [2] [v.; ~es, ~ed] adresera; rikta; tilltala

addre̲ssee [n.] mottagare

a̲dequate [adj.] lämplig, tillräcklig

a̲dequately [adv.] tillräckligt

ADHD [abbrev: atte̲ntion de̲ficit hyperacti̲vity diso̲rder] hyperaktivitetssyndrom

adhe̲sive ba̲ndage [n.] plåster

ad hoc [adj.; Latin: for this purpose] improviserad, för ändamålet, hjälp-, tilläggs-

adja̲cent [adj.] angränsande, intilligande

a̲djective [n.] adjektiv

adjo̲ining [adj.] angränsande

adju̲st [v.] anpassa

adju̲stment [n.] reglering; anpassning

admi̲nister [v.] sköta, administrera; ge, tilldela

administra̲tion [n.] styrelse

admi̲nistrative [adj.] administrativ

admi̲nistrator [n.] administratör, förvaltare, intendent

admira̲tion [n.] beundran

admi̲re [v.] beundra

admi̲ssion [n.] antagning; insläpp, inträde; erkännande; ~ **fee** inträdesavgift; ~ **requirements** inträdeskrav; ~ **test/exam** inträdesprov; ~ **ti̲cket** inträdesbiljett

admi̲t [v.; -tting, -tted] erkänna, bekänna; tillåta; rymma

admi̲ttance [n.] tillträde

admi̲ttedly [adv.] visserligen

adole̲scent [n.] tonåring

ado̲pt [v.] adoptera; anta, införa

ado̲pted child [n.] adoptivbarn

ado̲ption [n.] adoptering; antagande

ado̲ptive pa̲rents [n.pl.] adoptivföräldrar

ado̲rn [v.] pryda

ADP [abbrev: automa̲tic da̲ta pro̲cessing] automatisk databehandling (ADP)

adu̲lt [adj./n.] vuxen; ~ **educa̲tion** vuxenutbildning; ~**o̲nset dia̲betes** vuxendiabetes; **for ~s only** barnförbjuden

adva̲nce [1] [n.] framryckning, framsteg; ökning; **in ~** förhand, i förväg; ~ **bo̲oking** förhandsbeställning; ~ **pu̲rchase** förköp; ~ **reserva̲tion** förhandsbokning

adva̲nce [2] [v.] avancera, flytta fram; befordra

adva̲nced [adj.] framskriden, avancerad; ~ **course** fortsättningskurs; ~ **degre̲e** högra studier; ~ **pla̲cement** advancerade kurser

adva̲ntage [n.] fördel; företräde; **have/get the ~ o̲ver** ha/få övertag över; **take ~ of** utnyttja

advanta̲geous [adj.] fördelaktig

adve̲nture [n.] äventyr; ~ **film** äventyrsfilm

a̲dverb [n.] adverb

adve̲rse [adj.] fientlig, rakt emot

a̲dvertise [v.] annonsera, göra reklam; ~ **for** annonsera efter

adve̲rtisement [n.] annons

a̲dvertising [n.] reklam; ~ **ba̲nner** reklambanner

advi̲ce [n.] råd, rådgivning; tips; **a̲sking for ~** rådfrågning

advi̲se [v.] råda

advi̲ser [n.; also: **advisor**] konsulent

advi̲sory [adj.] rådgivande; ~ **se̲rvices** rådgivande tjänster

a̲dvocate [1] [n.] förespråkare

a̲dvocate [2] [v.] propagera, förespråka

Aegean Sea [n.] Egeiska havet
aesthetic [adj.; see: esthetic]
aesthetics [n.; see: esthetics]
affair [n.] affär, sak; händelse;
    current ~s aktuella frågor;
    foreign ~s utrikesärenden; love ~
    kärleksaffär
affect [v.] inverka på, drabba; göra
    intryck på
affection [n.] tillgivenhet; känslor
affiliate [v.] ansluta
affinity [n.; -ties] släktskap, likhet;
    sympati
afford [v.] ge, skänka; be able to ~
    ha råd med
Afghan [adj.] afghansk
AFL-CIO [abbrev: American Fed-
    eration of Labor - Congress of In-
    dustrial Organizations]
    landsorganisationen i USA
afraid [adj.] rädd; be ~ of vara rädd
    för; I'm ~ I can't come jag kan
    tyvärr inte komma
Africa [n.] Afrika
African [adj.] afrikansk
Afro [n.] afrofrisyr
Afro-American [adj.] afroamerikansk
after¹ [adv.] efter; efteråt, senare
after² [conj.] sedan, efter det att
after³ [prep.] efter; ~ all endå,
    egentligen; ~ some time så
    småningom; be ~ sthg sträva efter
    ngt, söka ngt
afternoon [n.] eftermiddag; good ~
    god middag; in the ~ på eftermid-
    dagen
aftershave lotion [n.] rakvatten
after-sun lotion [n.] efter-solkräm
afterward(s) [adv.] sedan, efteråt
again [adv.] åter, igen; om
against [prep.] mot, emot
age¹ [n.] ålder; tid, period; ~s
    evighet; for ~s i många herrans år
age² [v.] åldras; göra gammal
aged [adj.] åldrad; åldrig; the ~ de
    gamla
agency [n.; -cies] agentur, kontor;
    organ; medverkan
agenda [n.] dagordning
agent [n.] agent
aggregate [adj.] sammanlagd

aggression [n.] angrepp
aggressive [adj.] aggresiv
agitate [v.] uppröra, agitera; get ~d
    stressa
ago [adv.] sedan; 10 minutes ~ för
    10 minuter sedan; 2 weeks ~ för 2
    veckor sedan; 2 years ~ för 2 år
    sedan
agony [n.; -nies] skjälskval, plåga;
    dödskamp
agree [v.] samtycka; vara överens;
    ~ on/about komma överens om,
    hålla med om; ~ with someone
    about hålla med någon om; milk
    doesn't ~ with me jag tål inte mjölk
agreed (on) [adj.] ense (om)
agreement [n.] överenskommelse,
    avtal; in ~ about överens om
agricultural [adj.] jordbruks-; ~
    country jordbruksland; ~ policy
    jordbrukspolitik; ~ society jord-
    brukssamhälle; ~ university lant-
    bruksuniversitet; ~ worker
    lantarbetare
agriculture [n.] jordbruk
ahead [adv.] före, i förväg, framför,
    fram
ahead of [prep.] framför, före
AI [abbrev: Amnesty International;
    artificial insemination; artificial
    intelligence] Amnesty Internatio-
    nal; artificiell insemination; artifi-
    ciell intelligens
aid¹ [n.] bistånd; hjälpmedel; ~ to
    developing countries u-landshjälp
aid² [v.] bistå, hjälpa
AIDS [abbrev: acquired immune
    deficiency syndrome] förvärvat
    immunbristsyndrom (aids)
ailment [n.] sjukdom, krämpa
aim¹ [n.] mål, syfte; sikte
aim² [v.] sikta med, måtta på; sträva
    efter; ha för avsikt
ain't [v.; contr: are not; informal]
    är inte
aioli [n.] vitlökmajonnäs, aioli
air [n.] luft; ~ conditioning luft-
    konditionering; ~ filter luftfilter;
    ~ mattress luftmadrass; ~ pollution
    luftförorening; ~ pressure luft-
    tryck; ~ terminal flygterminal

air-conditioned [adj.] luftkonditionerad
aircraft [n.] flyg
airline [n.] flygbolag
airmail [n.] flygpost; luftpost; by ~
med flygpost
airplane [n.] flygplan
airport [n.] flygplats; ~ bus flygbuss; ~ tax flygplatsavgift
airsickness bag [n.] flygsjukpåse
airy [adj.] luftig
aisle [n.] gång, mittgång; ~ seat
plats vid gången
AK [abbrev: Alaska] Alaska [del-
stat i USA]
aka [abbrev: also known as] alias
AL [abbrev: Alabama; American
League] Alabama [delstat i USA];
American League [baseboll-liga i
USA]
Alabama (AL) [n.] Alabama [del-
stat i USA]
alarm¹ [n.] alarm; ~ clock väckarklocka
alarm² [v.] alarmera; skrämma
Alaska (AK) [n.] Alaska [delstat i
USA]
Albania [n.] Albanien
Albanian¹ [adj.] albansk
Albanian² (language) [n.] albanska
albeit [conj.] även om
album [n.] album; skiva
alcohol [n.] alkohol; ~ license vin-
och spriträttigheter
alcoholic¹ [adj.; beverage] alkoholhaltig; stark; non-~ alkoholfri
alcoholic² [n.] alkoholist
alcove [n.] alkov
alert¹ [adj.] alert, pigg, vaken
alert² [v.] larma, varna
algae [n.pl.] alger
Algeria [n.] Algeriet
Algerian [adj.] algerisk
Algiers [n.] Alger
alien¹ [adj.] främmande, utländsk
alien² [n.] främling, utlänning
alike [adv.] lik, likadan
alive [adj.] vid liv, levande
all¹ [adj./pron.] all, allt, alla; hel,
samtliga; ~ night hela natten; by
~ means för all del; best of ~ allra

bästa; ~ sorts of things allt möjligt;
~ the time jämt
all² [adv.] helt, alldeles; ~ but nästan; ~ too alltför
allegation [n.] anklagelse, påstående
allege [v.] förege, påstå, anföra
alleged [adj.] påståd, utpekad
allegedly [adv.] efter vad som påstås
allergic (to) [adj.] allergisk (mot)
allergy [n.; -gies] allergi
alley [n.] liten väg, gränd
alliance [n.] förbund, allians
allied [adj.] allierad, förbunden
all-in-one printer [n.] flerfunktionsskrivare, multifunktionsskrivare
all-night pharmacy [n.; -cies]
nattapotek
allocate [v.] tilldela, fördela, allokera
allocation [n.] tilldelning, fördelning, allokering
allow [v.] tillåta, låta; godkänna;
beräkna
allowed [adj.]: be ~ to få lov att
allowance [n.] hänsynstagande;
bidrag; ranson
all right¹ [adj.] någotsånär; tillåten;
oskadad
all right² [adv.] någotsånär; säkert,
gärna
all right³ [interj.] okej, visst; jaha, ja
allspice [n.] kryddpeppar
ally [n.; allies] bundsförvant,
allierad
almond [n.] mandel; ~ cake mandeltårta; ~ paste mandelmassa
almost [adv.] nästan, nära; i det
närmaste
alone [adj.] ensam; leave ~ lämna i
fred
along¹ [adv.] framåt
along² [prep.] längs
alongside¹ [adv.] långsides
alongside² [prep.] vid sidan av
aloud [adv.] högt
alphabet [n.] alfabet
alpine skiing [n.] utförsåkning
Alps [n.pl.] Alperna
already [adv.] redan
alright [adj./adv.; see: all right]
Alsace [n.] Elsass
also [adv.] också, även

Alta. [abbrev: Alberta] Alberta
  [Canadian prov.]
altar [n.] altare
alter [v.] ändra, förändra; revidera
alteration [n.] förändring, ändring
alternate route [n.] alternativ väg
alternating [adj.] omväxlande; ~
  current (AC) [n.] växelström
alternative [adj./n.] alternativ
alternatively [adv.] annars, för
  annars, i annat fall
alternator [n.] växelströmgenerator,
  omformare
although [conj.] fastän, trots att
altitude [n.] höjd (över havet)
altogether [adv.] totalt
aluminum [n.] aluminium; ~ **foil**
  foliepapper, aluminiumfolie
always [adv.] alltid, jämt
Alzheimer's disease [n.]
  Alzheimers sjukdom
a.m.[1] [abbrev: ante meridiem: before noon] förmiddagen (f.m.)
AM[2] [abbrev: amplitude modulation]
  amplitudmodulering
amateur [adj./n.] amatör
amaze [v.] förvåna, häpna
amazing [adj.] förbluffande,
  häpnadsväckande
Amazon River [n.] Amazonfloden
ambassador [n.] ambassadör
amber [n.] bärnsten
ambiguity [n.; -ties] tvetydighet,
  oklarhet
ambiguous [adj.] tvetydig, oklar
ambition [n.] ambition
ambitious [adj.] ärelysten; ambitiös
ambulance [n.] ambulans
amend [v.] göra ändring, förbättra
amendment [n.] rättelse, ändring
amenities [n.pl.] bekvämligheter
America [n.] Amerika
American[1] [adj.] amerikansk
American[2] [n.] amerikan
American Indian [n.] indian
amid(st) [prep.] mitt i, under
among(st) [prep.] bland; ~ **other**
  things bland annat (bl a)
amount [n.] summa, belopp
amount to [v.] uppgå till; vara detsamma som

amp. [abbrev: ampere; amplifier]
  ampere; förstärkare
ampersand (&) [n.] et-tecken,
  och-tecken
ample [adj.] rymlig, riklig
ampule [n.] kapsel
amputated [adj.] amputerad
amuse (oneself) [v.] roa (sig),
  underhålla
amusement [n.] nöje; ~ **park**
  nöjespark, nöjesfält
amusing [adj.] rolig, underhållande
an [indef.art.; see: **a**]
analog [adj.] analog
analogy [n.; -gies] analogi, jämförelse
analysis [n.; -ses] analys, undersökning
analyst [n.] analytiker
analyze [v.] analysera
anarchy [n.; -chies] anarki
ancestor [n.] förfader
anchor[1] [n.] ankare
anchor[2] [v.] ankra; förankra
anchorage [n.]: **no** ~ ankring
  förbjuden
anchovy [n.; -vies] sardell, ansjovis
ancient [adj.] forntida, urgammal
and [conj.] och, samt [formal]; ~ **so**
  forth (etc.) med mera (m.m.)
anesthetic [n.] bedövningsmedel;
  general ~ narkos
anew [adv.] på nytt, om
angel [n.] ängel
anger[1] [n.] vrede
anger[2] [v.] förarga
angina [n.] kärlkramp
angle [n.] vinkel; ~ **brackets (< >)**
  vinkelparentes
angrily [adv.] argt, ilsket
angry [adj.] arg, ilsken; ond
animal[1] [adj.] animalisk, djurisk
animal[2] [n.] djur; ~ **feed** djurfoder;
  ~ **rights** djurens rättigheter
animated [adj.] animerad
animation [n.] animering
ankle [n.] vrist
annexed [adj.] bifogad
anniversary [n.; -ries] jubileum
Anno Domini (A.D.) [adv.] efter
  Kristus (e.Kr.)

announce [v.] meddela; anmäla
announcement [n.] meddelande; anmälan; annons
annoy [v.] reta, irritera
annoyed [adj.] irriterad, förargad
annoying [adj.] förarglig
annual [adj.] årlig; ettårig; ~ income årsinkomst
annually [adv.] årligen
anonymous [adj.] anonym
anorak [n.] anorak
another [pron.] en annan/ett annat; en/ett till; ~ week en vecka till
answer[1] [n.] svar; ~ form svarsblankett
answer[2] [v.] svara
answering machine [n.] telefonsvarare
ant [n.] myra
Antarctica [n.] Antarktis
Antarctic Circle [n.] södra polcirkeln
Antarctic Ocean [n.] Södra ishavet
antibiotic [n.] antibiotisk medel; ~s antibiotika
antibody [n.; -dies] antikropp
anticipate [v.] förutse; räkna med
anticipation [n.] förväntan, förkänsla
antifreeze [n.] frostskyddsmedel, glykol
antiquated [adj.] föråldrad
antique[1] [adj.] antik
antique[2] [n.] antikvitet; ~ store antikaffär; antikvitetsaffär
antiseptic [n.] antiseptisk medel; ~ cream antiseptisk salva
anti-theft marking [n.] stöldmärkning
anti-virus program [n.] antivirusprogram
antler [n.] horn
anxiety [n.; -ties] oro, ängslan
anxious [adj.] ängslig, bekymrad; angelägen, ivrig
any[1] [adv.] något
any[2] [pron.] någon/något/några; vilken/vilket som helst; not ~ ingen/inget/inga
anybody [pron.] någon som helst, vem som helst
anyhow [adv.] hur som helst; i alla fall
anyone [pron.] någon

anything [pron.] någonting, något; vad som helst
anyway [adv.] i alla fall
anywhere [adv.] någonstans, var som helst
AP [abbrev: Associated Press; advanced placement] Associated Press [nyhetsbyrå i USA]; avancerade kurser [på gymnasieskolorna]
apart [adv.] isär, ifrån varandra; åt sidan
apart from [prep.] bortsett från
apartment [n.] lägenhet, våning; ~ building våningshus, hyreshus
APB [abbrev: all-points bulletin] efterlysning
aperture [n.] öppning; bländare [foto]
APEX [abbrev: Advance Purchase Excursion (air ticket)] APEX-biljett
apiece [adv.] per styck
apologize [v.] be om ursäkt
apology [n.; -gies] ursäkt, avbön
apostrophe (') [n.] apostrof(tecken)
appalling [adj.] förfärlig, hemsk
apparatus [n.; ~es] apparat, maskineri, anordning
apparent [adj.] synbar, uppenbar; skenbar
apparently [adv.] uppenbarligen, till synes
appeal[1] [n.] vädjan, upprop, appell; överklagande; lockelse, attraktion
appeal[2] [v.] vädja; appellera, överklaga; locka
appealing [adj.] vädjande; lockande
appear [v.] verka; visa sig; framgå
appearance [n.] utseende; uppträdande; ~s sken
appendicitis [n.] blindtarmsinflammation
appendix[1] [n.; ~es] blindtarm
appendix[2] [n.; -dices] tillägg, bilaga
appetite [n.] aptit, matlust; lust; loss of ~ aptitlöshet
appetizer [n.] aptitretare, förrätt
apple [n.] äpple; ~ cake äppelkaka; ~ fritters äppelringar; ~ juice äppelmust; ~ pie äppelpaj
applet [n.] appletprogram, miniprogram [IT]

appliance [n.] apparat, redskap;
domestic ~s hushållsapparater
applicable [adj.] tillämplig,
användbar
applicant [n.] sökande
application [n.] ansökan; tillämpning, användning; applikation,
tillämpningsprogram [IT]; ~ form
ansökansblankett; submit an ~
applicera
applied [adj.] praktisk, tillämpad
apply [v.; -plies, -plied] anbringa,
lägga på; använda; ansöka, söka
in, applicera
appoint [v.] utnämna; bestämma
appointed [adj.] bestämmd
appointment [n.] beställning; tid,
tidsbeställning; make an ~ stämma
möte, beställa tid
appraisal [n.] värdering, bedömning
appreciate [v.] uppskatta; förstå;
stiga
appreciation [n.] uppskatning,
förståelse, värdering; ökning i
värde
approach¹ [n.; ~es] sätt att se på
eller företa en sak; närmande
approach² [v.; ~es, ~ed] närma sig
appropriate [adj.] lämplig;
passande
approval [n.] gillande; godkännande; on ~ till påseende, på prov
approve [v.] gilla; godkänna
approved [adj.] godkänd; beprövad
approximate [adj.] ungefärlig
approximately (approx.) [adv.]
approximativt; ungefär, cirka
APR¹ [abbrev: annual percentage
rate] årlig ränta
Apr.² [abbrev: April] april
apricot [n.] aprikos
April [n.] april
apron [n.] förkläde
apse [n.] absid
apt¹ [adj.] träffande; dyktig
apt.² [abbrev: apartment] lägenhet
aptitude test [n.] anlagstest
aquarium [n.; ~s] akvarium
Aquarius [n.] Vattumannen [zodiac]
aquavit [n.] aqvavit
AR [abbrev: Arkansas] Arkansas
[delstat i USA]

Arab [n.] arab
Arab League [n.] Arabförbundet
Arabia [n.] Arabien
Arabian [adj.] arabisk
Arabic (language) [n.] arabiska
arbitrary [adj.] godtycklig,
egenmäktig
arc [n.] cirkelbåge, båge
arcade game [n.] arkadspel,
spelautomat
arch¹ [n.; ~es] valv, båge; hålfot
arch² [v.; ~es, ~ed] välva, kröka
archbishop [n.] ärkebiskop
archeological [adj.] arkeologisk
archeologist [n.] arkeolog
archeology [n.; -gies] arkeologi
archipelago [n.; ~s/~es] skärgård
architect [n.] arkitekt
architectural [adj.] arkitektonisk,
byggnads-
architecture [n.] arkitektur
archive [n.] arkiv
arctic¹ [adj.] arktisk; Arctic Circle
norra polcirkeln; ~ Ocean Norra
ishavet; ~ region [n.] Nordpolsområdet
Arctic² [n.] Arktis
are [v.: be] är; finns; the books ~
old böckerna är gamla; there ~
plates in the cupboard det finns
tallrikar i skåpet; ~ there (any)
old books on the table? finns det
gamla böcker på bordet?
area [n.] område, terräng, trakt;
yta, areal; ~ code riktnummer; ~
of application användningsområde; ~ of learning [discipline]
vetenskapsgren, disciplin
arena [n.] arena
aren't [contr: are not; see: be]
är inte
Argentinian, Argentine [adj.]
argentinsk
argue [v.] bråka, tvista; argumentera;
diskutera
argument [n.] gräl, dispyt; argument;
resonemang
Aries [n.] Väduren [zodiac]
Arizona (AZ) [n.] Arizona [delstat
i USA]
arise [v.; arose, arisen] uppstå,
framträdda

arithmetic [n.] räkning
Arkansas (AR) [n.] Arkansas [delstat i USA]
arm[1] [n.] arm; ~s vapen; ~s race kapprustning
arm[2] [v.] beväpna, rusta
armchair [n.] fåtölj
armed [adj.] beväpnad, utrustad; ~ forces försvarsmakten; ~ robbery väpnat rån
Armenia [n.] Armenien
Armenian[1] [adj.] armenisk
Armenian[2] (language) [n.] armeniska
armistice [n.] stillestånd
armor [n.] rustning; pansar
armory [n.; -ries] rustkammare
armpit [n.] armhåla
arms [n.pl.; see: arm]
army [n.; -mies] armé
around[1] [adv.] runt omkring; om
around[2] [prep.] kring, omkring, runt; om; vid; ~ half past eight vid halv 9-tiden
arouse [v.] uppväcka, rycka upp
arr. [abbrev: arranged by; arrival] arrangerad av; ankomst
arrange [v.] ordna, arrangera
arrangement [n.] uppläggning, uppställning; regi
array [n.] samling; matris
arrest[1] [n.] anhållande, arrestering; hejdande; cardiac ~ hjärtestillstånd; under ~ arresterad
arrest[2] [v.] anhålla, arrestera; stoppa; fånga
arrival [n.] ankomst; ankommande [person]; ~ time ankomsttid
arrive [v.] komma fram, anlända; ~ at [place] ankomma till; have ~d vara framme
arrow [n.] pil; ~ key piltangent
art [n.; see also: arts] konst; ~ dealer konsthandlare; ~ gallery konstgalleri; ~ museum konstmuseum; ~ nouveau jugendstil; ~ object konstföremål; work of ~ konstverk; the fine ~s de sköna konsterna
artery [n.; -ries] artär

arthritis [n.] artrit, ledinflammation
artichoke [n.] kronärtskocka; ~ hearts kronärtskocksbotten
article [n.] sak, vara; artikel; ~ of clothing klädesplagg
articulate [v.] artikulera, uttala
artificial [adj.] konstgjord, artficiell; ~ intelligence artificiell intelligens; ~ sweetener sötningsmedel
artist [n.] konstnär
artistic [adj.] konstnärlig, artistisk
arts [n.pl.] humaniora; ~ and crafts konsthantverk; ~ and letters humaniora; ~ page kultursida; liberal ~ humaniora; the fine ~ de sköna konsterna; visual ~ bildkonst
as[1] [adv.] så, lika; som; ~ big ~ you lika stor som du; not ~ big ~ you inte så stor som du; ~ far ~ I know såvitt jag vet; ~ of (date) från och med; ~ soon ~ possible så snart som möjligt; ~ it were liksom; ~ well även
as[2] [conj.] såsom, eftersom
ASA [abbrev: American Standards Association] ASA [standardiseringsorganen i USA]
ASAP [abbrev: as soon as possible] så snart som möjligt, snarast möjligt
ascend [v.] bestiga; stiga
ascending order [n.] stigande ordning
ascent [n.] bestigning; stigning
ascertain [v.] förvissa sig om; få reda på; fästställa
ASCII [abbrev: American Standard Code for Information Interchange] ASCII-kod
ASEAN [abbrev: Association of Southeast Asian Nations] ASEAN [de sydöstasiatiska staternas samarbetsorganisation]
ash [n.; ~es] aska; ask [tree]
ashamed [adj.] skamsen, generad
ashore [adv.] i land
ashtray [n.] askfat, askkopp
Asia [n.] Asien
Asian[1] [adj.] asiatisk

Asian² [n.] asiat
aside [adv.] avsides, åt sidan, undan
aside from [adv.] bortsett från
ask [v.] fråga; be; ~ **about** fråga efter; ~ **at the front desk** fråga vid receptionen; ~ **for** be om; ~ **for assistance** fråga om hjälp
asleep [adj./adv.] sovande; **be** ~ sova; **fall** ~ somna
asparagus [n.; ~es] sparris; ~ **soup** sparrissoppa; ~ **tip** sparrisknopp; **cream of** ~ **soup** redd sparrissoppa
aspect [n.] aspekt, synpunkt; utsikt; ~ **ratio** bredd/höjdförhållande
aspic [n.] aladåb
aspiration [n.] strävan; aspiration
aspire [v.] sträva efter
aspirin [n.] aspirin
ass [n.; ~es; colloq.] arsle [body part, vul.]; åsna [animal]
assassination [n.] mord, lönnmord
assault¹ [n.] anfall, stormning; olaga hot; misshandel; **sexual** ~ sexuellt övergrepp
assault² [v.] anfalla; storma; överfalla, misshandla
assemble [v.] sammankalla, samla; montera
assembler : [n.] ~ **code** assembler [IT]; ~ **language** assembler [IT]
assembly [n.; -lies] sammankomst, möte; församling; montering
assert [v.] hävda, påstå
assertion [n.] påstående
assess [v.; ~es. ~ed] värdera; beskatta
assessment [n.] bedömning, värdering; beskattning
asset [n.] tillgång; ~**s and liabilities** tillgångar och skulder, aktiva och passiva
asshole [n.; vul.] arsle [vul.], fåntratt [colloq.], stolle [colloq.]
assiduously [adv.] flitigt
assign [v.] ange, anföra; avträda; bestämma; anslå
assignment [n.] uppgift; beting, läxa; tilldelning
assist [v.] hjälpa, bistå; hjälpa till
assistance [n.] hjälp, bistånd
assistant¹ [adj.] biträdande; ~ **professor** universitetsadjunkt, forskarassistent

assistant² [n.] medhjälpare, assistent
assisted-living apartments [n.pl.] servicehus
Assoc. [abbrev: association; associate] förening; associerad
associate¹ [n.] delägare; kollega; ~ **professor** universitetslektor, docent; ~**s degree** högskolediplom [efter 2 års studier]
associate² [v.] förbinda; associera; uppta
associated [adj.] förbunden, associerad; ~ **with** knuten med, ansluten till
association [n.] förening, sammanslutning; förbund; association
assorted [adj.] blandad
assortment [n.] sortiment, varusortiment; urval
asst. [abbrev: assistant] adjunkt
assume [v.] anta, förmoda; tillträda
assuming that [conj.] förutsatt att
assumption [n.] antagande, förutsättning; övertagande
assurance [n.] försäkring, säkerhet; självförtroende
assure [v.] försäkra, förvissa; trygga
asterisk (*) [n.] asterisk, stjärntecken
asthma [n.] astma
astonish [v.; ~es. ~ed] förvåna, överraska
astonished [adj.] förvånad
astonishing [adj.] förvånande
astonishment [n.] förvåning
astound [v.] förvåna
astray [adv.] vilse
astronaut [n.] astronaut
astronomical [adj.] astronomisk
astronomy [n.; -mies] astronomi
asylum [n.] asyl
asynchronous [adj.] asynkron
at [prep.] vid, på, hos; ~ **the breakfast table** vid frukostbordet; ~ **the hotel** på hotellet; ~ **the office** på kontoret; ~ **Jan's place** hos Jan
A-team [abbrev: first team] topplag, A-lag
Athens (Greece) [n.] Aten
athlete [n.] idrottsman
athletic [adj.] idrotts-, atletisk
athletics [n.] friidrott; idrott; ~ **club** idrottsklubb

Atlantic Ocean [n.] Atlanten
atlas [n.; ~es] atlas, kartbok
ATM [abbrev: automated teller machine] bankomat
atmosphere [n.] atmosfär; stämning
atmospheric [adj.] atmosfärisk
atom [n.] atom
atomic [adj.] atomisk
at-sign (@) [n.] snabel-a (@)
att. [abbrev: attention, attorney, attached] tillhanda; advokat; bifogad
attach [v.; ~es, ~ed] fästa, sätta fast; bifoga
attached [adj.] knuten till; bifogad; fäst vid
attachment [n.] tillgivenhet; fästanordning; bilaga, tillägg
attack[1] [n.] anfall, angrepp, attack
attack[2] [v.] anfalla, angripa; drabba
attacker [n.] angripare
attain [v.] uppnå, förvärva
attainment [n.] uppnående; ~s kunskaper
attempt[1] [n.] försök; attentat
attempt[2] [v.] försöka
attempted murder [n.] mordförsök
attend [v.] delta i, gå på, bevista; sköta, behandla; ledsaga
attendance [n.] närvaro; publik; betjäning; ~ **list** närvarolista
attention [n.] uppmärksamhet, kännedom; omsorg
attest [v.] vittna om; attestera, vidimera
attitude [n.] ställning, hållning
attn. [abbrev: attention] tillhanda
attorney [n.] advokat
Attorney General justitiekansler, riksåklagare
attract [v.] dra till sig, locka
attraction [n.] dragningskraft; attraktion
attractive [adj.] lockande, tilltalande; snygg
attribute [n.] attribut, utmärkande drag
attribute to [v.] tillskriva, tillräkna
atty. [abbrev: attorney] advokat
auburn-colored [adj.] kastanjefärgad
auction [n.] auktion
audience [n.] publik
audioguide [n.] audio-guide

audiovisual aids [n.pl.] AV-hjälpmedel
audit[1] [n.] revision
audit[2] [v.] revidera, granska
audition [n.] prov
auditor [n.] revisor; åhörare
Aug. [abbrev: August] augusti
augment [v.] öka, förstärka
August [n.] augusti
aunt [n.] [maternal] moster, tant; [paternal] faster, tant
aurora borealis [n.] norrsken
austere [adj.] sträng; stram
Australia [n.] Australien
Australian[1] [adj.] australiensisk, australisk
Australian[2] [n.] australier
Austria [n.] Österrike
Austrian [adj.] österrikisk
authentication [n.] äkthetsbevisning; autentisering, verifiering
author [n.] författare
authoring tool [n.] författarverktyg
authority [n.; -ties] myndighet; befogenhet
authorization [n.] bemyndigande; tillåtelse
authorize [v.] auktorisera, bemyndiga; tillåta
authorized [adj.] tillåten, auktoriserad
auto [n.] car; ~ **train** biltåg
automated teller machine (ATM) [n.] uttagsautomat, bankomat
automatic [adj.] automatisk; ~ **door** automatisk dörr; ~ **transmission** automatlåda, automatväxel
automatically [adv.] automatiskt; av sig själv
automobile [n.] bil; ~ **accident** bilolycka; ~ **ferry** bilfärja; ~ **inspection** bilprovning; ~ **insurance** trafikförsäkring; ~ **tax** bilskatt
autonomous [adj.] autonom, självstyrande
autonomy [n.; -mies] autonomi, självstyre
autumn [n.] höst; **late** ~ senhöst
auxiliary[1] [adj.] hjälp-; ~ **verb** hjälpverb
auxiliary[2] [n.; -ries] hjälpare

AV [abbrev: audiovisual]
audiovisuell
availability [n.; -ties] tillgänglighet, tillgång
available [adj.] ledig, tillgänglig,
disponibel
avalanche [n.] lavin
Ave. [abbrev: Avenue] aveny
avenue [n.] aveny
average[1] [adj.] genomsnittlig,
medel-, mellan-; of ~ difficulty
mellansvår
average[2] [n.] genomsnitt, medeltal;
on ~ i medeltal
average[3] [v.] beräkna genomsnittet
för; i genomsnitt uppgå till; ~ out
jämna ut sig
aviation [n.] flygning, flyg;
flygväsen
avocado [n.; ~s/~es] avokado
avoid [v.] undvika, undgå; slippa;
sky
await [v.] vänta, avvakta
awake[1] [adj.] vaken
awake[2] [v.; awoke, awoken] väcka
[trans.]; vakna [intrans.]
awaken [v.] väcka [trans.]; vakna
[intrans.]
award[1] [n.] pris, belöning;
skadestånd

award[2] [v.] tilldela, belöna med
awarding of prizes [n.] prisutdelning
aware [adj.] medveten, uppmärksam
awareness [n.] medvetenhet,
uppmärksamhet
away [adv.] bort; i väg; borta; go ~!
stick!
awe [n.] vördnad, fruktan
awesome [adj.] fantastisk, väldig
awful [adj.] fruktansvärd; hemsk,
förfärlig
awfully [adv.] hemskt
awkward [adj.] besvärlig, krånglig;
generad, klumpig
AWOL [abbrev: absent without
leave] (ta) permis utan tillstånd
awry [adv.] galet, snett
axe [n.] yxa
axiom [n.] axiom, självklar sats
axis [n.; axes] axel
axle [n.] hjulaxel
ayatollah [n.] ayatollah
aye [interj.] ja
AZ [abbrev: Arizona] Arizona
[delstat i USA]
Azerbaijan [n.] Azerbajdzjan
Azerbaijani [adj.] azerbajdzjansk
Azeri (language) [n.] azerbajdzjanska
AZT [abbrev: azidothymidine]
AZT [läkemedel mot aids]

B

b.[1] [abbrev: born] född
B[2] [abbrev: second-highest mark in school] betyg bättre än medel
B.A. [abbrev: Bachelor of Arts] kandidat
baby [n.; -bies] baby, spädbarn; ~ **bottle** nappflaska; ~ **carriage** barnvagn; ~ **carrier** bärsele; ~ **food** barnmat; ~ **monitor** babylarm; ~ **wipes** våtservetter för barn; **expect a** ~ vänta barn; **have a** ~ få barn
babysit [v.] sitta barnvakt
babysitter [n.] barnvakt
babysitting service [n.] barnvaktsservice
babywear [n.] spädbarnskläder
Bachelor of Science/Arts (B.S./B.A.) [n.] filosofie kandidat (fil.kand.)
bachelor's degree [n.] kandidat
back[1] [adj.] bak-; ~ **door** bakdörr; ~ **wheel** bakhjul
back[2] [adv.] bak; åter, tillbaka; **all the way** ~ längst bak; **to the** ~ bakåt
back[3] [n.] rygg; ryggstöd [of chair]; baksida; ~ **pain** ryggsmärta
back[4] [v.] backa; ~ **up** [support] backa upp
backache [n.] ont i ryggen, ryggont
backbone [n.] stamnät
background [n.] bakgrund, fond; skrivbordsunderlägg [IT]
backing [n.] understöd, hjälp; backning
backlit [adj.] bakgrundsbelyst
backpack [n.] ryggsäck
backseat [n.] baksäte
backslash (\) [n.; ~es] bakstreck, omvänt snedstreck [IT]
backspace [v.] bakstega [IT]
backstairs [n.pl.] baktrappa
backup copy [n.; -pies] reservkopia, säkerhetskopia
backup lights [n.pl.] bakljus
backward[1] [adj.] bakåtriktad; underutvecklad; reaktionär
backward(s)[2] [adv.] bakåt, bak-

länges; ~ **compatible** bakåtkompatibel; **go** ~ backa
bacon [n.] bacon
bacteria [n.pl.] bakterier
bad[1] [adj.; worse, worst] illa; ond; dålig; skämd; ~ **luck** elände, otur
bad[2] [adv.; worse, worst] dåligt, illa; **not** ~ inte dåligt, inte farligt; **too** ~ synd, tråkigt
badge [n.] emblem, märke; kännetecken
badly [adv.] dåligt, illa; **take something** ~ ta illa upp
badminton [n.] badminton
bad-tempered [adj.] vresig, sur, på dålig humör
bag [n.] påse; väska
baggage [n.] resgods, bagage; ~ **cart** bagagekärra, bagagevagn; ~ **check** bagagekvitto; ~ **check-in** bagageincheckning; ~ **checkroom** effektförvaring, resgodsinlämning; ~ **claim** bagageutlämning; ~ **claim area** bagagehall; ~ **counter** resgodsexpedition; ~ **locker** förvaringsbox, förvaringsfack
Baghdad [n.] Bagdad
bag-snatcher [n.] väskrykare
bail [n.] borgen
bait [n.] bete
bake [v.] baka; grädda
baked [adj.] bakad; ~ **beans** bruna bönor; ~ **potato** bakad potatis; **freshly** ~ nybakad
baker [n.] bagare
bakery [n.; -ries] bageri
baking pan [n.] bakform, kakform, bakplåt
balance[1] [n.] balans, jämvikt; saldo [bank]; ~ **brought forward** ingående saldo; ~ **carried forward** utgående saldo
balance[2] [v.] balansera; vara i jämvikt; bringa i jämvikt; motväga
balanced [adj.] balanserad, i jämvikt, stabil; allsidig
balcony [n.; -nies] balkong
bald [adj.] (flint)skallig
balding [adj.] tunnhårig

Balkans [n.pl.] Balkan
ball [n.] boll; kula; bal [dance]; ~
   game match; ~**s** [vul.] ballar; ~**s!**
   [vul.] fan!
ballet [n.] balett
balloon [n.] ballong
ballot [n.] valsedel; ~ **box** valurna
ball-playing [n.] bollspel
ballpoint pen [n.] kulspetspenna
ballroom dancing [n.] sällskapsdans
balsamic vinager [n.] balsam-
   vinäger
Baltic [n.]: ~ **area** Baltikum; ~ **Sea**
   Östersjön; ~ **states** Baltikum
ban¹ [n.] förbud
ban² [v.; banning, banned, banned]
   förbjuda
banana [n.] banan
band [n.] band
bandage [n.] bandage, förband,
   binda
bandwidth [n.] bandbredd
bang¹ [n.] smäll, knall
bang² [v.] smälla, slå
banish [v.; ~es, ~ed] förvisa; slå bort
banister [n.] räcke
bank¹ [n.] bank; strand; ~ **account**
   bankkonto; ~ **card** bankkort; ~
   charges bankutgifter; ~ **clerk**
   banktjänsteman; ~ **statement**
   kontoutdrag
bank² [v.] sätta in pengar; dosera;
   banka; ~ **with** ha bankkonto hos
bankbook [n.] bankbok
banker [n.] bankir
banking [n.] bankväsen
bankrupt [adj.] bankrutt
bankruptcy [n.; -cies] konkurs
banner [n.] banderoll, fana; banner
   [IT]
banquet [n.] festmåltid, bankett
baptize [v.] döpa
baptized [adj.] döpt
bar¹ [n.] bar; stång; bom; domstol;
   the ~ advokatsamfundet, ad-
   vokatyrket; ~ **chart** stapeldiagram;
   ~ **code** streckkod; ~ **counter**
   bardisk; ~ **service** barservering
bar² [v.; barring, barred, barred]
   blockera, hindra, avstänga
barbecue¹ [n.] grillning, grillfest

[party]; ~ **area** grillplats
barbecue² [v.] grilla
barbed wire [n.] taggtråd
barber [n.] frisör, herrfrisör
barbershop [n.] frisörsalong
bare [adj.] bar, naken; kal
barely [adv.] knappt; torftigt
bargain¹ [n.] bra köp, fynd; ~ **price**
   vrakpris
bargain² [v.] förhandla; **more than**
   I had ~ed for mer än jag hade
   räknat med
bark¹ [n.] bark [tree]; skall [dog]
bark² [v.] skälla [dog]; ryta
barley [n.] korn
barn [n.] lada, ladugård
baroque [adj.] barock; bisarr
barrel [n.] tunna, fat
barrier [n.] spärr, hinder, barriär;
   ~**free** utan hinder
base¹ [n.] bas; sockel; **get to first** ~
   komma en bit på vägen
base² [v.] basera, grunda
baseball [n.] baseboll [slagbollspel
   i USA som liknar brännboll]
basement [n.] källare
basic [adj.] grund-, bas-; ~ **education**
   grundutbildning; ~ **training**
   grundutbildning
basically [adv.] egentligen, i grund
   och botten
basil [n.] basilika
basin [n.] bäcken, bassäng
basis [n.; bases] grund, bas, basis;
   on the ~ of beroende på
basket [n.] korg
basketball [n.] basketboll
bass [n.; ~es] bas [voice]; havsaborre [fish]
bastard [n.] utomäktenskapligt
   barn; knöl [vul.]
bat [n.] fladdermus; slagträ
batch [n.; ~es] hop, hög; sats; ~
   processing satsvis bearbetning
bath [n.] bad; badkar; badhus; ~
   towel badhandduk, badlakan
bathe [v.] bada; badda
bathing [adj.]: ~ **cap** badmössa; ~
   hut badhytt; ~ **shoes** badskor
bathrobe [n.] badrock, badkappa
bathroom [n.] badrum; toalett;

~ **cabinet** badrumsskåp; ~ **mat** badrumsmatta

bathtub [n.] badkar

batter [v.] slå; misshandla; hamra

battered [adj.] sönderslagen, illa medfaren; utsatts för misshandel

battery [n.; -ries] batteri; ~ **charger** batteriladdare

battle¹ [n.] strid, slag

battle² [v.] kämpa

battlements [n.pl.] tinnar

baud [n.] baud [IT]

bay [n.] vik, bukt; utrymme; last-plats, hållplatsläge; ~ **leaf** lagerblad

B&B [abbrev: bed and breakfast] rum inklusive frukost

BBQ [abbrev: barbecue] grillfest

B.C. [abbrev: before Christ; British Columbia; Boston College] före Kristus; British Columbia [Canadian prov.]; Boston College

B.C.E. [abbrev: before Common Era] före Kristus

be [v.; am, is, are; was, were; been] vara, bli; finnas; **there is/are** det finns

beach [n.; ~es] badstrand, strand, badplats

beach shoes [n.pl.] strandskor, badskor

bead [n.] pärla; droppe

beam¹ [n.] stråle; bjälke; **high** ~ helljus; **low** ~ halvljus

beam² [v.] utstråla, sända ut

bean [n.] böna; ~ **sprouts** bönskott; **green** ~ gröna bönor, haricots verts; **runner** ~ rosenbönor; **spring** ~ brytbönor

bear¹ [n.] björn; ~ **market** baisse

bear² [v.; bore, borne/born] bära; tåla, tolerera

bearable [adj.] uthärdlig

beard [n.] skägg

bearing [n.] hållning; betydelse; riktning

beast [n.] djur; odjur

beat¹ [n.] slag, takt; rond

beat² [v.; beat, beaten] slå ; vispa; trampa; ~ **it!** stick!; ~ **s.o. up** klå upp ngn.; ~ **children** aga barn

beater [n.] visp

beating [n.] stryk, omgång; nederlag

beautiful [adj.] vacker, skön; fin

beautifully [adv.] härligt, vackert

beauty [n.; -ties] skönhet; ~ **care** skönhetsbehandling; ~ **parlor** damfrisering, skönhetssalong

because [conj.] därför att, eftersom, för att

because of [prep.] på grund av (p.g.a.)

become [v.; became, become] bli; anstå, klä

becoming [adj.] klädsam, passande

bed [n.] säng; **go to** ~ lägga sig, gå till sängs

bedcover [n.] sängtäcke

bedding [n.] sängkläder

bedroom [n.] sovrum

bedsheet [n.] lakan

bedside table [n.] nattduksbord, sängbord

bedspread [n.] överkast

bee [n.] bi

beef [n.] biff, biffkött, nötkött, oxkött; ~ **meatball** oxjärpe; ~ **stew** ragu; ~ **tongue** oxtunga

beer [n.] öl; ~ **on tap** fatöl; **dark** ~ mörkt öl; **strong** ~ starköl

beet [n.] rödbeta

before¹ [adv.] före, förr, förut

before² [conj.] innan, förrän

before³ [prep.] framför, före, förr; ~ **meals** före måltiden

beforehand [prep.] på förhand, i förväg

beg [v.; begging, begged, begged] tigga, be

begin [v.; beginning, began, begun] börja

beginner [n.] nybörjare; ~**'s course** nybörjarkurs

beginning [n.] början; **in the** ~ i början

begun [adj.] börjad

behalf [n.]: **on Jan's** ~ för Jans skull, i Jans ställe

behave [v.] uppföra sig, bete sig, förhålla sig, uppträda; uppföra sig väl

behavior [n.] beteende, uppförande, förhållande

behind¹ [adv.] bakom; bakåt, till-baka; efter; **from** ~ bakifrån

behind² [prep.] bakom, efter

beige [adj./n.] beige

being[1] [v.]: **for the time ~** för närvarande

being[2] [n.] tillvaro; väsen

Belarus [n.] Vitryssland

Belgian [adj.] belgisk

Belgium [n.] Belgien

belief [n.] tro, övertygelse, tilltro

believe (in) [v.] tro (på)

bell [n.] klocka

bellboy [n.] piccolo

belles lettres [n.pl.] skönlitteratur

belly [n.; -llies] buk, mage

belong [v.] höra (hemma); **~ to** tillhöra, höra till; **~ together** höra ihop

belongings [n.pl.] tillhörigheter, grejer

below [adv./prep.] under, nedanför; **stated ~** nedanstående

belt [n.] skärp, bälte

bench [n.; ~es] bänk; **the ~** domarkåren

bend[1] [n.] böjning, kurva

bend[2] [v.; bent, bent] böja; luta

bending [n.] böjning

beneath [prep.] under

beneficial [adj.] välgörande, nyttig; hälsosam

beneficiary [n.; -ries] förmånstagare, betalningsmottagare

benefit[1] [n.] förmån, fördel; bidrag; **for Jan's ~** till förmån för Jan

benefit[2] [v.] vara till nytta; nytta av

bequeath [v.] testamentera

bequest [n.] testamente; legat

berry [n.; berries] bär; **~-picking expedition** bärutflykt

berth [n.] sovplats, bädd; kajplats

beside [prep.] bredvid, intill

besides[1] [adv.] dessutom; för resten

besides[2] [prep.] utom; **~ the fact that** bortsett från

best[1] [adj./adv.; superl.: good] bäst; toppen [colloq.]; **~ of all** allra bäst; **~ before (date)** bäst före (datum); **~ wishes** varma lyckönskningar

best[2] [n.] (det) bästa; **all the ~** allt gott

bet[1] [n.] vad

bet[2] [v.; betting, bet, bet] slå vad; **you ~!** var så säker!

beta blocker [n.] betablockare

beta version [n.] betaversion [IT]

betray [v.] förråda, svika; avslöja

better[1] [adj./adv.comp.: good] bättre; **we had ~ go** det är bäst att vi går; **~ late than never** bättre sent än aldrig; **get ~** tillfriskna

better[2] [n.] **one's ~s** folk som är förmer; **for the ~** till det bättre; **get the ~ of s.o.** få övertaget över någon; **for ~ or for worse** i nöd och lust, i med- och motgång; **so much the ~** desto bättre; **the sooner the ~** ju förr desto bättre

betting [n.] vadhållning, vadslagning

between[1] [adv.] emellan, mitt emellan

between[2] [prep.] mellan, emellan

beverage [n.] dryck

beware [v.] akta sig; **~ of dog** varning för hunden

bewildered [adj.] förvirrad

beyond[1] [adv.] bortom; mera

beyond[2] [prep.] bortom; efter; utom

bias [n.; ~es] benägenhet, fördom

Bible [n.] bibel

bibliography [n.; -phies] bibliografi, litteraturförteckning

bicycle [n.] cykel; **~ path** cykelbana, cykelspår; **~ racing** cykeltävling; **~ seat** sadel

bid[1] [n.] bud, försök; **no ~** [cards] pass

bid[2] [v.; bidding, bade/bid, bid] bjuda

bidirectional [adj.] dubbelriktad

big [adj.] stor; **~ brother** storebror; **~ brother attitude** storebrorsfasoner; **~ city** storstad; **Big Apple** New York City

bigger [adj.comp.: big] större; **make ~** öka

biggest [adj.superl.: big] störst

bike [n.; see: **bicycle**]

bikini [n.] bikini

bile [n.] gala; ilska

bill [n.] räkning, nota; lagförslag; affisch; sedel [currency]; **~ of sale** köpebrev

billion [num.; US billion = thousand millions] miljard

bin [n.] lår, binge; låda
binary [adj.] binär; ~ **numbers**
binära tal
bind [v.; bound, bound] binda
binding[1] [adj.] bindande
binding[2] [n.] bindning; band; **ski ~**
skidbindning
binoculars [n.pl.] kikare
biography [n.; -phies] biografi
biological [adj.] biologisk
biologist [n.] biolog
biology [n.] biologi
biotech [n.; see: **biotechnology**]
biotechnology [n.; -gies] bioteknik
birch [n.; ~es] björk
bird [n.] fågel; ~ **of passage** flyttfågel; **migratory ~** flyttfågel; ~
reserve fågelreservat; ~**'s egg**
fågelägg; ~**'s nest** fågelbo
birdcage [n.] fågelbur
birth [n.] födelse; ~ **certificate**
födelse; ~ **control** barnbegränsning; **country of ~** födelseland;
date of ~ födelsedatum; **place of**
~ födelseort; **year of ~** födelseår
birthday [n.] födelsedag; ~ **card**
gratulationskort; **happy ~** gratulerar på födelsedagen; **have one's**
~ **fylla år**
biscuit [n.] kex
bishop [n.] biskop; löpare [chess]
bishopric [n.] biskopssäte
bit[1] [n.] **a ~** lite, lite grann; tag
[time]; **a ~ of each/everything**
lite av varje; **not a ~** inte ett dugg;
quite a ~ en hel del
bit[2] [n.] bit, stycke; bit [IT]
bitch[1] [n.; ~es] hyna [animal]; häxa,
slyna [vul.]; **son of a ~** jävla knöl
[vul.]
bitch[2] [v.; colloq.; ~es, ~ed, ~ed]
krångla, klaga
bitchy [adj.] elak, spydig
bite[1] [n.] bett, stick; munsbit
bite[2] [v.; bit, bitten] bita; nappa [fish]
bitmap [n.] bitkarta [IT]
bitmapped [adj.] bitmappad [IT];
~ **font** bitkartafont, rasterfont [IT]
bitten [adj.] stucken
bitter [adj.] bitter, besk; bittande
bitterly [adv.] bittert; bittande

bizarre [adj.] bisarr
black [adj.] svart; ~ **currants** svarta
vinbär; ~ **grapes** blåa vindruvor;
~ **grouse** orre; ~ **market** svarta
börsen; ~ **pepper** svartpeppar
black [n.] svart; ~**s** de svarta
black-and-white film [n.] svartvit
film
blackberries [n.pl.] björnbär
blackboard [n.] (svart) tavla
blackmail [v.] utöva utpressning
mot
Black Sea [n.] Svarta havet
bladder [n.] blåsa, urinblåsa
blade [n.] blad
blame[1] [n.] skuld, klander; **take the**
~ **on oneself** ta på sig skulden
blame[2] [v.] klandra, lägga skulden
på; **have oneself to ~** skylla sig
själv
blank[1] [adj.] tom, blank
blank[2] [n.] lucka; **fill-in-the-blanks
test** lucktest
blanket [n.] filt, täcke
blast[1] [n.] vindstöt; explosion; stöt
blast[2] [v.] spränga; skövla
blatant [adj.] påfallande, skriande
blaze[1] [n.] låga; brand; starkt sken
blaze[2] [v.] flamma, brinna
blazer [n.] blazer
bldg. [abbrev: **building**] byggnad,
hus
bleach [n.; ~es] blekning; klormedel
bleaching [n.] blekning
bleak [adj.] kal; kylig; trist
bleed [v.; bled, bled] blöda
bleeding [n.] blödning
bless [v.; ~es, ~ed, ~ed] välsigna
blessing [n.] välsignelse
blind[1] [adj.] blind; ~ **copy (bcc)**
hemlig kopia; ~ **person** blind
person
blind[2] [v.] göra blind, blända
blinds [n.pl.] rullgardin
blink [v.] blinka
blinker [n.] blinkljus
blinking [adj.] blinkande
bliss [n.; ~es] lycksalighet, lycka
blister [n.] blåsa, skavsår
blithe [adj.] bekymmerslös; glad,
munter

blizzard [n.] snöstorm
block[1] [n.] kvarter; stockning; block; hinder; ~ **letter** tryckbokstav, stor bokstav
block[2] [v.] blockera, hindra, spärra av
blockage [n.] stopp
blog [abbrev: web log] blogg
blond [adj.] blond
blood [n.] blod; ~ **poisoning** blodförgiftning; ~ **pressure** blodtryck; ~ **sausage** blodpudding; ~ **test** blodprov; ~ **type** blodgrupp; **lose** ~ blöda
bloody [adj.] blodig
bloom [v.] blomma, slå ut i blom; blomstra
blouse [n.] blus
blow[1] [n.] slag, stöt
blow[2] [v.; blew, blown] blåsa; ~ **one's nose** snyta sig; ~ **up** spränga; förstora [photo]
blow-dry (one's hair) [v.] föna (håret)
blow-drying [n.] föning
blue[1] [adj.] blå; ~ **cheese** grönmögelost, ädelost
blue[2] [n.] blå
blueberry [n.; -ries] blåbär
blues [n.pl.] blues
bluff [v.] bluffa
blunder [n.] blunder
blurred [adj.] suddig
blush[1] [n.; ~es] rodnad; rosévin [wine]
blush[2] [v.; ~es, ~ed] rodna
blvd. [abbrev: boulevard] boulevard, esplanad
BO [abbrev: body odor] svettlukt
board [n.] bräde, bräda; tavla; kost; styrelse; ~ **of directors** styrelse; **full** ~ [all meals] helpension; **on** ~ ombord
board [v.] borda, gå ombord på, stiga på; brädfordra
boarding [n.] bordning [boat], påstigning [train, air]; ~ **assistance** påstigningshjälp; ~ **pass** boardingkort; ~ **school** internatskola
boardinghouse [n.] pensionat
boast [v.] skryta

boat [n.] båt; ~ **tour** båttur; ~ **trip** båtkryssning, båtresa
bodily [adj.] kropslig; fysisk
body [n.; -dies] kropp; lik; huvuddel; organ; samling; ~ **shop** reparationsverkstad; **part of the** ~ kroppsdel
bodyguard [n.] livvakt
bog [n.] mosse, mossmark, myr
Bohemian [adj.] böhmisk, bohemisk
boil[1] [n.] kokning, kokpunkt; böld
boil[2] [v.] koka
boiled [adj.] kokad, kokt
boiler [n.] varmvattenberedare; panna
boilerplate [n.] standardtext
bold[1] [adj.] djärv, modig; fräck
bold[2] [n.] fet text, fetstil
boldface [n.] fetstil [IT]
boletus mushroom [n.] karljohanssvamp
bolognese sauce [n.] köttsås
bolt [n.] bult, skruv; regel
bomb[1] [n.] bomb
bomb[2] [v.] bomba
bomber [n.] bombplan; bombattentatsman; **suicide** ~ självmordsbombare
bombing [n.] bombning; bombattentat
bon appetit! [phrase] smaklig måltid!
bon voyage! [phrase] trevlig resa!
bond[1] [n.] band; förbindelse, borgen; obligation; bindning
bond[2] [v.] fästa (ihop), binda; fästa sig; sitta ihop
bone[1] [n.] ben
bone[2] [v.] bena
bonus [n.; ~es] bonus
book[1] [n.] bok; telefonkatalog; libretto; **recorded** ~ ljudbok
book[2] [v.] beställa; boka; engagera
bookcase [n.] bokhylla, bokskåp
booking [n.] bokning, beställning
booklet [n.] häfte; ~ **of tickets** biljetthäfte
bookmark [n.] bokmärke
book-on-tape [n.] ljudbok
bookshelf [n.; -shelves] bokhylla
bookshop [n.] bokhandel
bookstore [n.] bokhandel

Boolean logic [n.] boolesk logik
boom[1] [n.] bom [pole]; dån [noise];
uppsving [economy]; ~ period
högkonjunktur
boom[2] [v.] dåna, dundra
boost[1] [n.] puff uppåt; lyft; ökning
boost[2] [v.] förstärka, öka; hjälpa
upp/fram; puffa för
boot[1] [n.] känga, stövel, pjäxa;
hjullås [parking punishment]
boot[2] [v.] starta [IT]
booth [n.] kiosk; hytt
border[1] [n.] gräns; kant
border[2] [v.] gränsa, dela gräns med
bore[1] [n.] tråkmåns
bore[2] [v.] borra; tråka ut; [see: bear]
bored [adj.] uttråkad, ointresserad,
less
boredom [n.] leda, tråkighet
boring [adj.] långtråkig, tråkig
born[1] [adj.] född; be ~ födas, vara
född
born/borne[2] [v.; see: bear]
borrow [v.] låna; can I ~ some
money from you? kan jag få låna
pengar av dig?
borrower [n.] låntagare
Bosnia [n.] Bosnien
Bosnian [adj.] bosnisk
Bosphorus [n.] Bosporen
boss [n.; ~es] chef, arbetsledare
botanical [adj.] botanisk; ~ garden
botanisk trädgård
botany [n.; -nies] botanik
both[1] [conj.] både; ~ Jan and Peter
både Jan och Peter
both[2] [pron.] båda, bägge
bother[1] [n.] besvär, bråk, plåga
bother[2] [v.] besvära (sig), oroa (sig);
~ about bry sig om
bottle [n.] flaska; ~ opener flasköppnare, kapsylöppnare; ~ recycling bin flaskbank; ~ top kapsyl;
~ warmer flaskvärmare
bottled [adj.]: ~ water buteljerat
vatten; ~ beer flasköl; ~ gas gasol;
locally ~ wine härtappning
bottom[1] [adj.] nedersta, understa,
sista
bottom[2] [n.] botten; bak, stjärt; ~s
up! botten upp!; from top to ~
uppifrån och ned

bough [n.] (stor) trädgren
boulder [n.] stenblock, bumling
bounce [v.] studsa; ej accepteras
[check]; ~ back återhämta sig
boundary [n.; -ries] avgränsning;
gräns
bouquet [n.] bukett
bourgeois [adj.] medelklassig,
borgerlig
bout [n.] dust, kamp; anfall, attack
bow[1] [n.] bugning, bockning; båge,
böjning; rosett; stråke; ~ tie fluga
bow[2] [v.] bocka, buga (sig); böja;
spela med stråke på
bowel [n.] tarm; ~ movement
avföring
bowl[1] [n.] djup tallrik, skål; stadium
[football]
bowl[2] [v.] spela bowling; ~ over slå
omkull; förbluffa
bowler [n.] bowlare; kubb [hat]
bowling [n.] bowling; ~ alley
bowlingbana
bow-wow [n.; dog sound] vov
box[1] [n.; ~es] ask, låda; ruta
[graphic]; box [post office]; loge
[theater]; ~ lunch matsäck; ~ office biljettkontor; bank ~ bankfack; post office ~ postbox
box[2] [v.; ~es, ~ed, ~ed] boxa
boxer [n.] boxare
boxing [n.] boxning
boy [n.] pojke, kille
boyfriend [n.] pojkvän
b.p.[1] [abbrev: boiling point] kokpunkt
BP[2] [abbrev: blood pressure;
British Petroleum] blodtryck;
British Petroleum
bps [abbrev: bits per second] bits i
sekunden
Br. [abbrev: Brother (religious
title)] Broder
bra [n.; abbrev: brassiere] behå
(bh) [abbrev: bysthållare]
bracelet [n.] armband
braces [n.pl.; dental] tandställning
bracket [n.] vinkeljärn, konsol;
grupp; curly ~ ({}) klammer;
square ~ ([]) hakparantes
braille [n.] punktskrift
brain [n.] hjärna; ~ tumor hjärntumör

brain-dead [adj.] hjärndöd
braised [adj.] bräserad
brake[1] [n.] broms; ~ fluid bromsvätska; ~ horsepower bromskrafter; ~ pads bromsbelägg
brake[2] [v.] bromsa
brakelight [n.] bromsljus
braking [n.] inbromsning
branch[1] [n.; ~es] gren, kvist; för-
grening; filial; hopp [IT]
branch[2] [v.; ~es, ~ed, ~ed] dela sig
brand[1] [n.] märke, ~ name
varumärke; ~name clothing
märkeskläder
brand[2] [v.] brännmärka
brand-new [adj.] helt ny
brandy [n.; -dies] konjak
brass [n.; ~es] mässing
brassiere (bra) [n.] bysthållare (bh)
brave [adj.] modig, tapper
Brazil [n.] Brasilien
Brazilian [adj.] brasiliansk
breach[1] [n.; ~es] brytning, brott,
överträdelse; bräsch; ~ of contract kontraktsbrott
breach[2] [v.; ~es, ~ed, ~ed] bryta,
överträda
bread [n.] bröd; ~crumbs brödsmulor, skorpsmulor; slice of ~
brödskiva
breaded [adj.] panerad
break[1] [n.] brytning, brott; paus,
rast; uppehåll; lunch ~ lunchrast
break[2] [v.; broke, broken] bryta, slå
sönder; överträda; förstöra; ~
down gå sönder; ~ in [criminal]
göra inbrott; ~ off bryta
breakdown [n.] motorstopp [car];
analys [data]; nervsammanbrott
[psychological]; have a car ~ få
motorstopp
breakfast [n.] frukost; ~ buffet
frukostbuffé; ~ cereal flingor,
frukostflingor; ~ room frukostrum;
~ table frukostbord; have ~ äta
frukost
break-in [n.] inbrott
breaking point [n.] brytpunkt
breakthrough [n.] genombrott
bream [n.] braxen [fish]
breast [n.] bröst; ~ cancer bröst-
cancer

breast-feed [v.; -fed] amma
breath [n.] andetag; anda
breathe [v.] andas
breathing [n.] andning; ~ apparatus
andningsapparat; ~ difficulties
andningssvårigheter
breed[1] [n.] ras, avel; sort, släkte
breed[2] [v.; bred, bred] föda ungar;
odla; föda upp
breeding [n.] avel, uppfostran;
häckning; ~ ground grogrund
breeze [n.] bris, fläkt
brewery [n.; -ries] bryggeri
bribe [n.] muta
bribery [n.; -ries] mutning,
bestickning
brick [n.] tegelsten
bridal couple [n.] brudpar
bride [n.] brud
bridegroom [n.] brudgum
bridge [n.] bro; brygga [ship];
bridge [card game]
bridle [n.] betsel; ~ path ridväg
brief[1] [adj.] kort, kortvarig
brief[2] [n.] sammandrag, resumé
brief[3] [v.] orientera, instruera
briefcase [n.] portfölj
briefly [adv.] kort, i sammandrag
briefs [n.pl.] trosor
brigade [n.] brigad, kår
bright [adj.] ljus; lycklig; begåvad
brighten [v.] lysa upp
brill [n.] slätvar [fish]
brilliance [n.] glans
brilliant [adj.] lysande, strålande;
genial
bring [v.; brought, brought] ta med
sig, ha med sig, hämta; ~ about
förorsaka; ~ out framhäva; ~ up
uppfostra
brink [n.] rand, kant
brisk [adj.] rask; ~ breeze friskt
vind
brisket [n.] lammbringa [lamb];
oxbringa [beef]
Brit. [abbrev: Britain, British]
Britannien, brittisk
broad [adj.] bred; ~ beans bondbönor; ~ jump längdhopp
broadband [n.] bredband; ~ connection bredbandsuppkoppling;
~ modem bredbandsmodem; ~

network bredbandsnät
broadcast[1] [n.] rundsändning
broadcast[2] [v.] basunera ut; sända ut
broaden [v.] bli bredare, vidgas
[intrans.]; göra bredare, vidga
[trans.]
broadly [adv.] i stort sett, i huvudsak
brochure [n.] broschyr
broiled [adj.] grillad, bräserad
broken [n.] sönder, trasig; bruten
broker [n.] mäklare
bronchial tubes [n.pl.] bronker
bronchitis [n.] bronkit
bronze [n.] brons; ~ age bronsåldern
brooch [n.; ~es] brosch
broom [n.] kvast, sopborste
Bros. [abbrev: Brothers] Bröderna
broth [n.] buljong
brother [n.] bror; big ~ storebror;
little ~ lillebror
brother-in-law [n.] svåger
brow [n.] panna, ögonbryn
brown[1] [adj.] brun
brown[2] [n.] brunt
browned [adj.] brynt
browse [v.] beta; bläddra [IT]
browser [n.] bläddrare, webbläsare
[IT]; ~ window webbfönster [IT]
bruise[1] [n.] blåmärke; stötmärke
bruise[2] [v.] få blåmärken [intrans.];
ge blåmärken [trans.]
brunette [n.] brunett
brush[1] [n.; ~es] borste; pensel
brush[2] [v.; ~es, ~ed, ~ed] borsta
Brussels [n.] Bryssel; ~ sprouts
brysselkål
brutal [adj.] brutal
B.S. [abbrev: Bachelor of Science;
bullshit (vul.)] kand.fil.; nonsens
BSE [abbrev: bovine spongiform
encephalopathy, mad cow disease]
galna ko-sjukan
BTU [abbrev: British Thermal Unit]
BTU [enhet för energi]
BTW [abbrev: by the way] förresten
[IT]
BU [abbrev: Boston University]
Boston University
bubble [n.] blåsa; ~ bath bubbelbad
bubbling [adj.] mousserande
Bucharest [n.] Bukarest

bucket [n.] hink
bud [n.] knopp
Buddhist [n.] buddist
buddy [n.; buddies] kompis [colloq.]
budget [n.] budget
buffer [n.] buffert [IT]
buffet [n.] byffé; cold ~ smörgåsbord
bug[1] [n.] liten insekt, lus; defekt,
fel; bacill; avlyssningsapparat;
mani
bug[2] [v.] bugga; irritera
build[1] [n.] (kropps)byggnad;
version [IT]
build[2] [v.; built, built] bygga,
anlägga
builder [n.] byggare
building [n.] byggnad; fastighet
built [adj.] byggd; uppförd
built-in [adj.] inbyggd
bulb [n.] glödlampa; lök [plant];
light ~ glödlampa; flash ~
fotoblixt
Bulgaria [n.] Bulgarien
Bulgarian[1] [adj.] bulgarisk
Bulgarian[2] (language) [n.]
bulgariska
bulk [n.] omfång; huvudpart; in ~ i
lösvikt; the ~ of merparten; ~
storage massminne [IT]
bull [n.] tjur; nonsens; ~ market
hausse
bullet [n.] kula
bulletin [n.] bulletin; rapport; ~
board anslagstavla
bullshit (BS) [n.; vul.] nonsens,
skitsnack [colloq.]
bully[1] [n.; -lies] översittare, mobbare
bully[2] [v.; -lies, -lied, -lied] mobba,
trackasera; tvinga
bullying [n.] mobbning
bump[1] [n.] knöl, bula; stöt, gupp
bump[2] [v.] stöta; köra
bumper [n.] stötfångare, kofångare
bun [n.] bulle; ~s [colloq.] stjärt
bunch [n.; ~es] bunt, klase; ~ of
flowers bukett
bundle[1] [n.] bunt, knyte, knippa,
bylte
bundle[2] [v.] bunta; stuva
bungalow [n.] enplansvilla, stuga

bungee-jumping [n.] bungy-hopp
bunk [n.] brits, sovbänk; ~ bed
våningssäng
burbot [n.] lake [fish]
burden[1] [n.] börda, last
burden[2] [v.] betunga, belasta
burdensome [adj.] betungande
bureau [n.; ~s] byrå
bureaucracy [n.; -cies] byråkrati
bureaucrat [n.] byråkrat
bureaucratic [adj.] byråkratisk
burger [n.; abbrev: hamburger]
hamburgare
burglar [n.] inbrottstjuv; ~ alarm
inbrottsalarm, stöldskydd
burglary [n.; -ries] inbrott
Burgundy wine [n.] bourgognevin
burial [n.] begravning
Burma [n.; Myanmar] Burma
Burmese[1] [adj.] burmansk
Burmese (language)[2] [n.] burmanska
burn[1] [n.] brännskada, brännsår;
ointment for ~s salva mot
brännskador
burn[2] [v.] bränna [trans.]; brinna
[intrans.]; get ~ed bränna sig
burner [n.] brännare
burning [adj.] brännande, brinnande; ~ pain sveda
burst[1] [n.] bristning; utbrott
burst[2] [v.; burst, burst] brista,
spricka; spränga
bury [v.; buries, buried] begrava
bus [n.; ~es/-sses] buss; databuss
[IT]; ~ driver busförare, busschaufför; ~ fare bussavgift; ~ lane
bussfil; ~ route busslinje, bussväg;
~ station busstation, bussterminal;
~ stop busshållplats; ~ terminal
bussterminal; ~ ticket bussbiljett
bush [n.; ~es] buske; bush
business [n.; ~es] affär, kommers,
näringsliv; ~ administration
företagsadministration, management; ~ class affärsklass; ~ con-

tact affärskontakt, affärsvän; ~
discussion affärssamtal; ~ district
affärskvarter, affärscentrum; ~
graphics affärsgrafik; ~ hours
öppettider; ~ trip affärsresa; ~
world affärsvärld; place of ~ handelplats; store is going out of ~
affären upphör; travel on ~ resa i
affärer
businessman [n.; -men] affärsman
businesswoman [n.; -men]
affärskvinna
busy [adj.] upptagen; flitig; livlig;
be ~ with hålla på med, syssla med
but[1] [conj.] men
but[2] [prep.] utan; not Jan ~ Peter
inte Jan utan Peter
butane gas [n.] butangas
butcher [n.] slaktare; ~ shop
köttaffär
butcher-delicatessen [n.] charkuteri
butter [n.] smör; ~ beans vaxbönor
butterfly [n.; -flies] fjäril
buttermilk [n.] kärnmjölk
button [n.] knapp
buttress [n.; ~es] stöttepelare
buy [v.; bought, bought] köpa
buyer [n.] köpare
buying power [n.] köpkraft
by[1] [adv.] förbi; ~ and ~ så
småningom
by[2] [prep.] vid; av; ~ all means för
all del; ~ the aisle vid gången; ~
the way förresten; a play ~
Strindberg pjäs av Strindberg
bye [interj.] hej då
BYOB [abbrev: bring your own
bottle/booze] ta med egen dryck
bypass[1] [n.; ~es] kringfartsled,
omfartsled; ~ operation by-
passoperation
bypass[2] [v.; ~es, ~ed, ~ed] gå förbi,
undvika
byte [n.] byte

C

C¹ [abbrev: Centigrade; average grade (in school); cold water] Celsius; medelbetyg; kalt vatten
c² [abbrev: copyright; century; cubic; cup (1/4 l.)] upphovsrätt; århundrade; kubik; kopp
CA [abbrev: California; Central America] Kalifornien [delstat i USA]; Centralamerika
cab [n.] taxi, droska; förarhytt
cabaret [n.] kabaré
cabbage [n.] kål; ~ **soup** kålsoppa; **stuffed ~** kåldomar
cabin [n.] hytt, stuga; ~ **deck** hyttdäck; **double ~** dubbelhytt; **single ~** enkelhytt
cabinet [n.] kabinett, skåp; ministär
cable [n.] kabel; ~ **car** linbana, kabinlift; ~ **modem** kabelmodem; ~ **railway** bergbana; ~ **TV** kabel-tv
cache memory [n.; -ries] cacheminne [IT]
cached [adj.] cachad [IT]
CAD [abbrev: computer-aided design] datorstödd konstruktion
Caesarean section [n.] kejsarsnitt
café [n.] café, fik
cafeteria [n.] cafeteria
caffeine free [adj.] koffeinfri
cage [n.] bur
Cairo [n.] Kairo
cake [n.] kaka, bakelse, tårta
Cal Tech [abbrev: California Institute of Technology] California Institute of Technology
cal. [abbrev: calorie; caliber] kalori; kaliber
calcium [n.] kalcium
calculate [v.] räkna; beräkna
calculation [n.] beräkning
calculator [n.] kalkylator, räknare
calendar [n.] kalender, almanacka
calf [n.; calves] kalv; vad [lower leg]; ~'s **liver** kalvlever
calfskin [n.] kalvskinn
California (CA) [n.] Kalifornien [delstat i USA]
call¹ [n.] anrop, rop; fordran; utrop; samtal [telephone]; **on ~** jourha-

vande; **be on ~** ha jourtjänst; **make a phone ~** ringa ett samtal; ~ **center** teletjänstcentral
call² [v.] kalla; ringa, ringa upp/efter; ropa; **be ~ed** heta, kallas; ~ **back** ringa tillbaka; ~ **for** kräva; ~ **off** avbryta; ~ **on** uppfordra, göra visit; ~ **in sick** sjukanmäla (sig)
calm¹ [adj.] lugn, stilla
calm² [n.] lugn, stillhet, ro
calm³ [v.] lugna (sig); stilla; bedarra
calmly [adv.] lugnt
calorie [n.] kalori
Cambodia [n.] Kambodja
Cambodian [adj.] kambodjansk
camcorder [n.] camcorder
camera [n.] kamera; ~ **case** kamerafodral; ~ **store** fotoaffär
Cameroon [n.] Kamerun
Cameroonian [adj.] kamerunsk
camomile tea [n.] kamomillte
camp¹ [n.] läger, förläggning; koloni; ~ **bed** tältsäng
camp² [v.] tälta, campa
campaign [n.] kampanj; ~ **slogan** valspråk
camping [n.] tältning; ~ **equipment** tältutrustning
campsite [n.] campingplats
campus [n.; ~es] universitetsområde; campus
camshaft [n.] kamaxel
can¹ [n.] burk, konservburk; ~ **opener** konservöppnare
can² [v.modal; could] kunna
can³ [v.; canning, canned, canned] lägga in, konservera
Canada [n.] Kanada
Canadian [adj.] kanadensisk
canal [n.] kanal
cancel [v.] avbryta, annullera; avbeställa, avboka
canceled [adj.] annullerad, inställd
cancer¹ [n.] cancer
Cancer² [n.] Kräftan [zodiac]; **Tropic of ~** Kräftans vändkrets
candidate [n.] kandidat
candied fruit [n.] kanderad frukt
candle [n.] ljus, stearinljus

candlestick [n.] ljusstake
candy [n.; -dies] godis, karameller
cane [n.] käpp; ~ sugar rörsocker
canine [adj.] hund
canned [adj.] konserverad; ~ beer
burköl; ~ food konserv
cannot [v.; see: can (modal)] kan
inte
canoe [n.] kanot; ~ paddling
kanotpaddling
canoeing [n.] kanotsport
can't [contr: cannot] kan inte
canteen [n.] lunchrum, servering;
fältflaska
cap¹ [n.] mössa; bottle ~ kapsyl
cap² [v.; capping, capped, capped]
sätta tak för
capability [n.; -ties] förmåga,
möjlighet
capable [adj.] duglig, skicklig,
begåvad; be ~ of kunna, duga till
capacity [n.; -ties] plats, kapacitet;
egenskap; rymd; förmåga
cape [n.] udde; cape
capers [n.pl.] kapris
Capetown [n.] Kapstaden
capital¹ [adj.] stor; belagd med
dödsstraff; utmärkt; ~ city huvudstad; ~ letters stora bokstäver,
versaler; ~ punishment dödsstraff
capital² [n.] kapital; huvudstad
capitalism [n.] kapitalism
capitalist¹ [adj.] kapitalistisk
capitalist² [n.] kapitalist
Capricorn [n.] Stenbocken [zodiac];
Tropic of ~ Stenbockens vändkrets
capsule [n.] kapsel
Capt. [abbrev: Captain] kapten
captain [n.] kapten; kommendör
captive [adj.] fången, fängslad
capture¹ [n.] tillfångatagande,
erövring; fångst
capture² [v.] ta till fånga, fånga
car [n.] bil; vagn [train]; ~ alarm
billarm; ~ deck bildäck; ~ door
bildörr; ~ inspection bilbesiktning; ~ insurance bilförsäkring;
~ key bilnyckel; ~ mechanic
bilmekaniker; ~ number vagnsnummer [train]; ~ radio bilradio;
~ registration documents reg-

istreringsbevis, registreringspapper; ~ rental biluthyrning; ~ repair bilreparation; ~ window
bilruta; by ~ med bil
carafe [n.] karaff [about 2 glassfuls]
caramel [n.] kola; ~ sauce kolasås
carat [n.] karat
caravan [n.] karavan; husvagn
caraway [n.] kummin
carbon [n.] kol; ~ copy (cc) kopia;
~ dioxide koldioxid
carbonated [adj.] med kolsyra;
kolsyrad
carburetor [n.] förgasare
card [n.] kort; ~ catalog kortregis-
ter, kartotek; ~ game kortspel; ~
reader kortläsare
cardboard [n.] papp, kartong; ~
box kartong
cardiac [adj.] hjärt-; ~ arrest hjärt-
stillestand
cardinal [adj.] huvudsaklig, väsentlig
care¹ [n.] vård; omsorg; bekymmer;
take ~ of ta hand om, vara rädd
om; take ~! sköt om dig!, ha de
bra!
care² [v.] bry sig om; ~ about bry
sig om; ~ for vara intresserad av,
ha lust med, sköta om; ~ to ha lust
att; I don't ~ det gör mig detsamma; I couldn't ~ less det
struntar jag i; who ~s? vad spelar
det för roll?
career [n.] bana; karriär; ~ counseling yrkesrådgivning; ~ woman
yrkeskvinna
careful [adj.] försiktig, aktsam;
omsorgsfull, noggrann; be ~ vara
noga med, vara rädd om; be ~!
akta dig!, se upp!
carefully [adv.] noggrant
caregiver [n.] anhörigvårdare
careless [adj.] slarvig, oaktsam;
likgiltig; sorglös
cargo [n.; ~es/~s] last
caricature [n.] karikatyr, parodi
carousel [n.] karusell
carp [n.] karp
carpal tunnel syndrome [n.]
karpaltunnelsyndrom
carpenter [n.] snickare

carpentry [n.] snickeri; träslöjd

carpet [n.] matta

carpool [v.] samåka

carriage [n.] vagn

carrier bag [n.] bärkasse

carrot [n.] morot

carry [v.; -rries, -rried, -rried] bära; ~ **out** genomföra, verkställa

carry-all bag [n.] rymlig bag

carry-on baggage [n.] handbagage

cart [n.] kärra

carton [n.] kartong; limpa [of cigarettes]

cartoon [n.] karikatyr; ~ **film** tecknad film

carve [v.] skära

carving [n.] snideri

case [n.] fall; låda; kast, skiftläge [type]; **in any** ~ i varje fall; **in most** ~s oftast; **in that** ~ i så fall; **lower-~ letters** gemener; **upper-~ letters** versaler

cash¹ [n.] kontanter, reda pengar; ~ **card** kontantkort; ~ **flow** kassaflöde; ~ **machine** uttagsautomat, bankomat; ~ **on delivery (COD)** mot postförskott, mot efterkrav; **in** ~ kontant; **pay** ~ köpa kontant

cash² [v.; ~es, ~ed, ~ed] lösa, lösa in

cashier [n.] kassör, kassörska [female]; ~**'s desk** kassa

casino [n.] kasino

cask [n.] fat, tunna

casserole [n.] gryta; låda

cassette [n.] kassett; ~ **player** kassettbandspelare

cast¹ [n.] kast; ensemble, de medverkande; avgjutning

cast² [v.; cast] kasta

castle [n.] slott; torn [chess]

casual [adj.] nonchalant, ogenerad; ~ **dress** ledig klädsel

casualty [n.; -ties] offer; **casualties** förluster, förolyckade

cat¹ [n.] katt; ~ **food** kattmat; ~ **litter** kattsand

CAT² [abbrev: computerized axial tomography] datortomografi

CAT scan [n.] datortomografi

catacombs [n.pl.] katakomber

catalogue [n.] katalog, förteckning; mapp

catastrophe [n.] katastrof

catch¹ [n.; ~es] fångst; fälla, hake; lås

catch² [v.; ~es, caught, caught] fånga

category [n.; -ries] kategori

cater [v.] levera mat till; ordna för

catering [n.] servering av mat

caterpillar [n.] larv; ~ **tractor** bandtraktor

cathedral [n.] domkyrka, katedral

Catholic¹ [adj.] katolsk

Catholic² [n.] katolik

cattle [n.pl.] boskap, nötkreatur

caught [v.; see: **catch**]

cauliflower [n.] blomkål

causal [adj.] orsaks-; kausal

cause¹ [n.] orsak, grund

cause² [v.] förorsaka, föranleda

caution [n.] försiktighet; varning

cautious [adj.] försiktig, varsam

cave [n.] håla, grotta

cavity [n.; -ties] hål; håla

cayenne pepper [n.] cayennepeppar

CB [abbrev: Citizens Band] privat radio

CBS [abbrev: Columbia Broadcasting System] CBS [tv-bolag i USA]

CBW [abbrev: chemical and biological warfare] kemisk och biologisk krigföring

cc. [abbrev: carbon copy; cubic centimeters] kopia; kubikcentimeter

CCTV [abbrev: closed-circuit television] övervakningskamera, intern television

CD [abbrev: compact disc] cd-skiva; ~ **burner** cd-brännare; ~ **drive** cd-enhet; ~ **player** cd-spelare; ~ **reader** cd-läsare; ~ **recorder** cd-bränare; ~ **writer** cd-bränare

CD-R¹ [abbrev: compact disc-recordable] cd-r [skrivbar cd]

Cdr.² [abbrev: Commander] kommendör, kommendörkapten

CD-ROM [abbrev: compact disc read-only memory] cd-rom; ~ **disc** cd-romskiva; ~ **drive** cd-romläsare; ~ **reader** cd-romläsare, cd-romspelare

CD-RW [abbrev: compact disc-rewritable] CD-RW [skrivbar cd som kan raderas och återanvändas]

CDT [abbrev: Central Daylight Time] somartid inom centraltidzonen i USA
cease [v.] upphöra, sluta
ceasefire [n.] vapenvila
ceasing [n.] uppehåll; **without** ~ utan uppehåll
ceiling [n.] tak; ~ **light** taklampa
celebrate [v.] fira
celebrated [adj.] berömd
celebration [n.] firande; högtid
celebrity [n.; -ties] berömdhet; kändis
celeriac [n.] rotselleri
celery [n.; -ries] selleri; ~ **root** rotselleri
cell [n.] cell; element; ~ **phone** mobiltelefon
cellar [n.] källare
Celtic [adj.] keltisk
cement [n.] cement; bindemedel
cemetery [n.; -ries] begravningsplats, kyrkogård
censorship [n.] censur
census [n.; ~es] folkräkning
cent.[1] [abbrev: century] årshundrade
cent[2] [n.] cent [1/100 dollar]
center[1] [n.] centrum, center; mittpunkt, medelpunkt
center[2] [v.] ställa i mittpunkten, koncentrera; ha sin medelpunkt
centered [adj.] centrerad [IT]
Centigrade [n.] Celsius [temperature]
centimeter [n.; 0.4 in.] centimeter
central [adj.] central, mellersta; ~ **heating** centralvärme
Central America [n.] Mellanamerika
Central Europe [n.] Mellaneuropa
centrifuge [n.] centrifug
century [n.; -ries] sekel, århundrade; **19th** ~ 1800-talet; **turn of the** ~ sekelskifte
CEO [abbrev: chief executive officer] verkställande direktör
ceramics [n.sg. & pl.] keramik
cereal [n.] sädesslag; flingor; **hot** ~ gröt
ceremony [n.; -nies] ceremoni, akt; ceremoniel

cert. [abbrev: certified (mail)] (brev) med begäran om mottagningsbevis
certain [adj.] säker; viss
certainly [adv.] visst, säkert
certainty [n.; -ties] visshet, säkerhet
certificate [n.] intyg, attest, certifikat; betyg, diplom; ~ **of authenticity** äkthetsbevis; ~ **of completion** slutbetyg
certified [adj.] legitimerad, vidimerad
certify [v.; -fies, -fied] attestera, intyga; auktorisera
Cesarean section [n.] kejsarsnitt
ceteris paribus [Latin phrase: all things being equal] allt annat lika
cf. [abbrev: compare] jämför
CFC [abbrev: chlorofluorocarbon] klorfluorkol
cfi [abbrev: see: cif]
CFO [abbrev: chief financial officer] finansdirektör, finanschef
Chad [n.] Tchad
chain [n.] kedja, kätting; ~ **guard** kedjeskärm; ~ **letter** kedjebrev; **snow** ~**s** snökedjor
chair[1] [n.] stol; ordförandestol; professur; ~ **lift** stollift
chair[2] [v.] vara ordförande
chairman [n.; -men] ordförande; ~ **of the board** styrelseordförande
chalk [n.] krita
challenge[1] [n.] utmaning; protest
challenge[2] [v.] utmana; bestrida
chamber [n.] konferensrum; kammare; ~ **music** kammarmusik; ~ **music concert** kammarkonsert
champagne [n.] champagne
champion[1] [n.] mästare; förkämpe
champion[2] [v.] kämpa för
championship [n.] mästerskap
chance[1] [adj.] tillfällig
chance[2] [n.] tilfällighet, slump; chans; **take a** ~ chansa
chancellor [n.] kansler
change[1] [n.] (för)ändring; ombyte; växel, småpengar; ~ **of address** adresförändring; ~ **of life** klimakterium; **exact** ~ jämna pengar; **give** ~ ge växel; **keep the** ~! det är jämna pengar!, behåll växeln!

change² [v.] byta; (för)ändra; växla; ~ **a reservation** boka om; ~ **at** [transfer] byta vid; ~ **baby diapers** byta på babyn; ~ **clothes** byta om kläder, klä om sig; ~ **lanes** byta körfält; ~ **one's mind** ångra sig

changeable [adj.] föränderlig, omväxlande

changing [n.]: ~ **of the guard** vaktombyte; ~ **room** omklädningsrum, skötrum [for babies]; ~ **table** skötbord

channel [n.] kanal; segelled

chanterelle mushrooms [n.pl.] kantareller

chaos [n.] kaos

chaotic [adj.] kaotisk

chapel [n.] kapell

chaperone [n.] övervakande vuxen

chaplain [n.] kaplan

chapter [n.] kapitel

char [n.] röding [fish]

character [n.] karaktär, natur; personlighet; figur; tecken

characteristic¹ [adj.] karakteristisk

characteristic² [n.] kännemärke

characterize [v.] karakterisera, beteckna

charcoal [n.] träkol, grillkol

charcoal-grilled [adj.] kolgrillad

charge¹ [n.] pris, avgift; anklagelse; uppsikt; anfall; laddning; **be in** ~ leda; **no** ~ gratis, fri; ~ **per kilometer** kilometerpris; **take** ~ **of** ta hand om

charge² [v.] ta betalt; debitera; anklaga; ladda [battery]; storma fram; ~ **card** betalkort

charitable [adj.] medmänsklig, välgörande

charity [n.; -ties] välgörenhetsorganisation; välgörenhet, barmhärtighet

Charles [n.] Karl

charm [n.] charm; berlock; trollformel

charming [adj.] förtjusande, bedårande

chart¹ [n.] tabell, diagram; sjökort

chart² [v.] kartlägga; visa med en tabell

charter [n.] charter; stadga; ~ **flight** charterresa

chase¹ [n.] jakt; förföljande

chase² [v.] jaga; springa efter

chat¹ [n.] prat, småprat; pratstund

chat² [v.; -tted] prata, chatta

cheap [adj.] billig

cheaper [adj.comp.] billigare

cheat [v.] lura; fuska; bedra

check¹ [n.] kontroll; check; nota, räkning; ~ **box** kryssruta; ~ **sum** kontrollsumma

check² [v.] kontrollera, kolla; ~ **in** checka in; ~ **off** markera; ~ **out** checka ut

checkbook [n.] checkhäfte

checkered [adj.] rutad

checkers [n.sg.] damspel

check-in (desk) [n.; airport] incheckning

checking account [n.] checkkonto

checkmark [n.] bock

checkmate [n.] schackmatt

checkout counter [n.] kassa; utcheckning

checkroom [n.] garderob

cheek [n.] kind; fräckhet

cheer¹ [n.] bifallsrop; **be of good** ~ vara vid gott mod

cheer² [v.] muntra upp

cheerful [adj.] glad, munter

cheers! [phrase] skål!

cheese [n.] ost; ~ **cake** ostkaka; ~ **sandwich** ostsmörgås; **blue** ~ grönmögelost, ädelost; **soft** ~ mjukost

chef [n.] köksmästare

chemical¹ [adj.] kemisk

chemical² [n.] kemikalie

chemistry [n.; -ries] kemi; personkemi

Chernobyl [n.] Tjernobyl

cherry [n.; -ries] körsbär

chervil [n.] körvel

chess [n.] schack; ~ **set** schackspel

chest [n.] bröst, bringa; kista, låda; ~ **of drawers** byrå

chestnut [n.] kastanj

chew [v.] tugga; bita på

chewable [adj.; tablets] kan tuggas

chewing gum [n.] tuggummi

chicken[1] [adj.] feg, skraj
chicken[2] [n.] kyckling, höns; fegis;
~ **leg** kycklinglår; ~ **salad** kyck-
lingsallad; ~ **soup** kycklingsoppa;
cream of ~ **soup** redd kycklingsoppa; ~ **pox** vattenkoppar
chickpeas [n.pl.] kikärtor
chief[1] [adj.] huvud-, över-
chief[2] [n.] chef, ledare; ~ **executive**
verkställande direktör
chiefly [adv.] framför allt, huvudsakligen
child [n.; children] barn; ~ **abuse**
övergrepp mot barn; ~ **care**
barnomsorg; ~'s **seat** bilbarnstol
[car], barnsits [bicycle], barnstol
[high chair]; ~'s **bed** barnsäng; ~'s
ticket barnbiljett
childbirth [n.] barnsäng, förlossning
child-friendly [adj.] barnvänlig
childhood [n.] barndom; ~ **illness**
barnsjukdom
childish [adj.] barnslig
childproof cap [n.; on jars] barn-
säkert lock
children [n.pl.; see: child] barn;
not for ~ barnförbjuden; **suitable**
for ~ barnvänlig, barntillåten
children's [adj.] barn-; ~ **book**
barnbok; ~ **clinic** barnavårdscentral (BVC); ~ **clothing** barnkläder;
~ **discount** barnrabatt; ~ **food**
barnmat; ~ **lift** barnlift; ~ **menu**
barnmeny; ~ **party** barnkalas; ~
pool barnbassäng; ~ **portion** barnportion; ~ **program** barnprogram
Chile [n.] Chile
Chilean [adj.] chilensk
chili pepper [n.] chilipeppar
chill[1] [n.] kyla; **catch a** ~ förkyla
sig
chill[2] [v.] kyla; **be** ~**ed** frysa
chilled [adj.] kyld, kall
chilly [adj.] kylig
chime [v.] ringa; slå
chimney [n.; ~s] skorsten
chin [n.] haka
China [n.] Kina
Chinese[1] [adj.] kinesisk; ~ **check-**
ers kinaschack; ~ **restaurant**
kinarestaurang

Chinese[2] (**language**) [n.] kinesiska
chip[1] [n.] skiva; flisa; chips;
spelmark
chip[2] [v.; -pped] flisa, slå av
chiropractor [n.] kiropraktiker
chive [n.] gräslök
chlorine [n.] klor
chocolate [n.] choklad; ~ **bar** chokladkaka; ~ **cake** chokladkaka; ~
ice cream chokladglass; ~ **roll**
rulltårta; ~ **sauce** chokladsås; **box**
of ~**s** chokladask
choice [n.] val, alternativ
choir [n.] kor; kör
choke[1] [n.] choke
choke[2] [v.] kväva(s), strypa
cholera [n.] kolera
cholesterol [n.] kolesterol
choose [v.; chose, chosen] välja;
vilja
chop[1] [n.] kotlett; hugg
chop[2] [v.; -pped] hugga
chopped [adj.] hackad
chord [n.] ackord; korda; sträng
chore [n.] arbete, syssla; ~**s**
småsysslor
choreographer [n.] koreograf
chorus [n.;~es] refräng; kor; kör
chosen [adj.] utvald
Christ [n.] Kristus
christen [v.] döpa
Christian [adj./n.] kristen
Christianity [n.] kristendom
Christmas [n.; ~es] jul; ~ **buffet**
julbord; ~ **Day** Juldagen; ~ **deco-**
rations juldekorationer; ~ **Eve** Julafton; ~ **present** julklapp; ~ **tree**
julgran; ~ **vacation** jullov; **Merry**
~ God Jul
chromosome [n.] kromosom
chronic [adj.] kronisk
church [n.; ~es] kyrka; ~ **service**
gudstjänst; ~ **tower** kyrktorn; ~
wedding kyrklig vigsel
church-affiliated school [n.] skola
anknuten till kyrkan
churchyard [n.] kyrkogård
CIA [abbrev: Central Intelligence
Agency] federala underrättelsetjän-
sten i USA

cif [abbrev: cost, insurance and
freight] frakt och försäkring
cigar [n.] cigarr
cigarette [n.] cigarett; ~ butt fimp,
cigarettfimp; ~ lighter cigarettändare
C in C [abbrev: Commander in
Chief] högsta befälhavare
cinema [n.] bio, biograf [lokal];
filmindustrin
cinnamon [n.] kanel; ~ roll
kanelbulle
circle¹ [n.] cirkel, ring; krets; traffic ~ rondell; ~ of friends vänkrets
circle² [v.] gå omkring/runt; kretsa
circuit [n.] kretsgång, rond;
strömkrets; short ~ kortslutning
circular¹ [adj.] cirkelrund;
roterande
circular² [n.] cirkulär
circulate [v.] sprida; cirkulera
circulation [n.] omlopp, cirkulation;
spridning
circulatory disorder [n.] cirkulationsrubbning
circumstance [n.] omständighet;
~s förhållanden, omständigheter
circus [n.; ~es] cirkus
CIS [abbrev: Commonwealth of
Independent States] Oberoende
staters samvälde (OSS)
cit. [abbrev: citation, cited; citizen]
citat, citering; medborgare
citadel [n.] citadell, fästning
cite [v.] citera
citizen [n.] medborgare
citizenship [n.] medborgarskap;
medborgaranda
city [n.; -ties] stad; ~ bus stadsbuss;
~ center stadscentrum, city; ~
commissioner borgarråd; ~ desk
lokalredaktion; ~ hall rådhus; ~
park stadspark; ~ wall stadsmur
civic [adj.] medborgerlig
civics [n.sg.] samhällslära; samhällsorienterande ämnen
civil [adj.] hövlig; medborgerlig;
borgerlig; civil; ~ aviation civil-
flyg; ~ disobedience civilmot-
stånd; ~ engineer väg- och
vattenbyggnadsingenjör; ~ mar-

riage borgerlig vigsel; ~ registration folkbokföring; ~ rights
movement medborgarrättsrörelse;
~ servant statsanställd, statstjänsteman; ~ union registrerat partnerskap; have a ~ wedding
ceremony gifta sig borgerligt
civilian¹ [adj.] civil
civilian² [n.] civil(ist)
civilization [n.] civilisation
claim¹ [n.] fordran, krav
claim² [v.] påstå; göra anspråk på;
fordra, kräva
clam [n.] mussla
clap [v.; -pping, -pped, -pped] ap-
pládera; klappa; stoppa, sätta
clarify [v.; -fies, -fied] klargöra,
göra klar
clarity [n.; -ties] klarhet, skärpa
clash [n.; ~es] sammanstötning,
konflikt
clasp [v.] knäppa fast; omfamna,
hålla fast
class [n.; ~es] klass; lästimme, lektion; kurs; årgång, årskurs; ~
struggle klasskamp
classic¹ [adj.] klassisk
classic² [n.] klassiker
classical [adj.] klassisk; ~ antiquity antiken; ~ music klassisk
musik
classicism [n.] klassicismen
classics [n.pl.] klassiska språk och
litteratur; ~ scholar klassiker
classification [n.] klassifikation
classify [v.; -fies, -fied, -fied] klassificera, systematisera
classmate [n.] klasskamrat
classroom [n.] klassrum
clause [n.] sats; klausul
clay [n.] lera; ~ court grusbana
[tennis]
clean¹ [adj.] ren; anständig
clean² [v.] rengöra, putsa, städa;
rensa [fish]
cleaner [n.] lokalvårdare; tvättmedel;
~s kemtvätt; vacuum ~ dammsugare
cleaning [n.] städning; ~ agent
rengöringsmedel; ~ company
städfirma; ~ person städare; ~

solution rengöringsvätska; ~
woman städerska
clear¹ [adj.] klar, tydlig; ljus; ren
clear² [v.] göra klar, klara; frita;
befria; tömma; godkänna; ~ **the**
table duka av bordet; ~ **up**
[weather] klarna upp
clearance [n.] godkännande; saner-
ing; fri höjd; ~ **sale** utförsäljning
clearing [n.] röjning; glänta;
hygge; ~ **house** clearingcentral
clearly [adv.] klart, tydligen, säkert,
uppenbarligen
clench [v.; ~es, ~ed, ~ed] gripa hårt
om, knyta
clergy [n.pl.] präster(skap)
clergyman [n.; -men] präst
clerical [adj.] kontors-; prästerlig
clerk [n.] kontorist [office]; expedit
[store]
clever [adj.] duktig, begåvad,
klyftig; fiffig
click¹ [n.] klickande ljud; klick,
klickning
click² [v.] klicka till; tända till;
klicka; ~ **on** klicka på
client [n.] kund; klient; ~ **program**
klientprogram; **client/server**
klient-server
cliff [n.] klippa
climate [n.] klimat
climax [n.; ~es] klimax, höjdpunkt;
orgasm
climb¹ [n.] klättring, stigning
climb² [v.] klättra, kliva; bestiga;
stiga
climber [n.] klättrare, bestigare;
streber
climbing [n.] klättring; ~ **plant**
klätterväxt; ~ **region** klätterområde
cling [v.; clung, clung] klibba (sig)
fast, klänga (sig) fast; hålla fast
clinic [n.] klinik, vårdcentral
clinical [adj.] klinisk; objektiv
clip¹ [n.] klämma
clip² [v.; -pping, -pped, -pped]
klippa, klämma
cloakroom [n.] garderob
clock [n.] klocka, ur
clockwise [adv.] medurs

clogs [n.pl.] träskor
cloister [n.] klostergång, pelargång
clone¹ [n.] klon; kopia
clone² [v.] klona; göra en exakt
kopia
cloning [n.] kloning
close¹ [adj.] nära, intim; tät; slät
close² [adv.] nära, strax, tätt; ~ **to**
shops nära affär
close³ [v.] stänga; avsluta; stängas,
sluta
closed [adj.] stängd; ~ **down** nedlagd; ~ **for renovations/repairs**
stängd för reparation; ~ **for**
vacation semesterstängd; ~ **off**
avstängd; ~ **to traffic** stängd för
trafik
closed-circuit television (CCTV)
[n.] intern television
closely [adv.] nära; tätt; ingående
closing [n.] stängning; slut; ~ **tag**
sluttagg [IT]; ~ **time** stängningsdags
closure [n.] stängning; avstängning;
avslutning
clot [n.] klimp, klump; propp [blood]
cloth [n.] tyg; trasa; duk
clothe [v.] klä; täcka
clothes [n.pl.] kläder, klädsel; ~
bag kappsäk; ~ **closet** garderob; ~
hanger galge, klädhängare; ~ **line**
klädstreck
clothespin [n.] klädnypa, tvättklämma
clothing [n.] klädsel; ~ **size** konfektionsstorlek; ~ **store** klädaffär;
piece of ~ plagg
cloud [n.] moln, sky; svärm
cloudberry [n.; -ries] hjortron; ~
jam hjortronsylt
cloudburst [n.] skyfall
cloudy [adj.] molnig, mulen; oklar
clove [n.] kryddnejlika
clover [n.] klöver
clown [n.] clown
club [n.] klubb; klubba [stick];
klöver [cards]; ~ **member** klubb-
ansluten, klubbmedlem
clubhouse [n.] klubbhus
clue [n.] ledtråd, spår; nyckel(ord)
clumsy [adj.] klumpig

cluster¹ [n.] klase, klunga, samling
cluster² [v.] samlas i klungor
clutch¹ [n.; ~es] koppling; ~ pedal kopplingspedal
clutch² [v.; ~es, ~ed, ~ed] gripa, hålla fast
Cmdr. [abbrev: Commander] kommendör, kommendörkapten
CND [abbrev: Campaign for Nuclear Disarmament] kampanjen för kärnvapennedrustning
CNN [abbrev: Cable News Network] CNN (nyhetsorganisation i USA)
c/o¹ [abbrev: care of] c/o, adress
CO² [abbrev: Commanding Officer; Colorado; conscientious objector] befälhavare; Colorado [delstat i USA]; vapenvägrare
Co.³ [abbrev: company] bolag, företag
coach¹ [n.; ~es] tränare, handledare; (turist)buss; vagn; andraklass
coach² [v.; ~es, ~ed, ~ed] träna; preparera
coal [n.] kol; glöd
coalition [n.] koalition, block
coarse [adj.] grov
coarse-grained [adj.] grovkornig
coast [n.] kust; ~ guard sjöräddningen, kustbevakningen
coastal [adj.] kust-
coastline [n.] kustlinje
coat [n.] rock [man's]; kappa [woman's]
cobbler [n.] skomakare
cocaine [n.] kokain
cock [n.] tupp [rooster]; kuk [vul.]
cockles [n.] hjärtmusslor
cockroach [n.; ~es] kackerlacka
cocoa [n.] choklad
coconut [n.] kokosnöt
COD¹ [abbrev: cash on delivery] mot efterkrav, mot postförskott
cod² [n.] torsk; ~ roe torskrom
code¹ [n.] kod; kodex, lagsammling; area ~ riktnummer
code² [v.] koda; kryptera
coed [n.] studentska
coffee [n.] kaffe; ~ break kafferast; ~ cup kaffekopp; ~ filter melittafilter; ~ machine kaffeapparat,

kaffebryggare; ~ pot kaffepanna; ~ set kaffeservis; ~ shop konditori; ~ table soffbord; ~ thermos kaffetermos; have a ~ fika
coffin [n.] likkista
cognac [n.] konjak
cognitive [adj.] kognitiv
cohabit [v.] sammanbo
cohabiting partner [n.] sambo
coherent [adj.] sammanhängande
coil [n.] rulle; slinga; spiral
coin¹ [n.] mynt; ~s småpengar
coin² [v.] mynta; prägla
coincide [v.] sammanfalla; stämma överens
coincidence [n.] sammanträffande, slump
coincidentally [adv.] tillfälligtvis
Col.¹ [abbrev: Colonel] överste
col.² [abbrev: column] kolumn
cold¹ [adj.] kall; oberörd; ~ boot kallstart [IT]; ~ buffet kallskänk; ~ cuts kallskuret; ~ water kallvatten; be/feel ~ frysa; grow ~ kallna
cold² [n.] kyla; förkylning, snuva; have caught a ~ vara förkyld
coleslaw [n.] vitkålsallad
colic [n.] kolik
collaborate [v.] samarbeta; kollaborera
collaboration [n.] samverkan
collapse¹ [n.] sammanbrott; hopfallande
collapse² [v.] falla ihop, störta in; klappa ihop
collar [n.] krage; halsband; ~ size kragmått
colleague [n.] arbetskamrat, kollega
collect [v.] samla, samla på; hämta
collect call [n.] samtal som mottagaren betalar, ba-samtal
collection [n.] samling, tömning; avhämtning
collective [adj.] kollektiv, gemensam; ~ bargaining kollektivförhandlingar
collectively [adv.] kollektivt
collector [n.] samlare
college [n.] högskola; skola; ~ admission exam intagningsexamen till högskolan; ~ graduate

akademiker, person med akademisk
examen; ~ **years** studieår
collide [v.] kollidera, stöta ihop
collision [n.] krock, kollision;
  multiple ~ seriekrock
collusion [n.] maskopi, hemlig
  överenskommelse
Colorado (CO) [n.] Colorado
  [delstat i USA]
Cologne [n.] Köln
colon [n.] kolon
colonel [n.] överste
colonial [adj.] kolonial
colony [n.; -nies] koloni
color[1] [n.] färg; ~ **film** färgfilm; ~
  rinse färgsköljning; ~ **scheme**
  färgschema; ~ **television** färg-tv
color[2] [v.] färga
colored [adj.] färgad; ~ **pencil** färgpenna; **brightly** ~ färgglad
colorfast [adj.] färghållbar
colorful [adj.] färgglad
coloring book [n.] målarbok
column [n.] pelare, kolumn; ~
  header kolumnhuvud
com [abbrev: commercial
  organization (Internet address)]
  bolag, företag
comb[1] [n.] kam
comb[2] [v.] kamma
combat[1] [n.] kamp, strid
combat[2] [v.; -batting, -batted, -batted]
  bekämpa, strida mot
combination [n.] sammanställning;
  förening; förbindelse; kombination
combine [v.] förena, kombinera
combined [adj.] förenad, kombinerad
come [v.; came, come] komma; ~
  again återkomma; ~ **back** komma
  tillbaka, återvända, återkomma; ~
  inside stiga in; ~ **out** utgå; ~ **upon**
  hitta på
comeback [n.] återkomst, comeback
comedy [n.; -dies] komedi, lustspel
comfort[1] [n.] komfort; bekvämlighet; tröst
comfort[2] [v.] trösta
comfortable [adj.] bekväm;
  tillräcklig
comfortably [adv.] bekvämt; lätt
comic[1] [adj.] komisk, rolig; ~ **book**
  serietidning

comic[2] [n.] komiker; ~**s** serie(teckning)
coming[1] [adj.] kommande; lovande
coming[2] [n.] ankomst
comma [n.] komma
command[1] [n.] befallning; befäl;
  uppmaning; kommando; ~
  prompt kommandoprompt [IT]
command[2] [v.] befalla; föra;
  behärska; tjäna
commander [n.] befälhavare
commemorate [v.] fira minnet av
commence [v.] börja
comment[1] [n.] anmärkning,
  kommentar
comment[2] [v.] kommentera
commentary [n.] kommentar
commentator [n.] kommentator
commerce [n.] inrikeshandel,
  handel
commercial[1] [adj.] kommersiell,
  handels-; reklam-; ~ **at (@)**
  snabel-a (@); ~ **television** reklam-tv
commercial[2] [n.] reklam
commission[1] [n.] kommission;
  uppdrag; tjänst; expeditionsavgift;
  fullmakt; **out of** ~ ur tjänst
commission[2] [v.] beställa; ~**ed by**
  på uppdrag av
commissioner [n.] ombud; kom-
  missionsmedlem; chef
commit [v.; -tting, -tted, -tted]
  begå; binda, förplikta
commitment [n.] förpliktelse
committed [adj.] engagerad; **be** ~
  engagera sig
committee [n.] utskott, kommitté
commodity [n.; -ties] (handels)vara,
  artikel
common [adj.] vanlig; gemensam;
  allmän; ~ **law spouse** sambo; ~
  sense sunt förnuft; **in** ~ **with**
  gemensamt med
**Common Agricultural Policy
  (CAP)** [n.] Gemensamma jord-
  brukspolitiken (GJP)
**Common Foreign and Security
  Policy (CFSP)** [n.] Gemensamma
  utrikes- och säkerhetspolitiken
  (GUSP)
commonly [adv.] vanligtvis
commonwealth [n.] samvälde

communal [adj.] gemensam, kollektiv; kommunal

communicable [adj.] smittsam

communicate [v.] meddela; stå i förbindelse med, kommunicera med

communication [n.] kommunikation(er); meddelande; **means of ~** kommunikationsmedel

communicative [adj.] kommunikativ

Communism [n.] kommunism

Communist[1] [adj.] kommunistisk

Communist[2] [n.] kommunist

community [n.; -ties] samhälle; **~ center** kulturhus; **~ college** folkshögskola; **~ service** voluntärverksamhet

commute [v.] pendla, omvändla

commuter [n.] pendlare; **~ train** pendeltåg

compact[1] [adj.] kompakt; **~ car** kompaktbil; **~ disc (CD)** cd-skiva

compact[2] [n.] pakt; puderdosa

companion [n.] kamrat, sällskap

companionship [n.] kamratskap, sällskap

company [n.; -nies] bolag, firma, företag; sällskap; **keep someone ~** göra/hålla ngn sällskap

comparable [adj.] jämförlig, jämförbar

comparative [adj.] komparativ; relativ

comparatively [adv.] jämförelsevis

compare [v.] jämföra

comparison [n.] jämförelse

compartment [n.] avdelning; kupé [train]

compass [n.; ~es] kompass

compatible [adj.] förenlig; kompatibel

compel [v.; -lling, -lled, -lled] tvinga

compensate [v.] kompensera, ersätta

compensation [n.] kompensation, ersättning

compete [v.] tävla, konkurrera

competence [n.] kompetens, skicklighet

competent [adj.] kompetent, skicklig; tillräcklig

competing [adj.] konkurrerande

competition [n.] tävling; konkurrens; **unfair ~** illojal konkurrens

competitive [adj.] konkurrenskraftig; tävlingsbetonad

competitor [n.] medtävlare; rival, konkurrent

compile [v.] ställa samman; kompilera [IT]

compiler [n.] kompilator [IT]

complain [v.] beklaga sig; klaga; **~ about** klaga på

complaint [n.] klagomål

complement[1] [n.] komplement; betämning [gram]

complement[2] [v.] komplettera

complementary [adj.] kompletterande

complete[1] [adj.] fullständig; färdig

complete[2] [v.] avsluta, fullgöra; komplettera; fyla i

completed [adj.] avslutad, färdig; ifylld

completely [adv.] alldeles, fullt

completion [n.] avslutning; komplettering; ifyllande

complex[1] [adj.] komplicerad; sammansatt

complex[2] [n.; ~es] komplex

complexion [n.] hy, hudfärg; utseende

complexity [n.; -ties] komplexitet

compliance [n.] tillmötesgående; eftergivenhet

complicate [v.] komplicera

complicated [adj.] komplicerad, krånglig

complication [n.] komplikation, förveckling

compliment [n.] komplimang; **~s** hälsningar

comply [v.; -plies, -plied, -plied] lyda, iaktta

component [n.] beståndsdel, komponent

compose [v.] utarbeta; utgöra, komponera; lugna

composer [n.] kompositör

composite [adj.] sammansatt

composition [n.] komposition, sammansättning; uppsats

compound[1] [adj.] sammansatt; ~ **fracture** öppen fraktur; ~ **interest** ränta på ränta
compound[2] [n.] sammansättning
compound[3] [v.] blanda ihop; förvärra
comprehension [n.] förstånd; uppfattning
comprehensive [adj.] omfattande, allsidig; ~ **insurance** helförsäkring, allriskförsäkring
compress [v.; ~es, ~ed] komprimera, pressa ihop
compressed [adj.] komprimerad
compression [n.] sammantryckning; komprimering
comprise [v.] omfatta, inkludera
compromise[1] [n.] kompromiss
compromise[2] [v.] kompromissa, dagtinga; kompromottera
compulsive [adj.] tvångsmässig
compulsory [adj.] obligatorisk; ~ **education** allmän skolplikt; ~ **schooling** skolplikt
compute [v.] beräkna, kalkylera
computer[1] [n.] dator [IT]; ~ **animation** datoranimation; ~ **assistance** datorhjälp; ~ **assistance** **center** dataakut; ~ **assistance** **service** datorjour; ~ **consultant** datakonsult; ~ **crime** databrott; ~ **equipment** datautrustning; ~ **game** dataspel, datorspel; ~ **graphics** datorgrafik; ~ **monitor** dataskärm; ~ **mouse** datormus; ~ **music** datormusik; ~ **nerd** datanörd; ~ **program** dataprogram, datorprogram; ~ **protection** dataskydd; ~ **science** datateknik; ~ **screen** datorskärm; ~ **system** datasystem; ~ **terminal** dataterminal; ~ **tomography** datortomografi; ~ **virus** datavirus [IT]
computer-[2] [prefix] data- [IT]
computer-aided [adj.] datorstödd [IT]; ~ **design** datorstödd konstruktion; ~ **instruction** datorstödd utbildning [IT]
computer-based training [n.] datorstödd utbildning [IT]
computing [n.] databehandling; beräkning [IT]

comradeship [n.] kamratskap
con [abbrev: contra; confidence; convict] motskäl; bondfångeri; straffånge
conceal [v.] dölja, gömma
concede [v.] medge, erkänna
conceive [v.] tänka ut, hitta på; bli gravid
concentrate [v.] koncentrera
concentration [n.] koncentrering; anrikning; **difficulties in** ~ koncentrationssvårigheter
concept [n.] begrepp
conception [n.] föreställning, begrepp; befruktning
conceptual [adj.] begreppsmässig
concern[1] [n.] bekymmer, omsorg; intresse; affär
concern[2] [v.] angå, beträffa; bekymra
concerned [adj.] bekymrad; intresserad
concerning [prep.] angående, med anledning av
concert [n.] konsert; ~ **hall** konserthus
concerted [adj.] gemensam
concerto [n.] konsert
concession [n.] medgivande; förmån
conclude [v.] avsluta, sluta; dra slutsatsen
conclusion [n.] slut, avslutning; slutledning; slutande
concrete[1] [adj.] verklig, konkret; betong-
concrete[2] [n.] betong
concussion [n.] hjärnskakning
condemn [v.] döma; kassera
condiments [n.pl.] smaktillsatser
condition [n.] tillstånd; villkor; ~**s** förhållande
conditional [adj.] villkorlig, beroende; kontitional
condo [abbrev: condominium] andelslägenhet
condom [n.] kondom
condominium apartment [n.] andelslägenhet
conduct[1] [n.] uppträdande, hållning; förvaltning
conduct[2] [v.] föra, leda; förvalta; dirigera; ~ **oneself** uppföra sig

conductor [n.] dirigent [orchestra]; konduktör [train]; ledare
cone [n.] kon; strut [ice cream]
confer [v.; -rring, -rred, -rred] konferera; tilldela
conference [n.] konferens; ~ **room** konferensrum
confess [v.; ~es, ~ed, ~ed] erkänna; bikta
confession [n.] bekännelse; bikt
confide [v.] anförtro
confidence [n.] förtroende
confident [adj.] tillitsfull, säker; självsäker
confidential [adj.] förtrolig; konfidentiell
configuration [n.] gestalt, form
confine [v.] begränsa, stänga in
confirmation [n.] bekräftelse; konfirmation
confiscate [n.] beslagta, konfiskera
conflict[1] [n.] konflikt, motsättning; ~ **of interests** intressekonflikt
conflict[2] [v.] vara oförenlig; strida
conform [v.] överensstämma; anpassa sig
confront [v.] konfrontera; möta
confrontation [n.] konfrontation
confuse [v.] förvirra; förväxla
confusing [adj.] virrig; förvirrad
confusion [n.] förvirring; förväxling
congestion [n.] stockning, överbefolkning; kongestion; **nasal** ~ nästäppa
Congo [n.] Kongo
congratulate [v.] gratulera, lyckönska
congratulation [n.] gratulation, lyckönskning; ~**s!** varma/hjärtliga gratulationer, gratulerar, grattis
congregation [n.] församling
congress [n.; ~es] kongress
conjunction [n.] sammanträffande; konjunktion [gram., astron.]
Connecticut (CT) [n.] Connecticut [delstat i USA]
connect [v.] förbinda, ansluta, koppla; ~ **to** koppla till
connected [adj.] ansluten, kopplad, uppkopplad
connection [n.] förbindelse, anknytning, anslutning, uppkop-

pling; ~ **speed** uppkopplingshastighet; **in** ~ **with** i anslutning till, i samband med
connectivity [n.; -ties] uppkopplingsmöjlighet, anslutningsbarhet
connector [n.] anslutningskontakt
conquer [v.] erövra, besegra
conquest [n.] erövring, seger
conscience [n.] samvete
conscientious [adj.] samvetsgrann, plikttrogen
conscious [adj.] medveten; vid medvetande
consciousness [n.] medvetande
consensus [n.; ~es] samförstånd
consent[1] [n.] samtycke, bifall
consent[2] [v.] samtycka
consequence [n.] följd, konsekvens; betydelse
consequent [adj.] följande, som följer (på)
consequently [adv.] följaktligen
conservation [n.] bevarande, konservering; skydd, vård; ~ **area** ekologiskt område
conservationist [n.] naturvårdare
conservative[1] [adj.] konservativ; försiktig
conservative[2] [n.] konservativ
consider [v.] tycka; fundera på; anse
considerable [adj.] betydande, avsevärd
considerably [adv.] avsevärt
consideration [n.] övervägande; hänsyn; **show** ~ **to** visa hänsyn mot; **take into** ~ ta hänsyn till
considering [conj./prep.] med hänsyn till
consist [v.] bestå (av)
consistency [n.] konsekvens, följdriktighet; konsistens
consistent [adj.] konsekvent, följdriktig; jämn; överensstämmande
consistently [adv.] konsekvent, ständigt
consolidate [v.] konsolidera; slå samman
consommé [n.] (kött)buljong
consonant [n.] konsonant
consortium [n.; ~s/-tia] konsortium

conspiracy [n.; cies] konspiration, komplott
constant [adj.] ständig, konstant; stadig
constantly [adv.] jämt, ständigt
constipated [adj.] hård i magen
constipation [n.] förstoppning
constituency [n.; -cies] valkrets
constituent [n.] beståndsdel; valman
constitute [v.] utgöra, bilda, konstituera
constitution [n.] författning, konstitution, grundlag
constitutional [adj.] författningslig, konstitutionell
constrain [v.] tvinga; begränsa
constraint [n.] tvång, restriktion
construct [v.] konstruera, bygga
construction [n.] konstruktion, byggnad; tolkning; ~ site byggarbetsplats; ~ worker byggnadsarbetare; under ~ under byggnad
constructive [adj.] konstruktiv
consulate [n.] konsulat
consult [v.] rådfråga, konsultera
consultant [n.] konsulent; specialistläkare
consultation [n.] överläggning, rådpläggning; ~ room mottagning
consulting [adj.] rådgivande, konsult-
consume [v.] förbruka, konsumera; förtära
consumer [n.] konsument; ~ goods konsumtionsvaror; ~ price index (CPI) konsumentprisindex
consumption [n.] konsumtion, förtäring, bruk
cont. [abbrev: continued] fortsatt
contact[1] [n.] kontakt; ~ information kontaktinformation; ~ lenses kontaktlinser; ~ person kontaktperson
contact[2] [v.] kontakta, ta kontakt med
contagious [adj.] smittsam
contain [v.] innehålla, behärska; hålla
container [n.] behållare; container
contaminated [adj.] förorenad
contemplate [v.] fundera; räkna med

contemporary[1] [adj.] samtida, nutida, modern
contemporary[2] [n.; -ries] samtida
contempt [n.] förakt
contend [v.] strida; sträva; tvista
content[1] [adj.] nöjd
content[2] [n.] innehåll; ~ filter spärrfunktion [IT]
contents [n.pl.] innehåll
contest[1] [n.] tävling, strid
contest[2] [v.] bestrida; tävla om, kämpa om
context [n.] sammanhang, kontext; omgivningar
context-sensitive help [n.] sammanhangsberoende hjälp
continent [n.] kontinent, fastland; världsdel
continental [adj.] kontinental
contingent [adj.] eventuell; villkorlig
continual [adj.] ständig, ihållande
continuation [n.] fortsättning; förlängning
continue [v.] fortsätta, förlänga; fortfara; förbli; ~ one's education/ training vidareutbilda sig
continued [adj.] fortsatt, oavbruten
continuing [adj.] fortsatt; ~ education vidareutbildning
continuity [n.; -ties] kontinuitet; scenario; skripta
continuous [adj.] kontinuerlig, oavbruten, ständig; utan uppehåll
continuously [adv.] oavbrutet, ständigt
contraceptive [n.] preventivmedel; ~ pills p-piller
contract[1] [n.] avtal, kontrakt
contract[2] [v.] avtala, avsluta; ingå, sluta; dra ihop
contraction [n.] sammandragning, förkortning
contractor [n.] leverantör, entreprenör
contractual [adj.] kontrakts-
contradict [v.] motsäga; bestrida
contradiction [n.] motsägelse, bestridande; ~ in terms självmotsägelse
contrary[1] [adj.] motsatt, trotsig

contrary² [n.; -ries] motsats; **on the ~** tvärtom
contrast¹ [n.] kontrast, motsättning
contrast² [v.] ställa upp som motsats, jämföra; kontrastera
contribute [v.] bidra med; ge bidrag
contribution [n.] bidrag, inlägg, insats
control¹ [n.] kontroll, uppsikt; **arms ~** vapenkontroll; **~ key (Ctrl)** kontrolltangent (Ctrl) [IT]; **~ panel** kontrollbord
control² [v.] kontrollera, behärska; revidera
controlled [adj.] kontrollerad
controller [n.] kontrollör, övervakare, revisor; kontroller [IT]; **~ card** kontrollerkort, styrkort [IT]; **air-traffic ~** flygledare
controversial [adj.] omtvistad, kontroversiell; polemisk
controversy [n.] kontrovers, tvist
contusion [n.] kontusion, blåmärke
convenience [n.] bekvämlighet, fördel; **~ store** närbutik
convenient [adj.] lämplig, bekväm, behändig
conveniently [adv.] bekvämt, lämpligen
convent [n.] kloster
convention [n.] konvention; sammankomst; **~ hall** kongresshall
conventional [adj.] konventionell
conversation [n.] samtal, konversation; **carry on a ~** föra samtal
converse [v.] samtala
conversely [adv.] omvänt
conversion [n.] omvandling, ombyggnad, omläggning; konvertering; **~ rate** omräkningskurs
convert [v.] förvandla, omsätta; konvertera
converter [n.] omvandlare
convey [v.] meddela, uttrycka; leda; medföra, framföra
convict¹ [n.] straffånge, förbrytare
convict² [v.] fälla
conviction [n.] fällande; övertygelse
convince [v.] övertyga
convinced [adj.] övertygad
convincing [adj.] övertygande
cook¹ [n.] kock, köksmästare

cook² [v.] koka, laga, steka; **~book** kokbok
cooked [adj.] kokad, färdigkokt; **~ in white sauce** stuvad
cookie [n.] (små)kaka, kex; cookie [IT]
cooking [n.] matlagning, tillagning; mat; **~ facilities** kokmöjligheter; **~ instructions** rekommenderad tillagning
cool¹ [adj.] sval, kylig; lugn; cool
cool² [v.] kyla, svala av; svalna
coolant [n.] kylvätska
cooler [n.] kylväska; kylare
cooling [n.] avkylning; **~ fluid** kylvätska; **~ system** kylsystem; **~ water** kylarvatten
co-op [abbrev: cooperative] kooperativ, konsum, bostadsrätt
cooperate [v.] samarbeta, samverka
cooperation [n.] samarbete, samverkan
cooperative [adj.] samarbetsvillig; kooperativ; **~ apartment** bostadsrättslägenhet
coordinate [v.] samordna, koordinera
cop [n.] polis
cope [v.] klara det, orka
Copenhagen [n.] Köpenhamn
copier [n.] kopiator
copper [n.] koppar
copy¹ [n.; -pies] kopia, exemplar; **make copies** göra kopior
copy² [v.; -pies, -pied, -pied] kopiera; **~ protection** kopieringsskydd
copying [n.] kopiering
copyright [n.] upphovsrätt
cord [n.] rep, snöre; sträng; **spinal ~** ryggmärg; **umbilical ~** navelsträng; **vocal ~s** stämband
CORE¹ [abbrev: Congress of Racial Equality] kongressen för rasjämlikhet i USA
core² [adj.] innersta, central
core³ [n.] kärna; reaktorhärd; **to the ~** alltigenom
cork [n.] kork
corked [adj.] med korksmak [wine]
corkscrew [n.] korkskruv
corn [n.] majs; **~ oil** majsolja; **~ on the cob** majskolv

corner [n.] hörn, gathörn; vinkel;
hörna [soccer]; ~ shop näröppet;
~ table hörnbord
cornerstone [n.] hörnsten
cornflakes [n.pl.] (majs)flingor
coroner [n.] obducent, rättsläkare
Corp. [abbrev: corporation]
aktiebolag
corporate [adj.] bolags-; gemensam, kollektiv
corporation (Corp., Inc.) [n.]
aktiebolag (AB)
corps [n.; ~] kår
corpse [n.] lik
correct¹ [adj.] riktig, rätt; passande;
be ~ stämma
correct² [v.] rätta till, korrigera
correction [n.] rättning, korriger-
ing; bestraffning
correctly [adv.] riktigt, med rätta
correlate [v.] sätta i relation (till)
correlation [n.] korrelation
correspond [v.] motsvara; brevväxla
correspondence [n.] motsvarighet;
brevväxling
correspondent [n.] korrespondent;
brevskrivare
corresponding [adj.] motsvarande
corridor [n.] korridor
corrupt [adj.] korrumperad; skadad
corrupted [adj.] korrumperad
corruption [n.] korruption, mutning; fördärvande; förvanskning
cosmetics [n.pl.] kosmetika: apply
~ sminka (sig)
cost¹ [n.] kostnad, pris
cost² [v.; ~, ~] kosta
costly [adj.] dyr
costume [n.] dräkt; kostym; ~
jewelry bijouterier
cosy [adj.] trävlig, mysig, behaglig
Côte d'Ivoire [n.] Elfenbenkusten
cottage [n.] stuga; villa; ~ cheese
keso, kvark; ~ industry hem-
industri
cotton [n.] bomull; ~ balls bomullsvadd; ~ swab bomullspinne
cottonseed oil [n.] bomullsfröolja
couch [n.; ~es] dyscha, soffa
couchette berth [n.] liggvagnsplats
couchette car [n.] liggvagn

cough¹ [n.] hosta; ~ medicine
hostmedicin
cough² [v.] hosta
coughing [adj.] hostig
could [v.modal past; see: can]
council [n.] råd; styrelse
Council of Europe [n.] Europarådet
Council of the European Union
[n.] EU-rådet
councillor [n.] rådsmedlem
counsel¹ [n.] råd, maning; advokat;
defense ~ försvarsadvokat
counsel² [v.] råda; mana till
counselling [n.] rådgivning
counsellor [n.] rådgivare
count¹ [n.] räkning; anklagelsepunkt;
värde; greve
count² [v.] räkna
countable [adj.] räknebar
counter¹ [adj.] mot-, kontra-
counter² [n.] disk; köksbänk;
räknare, webbräknare [IT]
counter³ [v.] motarbeta; besvara
counterclockwise [adv.] moturs
counterfeit [adj.] förfalskad
counterindications [n.pl.]
kontraindikationer
counterpart [n.] motstycke, mot-
part; kollega
countless [adj.] otalig
country [n.; -ries] land, terräng;
~ code landsnummer [telephone];
~ inn gästgivargård, värdshus; ~
road landsväg
countryside [n.] landsbygd, natur;
in the ~ på landet
county [n.; -ties] län; ~ administration länstyrelse; ~ council
landsting
coup [n.] kupp
couple¹ [n.] par
couple² [v.] koppla, förbinda
coupon [n.] kupong
courage [n.] mod
course [n.] kurs; maträtt; ~ of action tillvägagångssätt; ~ of study
studiekurs, studieväg; first ~ förrätt; main ~ huvudrätt; of ~ förstås,
(ja) visst, naturligtvis
court [n.] domstol, rätt; hov [royal];
~ of appeals hovrätt

courteous [adj.] artig, hövlig
courtesy [n.; -sies] artighet, hövlighet
courthouse [n.] domstolsbyggnad
courtyard [n.] gård
cousin [n.] kusin; second ~ syssling
covenant [n.] avtal, pakt
cover[1] [n.] täcke; lock; pärm; skydd; kuvert [restaurant]; ~ charge kuvertavgift
cover[2] [v.] täcka, skydda
coverage [n.] täckning, spridning
covered market [n.] övertäckt marknad
covering [n.] täcke, täckning
cover-up [n.] mörkläggning
coveted [adj.] eftertraktad
cow [n.] ko; mad ~ disease galna ko-sjukan
cowardly [adj.] feg; gemen
coworker [n.] medarbetare, kollega
CPA [abbrev: Certified Public Accountant] auktoriserad revisor
CPI [abbrev: consumer price index] konsumentprisindex
cpl. [abbrev: corporal] korpral
CPU [abbrev: central processing unit] centralenhet, centralprocessor (CPU)
cr. [abbrev: credit] tillgodohavande, kredit
crab [n.] krabba
crack[1] [n.] knackande, knall; spricka; crack [drugs]
crack[2] [v.] knacka; spricka, knäcka; kollapsa
cracked [adj.] sprucken
cracker [n.] kex
craft [n.] hantverk, slöjd; fartyg; arts and ~s konsthantverk
craftsman [n.; -men] hantverkare, yrkesman
cram [v.; cramming, crammed, crammed] proppa; plugga
crammed [adj.] överfull
cramp [n.] kramp; menstrual ~s menssmärtor
cranberries [n.pl.] tranbär; wild ~ lingon
crap [n.] skit; skitsnack; take a ~ skita [vulg.]

crane [n.] trana; kran
crash[1] [n.] ~es brak, krasch; olycka, krock; systemkrasch [IT]; ~ helmet störthjälm
crash[2] [v.; ~es, ~ed, ~ed] braka; krocka; störta; krascha
crate [n.] spjällåda, back
crawl [v.] krypa, kravla
crayfish [n.; ~] kräfta, langust
crayon [n.] färgkrita
crazy [adj.] galen, inte klok, tokig
cream[1] [adj.] krämfärgad
cream[2] [n.] grädde [dairy]; kräm [lotion]; ~ cheese färskost; ~ sauce grädsås; heavy ~ tjock grädde, vispgrädde; light ~ gräddmjölk; sour ~ gräddfil
creamed potatoes [n.pl.] stuvad potatis
create [v.] skapa, upprätta
creation [n.] skapande; skapelse, verk
creative [adj.] skapande, kreativ
creativity [n.; -ties] kreativitet
creator [n.] skapare
creature [n.] varelse, individ; kreatur; djur
credentials [n.pl.] betyg; identitetspapper; kreditivbrev
credibility [n.; -ties] trovärdighet
credible [adj.] trovärdig, trolig
credit[1] [n.] kredit, tillgodohavande; ära; tilltro; poäng [see: credit hours]; ~ card kreditkort; ~s eftertexten [film]
credit[2] [v.] tilltro; tillskriva; ge äran till
credit hours [n.pl.] poäng [3-poängs kurs i USA innebär 3 timmar i veckan]
creditor [n.] kreditor
creed [n.] trosbekännelse, troslära; credo
creep[1] [n.] äckel
creep[2] [v.; crept, crept] krypa, smyga (sig)
creeper [n.] klätterväxt, klängväxt
crème caramel [n.] brylépudding
Crete [n.] Kreta
crew [n.] besättning, manskap, personal, arbetslag; ~ cut snagg

crib [n.] babysäng
cricket [n.] syrsa; kricket [sport]
crime [n.] brott, kriminalitet; ~ fiction kriminalromaner; ~ prevention brottsförebyggande verksamhet; ~ rate antal brott; violent ~ våldsbrott
criminal[1] [adj.] brottslig, kriminell; kriminal-; ~ investigation department kriminalpolisen
criminal[2] [n.] brottsling, förbryttare
crisis [n.; crises] kris; ~ management krishantering
crisp [adj.] knaprig, mör, spröd; fräsch; koncis, markerad
crispbread [n.] knäckebröd
criterion [n.; -teria] kriterium
critic [n.] kritiker
critical [adj.] kritisk; livsviktig
criticism [n.] kritik, bedömning
criticize [v.] bedöma, kritisera
critique [n.] recension; do a ~ recensera
Croatia [n.] Kroatien
Croatian[1] [adj.] kroatisk
Croatian[2] (language) [n.] kroatiska
crochet [n.] virkning
crockery [n.; -ries] porslin, lergods
crook [n.] svindlare, tjuv; herdestav
crooked [adj.] krokig; sned, skev; oärlig
crop[1] [n.] skörd, gröda; samling
crop[2] [v.; -pping, -pped, -pped] skära av, stubba
cross[1] [adj.] arg, sur; kors-; mark with a ~ kryssa
cross[2] [n.; ~es] kors; bomärke; ~ street tvärgata
cross[3] [v.; ~es, ~ed, ~ed] fara över/genom; korsa, kryssa; körsa över; ~ out stryka
cross-country [adj.] terräng-, längd-; ~ skiing längdskidsåkning; ~ skis löparskidor
crossing [n.] korsning; övergång, överfart
crosslinked cable [n.] korsad kabel [IT]
crossover cable [n.] korsad kabel [IT]
cross-platform [adj.] plattforms-oberoende [IT]

crossware [n.] korsprogramvara [IT]
crossword puzzle [n.] korsord; do a ~ lösa korsord
crouch [v.; ~es, ~ed, ~ed] huka sig ned
crow [n.] kråka; as the ~ flies fågelvägen
crowd[1] [n.] (folk)massa, (folk)trängsel
crowd[2] [v.] trängas; packa full
crowded [adj.] fullt med folk, överfull
crowding [n.] trängsel
crown[1] [n.] krona; krans; topp; ~ jewels kronjuvel
crown[2] [v.] kröna
crucial [adj.] avgörande, kritisk
crucifix [n.; ~es] krucifix
crude [adj.] rå, grov; primitiv; ~ oil råolja
cruel [adj.] grym, gräslig
cruelty [n.; -ties] grymhet; misshandel
cruise[1] [n.] kryssning, tur; ~ missile kryssningsrobot; ~ ship kryssningsfartyg
cruise[2] [v.] kryssa; glida fram
crush [v.; ~es, ~ed, ~ed] krossa; trycka
crust [n.] skorpa, skalk
crutch [n.; ~es] krycka
cry[1] [n.; cries] rop, skrik; gråtstund
cry[2] [v.; cries, cried, cried] gråta; ropa, skrika
crypt [n.] krypta, gravvalv
crystal [n.] kristall; kristallglas
CST [abbrev: Central Standard Time] normaltid i centralzonen i USA
ct[1] [abbrev: cents; carat] cent; karat
CT[2] [abbrev: Connecticut] Connecticut [delstat i USA]
CTS [abbrev: carpal tunnel syndrome] karpaltunnelsyndrom
cu. [abbrev: cubic] kubik
Cuba [n.] Kuba
Cuban [adj.] kubansk
cubicle [n.] hytt, bås; sovcell
cubism [n.] kubism
cucumber [n.] gurka
cuddle [v.] krama, omfamna

cue [n.] stikreplik, signal, klartecken; biljardkö
cuff links [n.pl.] manschettknappar
cult [n.] kult, sekt
cultivate [v.] bearbeta, odla; bilda
cultivated [adj.] kultiverad, bildad; odlad
cultivation [n.] bearbetning; odling; bildning
cultural [adj.] kulturell; ~ arts center kulturhus
culture [n.] kultur; bildning; odling
cultured [adj.] kultiverad, bildad; odlad; ~ milk products fermenterade mjölkprodukter
cumbersome [adj.] besvärlig, ohanterlig
cumin [n.] kummin
cum laude [Latin phrase: with praise] "med beröm" [betygsgraden över godkänd]
cumulative [adj.] kumulativ, hopad
cunt [n.; vul.] fitta [vul.]
cup¹ [n.] kopp; pokal; ~ final cupfinal; ~ match cupspel
cup² [v.; -pping, -pped, -pped] kupa
cupboard [n.] skåp
cupola [n.] kupol
curator [n.] kurator
curds [n.pl.] ostmassa; kvark
cure¹ [n.] botemedel; kur
cure² [v.] bota; konservera, lägga in, torka, röka
curiosity [n.; -ties] nyfikenhet; kuriositet
curious [adj.] nyfiken; underlig
curiously [adv.] underligt, kuriöst
curl¹ [n.] lock; ring; ~s lockar, ringlar
curl² [v.] krulla, locka,
curlers [n.pl.] hårspolar
curling [n.] curling
curly [adj.] lockig, krullig; ~ brackets ({}) klammerparentes, spetsparentes [IT]
currants [n.pl.] vinbär; black ~ svarta vinbär; red ~ röda vinbär
currency [n.; -cies] valuta; utbredning, spridning; ~ exchange valutaväxel; valutaväxling; ~ exchange office växelkontor, växlingskontor

current¹ [adj.] aktuell; innevarande, gällande; ~ affairs aktuella frågor
current² [n.] ström; tendens
currently [adv.] för närvarande
curriculum [n.; ~s/-cula] studieplan
curriculum vitae (CV) [n.; Latin: course of life] levnadsbeskrivning
curry [n.; -rries] curry; curryrätt; ~ soup [mulligatawney] currysoppa
curse [v.] förbanna; svära; plåga
cursor [n.] markör [IT]; ~ movement key piltangent [IT]
curtain [n.] gardin; ridå [theater]
curve¹ [n.] kurva
curve² [v.] böja, kröka
curved [adj.] böjd, krökt
cushion [n.] kudde
custard [n.] äggkräm
custody [n.; -dies] vårdnad; förvar; take into ~ anhålla
custom¹ [adj.] gjord på beställning
custom² [n.] vana, bruk
customary [adj.] sedvanlig
customer [n.] kund; ~ information kundinformation; ~ parking kundparkering; ~ service kundservice, kundtjänst
customs [n.pl.] tull; ~ control tullkontroll; ~ declaration tulldeklaration; ~ duties tullavgifter; ~ officer tulltjänsteman
cut¹ [n.] skära; hugg; klippning; reduktion; ~ glass slipat glas
cut² [v.; ~, ~] skära; klippa (ut); skåra; ~ down skåra ner; ~ off bruten; ~ out klippa ut
cutlery [n.] matbestick
cutlet [n.] kotlett
cut-rate [adj.] lågpris-
cutting board [n.] skärbräda
cutting-edge [adj.] spjutspets-
CV [abbrev: curriculum vitae] kort levnadsbeskrivning, meritförteckning, CV
C&W [abbrev: country-and-western music] country and western musik
cyberspace [n.] cyberrymd
cycle¹ [n.] cykel, krets; takt [motor]; two-~ engine tvåtaktsmotor

cycle[2] [v.] cykla
cycling [n.] cykelsport, cykling; ~
  helmet cykelhjälm; ~ tour
  cykeltur
cylinder [n.] cylinder, vals
cynical [adj.] cynisk

Cypriot [adj.] cypriotisk
Cyprus [n.] Cypern
Czech[1] [adj.] tjeckisk
Czech[2] (language) [n.] tjeckiska
Czech Republic [n.] Tjeckiska
  republiken

D

'd¹ [contr: had; should, would]
hade; skulle
D² [abbrev: lowest passing grade]
godkänd
DA [abbrev: district attorney]
allmän åklagare
dabble (in) [v.] syssla lite, fuska
dad [n.] pappa, farsa [colloq.]
daddy [n.; -dies] pappa, farsa
[colloq.]
daily¹ [adj.] daglig; ~ **occupation**
dagssyssla; ~ **newspaper** dagstidning; ~ **program** dagsprogram
daily² [adv.] dagligen
dairy [n.; -ries] mejeri; ~ **products**
mejeriprodukter, mejerivaror
daisy [n.; -sies] tusensköna
damage¹ [n.] skada; ~**s** skadeersätt-
ning
damage² [v.] skada
damaged [adj.] skadad; trasig; **be ~**
skadas
damaging [adj.] skadlig
Damascus [n.] Damaskus
dammit! [interj.; colloq.; see: **damn!**]
damn!¹ [interj.; colloq.] tusan!
[colloq.], sjuton! [colloq.]; fan! [vul.];
not give a ~ [colloq.] strunta i
damn² [v.] förbanna, fördoma
damned [adj.] förbaskad; jävla [vul.]
damp [adj.] fuktig
dance¹ [n.] dans; ~ **band** dansband;
~ **floor** dansgolv; ~ **theater**
dansteater
dance² [v.] dansa
dancer [n.] dansare
dancing [n.] dans; att dansa
dandruff [n.] mjäll
danger [n.] fara, risk; **without ~**
riskfri
dangerous [adj.] farlig, riskfull;
extremely ~ livsfarlig
Danish¹ [adj.] dansk; ~ **pastry**
wienerbröd
Danish² (**language**) [n.] danska
Danube River [n.] Donau
Dardanelles [n.pl.] Dardanellerna
dare [v.] våga
daring [adj.] djärv

dark [adj.] mörk; ~ **beer** mörkt öl;
~ **brown** mörkbrun
dark(ness) [n.] mörker
darling [n.] älskling, raring
darn! [interj.; colloq.] tusan!,
sjuton! [colloq.]
dart¹ [n.] pil, kastspjut, dart
dart² [v.] rusa, störta; kasta
dash¹ [n.; ~es] rusning; en aning,
några droppar [cooking];
tankestreck; ~**es** streckad linje
dash² [v.; ~es, ~ed, ~ed] störta,
kila; slänga
DAT [abbrev: digital audio tape]
DAT-band
data¹ [n.pl.] data, information [IT];
~ **acquisition** datainsamling; ~ **bus**
databuss; ~ **capture** datafångst;
~ **cell** datacell; ~ **communication**
datakommunikation; ~ **compres-**
sion datakomprimering; ~ **file**
datafil; ~ **mart** dataförråd, datalager; ~ **mining** datagruvdrift;
~ **processing department**
dataavdelning; ~ **processing sec-**
tor databransch; ~ **processing**
system datasystem; ~ **transfer**
dataöverföring; ~ **warehouse**
datalager; ~ **warehousing** datalagerhantering [IT]
data-² [prefix] data- [IT]
database [n.] databas, dataregister
[IT]; ~ **management** databashantering [IT]
date¹ [n.] datum, tid, årtal; dadlar
[fruit]; ~ **of birth** födelsedatum;
sell-by ~ försäljningsdatum;
what's the ~ today? vad är det
för datum i dag?
date² [v.] datera
datebook [n.] dagbok, almanacka
dated [adj.] daterad
daughter [n.] dotter
daughter-in-law [n.] svärdotter
dawn [n.] gryning
day [n.] dag; dygn [24 hour period];
~ **guest** [n.] dagsbesökare; ~ **off**
ledig dag; ~ **pass** dagkort; ~ **plan-**
ner almanacka; ~ **trip** dagsutflykt;

~ **visitor** dagsbesökare; **all ~ long**
dygnet runt; **during the ~** under
dagen; **per ~** per dag; **the next ~**
dagen därpå
day care [n.] daglig tillsyn;
dagsjukvård; ~ **center** daghem,
barndaghem, dagis [colloq.]; ~
provider dagmamma [female]
day-to-day [adj.] daglig
daybed [n.] bäddsoffa
daylight [n.] dagsljus; ~ **savings
time (DST)** sommartid
daytime [n.] dagtid
db [abbrev: decibel] decibel
DBS [abbrev: direct broadcast
satellite] kommunikationssatellit
[IT]
DC [abbrev: District of Columbia;
direct current] District of Columbia (huvudstadsdistrikten i USA);
likström
D&C [abbrev: dilation and curet-
tage] skrapning
D-Day [abbrev: date of Normandy
invasion in WWII (June 6, 1944)]
dagen för invasionen i Normandie
under andra världskriget
DDS [abbrev: Doctor of Dental
Surgery] odontologie doktor
DE [abbrev: Delaware] Delaware
[delstat i USA]
dead[1] [adj.] död
dead[2] [adv.] jämn, absolut
Dead Sea [n.] Döda havet
dead-end street [n.] återvändsgata
deadline [n.] frist, termin
deadly [adj.] dödlig, livsfarlig
deaf [adj.] döv, med nedsatt hörsel;
~ **person** döv person
deaf-mute [adj.] dövstum
deal[1] [n.] affär; mängd; **a good ~** en
bra affär; **a good/great ~ of** mycket, en hel del
deal[2] [v.; dealt] tilldela; handla;
behandla; ~ **with** ha att göra med,
behandla, ta itu med, ta hand om
dealer [n.] handlande, -handlare;
langare [illicit]; givare [cards]
dealings [n.pl.] affärer,
förbindelser, handlande
dear [adj.] kär; **oh ~!** bevare mig
väl!; **my ~** kära du

death [n.] död; ~ **certificate** dödsattest; **beat to ~** slå ihjäl
debate[1] [n.] debatt, diskusion,
meningsutbyte
debate[2] [v.] diskutera, debattera;
fundera
debit [n.] debet; ~ **card** kontokort,
betalkort
debt [n.] skuld; **in ~** skyldig
debtor [n.] gäldenär, debitor
debugging [n.] avlusning, felsökning [IT]
debut [n.] debut
Dec. [abbrev: December] december
decade [n.] decennium; **the 1990s**
1990-talet
decaf [abbrev: decaffeinated]
koffeinfri
decaffeinated [adj.] koffeinfri, utan
kaffein
decay[1] [n.] förmultning; förfall
decay[2] [v.] multna, rottna; förfalla;
fördärva
deceive [v.] bedra; lura
December [n.] december
decent [adj.] passande, ordentlig;
hygglig
decentralization [n.] decentralisering
decentralize [v.] decentralisera
deception [n.] bedrägeri, list
deceptive [adj.] bedräglig
decibel [n.] decibel
decide [v.] avgöra, bestämma (sig),
besluta (sig); välja; ~ **to** besluta
sig för att
decimal [adj./n.] decimal; ~ **point**
(decimal) komma
deciphering [n.] dekryptering
decision [n.] avgörande, beslut
decision-making [n.] beslutsfat-
tande
decisive [adj.] avgörande;
beslutsam
deck [n.] däck; ~ **chair** däckstol,
solstol
declaration [n.] förklaring; deklaration; ~ **of value** värdedeklaration; **customs ~** tulldeklaration
declare [v.] förklara, deklarera;
förtulla [customs]
decline[1] [n.] avtagande, nedgång;
förfall; minskning

decline² [v.] avta, minska; avböja, tacka nej; sjunka
decoder [n.] avkodare [IT]
decoding [n.] avkodning [IT]
decompilation [n.] dekompilering [IT]
decompile [v.] dekompilera [IT]
decorate [v.] pryda; inreda
decoration [n.] dekorering, smyckning; dekoration; orden
decorative [adj.] dekorativ
decorator [n.] målare; dekoratör; **interior** ~ inredningsarkitekt
decrease¹ [n.] minskning, avtagande
decrease² [v.] minska, avta
decree [n.] dekret, förordning
decryption [n.] dekryptering [IT]
dedicate [v.] tillgna, dedicera
dedicated [adj.] hängiven, engagerad; ~ **computer** dedicerad dator [IT]
dedication [n.] hängivenhet; tillägnan; invigning
deed [n.] handling, gärning; bedrift; urkund
deem [v.] anse, mena
deep¹ [adj.] djup; ~ **breath** djupt andetag
deep² [adv.] djupt
deepfreezer [n.] frys
deep-fried [adj.] friterad
deep-frozen [adj.] djupfryst
deep-sea fishing [n.] havsfiske
deeply [adv.] djupt
deer [n.; ~] hjort, rådjur
default [n.] försummelse; grundvärde, standardinställning, standardalternativ [IT]; ~ **connection** standardanslutning [IT]; ~ **program** standardprogram [IT]; ~ **setting** standardinställning; ~ **value** förvalt värde, standardvärde
defeat¹ [n.] nederlag; omintetgörande
defeat² [v.] besegra; göra ned; omintetgöra
defect [n.] fel, brist, defekt; **speech** ~ talfel
defend [v.] försvara; värna; bestrida
defendant [n.] svarande
defender [n.] försvarare
defense [n.] försvar, skydd

defensive [adj.] defensiv, försvars-
deferred payment [n.] uppskjuten betalning
deficiency [n.; -cies] brist; ofullkomlighet; **vitamin** ~ vitaminbrist
deficit [n.] underskott, deficit, brist
define [v.] bestämma, begränsa; precisera
definite [adj.] klar; fästställd, uttrycklig, exakt; ~ **article** bestämd artikel
definitely [adv.] absolut, definitivt
definition [n.] definition; skärpa [image]; bestämmande
defragmentation [n.] defragmentering [IT]
defy [v.; -fies, -fied, -fied] trotsa; utmana
degree [n.] grad; examen; ~**s Centigrade** Celsius grader [-10°C=14°F, 0°C=32°F, 10°C=50°F, 20°C= 68°F, 30°C=86°F, 37°C=98.6°F, 100°C=212°F]
Delaware (DE) [n.] Delaware [delstat i USA]
delay¹ [n.] fördröjning, försening
delay² [v.] skjuta upp, dröja med
delayed [adj.] försenad; ~ **2 hours** 2 timmar försenad
delegate¹ [n.] delegat, ombud, representant
delegate² [v.] delegera
delegation [n.] delegering; delegation, deputation
delete [v.] radera, stryka, ta bort
deleted [adj.] borttagen
deletion [n.] strykning, borttagning
deli [abbrev: see: **delicatessen**]; ~ **counter** delikatessdisk
deliberate [adj.] överlagd; forsiktig
deliberately [adv.] avsiktligen
delicate [adj.] ömtålig; delikat; utsökt; fin
delicatessen [n.] delikatessaffär, delikatessbutik
delicious [n.] härlig; läcker
delight¹ [n.] nöje, glädje, fröjd
delight² [v.] glädja; finna nöje i
delighted [adj.] glad; förtjust
delightful [adj.] förtjusande, charmant

deliver [v.] överlämna; framföra; förlösa [baby]

delivery [n.; -ries] (ut)leverans, utbärning; nedkomst [baby]; ~ charge leveranskostnad; ~ time leveranstid; ~ van budbil; special ~ expressbefordran

Dem [abbrev: see: Democrat]

demand[1] [n.] begäran, fordran; efterfrågan

demand[2] [v.] fordra, kräva; begära

demanding [adj.] fordrande, krävande

demi-sec [adj.] halvtorr

demo [abbrev: demonstration] demonstration; demo

democracy [n.; -cies] demokrati

democrat [n.] demokrat

democratic [adj.] demokratisk

demolish [v.; ~es, ~ed] demolera; förstöra, krossa

demon [n.] demon

demonstrate [v.] demonstrera; bevisa

demonstration [n.] demonstration, bevisning

demonstrator [n.] demonstrant

denial [n.] förnekande; dementi; avslag

denial-of-service attack [n.] blockeringsattack [IT]

denim [n.] denim

Denmark [n.] Danmark

denominator [n.] nämnare; lowest common ~ (LCD) minsta gemensamma nämnare

denounce [v.] stämpla, kritisera; anmäla

dense [adj.] tät, kompakt; dum

density [n.; -ties] täthet; densitet

densly settled [adj.] tättbebyggd

dent [n.] buckla; hål

dental [adj.] tand- ; ~ care tandvård; ~ floss tandtråd

dentist [n.] tandläkare

denture [n.] tandprotes

deny [v.; -nies, -nied, -nied] neka, dementera; avvisa

deodorant [n.] deodorant

depart [v.] avresa, avgå, utgå

department [n.] avdelning; fakultet, institution; ~ store varuhus

Department of Agriculture [n.] Jordbruksdepartementet

Department of Defense [n.] Försvarsdepartementet

Department of Justice [n.] Justitiedepartementet

Department of State [n.] Utrikesdepartementet (UD)

departmental [adj.] avdelnings-, departements-

departure [n.] avgång, avresa; avsteg; ~ lounge avgångshall; ~ time avgångstid

depend (on) [v.] bero på; lita på

dependable [adj.] pålitlig, driftsäker

dependence [n.] beroende, avhängighet; drug ~ narkotikaberoende

dependency [n.; -cies] beroende, avhängighet

dependent[1] [adj.] beroende, hänvisad

dependent[2] [n.] beroende person, anhörig

depending on [prep.] beroende på

depict [v.] avbilda; skildra

deplete [v.] tömma, förbruka

deploy [v.] sprida; utvekla; placera

deposit[1] [n.] handpenning, insats; insättning; depositionsavgift; fyndighet [ore]; make a ~ deponera; no ~ ingen retur

deposit[2] [v.] sätta in

depot [n.] depå; vagnhall; järnvägsstation, busstation

deprecatory [adj.] avvärjande, nedsättande

depreciation [n.] värdeminskning; nedvärdering

depress [v.; ~es, ~ed, ~ed] deprimera; hämma; pressa ner, trycka ned

depressed [adj.] deprimerad

depressing [adj.] deprimerande

depression [n.] depression; nedtryckning; lågkonjunktur

deprivation [n.] berövande, förlust; sleep ~ sömnförlust

deprive [v.] beröva; förvägra

deprived [adj.] eftersatt, behövande

dept. [abbrev: see: department]

depth [n.] djup
deputy [n.; -ties] ställföreträdare, suppleant; vice-
derivative [n.] derivat
derive [v.] dra, få, erhålla; derivera
dermatologist [n.] hudläkare
descend [v.] gå ned, stiga ned; sjunka, sänka
descendant [n.] ättling, avkomling
descending sort [n.] fallande sortering [IT]
descent [n.] nedstigning; slutning; fall; härstamning
describe [v.] beskriva; beteckna
description [n.] beskrivning, skildring
deselect [v.] avmarkera [IT]
desert[1] [n.] öken, ödemark
desert[2] [v.] överge; desertera
deserted [adj.] övergiven; öde
deserve [v.] förtjäna; vara värd
design[1] [n.] formgivning, typ; ritning; mönster; plan
design[2] [v.] formge; planera; avse
designate [v.] beteckna; bestämma
designer [n.] formgivare, planerare; ~ jeans märkesjeans
desirable [adj.] önskvärd, attraktiv
desire[1] [n.] längtan; åtrå; begäran
desire[2] [v.] önska, åtrå, begära
desired [adj.] önskad
desk [n.] skrivbord; kassa, reception; ~ clerk portier; ~ drawer låda
desktop [n.] skrivbord [IT]; ~ computer bordsdator [IT]; ~ publishing (DTP) layoutprogram
despair [n.] förtvivlan
desperate [adj.] desperat, förtvivlad
desperation [n.] förtvivlan, desperation; in ~ förtvivlad
despite [prep.] trots
dessert [n.] dessert; ~ course efterrätt; ~ wine dessertvin
destination [n.] destination, resmål
destiny [n.; -nies] skickelse, bestämmelse, öde
destroy [v.] förstöra, kassera
destroyed [adj.] förstörd
destruction [n.] förstörelse, skada, förödelse
destructive compression [n.] förstörande komprimering [IT]

Det. [abbrev: Detective] kriminalare
detach [v.; ~es, ~ed, ~ed] lösgöra, ta loss, (av)skilja, avsöndra
detached [adj.] fristående, avskild; självständig, objektiv, oengagerad
detail [n.] detalj, enskildhet
detailed [adj.] detaljerad, utförlig, omständig; ~ figures detaljsiffror
detain [v.] försena, uppehålla, fördröja; anhålla [legal]
detect [v.] upptäcka, spåra
detection [n.] upptäckt
detective [n.] detektiv, kriminalare; ~ story deckare
detector [n.] detektor
detention [n.] försening, fördröjning; internering, arrest
deter [v.] avskräcka, avhålla, hindra
detergent [n.] rengöringsmedel, tvättmedel
deteriorate [v.] försämras, förfalla
determination [n.] beslutsamhet; bestämning, begränsning; beslut
determine [v.] bestämma (sig), besluta (sig)
determined [adj.] bestämd, besluten
deterrent[1] [adj.] avskräckande
deterrent[2] [n.] avskräckningsmedel
detest [v.] avsky
detour [n.] omväg, avvikelse; trafikomläggning
detox [abbrev: detoxification] avgiftning, detoxifiering; torken
detrimental [adj.] skadlig
devastating [adj.] ödeläggande, förödande
develop [v.] bygga ut; utveckla; framkalla [film]
developed country [n.; -ries] industriland (i-land)
developer [n.] utvecklare; spekulant; framkalare [photography]
developing country [n.; -ries] ukvecklingsland (u-land)
development [n.] utveckling; framkallning [film]; ~ assistance u-hjälp; ~ program utvecklingsprogram
deviation [n.] avvikelse; deviation
device [n.] anordning, apparat; påhitt; ~ driver styrrutin

devil [n.] djävul, fan
devise [v.] hitta på; uppfinna
devote [v.] ägna; ~ **oneself to** ägna
  sig åt
devoted [adj.] hängiven; ägnad
DEW [abbrev: distant early warn-
  ing] robotvarningssystem
diabetes [n.] diabetes, sockersjuka
diabetic[1] [adj.] sockersjuk
diabetic[2] [n.] diabetiker
diacritical mark [n.] accenttecken,
  diakritiskt tecken
diagnose [v.] diagnostisera
diagnosis [n.; -ses] diagnos
diagnostic program [n.] diagnosprogram [IT]
diagonally [adv.] snett; ~ **opposite**
  snett mittemot
diagram [n.] diagram, figur
dial [v.] slå; ~ **0 for the front desk**
  slå 0 till receptionen; ~ **a wrong**
  number ringa fel; ~ **number 345**
  slå nummer 345; ~ **tone** kop-
  plingston
dial-up connection [n.] uppringd
  anslutning, uppringd förbindelse
  [IT]
dialect [n.] dialekt
dialer [n.] uppringare, uppringningsprogram [IT]
dialogue [n.] dialog; ~ **box** dialogruta [IT]
diameter [n.] diameter
diamond [n.] diamant; ~s ruter
  [cards]
diaper [n.] blöja
diaphragm [n.] bländare [camera];
  mellangärde [chest]; pessar
  [contraceptive]
diarrhea [n.] diarré
diary [n.; -ries] dagbok, almanacka;
  keep a ~ föra dagbok
diced [adj.] i bitar, kluven
dichotomy [n.; -mies] delning;
  dikotomi
dick [n.] [vul.] kuk [vul.]; [colloq.]
  detektiv
dictate [v.] diktera, föreskriva
dictation [n.] diktamen
dictionary [n.; -ries] lexikon, ordbok
die [v.; dying, died, died] dö,
  avlida, omkomma

diesel [adj./n.] diesel
diet[1] [n.] diet; ~ **menu** meny för
  bantare
diet[2] [v.] hålla diet, banta
dietary [adj.] diet-; ~ **fats** fetter i
  kosten; ~ **fiber** kostfibrer; ~ **sup-**
  plements kosttillskott
dieter [n.] bantare
differ [v.] skilja sig; vara av olika
  mening
difference [n.] skillnad, avvikelse
different (from) [adj.] olik, annorlunda än
differential [n.] differential;
  differens
differentiate [v.] differentiera;
  skilja
differentiation [n.] differentiering
differently [adv.] annorlunda
difficult [adj.] svår, besvärlig,
  krånglig
difficulty [n.; -ties] svårighet
dig [v.; dug, dug] gräva
digest [v.] smälta; tänka över
digestion [n.] matsmältning
digital [adj.] digital; ~ **camera**
  digitalkamera; ~ **cash** digitala
  pengar; ~ **highway** elektroniska
  motorvägen; ~ **signature** digital
  signatur [IT]
digital-to-analog converter [n.]
  digital-analog-omvandlare [IT]
digitizer [n.] digitaliserare [IT]
dignity [n.; -ties] värdighet, höghet
dilemma [n.] dilemma
dill [n.] dill; ~ **sauce** dillsås
dilute [v.] spä ut; försvaga
dimension [n.] dimension, storlek;
  aspekt
diminish [v.; ~es, ~ed, ~ed] minska,
  försvaga
dimmed headlights [n.pl.] halvljus
dine [v.] äta middag
dining [adj.] mat-; ~ **car** restaurangvagn; ~ **nook** matvrå; ~ **room**
  matsal; ~ **table** matbord
dinner [n.] middag
dinosaur [n.] dinosaurie
dip[1] [n.] dopp, doppning; dipmix;
  nedgång; grop
dip[2] [v.; -pping, -pped, -pped]
  doppa; dyka

diphtheria [n.] difteri
diploma [n.] diplom; avgångsbetyg; studentexamen
diplomat [n.] diplomat
diplomatic [adj.] diplomatisk
dipper [n.]: Big Dipper Karlavagnen; Little Dipper Lilla Karlavagnen
direct¹ [adj./adv.] direkt; ~ current (D.C.) likström; ~ line direktlinje; ~ link direktlänk; ~ object ackusativobjekt; ~ service direktservice; ~ train direkttåg
direct² [v.] rikta; styra, dirigera; visa vägen; beordra
direction [n.] riktning, håll; regi [theater]; ~s vägbeskrivning, anvisningar
directive [n.] direktiv, föreskrift
directly [adv.] direkt, rakt; genast
director [n.] direktör, ledare; regissör [film]; dirigent [music]
directory [n.; -ries] adressförteckning; katalog, mapp [IT]; ~ assistance nummerbyrå; telephone ~ telefonkatalog
dirt [n.] smuts; jord; ~ road grusväg
dirty [adj.] smutsig; snuskig; ~ linen smutstvätt; ~ washing smutstvätt
disability [n.; -ties] funktionshinder, handikapp
disabled [adj.] handikappad, rörelsehindrad; suitable for the ~ handikappanpassad
disadvantage [n.] nackdel
disagree [v.] inte samtycka; inte vara överens; milk ~s with me jag tål inte mjölk
disagreement [n.] meningsskiljaktighet, oenighet
disappear [v.] försvinna
disappoint [v.] göra besviken; svika
disappointed [adj.] besviken
disappointing [adj.] nedslående
disappointment [n.] besvikelse
disapprove [v.] ogilla
disaster [n.] katastrof
disastrous [adj.] katastrofal, fatal
disc [n.] skiva
discard [v.] kasta bort, kassera; överge

discharge¹ [n.] frigivning; uttömning, utsläp; befrielse
discharge² [v.] släppa (ut); frige; ladda ur; skjuta; fullgöra
disciple [n.] elev, lärjunge
disciplinary [adj.] disciplinär
discipline¹ [n.] disciplin; vetenskapsgren
discipline² [v.] disciplinera
disclose [v.] avslöja; visa
disclosure [n.] avslöjande
disco [n.] disco; discomusik
disconnect [v.] koppla bort/loss/ur; stänga av
disconnected [adj.] osammanhängande; frånkopplad, lossnad
discontent [n.] missnöje
discontinue [v.] lägga ned
discotheque [n.] diskotek, disco
discount¹ [n.] rabatt; ~ store rabattvaruhus; ~ train röd avgång; holiday ~ helgrabatt; weekend ~ helgrabatt
discount² [v.] minska; bortse ifrån; rabattera; ~ed article reavara
discourage [v.] avskräcka, försöka hindra
discouraged [adj.] modlös, nedslagen
discourse [n.] tal, samtal
discover [v.] upptäcka
discovery [n.; -ries] upptäckt
discreet [adj.] diskret, taktfull
discrepancy [n.; -cies] avvikelse
discretion [n.] urskillning, omdöme; diskretion; handlingsfrihet
discriminate [v.] diskriminera; skilja
discriminating [adj.] skarpsinnig, kräsen
discrimination [n.] diskriminering; omdöme; skiljande
discuss [v.] diskutera
discussion [n.] diskussion, debatt; ~ group diskussionsforum, diskussionsgrupp
disdain [n.] förakt, ringaktning
disease [n.] sjukdom; sjuka
disguise [v.] förkläda, maskera; dölja, kamoflera
disgusting [adj.] äcklig, otäck

dish [n.; ~es] fat, karott, skål, assiett; maträtt; ~ **brush** diskborste; ~ **towel** torkhandduk; **dirty ~es** disk; **satellite** ~ parabolantenn
dishcloth [n.] disktrasa
dishonest [adj.] oheerlig, oärlig
dishonor [v.] vanära; skända
dishpan [n.] diskbalja
dishrag [n.] disktrasa
dishwasher [n.] diskmaskin
dishwasher-proof [adj.] diskmaskinsfast
dishwashing [n.] diskning; ~ **soap** diskmedel
dishwater [n.] diskvatten
disillusioned [adj.] desillusionerad
disinfect [v.] desinficera
disinfectant [n.] desinfektionsmedel
disintegrate [v.] sönderdela; desintegrera(s)
disk [n.] skiva; ~ **drive** diskettenhet, skivenhet [IT]; ~ **jockey** skivpratare; **hard** ~ hårddisk [IT]
diskette [n.] diskett [IT]
dislike¹ [n.] motvilja, antipati
dislike² [v.] tycka illa om
dislocated [adj.] ur led
disloyal [adj.] illojal
dismay [n.] bestörtning
dismiss [v.; ~es, ~ed, ~ed] avskeda; skicka bort; avfärda
dismissal [n.] avsked; bortskickande, frigivande
disobedient [adj.] olydig, ohörsam
disorder [n.] rubbning; orolighet; oreda
disorderly [adj.] oordentlig; orolig
disorganized [adj.] oordnad, oorganiserad
disparaging [adj.] nedsättande
disparity [n.; -ties] olikhet
disperse [v.] upplösa, sprida
dispersion [n.] kringspriddhet; dispersion
display¹ [n.] visning, skyltning, utställning; bildskärm; ~ **case** skyltskåp, vitrin; ~ **mode** visningsläge
display² [v.] förevisa, visa fram
displeased [adj.] missnöjd
disposable [adj.] engångs-, disponibel; ~ **camera** engångskamera; ~ **razor** engångsrakhyvel

disposal [n.] bortskaffande; avyttrande; **bomb** ~ bombröjning; **waste** ~ avfallshantering; **be at somebody's** ~ stå till någons förfogande
dispose of [v.] skaffa undan; göra sig av med
disposition [n.] läggning; tendens; arrangemang
dispute¹ [n.] dispyt, diskussion; tvist
dispute² [v.] diskutera; strida; kämpa om
disrupt [v.] splittra, upplösa
disruption [n.] splittring; upplösning
diss [v.; abbrev: disrespect; ~es, ~ed, ~ed] [colloq.] dissa, nonchalera, baktala
dissatisfied [adj.] missnöjd
dissect [v.] dissekera, noggrant granska
disseminate [v.] sprida
dissertation [n.] avhandling
dissolve [v.] lösa; ~ **in water** lösa i vatten
distance [n.] avstånd; sträcka; **keep one's** ~ hålla avstånd
distant [adj.] avlägsen, långt bort
distill [v.] bränna, destillera
distinct [adj.] olik, särskild; tydlig, klar
distinction [n.] betydelse; utmärkelse; åtskillnad
distinctive [adj.] utmärkande, särpräglad
distinguish [v.; ~es, ~ed] känneteckna; urskilja, skilja mellan; ~ **oneself** göra sig förtjänt
distinguished [adj.] framstående, lysande; distingerad
distort [v.] förvrida, förvränga
distortion [n.] förvridning, förvrängning
distract [v.] avleda, distrahera
distraction [n.] förvirring; avkoppling; vanvett
distress [n.; ~es] kval; trångmål
distribute [v.] dela ut; sprida
distributed [adj.] distribuerad; fördelad

distribution [n.] utdelning; spridning; ~ **of prizes** prisutdelning

distributor [n.] distributör; fördelare [auto]

district [n.] distrikt; stadsdel

disturb [v.] störa; rubba

disturbance [n.] störande; rubbning; oreda

disturbed [adj.] upprörd; störd

disturbing [adj.] störande, oroande

dithering [n.] ditrering [IT]

div. [abbrev: dividend; division] utdelning; avdelning, division

dive[1] [n.] dykning; simhopp

dive[2] [v.; dived/dove, dived] dyka

diver [n.] dykare

diverse [adj.] olika; mångfaldig

diversion [n.] avledande; tidsfördrift, nöje

diversity [n.] mångfald, skiljaktighet

divert [v.] avleda; underhålla

divide [v.] dela

divided [adj.] delad; skild, söndrad

dividend [n.] dividend; utdelning

divine [adj.] gudomlig; underbar; ~ **service** gudstjänst

diving [n.] dykning; **no** ~ dykning förbjuden; ~ **board** dyktrampolin, sviktbräde; ~ **equipment** dykarutrustning; ~ **mask** cyklopöga

divisible [adj.] delbar

division [n.] division, uppdelning

divorce[1] [n.] skilsmässa

divorce[2] [v.] skilja sig

divorced [adj.] skild, frånskild

DIY [abbrev: do it yourself] gör det själv

dizzy [adj.] yr

DJ [abbrev: disc jockey] discjockey, skivpratare

DJI [abbrev: Dow Jones Index] aktieindex i USA

DLL [abbrev: Dynamic Link Library] DLL [IT]

DMZ [abbrev: demilitarized zone] demiliteriserad zon

DNA [abbrev: deoxyribonucleic acid] deoxiribonukleinsyra (DNA)

do [v.; does, doing, did, done] göra

DOA [abbrev: dead on arrival] död vid ankomsten (till sjukhuset)

dob [abbrev: date of birth] födelsedatum

doc [abbrev: doctor; document] doktor; dokument

dock [n.] docka

docking station [n.] dockningstation [IT]

doctor [n.] läkare, doktor; ~'s **certificate** sjukintyg; ~'s **office** mottagning; ~'s **office hours** läkarmottagning; ~'s **wife** doktorinna; **visit to the** ~ läkarbesök

doctoral [adj.] doktors-; ~ **dissertation** doktorsavhandling

doctorate (Ph.D.) [n.] doktorat, doktorsgrad

Doctor of Laws [n.] juris doktor

Doctor of Philosophy (Ph.D.) [n.] Filosofie doktor (Fil.dr.)

doctrine [n.] doktrin, lära, dogm

document[1] [n.] dokument, handling; **Document Type Definition (DTD)** DTD [IT]

document[2] [v.] dokumentera

documentary film [n.] dokumentärfilm

documentation [n.] dokumentering

DOD [abbrev: Department of Defense] försvarsdepartementet

doe [n.] hind

does [v.present: do] gör

dog [n.] hund

doing [n] handling, verk

do-it-yourself store [n.] gör-det-själv varuhus

doll [n.] docka

dollar [n.] dollar

dolphin [n.] delfin

domain [n.] domän; ~ **address** domänadress [IT]; ~ **name** domännamn [IT]; ~ **name registration** domännamnregistrering [IT]

dome [n.] kupol

domestic [adj.] hem-; inrikes-; ~ **flight** inrikesflyg; ~ **help** hemhjälp; ~ **news** inrikesnyheter; ~ **policy** inrikespolitik; ~ **trade** inrikeshandel

dominance [n.] herravälde, dominans

dominant [adj.] dominerande; dominant

dominate [v.] dominera
domination [n.] herravälde, styre, dominans
Dominican Republic [n.] Dominikanska republiken
Donald Duck [n.] Kalle Anka
donate [v.] skänka
donated by [adj.] skänkt av
donation [n.] donation, gåva
done [adj.] gjord; färdigkokt, färdigstekt [food]
dongle [n.] hårdvarunyckel [IT]
donkey [n.] åsna
donor [n.] donator, givare
don't [contr: do not] gör inte, inte
donut [see: doughnut]
door [n.] dörr, port, ingång; ~ **code** dörrkod; ~ **handle** dörrhantag; ~ **width** dörrbredd
doormat [n.] dörrmatta
doorstep [n.] tröskel; ~**s** yttertrappa
doorway [n.] dörröppning
dormitory [n.; -ries] studenthem
DOS [abbrev: disk-operating system] skivoperativsystem [IT]
dosage [n.] dosering
dose [n.] dos
dot¹ [n.] punkt, prick; ~ **matrix printer** matrisskrivare [IT]
DOT² [abbrev: Department of Transportation] kommunikationsdepartementet
dots [n.pl.] prickar
dotted line [n.] prickar, streckad linje
double¹ [adj.] dubbel; ~ **bed** dubbelsäng; ~ **cabin** dubbelhytt; ~ **click** dubbelklicka [IT]; ~ **precision** dubbel precision [IT]; ~ **room** dubbelrum; ~ **slash** dubbla snedstreck [IT]; ~ **standard** dubbelmoral
double² [adv.] dubbelt
double³ [v.] fördubbla; lägga dubbel
doubles [n.pl.] dubbel
doubt¹ [n.] tvivel, tvekan
doubt² [v.] betvivla, tvivla på
doubtful [adj.] tveksam
doubtless [adv.] utan tvivel, säkert
dough [n.] deg; [colloq.] pengar
doughnut [n.] munk
down¹ [adj.] nere; **be** ~ vara nere;

~ **payment** handpenning
down² [adv.] ned, ner; nere; lodrät [crosswords]; **one flight** ~ en trappa ner
down³ [prep.] nedför; ~ **the stairs** nerför trappan
downhill skiing [n.] utförsåkning, alpin skidåkning
downlink [n.] downlink [IT]
download [v.] hämta hem, ladda ned [IT]
downloading [n.] nedladdning [IT]
download site [n.] programbibliotek [IT]
downstairs [adv.] nere
downstream [adv.] nedåtström
downtown [adv.] **live** ~ bo centralt
downtown area [n.] centrum, stadscentrum
downward [adj.] fallande, sjunkande
downward(s) [adv.] ner
downy [adj.] dunig
doze [v.] slumra
dozen [n.] dussin
Dr. [abbrev: Doctor; Drive] doktor; gata
draft¹ [n.] utkast, plan; inkallelse till militärtjänst; ~ **beer** öl på fat, fatöl
draft² [v.] göra utkast till, formulera; kalla in [military]; ta ut [liquid]
drafty [adj.] dragig
drag¹ [n.] hinder; tråkmåns; transvestitkläder
drag² [v.; -gging, -gged, -gged] dra, släpa
dragon [n.] drake
drain¹ [n.] dräneringsrör, avlopp
drain² [v.] avleda; dränera; tömma
drainage [n.] dränering, avvattning; avrinning
drama [n.] drama; dramatik
dramatic [adj.] dramatisk, teater-
drapes [n.pl.] draperi, gardiner
draw¹ [n.] oavgjord match [sports]
draw² [v.; drew, drawn] dra; rita, teckna
drawbridge [n.] vindbrygga
drawer [n.] låda; **chest of ~s** byrå
drawing [n.] teckning; dragning; ~ **pins** häftstift; ~ **program** ritprogram

dreadful [adj.] förskräcklig
dream[1] [n.] dröm
dream[2] [v.; dreamed/dreamt, dreamed/dreamt] drömma
dreamer [n.] drömmare, svärmare
dress[1] [n.; ~es] klänning; ~ circle första raden [theater seats]; ~ designer modedesigner
dress[2] [v.; ~es, ~ed] klä (sig); förbinda; get ~ed klä på sig
dressed [adj.] klädd (i)
dressing [n.] dressing; salva; ~ gown morgonrock
dressmaker [n.] sömmerska; ~'s skrädderi
dried [adj.] torkad, torr-; ~ fruit torkad frukt
drift[1] [n.] driva; ström; tendens
drift[2] [v.] driva, glida
drill[1] [n.] borr; exercis, övning
drill[2] [v.] borra; exercera
drink[1] [n.] dryck; drink [alcoholic], sup [hard liquor]; have some ~s supa
drink[2] [v.; drank, drunk] dricka; ~ up dricka ur
drinking water [n.] dricksvatten
drip[1] [n.] dropp
drip[2] [v.; -pping, -pped, -pped] droppa, drypa
drip-dry [adj.] strykfri
dripstone cave [n.] droppstens-grotta
drive[1] [n.] biltur; uppfartsväg; energi; kampanj; enhet [IT]; ~ specification enhetsbeteckning [IT]
drive[2] [v.; drove, driven] köra; driva; tvinga; ~ a car köra bil; ~ into köra på; ~ off the road köra av vägen; ~ on the right köra på höger sida; ~ out driva ut
driver [n.] chaufför, förare; driv-rutin [IT]; ~'s license körkort
driveway [n.] uppfartsväg
driving [n.] bilköring, körning; ~ lesson körlektion; ~ on the right högertrafik; ~ range driving-range [golf]; ~ school bilskola, trafikskola; ~ under the influence (DUI) rattfylleri
drizzle [n.] duggregn

drop[1] [n.] droppe; nedgång
drop[2] [v.; -pping, -pped, -pped] falla, sjunka; tappa, släppa, fälla ; ~ by/in titta in; ~ s.o. off släppa ngn
drop-down menu [n.] rullgardins-meny [IT]
drops [n.pl.] droppar
drown [v.] drunkna
drug[1] [n.] drog, läkemedel; narkotika; ~ addiction narkotika-beroende; ~ addict narkoman; ~ crime narkotikabrott; ~ dealer narkotikalangare; ~ dependence narkotikaberoende; ~ traffic narkotikahandel; ~ trafficker narkotikalangare
drug[2] [v.; -gging, -gged, -gged] droga, bedöva
drugs [n.pl.] droger, narkotika
drugstore [n.] apotek
drum [n.] trumma
drunk [adj.] berusad, full
dry[1] [adj. torr; ~ land fastland; ~ skin torr hud
dry[2] [v.; dries, dried, dried] torka
dry-cleaned [adj.] kemtvättad
dry cleaner [n.] kemtvätt
dry-cleaning [n.] kemtvätt
DST [abbrev: daylight savings time] sommartid
DTP [abbrev: desktop publishing] layoutprogram [IT]
DTs [abbrev: delirium tremens] delirium tremens
dual [adj.] dubbel; ~ boot dubbel start [IT]
dub [v.; -bbing, -bbed, -bbed] dubba
dubbed [adj.] dubbad [film]
dubious [adj.] tvivelaktig; tveksam
duck[1] [n.] anka
duck[2] [v.] dyka ned; böja sig
due [adj.] som ska komma, väntad; som ska betalas; tillbörlig; ~ date termin; be ~ to bero på, komma sig
due to [prep.] beroende på
DUI [abbrev: driving under the influence] rattfylleri
duke [n.] hertig

dull [adj.] tråkig, trist; matt; trög
duly [adv.] vederbörligen; i rätt tid
dumb [adj.] stum; dum
dummy variable [n.] fiktiv variabel
[IT]
dump[1] [n.] soptipp; håla; depå
dump[2] [v.] tippa, slänga
dumping [n.] tippning; **no ~** tippning förbjuden
dumpling [n.] klimp
duplex [adj.] tvåfaldig, duplex-
duplicate [n.] dubblett, duplikat
durable [adj.] hållbar, varaktig; **~
goods** varaktiga konsumtionsvaror
duration [n.] varaktighet, längd
during [prep.] under
dusk [n.] skymning
dust[1] [n.] damm, stoft; puder
dust[2] [v.] damma
dusty [adj.] dammig
Dutch[1] [adj.] nederländsk
Dutch[2] **(language)** [n.] holländska,
nederländska
duties [n.pl.] plikter

duty [n.; -ties] plikt; tjänst; avgift,
tull; **on ~** jourhavande; **be on ~** ha
jourtjänst
duty-free [adj.] tullfri, tax-fri; **~
goods** tax-fria varor, tullfria varor;
~ shop tax-fri affär, taxfreebutik
DVD [abbrev: digital video disc,
digital versatile disc] dvd-skiva
[IT]; **~ format** DVD-format [IT]
DVT [abbrev: deep-vein thrombo-
sis] djup ventrombos
dwelling [n.] bostad
DWI [abbrev: driving while intoxi-
cated] rattfylleri
dye [n.] färg, färgning
dyed [adj.] färgad
dying [adj.] döende
dynamic [adj.] dynamisk
dynamite [n.] dynamit
dynasty [n.; -ties] dynasti
dysentery [n.; -ries] dysenteri
dyslexic [adj.] dyslektisk, ordblind
dz. [abbrev: dozen (l2)] dussin

E

E¹ [abbrev: east, eastern] ost, öster

e-² [abbrev: electronic, Internet] elektronisk, Internet

ea. [abbrev: each] var, per styck

each [det./pron.] var, varje; per styck; **~ for himself** var och en för sig; **~ his own** var sin/sitt; **~ other** varandra; **$2 ~** 2 dollar per styck

eager [adj.] ivrig; angelägen

eagle [n.] örn

ear [n.] öra; **~ inflammation** öron-inflammation; **~, nose and throat (ENT) specialist** öron-näsa-hals-läkare

earache [n.] ont i örat, öronvärk

earlier¹ [adj.comp.] tidigare

earlier² [adv.comp.] förut, tidigare

early¹ [adj.] tidig

early² [adv.] tidigt; i god tid; bitti; **too ~** för tidigt; **as ~ as** redan

earn [v.] tjäna

earnings [n.pl.] intäkter [pl.], inkomster [pl.]

earphones [n.pl.] hörlurar [pl.]

earring [n.] örhänge

earth [n.] jord

earthquake [n.] jordbävning

ease¹ [n.] lätthet; välbehag, lugn

ease² [v.] lätta, minska; sakta (farten)

easily [adv.] lätt; mycket väl

east¹ [adj.] öster

east² [n.] öst

East Timor [n.] Östtimor

Easter [n.] Påsk; **~ Monday** annandag påsk; **~ Sunday** Påskdagen; **Happy ~!** Glad Påsk!

easterly [adj.] ostlig, östlig

eastern [adj.] öst-, öster

easy¹ [adj.] enkel, lätt; lugn, bekväm; **~ chair** fåtölj, vilstol

easy² [adv.] lätt; bekvämt; försiktigt; **take it ~** ta det lugnt

easy-going [adj.] lättsam

eat [v.; ate, eaten] äta, förtära; **~ at home** äta inne; **~ out** äta ute

ebony [n.] ebenholts

e-book [n.] elektronisk bok (e-bok) [IT]; **~ disc** läsplatta [IT]; **~ file** e-bokfil [IT]; **~ reader** bokdator [IT]

e-business [n.; ~es] e-handel [IT]

EC [abbrev: European Communities] Europeiska gemenskaperna

e-cash [n.] digitala pengar [pl.] [IT]

ECB [abbrev: European Central Bank] Europeiska centralbanken

ECG [abbrev: see: EKG]

echo¹ [n.; ~es] eko, genljud

echo² [v.; ~es, ~ed] återkasta

ECJ [abbrev: European Court of Justice] EG-domstolen

ecological [adj.] ekologisk

ecology [n.] ekologi

e-commerce [n.] näthandel, e-handel [IT]

econ. [abbrev: economics] ekonomi

economic [adj.] ekonomisk

Economic and Monetary Union (EMU) [n.] Ekonomiska och monetära unionen (EMU)

economical [adj.] ekonomisk; sparsam

economically [adv.] ekonomiskt

economics [n.] ekonomi

economist [n.] ekonom, civilekonom

economy [n.; -mies] ekonomi, näringsliv; **~ class** [n.] turistklass

eczema [n.] eksem

ed. [abbrev: edition; editor; education] upplaga; redaktör; undervisning, utbildning

edge [n.] kant, egg; fördel

edit [v.] redigera

edition [n.] upplaga, utgåva

editor [n.] redaktör, utgivare

editorial [n.] ledare

EDP [abbrev: electronic data processing] elektronisk data-behandling [IT]

EDT [abbrev: Eastern Daylight Time] sommartid i östliga USA

educate [v.] utbilda; undervisa

education [n.] utbildning, undervisning, fostran; utbildningsväsen, pedagogi

educational [adj.] undervisnings-, skol-, pedagogisk, läro-; **~ advisor** studierådgivare; **~ background** skolunderbyggnad

EEA [abbrev: European Economic

Area] Europeiska ekonomiska
samarbetsområdet
EEG [abbrev: electroencephalo-
gram] elektroencefalogram
eel [n.] ål
effect[1] [n.] effekt, verkan; inflytande; **~s** effekter, tillhörigheter
effect[2] [v.] verkställa, genomföra
effective [adj.] effektiv, verksam;
effektfull; faktisk
effectively [adv.] effektivt; i själva
verket
effectiveness [n.] effektivitet,
prestanda
efficiency [n.; -cies] effektivitet
efficient [adj.] effektiv, verksam,
duktig
efficiently [adv.] effektivt
effort [n.] ansträngning
EFL [abbrev: English as a foreign
language] undervisning i engelska
som främmande språk
EFTA [abbrev: European Free
Trade Association] EFTA
e.g. [abbrev: exempli gratia: for
example] till exempel (t ex)
egg [n.] ägg, **~ cup** äggkopp; **~ dish**
äggrätt; **~ sandwich** äggsmörgås;
~ spoon äggsked; **~ white** äggvita;
~ yolk äggula
eggplant [n.] aubergine, äggplanta
ego [n.] jag, ego
Egypt [n.] Egypten
Egyptian [adj.] egyptisk
EIB [abbrev: European Investment
Bank] Europeiska investeringsbanken
eight [num.] åtta
eight-bit [adj.] åttaställig [IT]
eighteen [num.] arton
eighteenth [adj.] artonde
eighth [adj.] åttonde
eightieth [adj.] åttionde
eighty [num.] åttio
either[1] [adv.] heller; **not me ~** inte
jag heller
either[2] [conj.] antingen; **~ A or B**
antingen A eller B
either[3] [det./pron.] endera; vardera,
båda, vilken som helst
EKG [abbrev: electrocardiogram]
elektrokardiogram (EKG)

elaborate [adj.] raffinerad,
komplicerad
elastic bandage [n.] elastisk binda
elbow [n.] armbåge
elder[1] [adj.comp.: old] äldre
elder[2] [n.] (församlings)äldste
elderly [adj.] äldre, ganska gammal;
~ woman tant
eldest [adj.superl.: old] äldst
e-learning [n.] e-kurs, e-utbildning,
webbaserad utbildning, webbkurs
[IT]
elect [v.] välja
elected [adj.] vald
election [n.] val; **~ day** valdag; **~
poster** valaffisch; **~ result** valresultat
elective [adj.] valfri; **~ courses**
tillvalsämne, valfritt ämne
elector [n.] väljare
electoral [adj.] val-
electorate [n.] väljarkår
electric [adj.] elektrisk (el); **~
heater** värmeelement; **~ meter**
elektricitetsmätare, elmätare; **~
outlet** eluttag; **~ plug** stickkontakt; **~ wheelchair** elrullstol
electrical [adj.] elektrisk (el); **~
goods** elartiklar, elektriska varor;
~ outlet nätuttag
electricity [n.] elektricitet (el); **~
bill** elräkning
electrolyte solution [n.] vätskeersättning
electron [n.] elektron
electronic [adj.] elektronisk, e-; **~
flash** elektronisk blixt; **~ transfer**
elektronisk överföring [banking]
electronics [n.] elektronik
elegant [adj.] elegant, förnäm
element [n.] element
elementary [adj.] elementär, enkel;
~ school grundskola; **~ school
pupil** grundskoleelev; **~ school
teacher** grundskolelärare
elephant [n.] elefant
elevator [n.] hiss
eleven [num.] elva
eleventh [adj.] elfte
elf [n.; elves] älva, alf, troll
elicit [v.] locka fram, framkalla,
väcka

eligible [adj.] berättigad, kvalificerad; passande
eliminate [v.] eliminera; likvidera
elite [n.] elit
elk [n.] älg; ~ **cow** älgko; ~ **hunt** älgjakt; ~ **meat** älgkött; ~ **roast** älgstek
else [adv.] annan, annat, fler, mer; **or** ~ eller också; **something** ~? något annat?
elsewhere [adv.] annanstans
ELT [abbrev: English language teaching] undervisning i engelska som främmande språk
e-mail[1] [abbrev: electronic mail] e-brev, e-meddelande, e-post, mail, mejl [IT]; ~ **account** e-postkonto; ~ **address** e-adress, e-postadress; ~ **administration** e-posthantering; ~ **management** e-posthantering; ~ **message** e-postmeddelande; ~ **program** e-postprogram; ~ **service** e-posttjänst [IT]
e-mail[2] [v.] maila, mejla, e-posta [IT]
embark [v.] inskeppa, ta ombord; inskeppa sig, gå ombord; ~ **on** inlåta sig i, ge sig in på, sätta igång med
embarrass [v.; ~es, ~ed, ~ed] göra förlägen, göra generad
embarrassed [adj.] förlägen, generad
embarrassing [adj.] pinsam, penibel
embarrassment [n.] förlägenhet; besvär
embassy [n.; -ssies] ambassad
embed [v.; -dding, -dded, -dded] bädda in
embedded [adj.] inbäddad; ~ **system** inbyggt system [IT]
embody [v.; -dies, -died]] ge konkret form; innehålla
embrace[1] [n.] omfamning; anammade
embrace[2] [v.] omfamna; begagna; omfatta
embroider [v.] brodera
embroidery [n.; -ries] broderi, brodering
embryo [n.] embryo
em dash [n.] em-streck [IT]

emerald [n.] smaragd
emerge [v.] dyka upp; uppstå
emergence [n.] uppdykande, uppkomst
emergency[1] [adj.] reserv-, nöd-, tvångs-, akut-; ~ **brake** nödbroms; ~ **center** akuten; ~ **duty hours** jourtid; ~ **exit** nödutgång; ~ **landing** nödlandning; ~ **medical service** olyckfallsavdelning; ~ **repair disk** reparationsdiskett [IT]; ~ **room** akutmottagning, sjukhusakuten; ~ **service** jourtjänst; ~ **treatment** akutvård
emergency[2] [n.; -cies] nödläge, nödsituation
emigrant [n.] emigrant, utvandrare
emigrate [v.] emigrera, utvandra
emigration [n.] utvandring
emission [n.] utsläpp, utstrålning
emoticon [n.] emotikon [IT]
emotion [n.] sinnesrörelse; känsla, emotion
emotional [adj.] känslo-; känslig
emperor [n.] kejsar
emphasis [n.; -ses] betoning, emfas
emphasize [v.] betona
empire [n.] kejsarrike, världrike, imperium
empirical [adj.] empirisk
employ [v.] anställa; använda
employee [n.] anställd, arbetstagare; ~**s' organization** arbetstagarsorganisation
employer [n.] arbetsgivare; ~**s' association** arbetsgivarorganisation
employment [n.] ställning; anställning; ~ **ad** platsannons; ~ **office** Arbetsförmedlingen (AF); ~ **status** anställningsform
empress [n.; -sses] kejsarinna
empty[1] [adj.] tom, slut; ~ **bottle** tomglas; **on an** ~ **stomach** på fastande mage
empty[2] [v.; -ties, -tied, -tied] tömma
EMS [abbrev: European Monetary System] Europeiska monetära systemet
EMU [abbrev: Economic and Monetary Union] Ekonomiska och monetära unionen

enable [v.] göra det möjligt, tillåta
enamel [n.] emalj
encl. [abbrev: enclosed, enclosure]
bilaga
enclose [v.] bifoga; omgärda, omge
enclosure [n.] bilaga; stängsel
encode [v.] koda in [IT]
encompass [v.; -sses, -ssed, -ssed]
omfatta; omge
encore!¹ [interj.] dakapo!
encore² [n.] extranummer
encounter¹ [n.] möte
encounter² [v.] röka, träffa, möta
encourage [v.] uppmuntra, gynna
encouragement [n.] uppmuntran;
främjande
encouraging [adj.] uppmuntrande,
hoppingivande
encroachment [n.] intrång
encryption key [n.] krypteringsnyckel [IT]
encyclopedia [n.] encyklopedi,
uppslagsbok
end¹ [n.] slut, ända; uppehåll; ändamål; ~ tag sluttagg [IT]; at/in
the ~ till sist, till slut, slutigen
end² [v.] sluta, ta slut
ending [n.] avslutning; ändelse
[gram]
endive [n.] endiv
endless [adj.] oändlig, gränslös
endorse [v.] skriva under på; stödja;
endossera
endowment [n.] donation; begåvning
endure [v.] vara; tåla, lida
enemy [n.; -mies] fiende
energetic [adj.] energisk
energy [n.; -gies] energi; ork; have
the ~ to orka
enforce [v.] upprätthålla respekten
för; tvinga fram
enforcement [n.] upprätthållande;
framtvingande
eng. [abbrev: engineering] teknik,
ingenjörsvetenskap
engage [v.] engagera, anställa,
uppta; delta i
engaged [adj.] engagerad; förlovad;
get ~ förlova sig
engagement [n.] förbindelse;
förlovning; engagemang

engine [n.] motor; lokomotiv
engineer [n.] ingenjör, tekniker;
maskinist
engineering [n.] ingenjörvetenskap;
teknik
England [n.] England
English¹ [adj.] engelsk; ~ woman
engelska
English² (language) [n.] engelska
English-speaking [adj.]
engelsktalande
Englishman [n.; -men] engelsman
engrave [v.] gravera
engraving [n.] gravyr
enhance [v.] intensifiera, öka;
förbättra
enhanced [adj.] förbättrad, utökad
enjoy [v.] njuta, njuta av; ~ oneself
ha det roligt
enjoyable [adj.] njutbar, trevlig
enjoyment [n.] njutning, nöje
enlarge [v.] förstora
enormous [adj.] enorm, väldig
enormously [adv.] enormt, kolossalt
enough [adv.] tillräckligt, lagom;
nog; ~ of tillräckligt med; that's ~
det räcker
enquire/enquiry [see: inquire/
inquiry]
enroll in [v.] skriva sig in, anmäla
sig till
ensue [v.] följa
ensure [v.] tillförsäkra
ENT [abbrev: ear, nose and throat
care] öron-, näs- och halsvård
entail [v.] medföra
enter [v.] gå/komma in, stiga in;
beträda; ~ your PIN slå in PIN
numret
Enter key [n.] Retur tangent [IT]
enterprise [n.] företag; företagsamhet
entertain [v.] underhålla; ha gäster
entertainer [n.] underhållare
entertaining [adj.] underhållande,
roande
entertainment [n.] underhållning,
nöje
enthusiasm [n.] entusiasm
enthusiast [n.] entusiast
enthusiastic [adj.] entusiastisk
entire [adj.] hel, total, intakt

entirely [adv.] helt och hållet
entitle [v.] berättiga
entitlement [n.] berättigande, rätt
entity [n.; -ties] enhet; begrepp
entrance [n.] ingång, entré; uppgång; inträde, tillträde; ~ **test** tillträdesprov
entry [n.; -ries] tillträde, åtkomst; inresa [into country]; **date of** ~ **into functions** tillträdesdag; **no** ~ **unless authorized** obehöriga äga ej tillträde
envelope [n.] kuvert
enviable [adj.] avundsvärd
envious [adj.] avundsjuk
environment [n.] miljö; ~ **friendly** miljövänlig
environmental [adj.] miljö-; ~ **pollution** miljöförstöring; ~ **protection** miljövård
environmentalist [n.] miljövän
environs [n.pl.] omgivning
envisage [v.] betrakta, förutse
enzyme [n.] enzym
epic[1] [adj.] episk
epic[2] [n.] epos
epilepsy [n.; -sies] epilepsi
epileptic [n.] epileptiker
episode [n.] episod, händelse
epoch [n.] epok
epoch-making [adj.] epokgörande
equal[1] [adj.] jämlik, lika
equal[2] [v.] vara lik (med)
equality [n.; -ties] jämlikhet
equally [adv.] lika, likaså
equal(s) sign (=) [n.] likhetstecken
equation [n.] ekvation
equator [n.] ekvatorn
equilibrium [n.; ~s/-bria] jämvikt(släge)
equip [v.; -pped] utrusta; ekipera
equipment [n.] utrustning
equity [n.; -ties] rättfärdighet; ~ **capital** eget kapital; **equities** stamaktier
equivalent[1] [adj.] likvärdig, jämförlig
equivalent[2] [n.] motsvarande värde; motsvarighet, ekvivalent
ER [abbrev: emergency room] akutmottagning

era [n.] tidsperiod
erase [v.] radera, sudda ut
eraser [n.] radergummi
erect [v.] resa, uppföra
erected [adj.] uppförd
erode [v.] fräta bort
erosion [n.] bortfrätande, erosion
errand [n.] ärende
error [n.] fel; ~ **handler** felhanterare [IT]
escalator [n.] rulltrappa
escape[1] [n.] rymning, flykt; utströmning; **Escape key (Esc)** escape-tangent [IT]
escape[2] [v.] fly, rymma; slippa, undkomma; ~ **from** fly
escort[1] [n.] eskort; kavalier
escort[2] [v.] ledsaga, eskortera
eskimo [n.] eskimå
ESL [abbrev: English as a second language] undervisning i engelska som främmande språk
ESOL [abbrev: English for speakers of other languages] undervisning i engelska som främmande språk
ESP[1] [abbrev: extrasensory perception] utomsinnlig varseblivning, extrasensorisk perception
esp.[2] [abbrev: especially] i synnerhet
especially [adv.] speciellt, i synnerhet, särskilt
Esq. [abbrev: Esquire (honorific added after lawyer's name)] advokat
essay [n.] uppsats; försök
essence [n.] innersta väsen; essens
essential [adj.] väsentlig, nödvändig; verklig
essentially [adv.] väsentligen, i huvudsak
EST[1] [abbrev: Eastern Standard Time] normaltid i östligaste USA
est.[2] [abbrev: established; estimated] etablerad, grundad; beräknad
establish [v.] upprätta, etablera, instifta
established [adj.] fästställd, etablerad; bevisad
establishment [n.] upprättande, etablering; företag; institution; **the** ~ det etablerade samhället

estate [n.] lantegendom, gods; dödsbo; **real** ~ fast egendom
estimate[1] [n.] uppskattning, värdering; bedömning
estimate[2] [v.] uppskatta, värdera; beräkna
estimated [adj.] beräknad; ~ **time of arrival (ETA)** beräknad ankomsttid; ~ **time of departure (ETD)** beräknad avgångstid
Estonia [n.] Estland
Estonian[1] [adj.] estländsk
Estonian[2] **(language)** [n.] estländska
et al. [abbrev: et alii: and others] och andra
et cetera (etc.) [adv.] med mera (mm), och dylikt (o d), och så vidare (osv)
et seq. [abbrev: et sequens: and following (pages, words)] och följande (sidor, ord)
ETA [abbrev: estimated time of arrival] beräknad ankomsttid
etc. [abbrev: et cetera] och dylikt (o.d.), och så vidare (osv.)
etching [n.] etsning, kopparstick
ETD [abbrev: estimated time of departure] beräknad avgångstid
eternal [adj.] evig, oändlig
eternity [n.; -ties] evighet
ethical [adj.] etisk, moralisk
ethics [n.] etik, moral
Ethiopia [n.] Etiopien
Ethiopian [adj.] etiopisk
ethnic [adj.] etnisk; ~ **cleansing** etnisk rensing
EU [abbrev: European Union] Europeiska unionen (EU)
EU citizen [n.] EU-medborgare
Euratom [abbrev: European Atomic Energy Community] Europeiska atomenergigemenskapen (Euratom)
euro [n.] euro [currency]
Euro directive [n.] EU-direktiv
Europe [n.] Europa
European [adj.] europeisk; ~ **championship** europamästerskap (EM)
European Commission [n.] EU-kommissionen

European Communities (EC) [n.pl.] Europeiska gemenskaperna (EG) [pl.]
European Economic Area (EEA) [n.] Europeiska ekonomiska samarbetsområdet (EES)
European Parliament [n.] Europaparlamentet
European Union (EU) [n.] Europeiska unionen (EU)
evaluate [v.] utvärdera, evaluera
evaluation [n.] utvärdering, evaluering
evasion [n.] undvikelse; **tax** ~ skattefusk
evasive [adj.] undvikande, svävande: **be** ~ slingra sig, komma med undanflykter
even[1] [adj.] jämn, slät; **get** ~ **with sbdy** bli kvitt med ngn, ta revansch på ngn
even[2] [adv.] även; till och med (t o m); ~ **if** om än, även om
evening [n.] kväll, afton; ~ **class** kvällskurs; ~ **dress** aftonklänning; ~ **newspaper** kvällstidning; ~ **service** [church] aftonsång; ~ **student** kvällsstuderande; ~ **wear** aftonkläder; **good** ~ god kväll; **in the** ~ på kvällen; **this** ~ i kväll
evenly [adv.] jämnt, lika; lugnt
event [n.] händelse, evenemang, attraktion; ~ **handler** händelsehanterare [IT]
eventual [adj.] slutlig; därav följande
eventually [adv.] så småningom
ever [adv.] någonsin; ~ **since** alltsedan
every [adj.] var(t), varenda, varje; ~ **other** varannan/vartannat; ~ **other day** varannan dag; ~ **third** var tredje
everybody [pron.] alla
everyday [adj.] daglig, vardags
everyone [pron.] alla
everything [pron.] allting, allt; ~ **possible** allt möjligt
everywhere [adv.] överallt
evidence [n.] bevis, stöd; vittnesmål
evident [adj.] tydlig, uppenbar, självklar

evidently [adv.] tydligen
evil[1] [adj.] ond, elak; skadlig
evil[2] [n.] ont, det onda; **the lesser** ~ det minst onda
evoke [v.] väcka, framkalla
evolution [n.] utveckling; **theory of** ~ utvecklingslära
evolutionary [adj.] utvecklings-, evolutions-
evolve [v.] utveckla (sig); frambringa
ex-[1] [prefix] före detta
ex.[2] [abbrev: example] exempel
ex[3] [n.]: **my** ~ min före detta fru/man
exacerbation [n.] irritation; förvärrande
exact [adj.] exakt; ~ **amount** exakt belopp; ~ **change** exakt växel, jämna pengar; ~ **fare** exakt belopp; ~ **payment** jämna pengar
exactly [adv.] exakt, jämnt, precis, just det; **not** ~ inte precis
exaggerate [v.] överdriva
exaggerated [adj.] överdriven
exaggeration [n.] överdrift
exam [n.; see: examination]
examination [n.] tentamen, examen, prov; undersökning; **without** ~ examensfri
examine [v.] undersöka; förhöra
examining room [n.] undersökningsrum
example [n.] exempel; **for** ~ (e.g.) till exempel (t ex)
excavation [n.] utgrävning
exceed [v.] överskrida
excellence [n.] förträfflighet, utmärkthet
excellent [adj.] utmärkt
except[1] [conj.] utom att
except (for)[2] [prep.] utom
exception [n.] undantag; **without** ~ utan undantag; ~ **error** undantagsfel [IT]
exceptional [adj.] ovanlig, exceptionell
exceptionally [adv.] ovanligt, exceptionellt
excess[1] [adj.] över-, överskotts-; ~ **baggage** övervikt, överviktsbagage; ~ **fat** överflödigt fett
excess[2] [n.] överdrift; omåttlighet; överskridande; överskott

excessive [adj.] orimlig, omåttlig
exchange[1] [n.] utbyte, byte; ~ **of views** meningsutbyte; ~ **rate** valutanotering, växelkurs; ~ **student** utbytesstudent; **right to** ~ bytesrätt
exchange[2] [v.] byta, byta ut
excite [v.] egga upp; stimulera; väcka
excited [adj.] ivrig
excitement [n.] sinnesrörelse, spänning
exciting [adj.] spännande
exclaim [v.] skrika, ropa, utropa
exclamation [n.] utrop; ~ **point (!)** utropstecken (!)
exclude [v.] utesluta
excluding [prep.] exklusive
exclusion [n.] uteslutande, utestängande
exclusive [adj.] exclusiv, sluten; odelad, särskild
exclusively [adv.] uteslutande, enbart
ex-con [abbrev: ex-convict] straffånge
excursion [n.] utflykt, rundtur
excuse[1] [n.] ursäkt, bortförklaring, förevändning
excuse[2] [v.] förlåta, ursäkta, rättfärdiga; ~ **me** förlåt (mig), ursäkta
exec. [abbrev: executive] chef, företagsledare
executable [adj.] exekverbar, körbar [IT]
execute [v.] avrätta; utföra, verkställa, expediera; exekvera
executed [adj.] utförd [IT]
execution [n.] avrättning; utförande; exekvering
executive[1] [adj.] verkställande; ~ **committee** styrelse; ~ **director** arbetande styrelsemedlem, verkställande direktör
executive[2] [n.] företagsledare, chef; styrelse
exemption [n.] befrielse, frikallelse; undantag, dispens
exercise[1] [n.] motion, övning; utövning; ~ **bike** motionscykel; ~ **book** skrivbok; ~ **room** motionsrum; **do** ~ gymnastisera

exercise[2] [v.] motionera; öva; utöva
exert [v.] utöva, bruka, utvekla; ~ oneself anstränga sig
exhaust[1] [n.] avgas; ~ pipe avgasrör
exhaust[2] [v.] uttömma, suga ut; utmatta
exhausted [adj.] uttröttad; slut
exhibit [v.] förevisa, ställa ut; visa
exhibition [n.] utställning, visning, mässa; ~ catalog utställningskatalog
exile [n.] landsförvisning; exil
exist [v.] existera; förekomma; still ~ finnas kvar
existence [n.] tillvaro, existens, förekomst
existing [adj.] existerande, nuvarande, befintlig
exit[1] [n.] utgång [way out]; avfart [highway]; utfart [vehicles from building]; utresa [leaving country]
exit[2] [v.] gå ut; avsluta [IT]
exotic [adj.] exotisk
expand [v.] utvigda; breda ut; utveckla
expanded memory [n.] expanderat minne [IT]
expansion [n.] utbredande; expansion; ~ board expansionskort, utbyggnadskort [IT]
expect [v.] vänta, räkna med; be ~ing vänta barn
expectation [n.] väntan, förväntning
expected [adj.] förväntad, förmodad
expedition [n.] expedition
expel [v.; -lled] driva ut; utvisa, avstänga
expenditure [n.] utgift; förbrukning
expense [n.] kostnad, utgift
expensive [adj.] dyr
experience[1] [n.] erfarenhet, vana, upplevelse
experience[2] [v.] uppleva, undergå
experienced [adj.] erfaren, rutinerad
experiment[1] [n.] försök, experiment
experiment[2] [v.] experimentera, göra försök
experimental [adj.] försöks-, experimental
expert[1] [adj.] sakkunnig; skicklig;

förfaren; ~ system expertsystem [IT]
expert[2] [n.] expert, specialist, fackman
expertise [n.] sakkunskap, expertis
expiration date [n.] utlöpande datum
expire [v.] löpa ut, gå ut
explain [v.] förklara
explanation [n.] förklaring
explicit [adj.] tydlig, klar, uttrycklig
explicitly [adv.] tydligt
explode [v.] explodera
exploit [v.] utnyttja, bearbeta, exploatera
exploitation [n.] exploatering
exploration [n.] utforskning
explore [v.] utforska
Explorer [n.] Utforskare [IT]
explosion [n.] explosion, sprängning; utbrott
explosive [adj.] explosiv, spräng-
export[1] [n.] exportvara; export
export[2] [v.] exportera
expose [v.] utsätta, lämna oskyddad; exponera; röja; ~ to utsätta för
exposed [adj.] utsatt
exposure [n.] utsatthet; avslöjande; exponering; ~ meter exponeringsmätare
express[1] [adj.] uttrycklig, direkt; express-; ~ checkout snabbkassa; ~ mail expresspost; ~ shipment [goods, money] express; ~ train direkttåg, expresståg, snälltåg
express[2] [v.; -es, -ed] uttrycka (sig); ~ one's views uttala sig
expression [n.] uttryck; fras
expressionism [n.] expressionism
exquisite [adj.] utsökt, fin; utomordentlig
extend [v.] sträcka sig; förlänga, sträcka ut
extended [adj.] utsträckt; förlängd, utvigdad
extension [n.] förlängning; ~ cord förlängningsladd
extensive [adj.] vidsträckt, omfattande, extensiv
extensively [adv.] i stor utsträckning

extent [n.] utsträckning, omfång; område

exterior¹ [adj.] yttre, ytter; utomhus-

exterior² [n.] utsida, yttre; exteriör

external [adj.] extern, utvärtes; ~ **memory** externminne [IT]

extinct [adj.] slocknad; utdöd

extinction [n.] utsläckande; utdöende

extra¹ [adj./adv.] extra; ~ **charge** tillägg; ~ **time** förlängning; ~ **week** extravecka; **be** ~ tillkomma

extra² [n.] extra sak; extraavgift; extrahjälp; extranummer

extract¹ [n.] extrakt; utdrag

extract² [v.] dra ut; extrahera; tvinga fram

extraordinary [adj.] utomordentlig

extreme¹ [adj.] ytterst, extrem

extreme² [n.] ytterlighet

extremely [adv.] ytterst, oerhört, synnerligen

extroverted [adj.] utåtriktad

eye¹ [n.] öga; ~ **disease** ögonsjukdom; ~ **doctor** ögonläkare; ~ **drops** ögondroppar

eye² [v.] betrakta

eyebrow [n.] ögonbryn

eyeglasses [n.pl.] glasögon

e-zine [n.] nyhetsbrev [IT]

F

F [abbrev: Fahrenheit; fail (school mark)] Fahrenheit [temperaturskalan]; icke godkänd

fabric [n.] tyg; struktur, textur

fabulous [adj.] sagolik, fantastisk

facade [n.] fasad, min

face¹ [n.] ansikte; ~ cream ansiktskräm; ~ mask ansiktsskydd

face² [v.] möta; vända sig mot

face-saving [adj.] som räddar ansiktet

facial [n.] ansiktsbehandling

facilitate [v.] underlätta, främja

facility [n.; -ties] lätthet; facilities bekvämligheter, resurser

facing [prep.] mot

fact [n.] faktum, uppgift, företeelse; in ~ faktiskt; ~ sheet faktablad

fact-finding [adj.] undersöknings-

faction [n.] fraktion, klick

factor [n.] faktor

factory [n.; -ries] fabrik; ~ outlet försäljningsställe

factual [adj.] saklig, objektiv; verklig

faculty [n.; -ties] fakultet; lärarstab; förmåga; ~ adviser studierådgivare

fad [n.] modefluga

fade [v.] vissna, blekna; ~ out tona bort

fag [n.; vul.] homofil, bög [colloq.]

fail¹ [n.; school mark] icke godkänd (IG); without ~ säkert, ofelbart

fail² [v.] misslyckas, stranda; bli icke godkänd; göra bankrott; svika

failure [n.] misslyckande; funktionsavbrott [IT]; be a ~ vara misslyckad; crop ~ felslagen skörd; engine ~ motorstopp; heart ~ hjärtsvikt; power ~ strömavbrott

faint¹ [adj.] svag; matt, otydlig; feel ~ bli svimfärdig

faint² [n.] svimning

faint³ [v.] svimma; ~ing spell svimning

fair¹ [adj.] rättvis, just; klar; lovande; ljus

fair² [adv.] rättvist, tydligt, rent

fair³ [n.] mässa; marknads-; nöjesfält; ~ ground nöjesfält

fairly [adv.] ganska, relativt; rättvist

fairy [n.-ries] fe, älva; ~ tale fe saga

faith [n.] tro, förtroende

faithful [adj.] trogen; trovägen; exakt

faithfully [adv.] troget; uppriktigt; exakt

fake [adj.] förfalskad, falsk

fall¹ [n.] fall, sjunkande; höst; ~s vattenfall; ~ semester/term hösttermin; this/next ~ till hösten

fall² [v.; fell, fallen] falla, ramla; sänka sig; avta; bli

fallacious [adj.] falsk, vilseledande

fallacy [n.; -cies] misstag; falsk slutledning

fallback [n.] reservutväg

fallibility [n.] felbarhet

fallout [n.] nedfall; biverkningar

false [adj.] falsk, felaktig; oäkta; ~ start tjuvstart, felaktig start

falsehood [n.] lögn, oärlighet

fame [n.] ryktbarhet, berömmelse

familiar [adj.] bekant, känd; kamratlig; otvungen; be ~ with känna till

family [n.; -lies] familj, släkt; ~ allowance barnbidrag; ~ entertainment familjenöje; ~ planning barnbegränsning; ~ with children barnfamilj

famine [n.] hungersnöd, svält

famous [adj.] berömd, känd

fan¹ [n.] fan, entusiast; fläkt [breeze]; ~ belt fläktrem

fan² [v.] fläkta på; underblåsa

fanatic [n.] fanatiker

fancy [adj.] speciellt utvald; ornerad, fasonerad; ~ goods prydnadssaker

fantastic [adj.] fantastisk, jättebra, suverän

fantasy [n.; -sies] fantasi

FAQ [abbrev: frequently asked questions] vanliga frågor

far¹ [adj.; further, furthest] fjärran, avlägsen

far² [adv.; further, furthest] långt, fjärran; as ~ as experience goes vad det beträffar erfarenhet; so ~

so good så långt är allt gott och
väll; **~ too much** alldeles för
mycket; **by ~** betydligt
far-sighted [adj.] långsynt
fare¹ [n.] biljettpris, taxa; kost
fare² [v.] ha det, klara sig
farewell! [interj.] adjö!, farväl!
farm¹ [n.] lantbruk, bondgård; **~
products** jordbruksprodukter; **~
subsidies** jordbruksstöd
farm² [v.] bruka; arrendera
farmer [n.] lantbrukare, bonde
farming [n.] jordbruk; odling
Faroe Islands [n.] Färöarna
fart¹ [n.; vul.] fjärt, prutt [colloq.]
fart² [v.; vul.] fjärta, prutta [colloq.]
fascinate [v.] fascinera
fascinated [adj.] fascinerad
fascinating [adj.] fascinerande
Fascist [adj.] fascistisk
fashion [n.] mode; **~ model** mannekäng; **~ show** modevisning
fashionable [adj.] fashionabel;
modern
fast¹ [adj.] fort, snabb; tvättäkt
[color]; **~ connection** snabb uppkoppling [IT]; **~ food** snabbmat;
~ food place snabbmatställe,
grillbar
fast² [adv.] fast, stadigt; fort, snabbt
fast³ [n.] fasta
fast⁴ [v.] fasta
fast-cooking [adj.] lätt att laga
fasten [v.] sätta fast, fästa
fat¹ [adj.] tjock; fet; **~ client** tjock
klient [IT]
fat² [n.] fett; **~ content** fettinnehåll;
~ substitutes fettersättningar
fat-free [adj.] fettfri
fatal [adj.] dödlig, dödande; ödes-
diger, fördärvlig, fatal; **~ error**
programkrasch [IT]
fate [n.] öde
father [n.] fader, far, pappa
father-in-law [n.] svärfar
fatigue [n.] trötthet; utmattning
fatty [adj.] fetthaltig, fet, oljig
faucet [n.] kran
fault [n.] defekt, fel
faultless [adj.] oklanderlig
favicon [n.] adressikon, adressymbol [IT]

favor¹ [n.] gunnst, ynnest; tjänst
favor² [v.] gilla; gynna
favorable [adj.] välvillig; gynnsam
favorite¹ [adj.] älsklings-, favorit; **~
place** älsklingsställe
favorite² [n.] favorit, gunstling
fax¹ [n.; ~es] fax
fax² [v.; ~es, ~ed] faxa
FBI [abbrev: Federal Bureau of In-
vestigation] federala polisen i USA
FDA [abbrev: Food and Drug Ad-
ministration] livs-och läkemedelsverket i USA
fear¹ [n.] fruktan, rädsla; ängslan
fear² [v.] frukta, vara rädd
fearful [adj.] rädd; fruktansvärd
fearless [adj.] orädd, utan fruktan
feasible [adj.] genomförbar, möjlig;
lämplig; sannolik
feast [n.] festmåltid; fröjd
feather [n.] fjäder
feature¹ [n.] grunddrag, kännemär-
cke, attribut, egenskap; **~ film**
långfilm
feature² [v.] demonstrera, visa,
presentera
Feb. [abbrev: February] februari
February [n.] februari
feces [n.] fekalier, skit [colloq.]
fed up: [adj] **be ~ with** vara trött
på, ha fått nog av
Fed. [abbrev: federal] federal
federal [adj.] förbunds-, federal
federation [n.] förening, förbund
fee [n.] avgift; honorar; **~ paid by
patient** patientavgift
feed¹ [n.] utfodring, matning; foder
feed² [v.; fed] fodra, föda; mata;
beta
feedback [n.] återkoppling [IT]
feeding bottle [n.] nappflaska
feel¹ [n.] känsel, känsla
feel² [v.; felt] känna; treva; tycka;
känna sig, må, vara; **~ like (doing)**
ha lust att; **~ sick** må illa; **how do
you ~?** hur mår du?
feeling [n.] känsel, känsla; mening;
stämning
feign [v.] hitta på; hyckla
fellow¹ [adj.] med-; **~ countryman**
landsman; **~ worker** arbetskamrat
fellow² [n.] karl, kille; kamrat

fellowship [n.] kamratskap;
sammanslutning
felony [n.; -nies] grövre brott
felt-tip pen [n.] tuschpenna
fem. [abbrev: female, feminine]
honlig, kvinnlig, feminin
female[1] [adj.] kvinnlig; ~ **connector**
honkontakt, hylskontakt
female[2] [n.] kvinna
feminine [adj.] kvinnlig, feminin
feminist [n.] feminist
fence[1] [n.] staket, stängsel
fence[2] [v.; sport] fäkta
fender [n.] stänkskärm
fennel [n.] fänkål
fermentation [n.] jäsning
ferry [n.; -rries] färja
fertile [adj.] bördig, fruktsam,
fertil, givande
fertility [n.] bördighet, fruktbarhet
festival [n.] festival, högtid
fetch [v.; ~es, ~ed, ~ed] hämta;
framkalla
fetus [n.; ~es] foster
feud [n.] fejd, strid, tvist
fever [n.] feber; ~ **thermometer**
febertermometer
feverish [adj.] febrig
few [adj./pron.] få; **a** ~ några
fewer [adj.comp.]: ~ **than** mindre än
ff. [abbrev: and following (pages)]
och följande sidor
fiancé [n.] fästman
fiancée [n.] fästmö
fiber [n.] fiber
fiber-optic cable [n.] fiberoptisk
kabel [IT]
fiction [n.] dikt; skönlitteratur [ro-
maner, noveller, diktning, drama]
fictional [adj.] uppdiktad
fiddle[1] [n.] fiol
fiddle[2] [v.] spela (på) fiol; leka med,
pyssla, fjanta; fiffla
field [n.] fält, mark, åker; område;
~ **hockey** landhockey; ~ **mushrooms** skogssvamp, vilda champinjoner; ~ **of study** disciplin
fierce [adj.] vild; häftig
FIFO [abbrev: first in - first out]
först in - först ut [IT]
fifteen [num.] femton

fifteenth [adj.] femtonde
fifth [adj.] femte
fiftieth [adj.] femtionde
fifty [num.] femtio
fig[1] [n.] fikon
fig.[2] [abbrev: figure; figurative]
figur; bildlig
fight[1] [n.] kamp, strid
fight[2] [v.; fought, fought] kämpa,
strida; bråka
fighter [n.] krigare; boxare; ~
plane jaktflygplan
figurative [adj.] bildlig
figure[1] [n.] figur; siffra; ~ **skating**
konståkning
figure[2] [v.] beräkna; anta; räkna
file[1] [n.] pärm, arkiv; fil [IT]; register; rad; ~ **allocation table (FAT)**
filallokeringstabell [IT]; ~ **extension** filtillägg [IT]; ~ **format**
filformat [IT]; ~ **manager** filhanterare [IT]; ~ **name** filnamn
[IT]; ~ **name extension** filnamnssuffix, filnamnstillägg,
filnamnsändelse [IT]; ~ **size** filstorlek [IT]
file[2] [v.] arkivera; lämna in
filet mignon [n.; see also: **fillet**]
filé
filet of beef [n.] oxfilé
File Transfer Protocol (FTP) [n.]
filöverföringsprotokoll (FTP) [IT]
filing cabinet [n.] förvaringsskåp,
dokumentskåp
filing system [n.] arkivsystem
Filipino [adj.] filippinsk
fill [v.] fylla; ~ **in** fylla i; ~ **up**
(with) fylla på
filled in [adj.] ifylld
fillet [n.; see: **filet**]
filling [n.] fyllning; plomb [tooth]
film[1] [n.] film; ~ **actor/actress**
filmskådespelare; ~ **clip** filmsnutt;
~ **director** filmregissör; **roll of** ~
filmrulle
film[2] [v.] filma
filter[1] [n.] filter; ~ **cigarettes** filtercigaretter
filter[2] [v.] filtrera
filthy [adj.] smutsig, skitig
final[1] [adj.] slutlig, sista, slutgiltig;

final; ~ **examination** slutexamen;
~ **station** slutstation
final[2] [n.] final
finally [adv.] till slut, äntligen,
slutligen
finance[1] [n.] finans; pengar, kapital;
~s finanser, ekonomi
finance[2] [v.] finansiera
financial [adj.] finansiell, finans-;
~ **year** räkenskapsår
find[1] [n.] fynd, upptäckt
find[2] [v.; found, found] finna, hitta;
~ **one's way** hitta vägen; ~ **one-self** befinna sig; ~ **out** ta reda på
findings [n.pl.] slutsats, utslag
fine[1] [adj.] bra, fin; **that's** ~ det går
bra; **I'm** ~ det går bra; ~ **arts**
sköna konsterna
fine[2] [adv.] bra, fint
fine[3] [n.] böter
fine[4] [v.] få böta
fine-grained [adj.] finkornig
finely [adv.] fint; skarpt; ~ **chopped**
finhackad
finger [n.] finger
fingernail [n.] fingernagel
fingerprint [n.] fingeravtryck
finish[1] [n.; ~es] slut; finish
finish[2] [v.; ~es, ~ed, ~ed] avsluta,
sluta (med), slutföra; ~ **eating** äta
färdigt
finished [adj.] över, slut
Finland [n.] Finland
Finn [n.] finne
Finnish[1] [adj.] finsk
Finnish[2] (**language**) [n.] finska
Finnish-speaking [adj.] finsktalande
fire[1] [n.] brand, eld; ~ **alarm** brand-
alarm; ~ **department** brandkår;
~ **door** branddörr; ~ **emergency**
brandfara; ~ **exit** brandutgång;
~ **extinguisher** brandsläckare;
~ **station** brandstation; ~ **truck**
brandbil; **light a** ~ göra upp eld;
in the event of ~ vid brandfara
fire[2] [v.] fyra av; antända; avskeda;
skjuta
firefighting [adj.] brandförsvars-,
brandsläcknings-
fireman [n.; -men] brandman
fireplace [n.] spis

firewall [n.] brandvägg
fireworks [n.pl.] fyrverkeri
firm[1] [adj.] fast; bestämd
firm[2] [n.] firma, företag
firmly [adv.] fast
firmware [n.] fast program [IT]
first[1] [adj.] första, förste; ~ **aid**
första hjälpen; ~ **aid kit** första-
hjälpenlåda; ~ **class** första klass;
~ **gear** ettan, ettans växel; ~ **grade**
första klassan; ~ **name** förnamn;
~ **team** A-lag; **at** ~ i början; ~ **in,**
~ **out (FIFO)** först-in-först-ut
first[2] [adv.] för det första
fiscal [adj.] fiskal, skatte-
fish[1] [n.; ~/~es] fisk; ~ **dish** fiskrätt;
~ **flour** fiskmjöl; ~ **mousse** fiskfärs; ~ **products** fiskprodukter;
~ **soup** fisksoppa; ~ **stall** fiskdisk;
~ **stick** fiskpinne; ~ **store** fiskaffär; **catch** ~ meta
fish[2] [v.; ~es, ~ed, ~ed] fiska
fishbone [n.] fiskben
fisherman [n.; -men] fiskare
fishing [n.] fiske; ~ **gear** fiskutrustning; ~ **license** fiskekort; ~
permitted fiske tillåtet; ~ **port**
fiskehamn; ~ **rod** metspö; ~
tackle fiskedon; ~ **village** fiskeby,
fiskeläge; **no** ~ fiske ej tillåtet,
fiske förbjudet
fishmonger [n.] fiskhandlare
fist [n.] näve
fit[1] [adj.] pigg, duglig, lämpad;
keep ~ hålla sig i form
fit[2] [n.] anfall, attack
fit[3] [v.; fit/fitted, fit/fitted] passa,
sitta bra; ~ **into** passa in i
fitness [n.] kondition; duglighet;
~ **center** gym; ~ **training**
konditionsträning
fitting[1] [adj.] passande
fitting[2] [n.] avpassning, provning;
~ **room** provrum, provhytt
five [num.] fem
fix [v.; ~es, ~ed, ~ed] fästa, rikta;
fixera; fixa
fixed [adj.] fastställd, bestämd;
fast; ~ **disk** fastskiva; ~ **rate** fastpris

fixed-term contract [n.]
visstidsanställning
fixture [n.] fast tillbehör; inredning
FL [abbrev: Florida] Florida
[delstat i USA]
flag [n.] flagga, fana; ~ **icon** flagg-
ikon [IT]
flambé [adj.] flamberad
flame [n.] flamma, låga
flap [n.] flik, lock; vingslag
flare¹ [n.] fladdrande låga; bloss,
signalljus
flare² [v.] fladdra, flamma upp;
bukta ut
flash¹ [n.; ~es] glimt, blixt; ~ **mem-**
ory fickminne, flashminne [IT]; ~
photography blixtfotografering
flash² [v.; ~es, ~ed, ~ed] glimta,
blinka; susa
flashing [adj.] blinkande
flashlight [n.] ficklampa
flat¹ [adj.] plan, platt; raklång; ~
bread tunnbröd; ~ **file** platt fil [IT];
~ **rate** fastpris; ~ **tire** punktering
flat² [adv.] precis; platt
flat³ [n.] platta; slätt; punktering
flatbed [adj.]: ~ **plotter** plankurvritare
[IT]; ~ **scanner** planskanner [IT];
~ **truck** flakvagn
flatten [v.] platta till
flatter [v.] smickra
flatulence [n.] gasbildning, flatulens
flavor [n.] smak, arom
flavoring [n.] smaksättning; ~
agents smakämnen
flea market [n.] loppmarknad
flee [v.; fled] fly, ta till flykten
fleet [n.] flotta
Flemish [adj.] flamländska
flesh [n.] kött
flexibility [n.] böjlighet
flexible [adj.] flexibel; böjlig; ~
working hours flexibel arbetstid
flick [n.] lätt slag, knäpp, släng
flight [n.] flyg, flygresa; ~ **atten-**
dant flygvärdinna [female], flygsteward [male]; ~ **information**
flyginformation; ~ **number** flygnummer; ~ **of stairs** trappa;
regular ~ reguljärflyg
fling [v.; flung] kasta, slänga

flip-flops [n.pl.] badsandaler
flippers [n.pl.] simfötter; simfenor
flirt [v.] flörta
float [v.] flyta
floating [adj.] flytande; rörlig; ~
point representation flyttalssystem [IT]
flock [n.] flock, skock
flood¹ [n.] högvatten, flod, ström
flood² [v.] översvämma; flöda över,
svämma över
floodlight [n.] strålkastare
floor [n.] golv; våning; ~ **lamp**
golvlampa; ~ **show** scenunderhållning; **first** ~ bottenvåningen;
on the second ~ på första våningen, på våningen en trappa upp
floppy disk [n.] diskett [IT]
Florida (FL) [n.] Florida [delstat i
USA]
florist [n.] blomsteraffär, blomsterhandel
flounder [n.] flundra, rödspätta
[fish]
flour [n.] mjöl
flourish [v.; ~es, ~ed, ~ed] blomstra
flow¹ [n.] rinnande, ström; tillflöde;
flod
flow² [v.] flyta, rinna; stiga
flowchart [n.] flödesdiagram
flower¹ [n.] blomma; blom; ~
bouquet blombukett; ~ **garland**
blomsterkrans; ~ **pot** blomkruka;
~ **show** blomsterutställning
flower² [v.] blomma, blomstra
fl.oz. [abbrev: fluid ounce] mått för
våta varor [ca. 0,3 dl.]
flu [abbrev: see: influenza]
fluctuation [n.] växling; tveksamhet
fluent [adj.] flytande, ledig
fluffy [adj.] luddig
fluid¹ [adj.] flytande; likvid
fluid² [n.] vätska
flunk [v.] köra, bli kuggad
flush [v.; ~es, ~ed, ~ed] spola; ~
the toilet spola i/på toaletten
flute [n.] flöjt
fly¹ [n.; flies] fluga
fly² [v.; flew, flown] flyga; rusa
flying¹ [adj.] flygande; flyg-; snabb;
~ **saucer** flyggande tefat; ~ **start**
rivstart

flying² [n.] flygning
FM [abbrev: frequency modulation]
frekvensmodulering (FM)
foam [n.] skum, fradga
f.o.b. [abbrev: free on board] fritt
ombord
focus¹ [n.; ~es] fokus; centrum
focus² [v.; ~es, ~ed, ~ed] fokusera;
ställa in
fog [n.] dimma; ~ **light** dimljus;
risk of ~ dimrisk
foggy [adj.] dimmig; oklar
foil [n.] folie; **aluminum/tin** ~
aluminiumfolie
fold¹ [n.] veck; vindning; vikning
fold² [v.] vika; fälla ihop
folder [n.] katalog, mapp; pärm; ~
structure mappstruktur [IT]
folding [adj.] vikbar; ~ **chair** fällstol; ~ **table** fällbord
foliage [n.] lövverk
folk [n.] folk; ~ **art** folkkonst; ~
costume folkdräkt; ~ **dance** folkdans; ~ **music** folkmusik; ~
musician spelman; ~ **song** folkvisa
folklore [n.] folklore
follow [v.] följa; ~ **someone** följa
efter någon
follower [n.] anhängare, efterföljare
following¹ [adj.] följande; ~ **wind**
medvind
following² [n.] följe; anhängarskara
following³ [prep.] till följd av; efter
fond (of) [adj.] förtjust i
font [n.] funt, teckensnitt [IT]; ~
manager teckensnittshantare [IT];
~ **size** teckenstorlek, textstorlek
[IT]
food [n.] mat, livsmedel, käk; ~
additives livsmedelstillsatser; ~
department matavdelning; ~
poisoning matförgiftning; ~ **preservative** konserveringsmedel; ~
shopping bag matkasse
foodstuff [n.] matvara, näringsmedel
fool¹ [n.] dåra, narr; **make a** ~ **of
s.o.** göra ngn löjlig
fool² [v.] skoja med, lura; ~ **around
with sthg** joxa med ngt
foolish [adj.] dum, narraktig, löjlig
foot [n.] fot; **on** ~ till fots; ~ **brake**

fotbroms; ~ **bridge** gångbro
football [n.; US; also see: **soccer**]
amerikansk fotboll
footer [n.] sidfot [IT]
footnote [n.] fotnot
footpath [n.] fotstig, stig
footstep [n.] fotsteg
footstool [n.] pall
for¹ [conj.] för
for² [prep.] åt, i, till; ~ **me** åt mig;
~ **my benefit** åt mig; ~ **5 days** i 5
dagar; ~ **2 hours** i 2 timmar; ~
example till exempel
forbid [v.; -dding, forbade/forbad,
-dden] förbjuda
forbidden [adj.] förbjuden
force¹ [n.] styrka, kraft; våld
force² [v.] tvinga; forcera, spränga
forced [adj.] tvungen
forecast¹ [n.] prognos; **weather** ~
väderrapport
forecast² [v.; ~] förutse
forehead [n.] panna
foreign [adj.] utländsk; främmande;
utrikes-; ~ **currency** utländsk
valuta; ~ **language** utländsk språk;
~ **news** utrikesnyheter; ~ **policy**
utrikespolitik; ~ **student** gäststuderande; ~ **trade** utrikeshandel
foreigner [n.] utlänning
foremost [adj.] främst; förnämst
forest [n.] skog; ~ **fire** skogsbrand
forested land [n.] skogsland,
skogsmark
forestry [n.] skogsvetenskap, skogs-
vård; ~ **worker** skogsarbetare
forever [adv.] för alltid
forge [v.] smida; förfalska
forgery [n.; -ries] förfalskning
forget [v.; -tting, forgot, forgotten]
glömma; **don't** ~ **to** glöm inte att
forging [n.] smide
forgive [v.; -gave, -given] förlåta
fork [n.] gaffel; vägskäl [in road]
form¹ [n.] form; formulär, blankett
form² [v.] bilda; utbilda; utveckla
formal [adj.] formell; högtidlig; ~
wear formell klädsel
formality [n.; -ties] formalitet;
formbundenhet
formally [adv.] formellt, högtidligt

format[1] [n.] format, uppställning
format[2] [v.] formatera [IT]
formation [n.] utformning; formering
formatting [adj.] formatering, ombrytning [IT]
former [adj.] tidigare; förra, förre, före detta
formerly [adv.] förut
formidable [adj.] kolossal; anskräckande
formula [n.] formel
formulate [v.] formulera
formulated [adj.] syntetisk
formulation [n.] formulering
fort [n.] fäste, skans; förläggningsort
forth [adv.] framåt, fram
forthcoming [adj.] (ut)kommande
forthright [adj.] rättfram, direkt
fortieth [adj.] fyrtionde
fortified [adj.] berikad
fortnight [n.] fjorton dagar
fortress [n.; ~es] borg, fästning
fortunate [adj.] lycklig
fortunately [adv.] lyckligtvis
fortune [n.] lycka; tur; förmögenhet
forty [num.] fyrtio
forty-five [num.] fyrtiofem
forum [n.] forum
forward[1] [adj.] främre; fram-; framskriden; indiskret
forward[2] [adv.] framåt, fram
forward[3] [v.] vidarebefordra, eftersända; **please** ~ för vidare befordran (fvb)
forwarding address [n.] eftersändningsadress
forward(s) [adv.] framåt
fossil [n.] fossil
foster [v.] vårda; utveckla, gynna
foul [adj.] stinkande, motbjudande; oren; ~ **play** ojust spel; brott
found [v.] grunda; gjuta
foundation [n.] stiftelse; grund; **lay the** ~ **of** grundlägga
founded [adj.] grundad
founder [n.] grundläggare
fountain [n.] fontän
four [num.] fyra
four-wheel drive [n.] fyrhjulsdrift
four-year college [n.] 4-års högskola

fourteen [num.] fjorton
fourteenth [adj.] fjortonde
fourth [adj.] fjärde
fox [n.; ~es] räv
foyer [n.] foajé
Fr. [abbrev: Father (religious title)] Fader
fraction [n.] bråkdel; bråk
fracture [n.] brytning; benbrott, fraktur
fractured [adj.] bruten
fragile [adj.] bräcklig, ömtålig
fragment [n.] stycke, bit; fragment
frail [adj.] bräcklig, svag
frame[1] [n.] ram; **~s technique** ramteknik [IT]
frame[2] [v.] rama in; tänka ut
framework [n.] stomme, ram
France [n.] Frankrike
franchise [n.] rösträtt; franchise
frank [adj.] öppen, ärlig, frank
frankfurter [n.] wienerkorv
frankly [adv.] öppet, uppriktigt sagt
frantic [adj.] desperat, hektisk
fraud [n.] bedrägeri; svek
free[1] [adj.] fri; gratis; ledig; ~ **admission** fritt inträde; ~ **agent** fritt handlande väsen; ~ **kick** frispark; ~ **of charge** avgiftsfri; ~ **program** gratisprogram [IT]; ~ **sample** gratisprov; ~ **trade** tullfrihet
free[2] [v.] befria, frige, frita
freeclimbing [n.] friklättring
freedom [n.] frihet; ~ **of choice** valfrihet; ~ **of expression/speech** yttrandefrihet; ~ **of the press** tryckfrihet
freelance [adj.] frilans-
freely [adv.] fritt
freeware [n.] freeware, gratisprogram [IT]
freeze[1] [n.] frost; frysning; **wage** ~ lönestopp
freeze[2] [v.; froze, frozen] frysa
freezer [n.] frys
freezing [adj.] bitande kall, iskall
freight [n.] fraktgods; frakt
French[1] [adj.] fransk; ~ **bread** franskbröd; ~ **roll** kuvertbröd; ~ **toast** fattiga ridare

French² (language) [n.] franska
french fries [n.pl.] pommes frites
Frenchman [n.; -men] fransman
Frenchwoman [n.; -men] fransyska
frequency [n.; -cies] frekvens
frequent [adj.] ofta förekommande,
allmän
frequently [adv.] ofta; ~ asked
questions (FAQ) vanliga frågor
fresco [n.; ~es] frescomålning
fresh [adj.] frisk, färsk; ~ air frisk
luft; ~ curd cheese kvark; ~
produce färskvaror; ~ snow nysnö;
~ water färskvatten
freshly [adv.] friskt; ~ painted
nymålad
freshman [n.; -men] recentior,
förstaårselev; ~ year förstaårskurs
Fri. [abbrev: Friday] fredag
Friday [n.] fredag
fridge [n.] kylskåp
fried [adj.] bräckt, stekt, stekt i
panna; ~ egg stekt ägg
friend [n.] vän, väninna [female],
kamrat; kompis [colloq.]
friendly [adj.] hygglig, vänlig
friendship [n.] vänskap
fright [n.] skräck, fruktan
frighten [v.] skrämma, förskräcka
frightened [adj.] rädd, förskräckt
frightening [adj.] skrämmande,
hemsk
fringe [n.] lugg, frans; marginal
frisbee [n.] frisbee
frog [n.] groda; ~'s legs grodlår
from [prep.] från, ur, av, ifrån; ~
above uppifrån; ~ below nerifrån;
~ home hemifrån; ~ Monday to
Friday från måndag till fredag;
~ more recent times från senare
tid; ~ where varifrån; Jan comes
~ Sweden Jan kommer ifrån
Sverige
front¹ [adj.] fram-, främre; ~ desk
receptionen; ~ door framdörr,
port; ~ light framljus; ~ seat
framsäte; ~ wheel framhjul
front² [n.] framsida, främre del;
front; at the very ~ längst fram;
from the ~ framifrån; in ~ of
framför, inför; in the ~ framtill

frontier [n.] gräns
frontside [n.] framsida
frost [n.] frost
frown¹ [n.] rynkad panna
frown² [v.] rynka pannan
frozen [adj.] frusen; djupfryst; bun-
den; ~ food djupfryst mat; ~ food
counter kyldisk; ~ foods
djupfrysta varor, fryst mat
fruit [n.] frukt; ~ bowl fruktskål;
~ drink saft; ~ juice fruktjos,
fruktjuice; ~ salad fruktsallad;
carbonated ~ drink fruktsoda
fruitful [adj.] fruktbar, bördig;
givande
frustrate [v.] frustrera; motverka
frustrated [adj.] frustrerad, besviken
frustrating [adj.] frustrerande
frustration [n.] frustration,
besvikelse
fry [v.; fries, fried, fried] steka
frying pan [n.] stekpanna
ft.¹ [abbrev: foot] fot
Ft.² [abbrev: Fort] befästning
FTP [abbrev: File Transfer Proto-
col] filöverföringsprotokoll (FTP)
[IT]
FTP-client (program) [n.] FTP-
klient [IT]
fuck¹ [n.; vul.]: not give a ~ skita i
[vul.]
fuck² [v.; vul.] knulla [vul.], ligga
med; ~ you! [vul.] dra åt helvete!
[vul.]
fucked [adj.; vul.] lurad, bedragad
fucking [adj.; vul.] jävla [vul.]
fudge [n.] kola
fuel [n.] bränsle; ~ gauge bensinmätare; ~ pump bensinpump; ~
tank bensintank
fulfil [v.; -lled] uppfylla, infria,
utföra
full [adj.] full, utförlig; rik; dryg;
mätt [food]; fullbelagd [hotel]; ~
professor professor; ~ program
[school] heltidsprogram; ~ time
heltid
full-blown [adj.] fullt utslagen
full-bodied [adj.] fyllig, mustig
full-length film/feature [n.] långfilm

full-time¹ [adj.] heltids-; ~ **job**
heltidsjobb
full-time² [adv.] heltid
fully [adv.] fullt, helt
fumes [n.pl.] rök, avgaser, ångor
fun¹ [adj.] skojig, rolig, kul
fun² [n.] nöje, skoj; **have** ~ ha kul,
ha det roligt
function¹ [n.] funktion; ~ **key (Fn)**
funktionstangent [IT]
function² [v.] fungera
functional [adj.] funktionell,
fungerande
functionality [n.; -ties] funktionalitet
fund¹ [n.] fond, kapital; ~s pengar
fund² [v.] finansiera, kapitalisera
fundamental [adj.] grund-, fundamental, huvud-
fundamentally [adv.] i grunden,
fundamentalt
funding [n.] finansiering
funeral [n.] begravning
fungus [n.; -gi] svamp; ~ **infection**
svampinfektion
funicular [n.] bergbana
funny [adj.] rolig, skojig; konstig,
lustig, besynnerlig
fur [n.] päls, skinn; ~ **coat** päls
furious [adj.] rasande; häftig
furnace [n.] värmepanna
furnish [v.] inreda, möblera

furnished [adj.] möblerad; ~ **room**
inackorderingsrum
furniture [n.] möbel; ~ **mover**
flyttkarl; ~ **store** möbelaffär
furrier [n.] körsnär
furry [adj.] pälsbetäckt
further¹ [adj.comp.: far] vidare,
ytterligare
further² [adv.comp.: far] längre;
vidare; ~ **back** längre bak; ~
forward längre fram
furthermore [adv.] dessutom
furthest [adv.superl.: far] längst
fury [n.; -ries] raseri, ursinne
fuse¹ [n.] propp, säkring; tändrör,
stubintråd
fuse² [v.] smälta, gjuta samman
fusion [n.] sammansmältning;
fusion
fuss [n.; ~es] bråk, tjafs, väsen
fussy [adj.] bråkig, tjafsig, petig,
knusslig
futile [adj.] gagnlös, fruktlös, ytlig
future¹ [adj.] framtids-; framtidsplan
future² [n.] framtid
fuzzy [adj.] suddig; ~ **logic** oskarp
logik
FYI [abbrev: for your information]
för din kännedom

G

G¹ [abbrev: general (film rating); Gentlemen (toilet), men's room] barntillåten [film]; herrar [WC]

g² [abbrev: gram; 1000 dollars] gram; 1000 dollar

G8 [abbrev: Group of 8] G8 [grupp som består av de 8 rikaste länderna i världen]

GA [abbrev: Georgia; General Assembly] Georgia [delstat i USA]; generalförsamling [FN]

gable [n.] gavel

gain¹ [n.] vinst; ökning

gain² [v.] vinna, skaffa sig; forta sig

gal.¹ [abbrev: gallon] gallon [3,8 liter]

gal² [n.; colloq.] tjej

galaxy [n.; -xies] galax

gale [n.] storm, stormvind, kuling; ~ **warning** stormvarning

gall [n.] fräckhet, bitterhet

gallery [n.; -ries] galleri

galley [n.; airplane/boat kitchen] kabyss, pentry

gallon [n.] gallon [3,8 liter]

gallop [v.] galoppera, rasa

gallows [n.] galge

gambling [n.] hasardspel

game [n.] spel, lek; match, parti; vilt; viltträtt; ~ **control adapter** speladapter [IT]; ~ **paté** viltpaté; ~ **port** spelport; ~ **preserve** jaktvård; ~ **room** spelrum

games [n.pl.] sport, idrott; spel; ~ **arcade** spelarkad; **Olympic Games** Olympiska spelen

gang [n.] liga, band; gäng

gang up on [v.] mobba

gap [n.] öppning, hål; lucka

gape [v.] gapa

garage [n.] garage; bilverkstad

garbage [n.] sopor [pl.]; strunt; ~ **bag** soppåse; ~ **can** soptunna; **garbage in, garbage out [GIGO]** sopor in - sopor ut [IT]

garden [n.] trädgård; plantering; ~ **apartment** marklägenhet; ~ **center** plantskola; ~ **furniture** trädgårdsmöbel; ~ **party** trädgårdsfest

gardener [n.] trädgårdsmästare

gardening [n.] trädgårdsskötsel

gargoyle [n.] grotesk vattenkastare

garish [adj.] gräll, prålig

garlic [n.] vitlök; ~ **mayonnaise** aioli, vitlökmajonnäs

garment [n.] klädesplagg; ~**s** kläder

garnish¹ [n.; ~es] garnering

garnish² [v.; ~es, ~ed, ~ed] garnera

gas [n.; ~es/-sses] gas; bensin; ~ **bottle/canister** gasolflaska; ~ **cylinder** gascylinder; ~ **cartridge** gaspatron; ~ **gauge** bensinmätare; ~ **pedal** gaspedal; ~ **station** bensinmack, bensinstation; ~ **stove** gasspis; ~ **tank** bensintank; **put ~ in one's car** tanka; **run out of ~** få bensinstopp

gasoline [n.] bensin

gasp [v.] flämta

gastric [adj.] mag-

gastritis [n.] magkatarr, gastrit

gate [n.] port, grind, bom [RR], spärr; gate [airport]

gateway [n.] port, in/utgång; nätbrygga [IT]

gather [v.] samla, plocka; vinna

gathering [n.] samling; möte; hopsamling; ~ **place** samlingsplats

GATT [abbrev: General Agreement on Tariffs and Trade] GATT

gauge [n.] mätare; mått; spårvidd

gauze bandage [n.] gasbinda

gay [adj.] gay [homosexual]; sprittande, glad; ~ **club** gayklubb

gaze¹ [n.] blick, betraktande

gaze² [v.] stirra, blicka, spana

GB [abbrev: gigabyte; Great Britain] gigabyte; Storbritannien

GDP [abbrev: gross domestic product] bruttonationalprodukt (BNP)

gear [n.] växel [automobile]; redskap, utrustning; mekanism; tackel; **get into first ~** lägga in ettan; **get into reverse ~** lägga in backen

gearbox [n.] växellåda

gearshift lever [n.] växelspak

geek [n.] datanörd [IT]

gel [n.] gelé
Gemini [n.] Tvillingarna
gemstone [n.] ädelsten
gen. [abbrev: general; genitive]
allmän, general; genitiv
gender [n.] kön; genus [gram]; ~
equality jämställdhet; ~ **studies**
genusvetenskap
gene [n.] gen
gene-manipulated food [n.] gen-
manipulerad mat
general[1] [adj.] allmän, generell, vanlig; ~ **delivery** poste restante; ~
election riksdagsval; ~ **practitioner** allmänläkare, allmänpraktiserande läkare; ~ **public** den stora
allmänheten; ~ **rule** huvudregel;
~ **store** matbutik; ~ **subjects**
[school] orienteringsämnen (OÄ);
for ~ **audiences** [film] barntillåten;
in ~ överhuvudtaget
general[2] [n.] general
General Assembly (GA) [n.]
generalförsamling
generally [adv.] allmänt
generate [v.] alstra, frambringa,
generera
generation [n.] alstring, frambring-
ande; generation; ~ **gap** genera-
tionsklyfta
generator [n.] dynamo, generator
generic [adj.] allmän; marklös
generous [adj.] generös
genetic [adj.] genetisk
genetically [adv.] genetiskt; ~
modified genmodifierad
genetics [n.] genetik
Geneva [n.] Genève; ~ **Conventions**
Genèvekonventionerna
genital [adj.] genital, köns-
genitals [n.pl.] (yttre) könsorganer
genius [n.; ~es] geni, snille
genocide [n.] folkmord
genre [n.] genre, stil
gentle [adj.] mild, snäll
gentleman [n.; -men] herre; **gentlemen!** mina herrar!
gently [adv.] sakta, milt
genuine [adj.] äkta, autentisk,
genuin
genuinely [adv.] uppriktigt

geog. [abbrev: geography, geo-
graphical] geografi, geografisk
geographic(al) [adj.] geografisk
geography [n.; -phies] geografi
geological [adj.] geologisk
geology [n.; -gies] geologi
geometry [n.; -ries] geometri
Georgia (GA) [n.] Georgia [delstat
i USA]
germ [n.] bakterie
German[1] [adj.] tysk; ~ **measles**
röda hund
German[2] **(language)** [n.] tyska
Germany [n.] Tyskland
gerund [n.] gerundium
gesticulate [v.] gestikulera
gesture[1] [n.] gest; **make ~s**
gestikulera
gesture[2] [v.] gestikulera
get [v.; getting, got, got/gotten] få,
skaffa (sig); hämta; bli; ~ **in** ta sig
in; ~ **off** kliva av, stiga av; ~ **on**
stiga på, kliva på; ~ **on well** trivas;
~ **sick** bli sjuk; ~ **stuck** haka upp
sig; ~ **to** komma till; ~ **up** stiga
upp
gherkin [n.] liten gurka
ghost [n.] spöke, ande; skugga
GI [abbrev: government issue;
colloq: U.S soldier] stategendom,
vanlig soldat
giant[1] [adj.] jättelik, gigantisk
giant[2] [n.] jätte, gigant
gift [n.] begåvning, gåva, present;
~ **certificate** presentkort; ~ **shop**
presentshop, presentaffär
gigabyte (GB) [n.] gigabyte, Gbyte
[IT]
gigantic [adj.] jättelik
giggle [v.] fnittra, fnissa
GIGO [abbrev: garbage in - garbage out] sopor in - sopor ut [IT]
gilded [adj.] gyllene
ginger [n.] ingefära; ~ **cake/cookie**
pepparkaka
gingerbread house [n.] pepparkakshus
giraffe [n.] giraff
girl [n.] flicka; tjej [colloq.]
girlfriend [n.] flickvän
give [v.; gave, given] ge, skänka,

lämna; ~ **back** återlämna; **please**
~ **me** jag skulle vilja ha
given [adj.] bekant, given, bestämd
glacier [n.] glaciär, jökel
glad [adj.] glad
gladly [adj.] mycket gärna
glance¹ [n.] blick
glance² [v.] titta, kasta en blick
gland [n.] körtel
glare [n.] skarpt sken, glans
glass [n.; ~es] glas; ~**es** glasögon;
~ **painting** glasmålning
glassware [n.] glas
glassworks [n.pl.] glasbruk
glazed tile [n.] kakelplatta
glide [v.] glida; glidflyga
glider [n.] segelflygplan
gliding [n.] segelflygning
glimpse [n.] glimt, skymt, kort
inblick
global [adj.] global; ~ **warming**
global uppvärmning
globalization [n.] globalisering
globe [n.] jordglob
gloom [n.] mörker; dysterhet
gloomy [adj.] dyster
glorious [adj.] ärorik, lysande;
strålande; härlig, underbar
glory [n.; -ries] ära
glossy [adj.; photo] blank
glove [n.] handske; ~**s** handskar; ~
compartment handskfack
glow¹ [n.] glöd, sken
glow² [v.] glöda, lysa, stråla
glucose [n.] druvsocker
glue¹ [n.] lim
glue² [v.] limma, klistra
gluten free [adj.] glutenfri
GM [abbrev: General Motors]
General Motors
GMO [abbrev: genetically modified organism] genändrad organism, genmodifierad organism
GMT [abbrev: Greenwich Mean
Time] Greenwichtid
GNP [abbrev: gross national
product] bruttonationalprodukt
(BNP)
go [v.; go/goes, went, gone] gå; åka
[vehicle], resa, fara; ~ **astray** gå
vilse; ~ **away** åka bort; ~ **back** gå

tillbaka; ~ **by** passera; ~ **get**
hämta; ~ **in for** hålla på med; ~
off sticka; ~ **out** utgå; ~ **to** gå till;
~ **up to** komma fram till; ~ **with**
passa (till)
goal [n.] mål; ~ **keeper** målvakt
goat [n.] get; ~ **cheese** getost
goblin [n.] troll
god [n.] gud; **God** Gud
goddaughter [n.] guddotter
goddess [n.; ~es] gudinna
godfather [n.] gudfar
godmother [n.] gudmor
godson [n.] gudson
going¹ [n.] gång; väglag; fart
going² [v.cont.]: **be** ~ **to** komma att
(+ inf); **be** ~ **on** pågå; **get** ~ sätta
igång; **get sthg going** få igång
något
going-out-of-business sale [n.]
utförsäljning
gold¹ [adj.] guld-, gyllene
gold² [n.] guld; ~ **medal** guldmedalj;
~ **plate** gulddoublé; ~ **work**
guldarbete
golden [adj.] guld-, gyllene; ~ **age**
glansperiod, guldålder; ~ **star**
guldstjärna
goldsmith [n.] guldsmed
goldsmithing [n.] guldsmide
golf [n.] golf; ~ **club** golfklubba
[device]; golfklubb; ~ **course**
golfbana; **18-hole** ~ **course**
artonhålsbana
gondola [n.] gondol; ~ **lift** ägglift
gone [adj.] borta; **all** ~ slut
good [adj.; better, best] god, bra;
snäll; ~ **afternoon!** god dag!; ~
evening! god afton!; **Good Friday**
Långfredag; ~ **luck!** lycka till!; ~
morning! god morgon!; ~ **night!**
god natt!; **be** ~ **enough** duga
good-looking [adj.] snygg
goodbye! [interj.] adjö!
goodness [n.] godhet, vänlighet;
my ~! du store tid!, käre nå'n!; **for**
~ **sake!** för Guds skull!
goods [n.pl.] varor [pl.]
goodwill [n.] god vilja; gott anseende
Google [v.] googla
goose [n.; geese] gås; ~ **liver** gåslever

gooseberries [n.pl.] krusbär
GOP [abbrev: Grand Old Party,
U.S. Republican Party] Republikanska partiet
gorge [n.] klyfta
gorge oneself [v.] frossa
gorgeous [adj.] praktful; tjusig,
strålande
gosh [interj.] ojdå
gospel [n.] evangelium; ~ **music**
gospelmusik; **the ~ truth** absolut
sanning
gossip [n.] skvaller, småprat
Gothenburg [n.] Göteborg
Gothic [adj.] gotisk
goto instruction [n.] hopp [IT]
goulash [n.; ~es] gulasch
Gov. [abbrev: Governor] guvernör
[i delstat i USA]
govern [v.] härska, styra; kontrollera;
regera
government[1] [adj.] stats-, statlig;
~ **subsidy** statsbidrag, statsunderstöd; ~ **support** statsunderstöd
government[2] [n.] regering
governor [n.] guvernör [i delstat i
USA]
govt. [abbrev: government] regering
gown [n.] klänning, dräkt
goy [n.] icke-jude
GP [abbrev: general practitioner]
allmänpraktiker
GPA [abbrev: grade point average]
medelbetyg
GPO [abbrev: Government Printing
Office] offentlig tryckeri i USA
GPS [abbrev: global positioning
system] satellitbaserade system
för positionsbestämning (GPS)
grab [v.; -bbing, -bbed, -bbed]
gripa, rycka till sig
grace [n.] behag, charm; gunst;
takt; nåd
graceful [adj.] graciös
grade[1] [n.] grad, nivå; klass, sort;
årskurs; betyg; lutning, stigning
grade[2] [v.] gradera, sortera;
betygsätta; planera
gradient [n.] lutning
gradual [adj.] gradvis; långsam
gradually [adv.] successivt; så
småningom

graduate[1] [n.] elev som har gått ut
skolan, person med akademisk examen; ~ **degree** magistersexamen,
doktorsexamen; ~ **education** forskarutbildning; ~ **school** institution
för forskarutbildning vid ett universitet; ~ **student** forskarstuderande, doktorand; ~ **study**
forskarutbildning
graduate[2] [v.] avsluta sina studier,
gå ut skolan
grain [n.] korn, frö; säd; fiber,
ådring
gram [n.] gram [28.4 grams = 1 oz.]
grammar [n.] grammatik
grammatical [adj.] grammatisk
grand [adj.] stor, storslagen, ståtlig;
utmärkt
grandchild [n.; ~ren] barnbarn
granddaughter [n.] dotterdotter
[daughter's daughter], sondotter
[son's daughter]
grandfather [n.] morfar [maternal],
farfar [paternal]
grandmother [n.] mormor [maternal], farmor [paternal]
grandparents [n.pl.] morföräldrar,
farföräldrar
grandson [n.] dotterson [daughter's
son], sonson [son's son]
grant[1] [n.] anslag; stipendium,
bidrag; beviljande
grant[2] [v.] bevilja; medge
grape [n.] druva, vindruva; **table**
~**s** druvor; **wine** ~**s** vindruvor;
grapefruit [n.] grapefrukt
graph [n.] graf, diagram, kurva
graphic [adj.] grafisk; ~ **art** grafik;
~ **work** grafik
graphic(al) user interface (GUI)
[n.] grafiska användargränssnitt
[IT]
graphical [adj.] grafisk
graphics [n.pl.] grafik; ~ **card**
grafikkort [IT]
grasp[1] [n.] grepp; räckhåll; förståelse
grasp[2] [v.] fatta, gripa
grass [n.; ~es] gräs; **keep off the ~!**
gräsmattan får ej beträdas!, var
räd om gräsmattan!
grate [v.] riva; raspa
grated [adj.] riven

grateful [adj.] tacksam
gratin [n.] gratäng; **au ~ gratinerad**
gratuity [n.; -ties] dricks
grave[1] [adj.] allvarsam, viktig; dyster; grav; **~ accent (`)** grav accent
grave[2] [n.] grav
gravel [n.] grus; **~ road** grusväg; **~ walk** grusgång
gravestone [n.] gravsten
graveyard [n.] kyrkogård, begravningsplats
gravity [n.; -ties] tyngdkraft, gravitation; tyngd; allvarlighet
gravy [n.; -vies] sky
gray [adj./n.] grå; **~ scale** gråskala
gray-haired [adj.] gråhårig
graze [n.] skrubbsår
GRE [abbrev: Graduate Record Examination] studiebegåvningstest [för sökande till intagning på doktorandstudier]
grease[1] [n.] fett
grease[2] [v.] smörja
greasy [adj.] fet, oljig; flottig; **~ hair** fett hår
great [adj.] stor; framstående; underbar, fantastisk, jättebra; **~ power** stormakt
Great Britain [n.] Storbritannien
greater-than sign (>) [n.] större-än-tecken
greatgrandfather [n.] farfarsfar, farmorsfar [on father's side]; morfarsfar, mormorsfar [on mother's side]
greatgrandmother [n.] mormorsmor, morfarsmor [on mother's side]; farmorsmor, farfarsmor [on father's side]
greatly [adv.] mycket, i hög grad
Greece [n.] Grekland
greedy [adj.] girig, lysten
Greek[1] [adj.] grekisk
Greek[2] [n.] grek
Greek[3] **(language)** [n.] grekiska
green [adj./n.] grön; **~ beans** brytbönor, haricots verts; **~ fee** greenfee [golf]; **~ peas** spritärter
Green Party [n.] miljöpartiet
greengrocer [n.] grönsaksaffär
greenhouse [n.] växthus

Greenland [n.] Grönland
greet [v.] hälsa, välkomna; möta
greeting [n.] hälsning
grid [n.] nät, system, plan; **~ computing** griddteknik [IT]; **~ technology** griddteknik [IT]
grief [n.] sorg, bedrövelse; **good ~!** du store tid!
grill[1] [n.] grill, halster
grill[2] [v.] grilla, halstra
grilled [adj.] grillad, från grillen, grill-; **~ fish** halstrad fisk; **~ sausage** grillkorv
grim [adj.] sträng; grym; obehaglig
grin[1] [n.] grin, flin
grin[2] [v.; -nning, -nned, -nned] grina, flina
grind [v.; ground, ground] slipa, mala
grip[1] [n.] grepp, tag; handtag
grip[2] [v.; -pping, -pped, -pped] gripa, fatta tag i; fångsla
groan [v.] stöna, jämra sig
grocery store [n.] livsmedelsaffär, livsmedelsbutik, matbutik
grope for [v.] treva efter, söka
gross [adj.] fet; brutto-; **~ national product (GNP)** bruttonationalprodukt (BNP)
grotesque [adj.] grotesk
grotto [n.; ~s/~es] grotta
ground[1] [adj.] malen; **freshly ~** nymalen
ground[2] [n.] mark, jord; grund; **~ floor** bottenvåning, gatuplan
groundcloth [n.] tältunderlag
group[1] [n.] grupp; **~s are welcome!** grupper välkomna!
group[2] [v.] gruppera (sig)
groupware [n.] gruppprogram [IT]
grove [n.] lund
grow [v.; grew, grown] växa; öka; bli; odla
growing [adj.] växande, levande
growl [v.] morra, brumma
grown [adj.] uppvuxen
grown-up [n.] vuxen
growth [n.] växt, ökning, utveckling
gruel [n.] välling
GSM [abbrev: Global System for Mobile Communications] digitalt mobiltelfonsystem (GSM)

guarantee[1] [n.] borgen, garanti
guarantee[2] [v.] garantera
guaranteed [adj.] garanterad
guard[1] [n.] vakt; skydd; gard;
  changing of the ~ vaktavlösning;
  on ~! en garde!
guard[2] [v.] skydda, väkta
guardian [n.] beskyddare; målsman
Guatemala [n.] Guatemala
Guatemalan [adj.] guatemalansk
guerrilla [n.] gerillasoldat
guess[1] [n.; ~es] gissning
guess[2] [v.; ~es, ~ed, ~ed] gissa,
  uppskatta
guest [n.] gäst; ~ book gästbok; ~
  house gäststuga, turisthotell,
  pensionat; ~ room gästrum
GUI [abbrev: graphical user inter-
  face] grafiskt användargränssnitt
  [IT]
guidance [n.] handledning; ~ counselor (studie)rådgivare
guide[1] [n.] guide; handledning; ~
  dog ledarhund
guide[2] [v.] leda, styra; guida
guidebook [n.] guidebok, turistbok
guided [adj.] guidad; ~ tour guidetur

guidelines [n.pl.] riktlinje
guild [n.] gille, skrå
guilt [n.] skuld
guilty [adj.] skyldig; skuldmedveten
guinea fowl [n.] pärlhöns
guitar [n.] gitarr
guitarist [n.] gitarrist
Gulf Stream [n.] Golfströmmen
gum [n.] tandkött; tuggummi
gun [n.] kanon, gevär, bössa, pistol
gunman [n.; -men] gangster, bandit
gust of wind [n.] vindstöt
gut [v.] rensa [fish]
guts [n.pl.] innanmäte; mod, kurage
gutter [n.] rännsten; takränna
guy [n.; colloq.] kille [colloq.],
  grabb [colloq.]; stötta; ~ rope
  tältlina
gym [n.] gym
gymnasium [n.; -s] idrottshall
gymnastics [n.] gymnastik
gyn. [abbrev: gynecology]
  gynekologi
gynecologist [n.] gynekolog,
  kvinnoläkare
Gypsy [n.; -sies] romani

H

H [abbrev: hot water] varmt vatten
ha [interj.] ha, ah
habit [n.] vana; beroende; **be in the ~ of** bruka
habitat [n.] naturlig miljö
hack [v.] hacka, hugga; hacka [IT]
hacker [n.] hackare [IT]
haddock [n.] kolja [fish]
Hague [n.]: **The Hague** Haag
hail¹ [n.] hagel
hail² [v.] hälsa; kalla på
hailstones [n.pl.] hagel
hair [n.] hår; **~ care** hårvård; **~ conditioner** hårbalsam; **~ gel** hårgelé; **~ mousse** hårmousse; **~ shampoo** hårschampo; **~ spray** hårspray; **do someone's ~** frisera håret på någon
hairband [n.] hårsnodd
hairbrush [n.; ~es] hårbörste
haircare products [n.pl.] hårvård-produkter
haircut [n.] klippning, frisyr; **get a ~** klippa sig
hairdresser [n.] frisör [male], frisörska [female], hårfrisör, frissan [colloq.]; **~ for women** damfrisör [male], damfrisörska [female]
hairdresser's [n.] frisörsalong, salong
hairdryer [n.] hårtork
hairpiece [n.] tupé
hairpins [n.pl.] hårnålar
hairstyle [n.] frisyr
hairy [adj.] hårig; hårresande
hake [n.] kummel [fish]
half¹ [adj.] halv; **~ a bottle** halv-flaska; **~ hour** halvtimme; **~ past 8** halv 9; **~ price** halva priset; **~ year** halvår
half² [adv.] halvt, halv-
half³ [n.; halves] halva, hälft
half-timbered [adj.] halft timrad
half-time [n.] halvtid
halfway [adv.] halvvägs
halibut [n.] hälleflundra [fish]
hall [n.] sal, hall, aula; vestibul; **city ~** stadshus; **concert ~** conserthus

halt¹ [n.] halt, rast, paus
halt² [v.] stanna, göra halt
ham [n.] skinka; **~ sandwich** skinksmörgås; **baked ~** julskinka
hamburger [n.] hamburgare; **~ beef** hackad biff
hammer¹ [n.] hammare
hammer² [v.] hamra
hammock [n.] hängmatta
hand¹ [n.] hand; **~ controls** hand-reglage; **~ lotion** handkräm; **~ luggage** handbagage; **~s off!** bort med händerna!
hand² [v.] räcka, lämna, ge; **~ in** lämna in; **~ over** räcka över
handbag [n.] handväska
handball [n.] handboll
handbook [n.] handbok
handbrake [n.] handbroms
handful [n.] handfull, näve
handheld computer [n.] fickdator [IT], handdator [IT]
handicap¹ [n.] handikapp; **~(ed) access** tillgång för människor med funktionsnedsättning; **~ vehicle** handikappfordon
handicap² [v.; -pping, -pped, -pped] handikappa
handicapped [adj.] funktionshin-drad, rörelsehindrad; **toilet for the ~** handikapptoalett
handicrafts [n.] hemslöjd
handkerchief [n.] näsduk
handle¹ [n.] handtag
handle² [v.] hantera; sköta; behandla
handlebars [n.pl.] styrstång
handler [n.] hanterare [IT]
handling [n.] hantering, behand-ling; **~ charge** expeditionsavgift
handmade [adj.] handgjord
handrail [n.] ledstång
hand-sewn [adj.] handsydd
handshaking [n.] handskakning
handsome [adj.] vacker, stilig, ståtlig
hand-woven [adj.] handvävd
handwriting [n.] handstil, skrift
hand-written [adj.] handskriven
handy [adj.] praktisk; till hands
hang [v.; hung/hanged, hung/hanged

(hanged for death penalty)]
hänga; ~ **out** hålla till, vara med;
~ **up** haka upp sig [IT], lägga på
[telephone]
hang gliding [n.] drakflygning,
hängflygning
hanger [n.] klädhängare
hanging indent [n.] hängande
indrag [IT]
hangover [n.] baksmälla
hangup [n.] fixering, hinder
happen [v.] hända, ske; komma
sig; ~ **to (do)** råka
happily [adv.] lyckligtvis; gärna
happiness [n.] lycka, glädje
happy [adj.] glad, lycklig; **be** ~
trivas; **make** ~ glädja
Happy New Year! [interj.] Gott
nytt år!
harass [v.; ~es, ~ed, ~ed] plåga,
trakassera
harassment [n.] trakasseri, mobbning; **sexual** ~ sexuella trakasserier
[pl.]
harbinger [n.] förebud
harbor [n.] hamn; ~ **area** hamnområde; ~ **master** hamnkapten;
guest ~ gästhamn
hard[1] [adj.] hård; svår; stark [alco-
hol]; ~ **disk** hårddisk [IT]; ~ **drive**
hårddisk [IT]; ~ **hyphen** hårt
bindestreck [IT]; ~ **liquor** starksprit, brännvin; ~ **space** fast mellanslag, hårt mellanslag [IT]
hard[2] [adv.] hårt, skarpt, flitigt,
svårt
hard-boiled [adj.] hårdkokt
hard-wired program [n.] fast program [IT]
hard-working [adj.] arbetsam
hard/soft contact lenses [n.pl.]
hårda/mjuka kontaktlinser
harden [v.] göra hård; förhärda
hardly [adv.] knappast, knappt
hardship [n.] vedermöda, lidande
hardware [n.] järnvaror [pl.]; materiel; hårdvara, maskinvara,
datorutrustning [IT]; ~ **key** hårdvarunyckel [IT]; ~ **store**
järnhandel
hare [n.] hare; **roast** ~ harstek

harm[1] [n.] skada, ont
harm[2] [v.] skada, göra ont
harmful [adj.] skadlig, farlig; ~ **for**
the environment miljöfarlig
harmless [adj.] oskadlig, ofarlig
harmony [n.; -nies] harmoni
harpoon [n.] harpun
harsh [adj.] hård, sträv; frän, skarp
harvest [n.] skörd, gröda, vinst;
bad ~ **year** missväxtår
hash [n.] pyttipanna, hackmat
hash browns [n.pl.] potatiskroketter
[pl.]
hassle[1] [n.] krångel, trubbel
hassle[2] [v.] trakassera
hastily [adv.] skyndsamt
hat [n.] hatt; ~ **rack** hatthylla; ~
shop modist
hate [v.] hata, avsky
hatred [n.] hat, avsky
haughty [adj.] högdragen, snorkig
haul [v.] dra, hala, släpa
haunt [v.] spöka
haunted [adj.] spök; skrämd
haunting [adj.] oförglömlig
have [v.; has, had] ha; få; ~ **to** få,
måste, behöva
Hawaii (HI) [n.] Hawaii [delstat i
USA]
hay [n.] hö; ~ **fever** hösnuva
hazard [n.] risk, fara; hasard; ~
warning lights varningsblinkers
hazardous [adj.] riskfylld, riskabel
hazelnuts [n.pl.] hasselnötter
H-bomb [abbrev: hydrogen bomb]
vätebomb
HDL [abbrev: high-density lipopro-
tein] HDL-kolesterol [det goda
kolesterolet]
hdqtrs. [abbrev: headquarters]
högkvarter, huvudkontor
HDTV [abbrev: high definition
television] högupplösnings-tv
HE[1] [abbrev: His/Her Excellency;
high explosive] Hans/Hennes
Excellens; högexplosiv
he[2] [pron.; his, him] han
head[1] [n.] huvud; chef; ~ **of state**
statschef; ~ **cheese** pressylta; ~
office huvudkontor
head[2] [v.] anföra, leda; sätta kurs,
gå till

head-on collision [n.] frontalkrock
headache [n.] huvudvärk; ~ **pills**
huvudvärkstabletter
header [n.] huvud [IT]; nickning
[sports]; ~ **cell** rubrikcell [IT]
heading [n.] rubrik
headlight [n.] framljus, billykta,
strålkastare
headline [n.] rubrik
headmaster [n.] rektor
headphones [n.pl.] hörlurar [pl.]
headquarters [n.pl.] högkvarter,
huvudkontor
headroom [n.; space to stand in] fri
höjd
headwaiter [n.] hovmästare
headwind [n.] motvind
heal [v.] bota, läka
health [n.] hälsa; ~ **care** hälsovård;
~ **check** hälsokontroll; ~ **club** gym;
~ **condition** hälsotillstånd; ~ **food**
hälsokost; ~ **food store** hälsokostaffär; ~ **insurance** sjukförsäkring;
to your ~! skål!
healthy [adj.] frisk, sund
heap [n.] hög
hear [v.; heard] höra; ~ **about/of**
höra talas om
hearing [n.] hörsel; utfrågning; ~
defect nedsatt hörsel; ~ **loop**
hörslinga; **hard of** ~ hörselskadad
heart [n.] hjärta; ~ **attack** hjärtattack, hjärtinfarkt; ~ **condition**
hjärtproblem, hjärtfel; ~ **defect**
hjärtfel; ~ **disease** hjärtsjukdom; ~
trouble hjärtbesvär; **by** ~ utantill
heartburn [n.] halsbränna
hearts [n.pl.; cards] hjärter
hearty congratulations [n.pl.]
hjärtliga lyckoönskningar
heat[1] [n.] hetta, värme; ~ **sink**
kylfläns [IT]; ~ **wave** värmebölja
heat[2] [v.] värma, upphetta
heath [n.] hed
heathen [adj.] hednisk
heather [n.] ljung
heating [n.] uppvärmning, värme
heaven [n.] himmel
heavier [adj.comp.: heavy] tyngre
heaviest [adj.superl.: heavy] tyngst
heavily [adv.] tungt; starkt

heavy [adj.] tung; stark, stor; ~
snow tungt snöfall
Hebrew (language) [n.] hebreiska
he'd [contr: he had; he would] han
hadde; han skulle
hedge[1] [n.] häck; skydd
hedge[2] [v.] svara undvikande;
gardera sig
heel [n.] häl; klack [shoe]; sista del
height [n.] höjd, längd; ~ **above**
sea level höjd över havet
heir [n.] arvinge, arvtagare
held [v.; see: **hold**]
helicopter [n.] helikopter
he'll[1] [contr: he will] han ska
hell[2] [n.] helvete; **what/who the** ~
is that? [colloq.] vad/vem fan är
det? [vul.]
hello! [interj.] hallå! [telephone];
god dag!, hej!
helmet [n.] hjälm
help[1] [n.] hjälp; ~ **button** hjälpknapp [IT]; ~ **desk** dataakut, data-
jour, hjälpcentral [IT]; ~ **key**
hjälptangent [IT]; ~ **line** hjälplinje,
journummer; ~ **menu** hjälp-meny;
~ **screen** hjälpskärm [IT]; ~ **win-**
dow hjälpfönster
help[2] [v.] hjälpa; ~ **with** hjälpa till;
~ **yourself** var så god
help-wanted ad [n.] platsannons
helpful [adj.] hjälpsam; nyttig
helping [n.] portion
helpless [adj.] hjälplös
Helsinki [n.] Helsingfors
hemisphere [n.] hemisfär, halvklot
hemorrhoids [n.pl.] hemorrojder
hen [n.] höna
hence [adv.] härav
Henry [n.] Henrik
her [pron.obj./poss.] henne [obj.];
hennes [poss.]
herb [n.] ört, kryddväxt; ~ **butter**
aromsmör, kryddsmör; **medicinal**
~**s** läkeörter [pl.]
herbal tea [n.] örtte
herd [n.] hjord, flock
here [adv.] här [location], hit [mo-
tion]; ~ **you are!** var så god!
[offering something]; ~**'s to you!**
skål!; **from** ~ härifrån; **up** ~
häruppe

hereby [adv.] härmed
hereditary [adj.] arvs-
heredity [n.; -ties] ärftlighet; arv
heritage [n.] arv; kulturarv
hernia [n.] bräck
hero [n.; ~es] hjälte
heroic [adj.] heroisk
heroin [n.] heroin
heroine [n.] hjältinna
herring [n.] sill
herringbone [n.] sillben
hers [pron.poss.: she] hennes
herself [pron.refl.] sig; henne själv
he's [contr: he is/has] han är/har
hesitant [adv.] tveksam, osäker
hesitate [v.] tveka
hesitation [n.] tvekan
heterogeneous [adj.] heterogen
heterosexual [adj.] heterosexuell
hexadecimal [adj.] hexadecimal
[IT]
hey! [interj.] hej!; hallå!; ~ **Peter!**
hallå Peter! hör du, Peter!
HF [abbrev: high frequency]
högfrekvens-
HHS [abbrev: Department of
Health and Human Services]
socialdepartementet i USA
hi![1] [interj.] hej; ~ **there!** hejsan!
HI[2] [abbrev: Hawaii] Hawaii [del-
stat i USA]
hidden [adj.] dold, gömd, hemlig
hide [v.; hid, hidden] dölja
hierarchy [n.; -chies] hierarki,
rangordning
hi-fi [abbrev: high fidelity] hi-fi
high[1] [adj.] hög; ~ **chair** barnstol;
~ **jump** höjdhopp; ~ **resolution**
högupplösning; ~ **school** läroverk
[allmän skola for elever mellan 14
och 18 år]; ~ **school certificate**
avgångsbetyg; ~ **school diploma**
avgångsbetyg; ~ **school graduate**
en som har avgångsbetyg från
läroverket; ~ **season** högsäsong; ~
speed höghastighet; ~ **tide** flod; ~
voltage line högspänningsledning
high[2] [adv.] högt, starkt
high-beam headlights [n.] helljus
higher [adj.comp.] högre; ~
education högre utbildning

highest [adj.superl.] högst, de
högsta
high-level [adj.] högnivå; ~ **language** högnivåspråk [IT]
highlight[1] [n.] höjdpunkt; urval;
glansdagar; slingor
highlight[2] [v.] markera
highlighting [n.] markering
highly [adv.] högst
high-rise building [n.] höghus
high-tech [adj.; also: **hi-tech**]
högteknologisk
highway [n.] motorväg; ~ **entrance**
påfart; ~ **exit** avfart; ~ **interchange** motorvägskorsning; ~
police motorvägspolis; ~ **toll**
motorvägsavgift
hijacking [n.] kapning
hike [v.] vandra
hiker [n.] vandrare
hiking [n.] fotvandring; ~ **boots**
vandrarkängor; ~ **map** vandringskarta; ~ **trail** vandringsled
hill [n.] backe, kulle, höjd
hillside [n.] bergsluttning, backe
him [pron.obj.: he] honom
himself [pron.refl.] sig; honom
själv
Hindu [adj.] hinduisk
hint[1] [n.] vink, antydan, tips; aning
hint[2] [v.] antyda; låta ana
hip [n.] höft
hire [v.] hyra
his [pron.poss.: he] hans; sin
hiss [v.; ~es, ~ed, ~ed] väsa, fräsa,
brusa
historian [n.] historiker
historic [adj.] historisk; ~ **building**
historisk byggnad
historical [adj.] historisk; ~ **feature**
historisk sevärdhet; ~ **monument**
kulturminne
history [n.; -ries] historia
hit[1] [n.] slag, träff; succé, slagnum-
mer; träff [IT]
hit[2] [v.; hitting, hit, hit] slå; träffa;
stöta
hitchhike [v.] lifta
hitchhiking [n.] liftning
hither [adv.] hit
hitherto [adv.] hittills

HIV [abbrev: human immuno-deficiency virus] humant immun-bristvirus (hiv); ~ test hiv-test
HIV-positive [adj.] hiv-positiv
HM [abbrev: His/Her Majesty] Hans/Hennes majestät
hmm [interj.] jaha
HMO [abbrev: health maintenance organization] privat primärvårds-klinik
hoarse [adj.] hes
hoarseness [n.] heshet
hoax [n.; ~es] bluff; tidningsanka; ~ virus bluffvirus [IT]
hobby [n.; -bbies] fritidsintresse, hobby
hockey [n.] ishockey; landhockey
hold¹ [n.] tag, grepp; **get ~ of** skaffa sig, få tag på/i
hold² [v.; held, held] hålla; ha plats för; dröja [on telephone]; ~ **down** hålla ner [IT]; ~ **one's breath** hålla andan
holding [n.] hållande; värdepapper
hole [n.] hål
holiday [n.] helgdag, helg; lov
hollandaise sauce [n.] hollandaisesås
hollow [adj.] hålig, tom, ihålig
holly [n.; -llies] järnek
holy [adj.] helig; **Holy Communion** nattvarden; **Holy See (Vatican)** Vatikanstaten
home¹ [adv.] hem [motion]; hemma [location]
home² [n.] hem; ~ **address** hem-adress; ~ **coming** hemkomst; ~ **cooking** husmanskost; ~ **country** hemland; ~ **directory** hemkatalog [IT]; ~ **furnishings** heminredning; ~ **help** hemtjänst; ~ **nursing help** vårdbiträde; ~ **page** förstasida, hemsida, startsida [IT]; ~ **sickness** hemlängtan; ~ **town** bostadsort, hemstad; ~ **use** hemmabruk; ~ **visit** hembesök; **at ~** hemma, inne; **not at ~** ute; **on the way ~** på hemvägen
homeless [adj.] hemlös, bostadslös
homemade [adj.] hemgjord, hemlagad
homeward [adv.] hem

homework [n.; no plural] hemupp-gifter [pl.], läxor [pl.]; **do ~** göra läxan, läsa läxor
homogeneous [adj.] enhetlig
homosexual [adj.] homosexuell
Hon. [abbrev: Honorable; Hon-orary] välborna; heders-, honorär-
honest [adj.] ärlig, hederlig
honestly [adv.] ärligt; uppriktigt sakt
honey [n.] honung
honeydew melon [n.] honungsmelon
honeymoon [n.] smekmånad ; ~ **trip** bröllopsresa
honk the horn [v.] tuta
honor¹ [n.] ära, heder
honor² [v.] ära, hedra
honorable [adj.] hedervärd, ärofull
hood [n.] kapuschong, huva; motorhuv [auto]
hoof [n.; hooves/hoofs] hov
hook¹ [n.] hake, krok
hook² [v.] häkta, knäppa; fånga med
hooked rug [n.] ryamatta
hope¹ [n.] hopp, förhoppning
hope² [v.] hoppas
hopeful [adj.] hoppfull
hopefully [adv.] förhoppningsvis
hopeless [adj.] hopplös
horizon [n.] horisont
horizontal [adj.] horisontell
horn [n.] horn; signalhorn [auto]
horrible [adj.] fruktansvärd, hemsk
horror [n.] fasa, skräck ; ~ **movie** skräckfilm
hors d'oeuvres [n.pl.] smårätter
horse [n.] häst
horseback [adj.] rid-; ~ **ride** ridtur; ~ **riding** ridning
horseracing [n.] hästkapplöpning
horseradish [n.] pepparrot
hospital [n.] sjukhus, lasarett
hospitality [n.; -ties] gästfrihet
host¹ [n.] värd; ~ **computer** värddator [IT]
host² [v.] vara värd
hostage [n.] gisslan
hostess [n.; ~es] värdinna
hostile [adj.] fiende-, fientlig, ovänlig
hostility [n.; -ties] fientlighet, ovänlighet

hot [adj.] varm, het; upphetsad; högaktuell, po modet; kryddstark; ~ **boot** varmstart [IT]; ~ **dog** varm korv; ~ **key** snabbtangent [IT]; ~ **plate** kokplatta; ~ **water** varmvatten; **be in/get into** ~ **water** få svårigheter; **not so** ~ inget vidare

hot-dog stand [n.] korvkiosk, korvstånd

hotel [n.] hotell; ~ **lounge** hotellfoajé; ~ **room** hotellrum

hotline [n.] direktlinje

hot-tempered [adj.] hetlevrad

hour [n.] timme; **for 2** ~**s** under 2 timmar

hourly wage [n.] timlön

house¹ [n.] hus, villa; ~ **number** husnummer; ~ **wine** husets vin; **at Jan's** ~ hos Jan; **cook and clean** ~ **for oneself** sköta hushållet själv

house² [v.] skaffa bostad, härbärgera; rymma

houseboat [n.] husbåt

household [n.] hushåll; ~ **goods** hushållsartiklar; ~ **linen** hushållslinne; ~ **utensils** husgeråd

housekeeping [n.] hushåll; ~ **by tenant** självhushåll

housewife [n.; -wives] hemmafru

housework [n.] hushållsarbete

housing [n.] bostad; ~ **advertisement** bostadsannons; ~ **agency** bostadsförmedling; ~ **allowance** bostadsbidrag; ~ **area** bostadsområde

hover [v.] sväva, kretsa

hovercraft [n.] svävare

how [adv.] hur; så; ~ **is it going?** Hur står det till?; ~ **nice!** så skönt!, vad trevligt!

however¹ [adv.] hur ... än; ~ **possible** hur som helst

however² [conj.] emellertid, dock

hp [abbrev: horsepower] hästkraft

HQ [abbrev: headquarters] högkvarter, huvudkontor

hr. [abbrev: hour] timme

HRT [abbrev: hormone replacement therapy] hormonell substitutionsbehandling

ht. [abbrev: height] höjd

HTML [abbrev: hypertext markup language] HTML [språk för strukturerade hypertextdokument] [IT]; ~ **code** HTML-kod [IT]; ~ **editor** HTML-editor [IT]; ~ **tag** styrkod [IT]

HTTP [abbrev: hypertext transfer protocol] HTTP [ursprungliga överföringsprotokollet för webben] [IT]

hub [n.] centrum; nätnav [IT]

hubcap [n.] navkapsel

hug¹ [n.] kram, omfamning

hug² [v.; -gging, -gged, -gged] krama, klämma, omfamna

huge [adj.] jättestor

human¹ [adj.] mänsklig, människo-, human-; ~ **rights** mänskliga rättigheter

human² [n.] människa

humane [adj.] human, mänsklig; humanistisk

humanity [n.; -ties] mänskligheten; **the humanities** humaniora

humble [adj.] ödmjuk, underdånig

humid [adj.] fuktig

humor [n.] humor; **sense of** ~ sinne för humor

humorous [adj.] humoristisk, lustig

hundred [num.] hundra

hundredth [adj.] hundrade

Hungarian¹ [adj.] ungersk

Hungarian² (language) [n.] ungerska

Hungary [n.] Ungern

hunger [n.] hunger

hungry [adj.] hungrig

hunt¹ [n.] jakt

hunt² [v.] jaga

hunter [n.] jägare

hunting [n.] jakt; ~ **knife** dolk; ~ **law** jaktlag; ~ **license** jaktkort; ~ **season** jaktsäsong

hurdle [n.] häck

hurray!/hurrah! [interj.] hurra!; ~ **for Jan!** leve Jan!

hurricane [n.] orkan

hurry¹ [n.] brådska, jäkt; **be in a** ~ ha bråttom

hurry² [v.; -rries, -rried, -rried] skynda sig; skynda på

hurt[1] [adj.] skadad
hurt[2] [n.] skada
hurt[3] [v.; hurt, hurt] värka, göra ont;
~ oneself göra sig illa
husband [n.] man, make
hut [n.] hytta
hydroelectric power [n.]
vattenkraft
hydrofoil [n.] bärplansbåt, flygbåt
hydrogen [n.] väte
hygiene [n.] hygien; hälsovårdslära

hyperlink [n.] hyperlänk [IT]
hypertext [n.] hypertext [IT]
HyperText Markup Language
(HTML) [n.] HTML [IT]
hyphen (-) [n.] bindestreck
hyphenation [n.] avstavning
hypocritical [adj.]: be ~ hyckla
hypothesis [n.; -ses] hypotes,
antagande
Hz. [abbrev: Hertz] hertz

I

I[1] [pron.] jag

I-[2] [abbrev: Interstate highway] huvudmotorväg i USA

IA [abbrev: Iowa] Iowa [delstat i USA]

ibid. [abbrev: ibidem, in the same place] på samma plats

IC [abbrev: integrated circuit] integrerad krets

ICBM [abbrev: intercontinental ballistic missile] interkontinental robot

ICC [abbrev: International Criminal Court] Internationella brottmålsdomstolen

ice [n.] is; ~(d) coffee iskaffe; ~ cream glass; ~ cube isbit; ~ free isfri; ~ hockey ishockey; ~ pack kylklamp; ~ skate skridsko; ~(d) tea iste; ~ tray islåda; ~ water isvatten

ice-cold [adj.] iskall

iced [adj.] iskyld

Iceland [n.] Island

Icelandic[1] [adj.] isländsk

Icelandic[2] (language) [n.] isländska

icing [n.] nedisning [airplane]; glasyr [cake]

ICJ [abbrev: International Court of Justice] Internationella domstolen, Haagdomstolen

icon [n.] ikon, symbol; idol; ~ tray aktivitetsfält [IT]

ICU [abbrev: intensive care unit] intensivvårdsavdelning (IVA), intensiven

icy [adj.] iskall; isig

id.[1] [abbrev: idem, the same] det samma

ID[2] [abbrev: Idaho; identification/identity (papers, card)] Idaho [delstat i USA]; legitimation; ~ card [n.] id-bricka, ID-kort

I'd [contr: I had/would] jag hadde/skulle (vara)

Idaho (ID) [n.] Idaho [delstat i USA]

Idaho (potato) skins [n.pl.] klyftpotatis

IDD [abbrev: international direct dialing] automatkoppling till utlandet

idea [n.] idé, begrepp, syn; a good ~ en bra idé

ideal[1] [adj.] idealisk, önske-; drömd, utopisk

ideal[2] [n.] ideal

idealistic [adj.] idealistisk

ideally [adv.] idealiskt; i idealfallet

identical [adj.] identisk; precis samma

identification [n.] legitimation; identifiering; associering

identify [v.] identifiera; ~ oneself legitimera sig

identity [n.; -ties] identitet; egenart; ~ card identitetskort, legitimation; ~ documents identitetshandling; ~ number identitetsnummer; ~ papers identitetshandling; proof of ~ legitimation; prove one's ~ legitimera

ideological [adj.] ideologisk

ideology [n.] ideologi

idiom [n.] idiom

idiot [n.] idiot, dåre

idle [adj.] sysslolös, overksam; stillastående; lat

i.e. [abbrev: id est, that is] det vill säga (dvs)

if [conj.] om, ifall; huruvida; as ~ som om; ~ any om ens några; ~ necessary vid behov; ~ nothing else om inte annat; ~ only when om inte annat när; ~ so i så fall; ~ you feel pain vid smärta

ignition [n.] tändning; ~ key tändningsnyckel; ~ switch tändningslås

ignorance [n.] okunnighet, ovetenhet

ignore [v.] ignorera; inte låtsas om, strunta i

IL [abbrev: Illinois] Illinois [delstat i USA]

ill[1] [adj.] dålig, sjuk; illvillig

ill[2] [adv.] illa, dåligt; knappast

I'll [contr: I will] jag ska

illegal [adj.] illegal, olaglig

illegally [adv.] olagligt; svart

Illinois (IL) [n.] Illinois [delstat i USA]
illness [n.; ~es] sjukdom
illogical [adj.] ologisk
ill-tempered [adj.] argsint
ill-timed [adj.] illa beräknad, olämplig
ill-treat [v.] misshandla, behandla illa
illuminate [v.] lysa upp
illuminated [adj.] upplyst
illusion [n.] illusion, självbedrägeri; **optical** ~ synvilla
illustrate [v.] illustrera, åskådliggöra
illustration [n.] illustration, belysning; **by way of** ~ till belysning
ILO [abbrev: International Labor Organization] Internationella arbetsorganisationen
im- [prefix] o- [not]; in- [inward]
image [n.] bild, avbild; föreställning; ~ **editor** bildredigerare; ~ **file** bildfil; ~ **processing** bildbehandling, bildhantering
imagery [n.; -ries] bilder [pl.], bildspråk
imaginable [adj.] tänkbar
imaginary [adj.] inbillad; inbillnings-
imagination [n.] fantasi; inbillning
imaginative [adj.] fantasirik, fantasifull
imagine [v.] föreställa sig, tänka sig; gissa, tro; inbilla sig
imaging [n.] bildhantering [IT]
imam [n.] imam
IMF [abbrev: International Monetary Fund] Internationella valutafonden
IMHO [abbrev: in my humble opinion] enligt min ringa mening
imitate [v.] imitera, efterlikna
imitation [n.] imitation, efterbildning; kopia, förfalskning
immediate [adj.] omedelbar, omgående
immediately [adv.] omedelbart, genast
immense [adj.] ofantlig, enorm; storartad
immigrant [n.] invandrare, immigrant

immigrate [n.] invandra, immigrera
immigration [n.] invandring; ~ **aimed at reuniting families** anknytningsinvandring; ~ **center** flyktingförläggning; ~ **of refugees** flyktinginvandring; ~ **policy** invandrarpolitik
imminent [adj.] överhängande, hotande
immoral [adj.] omoralisk; osedlig
immune [adj.] immun; oemottaglig; skyddad
IMO [abbrev: in my opinion; International Maritime Organization] enligt min åsikt; Internationella sjöfartsorganisationen
impact [n.] inverkan, inflytande; stöt, anslag; ~ **printer** anslagsskrivare
impair [v.] försämra, skada; sätta ner, minska
impatient [adj.] otålig, häftig
impeccable [adj.] oklanderlig; felfri
impediment [n.] hinder, avbräck; **speech** ~ talfel
imperative[1] [adj.] ytterst viktig
imperative[2] [n.] oavvisligt krav; imperativ [gram]
imperialistic [adj.] imperialistisk
impersonal [adj.] opersonlig
implement [v.] genomföra, fullfölja, uppfylla, verkställa
implementation [n.] realiserande
implication [n.] innefattande, inbegripande; slutsats; inblandning
implicit [adj.] underförstådd, implicit
implicitly [adv.] underförstått
imply [v.; -plies, -plied] innebära, föra med sig; antyda
impolite [adj.] oartig, ohövlig
import[1] [n.] import, införsel; betydelse
import[2] [v.] importera
import/export company [n.] import- och exportfirma
importance [n.] betydelse, vikt
important [adj.] viktig, väsentlig, betydande; **it's not** ~ det spelar ingen roll
importantly [adv.] viktigt nog; huvudsakligen

impose [v.] lägga på, införa; tvinga
impossible [adj.] omöjlig; outhärdlig
impossibly [adv.] hopplöst, vansinnigt
impress [v.] göra intryck på; inprägla
impressed [adj.] imponerad
impression [n.] intryck, känsla; märke, prägel; tryckning
impressionism [n.] impressionism
impressive [adj.] imponerande, effektfull, gripande
imprison [v.] sätta i fängelse, stänga in
imprisonment [n.] fångenskap, fängelsestraff
improve [v.] förbättra, utveckla, stärka
improved [adj.] förbättrad
improvement [n.] förbättring; upprustning
impulse [n.] impuls; stöt, fart
IN[1] [abbrev: Indiana] Indiana [delstat i USA]
in.[2] [abbrev: inch] tum [2,5 cm]
in-[3] [prefix] o- [not]; in- [inward]
in[4] [adj.] inne, populär
in[5] [adv.] inne; inåt
in[6] [prep.] [space] i, på, vid; [time] om, på, under, inom; ~ 20 minutes om 20 minuter; ~ a week's time inom en vecka; ~ all inalles; ~ an hour om en timme; ~ any case i alla fall; ~ any way possible hur som helst; ~ case ifall; ~ detail ingående; ~ excess of mera än; ~ front framme; ~ Swedish på svenska; ~ the afternoon på eftermiddagen; ~ the country på landet; ~ the evenings på kvällarna; ~ the fall på hösten; ~ the morning på morgonen; ~ the room på rummet
inability [n.; -ties] oförmåga
inaccessible [adj.] oåtkomlig, otillgänglig
inadequate [adj.] olämplig, otillräcklig, inadekvat
inappropriate [adj.] olämplig, oändamålsenlig
inbox [n.] inkorg

Inc. [abbrev: incorporated] aktiebolag (AB)
incapable [adj.] oduglig, inkompetent; oförmögen
incentive [n.] drivfjäder, motivation, uppmuntran, stimulationsåtgärd
incessantly [adv.] utan avbrott, oavbrutet
inch [n.; ~es] tum [2,5 cm]
incidence [n.] förekomst, frekvens, omfattning
incident [n.] händelse, intermezzo
incidentally [adv.] tillfälligtvis; förresten, för övrigt
incl. [abbrev: including] inklusive
inclination [n.] lust, böjelse, tendens; lutning, böjning
incline [n.] stigning, lutning
inclined [adj.] benägen, böjd; lutande
include [v.] omfatta, inkludera, inräkna
included [adj.] inkluderad, inräknad; be ~ ingå; meals not ~ utan måltider
including [prep.] inklusive; not ~ utan, exklusive
inclusion [n.] inbegripande, medtagande
income [n.] inkomst(er); ~ declaration inkomstanmälan; ~ tax inkomstskatt; ~ tax return allmän självdeklaration, deklaration
incoming [adj.] inkommande, ankommande; ~ deliveries inleverans
incomparable [adj.] ojämförlig
incomparably [adv.] ojämförligt
incompatible [adj.] inkompatibel; oförenlig
incompetent [adj.] inkompetent
incomprehensible [adj.] obegriplig
inconsistent [adj.] inkonsekvent, ologisk; oförenlig
inconspicuous [adj.] omärklig, obemärkt
incorporate [v.] inkorporera, arbeta in, innehålla; blanda upp; uppta

incorporated (Inc.) [adj.]: ~ **company** aktiebolag (AB)
incorrect [adj.] oriktig, felaktig, inkorrekt
increase¹ [n.] ökning, förhöjning
increase² [v.] tillta, öka, stiga; höja
increased [adj.] ökad
increasing [adj.] ökande, stigande
increasingly [adv.] alltmer, mer och mer
incredible [adj.] otrolig; fantastisk
incredibly [adv.] fantastiskt
increment [n.] tillväxt, ökning, inkrementering [IT]
incur [v.; -rring, -rred, -rred] ådra sig, åsamka sig, utsätta sig för
indeed [adv.] verkligen, faktiskt; ~? jaså?
indefinite [adj.] obestämd, vag
indent [n.] indrag [IT]
independence [n.] oberoende, oavhängighet, självständighet
independent [adj.] oberoende, oavhängig, självständig
independently [adv.] oberoende, oavhängigt
index [n.; ~es/indices] förteckning, index, register, sakregister; ~ **page** indexsida [IT]
indexed search [n.] indexerad sökning [IT]
India [n.] Indien
Indian¹ [adj.] indisk; ~ **Ocean** Indiska oceanen; ~ **summer** sensommar
Indian² [n.] indier
Indian³ [n.]: **American** ~ indian
Indiana (IN) [n.] Indiana [delstat i USA]
indicate [v.] ange, antyda, visa, tyda på
indication [n.] angivande, tillkännagivande, antydan; tecken
indicator [n.] tecken, visare; blinker [auto]
indices [n.pl.; see: **index**]
indifferent [adj.] likgiltig
indigenous [adj.] infödd; naturlig; ~ **population** urbefolkning
indigestion [n.] magbesvär; dålig matsmältning

indirect [adj.] indirekt
indirectly [adv.] indirekt, på omvägar
indisputably [adj.] otvivelaktigt
individual¹ [adj.] individuell, personlig
individual² [n.] individ, person
individually [adv.] individuellt; personligt
Indonesia [n.] Indonesien
Indonesian [adj.] indonesisk
indoor [adj.] inomhus-; ~ **swimming pool** inomhusbassäng, simhall
indoors [adv.] inomhus
induce [v.] förmå, framkalla; medföra, framkalla
indulge [v.] skämma bort; ge fritt utlopp åt; ~ **in** hänga sig av
industrial [adj.] industriell, industri-; ~ **city** industristad; ~ **country** industriland; ~ **district** industriområde; ~ **society** industrisamhälle
industry [n.; -ries] industri, näringsliv; flit, arbetsamhet
inequality [n.; -ties] olikhet; otillräcklighet
inevitable [adj.] oundviklig, obligatorisk
inevitably [adv.] oundvikligen
inexpensive [adj.] billig
inexperienced [adj.] oerfaren
infallibly [adv.] ofelbart
infant [n.] spädbarn, småbarn; ~ **formula** bröstmjölksersättning; ~ **mortality** barnadödlighet
infantry [n.; -ries] infanteri
infect [v.] infektera, smitta
infected [adj.] infekterad, smittad
infection [n.] infektion, smitta
infectious [adj.] smittsam, infektiös, smittande
infer [v.; -rred] sluta sig till, dra slutsatsen, antyda
inference [n.] slutledning, slutsats
inferior [adj.] lägre, underlägsen, mindervärdig
infinite [adj.] oändlig, omätlig; ~ **loop** oändlig slinga [IT]
infinitive [n.] infinitiv [gram]

infirmary [n.; -ries] sjukhus
inflammation [n.] inflammation;
  upphetsning
inflation [n.] inflation; uppblåsning
inflict [v.] pålägga, ålägga, tilldela,
  tillfoga
influence[1] [n.] inflytande, påverkan;
  under the ~ spritpåverkad
influence[2] [v.] inverka, påverka
influential [adj.] inflytelserik
influenza [n.] influensa
info [abbrev: see: information] tips
inform [v.] meddela, underrätta,
  upplysa, informera
informal [adj.] informell, utan
  formaliteter
information [n.] information,
  uppgift, upplysning; telephone ~
  nummerupplysning; ~ and communications technology (ICT)
  informations- och kommunikationsteknik (IKT); for your ~ för
  din kännedom; ~ counter informationsdisk; ~ desk informatio-
  nen; ~ office informationskontor;
  ~ science informationsvetenskap;
  ~ technology (IT) informationsteknik (IT)
informative [adj.] upplysande,
  informativ; lärorik
infraction [n.] brott; överträdelse
infrastructure [n.] infrastruktur
ingenious [adj.] fyndig, påhittig
ingenuity [n.; -ties] fyndighet
ingredient [n.] beståndsdel,
  ingrediens
inhabit [v.] bo i, bebo
inhabitant [n.] invånare
inherent [adj.] inneboende, ingående
inherit [v.] ärva
inheritance [n.] arv
inhibit [v.] undertrycka, hämma,
  hindra
inhibition [n.] hämning; inhibition
initial[1] [adj.] begynnelse-, första,
  initial-
initial[2] [n.] initial
initialize [v.] initialisera
initially [adv.] i början
initiate [v.] påbörja, inleda; uppta;
  inviga, lära

initiative [n.] initiativ
inject [v.] spruta in; ingjuta
injection [n.] spruta; insprutning
injunction [n.] förbudsföreläggande;
  befallning
injure [v.] skada, såra; förorätta
injured [adj.] skadad, sårad
injury [n.; -ries] skada
ink [n.] bläck; ~ cartridge bläckpatron [IT]
ink-jet printer [n.] bläckstråleskrivare [IT]
inland [adj.] inlands-, inrikes-
in-law [n.] släkting genom giftermål
inline skates [n.] inlines
inn [n.] gästgivargård, värdshus
innate [adj.] medfödd, naturlig
inner [adj.] inre, inner-; ~ tube innerslang
innocence [n.] oskuld; naivitet
innocent [adj.] oskyldig; naiv;
  harmlös; find ~ frikänna
innovation [n.] innovation; in-
  novering
innovative [adj.] uppfinningsrik,
  innovativ
input[1] [n.] insats; inmatning, input
  [IT]
input[2] [v.] mata in [IT]
inquest [n.] undersökning, förhör
inquire [v.] fråga, höra sig för; undersöka; fråga om/efter
inquiry [n.] efterfrågning; undersökning, förfrågning
INS [abbrev: Immigration and Nat-
  uralization Service] migrationsverket i USA
insane [adj.] vansinnig, psykiskt
  störd
inscription [n.] inskrift; dedikation
insect [n.] insekt; ~ bite insektsbett; ~ repellant insektsmedel
insecurity [n.] osäkerhet, otrygghet
insert[1] [n.] inlägg, inlaga, insticks-
  blad; ~ mode infogningsläge
insert[2] [v.] infoga; lägga in, sätta in
insertion point [n.] insättningspunkt [IT]
inset [adj.] nedbäddad [IT]
inside[1] [adj.] inre, inner-

inside² [adv.] inuti, inåt, in, inne
inside³ [n.] insida; ~s inälvor,
mage; ~ **out** ut och in, med insi-
dan ut
inside⁴ [prep.] inne i, inom
insider [n.] initierad person, insider
insight [n.] inblick, förståelse
insist [v.] insistera; vidhålla,
understryka
insistence [n.] hävdande, hållande;
yrkande, krav
insolent [adj.] oförskämd, fräck
insomnia [n.] sömnlöshet,
sömnsvårighet
inspect [v.] granska, inspektera,
besiktiga
inspection [n.] granskning, synande,
inspektion; **technical ~** [car]
kontrollbesiktning; **on closer ~**
vid närmare betraktande
inspector [n.] inspektör, kontrollant
inspiration [n.] inspiration,
ingivelse
inspire [v.] inspirera, fylla, inge
Inst. [abbrev: Institute] institut
install [v.] installera, insätta; lägga
in
installation [n.] installation; instal-
lering; ~ **file** installationsfil
installment [n.] avbetalning;
avsnitt
instance [n.] exempel; instans
instant¹ [adj.] ögonblicklig; snabb;
trängande; ~ **coffee** snabbkaffe;
~ **messaging** direktmeddelanden
instant² [n.] ögonblick
instantly [adv.] genast, omedelbart
instead [adv.] i stället
instead of [prep.] i stället för
instinct [n.] instinkt, sinne
institute [n.] institut, institution; ~
of technology teknisk högskola
institution [n.] institution, anstalt
institutional [adj.] institutions-,
institutionell; ~ **care** sjukhusvård
instruct [v.] undervisa, handleda;
instruera; informera
instruction [n.] undervisning;
handledning; instruktion [IT]; ~
set instruktionsmängd; ~s **for**
maintenance/care skötselråd; ~s
for use bruksanvisning

instructor [n.] lärare, instruktör;
högskoleadjunkt
instrument [n.] instrument, verktyg, redskap
instrumental [adj.] verksam, bidra-
gande; instrumentell
insufficient [adj.] otillräcklig,
bristande
insult¹ [n.] förolämpning, kränkning, skymf
insult² [v.] förolämpa, kränka,
skymfa
insulting [adj.] förolämpande,
kränkande, sårande
insurance [n.] försäkring; ~ **card**
försäkringskort, försäkringsbrev;
~ **company** försäkringsbolag; ~
for third party, fire and theft
halvförsäkring; ~ **policy**
försäkringsbrev
insure [v.] försäkra, assurera
intact [adj.] orörd, intakt, oskadad
intake [n.] intag; inmattning;
intagning
integer [n.] helt tal
integral [adj.] väsentlig; hel
integrate [v.] förena, integrera;
anpassa sig
integrated [adj.] integrerad; hel;
~ **circuit (IC)** integrerad krets
integration [n.] förening, införli-
vande; integration; ~ **policy**
integrationspolitik
integrity [n.] redbarhet; integritet
intellectual¹ [adj.] intellektuell
intellectual² [n.] intellektuell
intelligence [n.] begåvning, intelligens; upplysningar; ~ **quota (IQ)**
intelligenskvot
intelligent [adj.] intelligent,
skarpsinnig, begåvad
intend [v.] avse; ämna
intended [adj.] avsedd
intense [adj.] intensiv, stark, häftig,
våldsam
intensify [v.; -fies, -fied, -fied]
intensifiera, förstärka
intensity [n.; -ties] intensitet, kraft,
styrka
intensive [adj.] intensiv; ~ **care**
intensivvård
intent¹ [adj.] spänd; inriktad

intent² [n.] syfte, avsikt, uppsåt

intention [n.] avsikt, syfte (med); mening; **it was not my ~ that** det var inte meningen att; **with the ~ of** i avsikt att

intentionally [adv.] avsiktligen

inter alia [adv.] bland annat (bl a), med flera (m fl)

interact [v.] samspela, interagera, växelverka

interaction [n.] ömsesidig, växelverkan; **~s** interaktioner

interactive [adj.] interaktiv; **~ communication** interaktiv kommunikation

intercept [v.] genskjuta, spärra; snappa upp

intercity [adj.]: **~ bus** landsvägsbuss; **~ train** intercity tåg

intercourse [n.] umgänge; **sexual ~** sexuellt umgänge, samlag

interest¹ [n.] intresse; ränta; **~ rate** räntesats

interest² [v.] intressera

interested [adj.] intresserad, angelägen; **~ in** intresserad av

interesting [adj.] intressant; underhållande

interestingly [adv.] intressant nog

interface [n.] gränssnitt [IT]; **~ card** gränssnittskort [IT]

interfere [v.] ingripa, inskrida; gå emellan; mixtra

interference [n.] ingripande; hinder; störning; **~ with other drugs** konflikt med annan medicin

interim [adj.] interims-, provisorisk

interior¹ [adj.] inre, inomhus, inlands-

interior² [n.] inre, insida, interiör; inlandet

interlaced [adj.] sammanflätad [IT]

intermediate [adj.] mellan-; **~ level** mellannivå

intermission [n.] avbrott, paus

intern [n.] allmäntjänstgöring läkare (AT-läkare); praktikant

internal [adj.] inre; invärtes; intern; **~ disease** invärtes sjukdom; **~ medicine** invärtesmedicin; **~ memory** internminne [IT]; **for ~ use** för invärtes bruk

international [adj.] internationell, utrikes-; **~ call** utlandssamtal, utrikessamtal; **~ flight** utrikesflyg; **~ money order** utrikespostanvisning; **~ student** utbytesstudent; **~ student advisor** rådgivare till utbytesstudenter

internationally [adv.] internationellt

Internet [n.] Internet; **~ address** Internetadress; **~ bank** Internetbank; **~ café** Internet-café; **~ connection** Internetuppkoppling; **~ phone** Internettelefoni; **~ server** Internetserver; **~ service provider (ISP)** Internetleverantör; **~ subscription** Internetabonnemang

interoperability [n.; -ties] samkörningsmöjlighet [IT]

Interpol [abbrev: International Criminal Police Organization] Interpol

interpret [v.] tolka, tyda

interpretation [n.] tolkning, tydning

interpreter [n.] tolk; tolkare

interrogate [v.] förhöra

interrupt [v.] avbryta

interruption [n.] uppehåll, avbrott; **without ~** utan uppehåll

intersect [v.] korsa, skära

intersection [n.] vägkorsning, gatukorsning, korsning

interval [n.] mellanrum, mellantid; **at regular ~s** med jämna mellanrum

intervene [v.] komma emellan; intervenera, ingripa

intervention [n.] ingripande, intervention, mellankomst

interview [n.] intervju

interviewer [n.] intervjuare

intestine [n.] tarm; **~s** tarmar, inälvor

intimate [adj.] förtrolig, intim

intl. [abbrev: international] internationell

into [prep.] in i, in på

intolerable [adj.] odräglig, oacceptabel, olodlig

intonation [n.] intonation

intranet [n.] intranät [IT]

intravenously [adv.] intravenöst

intrigue [n.] intrig
intriguing [adj.] fängslande,
intressant
intrinsically [adv.] i sig, reellt
introduce [v.] introducera, presentera; införa; ~ **oneself** presentera
sig; **I want to ~ you to my wife**
jag vill presentera dig för min fru
introduction [n.] introduktion;
presentation
introductory course [n.] introduktionskurs (ITK)
intrusion [n.] intrång, störning,
inträngande
invade [v.] invadera, tränga in;
kränka
invalid[1] [adj.] ogiltig
invalid[2] [n.] sjukling, invalid
invaluable [adj.] ovärdelig
invariably [adv.] oföränderligt,
ständigt
invasion [n.] invasion, infall; intrång
invent [v.] uppfinna; hitta på
invention [n.] uppfinning;
uppfinnande
inventiveness [n.] fyndighet
inventor [n.] uppfinnare
invest [v.] investera, placera, satsa
investigate [v.] utforska, undersöka
investigation [n.] undersökning,
utredning
investigator [n.] forskare,
undersökare
investment [n.] investering,
placering
investor [n.] investerare, aktieägare
invigorating [adj.] stärkande
invisible [adj.] osynlig
invitation [n.] inbjudan, invitation,
erbjudande
invite [v.] bjuda, invitera; be; ~
home bjuda hem; ~ **in** bjuda in;
~ **someone for dinner** bjuda någon
på middag
invited [adj.] bjuden
invoice [n.] faktura
invoke [v.] åberopa, åkalla
involve [v.] medföra, involvera;
innebära; inveckla, dra in
involved [adj.] inblandad; inveck-
lad, engagerad

involvement [n.] inblandning, relation; förhållande
IOC [abbrev: International Olympic
Committee] Internationella
olympiska kommittén (IOK)
iodine [n.] jod
ion [n.] jon
IOU [abbrev: I owe you] skuldsedel,
jag är skyldig dig
Iowa (IA) [n.] Iowa [delstat i USA]
IP [abbrev: Internet protocol] pro-
tokollet i Internetkommunikatio-
nen [IT]
IQ [abbrev: intelligence quotient]
intelligenskvot
IRA [abbrev: individual retirement
account; Irish Republican Army]
pensionsförsäkringskonto med
skattefördel; Irländska republikanska armén
Iran [n.] Iran
Iranian[1] [adj.] iransk
Iranian[2] [n.] iranier
Iraq [n.] Irak
Iraqi [adj.] irakisk
irate [adj.] rasande
Ireland [n.] Irland
Irish[1] [adj.] irländsk
Irish[2] **(language)** [n.] irländska,
irska
Irishman [n.; -men] irländare
iron[1] [n.] järn; strykjärn; **Iron Age**
järnålder; ~ **ore** järnmalm
iron[2] [v.] stryka; ~ **out a problem**
utjämna ett problem
ironic [adj.] ironisk
ironically [adv.] ironiskt
ironing board [n.] strykbräde
ironwork [n.] järnsmide
irony [n.] ironi
irrational [adj.] oförnuftig, orimlig
irregular [adj.] oregelbunden,
ojämn
irrelevant [adj.] irrelevant, omotiverad, ej hörande till
irrespective of [prep.] oberoende av
irresponsible [adj.] oansvarig,
ansvarslös
irritate [v.] irritera, reta upp
irritated [adj.] irriterad
irritating [adj.] irriterande, retande

irrit**a**tion [n.] irritation, retning,
  förbittring
IRS [abbrev: Int**e**rnal R**e**venue S**e**r-
  vice] skatteverket i USA
is.¹ [abbrev: **i**sland] ö
is² [v.; see: **be**] är; ~/**are there?**
  finns det?
ISBN [abbrev: Intern**a**tional St**a**n-
  dard Book N**u**mber] ISBN [inter-
  nationellt standardnummer för
  böcker]
ISDN [abbrev: **I**ntegrated S**e**rvices
  D**i**gital N**e**twork] ISDN [standard
  för digital kommunikation över
  den digitala delen av telenätet]
Isl_**a**_**m** [n.] islam
Isl_**a**_**mic** [adj.] islamisk
Isl_**a**_**mist** [n.] islamist
island [n.] ö
isn't [contr: is not] är inte; ~ **he/she/**
  it? inte sant?
ISO [abbrev: Intern**a**tional Organi-
  z**a**tion for Standardiz**a**tion] Internationella standardiserings-
  organisationen (ISO)
isolate [v.] isolera
isolated [adj.] isolerad, avskild,
  ensam
isol_**a**_**tion** [n.] isolering
ISP [abbrev: **I**nternet s**e**rvice
  prov**i**der] internetoperatör [IT]
Israel [n.] Israel
Isr_**a**_**eli** [adj.] israelisk
issue¹ [n.] fråga, problem, sak, tvis-
  temål; utgivande; utgång; **be at ~**
  vara omstridd, vara under debatt

issue² [v.] sända ut, avge, utfärda;
  publicera; komma ut
it¹ [pron.] den (det)
IT² [abbrev: inform**a**tion techn**o**logy]
  informationsteknik [IT]
IT dep_**a**_**rtment** [n.] dataavdelning
  [IT]
it_**a**_**l.** [abbrev: it**a**lics] kursiv
It_**a**_**lian**¹ [adj.] italiensk
It_**a**_**lian**² **(l**_**a**_**nguage)** [n.] italienska
it_**a**_**licized** [adj.] kursiverad
it_**a**_**lics** [n.pl.] kursiv
Italy [n.] Italien
itch¹ [n.; ~es] klåda
itch² [v.; ~es, ~ed, ~ed] klia
item [n.] punkt, post, sak, artikel
itemized [adj.] specificerad
ITN [abbrev: Indep**e**ndent T**e**levi-
  sion News] ITN [brittiskt bolag
  för nyhetssändningar]
it's¹ [contr: it is, it has] den/det
  är/har
its² [poss.pron.: it] dess; sin/sitt/
  sina
its_**e**_**lf** [pron.] sig, sig själv; **in ~** per
  se, i sig själv
IU [abbrev: Indi**a**na Univ**e**rsity]
  Indiana University
IUD [abbrev: intra**u**terine dev**i**ce]
  spiral, intrauterint preventivmedel
IV [abbrev: intrav**e**nous] intravenös,
  dropp
IVF [abbrev: in v**i**tro fertiliz**a**tion]
  provrörsbefruktning
ivory [n.] elfenben

J

jack [n.] domkraft [auto]; knekt [cards]; jack [electr.]
jacket [n.] jacka, kavaj; omslag; skal
jacuzzi [n.] bubbelbad, jacuzzi
jail[1] [n.] fängelse, häkte
jail[2] [v.] sätta i fängelse
jam[1] [n.] sylt, marmelad
jam[2] [v.; -mmed] klämma, stoppa, pressa; blockera; hänga upp sig
jammed [adj.] packad, proppful; trasig
Jan. [abbrev: January] januari
janitor [n.] fastighetsskötare, lokalvårdare
January [n.] januari
Japan [n.] Japan
Japanese[1] [adj.] japansk
Japanese[2] (language) [n.] japanska
jar [n.] burk, kruka
jaundice [n.] gulsot
jaw [n.] käke, haka
jazz [n.] jazz
J.D. [abbrev: Jurum/Juris Doctor, Doctor of Laws] juris doktor (jur.dr)
jealous [adj.] svartsjuk, avundsjuk
jeans [n.pl.] jeans
jelly [n.; -llies] gelé, fruktgelé; ~ roll rulltårta
jellyfish [n.; ~/~es] manet
jerk [v.] slänga, rycka
jerry can [n.] vattendunk, bensindunk
jersey [n.] tröja
Jerusalem artichoke [n.] jordärtskocka
Jesus [n.] Jesus
jet [n.] stråle, ström; jet, jetplan; ~ lag rubbad dygnsrytm efter längre flygresa; ~ ski vattenskoter, jet-ski
jetty [n.; -tties] pir; brygga
Jew [n.] jude
jewel [n.] juvel, ädelsten
jeweler [n.] juvelerare
jewelry [n.] smycken, juveler; piece of ~ smycke
Jewish [adj.] judisk
JFK [abbrev: John F. Kennedy

International Airport (in NYC)] JFK (flygplats i NY)
job [n.] arbete; jobb, ställning; ~ interview anställningsintervju; ~ security anställningstrygghet; ~ training school yrkesförberedande skola
jobless [adj.] arbetslös
jockey [n.] jockej
jog [v.; -gging, -gged, -gged] jogga
jogging [n.] jogging; go ~ jogga; ~ pants joggingbyxor; ~ suit joggingoverall
John [n.] Johan
join [v.] förena, förbinda; följa med; ~ in vara med på, vara med; ~ someone göra/hålla sällskap
joint[1] [adj.] förenad, gemensam
joint[2] [n.] led; out of ~ ur led
jointly [adv.] gemensamt
joke[1] [n.] skämt, vits, skoj
joke[2] [v.] skämta, skoja
joker [n.] skämtare; joker [cards]
Jordan [n.] Jordanien
Jordanian [adj.] jordansk
jot down [v.; jotted] anteckna
journal [n.] tidskrift, tidning; dagbok
journalism [n.] journalistik
journalist [n.] journalist
journey [n.] resa
joy [n.] glädje, fröjd
joystick [n.] styrspak [IT]
J.P. [abbrev: justice of the peace] fredsdomare, underrättsdomare
Jr. [abbrev: junior] junior, den yngre
judge[1] [n.] domare, bedömare
judge[2] [v.] döma, avgöra; bedöma, anse
judg(e)ment [n.] bedömande; dom; omdömesförmåga
judicial [adj.] rättslig, juridisk, judiciell-
judicious [adj.] förståndig, välbetänkt
jug [n.] kanna, tillbringare, krus
juice [n.] saft, juice; orange ~ jos
juicy [adj.] saftig; pikant

Jul. [abbrev: July] juli
July [n.] juli
jump¹ [n.] hopp; höjning
jump² [v.] hoppa, skutta
jumper cables [n.pl.] startkablar
Jun. [abbrev: June] juni
junction [n.] korsning; koppling;
 förbindelse
juncture [n.] tidpunkt
June [n.] juni
jungle [n.] djungel
junior¹ [adj.] yngre, junior; lägre;
 ~ **college** förberedande högskola,
 2-års högskola; ~ **high school**
 grundskolans högstadium [elever
 mellan 12 och 15 år]
junior² [n.] junior; tredjeårsstudent,
 tredjeårselev [college, high school]
juniper berries [n.pl.] enbär
junk [n.] skrot, skräp; ~ **food**
 skräpmat; ~ **mail** skräppost
junk-mail filter [n.] skräppostfilter
 [IT]

junket [n.] utflykt; filbunke, kvarg
Jupiter [n.] Jupiter
jurisdiction [n.] jurisdiktion,
 domsrätt
jurisprudence [n.] juridik,
 jurisprudens
jury [n.; -ries] jury
just¹ [adj.] rättvis, riktig;
 välförtjänt; välgrundad
just² [adv.] just, precis; bara; ~ **behind** just bakom; ~ **fine** bara bra;
 ~ **outside** strax utanför; ~ **over**
 [quantity] dryg; ~ **right** lagom
justice [n.] rätt, rättvisa
justification [n.] försvar, rätt
justified [adj.] försvarlig, rättfärdig;
 ~ **text** justerad text
justify [v.; -fies, -fied] försvara,
 rättfärdiga; bevisa
JV [abbrev: junior varsity (second
 best sports team in school)] näst
 bäst skolidrottslag

K

K¹ [abbrev: Kelvin (temperature
scale)] kelvin
k² [abbrev: kilo; thousand] kilo;
tusen
kale [n.] grönkål
Kansas (KS) [n.] Kansas [delstat i
USA]
karaoke [n.] karaoke
kB [abbrev: kilobyte] kilobyte [IT]
kbps [abbrev: kilobits per second]
kilobits i sekunden [IT]
kcal. [abbrev: kilocalorie] kilo-
kalori
kebab [n.] kebab, grillspett
keen [adj.] ivrig, entusiastisk; skarp,
intensiv
keep [v.; kept] behålla, hålla, bevara, förvara; ~ **out!** tillträde förbjudet!; ~ **the change!** det är
jämnt!; ~ **the gate shut!** håll
grinden stängd!; ~ **up with** följa,
hänga med
keeper [n.] vårdare, väktare; -in-
havare; -vakt
Kentucky (KY) [n.] Kentucky
[delstat i USA]
Kenya [n.] Kenya
Kenyan [adj.] kenyansk
kerosene [n.] fotogen; ~ **lamp** fotogenlampa; ~ **stove** fotogenkök,
primuskök
ketchup [n.] ketchup
kettle [n.] kanna; kittel
key¹ [adj.] nyckel; ~ **industry** nyckel industri
key² [n.] nyckel; tangent [IT]; ~ **ring**
nyckelring; ~ **word** nyckelord
keyboard [n.] tangentbord [IT]
keyhole [n.] nyckelhål
keyword [n.] nyckelord
kg [abbrev: kilogram] kilogram
kHz [abbrev: kilohertz] kilohertz
[IT]
kick¹ [n.] spark; nöje
kick² [v.] sparka
kickoff [n.] avspark
kid [n.] unge; killing; getskinn
kidnap [v.; -pping, -pped, -pped]
kidnappa

kidney [n.] njure; ~ **bean** kidney-
böna; ~ **belt** njurbälte; ~ **stew**
hökarpanna; ~ **stone** njursten
kill [v.] döda, mörda, slå ihjäl
killer [n.] mördare, dråpare; ~
disease dödlig sjukdom
killing [n.] dödande, mord
kilobyte (kB) [n.] kilobyte (kbyte)
[IT]
kilogram (kg) [n.; 2.2 lbs.] kilogram (kg)
kilometer (km) [n.; 0.6 miles] kilometer (km)
kilometers per hour [n.; 0.6 MPH]
kilometer per timme
kind¹ [adj.] vänlig, snäll
kind² [n.] sort, slag; **a ~ of** ett slags;
what ~ of a dog is that? vad är
det för hund?
kindly¹ [adj.] vänlig, välvillig; mild,
välment
kindly² [adv.] vänligt; ~ **shut the
door** var snäll och stäng dörren
king [n.] konung, kung
kingdom [n.] kungarike; rike
kinky [adj.] pervers; krullig
kiosk [n.] kiosk
kiss¹ [n.; ~es] kyss, puss
kiss² [v.; ~es, ~ed, ~ed] kyssa, pussa
kit [n.] grejor, utrustning; **first-aid**
~ förbandslåda
kitchen [n.] kök; ~ **counter** köksbänk; ~ **equipment** köksmaskin;
~ **sink** diskbänk; ~ **table** köksbord
kitchenette [n.] kokvrå, pentry
kite [n.] drake; ~ **flying** drakflygning
kitten [n.] kattunge
KKK [abbrev: Ku Klux Klan] Ku
Klux Klan [vit rasistisk organisation i USA]
km [abbrev: kilometer] kilometer
knapsack [n.] ryggsäck
knee [n.] knä
kneel [v.; knelt] falla på knä
knife [n.; knives] kniv
knight [n.] riddare; springare [chess]
knit [v.; knitted/knit] sticka; ~ **together** knyta samman
knitting [n.] stickning; ~ **needle**
sticka

knock[1] [n.] slag, knackning, smäll, stöt
knock[2] [v.] slå; knacka; stöta
knot [n.] knut, knop
know [v.; knew, known] känna, känna till, veta; ~ **how** kunna; **get to** ~ lära känna; **you** ~ förstår du, alltså
knowledge [n.] kunskap; ~ **of Swedish** svenskkunskaper
known [adj.] känd
knuckle [n.] knoge, led
K.O. [abbrev: knockout (boxing)] knockout
Koran [n.] Koranen
Korea [n.] Korea
Korean[1] [adj.] koreansk
Korean[2] **(language)** [n.] koreanska

kosher [adj.] koscher
Kosovar [adj.] kosovoalbansk
Kosovo [n.] Kosovo
K.P. [abbrev: kitchen police (kitchen duty in military)] köksmalaj
KS [abbrev: Kansas] Kansas [delstat i USA]
Kurd [n.] kurd
Kurdish[1] [adj.] kurdisk
Kurdish[2] **(language)** [n.] kurdiska
kW [abbrev: kilowatt] kilowatt
kWh [abbrev: kilowatt-hour] kilowattimme
KY [abbrev: Kentucky] Kentucky [delstat i USA]
Kyrgyz [adj.] kirgizisk
Kyrgyzstan [n.] Kirgizistan

L

L¹ [abbrev: large; ladies' restroom]
stor; damer [WC]
l.² [abbrev: liter (1.06 qt.)] liter
LA [abbrev: Louisiana; Los Ange-
les] Louisiana [delstat i USA];
Los Angeles
lab [abbrev: laboratory; Labrador
(dog)] laboratorium, verkstad;
labrador
label¹ [n.] etikett, märke
label² [v.] etikettera, märka; stämpla
labeling [n.] märkning
labor¹ [n.] arbete; arbetskraft;
värkar; **organized** ~ fackfören-
ingsrörelsen; ~ **force** arbetskraft;
~ **immigration** arbetskraftsinvandring; ~ **market** arbetsmarknaden;
~ **movement** arbetarrörelse; ~
relations förhållandet mellan
arbetsmarknadens parter
labor² [v.] arbeta; bemöda sig,
anstränga sig
laboratory [n.] laboratorium,
verkstad
laborer [n.] arbetare, grovarbetare
lace [n.] spets; snöre, skosnöre
lack¹ [n.] brist; **for** ~ **of** av brist på
lack² [v.] sakna, lida brist på
lacking [adj.] otillräcklig; **be** ~
fattas, saknas
lad [n.] pojke
ladder [n.] stege, trappstege
ladies [n.pl.] damer; ~' **hairdresser**
damfrisör [male], damfrisörska
[female]; ~' **hairdresser's** damfrisering; ~' **restroom** damtoalett,
damer; ~ **section** [clothing]
damavdelning; ~' **wear** damkläder,
damkonfektion; ~ **and gentlemen!**
mina damer och herrar!
lady [n.; -dies] dam
lager beer [n.] lageröl
lake [n.] sjö
lamb [n.] lamm; lammkött [meat];
~ **chop** lammkotlett; ~ **shoulder**
lammbog; ~ **stew** lammgryta; **leg
of** ~ lammstek, lammlår; **roast** ~
lammstek
lamp [n.] lampa

LAN [abbrev: local area network]
lokalt nätverk [IT]
land¹ [n.] land; rike; mark; jord
land² [v.] landa; lägga till; hamna
på; råka in
landing [n.] trappavsats; landning;
emergency ~ nödlandning
landlady [n.; -dies] hyresvärdinna
landless [adj.] jordlös
landlord [n.] hyresvärd, husägare,
jordägare
landmark [n.] landmärke;
gränsmärke
landowner [n.] markägare
landscape [n.] landskap; ~ **mode**
liggande utskrift [IT]
lane [n.] gränd; körfält, fil; **bicycle**
~ cykelbana
language [n.] språk; ~ **advice**
språkrådgivning; ~ **consulting**
språkrådgivning; ~ **spoken at
home** hemspråk; ~ **teacher** språklärare; **foreign** ~ främmande språk;
sign ~ teckenspråk
lap [n.] knä, sköte
Lapland [n.] Lappland
Laplander [n.] same, lapp
Laplandish [adj.] lappländsk,
samisk
Lappish¹ [adj.] samisk, lappsk
Lappish² (language) [n.] samiska
laptop computer [n.] bärbar dator,
portföljdator [IT]
large [adj.] stor, rymlig; betydande
largely [adv.] till stor del, i stor
utsträckning
large-scale [adj.] i stor skala, mass-
laser [n.] laser; ~ **printer** laserskrivare [IT]
last¹ [adj.] sist; förra; ~ **call** sista
uppropet; ~ **Christmas** i julas;
~ **fall** i höstas; ~ **Monday** förra
måndagen, i måndags; ~ **name**
efternamn; ~ **night** i går kväll; ~
stop ändhållplats, ändstation; ~
time sista gången; ~ **winter** i
vintras
last² [adv.] sist; **at** ~ äntligen
last³ [v.] vara, hålla på; hålla; räcka

lasting [adj.] bestående; hållbar
lastly [adv.] till sist, slutligen
last-minute [adj.] i sista minuten
lat. [abbrev: latitude] latitud, breddgrad
late[1] [adj.] sen, försenad; avliden, förre; in ~ January i slutet av januari; be ~ komma sent, dröja
late[2] [adv.] sent
lately [adv.] på sista tiden, nyss
late-night [adj.] sen på natten
later [adj./adv.comp.: late] senare; a little ~ en stund senare
latest [adj./adv.superl.: late] senast
lather [n.] lödder
Latin [adj.] latinsk; latin-
Latin America [n.] Latinamerika
Latin American [adj.] latin-amerikansk
latitude [n.] breddgrad; handlings-frihet
latter [adj.] denne; sista
Latvia [n.] Lettland
Latvian[1] [adj.] lettisk
Latvian[2] (language) [n.] lettiska
laugh[1] [n.; pronounced: laff] skratt
laugh[2] [v.; pronounced: laff] skratta
laughter [n.] skratt
launch[1] [n.; ~es] avskjutning, start; motorbåt
launch[2] [v.; ~es, ~ed, ~ed] lansera, starta; skjuta av/upp; sjösätta
laundromat [n.] snabbtvätt, tvättomat
laundry [n.; -ries] tvätt [clothes & activity]; tvättinrättning [place]; ~ facilities tvättmöjligheter; ~ service tvättservice; do the ~ tvätta
lava [n.] lava
law [n.] lag, regel; rätt; juridik; polisen; ~ court domstol; ~ en-forcement upprätthållande av lag och ordning; ~ firm advokatbyrå; ~ student juris studerande
lawful [adj.] laglig, tillåten
lawless [adj.] laglös, rättlös
law-making [adj.] lagstiftande
lawn [n.] gräsmatta, gräsplan
lawsuit [n.] process, rättegång
lawyer [n.] advokat
laxative [n.] laxermedel, laxativ

lay[1] [adj.] lekmanna-, amatör
lay[2] [v.past; see: lie]
lay[3] [v.; laid, laid] lägga; ~ down lägga ned; ~ off lägga av; ~ on lägga på
layer [n.] lager, skikt
layered cut [n.] etappklippning
layout [n.] layout, uppläggning [IT]
lazy [adj.] lat, dåsig; be ~ lata sig
lb. [abbrev: pound] pund [0,45 kg]
LCD [abbrev: liquid crystal display] flytande kristaller
LDL [abbrev: low-density lipo-protein] LDL-kolesterol (det onda kolesterolet)
lead[1] [n.; pronounced: led] bly [metal]
lead[2] [n.; pronounced: leed] ledning, anförande; huvud; ~ part [theater] huvudroll; ~ story huvudnyhet
lead[3] [v.; pronounced: leed; led, led] leda, föra; gå före
leaded [adj.] blyad; ~ gasoline blybensin
leader [n.] ledare, anförare, chef
leadership [n.] ledarskap, ledning
leading [adj.] ledande, förnämst; ~ role huvudroll
leaf [n.; leaves] löv; blad
leaflet [n.] flygblad, broschyr
leaf through [v.] bläddra
league [n.] förbund; serie, liga
leak [v.] läcka
lean[1] [adj.] smal, tunn, mager
lean[2] [v.; leaned/leant] luta sig, stödja sig; ~ against luta mot; ~ out luta ut
leap[1] [n.] hopp, språng; ~ year skottår
leap[2] [v.; leapt/leaped] hoppa; öka dramatiskt
learn [v.; learned/learnt] lära sig; få höra; ~ about få reda på
learner [n.] elev; nybörjare; ~'s permit körkortstillstånd
learning [n.] studium; bildning
lease[1] [n.] arrende, uthyrande; arrendekontrakt
lease[2] [v.] arrendera, hyra
leased line [n.] fast anslutning [IT]

leash [n.; ~es] hundkoppel; **put on the** ~ koppla
leasing [n.] uthyrning, leasing
least [adj./adv.superl.: little] minst; **at** ~ åtminstone
leather [n.] läder, skinn; ~ **coat** skinnrock; ~ **goods** lädervaror; ~ **goods store** läderaffär; ~ **jacket** skinnjacka; ~ **pants** skinnbyxor
leave[1] [n.] lov, tillåtelse; permission
leave[2] [v.; left, left] lämna; avgå, ge sig iväg; ~ **him alone/in peace** lämna honom i fred
Lebanese [adj.] libanesisk
Lebanon [n.] Libanon
lecture [n.] föreläsning, föredrag; ~ **hall/room** föreläsningssal, aula
lecturer [n.] föreläsare; högskolelektor, universitetsadjunkt
LED [abbrev: light-emitting diode] lysdiod
leek [n.] purjolök
left[1] [adj.] vänster-; ~ **click** vänsterklicka [IT]; ~ **over** kvar; **be** ~ **over** kvarstå
left[2] [n.] vänster; **on the** ~ till vänster; **to the** ~ **of** till vänster om
left-hand [adj.] vänster-
left-handed [adj.] vänsterhänt
left-justified text [n.] vänsterjusterad text [IT]
left-justify [v.] vänsterställa [IT]
left-wing [adj.] vänsterbetonad, radikal
leg [n.] ben; lår [meat cut]
legacy [n.; -cies] arv
legal [adj.] laglig; juridisk; tillåten; ~ **blood alcohol limit** promillegräns; ~ **tender** lagligt betalningsmedel
legally [adv.] lagligt
legend [n.] legend, saga; inskrift
legendary [adj.] legendarisk
leggings [n.pl.] leggings [pl.]; överdragsbyxor [pl.]
legislation [n.] lagstiftning
legislative [adj.] lagstiftnings-, lagstiftande
legislature [n.] legislatur
legitimate [adj.] legitim, laglig; välgrundad

leisure [n.] fritid; lägligt tillfälle; ~ **activity** fritidsaktivitet; **at your** ~ när du får tid
lemon [n.] citron; ~ **juice** citronjuice; ~ **mousse** citronfromage; ~ **sole** rödtunga [fish]
lemonade [n.] lemonad, sockerdricka
lend [v.; lent] låna; skänka, ge
lender [n.] långivare
length [n.] längd; sträcka; stycke; **at** ~ slutligen; utförligt
lengthy [adj.] lång; utförlig
lenient [adj.] mild, eftergiven
lens [n.] lins, objektiv; glas [eyeglasses]; ~ **cap** linsskydd
lent[1] [adj.] utlånad
Lent[2] [n.] fastan, fastlagen
lentils [n.pl.] linser
lentil soup [n.] linssoppa
Leo [n.] Lejonet [zodiac]
lesbian[1] [adj.] lesbisk
lesbian[2] [n.] lesbisk kvinna
less [adv.comp.: little] mindre
lesser [adj.comp.: little] mindre
lesson [n.] lektion; timme; läxa
less-than sign (<) [n.] mindre-äntecken [IT]
let [v.; let] låta, tillåta; släppa; ~ **me help you!** får jag hjälpa dig?; ~**'s go!** så går vi!; ~ **s.o. know** säga till någon
lethargy [n.; -gies] letargi, dvala
letter [n.] brev [mail]; bokstav [alphabet]
lettuce [n.] sallad, salladshuvud, grönsallad
level[1] [adj.] jämn, slät; vågrätt; ~ **crossing** järnvägsövergång; ~ **teaspoon** en struken tesked
level[2] [n.] nivå; plan; höjd
level[3] [v.] jämna, planera; göra vågrätt, jämna ut
lever [n.] hävstång, spak
leverage [n.] inflytande; hävstångsmakt
levy [v.; -vies, -vied] uttaxera, lägga på
lexical [adj.] lexikalisk
lg. [abbrev: large] stor
lge. [abbrev: large] stor

L.I. [abbrev: Long Island] Long
Island
liability [n.; -ties] ansvar;
skyldighet; handikapp
liable [adj.] ansvarig, disponerad;
förpliktad, skyldig
liaison [n.] förbindelse, samband;
liaison
lib. [abbrev: library] bibliotek
liberal [adj./n.] liberal; ~ arts
humaniora
liberalism [n.] liberalism
liberate [v.] befria, lösa, frige
liberation [n.] befrielse, frigörelse;
~ movement befrielserörelse
liberty [n.; -ties] frihet; take liber-
ties ta sig friheter
Libra [n.] Vågen [zodiac]
librarian [n.] bibliotekarie
library [n.; -ries] bibliotek; ~ card
lånekort; ~ science biblioteksveten-
skap
Libya [n.] Libyen
Libyan [adj.] libysk
license [n.] licens; ~ agreement
licensavtal; ~ holder licensinnehavare; ~ plate nummerplåt, nummerskylt, registreringsskylt; ~
plate number registreringsnummer
licensee [n.] licensinnehavare
lick [v.] slicka
lid [n.] lock; stopp
lie¹ [n.] lögn, osanning
lie² [v.; lying, lay, lain; (on bed/
ground)] ligga; ~ down ligga ner
lie³ [v.; lying, lied; (tell a lie)] ljuga
lieutenant [n.] löjtnant
life [n.; lives] liv, levnad; ~ belt
livbälte; ~ expectancy medellivslängd; ~ insurance livsförsäkring;
~ jacket flytväst, livväst, räddningsväst; ~ raft räddningsflotte; ~
sentence livstidfängelse; ~ span
livslängd
lifeboat [n.] livbåt
life-drawing [n.] kroki
lifeguard [n.] badvakt, livvakt
lifestyle [n.] livsstil
life-support system [n.] livsupp-
hållande apparat, respirator
lifetime [n.] livstid

lift¹ [n.] skidlift; skjuts; lyftande; ~
pass liftpass
lift² [v.] lyfta; häva
lifting ramp [n.] lyftramp
ligament [n.] ligament, ledband;
torn ~ ledbandskada
light¹ [adj.] lätt; ljus; ~ beer folköl,
ljust öl, lättöl; ~ blue klarblå, ljusblå; ~ sauce tunn sås; ~ theater
revy
light² [n.] ljus; lampa; ~ emitting
diode (LED) lysdiod [IT]; ~
meter ljusmätare; ~ pen ljuspenna
[IT]; ~ sensitivity ljuskänslighet;
~ switch lampkontakt; turn the
~s on tända ljuset; can you give
me a ~? kan jag få eld?
light³ [v.; lighted, lighted / lit, lit]
tända; belysa
lighten [v.] lätta
lighter [n.] tändare
lighthouse [n.] fyr
lighting [n.] belysning
lightly [adv.] lätt
lightning [n.] blixtrande, blixt
light-rail train [n.] rälsbuss
like¹ [adj.] lik; be ~ vara lik, likna
like² [adv.] liksom; så, sådan; ~ this
så här; two ~ that två sådana
like³ [conj.] som
like⁴ [prep.] som
like⁵ [v.] tycka om, gilla; vilja; I
would ~ jag skulle vilja (ha)
likelihood [n.] sannolikhet
likely¹ [adj.] trolig; lämplig
likely² [adv.] troligen
likewise [adv.] likaledes; tillika
lima beans [n.] limabönor
limb [n.] gren [tree]; arm/ben [body]
lime [n.] lime
limestone [n.] kalksten
limit¹ [n.] gräns
limit² [v.] begränsa, inskränka
limitation [n.] begränsning
limited [adj.] begränsad; ~ load
begränsad last
limousine [n.] limousine
limp¹ [adj.] mjuk, slapp
limp² [v.] linka, halta
line¹ [n.] linje, streck; lina; ledning;
rad; kö; ~ break radbrytning [IT];

~ **feed** radframmatning, radmatning [IT]; **stand in** ~ stå i kö
line² [v.] ordna i linje; kanta; stoppa full; ~ **up** ställa sig i kö
linear [adj.] linje-, linjär, linear-
linen [n.] linne
linger [v.] dröja kvar, stanna kvar
lingerie [n.] damunderkläder
linguist [n.] språkkunnig person; lingvist
linguistic [adj.] språk-, lingvistisk
linguistics [n.] lingvistik, språkvetenskap
link¹ [n.] länk; **create a** ~ länka
link² [v.] länka, förbinda
linked to [adj.] associerad med
lion [n.] lejon
lip [n.] läpp; ~ **balm** läppbalsam; ~ **gloss** läppglans
lipstick [n.] läppstift
liquefied petroleum gas (LPG) [n.] gasol
liqueur [n.] likör
liquid¹ [adj.] flytande, i vätskeform; likvid; ~ **crystal display (LCD)** flytande kristaller
liquid² [n.] vätska
liquidity [n.; -ties] likviditet
liquor [n.] spritdryck; **hard** ~ sprit
liquorice [n.] lakrits
Lisbon [n.] Lissabon
list¹ [n.] lista, förteckning; ~ **arrow** listpil [IT]; ~ **box** listruta [IT]; ~ **of data** dataregister [IT]; ~ **of references** litteraturförteckning
list² [v.] lista, skriva upp på listan
listed building [n.] noterad byggnad
listen [v.] lyssna, höra på; ~ **to** lyssna på
listener [n.] hörare
lit. [abbrev: literature; literary] litteratur; litterär
lite [abbrev: light; see: **light** (adj.)]
liter [n.; 1.06 qt.] liter
literacy [n.; -cies] läs- och skrivkunnighet
literal [adj.] ordagrann, exakt; bokstavlig
literally [adv.] ordagrant; bokstavligt
literary [adj.] litterär; litteratur-; ~ **works** skönlitteratur

literature [n.] litteratur
lithium ion battery [n.] litiumjonbatteri
lithograph [n.] litografi
lithography [n.] litografi
Lithuania [n.] Litauen
Lithuanian¹ [adj.] litauisk
Lithuanian² (language) [n.] litauiska
litigation [n.] rättstvist, process
litter [n.] skräp, avfall; **cat** ~ kattsand
littering [phrase] **no** ~ skräpa inte ner
little¹ [adj.; smaller, smallest] liten/litet, lill-, lilla-, små [pl.]
little² [adv.; less, least] lite; **a** ~ **more** lite mer; **a** ~ **past 5** lite över 5
live¹ [adj.; rhymes with: dive] levande; direkt; oanvänd; ~ **music** livemusik
live² [adv.; rhymes with: dive] direkt
live³ [v.; rhymes with: give] bo; leva, vistas; ~ **together as a couple** sammanbo; **start living together** flytta ihop
lived [adj.] levt
livelihood [n.] uppehälle, levebröd
lively [adj.] livlig; livfull; glad
liver [n.] lever; ~ **paté** leverpastej
liverwurst [n.] leverkorv
living¹ [adj.] levande, i livet
living² [n.] liv; livsuppehälle, levebröd; **earn one's** ~ fortjäna sitt uppehålle; **make a** ~ **from** ägna sig åt; **what do you do for a** ~? vad arbetar du med?; ~ **room** vardagsrum; **standard of** ~ levnadsförhållande, levnadsstandard
lizard [n.] ödla
'll [contr: will, shall] ska, kommer att [futurum]
LLB [abbrev: Bachelor of Laws] jur.kand.
LLC [abbrev: limited liability company] bolag med begränsad ansvarlighet
LLD [abbrev: Doctor of Laws] jur.dr
load¹ [n.] last, börda; belastning; ~**s of** massor

load² [v.] lasta, lägga in; belasta;
ladda
loading [n.] last-
loaf [n.; loaves] limpa, bröd
loan [n.] lån, kredit; on ~ till låns
loaned out [adj.] utlånad
lobby [n.; -bies] vestibul, hall;
intressegrupp
lobster [n.] hummer
local [adj.] lokal; orts-, när-; ~
anesthesia lokalbedövning; ~ authorities de lokala mydigheterna
[pl.], kommunen ~ call lokalsamtal; ~ environment närmiljö; ~
government kommun; ~ network
lokalnätverk; ~ shop närbutik; ~
traffic lokaltrafik; ~ train lokaltåg
locality [n.] lokalitet, plats;
belägenhet
locally [adv.] lokalt
locate [v.] lokalisera; placera,
förlägga
location [n.] lokalisering; läge,
belägenhet
loc.cit. [abbrev: loco citato: in the
place cited] på anfört ställe
lock¹ [n.] lås; säkring; sluss; lock
[hair]
lock² [v.] låsa, stänga; ~ out låsa ut
locker [n.] skåp, förvaringsfack
locomotive [n.] lokomotiv
lodge [v.] framföra; hyra, bo
loft [n.] vind, loft; vindsvåning
log¹ [n.] stock, stam, kubb
log² [v.; -gged] registrera; ~ in/on
logga in; ~ out/off logga ut
log-in information [n.] inloggningsuppgifter [pl.]
logic [n.] logik
logical [adj.] logisk
logo [n.] logotyp
loin of pork [n.] karré
lone [adj.] enslig, ensam
lonely [adj.] ensam, enslig; ensam
och övergiven
long.¹ [abbrev: longitude] longitud,
längdgrad
long² [adj.] lång; for a ~ time länge;
~ vehicle långt fordon; in the ~
term i längden
long³ [adv.] långt; för länge sedan;

~ live the king! leve kungen!;
how ~ hur länge, hur långt tid
long⁴ [v.] längta; ~ to längta efter
long-distance [adj.] fjärr-, lång-; ~
bus långfärdsbuss; ~ call fjärrsam-
tal, inrikessamtal, rikssamtal; ~
train fjärrtåg
longer [adj./adv.comp.: long] längre
longest [adj./adv.superl.: long]
längst
long-haired [adj.] långhårig
long-sleeved [adj.] långärmad
long-standing [adj.] gammal,
långvarig
long-term [adj.] långfristig, långsiktig, långtids; ~ care långvård; ~
parking långtidsparkering
look¹ [n.] blick; ~s utseende
look² [v.] titta; ~ after hålla reda
på; ~ after oneself sköta om sig;
~ around se sig omkring, titta
runt; ~ at titta på; ~ for leta, söka,
leta efter; ~ like se ut som, se ut;
~ up slå upp; be ~ed after skötas
loop [n.] slinga
loose [adj.] lös, slak; ~ page lösblad;
get ~ lossna
loosely [adv.] löst
loosen [v.] lossa, lösa upp, mildra;
lossna
lope [v.] luffa
lord [n.] herre; Lord's Supper
nattvarden; good Lord! herre Gud!
lose [v.; lost] förlora, tappa, bli av
med; ~ one's way gå vilse
loser [n.] förlorare
loss [n.; ~es] förlust
lossless compression [n.] förlustfri
komprimering [IT]
lossy compression [n.] förstörande
komprimering [IT]
lost [adj.] förlorad; vilsegången; ~
and found office hittegodsmagasin, hittegodsexpedition; get ~
gå/komma vilse
lot [n.] tomt; massa , mängd; lott;
andel; a ~ mycket; a ~ of massa;
have ~s of ha gott om
lottery [n.; -ries] lotteri; ~ ticket
lott
lotto [n.] lotto

loud¹ [adj.] hög, stark; gräll, vulgär
loud² [adv.] högt; **out** ~ högt, med
 hög röst
louder [adj./adv.comp.: loud] högre
loudly [adv.] högt
loudspeaker [n.] högtalare
Louis [n.] Ludvig
Louisiana (LA) [n.] Louisiana
 [delstat i USA]
lounge [n.] vänthall; sällskapsrum,
 salong
love¹ [n.] kärlek; hälsningar; **in** ~
 förälskad, förtjust i; **fall in** ~ **with**
 bli kär i, förälska sig i; **make** ~
 ligga med varandra; **my** ~! min
 älskade!; ~ **affair** kärleksaffär
love² [v.] älska; tycka om, vara
 förtjust i
lovely [adj.] jättefin, skön, tjusig,
 härlig
lover [n.] älskare; beundrare
low¹ [adj.] låg; obetydlig; vulgär;
 mager; ~ **beam** halvljus; ~ **calorie**
 kalorifattig; ~ **rent** billig hyra; ~
 tide ebb
low² [adv.] lågt; tyst; knappt
low-alcohol beer [n.] lättöl
lower¹ [adj.comp.: low] lägre,
 nedre; ~ **berth** underbädd; ~ **edge**
 nederkant
lower² [v.] sänka; dämpa
lower-case letters [n.pl.] gemener
lowered [adj.] nedsatt
low-fat milk [n.] lättmjölk
low-level [adj.] på låg nivå
loyal [adj.] lojal, solidarisk, pålitlig
loyalty [n.; -ties] lojalitet, trofasthet
LP [abbrev: long-playing (record)]
 LP-skiva

LPG [abbrev: liquefied petroleum
 gas] gasol, kondenserad petroleum-
 gas
LPN [abbrev: licensed practical
 nurse] legitimerad undersköterska
LSD [abbrev: lysergic acid diethyl-
 amide] LSD
Lt. [abbrev: lieutenant] löjtnant
Ltd [abbrev: limited (company)]
 aktiebolag (AB)
luck [n.] lycka; tur; **what bad** ~!
 vilken otur!; **what (good)** ~!
 vilken tur!; **good** ~! lycka till!
luckily [adv.] lyckligtvis
lucky [adj.] lyckad; **be** ~ ha tur
luggage [n.] bagage; resväska; ~
 allowance tillåtet bagage
Luke [n.] Lukas
lull [n.] stiltje, vindstilla
lumbago [n.] ryggskott
lumber [n.] virke, timmer; ~ **track**
 timmerväg
lump [n.] klump; bit; knöl; ~ **sugar**
 bitsocker
lunch [n.; -es] lunch; **have** ~ äta
 lunch
lunchtime [n.] lunchtid; **around** ~
 vid lunchtid
lung [n.] lunga; ~ **disease**
 lungsjukdom
lush [adj.] yppig, saftig; lyxig
luster [n.] glans
Lutheran [adj.] lutersk
luxurious [adj.] luxuös, lyxig
luxury [n.; -ries] lyx, överdåd
LW [abbrev: long wave] långvåg
lynx [n.; ~es] lodjur
lyric¹ [adj.] lyrisk; ~ **poem** lyrik
lyric² [n.] lyrisk dikt

M

M¹ [abbrev: medium] medelstor
m.² [abbrev: meter; million] meter;
miljon
M&A [abbrev: mergers and acqui-
sitions] fusioner och förvärv
MA¹ [abbrev: Master of Arts; Mas-
sachusetts] fil. mag.; Massachusetts [delstat i USA]
mA² [abbrev: milliamperes] mil-
liAmpere (mA)
ma³ [n.; colloq.] mamma
ma'am [colloq: madam] frun
Maastricht Treaty [n.; EU]
Maastrichtfördraget
macaroni [n.] makaroner [pl.]
Macedonia [n.] Makedonien
Macedonian¹ [adj.] makedonsk
Macedonian² (language) [n.]
makedonska
machine [n.] maskin, apparat; ~
code maskinkod; ~ gun kulspruta,
maskingevär; ~ instruction
maskininstruktion [IT]; ~ wash-
able maskintvätt
machine-readable [adj.] maskin-
läsbar [IT]
machinery [n.; -ries] maskiner
[pl.]; maskineri
mackerel [n.; ~/~s] makrill [fish]
macro [n.] makro [IT]
macroeconomics [n.] makroekonomi
mad [adj.] arg, rasande; galen; ~
cow disease (BSE) galna ko-sjukan
(BSE)
madam [n.] fru
made [adj.] gjord, tillverkad; ~ in
Sweden av svenskt fabrikat; ~ of
av; ~ to order [clothing] beställningssytt
madman [n.; -men] dåre, galning
madness [n.; ~es] vansinne; raseri
magazine [n.] tidskrift, tidning;
magasin, kassett
magic¹ [adj.] magisk; förtrollad
magic² [n.] magi, trolleri; do ~
tricks trolla
magical [adj.] magisk, fantastisk
magnetic [adj.] magnetisk;
tilldragande

magnificent [adj.] storslagen,
praktful
magnitude [n.] storlek, omfattning;
betydelse
maid [n.] hembiträde, städerska,
tjänsteflicka; old ~ gammal
ungmö
maiden [n.] flicka; jungfru; ~
name flicknamn
mail¹ [n.] post; postverk; ~ merge
mottagaranpassning av dokument/
brev [IT]; by ~ per post; by return ~ omgående; put in the ~
posta; send by ~ posta
mail² [v.] sända med posten, posta
mailbox [n.] brevlåda, postlåda
mailing [n.] postande; ~ address
postadress; ~ list distributions-
lista, postlista, sändlista
mailman [n.; -men] brevbärare
mail-order [adj.] postorder-
main [adj.] huvud-; ~ course varmrätt; ~ post office huvudpostkontor; ~ road huvudväg, landsväg;
~ station centralstation; ~ street
huvudgata
Maine (ME) [n.] Maine [delstat i
USA]
mainframe [n.] stordator [IT]
mainland [n.] fastland
mainly [adv.] huvudsakligen, mest
mainstream¹ [adj.] traditionell;
strömlinjeformad
mainstream² [n.] huvudströmning,
ledande riktning
maintain [v.] upprätthålla; underhålla; hävda; påstå
maintenance [n.] underhåll; ~
allowance underhållsbidrag
Maj. [abbrev: major] major
majesty [n.; -ties] majestät
major¹ [adj.] större, stor, betydelsefull; dur [music key]; ~ road
riksväg
major² [n.] major [mil.]; huvudämne
[college]
majority [n.; -ties] majoritet; the ~
of de flesta
make¹ [n.] fabrikat

make² [v.; made, made] göra,
tillverka; tvinga att; förtjäna; ~
the bed bädda sängen; ~ a difference göra någon skillnad; ~ an
appointment boka en tid; ~ an
effort anstränga sig; ~ smaller
förminska; ~ sure kolla; ~ o.s. up
sminka sig
maker [n.] tillverkare, fabrikant;
decision ~ beslutsfattare
makeup [n.] smink, kosmetika;
sammansättning; extraprov,
omprov
making [n.] tillverkning, tillagande
malaria [n.] malaria
Malaysia [n.] Malaysia
Malaysian [adj.] malaysisk
male¹ [adj.] manlig, mans-, han-;
~ connector hankontakt
male² [n.] mansperson; hane; ~
chauvinist manschauvinist
male-dominated society [n.]
manssamhälle
malicious [adj.] illvillig, elak; ~
software fientlig programvara
[IT]
malnutrition [n.] undernäring,
felnäring
maltreat [v.] misshandla
malware [n.] fientlig programvara
[IT]
mama [n.] mamma
mammal [n.] däggdjur
man [n.; men] man, karl, herre;
människa; ~'s suit herrkostym
manage [v.] hantera, ta hand om;
klara; klara sig; ~ in time hinna
manageable [adj.] överkomlig,
lätthanterlig
management [n.] skötsel; ledning;
styrelse, regi
manager [n.] chef, direktör; hanterare [IT]
managerial [adj.] styrelse-
managing director [n.] verkställ-
lande direktör (vd)
Manchuria [n.] Manchuriet
mandate [n.] mandat; fullmakt
mandatory [adj.] obligatorisk,
befallande
maneuver¹ [n.] manöver

maneuver² [v.] manövrera
mango [n.; ~s/~es] mango
manic-depressive [adj.]
manodepressiv
manicure [n.] manikyr
manifest [v.] bevisa; visa
manifestation [n.] manifestation,
uttryck, utslag
manipulate [v.] manipulera,
hantera
manipulation [n.] manipulation
mankind [n.] mänskligheten
manner [n.] sätt, håll
mannerism [n.] manierism
manor [n.] herrgård, gods
manpower [n.] arbetskraft
mansion [n.] herrgård
manual¹ [adj.] manuell; ~ gearshift
manuell växelspak
manual² [n.] handbok
manufacture¹ [n.] fabrikation;
fabrikat
manufacture² [v.] tillverka,
producera
manufacturer [n.] fabrikant,
producent
manufacturing¹ [adj.] fabriks-
manufacturing² [n.] fabrikation,
tillverkning
manuscript [n.] manuskript, handskrift
many [adj.] många; how ~? hur
många?
map¹ [n.] karta (över); on the ~ på
kartan
map² [v.; -pping, -pped, -pped]
kartlägga; göra upp; ~ out planera
mapping [n.] kartläggning;
avbildning
Mar. [abbrev: March] mars
marathon [n.] maratonlopp
marble [n.] marmor [stone]; kula
[little ball]
March¹ [n.] mars
march² [n.; ~es] marsch, tåg
march³ [v.; ~es, ~ed, ~ed] marschera
margarine [n.] margarin
margin [n.] marginal, kant; ~ of/for
error felmarginal
marginal [adj.] marginell, mindre,
marginal-

marginally [adv.] i marginalen,
marginellt
marijuana [n.] marijuana
marinated [adj.] gravad, inlagd,
marinerad; ~ **roast beef** surstek;
~ **salmon** gravlax
marine[1] [adj.] marin-, havs-, sjö-
marine[2] [n.] marinsoldat; **merchant**
~ handelsflottan
marital status [n.] civilstånd
marjoram [n.] mejram
Mark[1] [n.] Markus
mark[2] [n.] märke; tecken; betyg
mark[3] [v.] märka, anteckna; markera; betäckna
marked [adj.] markerad
marker [n.] markör; märkpenna
market[1] [n.] marknad; torg; ~
economy marknadsekonomi; ~
share marknadsandel; ~ **stall**
torgstånd; ~ **trade** torghandel;
indoor ~ saluhall
market[2] [v.] marknadsföra; sälja
marketing [n.] marknadsföring; ~
department marknadsavdelning;
~ **director** marknadschef
marketplace [n.] torg
market-trader [n.] försäljare
marking [n.] märkning, markering
marmalade [n.] marmelad
marquee [n.] baldakin; rullande
text [IT]
marriage [n.] giftermål, äktenskap;
~ **ceremony** vigsel
married [adj.] gift; ~ **couple** äkta
par; ~ **to** gift med; **get** ~ **(to)** gifta
sig (med); **newly** ~ nygift; **not** ~
ensamstående, ogift
marrow [n.] märg
marry [v.; -ries, -rried, -rried] gifta
sig med
Mars [n.] Mars
marsh [n.; ~es] myr, sumpmark,
träsk
martial arts [n.pl.] kampsporter [pl.]
marvelous [adj.] underbar
Marxist [adj.] marxistisk
Mary [n.] Maria
Maryland (MD) [n.] Maryland
[delstat i USA]
marzipan [n.] marsipan

masc. [abbrev: masculine] maskulin
mascara [n.] mascara
masculine [adj.] manlig, maskulin
mash [n.; ~es] mos
mashed [adj.] -mos; ~ **potatoes**
potatismos; ~ **turnips** rotmos
mask[1] [n.] mask
mask[2] [v.] maskera; dölja
mass [n.; ~es] massa, mängd;
mässa [rel.]; ~ **media** massmedia;
~ **storage** massminne [IT]
Massachusetts (MA) [n.] Massachusetts [delstat i USA]
massacre [n.] massaker, massmord
massage [n.] massage
masseur [n.] massör
masseuse [n.] massös
massive [adj.] massiv, tung, kraftig
master[1] [n.] härskare; mästare; ~'s
degree magisterexamen; **Master**
of Business Administration
(MBA) magisterexamen i affärs-
mannaskap/företagsekonomi
(MBA); **Master of Art (MA)**
filosofie magister (fil.mag.);
Master of Science (MS) filosofie
magister (fil.mag.); ~'s **thesis**
magistersavhandling
master[2] [v.] behärska, bemästra
masterpiece [n.] mästerstycke
mat [n.] matta
match[1] [n.; ~es] tändsticka; tävling,
match; jämlike, motstycke, make
match[2] [v.; ~es, ~ed, ~ed] matcha,
anpassa; passa, motsvara
matching [adj.] matchande
mate [n.] make [m.], maka [f.];
schackmatt [chess]
material[1] [adj.] materiell; substantiell
material[2] [n.] material, tyg, stoff;
~s materiell
maternal [adj.] moderlig; på
mödernesidan
maternity [n.] moderskap; ~ **ward**
barnbördsavdelning (BB)
math [n.; colloq.] matte (colloq.)
mathematical [adj.] matematisk
mathematics [n.] matematik
matinée [n.] matiné
matrix [n.; ~rices] matris
matte [adj.] matt

matter¹ [n.] ämne, sak; **what's the ~?** vad är det?

matter² [v.] betyda; **it doesn't ~** det gör ingenting, det spelar ingen roll, det gör mig det samma

Matthew [n.] Matteus

mattress [n.; ~es] madrass

mature¹ [adj.] mogen; vuxen

mature² [v.] mogna

maturity [n.; -ties] mognad; mogen ålder

mausoleum [n.; ~s] mausoleum

mauve [adj.] lila

maximum¹ [adj.] maximal, högst, störst

maximum² [n.; -ma/~s] maximum, höjdpunkt

May¹ [n.] maj; **~ Day** Första maj

may² [v.modal; may, might] må, få; **~ I pay?** får jag betala?

maybe [adv.] kanske

mayonnaise [n.] majonnäs

mayor [n.] borgmästare

maypole [n.] majstång

MB [abbrev: megabyte; Manitoba] megabyte; Manitoba [Canadian prov.]

MBA [abbrev: Master of Business Administration] MBA (magisterexamen i företagsekonomi)

mbps [abbrev: megabits per second] megabits i sekunden

MC [abbrev: master of ceremonies] ceremonimästare, klubbmästare

MD [abbrev: Medical Doctor, Doctor of Medicine; Maryland] medicine doktor (med. dr); Maryland [delstat i USA]

mdse. [abbrev: merchandise] varor

MDT [abbrev: Mountain Daylight Time] sommartid i Klippiga bergen-zonen i USA

ME¹ [abbrev: Maine] Maine [delstat i USA]

me² [pron.obj.: I] mig

meadow [n.] äng

meal [n.] måltid; **after ~s** efter måltid; **enjoy your ~** smaklig måltid

mean¹ [adj.] otäck, gemen, ful; låg, dålig; medel-

mean² [n.] medelvärde, medelväg

mean³ [v.; meant, meant] betyda, mena; avse; innebära

meaning [n.] betydelse, betydning, mening

meaningful [adj.] meningsfull

meaningless [adj.] meningslös

means [n.pl.] medel, möjligheter [pl.], resurser [pl.]; **~ of transportation** kommunikationsmedel; **by all ~!** gärna!, för all del!

meantime [n.] mellantid; **in the ~** under mellantiden

meanwhile [adv.] under mellantiden

measles [n.] mässling

measure¹ [n.] mått; åtgärd; mån; **made to ~** skräddarsytt; **in some ~** i viss mån

measure² [v.] mäta, ta mått

measurement [n.] mätning; mått

measuring cup [n.] doseringsmått; kopp

meat [n.] kött; **~ casserole** köttgryta; **~ counter** köttdisk; **~ dish** kötträtt; **~ loaf** köttfärslimpa; **~ pie** köttpaj; **~ product** köttvara

meatball [n.] köttbulle

Mecca [n.] Mecka

mechanic [n.] mekaniker

mechanical [adj.] mekanisk; **~ engineer** maskintekniker

mechanics [n.] mekanik

mechanism [n.] mekanik; teknik

med. [abbrev: medium (size); medical] medelstor, medel-, mellan-; medicinsk

medal [n.] medalj

media [n.pl.] media

medical [adj.] medicinsk, läkar-; **~ care** sjukvård, läkarvård; **~ care system** sjukvårdssystem; **~ center** läkargrupp, vårdcentral; **~ certificate** läkarintyg; **~ insurance** sjukförsäkring; **~ insurance certificate** sjukförsäkringsintyg; **~ student** medicine studerande; **~ treatment** sjukvård; **put on ~ leave** sjukskriva; **on ~ leave** sjukskriven

medication [n.] läkemedel, medicin

medicine [n.] medicin

medieval [adj.] medeltida

mediocre [adj.] medelmåttig
meditate [v.] grubbla, meditera
meditation [n.] meditation
Mediterranean Sea [n.] Medelhavet
medium[1] [adj.] lagom; mittemellan;
~ **rare** halvblodig
medium[2] [n.; ~s/media] medium,
medel; medelväg
meet [v.; met] möta, träffa; mötas,
samlas; ~ **one another** träffas
meeting [n.] möte, sammanträde;
~ **place** mötesplats
megabyte (Mb) [n.] megabyte
(Mbyte) [IT]
megahertz [n.; ~] megahertz [IT]
megaton [n.] megaton
megawatt (MW) [n.] megawatt
(MW)
melancholy [adj.] melankolisk
melody [n.; -dies] melodi
melon [n.] melon
melt [v.] smälta
member [n.] medlem, ledamot;
lem, kroppsdel; ~ **of Parliament**
riksdagsledamot
membership [n.] medlemskap
membrane [n.] membran
memo [abbrev: memorandum]
promemoria (PM)
memoir [n.] memoar(er)
memorable [adj.] minnesvärd
memorandum [n.; ~s/-da]
promemoria
memorial [n.] minnesmärke
memorize [v.] memorera, lära sig
utantill
memory [n.; -ries] minne; ~
allocation minnestilldelning [IT];
~ **card** minneskort [IT]; ~ **dump**
minnesdump [IT]; **in ~ of** till
minne av
men [n.pl; see: **man**] män, herrar;
~**'s restroom** herrtoalett
mend [v.] laga, reparera; ställa till
rätta; bli bättre
meningitis [n.] hjärnhinneinflammation
menstruation [n.] menstruation,
mens
menswear [n.] herrkläder

mental [adj.] mental, psykisk; ~
illness psykisk sjukdom
mentally [adv.] mentalt, psykiskt; ~
handicapped psykiskt funktionshindrad, förståndshandikappad;
~ **ill** psykiskt störd
mention[1] [n.] omnämnande
mention[2] [v.] omnämna, tala om;
don't ~ it! ingen orsak!, för all del
menu [n.] matsedel; meny; ~ **bar**
menyrad [IT]; ~ **of the day** dagens
meny; **set ~ for 30 dollars** meny
för 30 dollar
meow [expr.] miau
merchant [n.] köpman, detaljhand-
lare; ~ **marine** handelsflotta
merciful [adj.] barmhärtig, nådig
mercury[1] [n.] kvicksilver
Mercury[2] [n.] Merkurius
mercy [n.; -cies] barmhärtighet, nåd
mere [adj.] blott, ren, bara; **a ~**
child bara ett barn
merely [adv.] endast, bara
merge [v.] slå ihop, sammanfoga
merge printing [v.] kopplad utskrift
[IT]
merger [n.] sammanslagning; ~**s**
and acquisitions (M&A) fusioner
och förvärv
meringue [n.] maräng; ~**s with**
whipped cream marängsviss
merit [n.] merit, förtjänst, värde
merry [adj.] glad, munter; **Merry**
Christmas! god Jul!; **the more**
the merrier ju fler desto roligare
mess[1] [n.; ~es] röra, oordning, oreda,
sjabbel, villervalla
mess[2] [v.; ~es, ~ed, ~ed]: ~ **about/**
around röra till saker och ting,
kladda; ~ **up** förstöra, sabba,
trassla till; ~ **with** lägga sig i
message [n.] meddelande, budskap;
~ **board** anslagstavla; ~ **box** meddelanderuta [IT]; ~ **verification**
[IT] meddelandeverifiering; **could**
you take a ~ for him? kan du
framföra något til honom?
messenger [n.] bud, budbärare
Messiah [n.] Messias
Messrs. [abbrev: pl. of Mr.] herrarna
messy [adj.] stökig; smutsig

Met. [abbrev: Metropolitan Museum; Metropolitan Opera] Met [konstmuseum i New York]; Met [operan i New York]
metadata [n.pl.] metadata [IT]
metal [n.] metall; ~ **industry** metallindustri
metalwork [n.] metallsmide, metallslöjd
metaphor [n.] metafor
metatag [n.] metatagg [IT]
meteorology [n.] meteorologi
meter [n.] mätare [device]; meter [3.3 feet]
method [n.] metod; system
methodology [n.; -gies] metodologi
methylated spirits [n.pl.] denaturerad sprit
metric ton [n.; ca. 1.1 US (short) tons] ton [1000 kg.]
metro [n.] tunnelbana
metropolitan [adj.] storstads-
Mexican [adj.] mexikansk
Mexico [n.] Mexiko
MFA [abbrev: Master of Fine Arts] magisterexamen i de sköna konsterna
mg [abbrev: milligram] milligram [1/1000 gram]
mgr. [abbrev: manager] direktör, föreståndare
MHz [abbrev: megahertz] megahertz
MI[1] [abbrev: Michigan] Michigan [delstat i USA]
mi.[2] [abbrev: mile] mile [1,6 km]
MIA [abbrev: missing in action] saknad i strid
Michigan (MI) [n.] Michigan [delstat i USA]
Mickey Mouse [n.] Musse Pigg
microfiche [n.] mikrofilmkort
microphone [n.] mikrofon
microprocessor [n.] mikroprocessor [IT]
microscope [n.] mikroskop
microwave [n.] mikro; ~ **oven** mikrougn, mikrovågsugn
mid [adj.] mitt-, mellan-, mid-
midday [n.] middagstid, middag
middle[1] [adj.] mellersta, mellan-, medel-; ~ **age** medelålder; ~ **class**

medelklassen; ~ **school** skola för barn i åldern 11-14 år
middle[2] [n.] mitt; **in the** ~ **of** mitt i
middle-aged [adj.] medelålders
Middle Ages [n.pl.] medeltiden
middle-class [adj.] borgerlig, medelklass-
Middle East [n.] Mellanöstern
middleware [n.] anpassningsprogram [IT], mellanprogram [IT], mellanvara [IT]
midnight [n.] midnatt; ~ **sun** midnattssol
midsummer [n.] midsommar
midterm examination [n.] mitterminsprov
midwife [n.; -wives] barnmorska
midwinter [n.] midvinter
might [v.modal.past; see: **may**] kunde, skulle
mighty [adj.] väldig, mäktig
migraine [n.] migrän
migrate [v.] utvandra; flytta
migration [n.] vandring, migration
Milan [n.] Milano
mild [adj.] mild, svag, lindrig
mile [n.] mile [1,6 km]
militant [adj.] militant, aggressiv
militaristic [adj.] militaristisk
military [adj.] militär; ~ **alliance** militärallians; ~ **forces** militär; ~ **man** militär; ~ **service** militärtjänst, värnpliktstjänstgöring, lumpen; ~ **service obligation** värnplikt, lumpen [colloq.]; **compulsory** ~ **service** allmän värnplikt; **do one's** ~ **service** göra lumpen; **time spent in** ~ **service** värnpliktstid
milk [n.] mjölk, bröstmjölk [human]; ~ **shake** milkshake; ~ **substitutes** mjölkersättningar
Milky Way [n.] Vintergatan
mill [n.] kvarn; spinneri
millimeter [n.] millimeter [1/25 inch]
milliner [n.] modist
million [n.] miljon
millionaire [n.] miljonär
min. [abbrev: minute] minut
minced [adj.] mald; hackad; ~ **meat** köttfärs

mind[1] [n.] sinne, förstånd, fantasi; mening, tanke; lust
mind[2] [v.] ge akt på, se till; akta sig för; se efter; ha något emot; **never** ~ det spelar ingen roll
mine[1] [n.] gruva; mina [military]; ~ **clearance** minröjning
mine[2] [pron.poss.: I] min/mitt/mina
mine[3] [v.] bryta, bearbeta
miner [n.] gruvarbetare
mineral [n.] mineral; ~ **deposit** mineralfyndighet; ~ **water** mineralvatten
mini-apartment [n.] övernattningsrum
miniature [adj.] miniatyr-
minibar [n.] minibar
minigolf [n.] minigolf
minimal [adj.] minimal, lägst
minimart [n.] närbutik
minimize [v.] minimera
minimum[1] [adj.] lägsta, minsta, minimi-; ~ **age** minimiålder; ~ **charge** minimipris; ~ **wage** minimilön
minimum[2] [n.; -ma/~s] minimum
mining [n.] gruvdrift, brytning, bergs-
minister [n.] minister, statsråd [govt.]; pastor [church]
ministerial [adj.] minister-, regerings-
Minister of Justice [n.] Justitieminister
ministry [n.; -ries] departement; prästerlig verksamhet
Ministry of Education [n.] Utbildningsdepartement
Minnesota (MN) [n.] Minnesota [delstat i USA]
minor[1] [adj.] mindre, smärre; omyndig; moll [music]; ~ **field** tillvalsämne
minor[2] [n.] omyndig person; tillvalsämne; moll [music]
minority [n.; -ties] minoritet
mint [v.] mynta, prägla
minus[1] [adj./prep.] minus, utan; ~ **sign (-)** minustecken (-)
minus[2] [n.; ~es] minus, brist
minute[1] [adj.] ytterst liten, minutiös
minute[2] [n.] minut; ögonblick; **just a ~!** ett ögonblick!

miracle [n.] mirakel, under
mirror [n.] spegel
mirroring [n.] spegling [IT]
misbehave [v.] bära/uppföra sig illa
misc. [abbrev: miscellaneous] blandad, varjehanda
miscarriage [n.] missfall
mischief [n.] ofog, rackartyg; okynne
miserable [adj.] trist
misery [n.; -ries] elände, olycka; nöd
misfortune [n.] olycka; otur
misleading [adj.] vilseledande, missvisande
miss[1] [n.; ~es] miss, bom; ung dam, fröken
miss[2] [v.; ~es, ~ed, ~ed] missa; försumma; sakna; ~ **out on** gå miste om
missile [n.] robot, missil, raket
missing [adj.] borta; försvunnen; **be ~** komma bort, fattas, saknas
mission [n.] uppdrag, mission, delegation; uppgift
Mississippi (MS) [n.] Mississippi [delstat i USA]
Missouri (MO) [n.] Missouri [delstat i USA]
misspelled [adj.] felstavad
mist [n.] dimma, töcken
mistake[1] [n.] misstag, fel
mistake[2] [v.; -took, -taken] missförstå, ta miste; förväxla
mistress [n.; ~es] älskarinna; härskarinna
misunderstand [v.; -stood] missförstå
misunderstanding [n.] missförstånd
misuse [v.] missbruka, använda felaktigt
MIT [abbrev: Massachusetts Institute of Technology] Massachusetts Institute of Technology
mitigate [v.] mildra, minska
mix[1] [n.; ~es] blandning, mix
mix[2] [v.; ~es, ~ed, ~ed] röra, blanda
mixed [adj.] blandad; ~ **herbs** bouquet garni; ~ **salad** blandad sallad
mixture [n.] blandning; mixtur
mix-up [n.] förväxling, misstag, förvirring

ml [abbrev: milliliter] milliliter
[1/30 fl.oz.]
mm [abbrev: millimeter] millimeter
[1/25 inch]
MN [abbrev: Minnesota] Minnesota [delstat i USA]
MO [abbrev: Missouri] Missouri
[delstat i USA]
moan [v.] jämra sig, stöna; beklaga
sig
moat [n.] vallgrav
mob [n.] pöbel, mobb; maffian
mobile[1] [adj.] rörlig, mobil; ~ **home**
husbil; ~ **phone** mobiltelefon
mobile[2] [n.] mobil
mobility [n.; -ties] rörlighet
mock [v.] förlöjliga; parodiera
modal [adj.] modal
mode [n.] sätt, metod; läge; bruk;
tonart
model[1] [adj.] modell-; mönster-
model[2] [n.] modell; mönster
model[3] [v.] visa; modellera; rita
modem [n.] modem [IT]; ~ **cable**
modemkabel [IT]; ~ **hijacking**
modemkapning [IT]
moderate [adj.] måttlig, moderat;
medelmåttig
moderation [n.] måtta; **in** ~ med
måtta, inom rimliga gränser
modern [adj.] modern; ~ **art** modern konst
modernize [v.] modernisera
modest [adj.] blygsam; anspråkslös,
försynt; anständig
modification [n.] förändring;
modifikation
modify [v.] förändra; modifiera;
anpassa
modular programming [n.] modulär programmering [IT]
module [n.] modul
modus operandi [n.; method of
operating] arbetsmetod
mogul slope [n.] puckelpist
Mohammed [n.] Muhammed
moist [adj.] fuktig
molasses [n.] melass, sirap
mold[1] [n.] form; mönster; mögel
[fungus]
mold[2] [v.] gjuta, forma

Moldavia [n.] Moldavien
molding [n.] gjutning
moldy [adj.] möglig
mole [n.] mullvad
molecular [adj.] molekyl-, molekylär-
molecule [n.] molekyl
molest [v.] uttsätta för sexuella
övergrepp; störa
mom [n.] morsa [colloq.]
moment [n.] ögonblick; **in a** ~ strax
momentary [adj.] ett ögonblicks,
kortvarig
momentum [n.; -ta/~s] fart, styrka,
kraft
Mon. [abbrev: Monday] måndag
monarch [n.] monarch
monarchy [n.; -chies] monarki
monastery [n.; -ries] kloster
Monday [n.] måndag
monetary [adj.] monetär, mynt-
money [n.; -nies] pengar [pl.]; ~
order postanvisning
Mongolia [n.] Mongoliet
Mongolian [n.] mongol
monitor[1] [n.] bildskärm [IT];
dosmätare; övervakare
monitor[2] [v.] övervaka, kontrollera,
följa
monk [n.] munk
monkey [n.] apa, markatta; ~ **wrench**
skiftnyckel
monkfish [n.; ~/~es] marulk [fish]
monochromatic [adj.] enfärgad,
monokrom
monopoly [n.; -lies] monopol
monster [n.] monster, odjur
Montana (MT) [n.] Montana [delstat i USA]
month [n.] månad
monthly [adj.] månatlig, varje
månad; ~ **charge** månadsavgift;
~ **salary** månadslön; ~ **ticket**
månadskort
monument [n.] minnesmärke,
monument
moo [v.] böla, råma
mood [n.] stämning, humör
moon [n.] måne
moonlight [n.] månsken, månljus
moor [n.] hed
moped [n.] moped

moral [adj.] moralisk
morale [n.] moral, stridsmoral
morality [n.; -ties] moral, sedelära; sedlighet
morals [n.pl.] moral, sedlighet
more [adj./adv.comp.: much, many] fler, mer; **no** ~ inte mera; **one** ~ en till; **the** ~ **the merrier** ju mer desto bättre; **there is/are no** ~ det är slut på
morel mushroom [n.] murkla; ~ **sauce** murkelsås
moreover [adv.] dessutom, vidare
morning [n.] morgon, förmiddag; ~ **coffee** förmiddagskaffe; ~ **newspaper** morgontidning; **during the** ~ i förmiddags; **good** ~! god morgon!; **in the** ~ på morgonen; **the next** ~ morgonen därpå; **this** ~ i morse, nu på morgonen
Moroccan [adj.] marockansk
Morocco [n.] Marocko
moron [n.] idiot
mortal [adj.] dödlig; förgänglig, jordisk; ~ **danger** livsfara
mortality [n.; -ties] dödlighet; mortalitet
mortally [adv.] dödligt
mortgage[1] [n.] inteckning, hypotek
mortgage[2] [v.] inteckna, belåna
mosaic [n.] mosaik
Moscow (Russia) [n.] Moskva
Moslem [see: **Muslim**]
mosque [n.] moské
mosquito [n.; ~es/~s] moskit, mygga; ~ **bite** myggbett; ~ **net** myggnät; ~ **repellant** myggmedel
most[1] [adj.superl.: many] mest, flest, det mesta [sing.], de flesta [pl.]
most[2] [adv.superl.: much] mest; i högsta grad, synnerligen; **at** ~ högst; ~ **of all** helst
mostly [adv.] mest, för det mesta
motel [n.] motell
mother [n.] mor, moder, mamma; ~ **board** moderkort [IT]; ~ **of pearl** pärlemor; ~ **tongue** modersmål
mother-in-law [n.; mothers-in-law] svärmor
Mother's Day [n.] Morsdag [usually last Sunday in May]

motif [n.] motiv, tema
motion [n.] rörelse, gest; förslag; ~ **sickness** åksjuka
motivate [v.] motivera; skapa intresse hos
motivation [n.] motivering
motive [n.] motiv, drivfjäder
motor [n.] motor; ~ **boat** motorbåt; ~ **oil** motorolja; ~ **sport** motorsport; ~ **vehicle** motorfordon
motorbike [n.] motorcykel
motorcycle [n.] motorcykel
motorist [n.] bilist
motto [n.] motto, tänkespråk; överskrift
mount [v.] sätta upp, installera, montera; stiga upp
mountain [n.] berg, fjäll; ~ **area** fjälltrakt; ~ **bike** mountainbike, terrängcykel; ~ **chain** bergskedja; ~ **hiking** fjällvandring; ~ **pass** bergspass; ~ **railway** bergbana; ~ **range** bergskedja; ~ **village** bergsby
mountaineering [n.] klättring
mouse [n.; mice] mus; ~ **button** musknapp [IT]; ~ **pad** musmatta [IT]; ~ **pointer** muspekare [IT]
mousse [n.] mousse; fromage
moustache [n.] mustasch
mouth [n.] mun, mynning
mouthful [n.] munfull, munsbit, smula
mouthwash [n.; ~es] munvatten
move[1] [n.] flyttning, drag; åtgärd
move[2] [v.] flytta, röra; rubba; röra sig; ~ **in with each other** flytta ihop; ~ **to** flytta till
movement [n.] rörelse
movie [n.] film; ~ **screen** filmduk; ~ **theater** bio, biograf
movies [n.pl.] bio
moving[1] [adj.] rörande, stämningsfull
moving[2] [n.] flyttning; ~ **van** flyttbil
MP3 player [n.] MP3-spelare
mpg [abbrev: miles per gallon] 'miles' körda med 3,8 liter bensin [20 mpg = 11,8 liter per 100 km]
mph [abbrev: miles per hour] 'miles' i timmen [10 mph = 16 km i timmen]

Mr. [abbrev: Mister] herr (hr)
Mrs. [abbrev: Mistress (pronounced: 'missiz'; title for married women)] fru
MS¹ [abbrev: Master of Science; Mississippi] filosofie magister i naturvetenskapliga ämnen; Mississippi [delstat i USA]
Ms.² [title for women, replaces Mrs. and Miss, pronounced: miz] fru/fröken
ms.³ [abbrev: manuscript] handskrift, manuskript
M/S⁴ [abbrev: motor ship] motorfartyg
MSG¹ [abbrev: monosodium glutamate (food seasoning)] natrium glutamat
msg.² [abbrev: message] meddelande
Msgr. [abbrev: Monsignor (Roman Catholic religious title)] Monsignore
MST [abbrev: Mountain Standard Time] normaltid i Klippiga bergen-zonen i USA
MSU [abbrev: Michigan State University] Michigan State University
MSW [abbrev: Master of Social Work] magisterexamen i socialt arbete
MT¹ [abbrev: Montana] Montana [delstat i USA]
mt.² [abbrev: mount, mountain; megaton] berg; megaton
mtg. [abbrev: meeting] möte
much [adv.] mycket; **how ~?** hur mycket?
mud [n.] gyttja, dy; smuts
muddle [n.] röra, oreda, virrvarr
muddy [adj.] smutsig, lerig
muesli [n.] müsli
muffled [adj.] dämpad, dov
muffler [n.] ljuddämpare; halsduk
mug [n.] mugg
mugged [adj.] överfallad
mugging [n.] rånöverfall
muggy [adj.] kvav
mulberry [n.; -ries] mullbär
mulla [n.] mulla
mulled wine [n.] glödgat vin
mullet [n.] multe [fish]

mulligatawney [n.; Indian curry soup] currysoppa
multicasting [n.] flersändning [IT]
multicultural [adj.] mångkulturell
multifunctional printer [n.] flerfunktionsskrivare [IT], multifunktionsskrivare [IT]
multimedia [adj.] multimedie-
multinational [adj.] multinationell
multipack [adj.] flerpacketerat
multiple¹ [adj.] mångahanda, mångsidig; **~ sclerosis (MS)** multipel skleros
multiple² [n.] mångfald, multipel
multiplex cinema [n.] mångbiograf, biopalats
multiplication [n.] multiplikation
multiplied by [adj.] gånger
multiply [v.; -plies, -plied, -plied] multiplicera, öka; flerdubblas
multiprocessing [n.] parallellbearbetning [IT], parallellkörning [IT]
multitasking [n.] fleruppdragskörning [IT], multikörning [IT]
multithreading [n.] flertrådsteknik [IT]
mumble [v.] mumla
mumps [n.] påssjuka
Munich [n.] München
municipal [adj.] kommunal; **~ council** kommunalfullmäktige, kommunstyrelse; **~ commissioner** kommunalråd; **~ library** stadsbibliotek
municipality [n.; -ties] kommun
mural [n.] väggmålning
murder¹ [n.] mord
murder² [v.] mörda
murdered [adj.] mördad; **be ~** mördas
murderer [n.] mördare
murmur [v.] sorla, susa; mumla
muscle [n.] muskel
museum [n.] museum; **~ village** museiby
mushroom [n.] svamp, champinjon; **~ sauce** svampsås; **~ soup** champinjonsoppa; **cream of ~ soup** redd champinjonsoppa
music [n.] musik; **~ file** musikfil [IT]; **~ hall** varieté; **~ program**

musikprogram; ~ **shop** musikaffär; ~ **store** musikhandel; **make** ~ musicera

musical[1] [adj.] musikalisk, melodisk; musik-

musical[2] [n.] musikal

musician [n.] musiker, musikant

Muslim[1] [adj.] muslimsk

Muslim[2] [n.] muslim

mussels [n.pl.] musslor, blåmusslor

must [v.modal; must] måste

mustard [n.] senap; ~ **plant** senapsväxt

mutant [n.] mutant, mutationsform

mutation [n.] förändring; mutation

mute [adj.] stum

mutter [v.] muttra, mumla; knorra

mutton [n.] får, fårkött; **roast** ~ fårstek

mutual [adj.] ömsesidig, inbördes; gemensam

MV [abbrev: motor vessel] motorfartyg

MVP [abbrev: most valuable player] den högst värderade spelaren i matchen

MW [abbrev: megawatt; medium wave] megawatt; mellanvåg

my [pron.poss.: I] min/mitt/mina

Myanmar [n.] Burma

myself [pron.refl.] mig, mig själv

mysterious [adj.] mystisk, hemlighetsfull; mysteriös

mystery [n.; -ries] gåta, hemlighet; deckare [novel]; ~ **film** kriminalfilm

mystic [n.] mystiker

myth [n.] myt

mythical [adj.] mytisk

mythology [n.; -gies] mytologi

N

N[1] [abbrev: north] norr, nord

n[2] [abbrev: noun; neuter] substantiv; neutrum

NAACP [abbrev: National Association for the Advancement of Colored People] Nationalsamling för färgades avancemang (NAACP)

NAFTA [abbrev: North American Free Trade Association] NAFTA [frihandelsområde bestående av Kanada, USA och Mexiko]

nail[1] [n.] nagel; spik; ~ **clipper** nagelklippare; ~ **file** nagelfil; ~ **polish** nagellack; ~ **polish remover** nagellackborttagningsmedel; ~ **scissors** nagelsax

nail[2] [v.] spika fast; avslöja; fängsla

naked [adj.] naken, bar; kal

name[1] [n.] namn, benämning; skällsord; rykte; ~ **plate** namnskylt; ~ **resolution** namnupplösning [IT]; **first** ~ förnamn; **last** ~ efternamn; **what is your ~?** vad heter du? hur var namnet?

name[2] [v.] nämna; bestämma

named after [adj.] uppkallad efter

namely [adv.] nämligen

nanotechnology [n.] nanoteknologi

nap [n.] tupplur; **take a** ~ ta sig en tupplur, sova middag

nape [n.; back of neck] nacke

napkin [n.] servett; **sanitary** ~ dambinda

Naples [n.] Neapel

narcotic [adj.] narkotisk, bedövande; ~ **drugs** narkotika

narrative[1] [adj.] berättande, narrativ

narrative[2] [n.] berättelse

narrator [n.] berättare

narrow[1] [adj.] smal, trång; knapp; noggrann; ~ **road** smal väg

narrow[2] [v.] göra trängre; bli trängre

narrower [adj.comp.] smalare, trängre

narrowly [adv.] smalt; nätt och jämt

NASA [abbrev: National Aeronautics and Space Administration] NASA [rymdflygstyrelsen i USA]

NASDAQ [abbrev: National Association of Security Dealers Automated Quotation] NASDAQ [börs för handel med aktier huvudsakligen i högteknologiska företag]

nasty [adj.] otäck, otrevlig, elak, ful, ruskig, farlig

nation [n.] nation; ~ **state** nationalstat

national [adj.] nationell, statlig; ~ **anthem** nationalsång; ~ **costume** nationaldräkt; ~ **debt** statsskuld; ~ **news** inrikesnyheter; ~ **park** nationalpark

nationalism [n.] nationalism

nationalist [n.] nationalist

nationalistic [adj.] nationalistisk

nationality [n.; -ties] nationalitet

nationally [adv.] nationellt, över hela landet

National Security Council (NSC) [n.] Nationella säkerhetsrådet i USA

nationwide[1] [adj.] nationell, landsomfattande

nationwide[2] [adv.] över hela landet

native [adj.] födelse-, hem-; medfödd; infödd; ~ **country** hemland; ~ **language** modersmål; ~ **speaker** infödd talare

native [n.] infödd

natl. [abbrev: national] nationell

NATO [abbrev: North Atlantic Treaty Organization] NATO [Atlantpaktsorganisationen]

natural [adj.] naturlig, natur-; omedelbar, självklar; ~ **gas** naturgas; ~ **history** naturhistoria; ~ **history museum** naturhistorisk museum; ~ **resource** naturtillgång; ~ **science** naturvetenskap

naturally [adv.] naturligtvis, för all del

nature [n.] natur; väsen; sort; ~ **conservancy** naturvård; ~ **reserve** naturreservat; ~ **study** naturkunskap; ~ **trail** naturstig

naughty [adj.] styg, elak; oanständig

nausea [n.] kväljningar [pl.], illamående

nauseous [adj.] illamående
naval [adj.] sjö-, marin-, fartygs-;
~ **forces** sjöstridskrafter
nave [n.] mittskep
navel [n.] navel
navigation [n.] navigation; sjöfart;
~ **button** navigeringsknapp [IT]
navy [n.; -vies] flotta, marin
Nazi [adj.] nazistisk
NB[1] [abbrev: New Brunswick]
New Brunswick
n.b.[2] [abbrev: nota bene, take note]
nota bene, observera (obs!), mark
väl
NBA [abbrev: National Basketball
Association] National Basketball
Association [basketbolliga i USA]
NBC [abbrev: National Broadcasting Company] NBC [tv-bolag i
USA]
NBC weapons [abbrev: nuclear,
biological and chemical weapons]
ABC-stridsmedel
NC [abbrev: North Carolina] North
Carolina [delstat i USA]
NCO [abbrev: noncommissioned
officer] underofficer
ND [abbrev: North Dakota] North
Dakota [delstat i USA]
NE [abbrev: northeast; Nebraska]
nordost; Nebraska [delstat i USA]
near[1] [adj.] nära
near[2] [adv.] nära; **get ~** närma sig
near[3] [prep.] nära; ~ **the sea** nära
havet; ~ **to** nära
near[4] [v.] närma sig
nearby[1] [adj.] närbelägen
nearby[2] [adv.] i närheten
nearest [adj.superl.] närmast
nearly [adv.] i det närmaste, nästan
near-sighted [adj.] närsynt
neat [adj.] ordentlig, snygg
Nebraska (NE) [n.] Nebraska [del-
stat i USA]
necessarily [adv.] nödvändigtvis
necessary [adj.] nödvändig
necessity [n.; -ties] nödvändighet,
behov; tvång; nödvändig sak
neck [n.] hals
necklace [n.] halsband, collier
nectarine [n.] nektarin

need[1] [n.] behov, krav, nöd
need[2] [v.] behöva
needed [adj.] nödvändig; **be ~**
behövas
needle [n.] nål; visare; **hypodermic**
~ kanyl, spruta
needless [adj.] onödig, överflödig
needlework [n.] handarbete, syarbete
needy [adj.] behövande, fattig
negative[1] [adj.] negativ; nekande
negative[2] [n.] negativ
neglect[1] [n.] försummelse;
vanskötelse
neglect[2] [v.] försumma; slarva med
negligence [n.] vårdlöshet, försum-
lighet, slarv
negligible [adj.] negligerbar
negotiable [adj.] förhandlingsbar;
säljbar; farbar, överkomlig
negotiate [v.] förhandla, under-
handla
negotiation [n.] förhandling,
underhandling
neigh [v.] gnägga
neighbor [n.] granne
neighborhood [n.] grannskap, trakt,
kvarter; ~ **restaurant** kvarterskrog
neighboring [adj.] grann-, närbelägen; ~ **house** grannhus
neither[1] [adv./conj.] varken; ~ **yesterday nor today** varken igår
eller idag
neither[2] [pron.] ingen/inget
neon light [n.] neonljus
nephew [n.] brorson [brother's son],
systerson [sister's son]
nephritis [n.] njurinflammation
Neptune [n.] Neptunus
nerd [n.] nörd; **computer** ~ datanörd
nerve [n.] nerv; ~**s** nerver; **have the**
~ **to** ha mod nog att [positive], ha
fräckheten att [negative]
nervous [adj.] nerv-, nervös; ~
breakdown nervsammanbrott; ~
system nervsystem; ~ **wreck**
nervvrak
nest[1] [n.] bo, rede, näste
nest[2] [v.] bygga bo; kunna staplas
nesting chairs [n.] stapelbara stolar
net[1] [adj.] netto-; slut-; ~ **income**
nettoinkomst; ~ **weight** nettovikt

net² [n.] nät, håv; nätverk
Netherlands [n.] Nederländerna [pl.]
netiquette [n.] nätikett [IT], nätvett [IT]
nettle [n.] nässla; ~ **soup** nässelsoppa
network¹ [n.] nätverk; ~ **cable** nätverkskabel [IT]; ~ **card** nätverkskort [IT]; ~ **connection** nätverksanslutning [IT]; ~ **service provider** nättjänstleverantör [IT]
network² [v.] skapa ett kontaktnät
netzine [n.] net-zine [IT]
neural network [n.] artificiellt neuronnät [IT], neuronnätt [IT]
neurotic [adj.] neurotisk
neutral [adj.] neutral
neutrality [n.; -ties] neutralitet
neutron [n.] neutron
Nevada (NV) [n.] Nevada [delstat i USA]
never [adv.] aldrig
nevertheless [adv.] trotts det, ändå
new [adj.] ny, färsk; ~ **releases** nya utgåvor; ~ **titles** nya titlar
newcomer [n.] nykomling
New Hampshire (NH) [n.] New Hampshire [delstat i USA]
New Jersey (NJ) [n.] New Jersey [delstat i USA]
newly [adv.] nyligen, ny-; ~ **trained** nyutbildad; ~ **wed/married** nygift
news [n.pl.] nyheter; ~ **broadcast** nyhetssändning; ~ **item** nyhet
newsgroup [n.] diskussionsforum [IT], diskussionsgrupp [IT], newsgrupp [IT]
newsletter [n.] nyhetsbrev, cirkulär
New Mexico (NM) [n.] New Mexico [delstat i USA]
newspaper [n.] tidning
newsstand [n.] tidningskiosk
New Year [n.] Nyår, Nyårshelg; ~'s **Day** Nyårsdagen; ~'s **Eve** Nyårsafton; Happy ~! Gott nytt år!
New York (NY) [n.] New York [delstat i USA]
New Zealand¹ [adj.] nyzeeländsk
New Zealand² [n.] Nya Zeeland
next¹ [adj.] nästa, följande; närmast; ~ **Monday** nästkommande

måndag; ~ **year** nästa år; ~ **door to** strax intill, alldeles bredvid
next² [adv.] därefter, sedan
next to [prep.] intill, vid, bredvid
NFL [abbrev: National Football League] National Football League [amerikansk fotbolliga i USA]
NGO [abbrev: nongovernmental organization] icke-statlig organisation
NH [abbrev: New Hampshire] New Hampshire [delstat i USA]
NHL [abbrev: National Hockey League] NHL [ishockeyliga i USA]
nibble [v.] knapra på, nagga, nafsa; nappa
nice¹ [adj.] trevlig, skön, hygglig; **have a ~ weekend!** trevlig helg!
nice² [adv.] ; ~ **to meet you!** trevligt att träffas!; **how ~!** vad trevligt!
nicely [adv.] utmärkt; ordentlig
nickname [n.] öknamn, smeknamn
nicotine [n.] nikotin
niece [n.] brorsdotter [brother's daughter]; systerdotter [sister's daughter]
night [n.] natt; **at ~** på natten; **good ~!** godnatt!; **per ~** per natt; **the other ~** häromkvällen; ~ **bell** nattklocka; ~ **club** nattklubb; ~ **owl** nattuggla; ~ **porter** nattportier; ~ **table** nattduksbord
nightgown [n.] nattdräkt
nightlife [n.] kvällsliv
nightly¹ [adj.] nattlig
nightly² [adv.] varje natt
nightmare [n.] mardröm
Nile River [n.] Nilen
nine [num.] nio
nineteen [num.] nitton
nineteenth [adj.] nittonde
ninetieth [adj.] nittionde
ninety [num.] nittio
ninth [adj.] nionde
nip [v.; -pping, -pped, -pped] nypa, knipa; bita
nipple [n.] bröstvårta; dinapp
nitrogen [n.] kväve
NJ [abbrev: New Jersey] New Jersey [delstat i USA]
NL [abbrev: Newfoundland and

Labrador] Newfoundland och
Labrador [Canadian prov.]
NM [abbrev: New Mexico] New
Mexico [delstat i USA]
no¹ [adj.] ingen, inte någon; ~ **admittance** ingen ingång; ~ **children under 5 years of age** inga
barn under 5 år; ~ **credit cards**
inga kreditkort; ~ **entry** ingen ingång; ~ **way** uteslutet
no² [adv.] nej, inte; ~ **more than**
högst
no.³ [abbrev: number] nummer (nr)
Nobel Prize [n.] nobelpris; ~ **winner** nobelpristagare
nobility [n.; -ties] adel; adelskap
noble [adj.] adlig; ädel
nobody [pron.; -dies] ingen
nocturnal [adj.] nattlig, natt-
nod¹ [n.] nick
nod² [v.; -dding, -dded, -dded]
nicka; halvsova
node [n.] nod
noise [n.] brus, buller, ljud, bråk
noisy [adj.] bullrig, högljudd,
störande
nomad [n.] nomad
nominal [adj.] nominell, formell
nominate [v.] nominera; utnämna
nomination [n.] nominering;
utnämning
non- [prefix] icke-, o-, -fri
noncommissioned officer (NCO)
[n.] underofficer
none¹ [adv.] inte
none² [pron.] ingen/inga; ~ **whatsoever** ingen som helst
nonetheless [adv.] trots allt, ändå
nonexistent [adj.] obefintlig
nonfiction [n.] facklitteratur,
sakprosa
nonprofit [adj.] icke vinstdrivande,
ideel
nonreturnable bottles [n.pl.] ej
retur [flaskor, glas]
nonsense [n.] nonsens, dumheter
[pl.]
nonsmoking [adj.] icke-rökare; ~
section icke-rökardel
nonstop [adj./adv.] nonstop
nonvolatile memory [n.] ickeflyk-
tigt minne [IT]

noodles [n.pl.] nudlar [pl.]
noon [n.] klockan tolv på dagen; **at**
~ mitt på dagen
no one [pron.] ingen, inte någon;
~ **whosoever** ingen som helst
nor [conj.] och inte; **neither** ... ~
varken ... eller
Nordic [adj.] nordisk; ~ **countries**
Norden [Scandinavia, incl.
Finland]
norm [n.] norm, det normala
normal [adj.] normal, vanlig; ~
skin normal hud
normally [adv.] normalt, i vanliga
fall
north¹ [adj.] nordlig, norra, nord
north² [adv.] norrut
north³ [n.] norr, nord; ~ **of** norr om
North African [adj.] nordafrikansk
North America [n.] Nordamerika
North Cape [n.] Nordkap
North Carolina (NC) [n.] North
Carolina [delstat i USA]
North Dakota (ND) [n.] North
Dakota [delstat i USA]
northeast [n.] nordost, nordöst
northern [adj.] nord-, nordlig, norra
Northern Ireland [n.] Nordirland
North Korea [n.] Nordkorea
North Pole [n.] Nordpolen
North Sea [n.] Nordsjön
North Star [n.] Polstjärnan
northwards [adv.] norrut
northwest [n.] nordväst
Norway [n.] Norge
Norwegian¹ [adj.] norsk
Norwegian² [n.] norrman
Norwegian³ (language) [n.] norska
nos. [abbrev: numbers] nummer
nose [n.] näsa; **blow one's** ~ snyta
sig
nosebleed [n.] näsblod
nostril [n.] näsborre
not¹ [adv.] icke, ej, inte; ~ **at all**
inte alls, absolut inte; ~ **for EU
citizens** inga EU-medborgare; ~
very inget vidare
not² [prefix] o-, icke-
nota bene [expres.: note well]
observera! (obs!)
notable [adj.] påfallande; framstående, betydande

notably [adv.] anmärkningsvärt; i synnerhet;

note[1] [expr.] nota bene (NB)

note[2] [n.] anteckning; kort brev; anmärkning, not; ton [music]

note[3] [v.] observera; notera

notebook [n.] anteckningsbok, block; ~ **computer** bärbar dator [IT]

nothing [pron.] inget, ingenting; ~ **but** ingenting annat än; ~ **special** inget särskilt; **for** ~ gratis

notice[1] [n.] notis, meddelande; anmälan; uppsägning; kännedom; ~ **board** anslagstavla

notice[2] [v.] lägga märke till, märka

noticeable [adj.] synlig; påfallande

notification [n.] uppsägning

notify [v.; -fies, -fied, -fied] underrätta, anmäla; kungöra

notion [n.] föreställning; uppfattning; aning; infall; ~s sybehör

notorious [adj.] ökänd, beryktad

noun [n.] substantiv

nourishment [n.] näring, föda

novel[1] [adj.] ny, nymodig

novel[2] [n.] roman

novelist [n.] romanförfattare

novella [n.] novell

novelty [n.; -ties] nyhet

November [n.] november

now [adv.] nu; ~ **and then** då och då; ~ **then** då så

nowadays [adv.] nuförtiden, numera

nowhere [adv.] ingenstans

NPR [abbrev: National Public Radio] NPR [reklamfri radiokanal i USA]

NRA [abbrev: National Rifle Association] National Rifle Association [nationellt vapeninnehavaresförbund i USA]

NS [abbrev: Nova Scotia] Nova Scotia

NSA [abbrev: National Security Agency] NSA [nationella säkerhetsorganen i USA]

NSC [abbrev: National Security Council] Nationella säkerhetsrådet i USA

NT [abbrev: Northwest Territories] Northwest Territories

nt.wt. [abbrev: net weight] nettovikt

NU [abbrev: Nunavut] Nunavut [Canadian prov.]

nuance [n.] nyans

nuclear [adj.] kärn-; atom- ; ~ **disarmament** kärnvapennedrusting; ~ **family** kärnfamilj; ~ **power** kärnkraft; ~ **power station** kärnkraftverk; ~ **reactor** kärnreaktor; ~ **waste** kärnkraftsavfall; ~ **weapons** kärnvapen

nuclear-free [adj.] kärnvapenfri

nucleus [n.; nuclei] kärna

nude[1] [adj.] naken, bar

nude[2] [n.] akt, nakenstudie

nudist beach [n.] nudiststrand

nuisance [n.] besvär, plåga, bråkstake; **what a ~!** så förargligt!

number[1] [n.] antal; nummer, tal; ~ **sign (#)** fyrkant, nummertecken [IT]; ~ **ticket** [in line at store] nummerlapp; ~s **game** lotto, lotteri

number[2] [v.] numrera; räkna

numeral [n.] siffra; räkneord

numerator [n.] täljare

numeric keypad [n.] numeriskt tangentbord [IT]

numerous [adj.] talrik

nun [n.] nunna

nunnery [n.] kloster

nurse[1] [n.] sjuksköterska, sköterska

nurse[2] [v.] sköta; amma

nursery [n.; -ries] daghem; handelsträdgård, plantskola; ~ **rhyme** barnvisa; ~ **school** daghem, dagis [colloq.]

nursing [n.] sjukvård; amning; ~ **home** servicehus; ~ **school** sjuksköterskaskola

nurture [v.] fostra; föda

nut [n.] nöt; mutter

nutcase [n.] dåre, galning

nutcracker [n.] nötknäppare

nutmeg [n.] muskot, muskotnöt

nutrient [n.] näringsämne

nutritional value [n.] näringsvärde

nutritious [adj.] näringsrik

nuts [adj.] knasig, knäpp

nutshell [n.] nötskal; **in a ~** i ett nötskal

NV [abbrev: Nevada] Nevada [delstat i USA]
NW [abbrev: northwest] nordväst
NWT [abbrev: see: **NT**]
NY [abbrev: New York] New York [delstat i USA]
NYC [abbrev: New York City] New York [staden]

nylon [n.] nylon; ~ **stockings** nylonstrumpor [pl.]
NYU [abbrev: New York University] New York University
NZ [abbrev: New Zealand] Nya Zeeland

O

oak [n.] ek
oar [n.] åra
oath [n.] ed; svordom
oats [n.pl.] havre
obedient [adj.] lydig
obelisk [n.] obelisk
obesity [n.] fetma, allvarlig övervikt
obey [v.] lyda, hörsamma
obituary [n.; -ries] dödsruna, dödsannons; nekrolog
object[1] [n.] föremål, objekt, sak;
syfte
object[2] [v.] ha invändningar, opponera sig, ha något emot
objection [n.] invändning, protest,
motvilja
objective[1] [adj.] objektiv
objective[2] [n.] mål; objektiv
object-oriented programming [n.]
objektorienterad programmering
[IT]
obligation [n.] förpliktelse,
skyldighet
oblige [v.] förplikta, tvinga
obliged [adj.] tvungen; tacksam
obscure[1] [adj.] mörk, skum; oklar;
dunkel; okänd
obscure[2] [v.] förmörka, fördunkla,
skymma
observation [n.] iakttagelse, observation; anmärkning
observatory [n.; -ries] observatorium
observe [v.] observera; iaktta, efter-
leva; fira
observer [n.] iakttagare
obsessed [adj.] besatt
obsession [n.] besatthet, fix idé,
fixering
obsolete [adj.] föräldrad, omodern
obstacle [n.] hinder
obtain [v.] skaffa sig; få tag i/på;
utvinna
obvious [adj.] tydlig, självklar
obviously [adv.] tydligen, självklart
occasion [n.] tillfälle; anledning
occasional [adj.] tillfällig, enstaka
occasionally [adv.] då och då,
emellanåt
occupant [n.] invånare; innehavare

occupation [n.] sysselsättning,
yrke; ockupation
occupational [adj.] arbets-, yrkes-
occupied [adj.] upptagen
occupy [v.; -pies, -pied, -pied] ockupera; inneha; bo i; uppta
occur [v.; -rring, -rred, -rred]
hända, inträffa, ske; förekomma
occurrence [n.] händelse, företeelse; förekomst
ocean [n.] hav, ocean
o'clock [adv.] klockan; it's 7 ~
klockan är 7
OCR [abbrev: optical character
recognition] optisk tecken-
igenkänning [IT]
Oct. [abbrev: October] oktober
octane [n.] oktan
October [n.] oktober
OD [abbrev: overdose] överdos
odd [adj.] underlig; ojämn; udda;
enstaka
oddly [adv.] underligt, konstigt
odds [n.pl.] odds [usually pl.],
utsikter [pl.], vinstchanser [pl.]
odometer [n.] vägmätare
odor [n.] lukt
OECD [abbrev: Organization for
Economic Cooperation and De-
velopment] OECD [ekonomiskt
samarbetsorgan]
OEM [abbrev: original equipment
manufacturer] ursprunglig kom-
ponenttillverkare [IT]
of [prep.] av; a cup ~ tea en kopp
te; the plays ~ Strindberg Strind-
bergs pjäser; ~ course givetvis
off[1] [adj./adv.] bort, i väg; avstängd,
frånkopplad; ~ duty inte i tjänst,
ledig; be ~ ge sig av; time ~
ledighet
off[2] [prep.] bort från, nerifrån; ~ the
record inofficiellt
offend [v.] såra; kränka
offender [n.] förbrytare
offense [n.] brott; anstött; take ~ ta
illa upp
offensive [adj.] stötande, kränkande;
offensiv, aggressiv; obehaglig

offer[1] [n.] erbjudande, anbud; offert
offer[2] [v.] erbjuda; utfästa; framföra, lägga fram, komma med
offered [adj.] erbjuden
offering [n.] offrande; offer
office [n.] kontor, byrå, expedition; ~ **automation** kontorsautomatisering [IT]; ~ **cleaning** kontorsstädning; ~ **hours** kontorstid; ~ **network** kontorsnätverk
officer [n.] officer; **police** ~ polisman
official[1] [adj.] officiell
official[2] [n.] tjänsteman
officially [adv.] officiellt
off-line [adj./adv.] frånkopplad [IT], inte ansluten [IT]
off-peak [adj.]: **at** ~ **hours** vid lågtrafik
off-road vehicle [n.] terränggående fordon
off-season [adj.] lågsäsongs-
offset [v.; -setting, -set, -set] uppväga, kompensera
offspring [n.] avkomma; ättling
often [adv.] ofta; **how** ~? hur ofta?
oh[1] [interj.] å!, äh!, oj!, äsch!, fy!; ~ **dear!/my!** oj!; ~ **yes** jodå
OH[2] [abbrev: Ohio] Ohio [delstat i USA]
Ohio (OH) [n.] Ohio [delstat i USA]
oil [n.] olja; ~ **change** oljebyte; ~ **filter** oljefilter; ~ **gauge** oljemätare; ~ **painting** oljemålning; ~ **rig** oljerigg; ~ **spill** oljeutsläpp; **cooking** ~ matolja; **olive** ~ olivolja
oily [adj.] oljig, fet; ~ **skin** fet hud
ointment [n.] salva; ~ **for cuts** sårsalva
OJ [abbrev: orange juice] apelsinsaft
OK [abbrev: okay; Oklahoma] OK, okej, bra; Oklahoma [delstat i USA]
okay [see: **OK**]
Oklahoma (OK) [n.] Oklahoma [delstat i USA]
old [adj.] gammal; ~ **age** ålderdom; ~ **age pension** ålderspension; ~ **maid** gammal ungmö/fröken; ~ **man** gubbe; ~ **people's home** ålderdomshem; ~ **town** gamla

stan/staden; **how** ~ **are you?** hur gammal är du?; **in the** ~ **days** förr i tiden
older [adj.comp.: old] äldre; **Scotia is** ~ **than Ashna** Scotia är äldre än Ashna
oldest [adj.superl.: old] äldst
old-fashioned [adj.] gammaldags
olive [n.] oliv; ~ **oil** olivolja
Olympic Games [n.pl.] Olympiska spelen (OS) [pl.]
ombudsman [n.; -men] ombudsman
omelet [n.] omelett
omission [n.] utlämnande; försummelse
omit [v.; omitted] utelämna, försumma
ON[1] [abbrev: Ontario] Ontario [Canadian prov.]
on[2] [adv.] på; vidare
on[3] [prep.] på; i; vid; ~ **foot** till fots; ~ **land** till lands; ~ **prescription** på recept; ~ **Sunday** på söndag; ~ **the map** på kartan; ~ **the telephone** i telefonen; ~ **the train** på tåget; ~ **the way** iväg; ~ **top** överst
on-call service [n.] jourtjänst
once[1] [adv.] en gång; förr; **for** ~ för en gångs skull; ~ **more** en gång till; **at** ~ genast
once[2] [conj.] en gång, när, så snart
oncoming [adj.] mötande; förestående; ~ **traffic** mötande trafik
one[1] [adj./num.] en/ett; ena; enda
one[2] [pron.] en; man; ~**'s** ens; ~ **after another** i rad; ~ **another** varandra; ~ **of them** den/det ena
one-day ticket/pass [n.] endagsbiljett
one-family house [n.] enfamiljsvilla
oneself [pron.refl.] sig; själv; **cook and clean house for** ~ sköta hushållet själv
one-story house [n.] enplansvilla
one-way street [n.] enkelriktad gata
one-way ticket [n.] enkel biljett, enkel resa
onion [n.] lök; ~ **soup** löksoppa
online[1] [adj.] direktansluten; ~

bank internetbank; ~ **help** direkthjälp; ~ **service** direkttjänst; ~
shopping näthandel
online² [adv.] direkt, på Internet
only¹ [adj.] enda; bara; **freight** ~
bara frakt; **the ~ thing** det enda
only² [adv./conj.] bara; endast
onset [n.] inträde, början
onto [prep.] på; **be ~ s.o.** inte låta
lura sig av någon
onward(s) [adv.] framåt, vidare
op. [abbrev: opus: work] opus, verk
op.cit. [abbrev: opere citato: in the
work cited] som är anfört arbete
OPEC [abbrev: Organization of
Petroleum Exporting Countries]
OPEC [organisation för stater
som är nettoexportörer av råolja]
op-ed [abbrev: opposite editorial
(article)] debattsida; ~ **piece**
debattartikel
open¹ [adj.] öppen; ledig; ~ **24
hours a day** öppen 24 timmar; ~
air friska luften; ~ **all night** nattöppen; ~ **architecture** öppen
uppbyggnad [IT]; ~ **in the evening**
kvällsöppen; ~ **market** torg; ~
source öppen källkod [IT]; **in the**
~ offentlig
open² [v.] öppna; få upp; ~ **here**
öppna här
open-air [adj.] ute-; ~ **café** uteservering; ~ **museum** friluftsmuseum; ~ **theater** friluftsteater
opener [n.] öppnare
opening [n.] öppning; ~ **hours**
öppettider; ~ **tag** starttagg [IT]
openly [adv.] öppet, offentligt
openness [n.; ~es] öppenhet
opera [n.] opera; ~ **house** operahus
operate [v.] operera
operating [adj.] arbets-, drifts-; ~
expenses driftskostnader [pl.]; ~
instructions bruksanvisningar [pl.];
~ **room** operationssal; ~ **system**
operativsystem [IT]
operation [n.] operation; **perform
an** ~ operera
operational [adj.] funktionsduglig;
drifts-
operations research [n.]
operationsanalys

operator [n.] operator
operetta [n.] operett
ophthalmologist [n.] ögonläkare
opinion [n.] mening, åsikt, uppfattning; ~ **formation** opinionsbildning; ~ **poll** opinionsundersökning;
~ **research** opinionsundersökning; **be of the** ~ anse; **public** ~
den allmänna opinionen
opponent [n.] motståndare,
motspelare
opportunity [n.; -ties] tillfälle,
möjlighet, chans; ~ **cost** marginal
kostnad
oppose [v.] opponera sig, motsätta
sig, bekämpa
opposed [adj.] motsatt, stridig
opposite¹ [adj.] mitt emot; motsatt
opposite² [n.] motsats; **just the** ~
tvärtom
opposite³ [prep.] mitt emot
opposition [n.] motstånd, opposition; ~ **party** oppositionsparti
oppression [n.] förtryck; bekläm-
ning; tryck
opt [v.] välja
optical [adj.] optisk; ~ **character
recognition (OCR)** optisk klartextläsning [IT]; ~ **fiber** optisk
fiber; ~ **illusion** synvilla
optician [n.] optiker
optimism [n.] optimism
optimistic [adj.] optimistisk
optimization [n.] optimering
option [n.] val; alternativ; option
optional [adj.] valfri, fakultativ
OR¹ [abbrev: Oregon; operating
room] Oregon [delstat i USA];
operationssal
or² [conj.] eller
oral [adj.] muntlig, oral; ~ **examination** muntlig examen [univ.],
oral undersökning [dentist]
orally [adv.] muntligen; oralt; **not
to be taken** ~ får ej tas oralt
orange [n.] apelsin [fruit]; brandgul, orange [color]; ~ **drink** apelsinsaft; ~ **juice** apelsinjos
orbit¹ [n.] bana, kretslopp
orbit² [v.] kretsa kring
orchestra [n.] orkester; ~ **seats**
parkett

orchestral [adj.] orkester-
orchid [n.] orkidé
ordeal [n.] svårt prov, pärs
order[1] [n.] ordning; order; beställning; uppdrag; orden; **in ~ to** för att; **out of ~** trasig, ur funktion
order[2] [v.] beordra; beställa
ordered list [n.] ordnad lista
ordinal [n.] ordningstal
ordinary [adj.] vanlig, vardags-
ore [n.] malm; **~ mining** malmbrytning
Oregon (OR) [n.] Oregon [delstat i USA]
organ [n.] organ; orgel [music]; **~ transplant** organtransplantation
organic [adj.] organisk; **~ foods** ekologiskt odlade varor [pl.]
organism [n.] organism
organization [n.] organisation; struktur
organizational [adj.] organisations-, företags-
organize [v.] organisera, ordna
organized [adj.] organiserad
organizer [n.] organisatör
Orient [n.] Orienten
orientation [n.] orientering; **sexual ~** sexuell läggning
orienteering [n.] orientering
origin [n.] ursprung; **country of ~** ursprungsland
original[1] [adj.] original, ursprunglig
original[2] [n.] original
originally [adv.] ursprungligen
originate [v.] ge upphov till; utgå från
ornament [n.] ornament, prydnad
ornithology [n.] ornitologi
orphan [n.] föräldralöst barn
orthodox [adj.] ortodox
orthopedics [n.] ortopedi
orthopedist [n.] ortoped
OSCE [abbrev: Organization for Security and Cooperation in Europe] Organisationen för säkerhet och samarbete i Europa (OSSE)
OTB [abbrev: off-track betting] toto, totalisator
OTC [abbrev: over the counter] receptfri, som säljs över disk

other [adj.] annan/annat; andra; ytterligare; **on the ~ hand** däremot; **the ~ night** häromkvällen; **and ~s** med flera
otherwise [adv.] annorlunda; annars
ouch! [interj.] aj!
ought [v.modal; ought] böra
ounce [n.] uns [28,4 g; 0,3 dl]
our(s) [pron.poss.: we] vår
ourselves [pron.refl.] oss; själv; **by ~** alena
out [adj./adv.] ute [place], ut [motion], utanför; borta; **~ loud** högt
outboard motor [n.] utombordsmotor
outbox [n.; ~es] utkorg
outbreak [n.] utbrott
outburst [n.] utbrott
outcome [n.] resultat, utgång
outdoor [adj.] ute-, utomhus-, ytter; **~ clothes** ytterkläder [pl.]; **~ pool** utomhusbassäng, utebassäng
outdoors [adv.] ute, utomhus; i det gröna
outer [adj.] ytter; **~ door** ytterdörr
outfit [n.] utstyrsel; utrustning
outgoing [adj.] utåtriktad; avgående; utgående
outing [n.] utflykt
outlet [n.] utlopp; uttag; **factory ~** försäljningsställe
outline[1] [n.] skiss, utkast; kontur; **~s** grunddrag; **~ font** vektorfont [IT]
outline[2] [v.] skissera
outliner [n.] idéprocessor [IT]
outlook [n.] utsikt, inställning
outmoded [adj.] omodern
out of [prep.] ut ur; utan; av; **~ doors** utomhus; **~ sight** utom synhåll; **~ one's mind** galen; **be ~ gas** vara utan bensin, ha bensinslut
out-of-date [adj.] föråldrad, gammal
outpatient clinic [n.] akuten, poliklinik
outpatient department [n.] akutmottagning
output [n.] tillverkning; uteffekt; utmatning [IT]
outrage [n.] harm, indignation; skandal; våld

outrageous [adj.] skändlig, kränkande; överdriven

outreach program [n.] uppsökande verksamhet

outset [n.] början

outside[1] [adj.] yttre, ytter-

outside[2] [adv.] ute [place], ut [motion]

outside[3] [n.] utsida; from ~ utifrån; on the ~ utanpå

outside (of)[4] [prep.] utanför, utom

outsider [n.] outsider, utomstående

outspoken [adj.] rättfram, frispråkig

outstanding [adj.] framstående; utestående

outward[1] [adj.] utåtriktad; yttre

outward(s)[2] [adv.] ut

outweigh [v.] uppväga

oval [adj.] oval

oven [n.] bakugn, ugn

oven-baked [adj.] ugnsbakad

oven-browned [adj.] ugnsbrynt

ovenproof [adj.] eldfast; ~ dish eldfast form

over[1] [adv.] över; ~ there där borta; talk ~ tala igenom

over[2] [prep.] över

overall[1] [adj.] total-, helhets-, samlad, generell

overall[2] [adv.] totalt. generellt

overalls [n.pl.] överdragskläder [pl.]

overboard [adv.] överbord

overcast [adj.] mulen

overcoat [n.] överrock

overcome [v.; -came, -come] övervinna, besegra; segra

overdrawn [adj.] övertrasserad [bank]

overdue [adj.] förfallen; försenad

overhead [n.] fasta utgifter

overheated [adj.]: get ~ gå varm [machine]

overlap[1] [n.] överlappning

overlap[2] [v.; -pped] överlappa; delvis täcka varandra

overlook [v.] erbjuda utsikt över; förbise

overnight [adv.] över natten

override [v.; -rode, -ridden] tillfälligt ersätta, åsidosätta

overseas[1] [adj.] utländsk, utrikes-

overseas[2] [adv.] utomlands

overt [adj.] uppenbar, offentlig

overtake [v.] köra förbi; hinna upp

over-the-counter drug [n.] receptfri medicin

overthrow [v.; -threw, -thrown] störta; vräka omkull

overtime [n.] övertid; förlängning [sports]

over-tired [adj.] överansträngd

overview [n.] översikt

overweight[1] [adj.] överviktig

overweight[2] [n.] övervikt

overwhelm [v.] överväldiga, överhopa; översvämma

overwhelming [adj.] överväldigande

overwrite mode [n.] överskrivningsläge [IT]

owe [v.] vara skyldig, ha att tacka för; how much do I ~? vad är jag skyldig?

owl [n.] uggla

own[1] [adj.] sin/sitt/sina; egen

own[2] [adv.] on one's ~ på egen hand

own[3] [v.] äga

owner [n.] ägare

ownership [n.] ägande, ägo

oxtail soup [n.] oxsvanssoppa

oxygen [n.] syre

oysters [n.pl.] ostron [pl.]

oz. [abbrev: ounce] uns [28,4 g; 0,3 dl]

ozone [n.] ozon

P							394							papers

P

P¹ [abbrev: parking] parkering
p.² [abbrev: piano (quiet); page]
piano, tyst; sida
p's and q's [exp.: manners, good
behavior, etiquette] **mind one's ~**
hålla tungan rätt i mun
PA¹ [abbrev: Pennsylvania; phy-
sician('s) assistant] Pennsylvania
[delstat i USA]; läkarassistent
pa² [n.] pappa
pace¹ [n.] steg, gång; hastighet,
tempo, takt
pace² [v.] gå fram och tillbacka; ~
oneself arbeta i sin egen takt
Pacific Ocean [n.] Stilla havet
pacifier [n.] tröstnapp
pack¹ [n.] packe, paket; grupp; ~ **of
cards** kortlek; ~ **of cigarettes**
paket cigaretter
pack² [v.] packa, packa ner, packa
in, lägga ned; ~ **up** packa ihop
package¹ [n.] kolli, paket; ~ **store**
spritbutik
package² [v.] förpacka, emballera
packaging [n.] förpackning,
packning
packed [adj.] packad, full; ~ **lunch**
matsäck
packet [n.] paket; ~ **switching**
paketförmedling [IT]
packing [n.] packning, emballage
pact [n.] fördrag, pakt
pad¹ [n.] skydd, dyna; skrivblock;
avskjutningsramp [missile]; kvart
[lodging]; **stamp ~** stämpeldyna
pad² [v.; -dded] vaddera, madrassera
paddle [n.] paddel
pagan [adj.] hednisk
page [n.] sida, blad; ~ **break** sidbrytning [IT]; ~ **style** formatmall
[IT]
pager [n.] personsökare
paid [adj.] betald; ~ **employment**
förvärvsarbete
pail [n.] hink, spann
pain [n.] smärta, värk; ont; **be in ~**
ha värk/ont/smärtor; **have a ~ in
the back** ha ont i ryggen; **be a ~
in the neck/ass** vara en plåga

painful [adj.] smärtsam, plågsam;
be ~ göra ont
painfully [adv.] pinsamt
painkiller [n.] smärtstillande medel,
värktablett
paint¹ [n.] färg; ~ **program**
målarprogram [IT]; **box of ~s**
färglåda; **wet ~!** nymålat!
paint² [v.] måla
painted [adj.] målad
painter [n.] målare
painting [n.] måleri; målning, tavla
pair [n.] par
pajamas [n.pl.] pyjamas
Pakistan [n.] Pakistan
Pakistani [adj.] pakistansk
pal [n.] kamrat, kompis [colloq.]
palace [n.] slott, palats
pale [adj.] blek; ~ **ale** ljust öl
Palestine [n.] Palestina
Palestinian [adj.] palestinsk
palm [n.] handflata; palm [tree]
Palm Sunday [n.] palmsöndagen
palmtop computer [n.] handdator,
fickdator
pamphlet [n.] broschyr
pan [n.] panna, form
Panama Canal [n.] Panamakanalen
pancake [n.] pannkaka
panel [n.] panel; ~ **discussion**
paneldiskussion
paneling [n.] panel
panic [n.] panik
panorama [n.] panorama
panties [n.pl.] trosor [pl.]
pants [n.pl.] byxor
panty [n.; -ties]: ~ **hose** strumpbyxor [pl.]; ~ **liners** trosskydd
papal [adj.] påvlig
paper¹ [n.] papper; tidning; dokument; uppsats; ~ **bag** kasse; ~ **clip**
gem, pappersklämma; ~ **goods**
pappersvaror; ~ **napkin** papper-
servett; ~ **tissue** pappersnäsduk;
~ **towels** hushållspapper
paper² [v.] tapetsera [wall]
paperback [n.] häftad bok, pocket-
bok
papers [n.pl.] handlingar, legitima-
tionshandlingar; tidningar

paperwork [n.] pappersarbete
paprika [n.] paprika
Papua New Guinea [n.] Papua Nya
Guinea
par [n.] del normala; par [golf]
parachute [n.] fallskärm
parachuting [n.] fallskärmshoppning
parade [n.] parad
paradise [n.] paradis
paraffin [n.] paraffin [wax]
paraglider [n.] flygskärm
paragliding [n.] skärmflygning
paragraph [n.] stycke
parallel[1] [adj.] parallell; ~ processing parallellkörning
parallel[2] [n.] parallel, motstycke;
breddgrad
paralysis [n.; -ses] förlamning
paralyze [v.] paralysera, lamslå
paramedic [n.] skjukvårdare,
ambulanspersonal
parameter [n.] parameter
paraplegic [adj.] paraplegisk,
ryggmärgsskadad
parasailing [n.] bogserskärmflygning
parasite [n.] parasit
parasol [n.] parasoll
parcel [n.] paket; del, lott
pardon[1] [n.] förlåtelse; benådning;
I beg your ~ förlåt
pardon[2] [v.] ursäkta; pardon? hur
sa?
parent [n.] förälder
parental [adj.] föräldra-; ~ control
Internetskydd för hem-pc styrad
av föräldrarna [IT]
parenthesis [n.; -ses] parentes,
parentestecken
parents-in-law [n.pl.] svärföräldrar
parent-teacher association (PTA)
[n.] föräldraförening
parent-teacher consultation [n.]
föräldramöte
parish [n.; ~es] socken, församling;
~ office pastorsexpedition; ~ registration kyrkobokföring
parity [n.; -ties] jämlikhet, paritet;
even ~ jämn paritet [IT]; odd ~
udda paritet [IT]
park[1] [n.] park; national ~ nationalpark

park[2] [v.] parkera
parking [n.] parkering; ~ fine parkeringsböter; ~ garage parkeringshus; ~ lot parkeringsplats; ~
meter parkeringsautomat, parkeringsmätare; ~ permitted parkering
tillåten; ~ prohibited parkerings-
förbud; ~ space parkeringsplats;
~ ticket parkeringsböter
Parliament [n.] Riksdagen; ~
building Riksdagshuset
parliamentary [adj.] parlaments-
parquet floor(ing) [n.] parkettgolv
parrot [n.] papegoja
parser [n.] textanalysator [IT]
parsley [n.] persilja
parsnip [n.] palsternacka
part[1] [n.] avsnitt, beståndsdel, del;
roll [theater]; bena [hair]; ~ number artikelnummer; ~ of speech
ordklass ; ~ of the country landsdel; ~ of town stadsdel, kvarter;
in ~ delvis
part[2] [v.] dela; skilja; bena [hair]
partial [adj.] partisk; partiell
partially [adv.] delvis
participant [n.] deltagare
participate [v.] delta, ha del i
participation [n.] deltagande
participle [n.] particip
particle [n.] partikel
particular[1] [adj.] speciell; kräsen;
kinkig
particular[2] [n.] detalj; in ~ i
synnerhet
particularly [adv.] speciellt
partitioning [n.] partitionering [IT]
partly [adv.] delvis
partner [n.] partner
partnership [n.] kompanjonskap
partridge [n.] rapphöna
part-time [adj.] deltids-
party [n.; -ties] fest, party; parti
[political]; ~ leader partiledare
pass[1] [n.; ~es] pass [mountain,
cards]; godkänd [school]
pass[2] [v.; ~es, ~ed, ~ed] passera;
räcka över; köra om [driving]; klara
[exam]; ~ through genomresa
passable [adj.] skaplig; framkomlig
passage [n.] genomfart

passenger [n.] passagerare, resenär;
~ car bil; sittvagn [railroad]
passing[1] [adj.] förbigående; över-
gående; ~ lane omkörningsfil
passing[2] [n.] omkörning; bortgång;
in ~ i förbigående; no ~ omkörning förbjuden
passion [n.] lidelse, passion, patos;
häftigt utbrott
passionate [adj.] passionerad; häftig
passive [adj.] passiv, övergiven
Passover [n.] Påsk
passport [n.] pass; ~ control passkontroll; ~ number passnummer
passport-size photo [n.] passfoto
password [n.] lösenord
past[1] [adj.] förfluten; förbi
past[2] [adv.] förbi
past[3] [n.] det förflutna; imperfekt
[gram]; in the ~ tidigare
past[4] [prep.] förbi; över [clock];
10 ~ 5 10 över 5
pasta [n.] pasta
paste [n.] deg; pasta, pastej; klister
paste in [v.] klistra in
pastel [n.] pastelkrita
pasteurized [adj.] pastöriserad
pastor [n.] pastor, präst
pastries [n.pl.] bakverk
pastry [n.; -ries] bakelse; smördeg;
~ shop finbageri, konditori
pasture [n.] bete, betesmark
PA-system [abbrev: public address
system] högtalaranläggning
pat [v.; -tting, -tted, -tted] klappa,
ge en klapp
patch[1] [n.; ~s] fläck; lapp; programfix [IT]; ~ cable mellankopplingskabel [IT]
patch[2] [v.; ~es, ~ed, ~ed] lappa,
laga; ~ up plåstra om, lappa ihop
paté [n.] pastej
patent [n.] patent; Patent Office
Patentverket
paternity [n.] faderskap; ~ leave
pappaledighet; ~ test faderskapstest
path [n.] gångstig, stig; sökväg [IT]
pathetic [adj.] patetisk, sorglig
patience [n.] tålamod
patient[1] [adj.] tålmodig, fördragsam
patient[2] [n.] patient; ~ card
patientbricka, patientkort

patrol[1] [n.] patrull
patrol[2] [v.] patrullera
patron [n.] beskyddare; kund; ~
saint skyddshelgon
pattern [n.] mönster; ~ recognition
mönsteridentifiering
pause[1] [n.] paus, avbrott
pause[2] [v.] pausa, göra en paus
pavement [n.] stenläggning; belagd
väg
pavilion [n.] paviljong
paving [n.] stenläggning
paw [n.] tass
pawn [n.] bonde [chess]
pay[1] [n.] betalning; lön; ~ raise
lönförhöjning
pay[2] [v.; paid, paid] betala; ~ phone
mynttelefon, telefonautomat
payable (to) [adj.] betalas (till)
payment [n.] betalning, utbetalning; means of ~ betalningsmedel
payroll tax [n.] arbetsgivaravgift,
socialavgift
pay-TV [n.] betal-tv
PBS [abbrev: Public Broadcasting
System] PBS [reklamfri tv-kanal i
USA]
PC [abbrev: personal computer;
politically correct] persondator
(PC); politiskt korrekt; ~ box/case
datorlåda [IT]
pct. [abbrev: percent] procent
pd. [abbrev: paid] betald
PDA [abbrev: personal digital as-
sistant] handdator
PDF [abbrev: portable document
format] pdf [portabelt dokument-
format] [IT]
PDQ [abbrev: pretty damn quick;
colloq.] fortare än kvikt
PDT [abbrev: Pacific Daylight
Time] sommartid på västkusten i
USA
PE[1] [abbrev: Prince Edward Island]
Prince Edward Island [Canadian
prov.]
P.E.[2] [abbrev: physical education]
idrott, gymnastik
pea [n.] ärt(a); ~ soup ärtsoppa
peace [n.] fred, ro; ~ movement
fredsrörelse; ~ prize fredspris; ~
process fredsprocess; in ~ i fred

peaceful [adj.] fridfull, stilla; freds-
peach [n.; ~es] persika
peak [n.] topp; at ~ hours under
　högtrafik
peanut [n.] jordnöt; ~ butter
　jordnötssmör
pear [n.] päron
pearl [n.] pärla
peas [n.pl.] ärter
peasant [n.] bonde, lant-
peat [n.] torv
pebbly [adj.] stenig
peculiar [adj.] egendomlig; märk-
　lig; särskild
pecuniary [adj.] pekuniär, penning-
pedagogy [n.; -gies] pedagogi
pedal [n.] pedal; ~ boat trampbåt
pedestrian [n.] fotgängare, gående;
　~ crossing övergång för fotgäng-
　are, övergångsställe; ~ overpass
　gångbro; ~ street gågata; ~ un-
　derpass gångtunnel
pediatric clinic [n.] barnsjukhus
pediatrician [n.] barnläkare
pedicure [n.] pedikyr
pee [v.; colloq.] kissa [colloq.]
peek [v.] kika, titta
peel¹ [n.] skal
peel² [v.] skala
peer¹ [n.] like
peer² [v.] kisa
peer-to-peer network [n.] jäm-
　likhetsnät [IT]
peg [n.] stång, pinne
PEI [abbrev: see: PE]
pelvis [n.] bäcken
pen¹ [n.] penna; ballpoint ~ kul-
　spetspenna; ~ reader läspenna [IT]
pen.² [abbrev: peninsula] halvö
penalty [n.; -ties] straff
pencil [n.] blyertspenna; ~ sharp-
　ener pennformerare, pennvässare
pendant [n.] hängsmycke
penetrate [v.] tränga igenom, bryta
　igenom; tränga in, penetrera
penicillin [n.] penicillin
peninsula [n.] halvö
penis [n.; ~es] penis
penknife [n.; -knives] pennkniv
Pennsylvania (PA) [n.] Pennsylva-
　nia [delstat i USA]

penny [n.; -nnies; 1/100 dollar]
　penny
pension [n.] pension; ~ fund
　pensionsfond
pensioner [n.] pensionär; ~s' asso-
　ciation pensionärsförening
people¹ [n.] folk
people² [n.pl.] folk, man; människor
pepper [n.] paprika [vegetable];
　peppar [spice]; ~ grinder/mill
　pepparkvarn; ~ shaker peppar-
　ströare; green ~ grön paprika; red
　~ röd paprika
per [prep.] per; ~ day per dag; ~
　kilo per kilo; ~ night per natt; ~
　week per vecka; ~ year om året;
　price ~ unit (kilo, liter) jämförs-
　pris
perceive [v.] märka; uppfatta
percent [adv./n.] procent
percentage [n.] procentandel
perceptible [adj.] märkbar
perception [n.] iakttagelseförmåga
perch [n.; ~es] abborre [fish]
perfect [adj.] perfekt, fulländad;
　fullständig
perfection [n.] fullkommande;
　fulländning
perfectly [adv.] perfekt
perform [v.] utföra; spela
performance [n.] föreställning;
　prestation
performer [n.] uppträdande (per-
　son), artist
perfume [n.] parfym; ~ shop
　parfymeri
perhaps [adv.] kanske
period [n.] period, tid; punkt; mens
　[menstruation]; ~ of notice upp-
　sägningstid; ~ of study studietid;
　~ of time stund; ~ pains mens-
　smärtor
periodical [n.] tidskrift
periodically [n.] tidvis
peripheral device [n.] periferien-
　het [IT]
perishables [n.pl.] färskvaror
permanent [adj.] permanent; fast;
　~ employment fast anställning,
　tillsvidareanställning; ~ residence
　permit permanent uppehållstill-
　stånd

permanently [adv.] beständigt
permission [n.] tillstånd; lov; ask ~
to be om lov att
permit[1] [n.] tillstånd; ~ required
tillstånd behövs; ~ holders only
tillstånd behövs
permit[2] [v.; -tting, -tted, -tted]
tillåta
permitted [adj.] tillåten; be ~ to få
perpetuity [adv.]: in ~ för all framtid
Persia [n.] Persien
Persian [adj.] persisk; ~ Gulf Per-
siska Viken
persist [v.] fortsätta, håla på
persistent [adj.] ihärdig; ståndaktig
person [n.] person, människa
personal [adj.] personlig; ~ cas-
sette/CD player freestyle; ~ computer (PC) persondator; ~ data
assistant (PDA) elektronisk almanacka, fickdator; ~ details
personuppgift; ~ organizer
planeringskalender; ~ reasons
familjeskäl; ~ use personlig bruk
personality [n.] personlighet
personally [adv.] personligen
personnel [n.] personal; ~ department personalavdelning
person-to-person call [n.] personligt samtal
perspective [n.] perspektiv, utsikt
persuade [v.] övertala, övertyga
persuasion [n.] övertalning,
övertygande
persuasive [adj.] övertalande,
övertygande
pessimistic [adj.] pessimistisk
pest [n.] skadedjur; plåga
pet [n.] husdjur; ~ food djurmat
petition [n.] ansökan
petty [adj.] obetydlig; småsint
pewter [n.] tenn
PG[1] [abbrev: parental guidance
(film rating)] tillåten för barn endast i vuxens sällskap
pg.[2] [abbrev: page] sida
PG-13 [abbrev: parental guidance
under 13] tillåten för barn under
13 endast i vuxens sällskap
pH [abbrev: measure of acidity] pH
[mått på surhet]
p&h [abbrev: postage and handling]

porto och expeditionskostnader,
frakt och emballage
pharmacy [n.; -cies] apotek
phase [n.] fas; stadium
PhD [abbrev: Doctor of Philosophy]
fil.dr
pheasant [n.] fasan
phenomenon [n.; -mena] företeelse,
fenomen
Philippine [adj.] filippinsk
Philippines [n.pl.] Filippinerna
philistine [adj.] kälkborgerlig
philosopher [n.] filosof
philosophical [adj.] filosofisk
philosophy [n.; -phies] filosofi
phishing [n.] nätfiske [IT]
phobia [n.] fobi
Phoenix (Arizona) [n.] Fenix
phone[1] [n.] telefon, telefonlur; ~
book telefonkatalog; ~ booth
telefonkiosk; ~ call telefonsamtal;
~ card telefonkort; ~ number
telefonnummer
phone[2] [v.] ringa, telefonera; ~ in
sick ringa och sjukanmäla sig
phonograph record [n.] platta
photo [n.] foto, bild, kort; ~ editor
bildredigerare [IT]; ~ op(portunity)
fototillfälle; ~ shop fotoaffär
photocopier [n.] kopiator
photograph[1] [n.] fotografi, foto;
take ~s fotografera
photograph[2] [v.] fotografera
photographer [n.] fotograf
photographic [adj.] fotografisk,
foto-; ~ materials fotoartiklar
photographing [n.] fotografering
photography [n.] fotografi; ~
course fotokurs
phrasal verb [n.] frasverb,
partikelverb
phrase [n.] fras, uttryck
physical [adj.] fysisk; ~ education
(PE) idrott, gymnastik; ~ handicap funktionshinder, fysiskt funktionshinder; ~ therapy sjukgymnastik; ~ training motionsgymnastik
physically [adv.] fysiskt
physician [n.] läkare
physics [n.] fysik
physiotherapist [n.] sjukgymnast

physiotherapy [n.; -pies] sjukgymnastik, fysioterapi
pianist [n.] pianist
piano [n.] piano; ~ player pianist
pick [v.] välja; plocka [flowers];
peta; hacka; ~ up hämta; get ~ed
up hämtas
pickle [n.] inlagd gurka
pickled [adj.] syltad; ~ beets in-
lagda rödbetor; ~ gherkins ättiks-
gurka; ~ herring inlagd sill
pickpocket [n.] ficktjuv
pickup [n.] avhämtning; ~ service
hämtservice; ~ truck varubil
picnic [n.] picknick; ~ area pick-
nickområde, rastplats [on high-
way]; ~ basket picknickkorg
picture[1] [n.] bild, tavla; ~ postcard
vykort
picture[2] [v.] avbilda, framställa;
skildra
picturesque [adj.] pittoresk
pie [n.] paj; ~ chart cirkeldiagram
[IT]
piece [n.] bit, stycke; a ~ per styck
pied-a-terre [n.] övernattningsrum
pier [n.] brygga, kaj, skeppskaj
piercing [adj.] genomträngande
pig [n.] gris, svin
pigeon [n.] duva
pike [n.] gädda [fish]
pile[1] [n.] trave, massa
pile[2] [v.] stapla upp, lägga upp i en
hög; ~ in pressa sig in
pilgrimage [n.] pilgrimsfärd; ~
church pilgrimskyrka; ~ site
vallfartsort
pill [n.] piller, tablett
pillar [n.] pelare
pillow [n.] kudde; ~ case örngott
pilot [n.] pilot
PIN[1] [abbrev: personal identification
number] personlig kod, PIN-kod;
~ code säkerhetskod, PIN-kod; ~
number PIN-kod
pin[2] [n.] nål
pin[3] [v.; -nning, -nned, -nned] nåla
fast; klämma fast
pinch [v.; ~es, ~ed, ~ed] nypa,
klämma; pina
pine [n.] tall, furu; ~ table furubord

pineapple [n.] ananas
ping-pong [n.] pingpong, bordtennis
pink [adj.] rosaröd; ~ slip
uppsägningsbrev
pinnacle [n.] höjdpunkt; tinne
pint [n.; 1/2 quart] halvliter
pioneer[1] [n.] banbrytare, pionjär
pioneer[2] [v.] bana väg för, vara
först med
pipe [n.] rör; pipa [tobacco, music]
pipeline [n.] rörledning, oljeled-
ning; in the ~ under planering
piquant [adj.] pikant, skarp
pirate [n.] pirat; ~ copying piratkopiering [IT]
pirating [n.] piratkopiering [IT]
Pisces [n.] Fiskarna [zodiac]
piss[1] [n.; vul.] piss [colloq.];
have/take a ~ pissa [colloq.]
piss[2] [v.; vul.; ~es] piss [colloq.]; ~
off [colloq.] förarga; get ~ed off
[colloq.] bli arg/rasande
pistachio [n.]: ~ ice cream [n.] pistachglass; ~ nut pistaschmandel
pit [n.] grop, hål; gruvhål; kärna;
be the ~s [colloq.] vara botten
pita bread [n.] pitabröd
pitch[1] [n.; ~es] tonhöjd; grad; lutning; beck
pitch[2] [v.; ~es, ~ed, ~ed] kasta,
slänga; ~ in hugga in, vara med;
~ a tent slå upp ett tält
pitcher [n.] tillbringare, kruka;
pitcher [bollkastaren i baseboll]
pity [n.; -ties] synd
pivot [v.] svänga; ~ table pivottabell [IT]
pixel [n.] bildpunkt, pixel [IT]
pizza [n.] pizza
pj's [abbrev: pajamas] pyjamas
pkg. [abbrev: package] paket
pkwy. [abbrev: parkway] aveny,
motorväg
pl. [abbrev: plural; place] plural;
plats, torg
place[1] [n.] ort, ställe; plats; ~ holder
plattshållare, plattsmarkering [IT];
~ to eat matställe; take ~ äga rum
place[2] [v.] placera, sätta
placement [n.] placering
plaice [n.] rödspätta, spätta [fish]

plaid [adj.] rutig
plain[1] [adj.] tydlig, enkel; uppriktig; ren; vanlig; ~ **food** husmanskost; ~ **text** [not encrypted] klartext [IT]
plain[2] [adv.] tydligt, klart; rent ut sagt
plain[3] [n.] slätt
plainly [adv.] klart
plaintiff [n.] kärande, målsagare
plan[1] [n.] plan; metod
plan[2] [v.; -nning, -nned, -nned] planera
plane [n.] flygplan; plan; hyvel [tool]; ~ **ticket** flygbiljett
planet [n.] planet
planetarium [n.; -ria/~s] planetarium
planned [adj.] planerad
planner [n.] planerare; planerings-kalender
planning [n.] planering
plant[1] [n.] växt; verk [factory]
plant[2] [v.] sätta, plantera
plantation [n.] odling, plantering
plasma [n.] plasma; ~ **display** plas-mabildskärm [IT]
plaster [n.] gips
plastic[1] [adj.] plast-; ~ **bag** plast-påse, kasse; ~ **wrap** plastfolie
plastic[2] [n.] plast; ~ **surgeon** plastikkirurg
plate [n.] tallrik, fat; platta, plåt
platform [n.] plattform; perrong [train]; tribun
platinum [n.] platina
plausible [adj.] plausibel, rimlig
play[1] [n.] pjäs, skådespel, teater-pjäs; spel; lek; **fair** ~ rent spel; **unfair/foul** ~ orent spel; ~ **group** lekgrupp
play[2] [v.] spela, leka; ~ **cards** spela kort; ~ **tennis** spela tennis
playback [n.] uppspelning
player [n.] spelare
playground [n.] lekplats
playmate [n.] lekkamrat
plea [n.] vädjan; svaromål; **guilty** ~ erkännande; **not guilty** ~ nekande
plead [v.; pled, pled/pleaded, pleaded] be, vädja; plädera
pleasant [adj.] angenäm, trevlig

please[1] [adv./interj.] tack; var god/ snäll/vänlig; ~ **come now** vill du vara snäll och komma nu; ~ **help yourself!** varsågod!; ~ **reply!** om svar anhålles!; ~ **ring the bell!** var god ring på klockan!; ~ **wait!** var god vänta!; ~ **wipe your feet!** var god torka av fötterna!
please[2] [v.] glädja, göra glad
pleased [adj.] nöjd; road; ~ **to meet you!** angenämt!, trevligt att träffas!
pleasure [n.] lust; nöje, glädje
pledge [v.] lova; förplikta; sätta i pant
plenty[1] [adv.] tillräckligt, ganska; ~ **of** gott om, massor av
plenty[2] [n.] mängd, massor; välstånd
pliers [n.pl.] tång
PLO [abbrev: Palestine Liberation Organization] PLO [palestinska befrielsefronten]
plot[1] [n.] komplott, intrig; jordbit [land]
plot[2] [v.; -tting, -tted, -tted] planera, anstifta; markera, rita in, kartlägga
plotter [n.] kurvritare [IT]
plow [v.] plöja
pls. [abbrev: please] var så snäll
pluck [v.] plocka
plug[1] [n.] kontakt, stickpropp; propp; **wall** ~ vägguttag
plug[2] [v.; -gging, -gged, -gged] plugga igen, stoppa till; ~ **in** ansluta, koppla in
plug-in [adj.] insticks-; ~ **card** in-stickskort [IT]; ~ **program** in-sticksprogram [IT]
plum [n.] plommon
plumber [n.] rörmokare
plunge[1] [n.] dykning, dopp; ras; sänkand
plunge[2] [v.] störta; stöta ner; rasa
plural [adj./n.] plural
plus [adj./n./prep.] plus; positiv; ~ **sign (+)** plustecken
PM[1] [abbrev: prime minister] premiärminister
p.m.[2] [abbrev: post meridiem: af-ternoon] eftermiddag (e.m.)
PMS [abbrev: premenstrual syn-drome] premenstruellt syndrom

pneumonia [n.] lunginflammation
P.O. Box [abbrev: post office box] postfack, postbox
poached [adj.] stuvad, pocherad; ~ **egg** förlorat ägg
pocket [n.] ficka; ~ **book** pocket-bok; ~ **calculator** miniräknare; ~ **computer** fickdator, handdator [IT]; ~ **knife** fickkniv; ~ **money** fickpengar
pocketbook [n.] plånbok
POE [abbrev: port of entry] tullhamn
poem [n.] dikt, vers, poem
poet [n.] diktare, poet
poetic [adj.] poetisk
poetry [n.] diktning, poesi
point[1] [n.] spets; poäng; komma [decimal]; punkt [font]; ~ **of view** uppfattning, utsiktspunkt; **no** ~ **in** ingen idé att; **decimal** ~ komma
point[2] [v.] peka; ~ **to** peka på
pointed [adj.] spetsig
pointing hand [n.] pekande hand
poison[1] [n.] gift; ~ **information center** giftinformation
poison[2] [v.] förgifta
poisoning [n.] förgiftning
poisonous [adj.] giftig
poke [v.] stöta, peta; röra om; stika; snoka; ~ **fun at** göra narr av
Poland [n.] Polen
Pole[1] [n.] polack
pole[2] [n.] stav, stång; pol; **North** ~ nordpolen; **South** ~ sydpolen
police [n.] polis; ~ **academy** polis-högskola; ~ **car** polisbil; ~ **checkpoint** poliskontroll; ~ **custody** häkte; ~ **officer** polis; ~ **report** polisrapport; ~ **station** polisstation
policeman [n.; -men] polis
policy [n.; -cies] politik, hållning, linje; **insurance** ~ försäkringsbrev
polio [n.] polio
Polish[1] [adj.] polsk
Polish[2] (**language**) [n.] polska
polish[3] [n.; ~es] polermedel, puts-medel, polityr; lack; **nail** ~ nagel-lack; **shoe** ~ skokräm
polish[4] [v.; ~es, ~ed, ~ed] slipa, putsa
polite [adj.] artig, hövlig

politely [adv.] hövligt
politeness [n.] hövlighet
political [adj.] politisk; ~ **prisoner** politisk fånge
politically [adv.] politiskt; ~ **correct** politiskt korrekt
politician [n.] politiker
politics [n.] politik
poll [n.] röstning; undersökning; ~ **ratings** opinionssiffror
pollen count [n.] pollenhalt
polling station [n.] vallokal
pollute [v.] förorena, förstöra
polluted [adj.] förorenad
pollution [n.] förorening; **air** ~ luftförorening; **water** ~ vatten-förorening
polymer [n.] polymer, makromolekyl
polytechnic [n.] högskola för teknisk yrkesutbildning
pomegranate [n.] pomegranat äppel
pond [n.] damm, tjärn
ponder [v.] överväga, fundera över
pony [n.; -nies] ponny, liten häst
pool [n.] bassäng; pool
poop[1] [n.; colloq.] skit [colloq.]
poop[2] [v.; colloq.] skita [colloq.]
pooped [adj.; colloq.] trött
poor [adj.] fattig; mager; dålig; ~ **guy!** stackars han!; ~ **road surface** dålig väg; ~ **visibility** dålig sikt
poorly[1] [adj.] klen, hängig
poorly[2] [adv.] dåligt
pop[1] [n.] knall, smäll [noise]; pop [music]; farsa [father]; läsk [drink]; ~ **art** popkonst; ~ **concert** pop-konsert; ~ **group** popgrupp; ~ **singer** schlagersångare; ~ **song** schlager
pop[2] [v.; -pping, -pped, -pped] smälla, knalla; dyka fram/ut; ~ **in** kila in
popcorn [n.] popcorn
Pope [n.] påve
POP server [n.; for incoming e-mail] POP-server [IT]
popular [adj.] folk-, allmän; pop-ulär; ~ **movement** folkrörelse; ~ **sport** massport
popularity [n.; -ties] popularitet

population [n.] befolkning
pop-up menu [n.] popup-meny, snabbmeny, snabbvalsmeny [IT]
pop-up window [n.] popup-fönster [IT]
porcelain [n.] porslin
pork [n.] fläsk, fläskkött, griskött; ~ **chop** fläskkotlett, griskotlett; ~ **filet** fläskfilé; ~ **knuckle** fläsklägg; ~ **loin** fläskkarré; ~ **pie** fläskpastej; ~ **roast** fläskstek; ~ **sausage** fläskkorv; **roast** ~ grisstek
porn [n.; colloq.] porr
porridge [n.] gröt
port [n.] hamn; portvin; ~ **authorities** hamnstyrelse
portability [n.] bärbarhet, portabilitet
portable [adj.] bärbar, portabel
portal [n.] portal [IT]
porter [n.] bärare
portfolio [n.] portfölj; mapp; utbud
porthole [n.] ventil
portion [n.] del; andel; portion
portrait [n.] porträtt; ~ **mode** stående utskrift [IT]
portray [v.] avbilda; skildra
Portugal [n.] Portugal
Portuguese[1] [adj.] portugisisk
Portuguese[2] **(language)** [n.] portugisiska
POS [abbrev: point of sale] försäljningsställe
pose [v.] framställa; posera
position[1] [n.] ställning, läge
position[2] [v.] placera; lokalisera
positive [adj.] positiv; bestämd; säker
positively [adv.] positivt, bestämt; säkert, absolut
possess [v.; ~es, ~ed, ~ed] äga, ha; behärska
possession [n.] besittning; egendom
possessive [adj.] hagalen; possesiv
possibility [n.; -ties] möjlighet; förutsättning
possible [adj.] eventuell, möjlig; ~ **delay** möjlig försening
possibly [adv.] eventuellt, möjligen, möjligtvis
post[1] [n.] plats, ställning; stolpe; ~

office post, postanstalt, postkontor; ~ **box** postbox
post[2] [v.] placera; sätta upp; affischera; ~ **an ad** införa en annons, annonsera
postage [n.] porto; ~ **and handling (p&h)** porto och expeditionskostnader; ~ **paid** fritt porto; ~ **stamp** frimärke
postal [adj.] post-; ~ **code** postnummer
postcard [n.] vykort
postdoctoral fellow [n.] forskarassistent, efter avlagd doktorsexamen
poster [n.] affisch
posterity [n.; -ties] efterkommande, eftervärlden
postgraduate [adj.] efter avlagd examen, doktorand-; ~ **studies** forskarutbildning
postmaster [n.] e-postansvarig, e-postmästare [IT]
postmortem [n.] obduktion; efterhandsundersökning
postnatal [adj.] efter födelsen
postpone [v.] skjuta upp, senarelägga
postwar [adj.] efterkrigs-
pot [n.] burk, gryta; [colloq.] marijuana; ~ **roast** grytstek
potassium [n.] kalium
potato [n.; ~es] potatis; ~ **chips** chips, potatischips; ~ **soup** potatissoppa; ~**es au gratin** potatisgratäng; **mashed** ~**es** potatismos
potential[1] [adj.] potentiell, eventuell
potential[2] [n.] möjligheter [pl.]
potentially [adv.] eventuellt
pothole [n.] grop, tjälskott
potholed [adj.] gropig
potted plant [n.] krukväxt
potter [n.] krukmakare; ~'s **workshop** krukmakeri
pottery [n.; -ries] lergods; keramik; krukmakeri
poultry [n.; -ries] fjäderfä, fågel
pound[1] [n.] pund [0,45 kg]; ~ **sign** (#) fyrkant, nummertecken [IT]
pound[2] [v.] dunka, hamra; klampa
pour [v.] hälla, ösa; strömma
poverty [n.; -ties] fattigdom; brist

POW [abbrev: prisoner of war] krigsfånge

powder [n.] puder; pulver; ~ **compact** puderdosa; ~ **snow** nysnö, pudersnö

powdered sugar [n.] pudersocker

power[1] [n.] makt, kraft; ~ **failure** strömavbrott; ~ **grid** elnät; ~ **station** kraftverk; ~ **supply** strömförsörjning [IT]; ~ **user** superanvändare [IT]

power[2] [v.] driva

powerful [adj.] kraftig

powerless [adj.] maktlös

pp. [abbrev: pages] sidor

PQ [abbrev: see: **QC**]

PR [abbrev: public relations] public relations (PR)

practical [adj.] praktisk

practically [adv.] praktiskt taget

practice[1] [n.] praktik; praxis; övning

practice[2] [v.] öva; praktisera; utöva; öva sig i

pragmatic [adj.] pragmatisk

Prague [n.] Prag

praise[1] [n.] beröm, lov

praise[2] [v.] berömma, prisa, lova

prawns [n.pl.] räkor [pl.]

pray [v.] be, bönfalla

prayer [n.] bön

preach [v.; ~es, ~ed] predika

precaution [n.] försiktighet

precede [v.] föregå, gå före; inleda

precedence [n.] företräde

precedent [n.] precedensfall

precious [adj.] dyrbar, kostbar; affekterad

precipitation [n.] nederbörd

precise [adj.] exakt, noggrann

precisely [adv.] just, precis

precision [n.] precision, noggrannhet

predator [n.] rovdjur; rövare

predecessor [n.] företrädare; förfader

predict [v.] förutsaga

predictable [adj.] förutsagbar

prediction [n.] förutsagelse

predoctoral fellow [n.] doktorandanställning

predominantly [adv.] för det mesta

prefabricated [adj.] prefabricerad, monteringsfärdig

prefer [v.; -rring, -rred, -rred] föredra; skulle hellre; ~ **A to B** föredra A framför B

preferably [adv.] företrädesvis, helst

preference [n.] förkärlek, företräde; preferens; **sexual** ~ sexuell läggning

preferred [adj.] som är att föredra

prefix [n.; ~es] prefix [gram.]

pregnancy [n.; -cies] graviditet

pregnant [adj.] gravid, havande

prehistoric [adj.] förhistorisk; ~ **times** urtiden

prejudice [n.] fördom, motvilja; förfång

preliminary [adj.] preliminär, förhands-

premature [adj.] för tidig; förhastad

premier[1] [adj.] främsta, förnämsta

premier[2] [n.] premiärminister, statsminister

premiere [n.] premiär

premises [n.pl.] lokal

premium [n.] premie; extra belopp; ~ **gasoline** högoktanig bensin

preoccupation [n.] sysslande; tankfullhet

preoccupied [adj.] helt upptagen av; förströdd

preparation [n.] förberedelse; tillagning; preparat

prepare [v.] förbereda; laga

prepared [adj.] förberedd, beredd

preposition [n.] preposition [gram.]

Pres. [abbrev: President] president

preschool [n.] förskola; ~ **teacher** förskolelärare

prescribe [v.] ordinera; föreskriva

prescription [n.] ordination, recept; ~ **drug** receptbelagt läkemedel; ~ **for** recept på; **available only on** ~ receptbelagd; **available without** ~ receptfri

presence [n.] närvaro; **in the** ~ **of** i närvaro av

present[1] [adj.] nuvarande, aktuell; föreliggande

present[2] [n.] present, gåva; presens

[gram.]; **at** ~ för närvarande, just nu
present[3] [v.] föreställa, presentera;
framföra
presentation [n.] presentation;
överlämnande
presenter [n.] presentatör
presently [adv.] snart; nu
preservation [n.] bevarande;
konservering
preserve[1] [n.] reservat; ~**s** sylt,
konserv; **game** ~ viltreservat
preserve[2] [v.] konservera, lägga in
preserved [adj.] konserverad,
syltad
preserving jar [n.] konservburk
presidency [n.; -cies] presidentskap
president [n.] president; verkställande direktör; rektor [college]
press[1] [n.; ~es] press; tryckeri;
trängsel; ~ **agency** pressbyrå; ~
conference presskonferens; ~
release pressrelease
press[2] [v.; ~es, ~ed, ~ed] trycka,
pressa; ~ **down** hålla ner [IT]; ~
on trycka på
pressure [n.] tryck; ~ **cooker** tryckkokare; ~ **group** påtryckningsgrupp; **low/high blood** ~ lågt/högt
blodtryck
prestige [n.] prestige, status
presumably [adv.] antagligen
presume [v.] anta, förmoda; tillåta
sig
pretend [v.] låtsas, hyckla
pretty[1] [adj.] söt, snygg, vacker;
skön
pretty[2] [adv.] ganska
prevail [v.] råda, segra
prevailing [adj.] rådande
prevalence [n.] allmän förekomst
prevalent [adj.] allmän, förharskande
prevent [v.] hindra, förhindra
prevented [adj.] förhindrad
prevention [n.] förhindrande
preview [v.] förhandsgranska
previous [adj.] föregående, förra
previously [adv.] förut
prey [n.] rov, byte; **bird of** ~ rovfågel
prey on [v.] jaga; plundra
price[1] [n.] pris; ~ **category** prisklass;
~ **control** priskontroll; ~ **freeze**

prisstopp; ~ **index** prisindex; ~ **of**
gasoline bensinpris; ~ **per liter**
literpris, pris per liter; ~ **per**
package pris per förpackning; ~
tag prislapp; **consumer** ~ **index**
(CPI) konsumentprisindex; **low** ~
lågpris
price[2] [v.] prissätta
prick[1] [n.] stick; [vul.] kuk
prick[2] [v.] sticka, sticka hål i; stinga
pride [n.] stolthet, högmod
priest [n.] präst
primarily [adv.] primärt; huvudsakligen
primary[1] [adj.] primär, första;
huvudsaklig; ~ **key** primärnyckel
[IT]; ~ **school** folkskola
primary[2] [n.; -ries] förberedande
valmöte
prime [adj.] främsta; förstklassig;
ursprunglig; ~ **minister** ministerpresident, statsminister; ~ **time**
bästa sändningstid
primitive [adj.] primitiv
prince [n.] prins
princess [n.; ~es] princessa
principal[1] [adj.] huvudsaklig,
huvud-; första; ~ **clause** huvudsats
[gram.]
principal[2] [n.] chef, rektor; kapital;
huvudperson
principally [adv.] huvudsakligen
principle [n.] prinsip, grund
print[1] [n.] tryck, stil; avtryck;
gravyr; kopia; **fine** ~ fin stil; **large**
~ stor stil; ~ **size** textstorlek [IT]
print[2] [v.] trycka; skriva ut [IT]; ~
on demand stycktrykning
printed [adj.] tryckt; ~ **circuit**
tryckt krets; ~ **matter** trycksaker
printer [n.] skrivare [IT]; tryckare
printing [n.] tryckning; ~ **on de-**
mand tryckning på begäran
printout [n.] utskrift [IT]
prior [adj.] föregående, förhands-
prior to [prep.] före
priority [n.; -ties] prioritet; före-
trädesrätt; förkörsrätt [driving]
pris fixe meal [n.] måltid/meny till
fast pris
prison [n.] fängelse

prisoner [n.] fånge
privacy [n.; -cies] avskildhet, privatliv; sekretess; ~ **policy** sekretesspolicy
private[1] [adj.] enskild, privat; ~ **car** personbil; ~ **college** privathögskola; ~ **detective** privatdetektiv; ~ **key** hemlig nyckel [IT]; ~ **motoring** privatbilism; ~ **property** privat område; ~ **room** privatrum; ~ **school** privatskola; ~ **university** privatuniversitet
private[2] [n.] menig [soldier]; **in** ~ privat; ~**s** könsdelar [pl.]
privately [adv.] privat, enskilt; personligt
privatization [n.] privatisering
privilege [n.] privilegium, rättighet; förmån
privileged [adj.] priviligerad, gynnad
prize [n.] pris, premie
prize-winning [adj.] prisbelönt
pro[1] [abbrev: professional] proffs
pro[2] [adv.] för
probability [n.; -ties] sannolikhet, probabilitet
probable [adj.] sannolik, trolig
probably [adv.] antagligen, förmodligen, troligen, troligtvis; nog, väl
probation [n.] prov; skyddstillsyn; **on** ~ [employment] provanställd
probationary employment [n.] provanställning
probe[1] [n.] undersökning; sond
probe[2] [v.] sondera; undersöka; tränga i
problem [n.] bekymmer, problem; fråga; **no** ~! inga problem! [pl.]; **what's your** ~? vad är det med dig?
procedure [n.] procedur; förfarande
proceed [v.] fortsätta; börja, övergå till
proceedings [n.pl.] åtgärder; handlingar
proceeds [n.pl.] intäkter [pl.], inkomster [pl.]
process[1] [n.; ~es] gång, förlopp; **be in** ~ vara i gång; **be in the** ~ **of** hålla just på med att

process[2] [v.; ~es, ~ed, ~ed] behandla
processing [n.] behandling
procession [n.] tåg
processor [n.] processor [IT]
proclaim [v.] proklamera, deklarera
produce[1] [n.] produkter [pl.]; **agricultural** ~ jordbruksprodukter [pl.]
produce[2] [v.] tillverka
producer [n.] producent, fabrikant; produktionsledare
product [n.] produkt, vara, fabrikat
production [n.] produktion, tillverkning; produkt; uppsättning [theater]
productive [adj.] produktiv, fruktbar; produktions-
productivity [n.; -ties] produktivitet, prestationsförmåga
profession [n.] yrke
professional[1] [adj.] yrkes-; professionell, proffs-; ~ **secrecy** tystnadsplikt
professional[2] [n.] yrkesman, fackman; professionell
professor [n.] professor; lärare
profile [n.] profil; porträtt
profit [n.] vinst, utbyte; nytta
profit from [v.] ha nytta av, tjäna på
profitable [adj.] nyttig, fruktbar; lönande, räntabel
profligate [adj.] slösande
profound [adj.] djup; djupgående; outgrundig
program [n.] program; ~ **file** programfil [IT]; ~ **in school** linje; ~ **library** programbibliotek [IT]; ~ **module** programmodul [IT]; ~ **of events** evenemangsprogramm; ~ **of study** kurs
program [v.; -mmed] programmera [IT]; planlägga
programmer [n.] programmerare [IT]
programming [n.] programmering; ~ **language** programmeringsspråk, programspråk [IT]
progress[1] [n.; ~es] framsteg, förlopp; **be in** ~ pågå
progress[2] [v.; ~es, ~ed, ~ed] göra framsteg, utvecklas

progression [n.] förflyttning
progressive [adj.] progressiv, framstegsvänlig; tilltagande
prohibit [v.] förbjuda; förhindra
prohibited [adj.] förbjuden
prohibition [n.] förbud; spritförbud [alcohol]
project[1] [n.] projekt, plan, uppslag
project[2] [v.] projektera, planera; framhäva; sticka fram
projection [n.] projektion; utstående del
projectionist [n.] maskinist
prolonged [adj.] långvarig
prominent [adj.] framstående, ledande; utstående
promise[1] [n.] löfte
promise[2] [v.] lova; förebåda
promising [adj.] lovande
promote [v.] främja, gynna; lansera; befordra; **be ~d** avancera, få befordran
promoter [n.] initiativtagare, upphovsman; främjare
promotion [n.] befordran; marknadsföring; främjande
prompt[1] [n.] uppmaning; kommandoprompt [IT], prompt [IT]
prompt[2] [adv.] snabb, skyndsam, omgående
prompt[3] [v.] driva; orsaka; uppmana
promptly [adv.] precis, på slaget
prone [adj.] benägen, utsatt; liggande på magen
pronoun [n.] pronomen
pronounce [v.] uttala; förklara
proof [n.] bevis, prov; normalstyrka [alcohol]
prop [v.; -pping, -pped, -pped] stötta, stödja
propaganda [n.] propaganda
propagation [n.] fortplantning, spridning
proper [adj.] rätt, riktig, ordentlig
properly [adv.] rätt, ordentligt, riktigt
property [n.; -ties] egendom, egenskap; **~ insurance** hemförsäkring; **large ~** lantegendom
proportion [n.] proportion; del
proportional [adj.] proportionell

proposal [n.] förslag; frieri
propose [v.] föreslå; lägga fram; **~ marriage** fria
proposed [adj.] tilltänkt, planerad
proposition [n.] påstående; förslag
proprietor [n.] ägare, innehavare
pros and cons [n.pl.] skälen för och emot [pl.]
prose [n.] prosa
prosecute [v.] åtala, beivra; fullfölja
prosecution [n.] åtal; åklagarsida; utförande
prosecutor [n.] åklagare
prospect [n.] utsikt, framtidsperspektiv; **~s** framtidsutsikter [pl.], möjligheter [pl.]
prospective [adj.] eventuell, framtida
prosperity [n.] välstånd, blomstring
prosperous [adj.] blomstrande, välbärgad, framgångsrik; **~ period** högkonjunktur
prostitute [n.] prostituerad, fnask
protect [v.] skydda; **~ oneself** skydda sig
protection [n.] skydd, beskydd
protective [adj.] skyddande, skydds-; beskyddande
protein [n.] protein, äggviteämne
protest[1] [n.] protest
protest[2] [v.] protestera; bedyra
Protestant[1] [adj.] protestantisk
Protestant[2] [n.] protestant
protester [n.] demonstrant
protocol [n.] protokoll
proton [n.] proton
prototype [n.] prototyp, urbild
proud [adj.] stolt; ståtlig
prove [v.; ~d, ~d/~n] bevisa, visa
proven [adj.] välkänd, beprövad
provide [v.] anskaffa, sörja för; ge, skänka; **~ for oneself** försörja sig
provided (that) [conj.] förutsatt att
provider [n.] leverantör; familjförsörjare; **Internet service ~ (ISP)** internetoperatör
province [n.] provins, landskap
provincial [adj.] regional; provinsiell
provision [n.] anskaffande; försörjning; bestämmelse; **~s** livsmedel, proviant

provisional [adj.] provisorisk
provoke [v.] framkalla; reta upp;
driva
proxy [n.; -xies] fullmakt; ~ **server**
mellanserver, proxyserver [IT]
prudent [adj.] klok, förståndig
prunes [n.pl.] katrinplommon [pl.]
PS [abbrev: post script] post scriptum
PST [abbrev: Pacific Standard
Time] normaltid på västkusten i
USA
pseudo [n.] bluff, posör
psychiatric [adj.] psykiatrisk
psychiatrist [n.] psykiater
psychological [adj.] psykologisk
psychologist [n.] psykolog
psychology [n.; -gies] psykologi
PT[1] [abbrev: physical training]
idrott, gymnastik
pt.[2] [abbrev: pint; part] halvliter; del
PTA [abbrev: parent-teacher asso-
ciation] föräldraförening
ptarmigan [n.] fjällripa, snöripa
PTO [abbrev: please turn over] var
god vänd
pub [n.] kvarterskrog, pub
public[1] [adj.] allmän, offentlig; ~
baths badhus; ~ **building** allmän
byggnad; ~ **garden** stadspark; ~
health folkhälsa; ~ **holiday** allmän
helgdag; ~ **key** öppen nyckel [IT];
~ **key encryption** kryptering med
öppen nyckel, öppen nyckel-kryptering [IT]; ~ **opinion** allmänna
opinion; ~ **relations** public relations; ~ **school** allmänn/kommu-
nal skola; ~ **service** allmän tjänst;
~ **toilet** allmän toalett; ~ **transportation** kollektivtrafik
public[2] [n.] allmänheten
publication [n.] publicering, skrift
publicity [n.; -ties] publicitet; reklam;
~ **brochure** reklambroschyr
publicly [adv.] offentligt, statligt
publish [v.; ~es, ~ed, ~ed] ge ut,
publicera; offentliggöra
publisher [n.] förläggare, utgivare
publishing [n.] förlagsverksamhet
pudding [n.] pudding, efterrätt
pull[1] [n.] drag; ~ **technology** pull-
teknik [IT]

pull[2] [v.] dra, slita; ~ **here** dra här;
~ **out** dra ut
pulled ligament/muscle [n.]
sträckning
pullover [n.] utanpåskjorta
pulp [n.] mos; massa; kött
pulpit [n.] predikstol, pulpet
pulsating [adj.] pulserande
pulse [n.] puls; **take someone's** ~
ta pulsen på någon
pump[1] [n.] pump
pump[2] [v.] pumpa
pumpkin [n.] pumpa
punch[1] [n.; ~es] slag; ; kraft;
hålslag
punch[2] [v.; ~es, ~ed, ~ed] klippa
till; slå hål i, klippa
punctual [adj.] punktlig
punctuation [n.] kommatering
puncture [n.] punktering; ~ **repair
kit** punkteringssats
punish [v.; ~es, ~ed, ~ed] straffa,
bestraffa
punishment [n.] straff, bestraffning
punk [n.] punk; skräp
pupil [n.] elev; pupill [eye]
purchase[1] [n.] inköp, köp
purchase[2] [v.] köpa
purchaser [n.] köpare
pure [adj.] ren
purely [adv.] rent
purified [adj.] renad
purity [n.; -ties] renhet
purple [adj.] mörklila
purpose [n.] syfte, avsikt; mål; **on**
~ med avsikt
purse [n.] portmonnä; handväska
pursue [v.] sträva efter, fortsätta
pursuit [n.] förföljelse; sysselsättning
push[1] [n.; ~es] knuff, puff; ~ **technology** push-teknik [IT]
push[2] [v.; ~es, ~ed, ~ed] trycka,
skjuta; knuffa; driva
pushdown list [n.] stack [n.] [IT]
put [v.; ~s, put, put] ställa, sätta,
lägga; ~ **on** [clothing] ta på sig;
~ **out** ställa ut; ~ **up at** ta in på
putter around [v.] pyssla
puzzle[1] [n.] bryderi; gåta; problem;
pussel

puzzle[2] [v.] förbrylla, grubbla
   på/över
puzzled [adj.] förbryllad, villrådig
puzzling [adj.] förbryllande, gåtfull
PVC [abbrev: polyvinyl chloride]
   polyvinylklorid (PVC)
Pvt. [abbrev: private (army rank)]
   menig
pyramid [n.] pyramid

Q

Q&A [abbrev: questions and answers] frågor och svar
QC [abbrev: Quebec] Quebec
QED [abbrev: quod erat demonstrandum, that which needed to be proved] vilket skulle bevisas (vsb)
q.t.[1] [abbrev: quiet (on the q.t.)] i hemlighet
qt.[2] [abbrev: quart] quart (0,95 liter)
quack [n.] kvacksalvare
quadrangle [n.] fyrkant
quail [n.] vaktel
qualification [n.] kvalifikation, merit; behörighet, utbildning; villkor; list of ~s meritförteckning
qualified [adj.] kvalificerad, meriterad, utbildad, behörig; reserverad
qualify [v.; -fies, -fied] kvalificera; begränsa
quality [n.; -ties] kvalitet; egenskap; förmåga; ~ control kvalitetskontroll
quantitative [adj.] kvantitativ
quantity [n.; -ties] kvantitet, mängd, mått; storhet
quantum [n.; -ta] kvantum, mängd; kvant; ~ mechanics kvantmekanik
quarrel[1] [n.] gräl, strid, tvist; invändning
quarrel[2] [v.] gräla, strida, tvista; klaga
quarry [n.; -ries] stenbrott; byte
quart [n.] quart [0,95 liter]
quarter [n.] fjärdedel; kvart [hour]; kvartal [3 months]; stadsdel, kvarter [town]; ~ past 7 kvart över sju; ~ to 8 kvart i åtta
quartet [n.] kvartett
quartz [n.; ~es] kvarts
queen [n.] drottning; dam [board games]

queer [adj.] underlig; homosexuell
quenelle [n.] quenell
query [n.; -ries] fråga, fundering; ~ language frågespråk [IT]
quest [n.] sökande, strävan
question[1] [n.] fråga; ~ mark frågetecken; ask a ~ ställa en fråga; that is out of the ~ det kommer inte på fråga
question[2] [v.] fråga; förhöra
questionable [adj.] tvivelaktig
questioning [n.] förhör
questionnaire [n.] frågeformulär
queue [n.] kö
quiche [n.] quiche
quick [adj.] snabb, hastig; hetsig; ~ fix lappning; ~ key snabbtangent [IT]; ~ search snabbsökning [IT]; ~ start rivstart [IT]
quick-frozen [adj.] snabbfrysen
quickly [adv.] fort, snabbt
quicksand [n.] kvicksand
quiet[1] [adj.] tyst, tystlåten
quiet[2] [n.] lugn, ro, stilla
quietly [adv.] lugnt, stilla
quilt [n.] täcke
quilted jacket [n.] täckjacka
quit [v.; quit] lämna; sluta, lägga av
quite [adv.] ganska; precis
quiz [n.; ~es] frågesport; förhör, lappskrivning; ~ show frågesportsprogram
quota [n.] kvot, tilldelning
quotation [n.] citat; kurs; ~ mark ("/") citationstecken
quote[1] [n.] citat
quote[2] [v.] citera, anföra
q.v. [abbrev: quod videt, check here for more information] se detta

R

R. [abbrev: river; restricted (film)] flod, älv; film ej tillåten för barn under 17

rabbi [n.] rabbin

rabbit [n.] kanin, hare

race[1] [n.] lopp, kapplöpning; ras, släkt; **in a ~** i kapp; **~ relations** rasrelationer

race[2] [v.] springa i kapp; springa fort, störta

racecourse [n.] kapplöpningsbana

racehorse [n.] kapplöpningshäst

racetrack [n.] kapplöpningsbana

racial [adj.] ras-; **~ discrimination** rasdiskriminering

racing bike [n.] tävlingscykel

racism [n.] rasism

racist [adj.] rasistisk

rack [n.] hylla; stativ

racket [n.] oväsen, larm; skoj, bluff, bedrägeri; racket [tennis]

radar speed check [n.] radarkontroll

radiation [n.] strålning

radiator [n.] värmeelement [house]; kylare [car]; **~ hose** kylarslang

radical[1] [adj.] radikal

radical[2] [n.] radikal; rot

radically [adv.] radikalt

radio [n.] radio; **~ set** radioapparat

radioactive [adj.] radioaktiv

radioactivity [n.; -ties] radioaktivitet

radish [n.; ~es] rädisa; **black ~** rättika

radius [n.; radii/~es] radie

rafting [n.] forsränning

rag [n.] trasa

rage[1] [n.] raseri

rage[2] [v.] rasa; storma

raid [n.] räd; razzia

rail [n.] stång; skena

railbus [n.; ~es] rälsbuss

railroad [n.] järnväg; **~ crossing** järnvägskorsning, järnvägsövergång; **~ line** järnvägslinje; **~ station** järnvägsstation

rain[1] [n.] regn; **~ check** ersättningsbiljett [vid uppskjutande på grund av dåligt väder t ex]; **~ forest** regnskog; **~ shower** regnskur

rain[2] [v.] regna; **~ heavily** ösregna

rainbow [n.] regnbåge

raincoat [n.] regnrock [man's]; regnkappa [woman's]

rainy [adj.] regnig

raise [v.] resa, lyfta; höja; födda upp, odla

raisin [n.] russin

raising [n.] uppfostran

rake [n.] räfsa [garden]

rally[1] [n.; -llies] möte; rally

rally[2] [v.; -llies, -llied] samla (ihop)

RAM[1] [abbrev: random access memory] RAM-minne

ram[2] [n.] bagge, gumse; bock

ramp [n.] ramp; uppfart, nerfart; trappa

random [adj.] på måfå, slumpmässig; **~ number generator** slumptalsgenerator

range[1] [n.] spis [kitchen]; rad, räcka; linje; omfång, avstånd; landområde; sortiment; **~ of goods** varusortiment; **shooting ~** skjutbana

range[2] [v.] klassificera; variera

rank[1] [n.] rang; grad

rank[2] [v.] räknas; ordna, placera

rap [n.] smäll, knackning; rap [music]

rape[1] [n.] våldtäkt

rape[2] [v.] våldta

rapid [adj.] hastig

rapids [n.pl.] fors

rappel [v.; -lled] fira sig ner med rep [mountain climbing]

rare [adj.] sällsynt, ovanlig, rar; blodig, lätt stekt [undercooked]

rarely [adv.] sällan

rash[1] [adj.] överilad

rash[2] [n.; ~es] utslag

raspberry [n.; -rries] hallon

rat [n.] råtta

rate[1] [n.] hastighet, takt; frekvens; kurs; pris

rate[2] [v.] uppskatta; räkna

rather [adv.] hellre; ganska

rating [n.] uppskattning; siffror [pl.]; klassificering

ratio [n.] förhållande

ration [n.] ranson, portion

rational [adj.] rationell

rationale [n.] grund, bevekelse, skäl
rattle [v.] skramla, slamra; rabbla
ravine [n.] klyfta, ravin
raw [adj.] rå, obearbetad; otränad;
blodig; ~ **material** råmaterial,
råvara; ~ **vegetables** råkost
ray [n.] stråle; rocka [fish]; ~ **tracing**
strålföljning, strålgång [IT]
razor [n.] rakkniv; rakapparat; ~
blade rakblad; **safety** ~ rakhyvel
R&B [abbrev: rhythm and blues]
rhythm and blues musik
RC [abbrev: Roman Catholic]
romersk-katolsk
R&D [abbrev: research and devel-
opment] forskning och utveckling
Rd. [abbrev: road] väg
RDA [abbrev: recommended daily
allowance] rekommenderad daglig
tillförsel
re [prep.; Latin: in re: in the matter
of] beträffande
reach[1] [n.; ~es] räckhåll, omfång;
gripande; **out of** ~ oåtkomlig
reach[2] [v.; ~es, ~ed, ~ed] nå, komma
till; sträcka; räcka
react [v.] reagera
reaction [n.] reaktion; opposition
reactor [n.] reaktor
read [v.; read (pronounced: red)] läsa;
~ **through** läsa igenom, skumma
reader [n.] läsare
readily [adv.] gärna; snabbt
reading [n.] litteratur, läsmaterial,
lektyr; ~ **comprehension** läsförståelse; ~ **knowledge** läsförmå-
gan [främmade språk]; ~ **light**
läslampa
ready [adj.] klar, färdig, redo;
beredd; ~ **to leave** resklar
ready-to-wear clothing [n.]
konfektion
real [adj.] verklig, egentlig; sann;
äkta; ~ **estate** fastighet; ~ **estate
agent** mäklare; ~ **time** realtid [IT]
realignment [n.] uträttning;
omgruppering
realism [n.] realism
realistic [adj.] realistisk
reality [n.; -ties] realitet, verklighet
realize [v.] inse, fatta; förverkliga
really [adv.] verkligen, egentligen;

absolut; gärna; rätt; jätte-; ~ **awful**
urdålig
realm [n.] rike, värld
rear[1] [adj.] bakre, bak; ~ **door**
bakdörr; ~ **light** bakljus
rear[2] [n.] baksida, bakre del
rear[3] [v.] föda upp; resa sig
rearmament [n.] upprustning
rearrangement [n.] omläggning
rearview mirror [n.] bakspegel
reason [n.] grund, orsak, skäl; **for
that** ~ därför
reasonable [adj.] rimlig; hygglig
reasonably [adv.] skäligt; rimligt
reasoning [n.] resonemang;
tankegång
reassure [v.] uppmuntra, lugna
rebel [n.] rebell
rebellion [n.] uppror
reboot [v.] omstarta [IT]
rebuild [v.] återuppbygga
rebuilt [adj.] ombyggd
recall [v.] kalla tillbaka; minnas
recd. [abbrev: received] mottagen
recede [v.] gå tillbaka
receipt [n.] kvitto; mottagande
receive [v.] ta emot
received [adj.] mottagen; allmänt
erkänd
receiver [n.] mottagare; hörlur
[telephone]
recent [adj.] ny, färsk, senare
recently [adv.] nyligen
reception [n.] reception; ~ **clerk**
portier; ~ **desk** mottagning
receptionist [n.] receptionist,
kundmottagare
recession [n.] konjunkturnedgång
recharge [v.] ladda om, ladda upp
recipe [n.] recept
recipient [n.] mottagare
reckon [v.] anse; räkna (med, ut)
recode [v.] koda om [IT]
recognition [n.] igenkännande
recognize [v.] känna igen
recommend [v.] rekommendera;
tillråda
recommendation [n.] rekommendation; **letter of** ~ rekommendationsbrev
recommended [adj.] rekommenderad
reconcile [v.] försona; förena

reconsider [v.] på nytt överväga;
right to ~ a purchase ångerrätt
reconstruct [v.] rekonstruera;
återuppbygga
reconstruction [n.] återuppbyg-
gande; ombildning
record[1] [n.] rekord, urkund, post;
skiva; ~ locking postlåsning [IT];
~ shop skivaffär
record[2] [v.] registrera, notera; spela
in
recorded book [n.] ljudbok
recorder [n.] inspelningsapparat;
blockflöjt
recording [n.] registrering;
inspelning
recount [v.] berätta; räkna igen
recover [v.] återvinna; hämta in;
tillfriskna
recovery [n.] tillfrisknande, bät-
tring; återvinnande; ~ room
uppvakningsrum
recreation [n.] fritidsaktivitet,
rekreation
recruit[1] [n.] rekryt
recruit[2] [v.] rekrytera; värva
recruitment [n.] rekrytering,
värvning
rectangular [adj.] fyrkantig,
rektangulär
rector [n.] kyrkoherde
rectum [n.] ändtarm
recur [v.; -rring, -rred, -rred] dyka
upp igen, upprepas
recursive [adj.] rekursiv
recycle [v.] återanvända, återvinna
red [adj.] röd; ~ cabbage rödkål;
Red Cross Röda Korset; ~ currants röda vinbär; ~ light rött
ljus; ~ pepper röd paprika; Red
Sea Röda Havet; ~ wine rödvin,
rött vin
redeem [v.] lösa ut; gottgöra
red-headed [adj.] rödhårig
red-hot [adj.] glödhet; intensiv
redness [n.] rodnad
reduce [v.] förminska, minska;
reducera; sänka; banta; ~ speed
sänka hastigheten
reduced [adj.] minskad, nedsatt; ~
price nedsatt pris

reduction [n.] minskning,
nedsättning
redundancy [n.; -cies] överflöd
redundant [adj.] överflödig
reel [n.] rulle, spola
reelection [n.] omval
refer [v.; ~rred] hänskjuta; hänvisa
till, åberopa (på), syfta på
referee [n.] domare
reference [n.] hänvisning; ~ book
uppslagsverk; ~s referenser [pl.]
referendum [n.; -dums/-da]
folkomröstning
referral [n.] hänskjutande;
remittering
reflect [v.] återkasta, reflektera,
återspegla; fundera
reflection [n.] reflexion, återkast-
ning; spegelbild
reflector [n.] reflektor; reflex
reflex [n.]: single-lens ~ (SLR)
camera reflexkamera
reflexive [adj.] reflexiv [gram.]
reform[1] [n.] reform
reform[2] [v.] reformera
reformation [n.] reformation
reformer [n.] reformator
refresh [v.] friska upp; uppdatera
[IT]; ~ oneself pigga upp sig;
läska sig
refreshments [n.pl.] förfriskningar
[pl.]
refrigerated display case [n.]
kyldisk
refrigerator [n.] kylskåp
refuge [n.] tillflyktsort; övernattningsstuga
refugee [n.] flykting; ~ camp flyktingläger; High Commissioner
for Refugees (UNHCR)
flyktingkommissariat
refund [n.] återbetalning; ersättning
refurbish [v.] putsa upp, snygga
upp; ombygga
refusal [n.] vägran, avslag
refuse[1] [n.] skräp, sopor; ~ separation
sopsortering
refuse[2] [v.] vägra, neka
regain [v.] återfå, återvinna
regard[1] [n.] avseende, hänseende;
with ~ to vad beträffar; ~s
hälsningar

regard² [v.] betrakta, anse
regarding [prep.] beträffande, angående
regardless [adv.] trots allt
regards [n.pl.] hälsningar [pl.]; **give Jan my ~** hälsa Jan åt mig, hälsa till Jan; **give one's ~ to** hälsa
regatta [n.] regatta
reggae [n.] reggae
regime [n.] regim; system
regiment [n.] regemente
region [n.] region, område
regional [adj.] regional, lokal-; **~ hospital** regionsjukhus
register¹ [n.] register, förteckning; **cash ~** kassaapparat
register² [v.] registrera; rekommendera
registered [adj.]: **~ letter** rekommenderat brev; **~ nurse (RN)** legitimerad sjuksköterska; **~ trademark** inregistrerat varumärke
registration [n.] registrering, inskrivning; **~ form** inskrivnings-blankett; **~ number** [car] bilregistreringsnummer
regret¹ [n.] ledsnad, sorg; **send one's ~s** hälsa att man tyvärr inte kan komma
regret² [v.] beklaga; ångra; **I ~** jag beklagar
regretful [adj.] ångerfull
regrettable [adj.] beklaglig
regular [adj.] regelbunden; stadig; korrekt; normal; **~ gas** normal-bensin
regularly [adv.] regelbundet; ordentlig
regulate [v.] reglera, justera
regulation [n.] reglering; regel
regulatory [adj.] reglerande
rehabilitation [n.] rehabilitering; återställande
rehearsal [n.] repetition; upprepning
rehearse [v.] repetera, öva in; upprepa
rehydration fluid [n.] vätskeersättning
reign¹ [n.] regering; regeringstid
reign² [v.] regera, härska
reindeer [n.] ren; **~ antlers** ren-

horn; **~ farmer** renskötare; **~ farming** renskötsel; **~ meat** renkött; **~ roast** renstek
reinforce [v.] förstärka
reinforced concrete [n.] armerad betong
reject [v.] förkasta, avslå, avvisa
rejection [n.] förkastande, avvisande
rejoinder [n.] replik
relate [v.] berätta; sätta i relation till; stå i relation till
related [adj.] besläktad, släkt; närliggande
relation [n.] relation, samband; **~s** förhållande
relational database [n.] relations-databas [IT]
relationship [n.] förhållande; släktskap
relative¹ [adj.] relativ
relative² [n.] släkting, släkt
relatively [adv.] relativt, jämförelsevis
relax [v.; ~es, ~ed] koppla av; släppa
relaxation [n.] avkoppling
relaxed [adj.] avspänd; avkopplande
release¹ [n.] frigivning; utsläpp; befrielse
release² [v.] frige
relevance [n.] relevans, samband
relevant [adj.] relevant, tillämplig
reliable [adj.] pålitlig, vederhäftig
reliance [n.] tillit, förtröstan
relief [n.] lättnad; hjälp, bistånd; relief [art]; **~ work** beredskapsar-bete
relieve [v.] lätta, avhjälpa; under-stödja; avlösa
religion [n.] religion
religious [adj.] religiös; **~ freedom** religionsfrihet
reluctance [n.] motsträvighet
reluctant [adj.] motvillig, ovillig
reluctantly [adv.] ogärna
rely on [v.; -lies, -lied, -lied] lita på; vara beroende av
REM [abbrev: rapid eye movement] snabba ögonrörelser [fas i sömnen]
remain [v.] förbli; stå kvar, stanna kvar; finnas kvar

remainder [n.] rest
remaining [adj.] kvarvarande, övrig
remains [n.pl.] lämningar [pl.],
  rester [pl.]
remark¹ [n.] anmärkning
remark² [v.] anmärka, kommentera
remarkable [adj.] enastående,
  beaktansvärd
remarkably [adv.] synnerligen
remedy¹ [n.; -dies] botemedel
remedy² [v.; -dies, -died] bota,
  avhjälpa
remember [v.] komma ihåg, minnas
remind [v.] påminna
reminder [n.] påminnelse
remnant [n.] rest, slump
remote [adj.] avlägsen; bortkopplad [IT], distans-, fjärr-; ~ **access**
  fjärråtkomst [IT]; ~ **connection**
  fjärranslutning [IT]; ~ **control**
  fjärrkontroll; ~ **possibility** ytterest
  liten möjlighet
removable [adj.] urtagbar; flyttbar;
  ~ **disk** löstagbar disk [IT]
removal [n.] avlägsnande, bort-
  förande; flyttning
remove [v.] föra bort, ta bort, röja
  undan; ta av
remuneration [n.] ersättning,
  belöning
renaissance [n.] renässans
rename [v.] döpa om
render [v.] göra; erlägga
renew [v.] förnya; ~ **a loan** låna om
renewable energy [n.] förnyelsebar
  energi
renewal [n.] förnyande; förlängning
renounce [v.] avsäga sig
renovate [v.] renovera
renovated [adj.] renoverad
renovation [n.] renovering; ~ **work**
  renoveringsarbete
rent¹ [n.] hyra; **for** ~ att hyra, uthyres
rent² [v.] hyra; ~ **out** hyra ut
rental [adj.] hyres-; ~ **agreement**
  hyreskontrakt; ~ **apartment**
  hyreslägenhet; ~ **car** hyrbil
rented [adj.] hyrd; ~ **out** uthyrd
rep¹ [abbrev: repertory theater; reputation; representative] reper-
  toarteater; rykte; representant,
  ombud

Rep.² [abbrev: Republican]
  republikan
repaint [v.] måla om
repainted [adj.] ommålad
repair¹ [n.] reparation; ~ **shop**
  reparationsverkstad, verkstad; ~
  work renoveringsarbete
repair² [v.] reparera; laga; ~ **cars**
  meka [colloq.]
repay [v.; repaid] återbetala; ersätta
repayment [n.] återbetalning;
  ersättning
repeat¹ [n.] upprepning; repris
repeat² [v.] upprepa; säga om;
  repetera
repeatedly [adv.] upprepade gånger
repercussion [n.] återverkning
repertoire [n.] repertoar
repetition [n.] upprepning,
  repetition
replace [v.] ställa tillbaka; ersätta
replacement [n.] återställande, ersättning, utbyte; ~ **part** reservdel;
  hip ~ höftledsoperation
replication [n.] replikering
reply¹ [n.; -lies] svar
reply² [v.; -lies, -lied, -lied] svara;
  ~ **all** svara alla [IT]
report¹ [n.] rapport; referat; betyg;
  ~ **card** skolbetyg, terminsbetyg;
  ~ **to the police** polisanmälan
report² [v.] anmäla; berätta
reported speech [n.] indirekt tal
reporter [n.] reporter
reporting [n.] reportage
represent [v.] representera, stå för;
  framställa
representation [n.] framställning,
  bild; föreställning; representation
representative¹ [adj.] representa-
  tiv; föreställande
representative² [n.] representant,
  ombud; **House of Representatives** representanthuset [en av
  kammaren i Kongressen i USA]
reproduce [v.] reproducera;
  regenerera
reproduction [n.] reproducering,
  reproduktion
reptile [n.] reptil, kräldjur
republic [n.] republik
republican [n.] republikan

reput**a**tion [n.] rykte, anseende
requ**e**st[1] [n.] begäran; önskemål; efterfrågan
requ**e**st[2] [v.] anhålla om, begära; be
requ**i**re [v.] behöva, erfordra
requ**i**red [adj.] erforderlig, obligatorisk: be ~ erfordras, fordras
requ**i**rement [n.] behov; krav, fordran
r**e**quisite [adj.] erforderlig, nödvändig
r**e**scue[1] [n.] räddning, bärgning
r**e**scue[2] [v.] rädda, bärga
res**e**arch[1] [n.] forskning, undersökning; ~ ass**i**stant forskningsassistent; ~ p**a**per forskningsavhandling; ~ trip forskningsresa
res**e**arch[2] [v.] forska
res**e**archer [n.] forskare
resembl**a**nce [n.] överensstämmelse, likhet
res**e**mble [v.] likna, påminna om
res**e**nt [v.] bli förnärmad över
res**e**ntment [n.] harm, förbittring
reserv**a**tion [n.] bokning, reservation; ch**a**nge in ~ ombokning
res**e**rve[1] [n.] reserv; reservat; tillbakadragenhet
res**e**rve[2] [v.] reservera, boka, beställa; förbehålla sig
res**e**rved [adj.] reserverad; tillbakadragen; ~ l**a**ne reserverad fil
res**e**rvoir [n.] reservoar
res**e**t [v.; -setting, -set, -set] ställa om; återställa [IT]
r**e**sidence [n.] vistelse, uppehåll; hemvist; bostad; ~ p**e**rmit uppehållstillstånd (UT); pl**a**ce of ~ bostadsort
r**e**sident[1] [adj.] bofast, bosatt
r**e**sident[2] [n.] bofast person, invånare
resid**e**ntial [adj.] bostads-; ~ **a**rea bostadskvarter
r**e**sidue [n.] återstod, rest
res**i**gn [v.] avgå, träda tillbaka; avsäga sig, sluta
resign**a**tion [n.] avsägelse; resignation
res**i**st [v.] motstå, motsätta sig; göra motstånd
res**i**stance [n.] motstånd
resol**u**tion [n.] beslut; lösning
res**o**lve [v.] lösa; besluta sig

res**o**rt [n.] rekreationsort; tillflykt
res**o**rt to [v.] ta sin tillflykt till
res**o**urces [n.pl.] resurser [pl.]
resp. [abbrev: resp**e**ctively] respektive
resp**e**ct[1] [n.] aktning; hänsyn; avseende; ~s hälsningar [pl.]
resp**e**ct[2] [v.] respektera; ta hänsyn till
resp**e**ctable [adj.] respektabel, aktad; hyfsad
resp**e**ctful [adj.] aktningsfull
resp**e**ctive [adj.] respective
resp**e**ctively [adv.] respektive
resp**o**nd [v.] svara
resp**o**ndent [n.] svarande
resp**o**nse [n.] svar; gensvar; ~ t**i**me svarstid
responsib**i**lity [n.] ansvar; t**a**ke ~ for ta ansvar för
resp**o**nsible [adj.] ansvarsfull; be ~ for ansvara för
rest[1] [n.] vila, rast, ro; rest, det övriga; ~ **a**rea rastplats; ~ h**o**stel raststuga
rest[2] [v.] vila (sig), ta igen sig
r**e**staurant [n.] restaurang; krog; l**u**xury ~ lyxrestaurang; ~ c**a**r restaurangvagn [train]
r**e**stless [adj.] rastlös, orolig
restor**a**tion [n.] restaurering, renovering; återställande
rest**o**re [v.] restaurera; återställa
rest**o**red [adj.] restaurerad
restr**a**in [v.] hindra; hålla tillbaka
restr**a**int [n.] återhållande; band
restr**i**ct [v.] inskränka, begränsa
restr**i**cted [adj.] begränsad, inskränkt
restr**i**ction [n.] inskränkning
restr**i**ctive [adj.] inskränkande
restr**u**cture [v.] omstrukturera
res**u**lt [n.] resultat, följd; as a ~ of till följd av
res**u**lt in [v.] resultera i
res**u**lting [adj.] som blir följden
r**e**sumé [n.] sammanfattning; levnadsbeskrivning
res**u**me [v.] återta; börja igen
r**e**tail[1] [adj.] detalj-, minut-; ~ pr**i**ce detaljhandelspris
r**e**tail[2] [v.] köpa/sälja i minut

retailer [n.] detaljist
retailing [n.] försäljning i minut
retain [v.] hålla kvar, behålla
retention [n.] kvarhållande;
bevarande
retire [v.] gå i pension; dra sig tillbaka; gå till sängs
retired [adj.] pensionerad; ~ **person**
pensionär
retirement [n.] pensionering;
tillbakadragenhet
retreat[1] [n.] reträtt; tillflykt
retreat[2] [v.] retirera, dra sig tillbaka;
sjunka
retrieval [n.] återvinnande; räddning;
hämtning
retrieve [v.] återvinna; hämta [IT];
rädda
retrospective [adj.] retrospektiv
return[1] [n.] återkomst, retur-;
återställande; utbyte; ~ **home**
hemkomst; **Return key** Retur [IT];
in ~ tillbaka; **tax** ~ självdeklaration
return[2] [v.] komma tillbaka, återvända; återlämna, lämna tillbaka
returnable bottle [n.] returglas
returned goods [n.] retur
Reuben sandwich [n.] smörgås
med salt kött, ost och surkål
reunion [n.] återförening;
sammankomst
reupholstered [adj.] omklädd
Rev.[1] [abbrev: Reverend (religious
title)] pastor, kyrkoherde
rev.[2] [abbrev: revised] reviderad
reveal [v.] avslöja, uppenbara, visa
revelation [n.] avslöjande;
uppenbarelse
revenge [n.] hämnd, vedergällning,
revansch
revenue [n.] inkomster [pl.]
reverse[1] [adj.] bak; ~ **gear** backen,
backväxel
reverse[2] [n.] motsats; baksida;
motgång
reverse[3] [v.] vända om, slå om;
ändra; backa
reverse-charges call [n.] ba-samtal,
samtal som betalas av mottagaren
revert to [v.] gå tillbaka till
review[1] [n.] granskning; recension;
överblick

review[2] [v.] granska; överblicka;
recensera
revise [v.] revidera, ändra
revised [adj.] reviderad
revision [n.] revidering, omarbetning; repetition
revival [n.] återupplivande; repris
revive [v.] återuppliva; ta upp igen
revolt [n.] uppror, resning; avfall
revolting [adj.] äcklig
revolution [n.] revolution; rotation;
kretslopp
revolutionary [adj.] revolutionär
revolve [v.] vrida sig, kretsa, snurra
runt
revue [n.] revy
reward[1] [n.] belöning, ersättning
reward[2] [v.] belöna, löna
rewarding [adj.] givande, lönande
rewritable [adj.] omskrivbar [IT]
rewrite [v.; -wrote, -written] skriva
om
RF [abbrev: radio frequency]
radiofrekvens
RFD [abbrev: rural free delivery
(mail address/delivery in rural
areas)] lantbrevbäring
RGB value [n.; red, green, blue]
RGB-värde [IT]
rhetoric [n.] retorik
Rh factor [abbrev: Rhesus factor]
Rh-faktorn
rheumatic disease [n.] reumatisk
sjukdom
rheumatism [n.] reumatism
Rhine (River) [n.] Rhen
Rhode Island (RI) [n.] Rhode Island [delstat i USA]
rhubarb [n.] rabarber
rhyme [n.] rim
rhythm [n.] rytm, takt
rhythmic [adj.] rytmisk
RI [abbrev: Rhode Island] Rhode
Island [delstat i USA]
rib [n.] revben
ribbon [n.] band; remsa
rice [n.] ris, risgryn; ~ **pudding**
risgrynsgröt, rispudding
rich [adj.] rik; riklig; mäktig, fet
[food]
riches [n.pl.] rikedom

rid [v.; rid/ridded] befria, rensa; **get ~ of** bli av med

ride¹ [n.] tur; skjuts, lift

ride² [v.; rode, ridden] åka [bus, train]; rida [horse]; cykla; **~ without paying** tjuvåka

rider [n.] åkare, passagerare

ridge [n.] rygg, kam, bergås

ridiculous [adj.] löjlig, absurd

riding school [n.] ridhus, ridskola

rifle [n.] gevär

rig [n.] rigg

right¹ [adj.] höger [not left]; riktig; **that's ~** det stämmer; **be ~** ha rätt

right² [adv.] riktigt, rätt; **~?** eller hur?; **~ away** genast, med detsamma; **~ click** högerklicka [IT]; **~ now** just nu; **~ up to our time** ända in i vår tid

right³ [n.] rättighet; rätt; höger [not left]; **~ of assembly** mötesfrihet; **~ of way** förkörsrätt; **~ to vote** rösträtt; **have the ~ to** ha rätt till; **on the ~** till höger; **to the ~** till höger; **driving on the ~** högerkörning

right-justified text [n.] högerjusterad text

right-justify [v.] högerställa

rightly [adv.] riktigt; med rätta

rigid [adj.] styv; sträng, rigorös

rigorous [adj.] rigorös, sträng; noggran

rim [n.] kant, rand; fälg

ring¹ [n.] ring, krans; ringning, klang, ton; **~ network** ringnät

ring² [v.; rang, rung] ringa

rink [n.] rink, isbana

rinse [v.] skölja; spola av

riot [n.] upplopp, tumult, bråk; **run ~** fara vilt fram

R.I.P. [abbrev: rest in peace] må han/hon vila i frid

rip [v.; -pping, -pped, -pped] riva, slita, skära upp

rip-off [n.] odrägligt dyr vara, blåsning

ripe [adj.] mogen, färdig

rise¹ [n.] stigning, höjd; framväxt; uppgång

rise² [v.; rose, risen] resa sig, stiga upp; öka

rising [adj.] stigande

risk¹ [n.] risk, fara

risk² [v.] riskera; våga, sätta på spel

risky [adj.] riskabel; vågad

ritual¹ [adj.] rituell

ritual² [n.] ritual

rival¹ [adj.] rivaliserande, konkurrerande

rival² [n.] rival, konkurrent

river [n.] älv, flod, ström; **~ bank** flodrand, flodstrand; **~ boat** kanalbåt; **~ cruise** flodkryssning; **~ running** forsränning

Riviera [n.] Rivieran

R.N. [abbrev: registered nurse] legitimerad sjuksköterska

roach [n.; ~es] mört [fish]; kackerlacka [insect]

road [n.] väg; **~ closed** vägen stängd; **~ conditions** väglag; **~ divider line** spärrlinje; **~ kill** överkört djur; **~ map (of)** vägkarta (över); **~ narrows** avsmalnande väg; **~ toll** vägavgift; **~ work** vägarbete

roadside [adj.] väg-; **~ emergency phone** vägtelefon; **~ restaurant** vägkrog

roadway [n.] körbana

roar [v.] ryta, vråla; dåna, brusa

roast¹ [adj.] stekt; **~ beef** rostbiff

roast² [n.] stek

roasted [adj.] stekt i ugn, ugnstekt; färdigstekt; **~ whole** helstekt

rob [v.; -bbing, -bbed, -bbed] plundra, råna; beröva

robbed [adj.] bestulen; rånad

robber [n.] rånare, rövare

robbery [n.; -ries] rån, plundring

robot [n.] robot

rock¹ [n.] klippa; sten; rock [music]; **~ climbing** bergsklättring, klippbestigning; **~ music** rockmusik; **whisky on the ~s** whisky med isbitar; **be on the ~s** vara pank, gå i kras

rock² [v.] gunga; skaka

rocket [n.] raket

rococo [adj.] rokoko

rod [n.] käpp, stång, stav

roe [n.; fish eggs] rom

role [n.] roll; **~ model** rollmodell

roll[1] [n.] bulle, småfranska; rulla,
lista; ~ **call** upprop
roll[2] [v.] rulla; kavla; ~ **up one's
sleeves** kavla upp ärmarna
rolled beef [n.] oxrulad
rolled oats [n.] havregryn
roller [n.] rulle; vals; hårspole; ~
skates rullskridskor [pl.]
rolling text [n.] rullande text
ROM [abbrev: read-only memory]
läsminne, ROM
Roman [adj.] romersk
romance [n.] romantik; romans
Romanesque [adj.] romansk; ~
style rundbågestil
Romania [n.] Rumänien
romantic [adj.] romantisk
romanticism [n.] romantiken
Romany [adj.] romani
Rome [n.] Rom
roof [n.] tak, yttertak, hustak
room [n.] rum; sal; plats; ~ **and
board** kost och logi; ~ **rate** pris
per rum; ~ **service** rumsbetjäning,
rumservice; ~ **temperature**
rumstemperatur
roommate [n.] någon som man
delar lägenhet med
roomy [adj.] rymlig
root[1] [n.] rot; grund; **square** ~
kvadratrot
root[2] [v.] slå rot, rota sig
rope [n.] rep, lina; tross
rose [n.] ros
rosé [n.] rosévin
rosemary [n.] rosmarin
rot [v.; -tting, -tted, -tted] ruttna
rotary [n.; -ries] rondell
rotate [v.] rotera; växla
rotation [n.] rotation, varv; **crop** ~
växelbruk
ROTC [abbrev: Reserve Officer
Training Corps] utbildningskår
för reservofficerare på univer-
siteterna i USA
rotten [adj.] rutten, skämd; urdålig
rough [adj.] grov, ojämn; svår,
hård, rå; ~ **seas** sjögång
roughly [adv.] grovt; ungefär
round[1] [adj.] rund; ungefärlig; ~
trip rundtur, retur

round[2] [n.] runda; omgång; ~ **of
golf** golfrunda; **play a** ~ **of golf** gå
en runda
round[3] [prep.]: runt; ~ **the clock**
dygnet runt
round[4] [v.] runda; göra rund
rounding off [n.] avrundning
round-trip [adj.] tur och retur, retur
rouse [v.] väcka; reta
route [n.] rutt, väg
router [n.] router [IT]
routine[1] [adj.] rutin-, rutinmässig
routine[2] [n.] rutin, praxis
row[1] [n.] rad, räcka; bänk; **in a** ~ i
rad; ~ **header** radhuvud [IT]
row[2] [v.] ro
rowanberry [n.] rönnbär
rowboat [n.] roddbåt
royal [adj.] kunglig; ~ **apartments**
kungliga våningen; ~ **couple**
kungapar; ~ **family** kungafamiljen;
~ **garden** kungsträdgård; **Royal
Palace** Kungliga slottet
RPI [abbrev: Rensselaer Polytechnic Institute] Rensselaer Polytechnic Institute
rpm [abbrev: revolutions per minute]
varv i minuten
R&R [abbrev: rest and recreation]
vila och rekreation, ledighet
RR [abbrev: railroad] järnväg
RRR (3 R's) [abbrev: reading,
(w)riting, and (a)rithmetic (basic
education)] grundläggande
skolämnen
RSVP [abbrev: répondez s'il vous
plaît, please respond] om svar
anhålles
Rt. [abbrev: route] landsväg,
huvudväg
RTF [abbrev: rich text format] RTF
[IT: dokumentfilformat som an-
vänds för överföring av formate-
rade dokument mellan olika
program och datorer]
rub [v.; -bbing, -bbed, -bbed]
gnida, gnugga, frottera
rubber [n.] gummi; ~ **boots** gummistövlar; ~ **dinghy** gummibåt;
~ **ring** gummiring; ~ **tire** gummiring
rubbish [n.] skräp, sopor [pl.]

ruby [n. -bies] rubin
rucksack [n.] ryggsäck
rudder [n.] roder
rude [adj.] ohövlig, grov; våldsam
rug [n.] matta
rugby [n.] rugby
ruin [n.] ruin; undergång, fall
rule¹ [n.] regel, ordningsregel, sed-
   vänja; föreskrift; styre; ~ of etiquette etikettsregel
rule² [v.] regera, styra; ~ out
   utesluta
ruler [n.] styresman; linjal
ruling¹ [adj.] regerande, gällande;
   dominerande
ruling² [n.] utslag
rum [n.] rom
rumor [n.] rykte
rumpsteak [n.] rumpstek
run¹ [n.] löpning, lopp; tendens
run² [v.; running, ran, run] springa,
   löpa; fly; rinna; ~ into köra på,
   stöta på; ~ out löpa ut, ta slut
rune [n.] runa; stone with ~s
   runsten
rung [n.] pinne
runner [n.] löpare

running¹ [adv.] i rad
running² [n.] löpning; ~ pants
   joggingbyxor; ~ shoes sportskor,
   träningskor; ~ text löpande text
   [IT]; ~ track motionsspår; ~
   water rinnande vatten
runny nose [n.] snuva; have a ~ ha
   snuva; with a ~ snuvig
runtime module [n.] körningsmodul
   [IT]
runway [n.] startbana, landningsbana
rural [adj.] lands-, lant-; ~ bus
   landsvägsbuss
rush¹ [n.] rusning; be in a ~ ha
   bråttom; ~ hour rusningstid
rush² [v.] rusa; störta
Russia [n.] Ryssland
Russian¹ [adj.] rysk
Russian² (language) [n.] ryska
rusty [adj.] rostig
rutabaga [n.] kålrot
RV [abbrev: recreational vehicle]
   husbil, campingbil
Rwanda [n.] Rwanda
Rx [abbrev; Latin: recipe: take!;
   prescription form] recept
rye [n.] råg; ~ bread rågbröd,
   limpa

S

S¹ [abbrev: south; small] syd, söder; liten

s.² [abbrev: second] sekund

's³ [contr: is; has; possessive marker (e.g. Peter's)] är; har; genetivmärke (Peters)

Sabbath [n.] sabbat

sack¹ [n.] säck, påse; säng; plundring; hit the ~ krypa till kojs

sack² [v.] plundra; ~ out krypa till kojs

sacred [adj.] helgad; helig; religiös

sacrifice¹ [n.] offer; uppoffrande

sacrifice² [v.] offra; uppoffra

sad [adj.] ledsen; sorglig

saddle [n.] sadel

sadly [adv.] sorgset; tråkigt

sadness [n.; ~es] sorgenhet

SAE [abbrev: stamped addressed envelope] frankerat svarskuvert

safe¹ [adj.] säker, trygg; riskfri; ~ for children barnsäker

safe² [n.] kassaskåp

safekeeping [n.] förvar

safely [adv.] säkert, tryggt, utan fara

safety [n.] säkerhet, trygghet; ~ belt bilbälte; ~ razor rakhyvel

safflower oil [n.] safflorolja

saffron [n.] saffran

sage [n.] salvia [herb]

Sagittarius [n.] Skytten

sail¹ [n.] segel; segling

sail² [v.] segla

sailboat [n.] segelbåt

sailing [n.] segling; ~ club segelklubb; ~ instructor seglingsinstruktör; ~ race kappsegling

sailor [n.] sjöman, matros

sailplane [n.] segelflygplan

sailplaning [n.] segelflygning

saint¹ [adj.] sankt, helige

saint² [n.] helgon; ~'s day namnsdag, helgondag

sake [n.] skull; for Jan's ~ för Jans skull

salad [n.] sallad; ~ bar salladsbuffé; ~ dressing salladssås; green ~ grönsallad

salami [n.] salami

salary [n.; -ries] lön; monthly ~ månadslön; weekly ~ veckolön

sale [n.] försäljning; realisation (rea); ~ item reavara; for ~ till salu; put up for ~ saluföra

sales [n.pl.] försäljning; ~ clerk expedit, affärsbiträde; ~ manager försäljningschef; ~ promotion kampanj

salesman [n.; -men] representant, säljare; expedit

saliva [n.] saliv

salmon [n.] lax; ~ trout laxöring; marinated ~ gravad lax

salon [n.] salong

SALT¹ [abbrev: Strategic Arms Limitation Talks] SALT [förhandlingar om begränsning av strategiska vapen]

salt² [n.] salt

salted [adj.] saltad; ~ salmon rimmad lax

saltshaker [n.] saltströare

salty [adj.] salt

salvage [n.] bärga, rädda

salvation [n.] frälsning, räddning

salve [n.] salva; botemedel

SAM [abbrev: surface-to-air missile] luftvärnsrobot

same¹ [adj.] samma; of the ~ age jämnårig; of the ~ sort likadan

same² [pron.] densamma/detsamma; it's all the ~ to me det gör mig detsamma; the ~ to you tack detsamma

Sami¹ [adj.] samisk, lappsk; ~ crafts sameslöjd

Sami² [n.] [native of Lappland] same, lapp

Sami³ (language) [n.] samiska

sample¹ [n.] prov, provexemplar; taking ~s [blood/urine] provtagning

sample² [v.] ta prov på; provsmaka; sampla

sampling [n.] sampling

sanction [n.] tillstånd; gillande; ~s sanktioner

sanctuary [n.; -ries] fristad, asyl, skydd; reservat; nature ~ naturskyddsområde

sand [n.] sand; ~ **castle** sandslott
sandals [n.pl.] sandaler [pl.]
sandbox [n.] sandlåda
sandpaper [n.] sandpapper
sandwich [n.; ~es] smörgås; **make a** ~ breda en smörgås
sandy [adj.] sandig; ~ **beach** sandstrand
sanitary [adj.] sanitär; ~ **facilities** sanitära bekvämligheter; ~ **napkin** dambinda
sans-serif [n.] linjärer [pl.; IT]; sans-seriffer [pl.; IT]
Santa Claus [n.] jultomte
sapphire [n.] safir
sarcastic [adj.] sarkastisk
sardines [n.pl.] sardiner [pl.]
SASE [abbrev: self-addressed stamped envelope] frankerat svarskuvert
Sask. [abbrev: Saskatchewan] Saskatchewan [Canadian prov.]
SAT[1] [abbrev: Scholastic Aptitude Test] studiebegåvningstest [för sökande till intagning på universitetet]
Sat.[2] [abbrev: Saturday] lördag
satellite [n.] satellit; ~ **TV** satellit TV
satiation [n.] mättnad
satisfaction [n.] belåtenhet; tillfredställande
satisfactory [adj.] tillfredställande, nöjaktig
satisfied [adj.] tillfreds, nöjd, belåten, mätt [food]; ~ **with** nöjd med
satisfy [v.; -fies, -fied, -fied] tillfredställa, gottgöra; stilla, släcka; övertyga
satisfying [adj.] tillfredställande
Saturday [n.] lördag; **last** ~ i lördags; **next** ~ på lördag; **this** ~ nu på lördag
Saturn [n.] Saturnus
sauce [n.] sås; mos
saucepan [n.] kastrull
saucer [n.] fat, tefat; **flying** ~ flygande tefat
Saudi Arabia [n.] Saudiarabien
sauerkraut [n.] surkål
sauna [n.] bastu

sausage [n.] korv
sautéed [adj.] smörfräst, bräckt, sauterad, stekt, brynt
savage [adj.] vild, barbarisk; grym
save [v.] rädda, bevara; spara; ~ **as** spara som [IT]
Save the Children [n.] Rädda Barnen
savings [n.pl.] besparing; ~ **account** sparkonto; ~ **bank** sparbank; ~ **book** sparbanksbok
saw [n.] såg
sawmill [n.] sågverk
say [v.; said] säga; ~ **again?** hur sa?; ~ **again** säga om; **that is to** ~ (i.e.) det vill säga (dvs)
saying [n.] ordspråk
SC [abbrev: South Carolina] South Carolina [delstat i USA]
scalable font [n.] skalbar font [IT]
scale [n.] skala; omfattning; ~**s** våg
scallops [n.pl.] kammussla, pilgrimsmusslor
scan [v.; -nned] granska; skumma; skanna [IT]
scandal [n.] skandal; skam
Scandinavia [n.] Skandinavien
Scandinavian [adj.] skandinavisk
Scania [n.] Skåne
scanner [n.] bildläsare, skanner [IT]
scanning [n.] avsökning; scanning [IT]
scar[1] [n.] ärr
scar[2] [v.; -rring, -rred, -rred] tillfoga ärr; märka
scarce [adj.] knapp; sällsynt
scarcely [adv.] knappt
scarcity [n.; -ties] knapphet, brist
scared [adj.] skrämd, rädd
scarf [n.; scarves] halsduk, scarf
scarlet [adj.] scharlakansröd; ~ **fever** scharlakansfeber
scary [adj.] hämsk, skrämmande
scatter [v.] sprida, strö ut; skingra
scattered [adj.] spridd, strödd, sporadisk
scenario [n.] scenario; **worst-case** ~ det värsta tänkbara scenariot
scene [n.] scen; plats; värld
scenery [n.; -ries] natur, landskap; scenbild

scent [n.] doft, lukt; spår
sceptical [adj.] skeptisk
sceptre [n.] spira
schedule[1] [n.] schema, tidtabell,
program
schedule[2] [v.] planera; registrera
scheduled [adj.]: as ~ enligt tidtabell; ~ working hours
schemalagd arbetstid
scheme [n.] system, ordning; plan;
intrig
Schengen Agreement [n.] Schengenavtalet [EU]
schnapps [n.] snaps
scholar [n.] forskare
scholarship [n.] stipendium;
lärdom
school [n.] skola; ~ bag skolväska;
~ child skolbarn; ~ children skolungdom; ~ health service skolhälsovård; ~ lunch skolmåltid; ~
marks skolbetyg; ~ supplies
skolmateriel; ~ system skolsystem; ~ trip skolresa; ~ vacation
skollov; ~ yard skolgård; ~ year
läsår, skolår; elementary ~ grundskola; go to ~ gå i skolan
schooling [n.] bildning; skolgång
schoolmate [n.] skolkamrat
sci-fi [abbrev: science fiction]
science fiction
sciatica [n.] ischias
science [n.] vetenskap; naturvetenskap; ~ fiction science fiction; ~
museum vetenskapsmuseum; ~
student vetenskapsstuderande
scientific [adj.] vetenskaplig; teknisk;
~ expedition forskningsresa; ~
notation exponentiellt skrivsätt
scientist [n.] vetenskapsman
scissors [n.pl.] sax
scoop [n.] skopa; skyffel; ice cream
~ glasskula
scooter [n.] sparkcykel; skoter
scope [n.] omfattning, omfång;
spelrum
score[1] [n.] ställning, läge; poäng;
partitur [music]; what's the ~?
[sports] vad står det?
score[2] [v.] få poäng, göra mål;
vinna; göra repor

scoreboard [n.] resultattavla
Scorpio [n.] Skorpionen [zodiac]
Scot [n.] skotte
Scotch whisky [n.] skotsk whisky
Scotland [n.] Skottland
Scottish [adj.] skotsk
scout [n.] spanare; scout
scramble [v.] kravla; rusa; kasta sig
i väg; blanda ihop
scrambled eggs [n.pl.] äggröra
scrap [n.] bit, stycke; skrot
scrape [v.] skrapa
scrape wound [n.] skrubbsår
scratch[1] [n.; ~es] rispa, skråma;
skrap
scratch[2] [v.; ~es, ~ed, ~ed] klösa,
rispa, riva; klia; ~ an itch klia sig;
~ pad kladdblock
scream[1] [n.] skrik; tjut
scream[2] [v.] skrika; tjuta
screen[1] [n.] skärm; filmduk
screen[2] [v.] skydda; skärma
screening [n.] visning; undersökning, kontroll
screenplay [n.] filmmanus
screw[1] [n.] skruv
screw[2] [v.] skruva; [colloq.] bedra;
[vul.] knulla [vul.]; be ~ed [col-
loq.] vara lurad/bedragad; get ~ed
[colloq.] bli lurad/bedragad; ~
you! [vul.] dra åt helvete! [vul.]
screwdriver [n.] skruvmejsel
script [n.] filmmanus; skript [IT];
~ language skriptspråk [IT]
scroll [v.] rulla
scroll bar [n.] rullningslist [IT]
scroll-down menu [n.] rullgardins-
meny [IT]
scrutiny [n.; -nies] fingranskning,
prövning
SCSI [abbrev: Small Computer
Systems Interface] SCSI [IT;
standard för anslutning av
kringutrustning]
scuba diving [n.] apparatdykning,
sportdykning
sculptor [n.] bildhuggare, skulptör
sculpture [n.] skulptur
SD [abbrev: South Dakota] South
Dakota [delstat i USA]
SE [abbrev: southeast] sydost

sea [n.] hav, sjö; **above** ~ **level** över havet (öh); **at** ~ till sjöss; **by** ~ sjövägen; **out at** ~ ute på havet; ~ **bass** havsaborre [fish]; ~ **bream** braxen [fish]; ~ **captain** sjökapten; ~ **crayfish** havskräfta [fish]; ~ **level** vattenstånd i havet, havsytan; ~ **urchin** sjöborre [fish]

seafood [n.] fisk och skaldjur; ~ **salad** västkustsallad

seal[1] [n.] sigill; prägel; säl [sea mammal]

seal[2] [v.] försegla, klistra igen; prägla; stoppa till

sealed [adj.] sluten, hermetisk

seamless [adj.] sömlös, skarvfri

seamstress [n.; ~es] sömmerska

search[1] [n.; ~es] sökande, spaning; **body** ~ kroppsvisitation

search[2] [v.; ~es, ~ed, ~ed] genomsöka, leta i; leta efter; utforska; ~ **and replace** sök och ersätt [IT]; ~ **box** sökruta [IT]; ~ **engine** sökmotor, sökverktyg [IT]; ~ **hit** sökresultat [IT]; ~ **string** söksträng [IT]; ~ **tool** sökverktyg [IT]; ~ **word** sökord

seascape [n.] havsmålning

seasick [adj.] sjösjuk

seasickness [n.] sjösjuka

seaside [n.] kust, strand; ~ **resort** badort

season[1] [n.] årstid; säsong; helg; ~'s **greetings!** jul- och nyårshälsningar!; ~ **ticket** säsongbiljett; **high** ~ högsäsong; **low** ~ lågsäsong

season[2] [v.] krydda, smaksätta

seasonal [adj.] säsongbetonad, säsongmässig

seasoning [n.] krydda; smaksättning

seat[1] [n.] sittplats, stol; sits; plats; ~ **belt** säkerhetsbälte; ~ **in legislature** mandat; ~ **number** platsnummer; ~ **reservation** platsbiljett

seat[2] [v.] sätta, placera

SEC[1] [abbrev: Securities and Exchange Commission] SEC [myndigheten i USA som utövar tillsyn över handeln med värdepapper]

sec.[2] [abbrev: secretary; second] sekreterare; sekund

second[1] [adj.] andra; en/ett till; ~ **class** andra klass; ~ **cousin** syssling; ~ **gear** tvåan

second[2] [n.] sekund

secondary [adj.] sekundär, underordnad, andrahands-; ~ **road** biväg; ~ **school** skola för elever mellan 11 och 16 år

secondhand [adj.] begagnad, andrahands-; ~ **goods** sekunda varor; ~ **store** second hand-affär

secondly [adv.] för det andra

secret[1] [adj.] hemlig, sekret, dold

secret[2] [n.] hemlighet

secretarial [adj.] sekreterar-

secretary [n.] sekreterare; minister; **Secretary-General** generalsekreterare; **Secretary of State** utrikesminister

secretion [n.] utsöndring

sect [n.] sekt

section [n.] del, avsnitt; stycke; sträcka; sektion

sector [n.] sektor, område; avsnitt

secular [adj.] världslig, profan; utomkyrklig

secure[1] [adj.] säker, trygg, skyddad

secure[2] [v.] befästa, säkra; skaffa sig

security [n.] säkerhet, trygghet; ~ **check** säkerhetskontroll; ~ **rope** säkerhetsrep

sedative [n.] lugnande medel

sediment [n.] sediment, avlagring

see [v.; saw, seen] se; titta på; förstå; ~ **also** se även; ~ **one another** ses; ~ **to** ta hand om, sköta om; ~ **you later!** vi ses!; ~ **you soon!** vi ses snart!; **able to be ~n** synas

seed [n.] frö, säd; kärna

seeing-eye dog [n.] ledarhund

seek [v.; sought, sought] söka; sträva efter

seem [v.] se ut, verka, tyckas

seemingly [adv.] skenbart, till synes

segment [n.] segment, del, avsnitt; klyfta

seize [v.] gripa, fatta; bemäktiga sig

seizure [n.] gripande; konfiskering; erövring; anfall

seldom [adv.] sällan
select[1] [adj.] vald, utvald, exklusiv
select[2] [v.] välja; markera [IT]
selected [adj.] vald; markerad [IT]
selection [n.] val; urval; markering
   [IT]
selective [adj.] selektiv
self [n./pron.; selves] sig själv; jag
self-awareness [n.] självkännedom
self-centered [adj.] självupptagen
self-confident [adj.] självsäker
self-discipline [n.] självdisciplin
self-employed [adj.]: **be** ~ vara
   egen företagare
selfish [adj.] självisk, egoistisk
self-respect [n.] självaktning
self-service [n.] självbetjäning,
   självservering, självservice; ~
   restaurant självservice restaurang
self-timer [n.] självutlösare [camera]
sell [v.; sold, sold] sälja
sell-by date [n.] sista försäljningsdag
seller [n.] försäljare
semantic [adj.] semantisk [gram.]
semester [n.] termin
semicolon [n.] semikolon
semiconductor [n.] halvledare
semidry [adj.] halvtorr
semifinal [n.] semifinal
seminar [n.] seminar, seminarium
Sen. [abbrev: Senator] senator
senate [n.] senat
senator [n.] senator
send [v.; sent, sent] skicka, sända;
   ~ **by e-mail** skicka/sända med
   e-post; ~ **by mail** posta; ~ **for**
   tillkalla
sender [n.] avsändare
sending [n.] expedition
senior[1] [adj.] äldre, senior; ~ **citizen**
   pensionär; ~ **high school** gymnasieskola; ~ **lecturer** universitetslektor, docent
senior[2] [n.] äldre person; pensionär,
   senior; fjärdeårsstudent [college]
sensation [n.] känsla, känsel;
   uppseende
sense[1] [n.] sinne; känsla; förnuft;
   mening, betydelse
sense[2] [v.] känna, märka, uppfatta
senseless [adj.] meningslös

sensible [adj.] klok, förnuftig
sensitive [adj.] känslig, mottaglig
sensitivity [n.] känslighet,
   sensibilitet
sent [adj.] skickad
sentence[1] [n.] sats, mening [gram.];
   dom
sentence[2] [v.] döma
sentiment [n.] stämning, uppfattning, mening
Seoul [n.] Söul
separate[1] [adj.] skild, särskild
separate[2] [v.] skilja, avsöndra,
   separera
separated [adj.] separerad
separately [adv.] var och en för sig
separation [n.] avskiljande;
   hemskillnad
Sept. [abbrev: September] september
sequence [n.] ordningsföljd, följd;
   sekvens
ser. [abbrev: series] serie
Serbia [n.] Serbien
Serbian[1] [adj.] serbisk
Serbian[2] **(language)** [n.] serbiska
sergeant [n.] sergeant, furir
serial [adj.] serie-, periodisk; ~ **access** sekventiell åtkomst [IT]; ~
   number serienummer; ~ **port**
   serieport [IT]
series [n.; ~] serie, rad, räcke
serifs [n.pl.] serif-teckensnitt [IT]
serious [adj.] allvarlig, farlig
seriously [adv.] på allvar
serum [n.; -rums/-ra] serum
servant [n.] tjänare; **civil** ~ statstjänsteman; **domestic** ~ hembiträde; ~ **girl** tjänsteflicka
serve [v.] servera; expediera; försörja; betjäna
server [n.] server, serverdator [IT];
   ~ **program** serverprogram
service [n.] tjänst; betjäning, service; ~ **charge** betjäningsavgift,
   expeditionsavgift; ~ **included**
   inklusive betjäning/serveringsav-
   gift; ~ **pack** servicepaket [IT]; ~
   station bensinstation; ~ **update**
   serviceuppdatering [IT]; **military**
   ~ militärtjänstgöring; **not in** ~ ej i
   trafik; **social** ~**s** socialvården

service-oriented [adj.] service-inriktad

serving [n.] portion; servering; ~ suggestions hur maten serveras

sesame oil [n.] sesamolja

session [n.] sammanträde

set[1] [adj.] fast, bestämd; stel, besluten; ~ menu måltid/meny till fast pris

set[2] [n.] uppsättning, sats; scenbild; läggning [hair]

set[3] [v.; setting, set, set] lägga, sätta, ställa; ~ foot on beträda; ~ free frige; ~ off ge sig iväg; ~ the table duka bordet; ~ to work on ta itu med; ~ up konfigurera

setting [n.] inställning; läggning

settle [v.] sätta till rätta; göra upp; avgöra; slå sig ner

settlement [n.] avgörande, lösning; betalning; bosättning

settler [n.] nybyggare, kolonist

seven [num.] sju

seven-bit [adj.] sjuställig [IT]

seventeen [num.] sjutton

seventeenth [adj.] sjuttonde

seventh [adj.] sjunde

seventieth [adj.] sjuttionde

seventy [num.] sjuttio

several [adj./pron.] flera; of ~ years flerårig

severe [adj.] sträng; hård, skarp; bister

sew [v.; sewed, sewn/sewed] sy

sewage [n.] avloppsvatten; ~ works reningsverk

sewing [n.] sömnad; ~ machine symaskin

sewn to order [adj.] beställningssytt

sex [n.] kön; sex, erotik; have ~ ha samlag

sexual [adj.] sexuell; ~ harassment sexuellt ofredande; ~ preferences sexuell läggning

sexuality [n.] sexualitet

sexy [adj.] sexig

SF [abbrev: San Francisco; science fiction] San Francisco; science fiction

SGML [abbrev: standard general markup language] SGML [IT; standard för dokumentutformning]

Sgt. [abbrev: sergeant] sergeant, furir

shade [n.] skugga; skärm; nyans

shadow[1] [n.] skugga

shadow[2] [v.] skugga

shady [adj.] skuggig

shaft [n.] skaft; trumma; schakt

shake [v.; shook, shaken] skaka, ruska; ~ hands with someone ta någon i hand

shaken up [adj.] omtumlad

shall [v.modal; should] ska

shallots [n.pl.] schalottenlök

shallow [adj.] grund, flat; ytlig; ~ end [pool] grunt

shame [n.] skam; what a ~! vad synd!, vilken otur!; it's a ~ that he couldn't come det är synd att han inte kunde komma

shampoo [n.] schampo

shank [n.] lägg

shape[1] [n.] form, fason; ordning; tillstånd

shape[2] [v.] forma

share[1] [n.] del, andel; aktie

share[2] [v.] dela, ha del i, få del av; ~ out dela ut

shared [adj.] delad

shareholder [n.] aktieägare

shareware [n.] shareware, sprid-program [IT]

sharing [n.] delning

shark [n.] haj

sharp[1] [adj.] skarp, vass; tvär

sharp[2] [adv.] på slaget [time]; skarpt

sharp[3] [n.] kors [music]

sharp-edged [adj.] vass

sharpen [v.] göra skarp, skärpa; formera

sharpness of vision [n.] synskärpa

shatter [v.] splittra, bryta sönder

shave [v.] raka sig

shaver [n.] rakapparat

shaving [n.] rak-; ~ brush rakborste; ~ cream rakkräm

shawl [n.] sjal

she [pron.] hon

she'd[1] [contr: she had/would] hon hade/skulle

shed[2] [n.] bod, skjul

shed[3] [v.; shed] fälla, tappa; ta/kasta av sig; gjuta, sprida

sheep [n.; sheep] får; ~'s (milk) cheese fårost

sheepskin [n.] fårskinn

sheer [adj.] ren, pur; skir; tvärbränt

sheet [n.] lakan; plåt, skiva; ark, blad [paper]; bottom ~ underlakan; top ~ överlakan

shelf [n.; shelves] hylla; continental ~ kontinentalhyllan

shell[1] [n.] skal; balja, skida; patron [gun]

shell[2] [v.] skala, rensa; bombardera

she'll[3] [contr: she will] hon ska

shellfish [n.] skaldjur

shelter[1] [n.] skydd; husrum; härbärge

shelter[2] [v.] skydda; ge tak över huvudet

shield[1] [n.] sköld; bricka

shield[2] [v.] skydda

shift[1] [n.] förändring, skifte, växling, övergång; skift; automatic ~ automatväxel; ~ key (Shift) skifttangent [IT]

shift[2] [v.] skifta, flytta; växla

shinbone [n.] skenben

shine [v.; shone/shined, shined] skina, lysa, glänsa; putsa, polera

shiny [adj.] skinande, glänsande

ship[1] [n.] båt, skepp, fartyg

ship[2] [v.; -pping, -pped, -pped] sända, skicka, transportera

shipment [n.] sändning, transport

shipping [n.] skeppning; sändande; ~ charge frakt

shirk [v.] smita från

shirt [n.] skjorta; tröja

shit[1] [n.; vul.] skit [colloq.]; ~! [vul.] fan! [vul.], jävlar! [vul.]; take a ~ [vul.] skita [colloq.]; not give a ~ [vul.] skita i

shit[2] [v.; vul.; shat, shat] skita [colloq.]

shiver[1] [n.] darrning, skälving, rysning

shiver[2] [v.] darra, skälva, rysa

shock[1] [n.] chock; stöt; ~ absorber stötdämpare

shock[2] [v.] chockera, ge en chock

shocked [adj.] chockerad

shocking [adj.] chockerande

shockproof [adj.] stötsäker

shock-resistant [adj.] stötsäker

shoe [n.] sko; ~ brush skoborste; ~ polish skokräm; ~ repair shop skomakare; ~ store skoaffär

shoelaces [n.pl.] skosnören [pl.]

shoot [v.; , shot, shot] skjuta; jaga; rusa; fotografera, filma

shooting [n.] skjutning; jakt; fotografering; ~ gallery/range skutbana

shop[1] [n.] butik, affär; ~ assistant affärsbiträde

shop[2] [v.; -pping, -pped, -pped] handla, shoppa

shopkeeper [n.] butiksinnehavare

shopper [n.] shoppare

shopping [n.] inköp, shopping; go ~ handla; ~ bag kasse, shoppingväska; ~ basket kundvagn, shoppingkorg, varukorg; ~ cart shoppingvagn; ~ center affärscentrum, köpcentrum, shoppingcenter; ~ mall galleria, shoppingcenter; ~ street affärsgata

shore [n.] strand, kust

short[1] [adj.] kort; knapp; be ~ of ha ont om; ~ circuit kortslutning; ~ film kortfilm; ~ story novell

short[2] [adv.] tvärt; otillräckligt

shortage [n.] brist, underskott

shortbread [n.] mördegskaka

shortcut [n.] genväg; ~ key kortkommando [IT]; ~ menu popupmeny, snabbmeny, snabbvalsmeny [IT]

shortly [adv.] kort, strax

shorts [n.pl.] shorts

short-term [adj.] kortfristig; ~ parking korttidsparkering

shot[1] [adj.] skjuten; ~ to death ihjälskjuten

shot[2] [n.] skott; spruta

should [v.modal] böra

shoulder [n.] axel; bog [meat cut]; vägren [road]; ~ bag axelväska; ~ pad axelvadd

shout[1] [n.] rop, skrik

shout[2] [v.] ropa, skrika

shove [v.] skuffa, skjuta, knuffa; stoppa

shovel [n.] skovel, spade

show¹ [n.] föreställning, utställning; show

show² [v.; showed, shown] visa; synas

shower [n.] dusch; ~ **curtain** duschdraperi; ~ **gel** duschtvål; ~ **room** duschrum; ~ **seat** duschstol; ~ **shoes** badskor; **take a** ~ duscha

showing [n.] visning; utställning

shrewd [adj.] skarpsinning, klyftig, smart

shrimp [n.] räka; ~ **cocktail** räkcocktail; ~ **sandwich** räksmörgås

shrink [v.; shrank, shrunk] krympa, minska; ~ **back from** skygga för

shrub [n.] buske

shrug [v.; -gging, -gged, -gged] rycka på axlarna

shudder [v.] rysa, bäva, huttra

shuffle [v.] gå släpigt; blanda [cards]

shun [v.; -nning, -nned, -nned] undvika, sky

shut¹ [adj.] stängd; **get something** ~ få igen något

shut² [v.; -tting, shut, shut] stänga, dra igen; ~ **in** stänga in; ~ **off** stänga av; ~ **out** stänga ute, utesluta

shutoff valve [n.] avstängningskran

shutter [n.] slutare

shuttle service [n.] skyttelservice

shy [adj.] blyg, skygg

Siberia [n.] Sibirien

sibling [n.] syskon

Sicily [n.] Sicilien

sick [adj.] sjuk; ~ **pay** sjuklön; **feel** ~ må illa

sickness [n.] sjukdom; illemående

side [n.] sida; ~ **dish** tillbehör; ~ **effect** biverkning; ~ **mirror** sidospegel; ~ **order** extra portion; ~ **road** avtagsväg; ~ **street** sidogata; **on the left/right** ~ på vänster/ höger sida

sideburns [n.pl.] polisonger

sidelight [n.] sidoljus

sidewalk [n.] trottoar

sideways [adv.] från sidan, sidledes, på snedden

SIDS [abbrev: sudden infant death syndrome] plötslig spädbarnsdöd (SIDS)

siege [n.] belägring

sieve [n.] sikt; såll

sigh¹ [n.] suck

sigh² [v.] sucka; susa

sight [n.] syn; sevärdhet; **catch** ~ **of** få syn på

sighted [adj.] **partially** ~ synskadad

sightseeing [n.] sightseeing, rundtur; ~ **tour** sightseeingtur

sign¹ [n.] skylt, tecken; **star** ~ stjärntecken; **traffic** ~ trafikmärke; ~ **language** teckenspråk

sign² [v.] underteckna, skriva under

signal¹ [n.] signal

signal² [v.] signalera, ge tecken

signature [n.] underskrift, signatur, namnteckning

significance [n.] betydelse

significant [adj.] betydelsefull, betydande; meningsfull

significantly [adv.] betydligt; betecknande

signify [v.; -fies, -fied, -fied] innebära; ge uttryck för; betyda

silage [n.] pressfoder

silence¹ [n.] tystnad, tystlåtenhet

silence² [v.] tysta

silent [adj.] tyst; **be** ~ tiga; **become** ~ tystna

silently [adv.] tyst, stilla

silk [n.] siden, silke; ~ **painting** sidenmåleri; **pure** ~ helsiden

silk-screen print [n.] screentryck

silly [adj.] dum, idiotisk

silver [adj./n.] silver; ~ **bowl** silverskål; ~ **plate** nysilver

silverware [n.] silversaker

SIM-card [abbrev: subscriber identity mobile card] SIM-kort [IT; för mobiltelefoner]

similar [adj.] lik; likadan; dylik; **be** ~ **to** likna

similarity [n.; -ties] likhet

similarly [adv.] likaledes, likadant

simple [adj.] enkel; enfaldig

simplicity [n.; -ties] enkelhet

simplify [v.; -fies, -fied] förenkla

simply [adv.] enkelt; rent av, bara

simulation [n.] simulering; förfalskning

simultaneous [adj.] samtidig, simultan

sin [n.] synd, försyndelse
since[1] [adv.] sedan dess; sedan
since[2] [conj.] sedan; eftersom
since[3] [prep.] sedan; ~ 8 this morning sedan kl 8 i morse
sincere [adj.] uppriktig, ärlig; hjärtlig
sincerely [adv.] uppriktigt,, verkligt; Yours ~ med vänlig hälsning, Din tillgivne
sing [v.; sang, sung] sjunga
singer [n.] sångare [male], sångerska [female]
single [adj.] enkel; enda; ensamstående [not married]; ~ cabin enkelhytt; ~ copy lösnummer; ~ file enfilig; ~ room enkelrum
singles [n.pl.] singel [sports]
singular [adj.] singular; ovanlig
sinister [adj.] olycksbådande; elak
sink[1] [n.] slask; diskho; handfat
sink[2] [v.; sank, sunk] sjunka; sänka sig
sinus [n.; ~es] bihåla
sinusitis [n.] bihåleinflammation
sip [v.; -pping, -pped, -pped] läppja; smutta
sir [n.] herrn
siren [n.] siren
sirloin steak [n.] utskuren biff
sis [abbrev: sister; colloq.] syster
sister [n.] syster; big ~ storasyster; little ~ lillasyster
sister-in-law [n.] svägerska
sit [v.; -tting, sat, sat] sitta; ~ down sätta sig, slå sig ner, ta plats; ~ down to lunch/dinner sätta sig till bords; ~ still sitta stilla
site [n.] plats; sajt [IT]; ~ map plattskarta, översikt
sitting [n.] servering [dining car]
situate [v.] placera, lägga, ställa
situated [adj.] be ~ ligga
situation [n.] läge, situation
SI-unit [abbrev: Système International unit] SI-enhet
six [num.] sex
sixteen [num.] sexton
sixteenth [adj.] sextonde
sixth [adj.] sjätte
sixtieth [adj.] sextionde

sixty [num.] sextio
size [n.] storlek, nummer
SK [abbrev: Saskatchewan] Saskatchewan [Canadian prov.]
skate[1] [n.] rocka [fish]
skate[2] [v.] åka skridskor
skateboard [n.] skateboard
skates [n.pl.] skridskor
skating [n.] skridskoåkning; ~ rink isbana, skridskobana
skeleton [n.] skelett
sketch[1] [n.; ~es] skiss, utkast; sketch; ~ pad skissblock
sketch[2] [v.; ~es, ~ed, ~ed] skissera
skewer [n.] grillspett
ski[1] [n.; see: skis]
ski[2] [v.; skis, skied, skied] åka skidor; ~ area skidort; ~ bindings skidbindningar; ~ boots pjäxor, skidpjäxor; ~ instructor skidlärare; ~ lesson skidlektion; ~ pants skidbyxor; ~ poles skidstavar; ~ resort skidort; ~ run skidspår; ~ school skidskola; ~ slope skidbacke; ~ tow släplift; ~ trail skidspår, piste; ~ wax skidvalla
skier [n.] skidåkare
skiing [n.] skidåkning; go ~ åka skidor; ~ competition skidtävling; ~ conditions skidföre; ~ equipment skidutrustning; ~ goggles skidglasögon; ~ season skidsäsong; ~ surface skidföre; ~ vacation skidlov
skill [n.] skicklighet; färdighet; ~s teknik
skilled [adj.] skicklig, duktig, kunnig
skillful [adj.] habil, skicklig, duktig
skim [v.; -mming, -mmed, -mmed] skumma; glida fram över
skim milk [n.] lättmjölk
skin [n.] hud, skinn; skal; ~ disease hudsjukdom; ~ moisturizer hudkräm
skip [v.; -pping, -pped, -pped] hoppa; hoppa rep; hoppa över, skippa
skipper [n.] skeppare, kapten
skirt [n.] kjol; ~s utkant
skis [n.pl.] skidor [pl.]

skull [n.] skalle
sky [n.; skies] himmel
slab [n.] platta; tjock skiva
slack [adj.] slapp; slak
slacken [v.] slappna; slakna; minska
slalom [n.] slalom; ~ skier
  slalomåkare; ~ slope slalombacke
slam [v.; -mming, -mmed, -mmed]
  slå igen, smälla igen
slang [n.] slang
slap [v.; -pping, -pped, -pped]
  smälla, slå
slash[1] [n.; ~es] hugg, slag; djup
  hack; snedstreck [IT]
slash[2] [v.; ~es, ~ed, ~ed] hugga
  upp/sönder/ner; reducera
slaughter [n.] slakt, massaker
slave [n.] slav [m.], slavinna [f.]
sled [n.] kälke, släde
sledding [v.] go ~ åka kälke
sleep[1] [n.] sömn
sleep[2] [v.; slept, slept] sova; ~ with
  ligga med
sleeper [n.; railroad car] sovvagn;
  ~ berth sovplats
sleeping [adj.] sov-; ~ bag sovsäck;
  ~ car sovvagn; ~ pill sömntablett
sleeplessness [n.] sömnlöshet
sleepy [adj.] sömnig
sleet [n.] snöglopp, snöslask
sleeve [n.] ärm; fodral
sleeveless [adj.] ärmlös
sleigh [n.] kälke, släde
slender [adj.] small, slank; ringa,
  knapp
slice[1] [n.] skiva; del
slice[2] [v.] skära upp
slick [adj.] gättad; smart
slide[1] [n.] rutschbana; glidning;
  diabild [photo]; ~ show bildspel
slide[2] [v.; slid, slid] glida; rutscha;
  smussla
slight [adj.] liten, obetydlig; späd
slightest [adj./adv.superl.] minsta
slightly [adv.] lätt, lindrigt, något
slim[1] [adj.] small, slank; liten
slim[2] [v.; -mming, -mmed, -mmed]
  banta
slip[1] [n.] stycke; fel, lapsus;
  underkjol
slip[2] [v.; -pping, -pped, -pped] glida;
  smyga; göra fel

slipped disc [n.] diskbråck
slippers [n.pl.] tofflor
slippery [adj.] hal, glatt, slirig; ~
  road surface slirig körbana; ~
  roads halt väglag
slogan [n.] slogan, slagord
slope [n.] lutning; backe; piste
slot [n.] smal öppning, slits; nich,
  lucka
Slovak[1] [adj.] slovakisk
Slovak[2] (language) [n.] slovakiska
Slovakia [n.] Slovakien
Slovene[1] [adj.] slovensk
Slovene[2] (language) [n.] slovenska
Slovenia [n.] Slovenien
slow[1] [adj.] långsam, sakta; be ~
  [clock] gå efter; ~ traffic långsam
  trafik
slow[2] [v.] sakta; sänka takten/farten
slowly [adv.] sakta, långsamt; more
  ~ långsammare
sluggish [adj.] lat, långsam, trög
sluice [n.] sluss; ränna
slump[1] [n.] plötsligt fall, nedgång;
  lågkonjunktur
slump[2] [v.] falla plötsligt; sjunka
  ner
slush [n.] blötsnö, snöslask; isdryck
sm. [abbrev: small] liten
smack [v.] smälla, daska; smacka
  med
small[1] [adj.] lilla, liten; ~ change
  växel
small[2] [n.] ~ of the back korsrygg
small-boat harbor [n.] småbåtshamn
smaller [adj.comp.] mindre
smallpox [n.] smittkoppor
smart [adj.] smart; stilig, flott;
  skarp; ~ card smartkort
smash [v.; ~es, ~ed, ~ed] slå sönder, krossa
smashed [adj.] sönderslagen, berusad
smear [v.] smeta; smörja
smell[1] [n.] lukt
smell[2] [v.] känna lukten, vädra;
  lukta på; lukta; stinka
smile[1] [n.] leende
smile[2] [v.] le, småle
smiley [n.] smiley [IT]
smith [n.] smed
smoke[1] [n.] rök; ~ alarm rökdetektor

smoke² [v.] ryka; röka; **may I ~?** får jag röka?
smoked [adj.] rökt, bräckt; **~ eel** rökt ål; **~ pork loin** kassler; **~ pork sausage** bräckkorv; **~ salmon** rökt lax; **lightly ~** lättrökt
smoker [n.] rökare
smoking [n.] rökning; **~ room/car** rökare; **no ~** rökning förbjuden
smooth¹ [adj.] slät, jämn, glatt; lugn, stilla; mjuk
smooth² [v.; ~s/~es, ~ed, ~ed] göra jämn, släta till
smoothly [adv.] jämnt
SMS [abbrev: short message services] SMS [IT]
SMTP server [n.; for outgoing e-mail] SMTP-server [IT]
SMU [abbrev: Southern Methodist University] Southern Methodist University
smuggle [v.] smuggla
snack [n.] matbit, munsbit; **~ bar** snackbar, barservering, byffé
snail [n.] snigel; **~ mail** snigelpost [IT]
snake [n.] orm
snakebite [n.] ormbett
snap [v.; -pping, -pped, -pped] nafsa, snappa; fräsa; knäckas; knappa
snatch [v.; ~es, ~ed, ~ed] rycka till sig; stjäla
sneak [v.; sneaked, sneaked/snuck, snuck] smyga (sig)
sneeze [v.] nysa
sniff [v.] vädra, lukta på
sniffles [n.pl.] snuva; **have the ~** vara täppt i näsan
snooty [adj.] snorkig
snorkel¹ [n.] snorkel
snorkel² [v.] snorkla
snow¹ [n.] snö; **~ tires** vinterdäck
snow² [v.] snöa
snowboard [n.] snowboard
snow-bound [adj.] insnöad
snowman [n.] snögubbe
snowmobile [n.] snöskoter
snowplow [n.] snöplog
snowrafting [n.] snowrafting
snowstorm [n.] snöstorm

so¹ [adv.] så, sålunda; **~ long!** hej så länge!; **is that ~?** jaså?
so² [conj.] så att; **~ far** hittills; **~ that** så pass att
soak [v.] blöta; göra genomvåt; **~ up** absorbera
so-and-so [n.] den och den; typ
soap [n.] tvål, såpa
soapsuds [n.pl.] tvållödder
soar [v.] flyga; stiga, svinga sig upp; skjuta i höjden
SOB¹ [abbrev: son of a bitch] jävla knöl
sob² [v.; -bbing, -bbed, -bbed] snyfta; **~ story** snyftreportage
sober [adj.] nykter
Soc. [abbrev: Society; socialist] förening; socialistisk
so-called [adj.] så kallad (sk.)
soccer [n.] fotboll; **~ field** fotbollsplan; **~ game** fotbollsmatch; **~ team** fotbollslag
social [adj.] social; **~ insurance number** FK-konto; **~ life** umgängsvana; **~ page** familjesida; **~ science(s)** samhällsvetenskap, samhällsorientande ämnen; **~ security** socialförsäkring, socialbidrag; **~ services** socialtjänst; **~ welfare** socialvård; **~ welfare administration** socialförvaltning; **~ work** socialt arbete, socialvård; **~ worker** socialarbetare, socialvårdare
socialism [n.] socialism
socialist¹ [adj.] socialistisk
socialist² [n.] socialist
socialize with [v.] umgås (med)
socially [adv.] socialt; på det sociala planet
society [n.; -ties] samhälle; förening
sociological [adj.] sociologisk
sociologist [n.] sociolog
sociology [n.; -gies] sociologi
sock [n.] socka, strumpa; slag, smäll
socket [n.] håla; sockel, fattning
soda [n.;] läsk; **~ water** sodavatten
sodium [n.] natrium
sofa [n.] soffa
soft [adj.] mjuk; dämpad; mild; lindrig; **~ drink** läsk, läskedryck; **~**

hyphen mjukt bindestreck [IT];
~ **shoulder** [road] ostadig vägren
soft-boiled [adj.] löskokt [egg]
soften [v.] mjuka upp; dämpa; lindra, försvaga
softball [n.] softboll [type of baseball]
software [n.] programvara [IT]; ~
engineer programmerare [IT]; ~
piracy piratkopiering av program
[IT]; ~ **reengineering** systemomarbetning [IT]
soil[1] [n.] grund, jord; botten, mark
soil[2] [v.] smutsa, solka
sojourn [n.] vistelse, uppehåll
solar [adj.] sol-; ~ **energy** solenergi; ~ **panel** solpanel; ~ **system** solsystem
solarium [n.; -ria/~s] solarium
sold [adj.] såld; ~ **out** slutsåld, utsåld
soldier [n.] soldat
sole[1] [adj.] enda, ensam; ~ **trader** egen företagare
sole[2] [n.] sula [shoe]; sjötunga [fish]
solely [adv.] ensam; endast
solemn [adj.] högtidlig, allvarlig
solid[1] [adj.] fast; massiv; mastig
solid[2] [n.] fast kropp; solid
solidarity [n.; -ties] solidaritet
solitary [adj.] ensam, enda; ~
confinement ensamcell
solo[1] [adj.] solo-, ensam-
solo[2] [n.] solo
soloist [n.] solist
soluble [adj.] lösbar
solution [n.] lösning
solve [v.] lösa; klara upp
solvent[1] [adj.] solvent
solvent[2] [n.] lösningsmedel
Somalia [n.] Somalia
some [adj./pron.] någon, något, några; viss; en del
somebody [pron.] någon; ~ **else** någon annan
somehow [adv.] på något sätt
someone [pron.] någon
something [pron.] något, någonting;
~ **else** något annat; ~ **worth**
seeing sevärdhet
sometime [adv.] någon gang, en gång

sometimes [adv.] då och då, i bland
somewhat [adv.] något, ganska, tämligen
somewhere [adv.] någonstans; ungefär
son [n.] son; ~ **of a bitch** jävla knöl
song [n.] låt, sång; ~ **festival** melodifestival
son-in-law [n.; sons-in-law] svärson
soon [adv.] snart, strax; ~ **after** strax efter; **as ~ as possible**
(ASAP) så snart som möjligt
sooner [adv.comp.] förr, tidigare; hellre; ~ **or later** förr eller senare
Sophia [n.] Sofia
sophisticated [adj.] sofistikerad, raffinerad, komplicerad
sophomore [n.] andraårsstuderande
sore [adj.] öm; sur; ~ **throat** ont i halsen, halsont
sorry [adj.] ledsen; **I'm** ~ förlåt, jag beklagar
sort[1] [n.] sort, slag; ~ **of** liksom; **and that ~ of thing** eller dylikt
sort[2] [v.] sortera
SOS [abbrev: Save Our Souls/Ship] SOS [nödsignal]
soufflé [n.] sufflé
soul [n.] själ; soul [music]
sound[1] [adj.] frisk, sund; klok; säker
sound[2] [n.] ljud; sund [geogr.]; ~
card ljudkort [IT]
sound[3] [v.] låta, tona; sondera; **that**
~**s good** det låter bra
soup [n.] soppa; ~ **plate** sopptallrik, djup tallrik; ~ **tureen** soppskål
sour [adj.] sur; ~ **cream** creme fraiche; ~ **milk** filmjölk
source [n.] källa; ~ **code** källkod [IT]
south[1] [adj./adv.] södra, syd-
south[2] [n.] syd, söder
South Africa [n.] Sydafrika
South America [n.] Sydamerika
South Carolina (SC) [n.] South Carolina [delstat i USA]
South Dakota (SD) [n.] South Dakota [delstat i USA]
southeast [adj./n.] sydost
South-East Asia [n.] Sydostasien
southern [adj.] sydlig, syd-, södra
southernmost [adj.] sydligaste

South Korea [n.] Sydkorea
South Pacific [n.] Söderhavet
South Seas [n.] Söderhavet
southwards [adv.] mot söder, söderut
southwest [adj./n.] sydväst
souvenir [n.] minne, souvenir; ~ shop souvenirbutik
sovereignty [n.] suveränitet
soy [n.]: ~ foods sojalivsmedel; ~ milk sojamjölk; ~ sauce sojasås
soybean oil [n.] sojabönsolja
soybean proteins [n.pl.] soya-proteiner
soybeans [n.pl.] sojabönor
space [n.] rymd, rum; plats; period; mellanslag [IT]; ~ bar mellanslags-tangent [IT]; ~ flight rymdfärd; ~ heater rumsuppvärmare; ~ shuttle rymdfärja; ~ station rymd-station; ~ walk rymdpromenad
spacecraft [n.] rymdskepp
spaceship [n.] rymdskepp
spacious [adj.] rymlig
spade [n.] spade; ~s [cards] spader
spaghetti [n.] spagetti
Spain [n.] Spanien
spam [n.] skräppost; ~ filter skräp-postfilter [IT]
Spaniard [n.] spanjor
Spanish[1] [adj.] spansk
Spanish[2] (language) [n.] spanska
spank [v.] ge smäll, daska till
spare[1] [adj.] extra, reserv-, fri-; ~ bed extrasäng; ~ part reservdel; ~ time fritid; ~ tire reservdäck; ~ wheel reservhjul
spare[2] [v.] undvara, avvara; skona, bespara
spareribs [n.pl.] revbensspjäll
spark [n.] gnista
sparkle [v.] gnistra; glittra
sparkling [adj.] pärlande, mouss-erande; ~ water sodavatten
sparkplug [n.] tändstift
sparse [adj.] gles
sparsely populated [adj.] glesbefolkad
spatial [adj.] rumslig, rymd
SPCA [abbrev: Society for the Pre-vention of Cruelty to Animals]

djurskyddsföreningen i USA
speak [v.; spoke, spoken] tala; ~ about prata/tala om; ~ to tala med
speaker [n.] talare, talman; högta-lare [device]
spear [n.] spjut, ljuster
special [adj.] särskild, speciell; extra-; ~ delivery expresspost; ~ discount price extrapris; ~ effects specialeffekter; ~ offer specialer-bjudande
specialist [n.] specialist, fackman
speciality [n.; -ties] specialitet; ut-märkande drag; ~ of the house husets specialitet
specialize [v.] specialisera
specialized [adj.] specialiserad, fack-
specially [adv.] särskilt, speciellt
specialty [n.; -ties] specialitet; local ~ specialitet för landsdelen
species [n.; ~] art; slag, typ, sort; ~ of plant växtart
specific [adj.] uttrycklig, bestämd; specifik
specifically [adv.] uttryckligen, bestämt
specification [n.] specificerande; ~s specifikation
specified [adj.] specificerad
specify [v.; -fies, -fied, -fied] specificera
specimen [n.] prov, exemplar
spectacle [n.] skådespel; anblick
spectacular [adj.] effektfull, prakt-full, imponerande
spectator [n.] åskådare
spectrum [n.; -tra/~s] skala; spektrum
speculate [v.] spekulera; fundera
speculation [n.] spekulation
speech [n.; ~es] tal; språk, mål; yttrande; give a ~ hålla tal; freedom of ~ yttrandefrihet; ~ therapist logoped
speechless [adj.] stum, mållös
speed[1] [n.] hastighet, fart, tempo; ~ check fartkontroll; ~ limit fart-gräns, hastighetsbegränsning; ~ trap hastighetskontroll
speed[2] [v., sped] rusa, hasta, jaga fram; köra för fort

speedometer [n.] hastighetsmätare
spell [v.; spelt, spelt/spelled, spelled]
  stava; ~ **out** bokstavera
spell-checker [n.] stavningskontroll
spelling [n.] stavning; rättskrivning;
  ~ **mistake** stavfel
spend [v.; spent, spent] lägga ut, ge
  ut [money]; använda, lägga ned
  [time]; ~ **the night** övernatta; ~
  time with tillbringa tid med
spending [n.] utgift; ~ **cut** nedskärning av utgifter; ~ **money**
  fickpengar
SPF [abbrev: sun protection factor]
  solskyddsfaktor
sphere [n.] sfär, klot, kula; område
spice [n.] krydda
spicy [adj.] kryddad; pikant
spider [n.] spindel; ~**'s web**
  spindelväv
spill [v.; spilt, spilt/spilled, spilled]
  spilla, stjälpa ut; rinna över
spin [v.; spun/span, spun] snurra
  runt, svänga runt; spinna; vinkla;
  ~ **doctor** nyhetsfrisör; ~ **dryer**
  centrifug
spinach [n.; ~es] spenat
spine [n.] ryggrad; tagg, pigg
spiral [n.] spiral,
spire [n.] spira
spirit [n.] ande, själ, kraft; anda,
  stämning; ~**s** humor, lynne; sprit
spiritual [adj.] andlig
spit [v.; spat, spat] spotta
spit-roasted [adj.] stekt på spett
spite [n.] ondska, illvilja; **in** ~ **of**
  trots
splash [v.; ~es, ~ed, ~ed] stänka ned,
  slaska ned; plaska med; plumsa
splendid [adj.] ståtlig, storartad,
  utmärkt
splendor [n.] glans, prakt
splinter [n.] flisa, skärva, sticka
split¹ [adj.] kluven, sprucken;
  delad; ~ **screen** delad skärm
split² [n.] klyvning, spricka
split³ [v.; -tting, split, split] splittra,
  klyva, spränga; dela upp
spoil [v.; ~ed, ~ed/~t, ~t] förstöra,
  fördärva; skämma bort
spoiled [adj.] förstörd, skämd
spoke [n.] eker; stegpinne

spoken [adj.] talad, muntlig;
  English ~ vi talar engelska
spokesman [n.] talesman, språkrör
sponge [n.] tvättsvamp; ~ **cake**
  sockerkaka
sponsor¹ [n.] sponsor, gynnare
sponsor² [v.] stå bakom, gynna;
  sponsra
sponsorship [n.] sponsorskap, stöd
spontaneous [adj.] omedelbar,
  spontan
spoof [n.] drift, parody; ~ **web site**
  bluffwebbplats [IT]
spool [n.] spole, rulle
spooler [n.] mellanlagrare [IT]
spoon [n.] sked
sport [n.] sport, idrottsgren; **pursue a** ~ sporta; ~ **utility vehicle
  (SUV)** city jeep
sporting goods store [n.] sportaffär
sports [n.pl.] idrott; ~ **association**
  idrottsförening; ~ **car** sportbil; ~
  center idrottshall; ~ **club** sportklubb; ~ **event** sportevenemang;
  ~ **field** idrottsplan, idrottsplats;
  ~ **hall** sporthall; ~ **jacket** blazer;
  kavaj
sportsman [n.; -men] idrottsman
sportswoman [n.; -men]
  idrottskvinna
spot¹ [n.] flack, prick; ställe, punkt
spot² [v.; -tting, -tted, -tted] fläcka
  ned, befläcka; få syn på, upptäcka,
  lägga märke till
spouse [n.] make [m.], maka [f.]
sprain [v.] vricka, sträcka
sprained [adj.] stukad
spray¹ [n.] stänk, skum; sprej
spray² [v.] spreja, spruta; stänka
spread¹ [n.] spridning; sträcka, omfång; bredbart pålägg [food]
spread² [v.; spread, spread] breda,
  sprida; sprida sig, sträcka sig
spreading [n.] spridning
spreadsheet [n.] kalkylblad [IT];
  ~ **program** kalkylprogram [IT]
spring¹ [n.] källa [water]; vår [sea-
  son]; hopp [jump]; fjäder [metal];
  ~ **equinox** [March 21] vårdagjämning; ~ **onion** vårlök, schal-
  lotenlök; ~ **semester** vårtermin

spring² [v.] hoppa, rusa; rinna,
spruta; dyka upp
sprinkle [v.] strö, stänka
sprint [v.] sprinta, spurta
sprout [n.] grodd; Brussels ~s
böngroddar
spruce [n.] gran
spur [n.] sporre
spurious [adj.] falsk
spy¹ [n.; spies] spion
spy² [v.; spies, spied, spied] spionera
spyware [n.] spionprogramvara [IT]
sq. [abbrev: square] kvadrat; torg
sq.ft. [abbrev: square foot] kvadrat
fot [0,1 kv. m.]
sq.in. [abbrev: square inch] kvadrat
tum [6,5 kv.cm.]
SQL [abbrev: structured query lan-
guage] SQL [fråge- och komman-
dospråk för hantering av databaser]
sq.mi. [abbrev: square mile]
kvadrat mile [2,6 kv.km.]
sq.yd. [abbrev: square yard] kvadrat
yard [0,85 kv.m.]
squab [n.] duva
squad [n.] grupp; patrull; trupp
squadron [n.] eskader [navy], division [air force]
squander [v.] slösa, ödsla bort
square¹ [adj.] fyrkantig, kvadratisk;
vinkelrät; ~ brackets ([])
hakparentes
square² [n.] kvadrat; fyrkant, ruta;
plats, torg
square³ [v.] göra kvadratisk, dela
upp i kvadrater; kvadrera; reglera,
utjämna
squash¹ [n.; ~es] trängsel; mos,
saft; squash [sport, vegetable]
squash² [v.; ~es, ~ed, ~ed] platta till
squeeze [v.] krama, klämma
squid [n.] bläckfisk [fish]
Sr. [abbrev: senior] senior, den äldre
Sri Lankan [adj.] lankesisk
SRO [abbrev: standing room only
(at public event)] bara ståplatser
kvar
SS [abbrev: steamship] ångfartyg
SSN [abbrev: social security num-
ber] personnummer
St. [abbrev: saint; street] sankt; gata

stab [v.; -bbing, -bbed, -bbed]
sticka, genomborra, knivhugga
stability [n.; -ties] stabilitet
stable¹ [adj.] stabil, fast
stable² [n.] stall
stack¹ [n.] trave, hög; stack [IT]
stack² [v.] stacka, trava, stapla
stadium [n.] stadion
staff¹ [n.] personal; stab; ~ room
personalrum
staff² [v.] bemanna, skaffa personal
stag [n.] kronhjort
stage [n.] stadium, steg; etapp; scen
stagger [v.] vackla, ragla; sprida
stain¹ [n.] fläck; bets
stain² [v.] fläcka; färga, bets
stained glass [n.] målat glas
stainless steel [n.] rostfritt stål
staircase [n.] trappa
stairs [n.pl.] trappa; trappuppgång;
up the ~ uppför trappan
stairwell [n.] trapphus
stake [n.] påle, stake; intresse, del,
andel; ~s insats; at ~ på spel
stakeholder [n.] intressent
stale [adj.] gammal, unken, för-
legad; övertränad
stalemate [n.] dödläge, stockning
stall¹ [n.] stand, kiosk; spilta, bås;
tjuvstopp [motor]
stall² [v.] slingra sig, komma med
undanflykter; tjuvstanna [motor]
stamina [n.] uthållighet, styrka
stamp¹ [n.] frimärke; ~ machine
frimärksautomat; put ~s on
frankera
stamp² [v.] stampa med/på, trampa
med/på; stämpla
stance [n.] ställning; inställning,
attityd
stand¹ [n.] stand, kiosk
stand² [v.; stood, stood] stå; ställa
sig; ~ up resa sig
stand-alone [adj.] fristående,
självständig
standard¹ [adj.] standard-, normal-;
~ charge standardpris; ~ deviation
standardavvikelse
standard² [n.] norm; standard; ~ of
living levnadsstandard
standby [adj.] reserv-, ersättnings-

stand-in [n.] ersättare, vikarie
standing [n.] ställning, status, anseende; ~ **room** ståplats; **no ~** stoppförbud
staple [n.] stapelvara, basvara; häftklammer
stapler [n.] häftapparat
star[1] [n.] stjärna; ~ **sign** stjärntecken
star[2] [v.; -rring, -rred, -rred] spela huvudrollen
stare [v.] stirra, glo
start[1] [n.] början, start; ~ **button** startknapp; ~ **menu** startmeny [IT]; ~ **page** startsida [IT]; ~ **tag** starttagg [IT]; **from the ~** från början
start[2] [v.] börja, starta; utgå; sätta igång; ~ **up** köra igång
starter [n.] startmotor; **for ~s** till att börja med; ~ **motor** startmotor
starting [prep.] från och med
startle [v.] skrämma, överraska
start-up [n.] nyetablering; igångsättning
starvation [n.] svält; uthungring
state[1] [n.] läge; stånd; tillstånd; stat, delstat; ~ **college** delstatsuniversitet; ~ **lottery** penninglotteri; ~ **property** statsegendom; ~ **school** statlig skola; ~ **secret** statshemlighet; ~ **subsidy** statligt stöd; ~ **university** delstatsuniversitet
state[2] [v.] uppge, pasta; framlägga; konstatera
stated below [adj.] nedanstående
State Department [n.] Utrikesdepartementet i USA
stateless [adj.] statslös
statement [n.] uttalande; rapport, redovisning; formulering; ~ **of account** kontoutdrag; **make a ~** rapportera
state-run [adj.] statlig
statesman [n.; -men] statsman
static [adj.] statisk; stagnerad
station [n.] station; ~ **manager** stationsansvarig; ~ **wagon** stationsvagn
stationary [adj.] stationär
stationer [n.] pappershandel
statistical [adj.] statistisk

statistics [n.] statistik
statue [n.] staty
status [n.; ~es] stånd; status; ~ **bar** statusfält, statusrad [IT]
statute [n.] lag, stadga
statutory [adj.] lagenlig; reglementerad
stay[1] [n.] upphåll, vistelse; upphov [legal]
stay[2] [v.] stanna; vistas; ~ **at** ta in på; ~ **the night** övernatta; ~ **to the left/right** hålla till vänster/höger
STD [abbrev.] **s**exually **t**ransmitted **d**isease] sexuellt överförd sjukdom
steadily [adv.] jämnt
steady [adj.] stadig, stabil; jämn, ständig; lugn
steak [n.] biffstek; ~ **tartare** råbiff
steal [v.; stole, stolen] stjäla; smyga
steam[1] [n.] ånga; imma
steam[2] [v.] ånga; koka med ånga
steamboat [n.] ångbåt
steamed [adj.] ångkokt
steamer [n.] ångfartyg
steel [n.] stål
steep [adj.] brant; ~ **descent/hill** brant backe
steeple [n.] kyrktorn
steer [v.] styra, manövrera
steering [n.] styrning; ~ **wheel** ratt
stem[1] [n.] stam, stängel; skaft
stem[2] [v.; -mming, -mmed, -mmed] stämma; hämma
step[1] [n.] steg; takt; åtgärd; trappsteg
step[2] [v.; -pping, -pped, -pped] trampa, stiga, kliva; ~ **in** kliva på, stiga på; ~ **inside** stiga in
stepchild [n.] styvbarn
stepdaughter [n.] styvdotter
stepfather [n.] styvfar
stepmother [n.] styvmor
stepson [n.] styvson
stereo [adj.] stereo-, stereofonisk, stereoskopisk; ~ **equipment** stereoanläggning
stereotype [n.] stereotyp
sterile [adj.] steril, ofruktbar
sterilizing solution [n.] steriliseringsvätska
stern[1] [adj.] sträng, bister, hård

stern² [n.] akter
steroid [n.] steroid
stew [n.] ragu, gryta; **beef ~** kalops
steward [n.] steward; hovmästare
stewed [adj.] kokt; **~ fruit** fruktkompott, kompott, kräm; **~
rhubarb** rabarberkompott
stick¹ [n.] pinne, kvist; kapp, stav;
klubba
stick² [v.; stuck] sticka, stoppa;
fästa; sitta fast, haka upp sig
sticky [adj.] klibbig; besvärlig,
omedgörlig; **~ space** fast mellanslag [IT]; **~ tape** tejp
stiff [adj.] styv; stel; trög; **have a ~
back/neck** vara stel i ryggen/
nacken
still¹ [adj.] stilla, tyst; **~ life** stilleben
still² [adv.] alltjämt, fortfarande, ännu
stimulate [v.] stimulera
stimulation [n.] stimulering
stimulus [n.; -li] stimulans, eggelse
sting¹ [n.] stick, styng, bett,
insektsbett
sting² [v.] sticka, stinga; plåga
stir [v.; -rring, -rred, -rred] röra;
väcka; vispa
stitch [n.; ~es] stygn; maska [knit-
ting]; håll [pain]
stochastic [adj.] stokastisk
stock [n.] lager; aktie; spad [broth];
~ exchange/market börsen
Stockholmer [n.] stockholmare
stockings [n.pl.] strumpor
stolen [adj.] stulen; **~ property**
tjuvgods
stomach [n.] mage, magsäck; **~ flu**
maginfluensa; **~ pain** magplåga;
~ ulcer magsår
stomachache [n.] magont, ont i
magen, magsmärtor
stone [n.] sten; **Stone Age** stenåldern
stoney [adj.] stenig
stool [n.] taburett, pall; avföring
[medical]; **~ sample** avföringsprov
stop¹ [n.] stopp; uppehåll; hållplats
[bus]; **~ sign** stopptecken; **last ~**
slutstation
stop² [v.; -pping, -pped, -pped]
stoppa, stanna; låta bli; sluta med,
lägga av; **~ at** stanna vid
stopover [n.] mellanlandning

stopper [n.] kork, propp
stopping [n.]: **no ~** stoppförbud
storage [n.] lagring, förvaring; **~
medium** lagringsmedium [IT]; **~
solution** [contact lenses] förvaringsvätska; **~ space** lagringsplats,
lagringsutrymme
store¹ [n.] affär, varuhus; lager; **~
clerk** expedit; **~ directory**
varuhusinformation; **~ window**
skyltfönster, vitrin
store² [v.] lagra, magasinera,
förvara
store-bought [adj.] butiksköpt
stored in cache memory [adj.]
cachad [IT]
storeroom [n.] förrådsrum;
lagerlokal
storey [n.; see: **story**]
storm¹ [n.] storm; **~ warning**
stormvarning
storm² [v.] rasa; storma
stormy [adj.] oväders-; stormig;
be ~ storma
story [n.; -ries] berättelse, saga;
historia; våning
stout [adj.] bastant, robust; kraftig,
tjok
stove [n.] spis; kamin
straight¹ [adj.] rak; i ordning; ärlig;
ren [no ice]; **~ cable** rak kabel
[IT]
straight² [adv.] rakt, rätt; **~ ahead**
rakt fram
straightedge [n.] linjal
straighten [v.] räta, rikta, ordna
straightforward [adj.] enkel,
okomplicerad; ärlig, direkt
strain¹ [n.] spanning, ansträngning,
utmattning
strain² [v.] anstränga, slita
strained muscle [n.] muskelsträckning
strait [n.] sund
strand [n.] sträng, slinga; strand
strange [adj.] obekant; konstig,
underlig
strangely [adv.] egendomligt,
märkvärdigt
stranger [n.] främling
strap [n.] rem, band; stropp
strategic [adj.] strategisk

str<u>a</u>tegy [n.; -gies] strategi
straw [n.] strå, halm; sugrör
str<u>a</u>wberry [n.; -rries] jordgubbe;
~ **cake** jordgubbstårta; **wild**
str<u>a</u>wberries smultron
stray [v.] ströva, irra; vandra
streak [n.] rand, streck; inslag
stream[1] [n.] bäck, ström, å; stråle;
strömning
stream[2] [v.] strömma, rinna; spruta ut
streamed v<u>i</u>deo [n.] direktuppspelad
video [IT]
str<u>ea</u>ming [n.] direktuppspelning
[IT]
str<u>ea</u>ming m<u>e</u>dia [n.] strömmande
media [IT]
street [n.] gata, väg; ~ **c<u>o</u>rner** gathörn; ~ **food stand** gatukök
strength [n.] styrka, kraft
str<u>e</u>ngthen [v.] stärka, styrka; bli
starkare
str<u>e</u>nuous [adj.] ansträngande;
energisk
stress[1] [n.; ~es] tryck, stress; vikt
stress[2] [v.; ~es, ~ed, ~ed] betona;
stressa
str<u>e</u>ssful [adj.] stressande
stretch[1] [n.; ~es] sträckning; sträcke;
~ **of road** vägsträcke
stretch[2] [v.; ~es, ~ed, ~ed] sträcka,
tänja
str<u>i</u>cken [adj.] drabbad, gripen; **be**
~ **with** drabbas av
strict [adj.] sträng, hård, rigorös
str<u>i</u>ctly [adv.] strängt; ~ **sp<u>ea</u>king**
egentligen
stride[1] [n.] steg, gång
stride[2] [v.; strode, stridden] skrida,
stega, kliva
strike[1] [n.] strejk
strike[2] [v.; struck, struck] slå;
drabba; träffa på
str<u>i</u>ker [n.] strejkare
str<u>i</u>king [adj.] påfallande, markant
string [n.] snore, band; sträng; rad;
~ **beans** brytbönor, skärbönor
strip[1] [n.] remsa; skena; serie
strip[2] [v.; -pping, -pped, -pped]
skrapa av; klä av
stripe [n.] rand, strimma; randning
striped [adj.] randig

strive [v.; strove, striven] sträva
(efter)
stroke[1] [n.] slag; slaganfall; sim-
sätt; streck
stroke[2] [v.] stryka, smeka; glätta
stroll[1] [n.] promenad
stroll[2] [v.] promenera, vandra
strong [adj.] stark, energisk; solid;
utpräglad
str<u>o</u>ngly [adv.] starkt; absolut
struck through [adj.] överstruken
[IT]
str<u>u</u>ctural [adj.] strukturell,
struktur-
str<u>u</u>cture[1] [n.] struktur, byggnad,
sammansättning
str<u>u</u>cture[2] [v.] strukturera
str<u>u</u>ggle[1] [n.] kamp, strid;
ansträngning
str<u>u</u>ggle[2] [v.] kämpa, strida,
anstränga sig; knoga
stub [n.] stump, nabb; **ticket** ~
talong
st<u>u</u>bborn [adj.] envis; besvärlig
stuck [adj.] fast; ~ **up** mallig; **be** ~
sitta fast; **be** ~ **together** sitta ihop;
get ~ haka upp sig, hänga sig
stud [n.] stift, dub, knapp; avels-
hingst
st<u>u</u>dent [n.] elev, student, studerande,
studentska [female]; ~ **card** studentkort; ~ **d<u>i</u>scount** studeranderabatt; ~ **d<u>o</u>rmitory** studentkorridor;
~ **f<u>i</u>nancing** studiemedel; ~ **h<u>ou</u>s-**
ing studentbostad; ~ **room**
studentrum
st<u>u</u>dies [n.pl.] studier, studium;
d<u>o</u>ctoral ~ doktorandstudier
st<u>u</u>dio [n.] ateljé, studio; ~ **ap<u>a</u>rt-**
ment enrumsvåning; ~ **couch**
bäddsoffa
st<u>u</u>dy[1] [n.; -dies] studier, studium;
studie; arbetsrum; ~ **grant**
studiebidrag
st<u>u</u>dy[2] [v.; -dies, -died, -died] läsa,
studera; undersöka; ~ **hard** plugga
stuff[1] [n.] saker; material; stoff
stuff[2] [v.] stoppa; packa, proppa in;
fylla
stuffed [adj.] stoppd; fylld; ~ **<u>a</u>ni-**
mal mjukisdjur [toy]

stuffing [n.] fyllning; stoppning
stuffy [adj.] kvav; täppt
stumble [v.] snubbla, stappla; staka sig
stun [v.; -nning, -nned, -nned] bedöva; överväldiga, chocka
stung [adj.] stucken
stunning [adj.] bedövande; raffig, jättesnygg
stunt [n.] konstnummer, trick
stupid [adj.] dum
stupidity [n.; -ties] dumhet
sturdy [adj.] kraftig, kraftigt byggd; orubblig
style [n.] stil, sätt, mode; format-mall [IT]; ~ **sheet** dokumentmall, stilmall [IT]
stylish [adj.] stilfull, flott
stylist [n.] stylist, hårfrisör
stylistic [adj.] stilistisk
sub [abbrev: submarine; substitute; submarine sandwich] ubåt; vikarie; lång dubbelmacka med kallskuret, ost och tomat
subdomain [n.] underdomän
subfolder [n.] undermapp [IT]
subject[1] [adj.] underlydande; lydande under, underkastad; ~ **to** utsättas för, lida av, beroende av; ~ **to duty/customs** tullpliktig
subject[2] [n.] ämne; motiv; subjekt; ~ **index** sakregister, ämnesindex, ämnesregister
subject[3] [v.] underkuva, utsätta för, belägga med
subjective [adj.] subjektiv
sublet [v.; -letting, -let] hyra ut i andra hand; ~ **apartment** andra-handslägenhet
submarine [n.] ubåt; lång dubbel-macka [med kallskuret, ost och tomat]
submenu [n.] undermeny [IT]
submission [n.] underkastelse; undergivenhet; framläggande, presentation
submit [v.; -tting, -tted, -tted] ut-sätta för; framlägga, presentera
subordinate [adj.] underordnad, lägre
subscribe [v.] prenumerera
subscriber [n.] abonnent

subscript text [n.] nedsänkt text [IT]
subscription [n.] prenumeration, abonnemang; ~ **fee** abonnemang-savgift
subsequent [adj.] följande
subsequently [adv.] därefter, sedan
subsidiary[1] [adj.] understöds-, sido-; ~ **company** dotterbolag
subsidiary[2] [n.; -ries] dotterbolag
subsidy [n.; -dies] subvention, bidrag
substance [n.] material; innehåll, tyngd; stadga
substantial [adj.] verklig, väsentlig; saklig
substantially [adv.] kraftigt; väsentligen
substantive [adj.] väsentlig
substitute[1] [adj./n.] vikarie, ersättning
substitute[2] [v.] använda i stället för; byta ut; ersätta med
substitution [n.] ersättande, utbyte
subtitled film [n.] textad film
subtitles [n.pl.] undertext; underti-tel; textremsa
subtle [adj.] subtil; hårfin, obestämbar
subtraction [n.] subtraktion
suburb [n.] förort
subversive [n.] omstörtande, subversiv
subway [n.] tunnelbana (T-bana); ~ **map** tunnelbanekarta; ~ **train** tunnelbanetåg
succeed [v.] lyckas, ha framgång; efterträda
success [n.; ~es] framgång; succé
successful [adj.] framgångsrik
successfully [adv.] med framgång
succession [n.] följd; succession
successive [adj.] följande, succes-sive, efter varandra
successor [n.] efterträdare; arvinge
succinct [adj.] koncis, kortfattad
such [adj./pron.] sådan, så; ~ **as** sådan som; **in ~ a way that** så pass att
suck [v.] suga; dia; vara botten
suckle [v.] dia, ge di; amma
suckling pig [n.] spädgris
sudden [adj.] plötslig, oväntad

s**u**ddenly [adv.] plötsligt
s**u**e [v.] stämma, åtala; bedja
s**u**ede [adj./n.] mocka
S**u**ez Can**a**l [n.] Suezkanalen
s**u**ffer [v.] lida; ~ **from** lida av
s**u**fferer [n.] lidande
s**u**ffering [n.] lidande, kval
s**u**ffice [v.] räcka; vara tillräcklig för
s**u**fficient [adj.] tillräklig
s**u**fficiently [adv.] tillräckligt
s**u**ffix [n.; ~es] suffix [gram]
s**u**ffrage [n.] rösträtt; univ**e**rsal ~
   allmän rösträtt
s**u**gar [n.] socker; ~ **bowl** sockerskål
s**u**gar-free [adj.] sockerfritt
sugg**e**st [v.] föreslå; antyda; påminna
   om; påstå
sugg**e**stion [n.] förslag; antydan;
   impuls; nyans
s**u**icide [n.] självmord; ~ **bomber**
   självmordsbombare
suit[1] [n.] kostym [man's], dräkt
   [esp. woman's]; rättegång,
   process; färg [cards]
suit[2] [v.] passa, klä; lämpa efter
s**u**itable [adj.] passande, lämplig;
   ~ **for** anpassad till; **be** ~ **for** passa
   till
s**u**itably [adv.] lämpligt, passande
s**u**itcase [n.] väska, resväska
s**u**ite [n.; pronounced: sweet] svit;
   paket [IT]
s**u**ited [adj.] lämplig, anpassad,
   klädsam
s**u**lfur [n.] svavel
s**u**ltry [adj.] kvav
sum[1] [n.] summa; belopp
sum[2] [v.; -mming, -mmed, -mmed]
   summera, addera; ~ **up** sammanfatta
s**u**mmarize [v.] sammanfatta,
   resumera
s**u**mmary [n.; -ries] sammanfattning,
   resumé
s**u**mmer [n.] sommar; ~ **house**
   sommarvilla; ~ **Olympics** sommarolympiaden; ~ s**e**ssion/**term**
   sommartermin; ~ **time** sommartid; ~ **timetable** sommartidtabell;
   ~ vac**a**tion sommarlov, sommarsemester, industrisemester;
   last ~ i somras

s**u**mmit [n.] bergstopp; ~ m**ee**ting
   toppmöte; ~ st**a**tion toppstation
s**u**mmon [v.] kalla samman; kalla
   in; uppmana; sammla
sun [n.] sol; ~ **chair** solstol; ~
   cream solskyddskräm; ~ **hat** sol-
   hat; ~ umbr**e**lla parasoll
Sun. [abbrev: S**u**nday] söndag
s**u**nbathe [v.] sola sig, solbada
s**u**nblock [n.] solskydd, solkräm
   med extra skydd; ~ f**a**ctor
   solskyddsfaktor
s**u**nburn [n.] solbränna, solsveda
s**u**ndae [n.] glasscoupe, sundae
S**u**nday [n.] söndag; ~ **church**
   s**e**rvice söndagsgudstjänst
s**u**ndeck [n.] soldäck
s**u**nglasses [n.pl.] solglasögon
s**u**nlight [n.] solljus
s**u**nny [adj.] solig
s**u**nrise [n.] soluppgång
s**u**nroof [n.] soltak
s**u**nset [n.] solnedgång
s**u**nshade [n.] solskydd, parasoll
s**u**nshine [n.] solsken
s**u**nstroke [n.] solsting
s**u**ntan l**o**tion [n.] solkräm
s**u**ntan oil [n.] sololja
S**U**NY [abbrev: State Univ**e**rsity of
   New York] State University of
   New York
s**u**per [adj.] toppen [colloq]
sup**e**rb [adj.] storartad
superf**i**cial [adj.] ytlig
superint**e**ndent [n.] intendent, ledare, chef; inspektor; kommissarie
sup**e**rior[1] [adj.] högre; förträfflig;
   överlägsen
sup**e**rior[2] [n.] överordnad, förman
sup**e**rlative [adj.] ypperlig, framstående; superlativ
s**u**permarket [n.] snabbköp
s**u**perscript [n.] upphöjd text [IT]
s**u**pertanker [n.] supertanker
sup**e**rvise [v.] övervaka, ha tillsyn
   över
superv**i**sion [n.] bevakning, uppsikt, tillsyn
sup**e**rvisor [n.] övervakare, förman; handledare
s**u**pper [n.] kvällsmat; supé
s**u**pplement[1] [n.] bilaga; tillägg

supplement² [v.] fylla ut, komplettera
supplementary [adj.] tilläggs-; ~ charge tilläggsavgift; ~ instruction stödundervisning; ~ pension tilläggspension
supplier [n.] leverantör
supply¹ [n.; -lies] anskaffning, tillgång, lager; utbud
supply² [v.; -lies, -lied] skaffa, leverera; täcka, ersätta
support¹ [n.] bidrag, försörjning
support² [v.] stötta, stödja, bära; bestyrka, biträda; ge support till [IT]
supporter [n.] anhängare, supporter; gynnare
supporting [adj.] stödjande, understöds-
suppose [v.] anta, förmoda; I ~ väl
supposed [adj.] förmodad, skenbar
supposedly [adv.] förmodligen, antagligen
suppositories [n.pl.] stolpiller
suppress [v.; ~es, ~ed, ~ed] undertrycka, kväva, tysta ned, dämpa; förtiga
supreme [adj.] högst, suverän; enastående, enorm
supt. [abbrev: superintendent] vicevärd, inspektor, chef
sure¹ [adj.] säker
sure² [adv.] för all del
surely [adv.] säkert, väl
surf [v.] surfa; ~ on surfa på
surface [n.] yta; sida; ~ mail vanlig post; ~-to-air missile luftvärnsrobot
surfboard [n.] surfbräda
surfing [n.] surfing; surfande [IT]
surgeon [n.] kirurg
surgery [n.; -ries] kirurgi
surgical [adj.] kirurgisk
surmise [v.] gissa, förmoda
surname [n.] efternamn, familjenamn
surplus¹ [adj.] överskotts-
surplus² [n.; ~es] överskott
surprise¹ [n.] överraskning, förvåning
surprise² [v.] överraska, förvåna
surprised [adj.] förvånad, överraskad

surprising [adj.] överraskande, förvånansvärd
surprisingly [adv.] förvånansvärt
surrealism [n.] surrealism
surrender [v.] överlämna, ge upp, utlämna
surround [v.] omge, omringa
surrounding [adj.] omgivande
surroundings [n.pl.] närmiljö, omgivning
surveillance [n.] bevakning, uppsikt, kontroll
survey¹ [n.] undersökning; översikt; granskning
survey² [v.] överblicka, ge en översikt över; granska
surveyor [n.] landmätare
survival [n.] överlevande; kvarleva
survive [v.] överleva, leva kvar
survivor [n.] överlevande (person)
suspect¹ [n.] misstänkt (person)
suspect² [v.] misstänka
suspected [adj.] misstänkt
suspend [v.] hänga upp; suspendera; tills vidare upphäva
suspense [n.] spanning, väntan
suspension [n.] fjädring [vehicle]; ~ bridge hängbro
suspicion [n.] misstanke, misstänksamhet; aning
suspicious [adj.] misstänksam, misstrogen; suspekt
sustain [v.] tåla, hålla upp; godkänna, acceptera
sustainable [adj.] hållbar, godtagbar
SUV [abbrev: sport utility vehicle] stadsjeep
SW [abbrev: southwest; short wave] sydväst; kortvåg
SWAK [abbrev: sealed with a kiss] stämplat med en kyss [letter]
swallow¹ [n.] svalg [bird]; sväljning
swallow² [v.] svälja
swamp¹ [n.] kärr, sumpmark
swamp² [v.] översvämma
swan [n.] svan
swap [v.; -pped] byta, utbyta
swap file [n.] växlingsfil [IT]
SWAT team [abbrev: special weapons and tactics team] terroristbekämpningsstyrka

sway [v.] svänga, gunga, kränga; ha makt/inflyttande över
swear [v.; swore, sworn] svära, bedyra
swearword [n.] svordom
sweat¹ [n.] svett
sweat² [v.] svettas
sweater [n.] kofta, tröja
sweating [n.] svettning
sweatshirt [n.] träningströja, sweatshirt
Swede [n.] svensk
Sweden [n.] Sverige
Swedish¹ [adj.] svensk; ~ crowns svenska kronor; ~ for immigrants svenska för invandrare (sfi); ~ woman svenska
Swedish² (language) [n.] svenska
sweep¹ [n.] sopning; svep, drag
sweep² [v.; swept] sopa; rusa, svepa
sweet [adj] söt; ~ and sour sauce sötsur sås; ~ corn majs; ~ potato sötpotatis
sweetbreads [n.] kalvbräss
sweets [n.pl.] godis, sötsaker [pl.]; karameller [pl.]
swell [v.; swelled, swollen] svälla, svullna
swelling [n.] svullnad
swerve [v.] vika av, svänga åt sidan
swift [adj.] snabb, hastig; snar
swim¹ [n.] simning, simtur, bad
swim² [v.; swam, swum] simma; ~ fins simfenor [pl.]
swimmer [n.] simmare
swimming [n.] simning; ~ area badplats; ~ belt/float simdyna; ~ instructor simlärare; ~ pool simbassäng; ~ school simskola; ~ trunks badbyxor; go ~ bada; no ~ badförbud

swimsuit [n.] baddräkt, badkläder
swindle [v.] bedra, lura
swing¹ [n.] svängning, sväng
swing² [v.; swung] svänga
Swiss [adj.] schweizisk
switch¹ [n.] strömbrytare, omkopplare; omställning; växel [railroad]
switch² [v.] koppla; växla; ~ off koppla av; ~ on slå på; ~ to växla till
Switzerland [n.] Schweiz
swollen [adj.] svullen
sword [n.] svärd
swordfish [n.; ~/~es] svärdfisk
syllable [n.] stavelse
symbol [n.] symbol
symbolic [adj.] symbolisk
symmetry [n.; -ries] symmetri
sympathetic [adj.] sympatisk
sympathy [n.; -thies] sympati
symphony [n.; -nies] symfoni
symptom [n.] symptom, tecken
synagogue [n.] synagoga
sync [abbrev: synchronization] synkronisering
syndrome [n.] syndrom
syntactic [adj.] syntaktisk [gram]
synthesis [n.; -ses] syntes
synthesized music [n.] datormusik [IT]
synthetic [adj.] syntetisk
Syria [n.] Syrien
Syrian [adj.] syrisk
syrup [n.] sirap; saft
system [n.] system; ~ file systemfil [IT]; ~ program systemprogram [IT]; ~ reengineering systemomarbetning [IT]; ~ tray meddelandefält [IT]
systematic [adj.] systematisk

tab 442 tbsp.

T

tab [n.] flik, lapp; nota; ~ **key** tabb-
tangent [IT]
table [n.] bord; tabell [in document];
~ **lamp** bordslampa; ~ **mat** karottunderlägg; ~ **service** bordservering; ~ **tennis** bordtennis; ~ **wine**
bordsvin; **set the** ~ duka bordet
tableau [n.] tablå
tablecloth [n.] bordduk
tablemat [n.] tablett, underlägg
tablespoon [n.] matsked
tablet [n.] tablett
taboo [adj.] tabu, förbjuden
tack¹ [n.] nubb, spik; kurs, hals
[sailing]
tack² [v.] spika, nubba
tackle [v.] tackla; klara av
tactic [n.] manöver; ~**s** taktik
tag [n.] lapp; tagg [IT]; ~ **question**
[gram.] eller-hur-fråga
tail [n.] stjärt, svans; baksida; ~
light bakljus
tailgate [v.]: **don't** ~ håll avstånd
tailor [n.] skräddare; ~**'s shop**
skrädderi
tailor-made [adj.] skräddarsydd
Tajik¹ [n.] tadzjikisk
Tajik² (**language**) [n.] tadzjikiska
Tajikistan [n.] Tadzjikistan
take [v.; took, taken] ta; föra; ~ **a**
taxi åka taxi; ~ **an exam** tenta; ~
care of sköta; ~ **in** ta emot; ~ **it**
easy ha det bra; ~ **notes** anteckna;
~ **off** ta av (sig), starta; ~ **out** ta ut,
ta med sig; ~ **part** delta, vara med
på
taken [adj.] upptagen
takeoff [n.] start; ~ **area** startplats;
~ **runway** startbana
take-out food [n.] take-away mat
takeover [n.] övertagande; ~ **bid**
uppköpsbud
tale [n.] berättelse, historia, saga
talent [n.] talang, begåvning
talented [adj.] begåvad
talk¹ [n.] samtal; prat; föredrag; ~
show pratshow
talk² [v.] prata, tala; ~ **to you later**
vi hörs

talking [n.] prat
tall [adj.] hög, lång
Talmud [n.] Talmud
tampon [n.] tampong
tan [n.] solbränna
tangerine [n.] mandarin
tangible [adj.] verklig, faktisk;
materiell
tank [n.] tank, reservoar
tanker [n.] tanker
tap¹ [n.] kran; knackning
tap² [v.; -pping, -pped, -pped]
knacka; trumma; avlyssna
tape [n.] band; tejp; ~ **recorder**
bandspelare
tapestry [n.] gobeläng, tapet
target¹ [n.] mål; skottavla
target² [v.] uppsätta som mål
tariff [n.] tariff, tull, taxa
tarragon [n.] dragon
tartar [n.] tandsten [dental]
task [n.] uppgift, uppdrag; ~ **bar**
aktivitetsfält [IT]; ~ **manager**
aktivitetshantare [IT]; ~ **pane**
åtgärdsfönster [IT]
taste¹ [n.] smak
taste² [v.] smaka
tasteful [adj.] smakfull
tasteless [adj.] smaklös
tasty [adj.] välsmakande
tattered [adj.] trasig
Taurus [n.] Oxen [zodiac]
tax¹ [n.; ~es] skatt; ~ **authority**
skattemyndighet; ~ **evasion** skatteflykt; ~ **return** självdeklaration
tax² [v.; ~es, ~ed] beskatta;
anstränga, betunga
taxation [n.] beskattning; ~ **at the**
source källbeskattning
taxi [n.] taxi; ~ **driver** taxichaufför;
~ **license** taxikort; ~ **lane** taxifil; ~
stand taxihållplats
taxpayer [n.] skattebetalare
TB [abbrev: tuberculosis] tuberkulos (tbc)
TBA [abbrev: to be announced]
datum/lokal ej bestämt
T-bone steak [n.] T-benstek
tbsp. [abbrev: tablespoon] matsked

tea [n.] te; ~ **bag** tepåse; ~ **cosy** tevärmare; ~ **cup** tekopp
teach [v.; taught, taught] lära, undervisa
teacher [n.] lärare [m.], lärarinna [f.]
teacher-training college [n.] lärarhögskola
teaching [n.] undervisning; ~s lära
team [n.] lag; grupp
teapot [n.] tekanna
tear[1] [n.] tår [weeping]; reva, hål [hole]; **in** ~**s** i tårar
tear[2] [v.; tore, torn] slita, riva; rusa; ~ **oneself away** slita sig ifrån
tease [v.] reta, förärga
teaspoon [n.] tesked
teat [n.] spene, napp
technical [adj.] yrkesinriktad, teknisk
technically [adv.] formellt sett
technician [n.] tekniker
technique [n.] teknik
technological [adj.] teknologisk
technology [n.] teknologi
teddy bear [n.] nalle
tedious [adj.] långtråkig, ledsam
tee [n.] tee [golf]
teenage [adj.] tonårs-
teenager [n.] tonåring
teens [n.pl.] tonår
teeny [adj.] mycket liten
TEFL [abbrev: teaching of English as a foreign language] undervisning i engelska som främmande språk
tel. [abbrev: telephone] telefon
telecommunications [n.] telekommunikationer
telecommuting [n.] distansarbete
telegram [n.] telegram
telephone[1] [n.] telefon; ~ **bill** teleräkning; ~ **book** telefonkatalog; ~ **booth** telefonkiosk; ~ **call** telefonsamtal; ~ **card** telefonkort, telekort; ~ **company** telefonbolag; ~ **directory** telefonkatalog; ~ **extension** anknytning; ~ **information** nummerbyrå; ~ **jack** telefonjack; ~ **line** telefonledning, telefonlinje; ~ **number** telefonnummer; ~ **operator** telefonist; ~ **receiver** lur; ~

service teletjänst; ~ **subscription** telefonabonnemang; **on the** ~ i telefon
telephone[2] [v.] ringa, telefonera
telephoto lens [n.] teleobjektiv
telescope [n.] teleskop
television [n.] television (tv), teve; ~ **lounge** tv-rum; ~ **set** tv-apparat
tell [v.; told] berätta; säga; tala om
temper [n.] humör, lynne
temperament [n.] temperament, sinnelag, humör
temperance [n.] nykterhet; ~ **movement** nykterhetsrörelse
temperature [n.] temperatur (tempen); feber; **what's the** ~ **today?** vad är det för temperatur i dag? [-10°C=14°F, 0°C=32°F, 10°C= 50°F, 20°C=68°F, 30°C=86°F, 37°C=98.6°F, 100°C=212°F]
template [n.] schablon, mall [IT]
temple [n.] helgedom; tempel; synagoga; tinning [head]
temporarily [adv.] temporärt; för tillfället
temporary [adj.] provisorisk, tillfällig; ~ **work** vakariat
tempt [v.] fresta, locka
temptation [n.] frestelse
ten [num.] tio
tenant [n.] hyresgäst
tend [v.] tendera; vårda, sköta
tendency [n.] tendens; benägenhet
tender [adj.] mjuk, mör, öm
tenderloin [n.] oxfilé
tendon [n.] sena
tenet [n.] grundsats, lära
Tennessee (TN) [n.] Tennessee [delstat i USA]
tennis [n.] tennis; ~ **court** tennisbana; ~ **player** tennisspelare; ~ **racket** tennisracket; ~ **stadium** tennisstadion
tense[1] [adj.] spänd, spännande
tense[2] [n.] tempus, tidsform [gram.]
tension [n.] spänning
tent [n.] tält; ~ **peg** tältpinne; ~ **pole** tältstake; **put up a** ~ tälta
tenth [adj.] tionde
term[1] [n.] tid, period, termin; ~ **of office** mandat; ~s villkor [see:

terms]; ~ **paper** terminsuppsats
term[2] [v.] benämna, kalla
terminal[1] [adj.] dödlig, obotlig
terminal[2] [n.] slutstation; terminal
[IT]
terminate [v.] avsluta; sluta
terminology [n.] terminologi; ~
advice/consulting termtjänst
terms [n.pl.] villkor; förhållande; ~
of agreement avtalsvillkor; ~ **of**
delivery leveransvillkor; ~ **of sale**
försäljningsvillkor, köpvillkor
terra-cotta [n.] terrakotta
terrace [n.] terrass
terrain [n.] terräng
terrible [adj.] förfärlig, hemsk
terribly [adv.] förskräckligt; jätte-;
~ **kind** jättesnällt
terrific [adj.] jättefin
terrify [v.; -fies, -fied] förskräcka,
skrämma
terrifying [adj.] fruktansvärd,
skrämmande
territorial [adj.] territorial; ~ **waters**
territorialvatten
territory [n.; -ries] område, land;
besittning
terror [n.] skräck, fasa
terrorism [n.] terrorism
terrorist [n.] terrorist
TESL [abbrev: teaching of English
as a second language] undervisning i engelska som främmande
språk
TESOL [abbrev: teaching of English to speakers of other languages]
undervisning i engelska som
främmande språk
test[1] [n.] prov, test, förhör; **nuclear**
~ kärnvapenprov
test[2] [v.] prova, testa, pröva
testament [n.] testamente
testimony [n.; -nies] vittnesmål;
bevis
tetanus [n.] stelkramp
Texas (TX) [n.] Texas [delstat i USA]
text [n.] text; ~ **editor** texteditor,
textredigerare [IT]; ~ **message**
textmeddelande, sms [IT]; ~
processing texthantering [IT]; ~
size textstorlek [IT]; ~ **wrap** radbrytning [IT]

textbook [n.] lärobok, skolbok,
handbok
textile [n.] vävnad, textilmaterial;
~**s** textilvaror
texture [n.] textur, struktur
TGIF [abbrev: thank God it's Friday]
tack vare Gud att det är fredag
Thai[1] [adj.] thailändsk
Thai[2] **(language)** [n.] thai
Thailand [n.] Thailand
than [conj./prep.] än [comparisons];
förrän
thank [v.] tacka; ~ **you** tack, tack
ska du ha; ~ **you very much** tack
så mycket
thanks [n.pl./interj.] tack; ~ **and**
the same to you tack, detsamma;
~ **for a nice evening** tack för i
kväll; ~ **for your help** tack för
hjälpen; ~ **to** tack vare
that[1] [adv.] så; ~ **much** så mycket
that[2] [conj.] att; **he said** ~ ... han sa
att ...
that[3] [pron.; those] den/det där,
den/det, denna/detta; ~ **is** det vill
säga
that[4] [rel.pron.] som, vilken; **the**
bus ~ **I took** bussen som jag åkte
med
thatched roof [n.] halmtak
thaw [v.] töa
the [det.] den/det; [postposed article: bok, boken; hus, huset]
theater [n.] teater; ~ **workshop**
teaterverkstad
theft [n.] stöld
their [pron.] deras, sin/sitt/sina
them [pron.obj.] dem [pronounced:
dom]
theme [n.] tema, ämne
themselves [pron.] sig, sig själva
then [adv.] därefter, då, sedan
theology [n.] teologi
theoretical [adj.] teoretisk
theorist [n.] teoretiker
theory [n.; -ries] teori, lära
therapeutic [adj.] terapeutisk
therapist [n.] terapeut
therapy [n.; -pies] terapi
there[1] [adv.] där; **from** ~ därifrån;
to ~ dit; **are we** ~? är vi framme?
there[2] [pron.] ~ **is/are** det finns

thereafter [adv.] därefter
thereby [adv.] därmed
therefore [adv.] därför; alltså
thermal [adj.] värme-, termisk
thermometer [n.] termometer
thermos [n.] termos; ~ **bottle** termosflaska
these [see: **this**]
thesis [n.; theses] tes; avhandling, doktorsavhandling
they [pron.] de [usually pronounced: dom]; man [generic]
thick [adj.] tjock, grov
thickness [n.] tjocklek, grovlek
thief [n.; thieves] tjuv
thigh [n.] lår
thin [adj.] tunn; mager; ~ **client** tunn klient [IT]
thing [n.] sak, ting, grej
think [v.; thought] tänka; tycka, tro; ~ **about** fundera på, tänka på; ~ **of** tänka på; ~ **up** hitta på
thinkable [adj.] tänkbar
thinking [adj./n.] tänkande
third[1] [adj.] tredje
third[2] [n.] tredjedel
third-party [adj.] tredjeparts-
thirsty [adj.] törstig
thirteen [num.] tretton
thirteenth [adj.] trettonde
thirtieth [adj.] trettionde
thirty [num.] trettio
this[1] [adj./pron.] den/det, denna/detta, den/det här; ~ **after-noon/year** i eftermiddag/år
this[2] [adv.] så; ~ **much** så mycket
thither [adv.] dit
Thor [n.] Tor
thorn [n.] törne, torn
thorough [adj.] grundlig, ingående
thoroughly [adv.] grundligt, alldeles
those [see: **that**]; **two of** ~ två sådana
though [adv./conj.] fast; **as** ~ som om; **even** ~ även om
thought [n.] tanke
thoughtful [adj.] tankfull, hänsynsfull
thoughtless [adj.] tanklös
thousand [num.] tusen; ~**s** tusentals
thousandth [adj.] tusende
thread [n.] tråd, garn

threat [n.] hot, fara
threaten [v.] hota
threatening [adj.] hotande
three [num.] tre
three-D (3-D) [abbrev: three di-mensional] tredimensionell (3-D)
three-quarter [adj.] trekvarts-
threshold [n.] tröskel
thrift [n.] sparsamhet
thrill[1] [n.] ilning, rusning
thrill[2] [v.] rysa
thrilled [adj.] överlycklig
thriller [n.] spännande bok/film; thriller
thrilling [adj.] spännande, gripande
thrive [v.] trivas
throat [n.] hals; strupe; ~ **infection** halsinfektion; ~ **lozenges** hals-tabletter; **clear one's** ~ harkla; **sore** ~ ont i halsen
throbbing [adj.] pulserande
throne [n.] tron, stol
throttle [n.] spjäll; **hand** ~ handgas
through[1] [adv.] igenom; direkt; slut; ~ **road** genomfartsväg; **may I come** ~, **please?** kan jag få komma förbi, tack?
through[2] [prep.] genom, igenom
throughout [adv./prep.] alltigenom
throughput [n.] produktion; sys-temkapacitet [IT]
throw[1] [n.] kast
throw[2] [v.; threw, thrown] kasta, slänga; ~ **away** kasta bort; ~ **out** slänga ut
thru [see: **through**]
thrust[1] [n.] stöt, knuff; angrep; syfte
thrust[2] [v.; thrust, thrust] sticka, stoppa; knuffa
thumb [n.] tumme
thumbnail image [n.] miniatyrbild, minibild [IT]
thunder[1] [n.] åska, dån
thunder[2] [v.] åska, dundra
thunderstorm [n.] åskväder
Thurs. [abbrev: Thursday] torsdag
Thursday [n.] torsdag
thus [adv.] så, så här; alltså
thyme [n.] timjan
Tibet [n.] Tibet

tick¹ [n.] fästing [insect]
tick² [v.] ticka; funka; pricka av;
  get ~ed off [colloq.] bli förbannad
ticket [n.] biljett; ~ agency biljettagentur; ~ checker biljettkontrollant; ~ collector konduktör; ~ cost
  biljettpris; ~ counter biljettdisk; ~
  holder biljettinnehavare; ~ machine biljettautomat; ~ office biljettkassa, biljettkontor; ~ window
  biljettlucka; number ~ [in line at
  store] kölapp
ticket-vending machine [n.]
  biljettautomat
tickle [v.] kittla, killa
tic-tac-toe [n.] luffarschack
tide [n.] tidvatten, ebb och flod;
  high ~ högvatten; low ~ lågvatten
tidy¹ [adj.] snygg, städad
tidy² [v.; -dies, -died, -died] städa;
  hyfsa
tie¹ [n.] slips [clothing]; band, länk;
  sliper [railroad]; ~ clip slipsklämma; ~ game oavgjord match
  [sports]
tie² [v.] binda, knyta
tier [n.] rad
Tierra del Fuego [n.] Eldsland
tiger [n.] tiger
tight¹ [adj.] trång, snäv
tight² [adv.] trångt; tätt
tighten [v.] spänna, dra åt
tighter [adj.comp.] trängre
tightly [adv.] fast, hårt, tätt
tights [n.pl.] strumpbyxor
tilde [n.] tilde [IT]
tile [n.] tegel, platta; ~ roof tegeltak
till [conj./prep.] till(s), ända till(s);
  ~ 5 o'clock till kl 5
timber [n.] timmer; virke
time¹ [n.] tid, dags; gång [occasion,
  repetition]; another ~ en annan
  gång; at any ~ när som helst; at
  the same ~ samtidigt; at what ~?
  hur dags?; for the ~ being tills
  vidare; for the first ~ för första
  gången; how many ~s? hur många
  gånger?; in/on ~ i tid; what ~ is
  it? hur mycket är klockan?; ~ immemorial urminnes tider; ~ sharing tidsdelning; ~ to go dags att gå

time² [v.] välja tidpunkten för;
  tajma
timely [adj.] läglig, lämplig, aktuell
times [n.pl.] gånger; 5 ~ a day 5
  gånger om dagen
timetable [n.] tidschema, turlista
timing [n.] val av tidpunkten,
  tajming
tin [n.] tenn; bleck, plåt; ~ foil
  aluminiumfolie
tincture of iodine [n.] jodsprit
tinder [n.] fnöske
tinsel [n.] glitter
T-intersection [n.] T-korsning
tint¹ [n.] färgton; toning
tint² [v.] tona, färga
tiny [adj.] mycket liten
tip¹ [n.] spets, tipp; dricks, serveringsavgift; tips
tip² [v.; -pping, -pped, -pped] tippa,
  stjälpa; ge dricks; ~ off tipsa, varna
tip-off [n.] tips; give someone a ~
  tipsa
tire¹ [n.] bildäck, däck
tire² [v.] trötta; tröttna
tired [adj.] trött, hängig; ~ of school
  skoltrött
tiredness [n.] trötthet
tiring [adj.] jobbig; tröttsam;
  ansträngande
tissue [n.] vävnad; mjukt papper; ~
  paper silkespapper
title [n.] titel, rubrik
TLC [abbrev: tender loving care]
  öm och kärleksfull omvårdnad
TM [abbrev: trademark; transcendental meditation] varumärke,
  firmamärke; transcendental
  meditation
TN [abbrev: Tennessee] Tennessee
  [delstat i USA]
TNT [abbrev: trinitrotoluene] trini-
  trotoluen (TNT)
to¹ [prep.] till, åt, för; i [clock]; [in-
  finitive marker] att; quarter ~
  two kvart i två
to² [adv.] igen; ~ and fro fram och
  tillbaka
toast [n.] rostat bröd
toasted [adj.] rostad
toaster [n.] brödrost

tobacco [n.] tobak
tobacconist [n.] tobaksaffär, tobakshandlare
today [adv.] i dag; ~'s **newspaper** dagens avis; ~'s **special** dagens rätt; **of** ~ nutida
toddler [n.] litet barn; ~s små barn
toe [n.] tå
together [adv./prep.] ihop; tillsammans; ~ **with** tillsammans med; **all** ~ allesammans
toggle [n.] omkopplare [IT]
toil [v.] slita
toilet [n.] toalett, WC; ~ **paper** toalettpapper
toiletries [n.pl.] toalettartiklar
token [n.] tecken, bevis; pollett, jetong; igenkänningstecken [IT]
tolerance [n.] tolerans
tolerate [v.] tolerera, tillåta
toll [n.] avgift, tull
tomato [n.; tomatoes] tomat; ~ **juice** tomatjuice; ~ **salad** tomatsallad; ~ **sauce** tomatsås; ~ **soup** tomatsoppa; **cream of** ~ **soup** redd tomatsoppa
tomb [n.] grav
tomorrow [adv.] i morgon; ~ **evening** i morgon kväll; ~ **morning early** i morgon bitti; **the day after** ~ i övermorgon
ton [n.] ton [1 US (short) ton = 0.9 metric tons]
tone [n.] ton, tonfall; signal
tongs [n.pl.] tång
tongue [n.] tunga; språk
tonic [n.] tonic
tonight [adv.] i natt, i kväll
tonsil [n.] mandel, tonsill
tonsillitis [n.] halsfluss, tonsillit
tonsils [n.pl.] tonsiller
too [adv.] också, även [also]; för [excess]; ~ **long** för länge; ~ **much** för mycket
tool [n.] verktyg; ~ **tip** verktygstips [IT]
toolbar [n.] verktygsfält [IT]
toolbox [n.] verktygslåda
tooth [n.] tand [pl. tänder]; ~ **decay** karies
toothache [n.] tandvärk

toothbrush [n.] tandborste
toothpaste [n.] tandkräm
toothpick [n.] tandpetare
top^1 [adj.] översta, över-, bästa; ~ **sheet** överlakan
top^2 [n.] topp, övre del; snurre [toy]
top^3 [v.] överträffa, slå
topic [n.] ämne, tema; ~ **of/for discussion** diskussionsfråga
top-level domain (TLD) [n.] toppdomän [IT]
toppings [n.pl.] pålägg [sandwich]
Torah [n.] Torah
torch [n.] fackla
torment [v.] plåga
torrent [n.] fors, störtflod
torso [n.] torso
torture^1 [n.] tortyr, kval
torture^2 [v.] tortera, plåga
toss [v.; ~es, ~ed, ~ed] kasta, slänga
total^1 [adj.] fullständig, total, slut-
total^2 [n.] slutsumma
totally [adv.] totalt
touch^1 [n.; ~es] beröring; kontakt; **get in** ~ **with** kontakta, ta kontakt med; **keep in** ~ **with** hålla kontakt med; **we'll be in** ~ vi hörs; ~ **screen** pekskärm
touch^2 [v.; ~es, ~ed, ~ed] röra, vidröra
touching [adj.] rörande
touch-sensitive [adj.] tryckkänslig [IT]
tough [adj.] besvärlig, jobbig, slitig; hård, tuff; seg [meat]
toupee [n.] tupé
tour^1 [n.] tur, rundtur, rundresa, rundvandring; visning; ~ **around the island(s)** örundtur; ~ **guide** resledare; ~ **of the city** stadsrundtur
tour^2 [v.] gå/resa runt; turnera
touring bike [n.] landsvägscykel
tourism [n.] turism
tourist [n.] turist; ~ **attraction** turistattraktion; ~ **dormitory** sommarhotell; ~ **group** turistgrupp; ~ **information** turistinformation; ~ **office** turistbyrå; ~ **pamphlet** turistbroschyr
tournament [n.] turnering, tävling
tow [v.] bogsera; ~ **lift** draglift; ~ **line**

bogserlina; ~ **truck** bärgningsbil
toward [prep.] mot
towel [n.] handduk
tower [n.] torn; borg
towing service [n.] bärgningsservice
town [n.] stad; ~ **center** centrum; ~
    dweller stadsbo; ~ **hall** stadshus;
    ~ **map** stadskarta
townsperson [n.] stadsbo, borgare
toxic [adj.] toxisk, giftig
toy [n.] leksak; ~ **store** leksaksaffär
trace¹ [n.] spår, märke
trace² [v.] spåra, följa
tracing paper [n.] kalkerpapper
track¹ [n.] spår
track² [v.] spåra
trackball [n.] styrkula [IT]
tracker [n.] webbräknare [IT]
trackpad [n.] styrplatta [IT]
tracksuit [n.] träningsoverall,
    joggingoverall
tractor [n.] traktor
trade¹ [n.] handel, affärer, kommers;
    fack; ~ **fair** mässa; ~ **school**
    yrkeskola; ~ **union** fackförening;
    member of a ~ union fackligt
    ansluten; ~ **unions** fackliga orga-
    nisationer; **Ministry of Trade**
    Handelsdepartementet
trade² [v.] handla, driva handel
trade-in [n.] inbyte
trade-off [n.] utbyte, kompromis
trader [n.] handlare; köpman
trade-union movement [n.]
    fackföreningrörelse
trading [n.] handel; ~ **firm**
    handelsfirma
tradition [n.] tradition, hävd
traditional [adj.] traditionell
traditionally [adv.] traditionellt
traffic [n.] trafik; ~ **accident** trafik-
    olycka; ~ **circle** rondell; ~ **jam**
    trafikstockning; ~ **lane** körfält, fil;
    ~ **light** trafikljus; ~ **police** trafikpo-
    lis; ~ **problems** trafiksvårigheter;
    oncoming ~ trafik från motsatt
    riktning
traffic-free zone [n.] trafikfri zon
tragedy [n.; -dies] tragedi
tragic [adj.] tragisk
trail¹ [n.] spår; led, stig

trail² [v.] släpa; spåra
trailer [n.] släp; husvagn; trailer
    [film]
train¹ [n.] tåg; ~ **schedule** tågtider;
    ~ **station** järnvägsstation, tågsta-
    tion; ~ **traveller** tågresenär
train² [v.] öva, träna; utbilda sig
trained [adj.] utbildad
trainee [n.] praktikant, lärling
trainer [n.] tränare, handledare
training [n.] utbildning, träning
trait [n.] karaktärsdrag, egenskap
traitor [n.] förrädare
tramp around [v.] luffa, vandra
    omkring
transaction [n.] affär, transaktion
transcript [n.] avskrift; betyg
    [school]
transcription [n.] avskrivning;
    avskrift; transkribering
transfer¹ [n.] överföring; ~ **bus**
    transferbuss; ~ **ticket** övergångs-
    biljett; ~ **time** överföringstid
transfer² [v.; -rring, -rred, -rred]
    flytta över; överföra; byta [train]
transform [v.] förvandla, omvandla
transformation [n.] förvandling,
    omvandling
transformer [n.] transformator
transfusion [n.] transfusion
transit [n.] genomresa; transport;
    kollektivtraffik; **in** ~ på genomresa
transition [n.] övergång
translate [v.] översätta
translation [n.] översättning
translator [n.] översättare
transmission [n.] vidarebefordran,
    överföring; växellåda; utsändning
    [radio]
transmit [v.] vidarebefordra,
    sprida, överföra; sända ut [radio]
transparent [adj.] genomskinlig
transplant [n.] plantera om;
    transplantera
transport¹ [n.] transport; transport-
    medel; trafik; ~ **service** färdtjänst
transport² [v.] transportera
transportation [n.] transport;
    kommunikation; **means of** ~
    transportmedel
trap¹ [n.] fälla, snara

trap² [v.; -pping, -pped, -pped]
fånga, snärja, ertrappa
trash [n.] skräp, sopor [pl.]; ~ **bag**
sopsäck, ~ **can** soptunna
trauma center [n.] akuten
traumatic [adj.] traumatisk
travel¹ [n.] resa; ~ **account** reseskildring; ~ **agency** resebyrå,
reseföretag; ~ **clock** reseur; ~
guide reseguide
travel² [v.] fara, resa, åka; färdas
traveler [n.] resande, resenär; ~'**s**
check resecheck
traveling [adj.] resande; rese-; ~
companion resekamrat; ~ **salesman** handelsresande, representant
tray [n.] bricka
tread [v.; trod, trodden] träda, stiga,
gå; trampa
treasure¹ [n.] skatt, klenod
treasure² [v.] värda; uppskatta
treasurer [n.] kassör, skattmästare
treasury [n.] skattkammare; finansdepartementet
treat¹ [n.] bjudning; nöje
treat² [v.] behandla; betrakta; trak-
tera, bjuda på
treatment [n.] behandling; ~ **room**
behandlingsrum
treaty [n.; -ties] fördrag, avtal
tree [n.] träd; ~ **line** trädgräns; ~
trunk trädstam
treeless [adj.] skoglös, kal
tremble [v.] darra, skaka; bäva
tremendous [adj.] kolossal, enorm;
fantastisk
tremendously [adv.] väldigt
trench [n.; ~es] skyttegrav; dike,
ränna
trend [n.] trend, tendens
trespassing [n.] intrång; **no** ~ tillträde förbjudet
trial [n.] prov, försök; rättegång,
process; ~ **version** provversion
triangle [n.] triangel
tribe [n.] folkstam, släkt
tribunal [n.] domstol, tribunal
tribute [n.] gärd, hyllning; tribut
trick¹ [n.] knep, list; konstgrepp,
trick
trick² [v.] lura
trigger¹ [n.] avtryckare, utlösare

trigger² [v.] starta, utlösa
trillion [n.] biljon [one million
millions]
trim¹ [n.] skick; putsning, klippning
trim² [v.; -mming, -mmed, -mmed]
klippa, putsa; dekorera [tree];
putsa [hair]
trimester [n.] period på tre må-
nader; termin [school; 3 ~s per
school year]
trimmings [n.pl.] garnityr; rester;
dekorationer
trinity [n.; -ties] trefaldighet
trio [n.] trio
trip¹ [n.] resa, tur; **have a good** ~
trevlig resa
trip² [v.; -pping, -pped, -pped]
snubbla, snava
triple [adj.] trefaldig, trippel-
tripod [n.] stativ
triumph [n.] triumf, seger
triumphal arch [n.] triumfbåge
trivial [adj.] obetydlig, banal
Trojan horse [n.] trojansk häst
trolley [n.] spårvagn; ~ **bus** trådbuss; ~ **stop** spårvagnshållplats
troop [n.] trupp; mängd
trophy [n.; -phies] trofé
tropical [adj.] tropisk
Tropic of Cancer [n.] Kräftans
vändkrets
Tropic of Capricorn [n.] Stenbockens vändkrets
trot [v.; -tting, -tted, -tted] trava
trouble¹ [n.] oro, bekymmer, besvär
trouble² [v.] oroa, bekymra, besvära
troublesome [adj.] besvärande,
krånglig
trousers [n.pl.] byxor, långbyxor
trout [n.] forell
truck [n.] lastbil; ~ **driver** lastbilschaufför; ~ **exit** utfart för lastbil
true [adj.] sann, riktig, äkta; trogen
truly [adv.] verkligt, riktigt; **Yours**
~ Högaktningsfullt
trumpet [n.] trumpet
truncate [v.] stympa, skära av
truncation [n.] avskärning, trunkering [IT]
trunk [n.] stam [tree]; koffert;
bagagelucka, bagageutrymme
trust [v.] lita på

trust**ee** [n.] förtroendeman; styrelsemedlem
truth [n.] sanning; ~ **table** sanningstabell
try[1] [n.; tries] försök
try[2] [v.; trying, tried, tried] försöka, pröva; ~ **on** prova; ~ **out** testa
trying [adj.] ansträngande, krävande, pressande
T-shirt [n.] T-skjorta, T-tröja
tsp. [abbrev: t**ea**spoon] tesked
tube [n.] rör, tub, slang
tuberculosis [n.] tuberkulos
tuck [v.] stoppa in/ner
Tues. [abbrev: T**ue**sday] tisdag
Tuesday [n.] tisdag
tuition [n.] undervisning; undervisningsavgift
tulip [n.] tulpan
tumble [v.] ramla; tumla
tumbler [n.] vattenglas
tumor [n.] tumör, svulst
tuna [n.] tonfisk
tune[1] [n.] melodi, låt; stämning
tune[2] [v.] stämma; ställa in
Tunisia [n.] Tunisien
Tunisian [n.] tunisisk
tunnel [n.] tunnel
turbot [n.] piggvar [fish]
turkey[1] [n.] kalkon
Turkey[2] [n.] Turkiet
Turkish[1] [adj.] turkisk; ~ **bath** turkiskt bad
Turkish[2] (**language**) [n.] turkiska
turn[1] [n.] vändning, varv; tur; ~ **signal** blinker; **it's your** ~ det är din tur
turn[2] [v.] skruva, svänga, vrida, vända; ~ **around** skruva sig om; ~ **down** skruva ned [radio]; ~ **left/right** svänga till vänster/höger, ta till vänster/höger; ~ **off** ta av [road], stänga [radio]; ~ **on** sätta på; ~ **on a light** tända; **please** ~ **over** var god vänd (vgv)
turnip [n.] rova, kålrot
turnkey [adj.] nyckelfärdig
turnout [n.] valdeltagande [election]
turnover [n.] omsättning [business]; knyte [pastery]
turquoise [n.] turkos

turret [n.] litet torn
turtle [n.] sköldpadda; ~ **soup** sköldpaddssoppa
turtleneck [n.] polokrage
tutor [n.] handledare; privatlärare
tutorial [n.] lektion, handledning
tutoring [n.] privata lektioner
tuxedo [n.] smoking
TV [abbrev: television] television (tv); ~ **antenna** tv-antenn; ~ **channel** tv-kanal; ~ **program** tv-program; ~ **socket** tv-uttag
TV-dinner [n.] färdiglagad måltid
tweezers [n.pl.] pincett
twelfth [adj.] tolfte; ~ **grade** tolfte klass [last year of high school]
twelve [num.] tolv
twentieth [adj.] tjugonde
twenty [num.] tjugo
twice [adv.] två gånger
twig [n.] kvist
twilight [n.] skymning
twin [n.] tvilling; ~ **beds** två enkelsängar
twine[1] [n.] snöre, garn
twine[2] [v.] tvinna, spinna; linda, knyta
twist[1] [n.] vridning; krök
twist[2] [v.] vrida, sno; tvinna
twisted [adj.] snodd, vriden; stukad [ankle]
two [num.] två
two-cycle engine mix [n.] tvåtaktsblandning
two-lane highway [n.] två-filig väg
two-room apartment [n.] tvårumslägenhet
two-way traffic [n.] dubbelriktad trafik, mötande trafik
two-year college [n.] förberedande college
TX [abbrev: Texas] Texas [delstat i USA]
type [n.] art, typ; stil, tryck
typewriter [n.] skrivmaskin
typhoid fever [n.] tyfoidfeber, tyfus
typhus [n.] fläcktyfus
typical [adj.] typisk
typically [adv.] typiskt

U

U- [abbrev: University of ...
(UConn = University of Connecticut)] delstatsuniversitetet i ...
UAE [abbrev: United Arab Emirates] Förenade arabemiraten
ubiquitous [adj.] överallt förekommande
UC [abbrev: University of California] University of California
UCLA [abbrev: University of California, Los Angeles] University of California i Los Angeles
UCSD [abbrev: University of California, San Diego] University of California i San Diego
UFO [abbrev: unidentified flying object] oidentifierat flygande föremål (ufo)
ugh [interj.] usch
ugly [adj.] ful; otrevlig; sur
UHF [abbrev: ultrahigh frequency] ultrahög frekvens (UHF)
UHT [abbrev: ultrahigh temperature, ultraheat treated, ultra-pasteurized] ultrahög temperatur (UHT)
UK [abbrev: United Kingdom] Förenade kungariket [Storbritannien och Nordirland]
Ukraine [n.] Ukraina
Ukrainian¹ [adj.] ukrainsk
Ukrainian² (language) [n.] ukrainska
ulcer [n.] sår; **gastric ~** magsår
ultimate [adj.] slut-; avgörande
ultimately [adv.] slutligen, till sist
ultrasound [n.] ultraljud
umbrella [n.] paraply, parasol
umpire [n.] domare
UN¹ [abbrev: United Nations] Förenta nationerna (FN)
un-² [prefix] o-
unable [adj.] **be ~ to go** inte kunna gå
unacceptable [adj.] oacceptabel
unaccustomed [adj.] ovan; ovanlig
unaffected [adj.] opåverkad; naturlig
unafraid [adj.] orädd
unaided [adj.] utan hjälp

unambiguous [adj.] entydig, otvetydig
unanimous [adj.] enhällig, enig
unanswered [adj.] obesvarad
unarmed [adj.] obeväpnad
unashamed [adj.] ogenerad; skamlös
unassailable [adj.] oangripbar, oantastlig
unattainable [adj.] ouppnåerlig
unattended [adj.] utan tillsyn, försummad; obesökt
unattractive [adj.] charmlös, osympatisk
unauthorized [adj.] obehörig
unavoidable [adj.] oundviklig
unaware [adj.] omedveten, okunnig
unawares [adv.] omedvetet; oväntat
unbalanced [adj.] obalanserad, sinnesförvirrad; ojämn; inte balanserad
unbearable [adj.] odräglig
unbelievable [adj.] otrolig
unbiased [adj.] fördomsfri, objektiv
unbounded [adj.] obegränsad, oinskränkt
unbroken [adj.] obruten; oavbruten; oöverträffad
unbuttoned [adj.] knäppad upp; oinskränkt
UNC [abbrev: University of North Carolina] University of North Carolina
uncanny [adj.] hemsk; förunderlig, otrolig
uncarbonated [adj.] utan kolsyra
uncertain [adj.] osäker
uncertainty [n.] osäkerhet
unchanging [adj.] oföränderlig, konstant
uncle [n.] morbror [maternal], farbror [paternal]
unclear [adj.] oklar, svårförståelig
uncomfortable [adj.] obekväm
uncommitted [adj.] oengagerad; neutral; opartisk
uncommonly [adv.] ovanligt, sällsynt

unconcerned [adj.] obekymrad,
   oberörd
unconditional [adj.] villkorslös;
   obetingad
uncongenial [adj.] motbjudande;
   olämplig
unconscious [adj.] medvetslös;
   omedveten
uncontrolled [adj.] okontrollerad,
   obehärskad
uncountable [adj.] oräknelig;
   oräknebar
uncover [v.] täcka av; avslöja
undeniably [adv.] onekligen
under [adv./prep.] under, nedanför,
   nere; mindre än
underclassmen [n.pl.] studerande i
   första och andra årskurserna
underdeveloped [adj.] underutvecklad
underestimate [v.] underskatta,
   undervärdera
undergo [v.; -goes, -went, -gone]
   genomgå, undergå; lida
undergraduate [n.] studerande,
   student; ~ education universitets-
   studier
underground [adj./adv.] under-
   jordisk; illegal; ~ garage underjordsgarage
underlie [v.; -lay, -lain] bilda un-
   derlaget till; vara grundvalen till
underline [v.] stryka under; betona
underlined [adj.] understruken [IT]
underlining [n.] understrykning
   [IT]
underlying [adj.] underliggande,
   bakomliggande; bärande
undermine [v.] underminera,
   undergräva
underneath [adv./prep.] under,
   inunder
underpants [n.pl.] kalsonger
underpass [n.] vägtunnel,
   gångtunnel
underscore[1] [n.] understreck [IT]
underscore[2] [v.] stryka under;
   betona
underscored [adj.] understruken
   [IT]; betonad
undershirt [n.] linne, undertröja

underside [n.] undersida
understand [v.; -stood, -stood]
   förstå, begripa, fatta
understandable [adj.] förståelig,
   begriplig
understanding [n.] förstående
undertake [v.; -took, -taken]
   företa; förbinda sig, ta på sig
undertaking [n.] företag;
   förbindelse; löfte
undertaker [n.] begravningsentre-
   prenör
underwater [adj.] undervattens-
underwear [n.] underkläder
underworld [n.] undre världen;
   kriminella kretsar; underjorden
underwriter [n.] försäkringsgivare,
   garant
undesirable [adj.] icke önskvärd,
   ovälkommen
undisguised [adj.] oförställd, öppen
undisputed [adj.] obestrid
undisturbed [adj.] ostörd, orörd,
   oberörd
undo [v.; -does, -did, -done] ångra
undoing [n.] fördärv, olycka,
   undergång
undoubted [adj.] otvivelaktig, obe-
   stridlig
undress [v.; ~es, ~ed, ~ed] klä av
   (sig)
undue [adj.] otillbörlig, obehörig;
   onödig, överdriven
unduly [adv.] onödigt; otillbörligt
unearth [v.] gräva upp, upptäcka
uneasiness [n.] oro, ängslan
uneasy [adj.] orolig, ängslig
uneducated [adj.] obildad,
   okultiverad
unemployed [adj.] arbetslös
unemployment [n.] arbetslöshet;
   ~ assistance kontant arbetsmarknadsstöd (KAS); ~ benefits arbetslöshetsersättning; ~ benefits office
   A-kassa (abbrev: arbetslöshetskassa)
unending [adj.] ändlös, evig
unequal [adj.] ojämn
unequivocal [adj.] otvetydig
UNESCO [abbrev: United Nations
   Educational, Scientific and Cultural Organization] UNESCO

[FN:s underorgan för främjande
av internationellt samarbete inom
områdena utbildning, vetenskap
och kultur]
uneven [adj.] ojämn; ~ **road surface** ojämn väg
unexpected [adj.] oväntad,
oförutsedd
unexpired [adj.] inte utlupen
unexplained [adj.] oförklarad
unfair [adj.] orättvis, ojust; ~ **competition** illojal konkurrens
unfaithful [adj.] otrogen, trolös
unfamiliar [adj.] obekant, okänd,
ovanlig
unfashionable [adj.] omodern
unfavorable [adj.] ogynnsam,
ofördelaktig
unfit [adj.] olämplig, oduglig, oförmögen, ovärdig
unfold [v.] veckla ut; utveckla,
uppenbara
unforeseen [adj.] oförutsedd
unforgivable [adj.] oförlåtlig
unfortunate [adj.] olyckligt lottad;
beklaglig, olycklig
unfortunately [adv.] tyvärr
unfriendly [adj.] ovänlig; skadlig
för
ungrateful [adj.] otacksam
unguarded [adj.] obevakad;
oförsiktig
unhappily [adv.] olyckligt
unhappiness [n.] olycka, elände
unhappy [adj.] olycklig, misslyckad,
olämplig
UNHCR [abbrev: United Nations
High Commission for Refugees]
UNHCR [FN:s flyktingkommis-
sariat]
unhealthy [adj.] ohälsosam, osund,
skadlig
unheard [adj.] ohörd; ~ **of** okänd,
oerhörd
unheroic [adj.] oheroisk
unhesitating [adj.] beslutsam,
tveklös
UNICEF [abbrev: United Nations
Children's Fund] UNICEF [FN:s
barnfond]
unification [n.] sammanslagning,
enande

unified [adj.] förenad
uniform[1] [adj.] likforming, enhetlig
uniform[2] [n.] uniform
uniformed [adj.] uniformsklädd
uniformity [n.] likformighet;
jämnhet
unify [v.; -fies, -fied] förena, föra
samman
unilateral [adj.] ensidig
unimaginative [adj.] fantasilös
unimportant [adj.] oviktig,
obetydlig
uninitiated [adj.] oinvigd
uninsured [adj.] utan försäkring
unintentionally [adv.] oavsiktligen
uninterested [adj.] ointresserad
uninteresting [adj.] ointressant
**uninterruptible power supply
(UPS)** [n.] avbrotsfri kraft
union [n.] förening; union; fackförening; förbindelse
unique [adj.] unik
unison [n.] samklang; endräkt,
samförstånd
unit [n.] enhet
unite [v.] ena, förena
united [adj.] förenad
United Arab Emirates [n.] Förenade arabemiraten
United Nations (UN) [n.] Förenta
Nationerna (FN)
United States (USA) [n.] Förenta
Staterna (USA)
unity [n.] enhet; helhet; endräkt
Univ. [abbrev: university]
universitet
universal [adj.] allmän, universell;
~ **suffrage** allmän rösträtt
universe [n.] universum, världsalltet
university [n.] högskola, universitet; ~ **department** institution; ~
examination tenta, tentamen; ~
town universitetsort
unjust [adj.] orättfärdig, orättvis
unjustified [adj.] oberättigad,
omotiverad
unkempt [adj.] okammad; vanskött
unkind [adj.] ovänlig, inte skonsam
unknown [adj.] okänd
unlawful [adj.] olaglig, olovlig,
otillåten

unleaded [adj.] blyfri; ~ gasoline
  blyfri bensin
unleash [v.; ~es, ~ed] släppa lös;
  utlösa
unleavened [adj.] ojäst
unless [conj.] om inte, utan att
unlike[1] [adj.] olik
unlike[2] [prep.] olikt, i motsats till
unlikely [adj.] osannolik, föga
  lovande
unlimited [adj.] obegränsad;
  gränslös
unload [v.] lossa; frigöra; ta ut
  patronerna ur (geväret)
unlock [v.] låsa upp
unlucky [adj.] oturlig; be ~ ha otur
unmarried [adj.] ogift
unmentionable [adj.] onämnbar
unmistakable [adj.] omisskännlig
unmoved [adj.] oberörd; orörd
unnatural [adj.] onaturlig
unnecessary [adj.] onödig
unnecessarily [adv.] onödigt;
  onödigtvis
UNO [abbrev: see: UN]
unofficial [adj.] inofficiell
unnoticed [adj.] obemärkt
unordered list [n.] oordnad lista
  [IT]
unorthodox [adj.] oortodox;
  okonventionell
unpack [v.] packa upp, packa ur
unpaid [adj.] obetald; utan lön
unpleasant [adj.] obehaglig, otrevlig
unpopular [adj.] impopulär
unprecedented [adj.] exempellös,
  utan motstycke
unpredictable [adj.] oförutsägbar;
  opålitlig
unprepared [adj.] oförberedd
unpretentious [adj.] anspråkslös
unprofitable [adj.] olönsam;
  ofruktbar
unquestioned [adj.] obestridd
unread [adj.] oläst [IT]
unreadable [adj.] oläsbar
unreal [adj.] overklig; inbillad
unrealistic [adj.] orealistisk
unreality [n.] overklighet
unreasonable [adj.] oförnuftig,
  orimlig

unreliable [adj.] opålitlig
unrest [n.] oro
unrewarding [adj.] föga givande,
  otacksam
unrivaled [adj.] makalös, utan like
unruffled [adj.] oberörd; stilla,
  slät; okrusad
unruly [adj.] ostyrig, besvärlig
unsaid [adj.] osagd
unsatisfactory [adj.] otillfredsstäl-
  lande
unsaturated fat [n.] omättat fett
unseen [adj.] osynlig, dold; okänd
unsettled [adj.] orolig, ostadig;
  oavgjord
unskilled [adj.] oerfaren, okunnig;
  outbildad; ~ labor outbildad
  arbetskraft, grovarbete
unsound [adj.] inte frisk; osund;
  ohållbar; orolig; osäker
unspeakable [adj.] outsäglig,
  namnlös; avskyvärd
unspoiled [adj.; also: unspoilt]
  ofördärvad, inte bortskämd
unspoken [adj.] outtalad
unstable [adj.] ostadig
unsteady [adj.] ostadig, vacklande;
  ombytlig; ojämn
unsuccessful [adj.] misslyckad
unsuitable [adj.] olämplig, inte
  passande
unsure [adj.] osäker, oviss, tveksam
unsuspecting [adj.] omisstänksam
unsustainable [adj.] ohållbar
unsympathetic [adj.] oförstående,
  osympatisk
untapped [adj.] outnyttjad
unthinkable [adj.] otänkbar
untidy [adj.] stökig
untie [v.] knyta upp, lossa
until [conj./prep.] tills, ända till, till
  dess; ~ further notice tills vidare;
  not ~ inte förrän
unto [prep.; see: to]
untold [adj.] omätlig, outsäglig
untouched [adj.] orörd, obeskadad
untrue [adj.] osann, falsk; illojal
unused [adj.] oanvänd; ovan
unusual [adj.] ovanlig
unvisited [adj.] obesökt
unwanted [adj.] oönskad

unwelcome [adj.] ej välkommen, oönskad
unwilling [adj.] ovillig
unwillingly [adv.] ogärna
unwise [adj.] oklok
unwittingly [adv.] oavsiktligt; aningslöst
unworthy [adj.] ovärdig
unwritten [adj.] oskriven
up[1] [adv.] upp [motion], uppåt; uppe [position]; ~ **there** där uppe; ~ **to** fram till; ~ **to and including** till och med (t o m); ~ **to now** hittills; **be** ~ [not in bed] vara uppe; **what's** ~? hur är läget?
up[2] [prep.] uppför, uppe på
upbringing [n.] barnuppfostran
update[1] [n.] uppdatering [IT]
update[2] [v.] uppdatera [IT]
updated [adj.] uppdaterad [IT]
upgrade[1] [n.] uppgradering [IT]
upgrade[2] [v.] uppgradera [IT]
uphold [v.] upprätthålla, vidmakthålla; godkänna, gilla
upholster [v.] polstra, klä
uplink [n.] uplink [IT]
upload [v.] överföra; lägga upp, uppladda [IT]
upon [prep.; see: **on**] på
upper [adj.] övre; ~ **berth** överbädd; ~ **body** överkropp; ~ **class** överklassen
upper-case letters [n.pl.] versaler
upperclassmen [n.pl.] studerande i tredje och fjärde årskurserna
upright [adj./adv.] upprätt, lodrät; hederlig
upset[1] [adj.] upprörd; ~ **stomach** dålig mage, mage i olag
upset[2] [v.; upset] stjälpa; bringa oordning; rubba, uppröra
upside down [adv.] upp och ned
upstairs [adv.] på övervåningen, uppe
upstream [adv.] uppströmmen, mot strömmen
up-to-date [adj.] à jour, aktuell
upward [adj.] uppåtriktad, stigande
upwards [adv.] uppåt, upp, uppför
uranium [n.] uran
Uranus [n.] Uranus

urban [adj.] stads-, urban
urge[1] [n.] lust
urge[2] [v.] försöka övertala, uppmana; tillråda; driva på
urgency [n.] angelägenhet; allvar
urgent [adj.] brådskande, angelägen; ivrig; ~ **shipment** ilgods; **be** ~ vara bråttom
urinary tract infection [n.] urinvägsinfektion
urinate [v.] urinera, kasta vatten
urine [n.] urin; ~ **test** urinprov
URL [abbrev: **u**niform **r**esource **lo**cater] webbadress, URL [adresstandard för resurser po Internet] [IT]
urologist [n.] urolog
US[1] [adj.; abbrev: **U**nited **S**tates, **American**] amerikansk
us[2] [pron.obj.: we] oss
USA [abbrev: **U**nited **S**tates of **A**merica] Förenta staterna (USA)
USAF [abbrev: **U**nited **S**tates **A**ir **F**orce] amerikanska flygvapnet
usage [n.] behandling; (språk)bruk
USB port [abbrev: **u**niversal **s**erial **b**us] USB-port [IT]
USC [abbrev: **U**niversity of **S**outhern **C**alifornia] University of Southern California
USCG [abbrev: **U**nited **S**tates **C**oast **G**uard] amerikanska sjöräddningen
USDA [abbrev: **U**nited **S**tates **De**partment of **A**griculture] Jordbruksdepartementet i USA
use[1] [n.; pronounced: yoos] bruk, användande; användning, nytta; **make** ~ **of** anlita; **it's no** ~ **to** det är ingen idé att; **no longer in** ~ nedlagd
use[2] [v.; pronounced: yooz] använda, bruka; ~ **up** förbruka; ~ **before** använd innan; ~ **chains or snow tires** använd kedjor eller vinterdäck; ~ **headlights** använd helljus; ~ **the underpass** använd gångtunneln
used [adj.] begagnad, använd; ~ **to smoke** brukade röka; **get** ~ **to** vara van vid, vänja sig
useful [adj.] användbar

useless [adj.] oduglig, oanvändbar; meningslös

user [n.] användare; ~ **agent** användaragent [IT]; ~ **assistance** användarhjälp [IT]; ~ **defined** användardefinierad [IT]; ~ **ID** användar-ID, användaridentitet, kontonamn [IT]; ~ **interface** användargränssnitt [IT]; ~ **license** användarlicens [IT]; ~ **name** användarnamn [IT]; ~ **support** användarstöd [IT]; ~'**s instructions** bruksanvisning

user-friendly [adj.] användarvänlig [IT]

USMC [abbrev: United States Marine Corps] amerikanska marinsoldatkåren

USN [abbrev: United States Navy] amerikanska flottan

USS [abbrev: United States Ship] amerkanskt örlogsfartyg

USSR [abbrev: Union of Soviet Socialist Republics] Sovjetunionen

usual [adj.] vanlig; **as** ~ som vanligt

usually [adv.] vanligen, vanligtvis; **I** ~ **drive** jag brukar åka bil

UT [abbrev: Utah] Utah [delstat i USA]

Utah (UT) [n.] Utah [delstat i USA]

utensils [n.pl.] matbestik

utility [n.] nytta; **public** ~ kommunalt affärsverk; ~ **program** hjälpprogram [IT]

utopian [adj.] utopisk

utter[1] [adj.] fullständig, absolut

utter[2] [v.] låta höra; yttra

utterance [n.] uttalande, yttrande

utterly [adv.] fullständigt, ytterst

u-turn [n.] u-sväng

UV [abbrev: ultraviolet] ultraviolett

UVA [abbrev: University of Virginia] University of Virginia

V

V [abbrev: volt] volt

VA [abbrev: Virginia; Veterans Administration] Virginia [delstat i USA]; krigsveteransverket i USA

vacancy [n.; -cies] ledigt rum; **no ~** fullbelagt; **job ~** ledig plats

vacant [adj.] ledig, tom; uttryckllös

vacation [n.] lov, semester; **~ camp grounds** semesterby; **~ cottage** semesterstuga; **~ resort** semesterort; **~ schedule** semesterschema; **go on ~** semestra

vaccinate [v.] vaccinera

vaccinated [adj.] vaccinerad

vaccination [n.] vaccinering; **~ card** vaccinationskort

vaccine [n.] vaccin

vacuum [n.] vakuum; **~ cleaner** dammsugare

vacuum-packed [adj.] vakuumförpackad

vague [adj.] vag, oklar, obestämd

vaguely [adv.] vagt

vain [adj.] fåfäng; **in ~** förgäves

valid [adj.] giltig, gällande; **be ~** gälla

validate [v.] bekräfta

validity [n.; -ties] giltighet; validitet

valley [n.] dal

valuable [adj.] värdefull; **~s** värdesaker

valuation [n.] värdering; värde

value[1] [n.] värde; valuta; **~s** värderingar

value[2] [v.] värdera, uppskatta

value-added tax (VAT) [n.] mervärdesskatt (moms); **~ included** moms inräknad; **~ receipt** moms-kvitto

valve [n.] ventil

van [n.] skåpbil; minibuss; **delivery ~** varubil

vanilla [n.] vanilj; **~ custard** vaniljsås

vanish [v.; ~es, ~ed, ~ed] försvinna

variable[1] [adj.] varierande

variable[2] [n.] variabel, växlande

variant [n.] variant

variation [n.] variation, avvikelse; variant

varied [adj.] omväxlande, varierande, skiftande

variety [n.; -ties] ombyte, omväxling; mängd; varietet, variant; **~ show** varieté

various [adj.] olika, diverse

vary [v.; -ries, -ried, -ried] variera, skifta; avvika

varying [adj.] varierande; **~ cloud cover** växlande molnighet

vase [n.] vas

vast [adj.] väldig, stor

VAT[1] [abbrev: value-added tax (sales tax)] mervärdesskatt (moms)

vat[2] [n.] fat, kar, tank

Vatican City [n.] Vatikanstaden

Vatican State [n.] Vatikanstaten

vault [n.] valv

VCR [abbrev: video cassette recorder/player] video

VD [abbrev: venereal disease] venerisk sjukdom (VS), könssjukdom

VDU [abbrev: visual display unit] bildskärmsterminal [IT]

V-E Day [abbrev: Victory in Europe Day (May 8, 1945)] segerdagen i Europa

veal [n.] kalvkött; **~ fillet** kalvfilé; **~ stew** kalvfrikassé; **roast ~** kalvstek

vector [n.] vektor

vector-based [adj.] vektorbaserad

vegan [adj.] vegan-

vegetable [n.] grönsak; **~ beef soup** köttsoppa; **~ plate** grönsakstallrik; **~ soup** grönsakssoppa

vegetarian[1] [adj.] vegetarisk

vegetarian[2] [n.] vegetarian

vegetation [n.] växtliv; vegeterande

veggies [abbrev: vegetables] grönsaker

vehicle [n.] fordon, vagn; medel, medium; **~ entrance** infart; **~ exit** utfart; **~ registration document** bilregistreringspapper; **~ traffic** motortrafik

veil [n.] slöja

vein [n.] ven, åder

Velcro [n.] kardborrband; ~ **faste-ning** kardborrknäppning
velocity [n.; -ties] hastighet
velvet [n.] sammet
vending machine [n.] automat
vendor [n.] säljare
venereal disease (VD) [n.] könssjukdom
vengeance [n.] hämnd
Venice [n.] Venedig
venison [n.] hjortkött, rådjurskött; **roast** ~ rådjurstek
ventilation [n.] luftväxling; ventilering
ventilator [n.] ventil; fläkt; respirator
venture[1] [n.] företag, projekt; risktagande; ~ **capital** riskkapital
venture[2] [v.] våga, försöka
venue [n.] plats, ställe
Venus [n.] Venus
veranda [n.] veranda
verbal [adj.] ord-, verbal; muntlig; verb-
verdict [n.] utslag; dom; **give a** ~ fälla utslag
verify [v.; -fies, -fied] kontrollera, verifiera
Vermont (VT) [n.] Vermont [delstat i USA]
versatile [adj.] mångsidig, mångkunnig
verse [n.] vers, poesi; strof
version [n.] version, variant
versus [prep.] mot; kontra
vertical [adj.] vertikal, lodrät; ~ **bar** lodstreck [IT]
very[1] [adj.] själva; allra
very[2] [adv.] mycket, jätte-, väldigt; ~ **big** jättestor; **not** ~ inte särskilt
vessel [n.] fartyg, skepp; kärl; **blood** ~ blodkärl
vest [n.] väst
vet [abbrev: veterinarian; veteran] veterinär; veteran
veteran [n.] veteran
veterinarian [n.] veterinär
veterinary inspection [n.] veterinärkontrollbesiktning
veto[1] [n.] veto
veto[2] [v.] inlägga veto mot

VFW [abbrev: Veterans of Foreign Wars] krigsveteransförbund i USA
VHF [abbrev: very high frequency] mycket höga frekvenser (VHF), ultrakortvåg (UKV)
via [prep.] genom, över
viable [adj.] genomförbar; livskraftig
vibration [n.] vibration; svängning, pendling
vicar [n.] kyrkoherde
vice versa [adv.] vice versa, och tvärtom
vice-president [n.] vicepresident; vice verkställande direktör
vicinity [n.; -ties] närhet; **in the** ~ **of** i närheten av
vicious [adj.] illvillig, brutal; ilsken; hemsk
victim [n.] offer; drabbad person
victory [n.; -ties] seger
video [adj./n.] video, videoapparat [IT]; ~ **camera** videokamera [IT]; ~ **card** videokort [IT]; ~ **clip** videosnutt [IT]; ~ **display unit (VDU)** bildskärm [IT]; ~ **game** videospel [IT]; ~ **on demand (VOD)** beställvideo [IT]; ~ **recorder** videospelare [IT]
videocassette [n.] videokassett [IT]
videotape [n.] videoband [IT]
videotaped [adj.] spelad in på video [IT]
view[1] [n.] läge, utsikt, vy; ~ **of the sea** havsutsikt, sjöutsikt
view[2] [v.] se på, betrakta
viewer [n.] visare; tittare [TV]
viewfinder [n.] sökare
viewing [n.] besiktning, visning; ~ **gallery** åskådarläktare
viewpoint [n.] utsiktspunkt
vigorous [adj.] kraftig, energisk
viking [n.] viking
village [n.] by; ~ **festival** byfest
villager [n.] bybo
villain [n.] bov, skurk
vinaigrette salad dressing [n.] vinägrettsås
vine [n.] vinranka, ranka
vinegar [n.] ättika [cider]; vinäger [wine]

violation [n.] brott, överträdelse, kränkning

violence [n.] våld; häftighet

violent [adj.] våldsam, häftig

violently [adv.] våldsamt

violet [n.] viol; violett

violin [n.] violin, fiol

VIP [abbrev: very important person] höjdare, högdjur, VIP

virgin [n.] jungfru

Virginia (VA) [n.] Virginia [delstat i USA]

Virgo [n.] Jungfrun [zodiac]

virtual [adj.] virtuell; ~ reality virtuell verklighet [IT]

virtually [adv.] faktiskt, i realiteten

virtue [n.] dygd; fördel

virus [n.] virus; ~ attack virusangrepp [IT]; ~ program virusprogram [IT]; ~ protection virusskydd [IT]

visa [n.] visum

viscous [adj.] viskös

visibility [n.; -ties] sikt; synlighet

visible [adj.] synlig; tydlig

vision [n.] syn

visit[1] [n.] besök; have a ~ from ha/få besök av

visit[2] [v.] besöka; hälsa på

visited [adj.] besökt [IT]

visiting hour(s) [n.] besökstid

visitor [n.] besökare

visor [n.] skärm

visual [adj.] syn-, visuell; ~ acuity synskärpa

visually impaired [adj.] synskadad

vital [adj.] livsviktig; livs

vitamin [n.] vitamin

vivid [adj.] livlig, livfull

V-J Day [abbrev: Victory in Japan Day (August 15, 1945)] segerdagen över Japan

V-necked [adj.] v-ringad i halsen

vocabulary [n.] vokabulär; ordlista

vocal [adj.] röst-, stäm-; muntlig; högljudd

vocalist [n.] sångare

vocational [adj.] yrkes-; ~ school yrkesförberedande skola; ~ training yrkesutbildning; ~ training course yrkeskurs

voice [n.] stämme, röst; ~ over Internet (VOI) Protocol Internettelefoni, IP-telefoni [IT]; ~ recognition röstigenkänning [IT]; ~ synthesis talsyntes [IT]

voice-mailbox [n.] röstbrevlåda [IT]

vol. [abbrev: volume] volym

volatile [adj.] flyktig, labil; ~ memory flyktigt minne [IT]

volcano [n.] vulkan

volleyball [n.] volleyboll

volt (V) [n.] volt (V)

voltage [n.] spänning, strömstyrka

volume [n.] volym

voluntarily [adv.] frivilligt

voluntary [adj.] frivillig; finansierad genom frivilliga bidrag

volunteer[1] [n.] frivillig, voluntär

volunteer[2] [v.] anmäla sig frivilligt; frivilligt erbjuda

vomit [v.] spy, kräkas

vomiting [n.] kräkning

vote[1] [n.] röst; röstertal; omröstning; rösträtt

vote[2] [v.] rösta; välja till; rösta för

voter [n.] väljare

voting [n.] omröstning, val; ~ district valdistrikt; confidentiality of ~ valhemlighet

voucher [n.] kupong, voucher

vowel [n.] vokal

voyage [n.] resa, färd

VP [abbrev: vice-president] vice-president, vice verkställande direktör

vs. [abbrev: versus (against)] mot, kontra

VT [abbrev: Vermont] Vermont [delstat i USA]

vulnerable [adj.] utsatt

VW [abbrev: Volkswagen] Volkswagen

W

W [abbrev: watt; west, w**e**stern; w**o**men's t**oi**let] watt; väster, väst; damer [toalett]

WA [abbrev: W**a**shington (state)] Washington [delstat i USA]

w_a_**ding pool** [n.] plaskdamm

w_a_**ffle** [n.] våffla

wag [v.; -gged] vifta (på)

wage [n.] lön; ~ **freeze** lönstopp; **m**_o_**nthly** ~ månadslön

w_a_**gon** [n.] vagn

waist [n.] midja, liv

w_a_**istcoat** [n.] väst

wait[1] [n.] väntan, väntetid

wait[2] [v.] vänta; ~ **and see** avvaktande; ~ **for** vänta på; ~ **staff** serveringspersonal

w_a_**iter** [n.] servitör, kypare; ~! hovmästarn!

w_a_**iting** [n.] väntan; ~ **list** väntelista; ~ **room** väntrum, väntsal

w_a_**itress** [n.] servitris; ~! fröken!

wake[1] [n.] vaka, minnestund; kölvatten

wake[2] [v.; woke/waked, woken/ waked] vakna [intr.]; väcka [tr.]; ~ **up** [intr.] vakna

w_a_**ke-up call** [n.] väckning

walk[1] [n.] promenad, vandring

walk[2] [v.] gå, promenera; vandra; ~ **on** beträda

w_a_**lker** [n.] fotvandrare; gåstol [babies], gåbock [handicapped]

w_a_**lking**[1] [adj.] gående, gång-; ~ **aid** gånghjälpmedel; ~ **route** vandringsled

w_a_**lking**[2] [n.] gång, fotvandring

walk-in m_e_**dical c**_e_**nter** [n.] akuten

w_a_**lkway** [n.] gångstig

wall [n.] mur, vägg; ~ **s**_o_**cket** vägguttag; c**i**ty ~s ringmur

w_a_**llet** [n.] plånbok

w_a_**lleyed pike** [n.] gös

w_a_**llpaper** [n.] tapet; skrivbordsunderlägg [IT]; **put up/hang** ~ tapetsera

w_a_**ll-to-w**_a_**ll c**_a_**rpeting** [n.] heltäckningsmatta

w_a_**lnut** [n.] valnöt

wand [n.] trollspö; läspenna [IT]

w_a_**nder** [v.] vandra omkring

w_a_**nna-be** [n.; colloq. someone who wants to be] en som drömmer att bli något

want[1] [n.] behov, önskning; brist; nöd

want[2] [v.] vilja, begära; behöva; sakna

w_a_**nted** [adj.] önskad; ~ [want to buy] köpes; **be** ~ önskas

war [n.] krig; **the Cold War** det kalla kriget; ~ **cr**_i_**minal** krigsförbrytar; ~ **mem**_o_**rial** krigsmonument; ~ **of liber**_a_**tion** befrielsekrig; **d**_u_**ring the** ~ under kriget; **wage** ~ föra krig

ward [n.] avdelning; distrikt; myndling

w_a_**rdrobe** [n.] garderob

w_a_**rehouse** [n.] lager, magasin

warm[1] [adj.] varm; hjärtlig; häftig

warm[2] [v.] värma (sig)

w_a_**rmly** [adv.] hjärtligt

warmth [n.] värme; hetsighet

warn [v.] varna; varsla

w_a_**rning** [n.] varning; ~ **light** varningsljus; ~ **sign** varningsmärke

w_a_**rrant** [n.] order; grund; **arr**_e_**st** ~ häktningsorder

w_a_**rranty** [n.; -ties] garanti

w_a_**rrior** [n.] krigare; ~ **king** krigarkung

W_a_**rsaw** [n.] Warszawa

w_a_**rship** [n.] krigsskepp

w_a_**rtime** [n.] krigstid

w_a_**ry** [adj.] varsam, vaksam

was [v.past: be] var

wash[1] [n.; ~es] tvättning; tvätt

wash[2] [v.; ~es, ~ed, ~ed] tvätta; ~ **by hand** handtvätta; ~ **d**_i_**shes** diska; ~ **s**_e_**parately** tvätta separat

w_a_**sh-and-w**_e_**ar** [adj.] strykfri

w_a_**shbasin** [n.] tvättställ, tvättfat, handfat

w_a_**shbowl** [n.] tvättställ, tvättfat, handfat

w_a_**shcloth** [n.] tvättlapp

w_a_**shing** [n.] tvättning; tvätt; ~

dishes diskning; **~ in water** vattentvätt; **~ machine** tvättmaskin
Washington (WA) [n.] Washington [delstat i USA]
washproof [adj.] tvättäkt
washrag [n.] tvättlapp
washroom [n.] tvättrum
washstand [n.] tvättställ
WASP¹ [abbrev: White Anglo-Saxon Protestant] person som hör till etablissemanget, borgarbracka
wasp² [n.] geting
waste¹ [adj.] avfalls-
waste² [n.] slöseri; avfall, sopor, skräp
waste³ [v.] slösa bort, kasta bort, förslösa; försitta
wastebasket [n.] papperskorg
wasteful [adj.] slösaktig, oekonomisk; **be ~** slösa
wastepaper basket [n.] papperskorg
watch¹ [n.; ~es] armbandsklocka, armbandsur; vakt
watch² [v.; ~es, ~ed, ~ed] se på, titta på; bevaka; passa på; **~ out for** akta sig för, se upp för
watchmaker [n.] urmakare; **~'s** uraffär
water¹ [n.] vatten; **~ bottle** vattenflaska; **~ can** vattendunk; **~ consumption** vattenförbrukning; **~ course** vattendrag; **~ faucet** vattenkran; **~ glass** vattenglas; **~ heater** varmvattenberedare; **~ mill** vattenkvarn; **~ skis** vattenskidor; **~ sports** vattensport; **~ tower** vattentorn; **~ wings** simdynor, armkuddar; **not drinking ~** ej dricksvatten
water² [v.] vattna
watercolor [n.] akvarell, vattenfärg
watercress [n.; ~es] källkrasse, krasse
waterfall [n.] vattenfall, fors
watering can [n.] vattenkanna
watermelon [n.] vattenmelon
waterproof [adj.] vattentät
water-ski [v.] åka vattenskidor
waterskiing [n.] vattenskidåkning; **go ~** åka vattenskidor
watt (W) [n.] watt

wave¹ [n.] våg; bölja
wave² [v.] vinka; bölja
wavy [adj.] vågig
waxing [n.] benvaxning [legs]
waxwork [n.] vaxfigur
way [n.] väg; sätt; **~ in** entré; **~ of life** livsstil; **~ out** utgång; **get in the ~** komma emellan; **this ~, please** den vägen
we [pron.] vi
weak [adj.] svag
weaken [v.] försvaga(s)
weakness [n.; ~es] svaghet
wealth [n.] förmögenhet, rikedom
wealthy [adj.] förmögen, rik
weapon [n.] vapen; **~s of mass destruction (WMD)** massförstörelsevapen
wear¹ [n.] användning, bruk; kläder; slitning
wear² [v.; wore, worn] ha på sig, bära; nöta(s), slita(s); **~ out** slita ut
wearing [adj.] klädd i
weary [adj.] trött
weather [n.] väder, väderlek; **~ forecast** väderleksutsikt, väderprognos, väderleksrapport
weave [v.; wove, woven] väva; flätta, binda
web [n.] väv, spindelväv; nät, webb- [IT]; **~ browser** webbläsare, surfbräda [IT]; **~ channel** webbkanal [IT]; **~ counter** webbräknare [IT]; **~ host** webbhotell [IT]; **~ page** webbsida [IT]; **~ services** webb services [IT]; **~ site** webbplats [IT]; **~ storage** webbaserad datalagring, webblagring [IT]; **~ surfer** nätsurfare [IT]
web-based [adj.] nätbaserad, webbaserad [IT]
webcasting [n.] webbutsändning, push-teknik [IT]
webmaster [n.] webbansvarig, webbmästare [IT]
webzine [n.] webbtidning [IT]
Wed. [abbrev: Wednesday] onsdag
wedded [adj.] gift, äkta; **~ husband** äkta man; **~ wife** äkta hustru
wedding [n.] vigsel, bröllop; **~ day** bröllopsdag

wedge [n.] kil
Wednesday [n.] onsdag
weed [n.] ogräs
week [n.] vecka; **in two ~s time** om fjorton dagar; **last** ~ i förra veckan; **per** ~ per vecka; **this** ~ den här veckan; ~ **pass** veckokort
weekday [n.] veckodag, vardag
weekend [n.] helg, veckoslut; ~ **cottage** semesterstuga, fritidshus; ~ **rate** helgtariff; **during the** ~ i helgen; **have a good** ~ trevligt helg
weekly[1] [adj.] vecko-; ~ **ticket** veckobiljett; ~ **magazine** vecko-tidning
weekly[2] [adv.] varje vecka
weep [v.; wept] gråta
weigh [v.] väga; tynga
weight [n.] vikt; ~ **training** styr-keträning; **try to lose** ~ banta
weird [adj.] underlig; kuslig
welcome[1] [adj.] välkommen; **you are** ~ ingen orsak, för all del, var så god
welcome[2] [n.] mottagande
welcome[3] [v.; ~d] välkomna, hälsa välkommen
welfare [n.] välfärd; socialarbete, socialvård; **be on** ~ leva på under-stöd; ~ **state** välfärdssamhället
well[1] [adj.; better, best] frisk, bra; **I am** ~ jag mår bra; **get** ~! krya på dig!
well[2] [adv.; better, best] bra, gott, noga, väl
well[3] [interj.] nåja, tja; nämen
well[4] [n.] brunn; källa
well-behaved [adj.] välartad, snäll
well-being [n.] välbefinnande
well-done [adj.] välgjord; genom-stekt, välstekt [meat]
well-equipped [adj.] välutrustad
well-known [adj.] välkänd
well-paid [adj.] välbetald
were [v.past: be] var, vore
west[1] [adj.; see: **western**]
west[2] [n.] väster
western[1] [adj.] väst-, västlig, västra
Western[2] [n.] västern [film]
West Virginia (WV) [n.] West Vir-ginia [delstat i USA]

wet[1] [adj.] våt; ~ **paint** nymålad; ~ **snow** blötsnö; ~ **suit** vätdräkt
wet[2] [v.; wet/wetted] väta, fukta
whale [n.] val
wharf [n.; -rves/~s] kaj
what[1] [interrog.pron.] vad, vilken/vilket/vilka; ~ **did you say?** vad sa du?; ~ **do you know!** nämen!; ~ **fun** vad kul; ~ **time is it?** Hur mycket är klockan?; **or** ~? eller hur?; ~ **a gorgeous day!** vilken härlig dag!
what[2] [rel.pron.] vad, den/det som
whatever [rel.pron.] vad som helst, vilken/vilket/vilka ... än
whatsoever [see: **whatever**]
wheat [n.] vete; ~ **flour** vetemjöl
wheel [n.] hjul; ratt; **steering** ~ ratt
wheelchair [n.] rullstol; ~ **accessi-ble** rullstolsanpassad; ~ **hike** rull-stolsvandring; ~ **lifting platform** rullstolslyft; ~ **ramp** rullstolsramp; ~ **suitable** rullstolsanpassad; ~ **user** rullstolsburen person
wheelchair-bound [adj.] rull-stolsbunden
when[1] [conj.] när, då; sedan
when[2] [interrog.adv.] när, hur dags; **by** ~ senast när; **from** ~ från vilken tid; **since** ~ sedan när
whence [adv.] varifrån
whenever [adv.] när som helst
where[1] [interrog.adv.] var; ~ **to** vart; ~ **is the dining room?** var finns matsalen?
where[2] [rel.adv.] där
whereas [conj.] medan; eftersom
whereby [adv.] varigenom, varmed
wherever [adv.] varhelst
whether [conj.] om, huruvida; ~ **he wants to or not** antingen han vill eller inte
whey cheese [n.] mesost, messmör
which[1] [interrog.pron.] vilken/vilket/vilka
which[2] [rel.pron.] som, vilken/vilket/vilka
whichever [rel.pron.] vilken/vilket/vilka ... än
while[1] [conj.] medan, så länge; ~ **you wait** medan ni väntar

while² [n.] stund, tag; **after a ~**
efter en stund
whining [adj.] grinig
whip¹ [n.] piska
whip² [v.; -pping, -pped, -pped]
vispa; rusa
whipped/whipping cream [n.]
vispgrädde
whirl [v.] virvla; rusa
whisk [n.] visp
whisky [n.] whisky
whisper¹ [n.] viskning, rykte
whisper² [v.] viska; susa
whistle¹ [n.] visselpipa, vissla
whistle² [v.] vissla; susa
white¹ [adj.] vit/vitt, blek; **~ beans**
vita bönor; **~ bread** vitt bröd; **~
cabbage** vitkål; **~ pages** vita
sidorna; **~ pepper** vitpeppar; **~
sauce** vitsås; **~ vinegar** ättika; **~
wine** vitt vin
white² [n.] vitfärg
whitebait [n.] småsill [fish]
white-collar worker [n.]
kontorsarbetare
whitefish [n.] sik
whither [interrog.adv.] vart
whiting [n.] vitling [fish]
WHO¹ [abbrev: World Health Or-
ganization] Världhälsoorganisa-
tionen
who² [interrog.pron.] vem
who³ [rel.pron.] som
whoever [pron.] vem som helst
whole¹ [adj.] hel, full-; **~ wheat
bread** fullkornsbröd; **~ wheat
flour** fullkornsmjöl
whole² [n.] helhet; **on the ~**
överhuvudtaget
wholesale [adv.] en gros
wholesaler [n.] grosshandlare,
grossist
wholly [adv.] helt, fullt
whom [pron.obj.: who] vem
whooping cough [n.] kikhosta
whose [pron.poss.: who] vars
why¹ [interrog.adv.] varför; **~ is
that?** hur kommer det?
why² [rel.adv.] varför
WI [abbrev: Wisconsin] Wisconsin
[delstat i USA]

wicked [adj.] ond, elak; stygg;
hemsk
wide¹ [adj.] bred, vid; felriktad
wide² [adv.] långt, vitt
widely [adv.] vitt, allmänt
widen [v.] utvidga, bredda
wider [adj.comp.] breddare
wide-ranging [adj.] vittomfattande
widespread [adj.] omfattande
widow [n.] änka; horunge [word
processing]
widower [n.] änkling
width [n.] bredd, vidd
wife [n.; wives] hustru, fru, maka
wig [n.] peruk
wiggly [adj.] slingrande, vågig
wild¹ [adj.] vild; stormig; tokig; **~
animal(s)** vilt; **~ boar** vildsvin; **~
duck** vildand; **~ West** Vilda
Västern
wild² [adv.] vilt
wildcard [n.] ersättningstecken,
jokertecken [IT]
wilderness [n.] vildmark, ödemark
wildlife [n.] djurliv
wildly [adv.] vilt
will¹ [n.] vilja; testamente
will² [v.; want] vilja
will³ [v.modal, future] ska, komma
att, vill
willing [adj.] villig
willingly [adv.] gärna
willingness [n.] villighet
wilted [adj.] vissen
win¹ [n.] seger; vinst
win² [v.; won, won] vinna, segra
wind¹ [n.] vind; **~ conditions** vindförhållanden; **~ force/strength**
vindstyrka; **the ~s** blåsinstru-
menten [music]
wind² [v.; wound] spola, slingra;
slingra sig
windbreak [n.] vindskydd
windbreaker [n.] vindtät jacka
winding [adj.] krokig
windmill [n.] väderkvarn
window [n.] fönster; lucka [post of-
fice]; **~ frame** fönsterkarm; **~
pane** fönsterruta; **~ seat** fönsterplats; **~ table** fönsterbord
windowsill [n.] fönsterbräde

windshield [n.] vindruta; ~ **clean-ing fluid** spolarvätska; ~ **washer** vindrutespolare; ~ **wiper** vindrutetorkare

windsurf [v.] vindsurfa

windsurfing board [n.] vindsurfingbräda

windy [adj.] blåsig; be ~ blåsa

wine [n.] vin; ~ list vinlista; ~ vinegar vinäger; red ~ rödvin; white ~ vitvin

wineglass [n.] vinglas

wing [n.] vinge; flygel [building]

winner [n.] vinnare, segrare

winning [adj.] vinnande

winter [n.] vinter; ~ darkness vintermörker; ~ season vintersäsong; ~ sports resort vintersportort; ~ schedule vinter tidtabell; ~ vacation vinterlov, vintersemester

wipe [v.] torka

wire[1] [n.] tråd, metalltråd; barbed ~ taggtråd

wire[2] [v.] telegrafera

Wisconsin (WI) [n.] Wisconsin [delstat i USA]

wisdom [n.] visdom; ~ tooth visdomstand

wise [adj.] vis, klok

wish[1] [n.; ~es] önskemål; ~ list önskelista

wish[2] [v.; ~es, ~ed, ~ed] önska

wit [n.] vett, klokhet; espri

witch [n.; ~es] häxa, käring

with [prep.] med

withdraw [v.; -drew, -drawn] dra tillbaka; ta bort; ta ut

withdrawal [n.] tillbakadragande; uttag

withhold [v.; -held] hålla inne; ~ing tax källskatt, A-skatt

within [adv.] inom, inuti, inne i; from ~ inifrån; ~ a week inom en vecka

without [prep.] utan, utan att

witness[1] [n.; ~es] vittne

witness[2] [v.; ~es, ~ed, ~ed] bevittna; vittna

witty [adj.] kvick, spirituell

wizard [n.] trollkarl; mästare; guide, vägvisare [IT]

WMD [abbrev: weapons of mass destruction] massförstörelsevapen

wolf [n.; wolves] varg, ulv

woman [n.; women] kvinna; kvinnlig; ~ writer kvinnlig författare

women's [n.pl.] kvinn-, dam-; ~ liberation kvinnorörelse; ~ magazine damtidning; ~ movement kvinnorörelse; ~ organization kvinnoförening

wonder[1] [n.] under; undran

wonder[2] [v.] undra

wonderful [adj.] underbar

won't [contr: will not] ska inte, kommer inte att

wood [n.] trä, ved; ~ carving träfigur, träsnideri; ~ grouse tjäder; ~ products industry träindustri; of ~ i trä; ~s skog

woodcock [n.] morkulla

woodcut [n.] träsnitt

wooden [adj.] trä-, i trä; ~ church träkyrka; ~ knife träkniv; ~ spoon träsked

woodland [n.] skogsmark

wool [n.] ull; ylle; all/pure ~ helylle

woolen [adj.] ull-; ylle-

word [n.] ord; löfte; ~ class ordklass; ~ order ordföljd; ~ processor ordbehandlare [IT]

wording [n.] formulering

word-processing program [n.] ordbehandlingsprogram [IT]

work[1] [n.] arbete, jobb, insats; verk; ~ experience arbetslivserfarenhet; ~ from home distansarbete; ~ permit arbetstillstånd (AT); ~ week arbetsvecka

work[2] [v.] arbeta, jobba; fungera; ~ hard slita

workbench [n.] arbetsbänk

workbook [n.] arbetsbok

worker [n.] arbetare; ~s' organization arbetstagarsorganisation

workforce [n.] arbetarkraft

working [adj.] arbetar-; ~ class district arbetarkvarter; ~ conditions arbetsförhållande; ~ day arbetsdag, vardag; ~ environment arbetsmiljö; ~ hours arbetstid

working-class [adj.] arbetar-
workings [n.pl.] verk; verksamhet
workload [n.] arbetsbörda
workman [n.; -men] arbetare
workplace [n.] arbetsplats
works [n.] fabrik, bruk; public ~
offentliga arbeten
workshop [n.] verkstad;
studiegrupp, seminarium
workstation [n.] arbetsstation [IT]
world [n.] värld, jord; ~ champion
världsmästare; ~ citizen världsmedborgare; ~ of work yrkesliv;
~ war världskrig
World Wide Web (www) [n.]
webben (www) [IT]
world-famous [adj.] världsberömd
worldwide¹ [adj.] världsomfattande,
global
worldwide² [adv.] över hela världen
worm [n.] mask, kryp
worn [adj.] sliten; trött
worried [adj.] bekymrad, orolig
worrisome [adj.] besvärlig,
plågsam; orolig
worry¹ [n.; -rries] oro, bekymmer
worry² [v.; -rries, -rried] oroa (sig),
bekymra (sig)
worse [adj./adv.comp.] sämre; värre
worship [n.] dyrkan; gudstjänst;
freedom of ~ fri religionsutövning
worst¹ [adj./adv.superl.] sämst,
värst
worst² [n.] the ~ den/det/de värsta
worth¹ [adj.] värd
worth² [n.] värde
worthwhile [adj.] värdefull, lönande
worthy [adj.] värdig; ~ of värd
would [v.modal] skulle; ville;
skulle vilja; brukade; ~ like to
skulle vilja
would-be [adj.] tilltänkt; så kallad
wound¹ [n.] sår, skada
wound² [v.] såra, skada
WP [abbrev: word processing]
ordbehandling [IT]
wpm [abbrev: words per minute]
ord i minuten

wrap [v.; -pping, -pped, -pped] slå
in, svepa in
wrapping [n.] inslagning, packning,
förpackning; ~ paper omslagspapper
wreath [n.] krans; slinga
wreck¹ [n.] vrak; ruin
wreck² [v.] förstöra, fördärva,
skrota
wreckage [n.] vrakdelar; ruin
wrench [n.; ~es] vridning;
skiftnyckel
wrist [n.] handled
wristwatch [n.; ~es] armbandsklocka, armbandsur
write [v.; wrote, written] skriva; ~
protect skrivskydda [IT]
writer [n.] författare; skrivare
writing [n.] skrift; skrivning; handstil; ~ pad skrivblock, block; ~
paper brevpapper
written [adj.] skriftlig, skriven; ~
test skriftlig prov
wrong¹ [adj.] fel, snett; ~ number
fel nummer; dial the ~ number
komma fel
wrong² [adv.] fel, orätt
wrong³ [n.] orätt, ont
wrongly [adv.] fel, orätt
wt. [abbrev: weight] vikt
WV [abbrev: West Virginia] West
Virginia [delstat i USA]
WWF [abbrev: Worldwide Fund
for Nature] Världsnaturfonden
WWI/II [abbrev: World War One/
Two] första/andra världskrigen
www [abbrev: World Wide Web]
webben
WY [abbrev: Wyoming] Wyoming
[delstat i USA]
Wyoming (WY) [n.] Wyoming
[delstat i USA]
WYSIWYG [abbrev: what you see
is what you get] skärmen visar
samma sak som en utskrift

X

X [abbrev: unknown person/thing; times; wrong answer; mark, cross] okänd person/sak; gånger; felaktig svar; kryss

x-axis [n.; -axes] x-axel

X-chromosome [n.] X-kromosom

xenophobia [n.] främlingshat, xenofobi

XL [abbrev: extra large] extra stor

X-mas [abbrev: Christmas] Jul

XML [abbrev: Extensible Markup Language] XML [standard för strukturmarkering av textbaserade elektroniska dokument]

xoxo [abbrev: hugs and kisses (closing in letter)] kyssar

X-rated [adj.; film/material with explicit sexual content or violence] ej lämplig för barn, brutal

x-ray[1] [n.] röntgenundersökning, röntgenbild

x-ray[2] [v.] röntga

XS [abbrev: extra small] extra liten

x-y plotter [n.] kurvritare

Y

Y [abbrev: see: **YMCA**]
y-axis [n.; -axes] y-axel
yacht [n.] yacht
yard [n.] gård, trädgård; yard [0,9 m]
yarn [n.] garn, tråd
yawn [v.] gäspa
yd. [abbrev: yard] yard [0,9 m.]
yeah [interj.] ja
year [n.] år; årtal; **a ~ from now**
om ett år; **last ~** i fjol; **this ~** i år
yeast [n.] jäst
yell [v.] skrika, tjuta
yellow[1] [adj.] gul; **~ fever** gula
febern; **~ pages** gula sidorna
yellow[2] [n.] gul färg
yep [interj.] ja
yes [interj.] ja; jo [in answer to a
negative question]; **~, of course**
javisst
yesterday [adv.] i går; **~ morning**
i går morse; **early ~** i går morse;
the day before ~ i förrgår
yet [adv.] dock; ännu; **not ~** inte
ännu
Yiddish [n.] jiddisch
yield[1] [n.] utbyte, vinst, avkastning
yield[2] [v.] ge, ge i avkastning,
lämna ifrån sig; **~ priority** lämna
företräde [traffic]; **obligation to ~**
väjningsplikt [traffic]
YMCA [abbrev: Young Men's
Christian Association] Kristliga
föreningen av unga män (KFUM)
yoga [n.] yoga

yogurt [n.] filmjölk, yoghurt
you [pron. sing & pl.] du/dig
[sing.subj/obj.], ni/er
[pl.subj./obj.]; man/en [generic,
"one"; subj./obj.]
you'd [contr: you had; you would]
du/ni hadde, du/ni skulle
you'll [contr: you will] du ska
young [adj.] ung, liten; **~ lady**
fröken, ung dam; **~ people** ungdom, de unga
younger [adj.comp.] yngre; **Ashna
is ~ than Scotia** Ashna är yngre
än Scotia
youngest [adj.superl.] yngst
youngster [n.] unge
your [pron.poss. sing. & pl.]
din/ditt/dina [sing.]; er(t) [pl.]
you're [contr: you are] du är
yours [pron.poss.; see: **your**]
yourself [pron.refl.] dig; själv
youth [n.] ungdom; **~ discount**
ungdomsrabatt; **~ hostel**
vandrarhem
you've [contr: you have] du har
yr. [abbrev: year] år
YT [abbrev: Yukon] Yukon
Yugoslav [n.] jugoslav
Yugoslavia [n.] jugoslavien
YWCA [abbrev: Young Women's
Christian Organization] Kristliga
förening för unga kvinnor
(KFUK)

Z

zero [num.] noll
zigzag[1] [n.] sicksack
zigzag[2] [v.; -gged] gå i sicksack,
  kryssa
zip[1] [n.] kraft, energi; ~ **code** postnummer
zip[2] [v.; -pping, -pped, -pped] susa;
  ~ **up** dra igen blixtlåset
zipper [n.] blixtlås
zodiac sign [n.] stjärntecken
zone [n.] zon

zoning [n.] stadsplanering,
  indelning
zoo [n.] djurpark, zoo
zoology [n.] zoologi
zoom [v.] rusa; zooma [IT]; ~ **in**
  zooma in [IT]; ~ **out** zooma ut
  [IT]
zucchini [n.] zucchini, courgette
zzz, z's [abbrev: sleep, snoring]
  sömn, snarking